Trial
By
Your
Peers

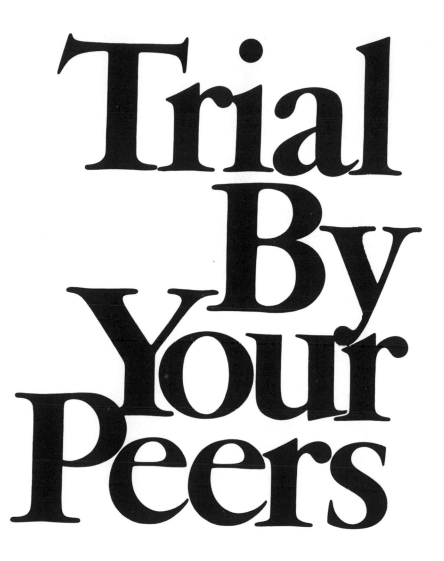

Trial By Your Peers

WILLIAM ZAMORA

A MAURICE GIRODIAS BOOK

DISTRIBUTED BY LYLE STUART INC.

© William Zamora, 1973
Published by Maurice Girodias Associates, Inc.
220 Park Avenue South, New York 10003, U.S.A.
Printed in the United States of America

L.C. 73-82687
ISBN 0-8184-0228-8

Trial
By
Your
Peers

PREFACE

We lived in a world filled with inside influences, which as the months passed by infringed upon our lives, and, to a certain extent, we were affected by other jurors' wishes and acts.

Anything any juror did had some effect upon the other jurors, and yet we kept to ourselves the thought that we had to find out how to live our own lives among these strangers, thrown together by law and custom of our land, but especially by our duties and our responsibilities as individuals. Yes, we were together but not close. We had to carry everyday in our heads the evidence presented in court. We could not discuss it among ourselves, not even voice an opinion in part or as a whole—all that evidence to share with, to talk about. We had to find out how to live with it, how to restrain ourselves from saying something. It was prohibited. Consequently, we had to find out how to live our own lives, use our own minds, and go on toward the end without letting the other jurors know how we felt and thought about the verdict we would finally render during the time of deliberation of the already-famous Manson trial.

But the truth, such being its nasty habit, refuses to coincide with our illusions. What we think is a candid picture of ourselves turns out to be either an idealized portrait or a libelous caricature. Of all the arts, that of describing a portrait of a person is unquestionably the cruelest of them all. As human as the jurors are, they will protest. They will denounce me as a miserable slanderer. When they read this book, they will view themselves and tell their relatives and acquaintances that what I wrote shares no similarity to the truth. They will say that I scarcely knew anything at all, that I twisted and distorted their behavior in my writing in order to take pride in knowing how good I am at judging people. It matters not how cunning, how intelligent, or how well informed I was; the truth is that I observed by the mere fact of being sequestered that people give up, and in time they become what they really are, all

7

I had to do was to focus and intensify my attention. I could not possibly have been able to write this book had it not been for the variety of characters, the different types and walks of life among the jurors, and especially their behavior. They made me discover the formula that I had been hunting for years—to use my mind, to write, to express my personal views—and thanks to the circumstances, I am able to write my own experiences while serving as a juror in the Tate-LaBianca murder case.

If some of the episodes seem to be less personal, please remember that it was the seemingly small events of a juror's life that made up the greater portion of my observations.

—WILLIAM M. ZAMORA
31st of July, 1971

One of the things for which I was popular while in the Army was the fact that my hometown was Hollywood—the movie capital and mecca of the world—the city where the movie stars dwelled. Everybody would ask me if I had seen or talked to a certain movie star. Most of the questions were in regard to how "they" reacted when I spoke to them and how "they" looked. Were the female stars as beautiful as they were shown on the screen? Were they friendly? Had I been to their homes? Were they real? For them, undoubtedly, the world of celluloid was a world of fantasy—a dream world—a world of stars. The actors and actresses were not people, but heroes and heroines. They would identify themselves with the roles their favorite actors had played on the screen and want to know if the movie stars were similar or closely related to characters they had performed in their real life.

As you may well know, it was a task for me to answer these questions. To begin with, I did not personally know any big movie star. True, I had seen some of them in person, talked a little, but beyond the usual greeting and perhaps a compliment or two about how good they had been in a movie, I had no knowledge of their private lives. And I'm sure, even if I had asked them, they would not have told me anything—it was not my business—and besides, they were not about to divulge any particulars of their private doings. No one does.

You can well imagine me trying to answer such demanding questions as, "Is it true that Marilyn Monroe wears nothing underneath?"—"Is it true that she sleeps in the nude?" Or perhaps, such provocative questions such as—"Is it true that Piper Lourie eats roses for breakfast?"

Anyway, I could not honestly answer, anymore than I could make any comments, as to the veracity of those questions.

Now in 1971, a new type of popularity has been built around me, I still live in Hollywood. I have once more become popular because of the nine and one-half months I had been sequestered as a juror on the Tate-LaBianca murder case. My friends and the people I meet often ask me questions as to what reaction I experienced while looking at photographs of the slain, beautiful, honey-blonde Sharon Tate.

They also asked me just what being sequestered did to you. "How long did it last?" "Did you like it?" "Did you get along with the rest of the jurors?" "I just can't imagine anyone doing that—especially you, so full of life and such an exciting individual—"why did you let them sequester you?" "Oh, by the way, what did you do for sex?" "Don't tell me that you spent nine and one-half months without sex? Not you, of all people. Who can?" "Why didn't you just walk out?" "Why", "why", "and", "why". Always the same question: "WHY?" Those were the questions that were most pertinent and most often unanswered about being **SEQUESTERED.**

To answer my family and friends' questions, and those who might be interested, I shall endeavor to describe, to the best of my ability, the sequence of the trial's events and life among the jurors beginning with its day of inception.

By mail, I had been instructed to: "Please appear June 22nd, 1970, at 8.25 A.M., Jury Assembly Room - Room 222, County Courthouse." On that day I was somewhere in Europe—in fact it had been a month—and I didn't return until a week later, June 29th. So I called their office to explain. The lady on the phone replied that she would mark my absence, but to appear at the same place, same time on the following Monday, July 6th. I thanked her and hung up.

"Good," I told myself, "that will give me a chance to return to work and break the news to my boss." As it happened, my squad leader did not mind. I guessed it was because we had just finished a project and were awaiting a new assignment. With a resigned look, as he lifted his legs onto the desk and folded his arms, my boss said, "If you have to go, you have to go." "Alright then, I will see you in thirty days," I answered.

On a balmy, warm morning in the summer of 1970, dressed in a light suit, I drove in my car to the Los Angeles County Courthouse. The sun was shining on my face—the traffic was heavy even though it was later than I usually drove. I got off at Grand Avenue, passed the music center on my left, and proceeded to the courthouse across the street. I parked my car and walked along with people who had also parked, and who obviously had been summoned for jury duty.

I looked on the second floor and went directly to Room 222. At the entrance door, a deputy sheriff was checking names that he had on his list. He also distributed a juror's manual to each person entering and advised them to

10

read and study the information contained therein prior to the commencement of his or her period of service.

I waited about five minutes. The courtroom held at least three-hundred summoned jurors. Another deputy sheriff stood up in front of all of us and announced that shortly a judge of the Los Angeles Superior Court would instruct us as to the performance of our duties as a juror. We waited, and the judge entered. The deputy sheriff said: "Please remain seated, Honorable Judge Albert J. Smith presiding."

The judge began by saying: "Dear citizens, you have been summoned to perform a most civil function as a juror". He explained that his primary intent was to assist the newly-chosen and inexperienced juror in the performance of his duties. He further explained that what he had to say would be helpful to those who have had previous experience because it would refresh their memories concerning the many intricate problems with which jurors are constantly confronted. Then he emphasized that our participation as jurors will help to preserve and perpetuate our fundamental democratic process, and that it was not only our right, but also our solemn obligation.

He explained that the length of time we were compelled to serve was four weeks, or twenty working days, in a given month. He spoke about the rudimentary proceedings in different aspects. He also mentioned two or three examples in which he brought laughter and joking—the tenseness was gone. Most of us felt at ease and even willing to participate because of his chummy, relaxing, and inviting attitude. His psychological approach endowed us to begin to accept our situation.

He urged us to wear tasteful conservative clothes. He reminded us that as jurors, we should be well-presented. "No juror will be dismissed because of the attire he or she wears in court", he said. "But then again," he continued, "you will be judges and as such, you should dress accordingly". "For those", he added, "who have any hardship or feel they should be excused and are unable to serve at this time, speak to the bailiff-in-charge". "But mind you", he stressed, "there will be no excuses accepted unless they are genuinely valid. You may be exempted at this time, but that does not mean necessarily that you will be legally excused. Eventually you will be recalled, and, for Heaven's sake, we do need you now, and, since you are here, you might as well serve and get it over with. That makes sense—doesn't it"? We all roared with laughter. "It isn't as bad as you may think", he assured us, "you may have to sit in court and listen to traffic citations which might appear to be boring, or some other lesser violations. But remember that a trial by jury is a basic right, which is the very essence of freedom under our constitution, and everyone

11

knows the importance of the court as an agency to settle legal disputes and to hear and determine charges against those accused of crimes". Then he explained that the function of the jury is to determine the truth, or the facts, and that the jury has no power to determine the application of the law, but must accept and apply the instructions of the judge as to what the law is, without regard to its individual opinions.

The judge finished by saying, "Thank you for your attention, and I hope that during the time you will serve you may be able to view a very interesting case". (Boy! Little did he know what I was going to get into—neither did I.)

As a final "p.s." he reminded each and everyone of us to make sure that our addresses given had remained the same; and, if anyone had moved since receiving their notice, to report the change in the assembly room. "It is important", he emphasized, "because that would determine the distance in miles you will be paid for driving each day to court, and, while we are on the subject of mileage", he continued, "if you do not have a Los Angeles County Courthouse parking permit, please inquire to the deputy for one. Thank you and good luck!" he concluded. The judge left the room.

Then, the same deputy who had previosly spoken to us, announced in a very loud voice: "Quiet please! Please be quiet! Do take your seats!" He continued, "If there is anyone with any hardship that would make him or her unable to serve, please remain seated. The rest will please follow the deputy at the entrance door where he will escort you to the assembly room, where you will wait until your name is called."

I had no hardship, and since I had served on two previous occasions as a juror, my attitude was solely to accept and wait until the time would come to return to work. I had twice been on civil cases, very shallow cases. I was on one for assault to commit murder, but it was a very, very simple case. It didn't get beyond any expectation. There was another, a homosexual case, but nothing significant, just a guy who had been apprehended by the vice squad in the Greyhound Bus station. In fact he was an actor. But the rest of them were just simple violations, and traffic tickets.

The bailiff escorted us to the assembly room; and, as we walked in, I noticed jurors who had already arrived—some playing cards, others working on jigsaw puzzles, others reading newspapers or paperback editions of novels, some watching television. Some were sitting, others were dozing, and still others were having coffee and donuts, which they purchased from a snack bar window adjacent to the assembly room.

I didn't want to sit, read, watch television, or any of the above to kill time, so I remained by the entrance and observed the range of ages among the jurors and looked for young attractive women, merely for companionship or whatever.

A short, uniformed bailiff, wearing a thick moustache, entered the room, accompanied by a tall, blonde, female bailiff. He called off forty names, including mine, and those who stood were instructed to line up, and again we were escorted by those two deputies. At first, I had thought they were going to take us somewhere in the building—that is, the Los Angeles County Courthouse.

Since I did not know anybody, I could not speak to anyone; so I just followed, but to my surprise I noticed that we were leaving the building, and even ordered to get into a Los Angeles County Sheriff's jail bus. Needless to mention, a jail bus is far from being comfortable, but just the same, we were driven not too long a distance. The bus stopped, and as we got out, I found out that the building was the Hall of Justice. We did not enter on the main entrance, but through a high, thick, mesh-wire, sliding electric gate which was operated by a guard deputy sheriff from a watchtower.

"They're taking us to jail", someone said jokingly. I had never been inside, nor had I seen this part of the building. The area between the Hall of Justice edifice and an adjacent dilapidated building form an open driveway—we walked towards the wall at the end of it where a huge sign "**BLOW HORN FOR GUARD**" was painted in red. I also noticed some prisoners washing garbage cans which had contained leftover food.

Bearing to the left and into a corridor inside the building, there was a line of three or four Los Angeles County Coroner's hearses, and in the background a walking ramp leading to a door with a sign that read: "Coroner's Receiving Room—Authorized Personnel Only."

The corridor was drafty and cool—a strong and repugnant odor permeated the atmosphere, making some of the prospective jurors hold their breaths. Suddenly, they made us turn to the left. More prisoners scattered around were told to move aside for us to pass and enter an elevator lobby.

Although there were three elevators, still there wasn't room enough for all of us. The two bailiffs divided us in two groups. One bailiff in charge of each group.

Inside the elevator we stood next to each other like sardines. The operator was a very heavy-built, likeable, black deputy—I chuckled as I watched his belly expand everytime he would breathe. Over the door a sign read: "**NO WEAPONS ALLOWED BEYOND THE 9TH FLOOR**".

Our group reached the ninth floor first, and proceeded out into a small

13

foyer, where we were told to wait. About fifteen feet further back, I noticed some prisoners in a cell with their hands on the bars, glancing intensely at the jurors going through. Behind a wooden counter two deputies sat. The youngest, a chubby deputy, walked from the counter and stepped in front of our escorting sheriff. He approached a door and looked through a small sliding-window to make sure it was free from traffic of prisoners, and then opened it with a large, unusual, square key.

We followed the bailiff, who, while escorting us, remained in silence to our questions as to where we were being taken...we walked down a hallway, bearing to the right at each turn, and for a moment it seemed as if we were going back to our point of origin or somewhere near the foyer.

Again we were asked to wait in front of a door— door number 104. The sheriff wanted to check if the group behind had caught up with us. He returned, and from a ring of keys, picked one, opened the door, and guided us down a zigzag narrow flight of stairs—at the bottom he opened two more doors, and led us into a crowded room. Eight large flourescent light fixtures, hanging from a high ceiling, brightly illuminated the courtroom, giving access for one to appreciate the rich wood paneling. A railing separated the judge's bench and the counsel tables from the rest of the room, which was divided by a central aisle in two sections.

As we walked in, I noticed at my left, seated on the jury box in the front row, an attractive red-headed lady. She was furiously knitting. Within the next two seats, there was a young man whose hair, fashioned modernly, covered his forehead and ears; oddly enough, the color of his hair was also red.

All this sight seeing was so different. If you've ever been on a jury, you know that normally it's monotonous. You meet certain people there, and some of them don't care. Most of them are retired people and they don't care to converse. And those who do converse are those who divulge everything, and so forth, and you couldn't care less, because it's the same thing. In other words tiresome people who have no friends, no nothing, and this is a great thing for them, to become involved. This was **different.**

But what caught my attention to take a look at my right was that someone behind me had softly whispered: "I'll be damned, it's the Manson trial."

Having seen him only in a photograph, I expected to see a much bigger man; however, his eyes were so intensifying that his height didn't matter. Manson sat and watched us parade as if he was screening us for a movie role. He had a constant smile on his face and looked pleased. His long, Jesus-like hair and beard made him look almost like a character drawn out of one of the El Greco paintings. He appeared like a target and we used our eyes as darts to watch him—he appeared so different from the rest of us.

"Just follow the line," said the bailiff, who had escorted us and shortly after I saw him giving the slip of paper with each of our names on it to a tall, bald man wearing a dark gold plaid jacket.

All the jurors had been ushered to sit in the spectators' section, except me. The last row, placed against the wall, had no central aisle between sections, and for lack of seating capacity, they sat me slightly off behind the section assigned to the prospective jurors.

"As soon as anyone is called," said unexpectedly the same tall, blonde, female bailiff who had escorted us, "would you please move to that seat?"

"I don't understand; what do you mean?" I inquired.

Leaning towards me, she smiled and said: "I mean when the court clerk pulls the name of a juror out of the box, he will get up and go to sit in the jury box, then you take the seat vacated by that juror—understand now?"

"Yes, I do," I responded.

"The reason," she offered the information, "is because we like to keep the jurors together."

Seated at my right was a very, very, chic, elegant and somewhat beautiful woman. She was attired in a chaste and simple, but tasteful, one-piece blue dress with a white cowl collar, which matched the color of her shoes, handbag, and gloves. As she sat with her legs crossed in a dignified manner, I noticed her legs were well-formed, well-shaped. But then, thinking of what the great American, Will Rogers, had once said: "I never met a man I didn't like," I said to myself: "I never met a woman whose legs I didn't like."

Inquisitively, I asked her: "Have you served before as a juror?" She didn't respond—just shook her head negatively. Again, I asked her, "You mean to tell me this is your first time?" "Yes," she said, "and you?" "This is my third time," I replied, "twice I served in Municipal Court, and now my first time in Superior Court," and then, half-smiling, I concluded by saying, "oh well, there's always a first time for everything." "Right," she agreed, also smiling.

"Quiet please!" shouted a lofty bailiff as the judge, wearing a black robe, entered the courtroom, and then continued, "remain seated, come to order, this Court is again in session."

The judge looked around and approaching a microphone placed on his desk, leaned forward and said: "All parties and counsel are present." Then, directing his attention to the court clerk, the tall bald-headed man whom I

15

had seen before and who was standing immediately at his right, the judge proceeded: "You may swear in the prospective jurors."

"Would you please stand up and raise your right hand," said the court clerk. We stood up.

He spoke: "You, and each of you, do solemnly swear that you will well and truly answer such questions as may be asked of you touching your qualifications to act as trial jurors in the cause now pending before this Court, so help you God."

"I do," we all said in unison when he finished, and then he told us: "Please be seated."

"Ladies and gentlemen," said the judge, "This is the case of the people of the state of California against Charles Manson, Susan Atkins, Patricia Krenwinkel and Leslie Van Houten.

"Mr. Manson, Miss Atkins, and Miss Krenwinkel have been charged with seven counts of murder and one count of conspiracy to commit murder. Miss Van Houten has been charged with two counts of murder and one count of conspiracy to commit murder."

Each of the accused, clad in denim prisoners' garb, was asked individually by the judge, to stand up and face the prospective jurors so they could be identified.

The judge, looking at us, asked: "Does anyone of you know personally Mr. Charles Manson?" While smiling and rubbing his beard, Charles Manson stood up—his bushy and long, unkempt hair made him appear somewhat taller than he actually was. None of the prospective jurors replied.

"You may sit down, Mr. Manson," said the judge. The prisoner obliged.

"Does anyone of you know personally Miss Susan Atkins?" inquired the judge. Dark-haired Susan Atkins stood up quickly, and gave us a defiant look. Again, no one replied. She sat without being told to do so.

"Does anyone of you know personally Miss Patricia Krenwinkel?" asked the judge. With her chestnut-colored long hair covering each side of her face, Patricia Krenwinkel stood up. While closing her eyes and tightening her thin lips, she forced a smile. Once again, no one replied.

"Does anyone know personally Miss Leslie Van Houten?" the judge said one more time. Tall and thin-looking, Leslie Van Houten stood up. She displayed two, prominent, rounded dimples as she smiled at us.

Since no one responded, the Court continued: "The names of the victims are as follows:

"Sharon Tate Polanski, a human being, female Caucasian.

"Abigail Folger, a human being, female Caucasian.

"Voityk Frykowski, a human being, male Caucasian.

"Jay Sebring, a human being, male Caucasian.

"Steven Parent, a human being, male Caucasian.

"Rosemary LaBianca, a human being, female Caucasian.

"Leno LaBianca, a human being, male Caucasian."

The judge asked us: "Did anyone of you know any of the victims personally?" No response.

"The defendants in this case have pleaded "not guilty" to these charges," said Judge Older. Then, as required by law to be given in every criminal case, he recited by memory the following instructions: "A defendant in a criminal action is presumed to be innocent until the contrary is proved, and in case of a reasonable doubt whether his guilt is satisfactorily shown, he is entitled to an acquittal, but the effect of this presumption is only to place upon the state the burden of proving him guilty beyond a reasonable doubt. Reasonable doubt is defined as follows:

It is not a mere possible doubt, because everything relating to human affairs and depending on moral evidence is open to some possible or imaginary doubt. It is that state of the case which, after the entire comparison and consideration of all the evidence, leaves the minds of jurors in that condition that they cannot say they feel an abiding conviction, to a moral certainty, of the truth of the charge!"

The Court proceeded to introduce the counsel—in the same manner as the defendants—each one of them stood up, facing the prospective jurors as their names were called.

"The People will be represented by Deputy District Attorney Mr. Vincent T. Bugliosi," said the Judge. I noticed that when Mr. Bugliosi stood up, though his last name sounded Italian-descent, he didn't look like a typical Italian as represented in American films; he looked Scandinavian.

"And, Deputy District Attorney Mr. Aaron Stovitz," the judge continued. Mr. Stovitz looked more like an Italian, though anybody having Aaron as a first name has to be other than Italian, for sure.

"Mr. Manson will be represented by Mr. Irving Kanarek." A short and stocky man stood up. He reminded me of the late Henry Armetta.

"Miss Atkins will be represented by Mr. Daye Shinn," A well-trimmed and dressed Oriental-descent man stood up.

"Miss Krenwinkel will be represented by Mr. Paul Fitzgerald." A tall young man stood up. His baby-face looks contradicted the circles under his eyes.

"And Miss Van Houten will be represented by Mr. Ira Reiner." A man,

17

big enough to be a football player, stood up. His looks and premature-gray, undulated hair stirred up some women in the audience to gasp for some air.

"Does anyone of you now personally or have had, any business deals with these counsel?" inquired the judge. None of us responded. The judge looked at his right and...

The court clerk. holding a brown tin box in front of himself, began to shake it vigorously to mix the contents. He stopped, and then pulled out a slip of paper, and with a majestic intonation, read: "Mrs. Deborah Hart, H-a-r-t."

"This is like a lottery," I confided to the lady to whom I had spoken before. She looked quickly at me and exclaimed: "That's me!" Without hesitation, she walked nervously toward the jury box.

"So that's her name," I said to myself. "Mrs. Deborah Hart."

The tall female deputy sheriff gave me a nod, and I complied by taking the seat vacated by Mrs. Hart.

"Mrs. Alice Jackson, J-a-c-k-s-o-n." A black lady stood up and took a seat in the jury box.

Later, the judge announced that he would interview, in his private chambers, the selection of prospective jurors in the presence of the defendants, the defense lawyers, and the prosecution lawyers. Shortly after, the judge left the room; the parties involved followed suit. The prisoners were escorted by two or three bailiffs and also a court reporter, carrying his tripod in one hand and his machine in the other.

That day, some twenty-odd names had been drawn out, but not mine. They had gone into the judge's chambers and had been excused for one reason or another, and on their way out of the courtroom, the court clerk had given to each one the slip of paper with his or her name on it, and had also instructed them to return it to the clerk-in-charge of the assembly room and to wait there until their names were called once more.

At 4:30 P.M., the judge adjourned the day's session until 9:30 A.M. of the following day.

Most of the prospective jurors wanted to walk out to their cars, but the bailiff didn't allow it. We were escorted around the same long route we came in, and driven back to the Los Angeles County Courthouse in an uncomfortable jail bus, even though the distance was only two blocks. Outside, the heat was boiling up, and the weather man had predicted an average of 90 degrees daily temperature with heavy smog for the entire week. The heat inside the bus, with no air conditioning and mesh wire blocking the windows, was

18

high enough to boil an egg.

The next morning, the bailiff had added some twenty new prospective jurors to join us in our short bus ride.

The judge introduced again the parties involved in the same manner as before. There were more names drawn out of the box, but not mine.

The selection of jurors in open court for that day began around eleven o'clock in the morning. Those seated in the jury box were examined by attorneys for both sides. One bailiff had brought a microphone to use in front of them, and they took turns in answering questions.

Mrs. Hart appeared composed, though her voice sounded a little nervous. She was subjected to an excruciating interrogation which periodically sent her to concentrate before answering the questions. She was brave. It was obvious she was not prepared to cope with all the tension surrounding her, but she controlled her emotions and maintained her stability, despite the personal questions imposed on her for answers. She was questioned more than anybody.

The judge and the rest of the parties resumed the interviews in private chambers and kept sending for more prospective jurors. My name still was not called.

I had given up the thought that the court clerk would ever draw my name out of the tin box. For a moment I even doubted my name was inside. They had already disqualified a considerable number of prospective jurors.

Two black jurors who had been seated in the jury box for over a week were suddenly excused. Everyone had expected them to have been accepted by the prosecution. For reasons unknown, the defense lawyers had not exercised their right to challenge or excuse a certain number of prospective jurors, but yet the prosecution was the only side making use of that right. Why? We couldn't figure it out.

"Mr. William M. Zamora, Z-a-m-o-r-a!" shouted, out loud, the court clerk. After I dashed across the railing gate held open by a bailiff, the court clerk wanted to know if he had pronounced my last name correctly. I nodded positively, and then he escorted me inside the judge's chambers.

The room was small and full of people. After introducing me to them, the court clerk swiftly left the room, closing the door behind me.

I stood still, almost petrified for a second, looking quickly at everybody from a higher level. I noticed everyone was seated except the bailiffs standing next to the defendants. For a moment, it seemed as if no one was going to say anything.

"Please have a seat, Mr. Zamora," said Judge Older, as he pointed to a

19

vacant chair next to his desk, placed in an identical position as the witness stand is located in the courtroom—except much closer. As I walked to the chair, I felt their eyes glued to my skin; they studied every movement I made. If they had told me that I had no blood on my face, I would have believed it. I felt no circulation nor feeling of any kind.

At first I didn't think I was going to qualify to stay put on the jury because this was a transcendental case where they would ask me questions...where they would evaluate my integrity as a prospective juror. Not that I have no integrity, but in the eyes of somebody else I might not appear honest and fair. But I went through with high flying colors. They had arranged the chairs so those who would sit could convey their attention and gaze toward the person being interviewed.

"A very strategical idea", I told myself.

Manson was seated almost opposite me—at his side were the three female defendants—behind were the counsel.

"Mr. Zamora, have you ever served as a juror in a criminal case?" asked Mr. Bugliosi. "No sir, I have not."

"Did you know Miss Sharon Tate or any of the victims?" asked again the prosecutor.

"I've seen Miss Sharon Tate in one film. I believe it was 'Beyond the Valley of the Dolls,' otherwise, I have no previous knowledge of either of the victims. Oh, yes..." I corrected myself, "I think I have read someplace about Jay Sebring being the barber for some movie stars, but that's all."

Then Mr. Fitzgerald asked: "Mr. Zamora, just because these defendants have been arrested, would you consider them guilty of the crimes with which they have been charged?"

They all waited. Manson leaned back and folded his arms as if to challenge my answer. Looking straight at Manson's eyes and then at the girls, I responded cautiously.

"The fact that some suspects are arrested and brought into court to be tried, the evidence against them is, by no means, conclusive."

After answering the last question, I couldn't recall who had asked me what—Charles Manson had kept, giving me up to that moment, a sort of an intimate look with his eyes—it bothered me to the point that he had become aware of my uneasiness. We were about three feet apart from each other. He smiled at me. I returned a subtle smile.

"Mr. Zamora, do you understand the question?" said Judge Older, who was the only person I could not see face-to-face. Turning slightly to my right to address him, I hesitated to answer for fear of not knowing what to

20

say, but somehow managed to utter some explanation: "Eh,....no sir, not quite."

"Repeat the question," said the judge to one of the counsellors.

"I'd be glad to, Your Honor," replied Mr. Kanarek.

"Could you tell us, Mr. Zamora, what you heard or read about this case?"

"Sir," I began by saying, "the only thing I know is that some crimes were committed back in August of 1969—I learned of them on TV or radio—I don't know which one of them, but one for sure. Then, on November 22nd of the same year, I left for one month's vacation in Europe—I believe the defendants were apprehended while I was gone. When I came back, the publicity had faded away—then, in June of 1970, or last month, I went back to Europe for one month. Again, I was not aware of the publicity given to this case."

Mr. Bugliosi then asked: "Mr. Zamora, did you at any time while you were gone on vacation read about this case?"

"No sir," I responded, "it's my policy, while going on vacation, to ignore any type of news."

"Didn't you read anything at all?" he insisted.

"Well, to tell you the truth, on the plane going over, I sort of flipped the pages of a 'Newsweek' magazine.." Then, half-smiling, I admitted to them that I had gone to sleep while looking at it.

Judge Older wanted to know if it would cause any inconvenience—my absence at work. I replied in the negative. Mr. Stovitz from the rear of the room asked: "Would it be an inconvenience for Mrs. Zamora if you were to be sequestered while serving on this trial?"

Smilingly I replied: "There's no Mrs. Zamora, I'm single." They all smiled as the Judge excused me. On my way out Manson winked at me, and the girls, still smiling, followed me with their eyes. A bailiff ushered me to a juror's chair—the first seat on the second row, seat number 7.

"Glad to have you," said the attractive, red-headed lady in front of me.

"Thank you, but I don't think they'd ever select me," I said.

"Don't knock it, you look like a juror already." We both laughed when she said that. I felt grateful for her kind, welcoming words. Somehow it relieved the pressure which I had gone through a few minutes before.

Fortunately, when the attorneys for both sides asked questions in open court, they didn't ask me too many personal questions. They confined themselves to the explanation of those only issues which we would expect during the process of the trial.

Mr. Ira Reiner, defense lawyer for Leslie Van Houten, asked us "for ins-

21

tance, if the prosecution brings evidence which proves to find guilty any other defendant," would that automatically influence any of us to vote "guilty" against his client?

Then, with a deep-toned voice, repeated the same question to each juror, as to separate his client from the other defendants.

"Do you understand that I am representing Miss Leslie Van Houten and only Miss Van Houten?"

His voice was so strong and distinctive, especially when using the microphone, he appeared to shout: "When I speak in this courtroom, I am speaking only for Leslie Van Houten."

A prospective juror, leaning over my shoulder, whispered to me, "He's been repeating that statement for the last week, yelling at everyone—no one is stopping him! He'll be dumped. You'll see."

"What do you mean?" casually I asked.

"I'll explain it later," she responded.

Her name was Donna, and at high noon on the ninth floor of the Los Angeles County Court cafeteria, she informed me, "Any prospective juror can be dismissed without cause, by one of the attorneys. Dismissing without cause could be hardship or bias and it must be proved by the attorney to the satisfaction of the judge. Each defense attorney has five peremptory challenges with which he can excuse a prospective juror without cause."

"Also," she continued, "the four defense attorneys have twenty additional peremptory challenges which they can only use collectively. If one decides against a collective challenge, none may do so."

Then she added, "by the same token, the prosecution also has a total of forty peremptory challenges."

"How come you know so much about it?" I inquired curiously.

"I happen to work as a legal secretary in a large, established, law firm, and you wanna know something? They won't accept me as a juror because my brother-in-law is a lawyer."

"But I still don't know why you think Mr. Reiner will be 'dumped' " I asked again.

"It's obvious," she exclaimed, as she finished eating a large plate of tuna and cottage cheese salad, "why is Reiner the only attorney of the defense exercising his five personal peremptory challenges while Fitzgerald, Kanarek, and Shinn refuse to exercise any of the twenty joint challenges? I'll tell you why. Something is fishy."

"The tuna in your salad," I pointed to her plate. She shook with laughter and evaded once more the same question on our way back to Department

22

of the Los Angeles Superior Court.

Leslie Van Houten stood up in court now and then, asking to be heard.

"Miss Van Houten, you must speak through your counsel," said Judge Older on one occasion. However Leslie Van Houten insisted many times, demanding to be heard, and Judge Older's temper was wearing thin, and, to get her off his neck, finally allowed her to address the court.

Defiantly, Leslie Van Houten stood up and spoke fiercely and clearly: "Your Honor, Mr. Reiner is not speaking for me, he's speaking for himself."

Then, looking at us jurors, Leslie continued: "His voice is not my voice. He can't speak for me."

"What's on your mind?" Judge Older asked again.

Leslie bent over slightly to hear what Patricia Krenwinkel was saying and, hesitantly, looked at Charles Manson in a flash of a second for assurance, and answered loudly: "Your Honor, I want Mr. Reiner removed as my attorney," and then with a satisfied and almost triumphant look, she announced, "I don't want him to represent me."

"Your request is denied. Let's proceed," firmly stated Judge Older.

For some reason, Mr. Reiner also asked each prospective juror: "If the evidence proves Leslie Van Houten 'not guilty', would you render that verdict even though she herself express a desire to be found guilty?"

I was thinking to myself "Why would she want to be found guilty? Maybe Mr. Reiner is following a pattern of questioning which she doesn't approve of—maybe she doesn't want to be sectioned off from the other defendants. Who knows? I'll soon find out."

Mr. Fitzgerald on the other hand emphasized that when he had put a question to a juror, that question would also be applicable to the rest of the jurors.

Mr. Bugliosi's definition of what "conspiracy" meant, in terms of easy comprehension, was done in such a fashion that left no one with a doubt as what "conspiracy" meant in legal terms. He would explain as follows: "Suppose that, we have three people—A, B and C. A plans to rob a bank, and he asks the aid of B and C. Ultimately, A sends B and C to commit the robbery. By law, A, though he didn't physically participate nor commit the robbery, is guilty as much as B and C."

One long week had passed by, and still I was seated in the jury box not knowing whether they'd accept me at the end or not. I just couldn't believe they would even consider me. However, gradually I began to feel confident they would select me as a juror.

The selection of jurors had begun the 15th of June—and yet, on that day, the 14th of July—they were still screening prospective jurors in the judge's private chambers. Many of them were excused when they reflected they might be prejudiced against the defendants. Some declared their beliefs against the death penalty. Others stated their religious background wouldn't allow them to sit and hear someone call himself Jesus Christ. Others were concerned about the effect of pictures of the victims. Still others would decline on account not wanting to listen to obscene language. Added to all those reasons above, there were also those who refused to serve because they couldn't be away from their homes or jobs for the length of time the judge and counsel had mentioned. It had to be more than just "no". It had to be hardship, or a plain decision that you just don't believe in the judicial system. But I wouldn't be able to do so because my conscience wouldn't have allowed me.

The jury selection process seemed interminable. There were 148 prospective jurors screened in the judge's private chambers.

At four o'clock on that afternoon, the judge walked in the court room preceded by the counsel—we expected more questions to be asked in open court—but, when the prosecutor and his assistant as well as the defense lawyers sat in court, they all gave us that special look as if to make sure we in the jury box were the panel they had finally decided to accept.

The prosecuting attorney swiveled his chair to face the jury box. With one hand under his chin, he looked at each one of us. His eyes reminded me of a typewriter carriage—moving from left to right. The jury, eventually selected, met Mr. Bugliosi's specifications. He got up and addressed the Court.

"Your Honor, the people accept the jury as it is presently constituted."

Rhythmically, one at a time, the defense attorneys stood up and accepted the panel of jurors in behalf of their clients.

Immediately after, Judge Older indicated to the court clerk to swear in the selected jury, which was ultimately composed of seven men and five women.

The sketch artists had been drawing every prospective juror who had sat in the jury box, but at that moment I noticed they were really busy drawing only the selected jurors.

"Will you raise your right hand and stand up please," said the court clerk. Everyone was watching us. Silence. Nothing was heard except the shuffling noise of the jurors rising from their chairs.

"You, and each of you, do solemnly swear that you will well and truly try the cause now pending before this Court, and a true verdict rendered therein according to the evidence and the instructions of the Court, so help you God."

When we all responded: "I do," we were all deeply held with the responsibi-

24

lity ahead of us. It was our first taste of American legal procedure. True, while we waited, we had thought of the possibility of being chosen, but now that we were legally accepted, and that we were to be the sole judges of the Tate-LaBianca murder trial, the "Crime of the Century," we became more concerned. Let's face it, how often does one have the opportunity to undergo the highest responsibility of mankind?

I thought it was the most important investment in anybody's life to be able to do. I was invested with the most powerful duty anybody can do, to judge another man's life. This was life; life and death ... to judge whether these people were right or wrong, whether they had committed these crimes. I felt terribly, terribly, invigorated with premonitions, responsibility, integrity; and I felt proud at the same time. And I thought, I'm not going to defeat the purpose with which I had been invested, and I want to do my best because I am not doing it for myself. I'm doing it for the entire world; for the whole community where I reside; for all the people. I could not help thinking that this was the most important thing that had ever been given to me ... a decision to make. I had never had this opportunity. And of course you read about it, and you see it in the movies and on television. But this ... another human being ... it was tremendous, a feeling of committing tremendously, a tremendous responsibility. At the time I was not concerned with my welfare, with the repercussions of this. I don't want to appear as a hero in this book. I want to be just genuine. I was just another citizen, citizen caught in circumstance and had to make a decision. But I was aware of these things.

Now, we jurors, thrown together, having planted upon us a special and unique responsibility to perform, that of being judges, would have to conform and follow Judge Older's orders: to live at the Ambassador Hotel, under the same roof while being sequestered, and eventually judge the lives of four human beings. We jurors had become "involved."

My last night as a free man I decided to spend with a good friend of mine —a versatile actress who has dominated many television starring roles. With a couple hours in advance, she had managed to get hold of a group of mutual friends, and we all congregated at Casa Escobar, a Mexican restaurant, for drinks and especially dancing, cheek-to-cheek, to the music of a talented combo featuring latin melodies. The environment was jovial and happy, supported by the flowing nectar of tequila margaritas. I left the night club a few minutes before closing time, armed with hopes and good wishes from my friends.

That night I couldn't sleep too well—my mind was full of thoughts—thoughts which would disappear as quickly as they would come. I wondered about

25

the task ahead of me, I visualized in a fast-blinking sequence the victims' pictures. Then I wanted to check what had been packed—did I leave something behind? Would I need this or that? It almost felt like I was planning a revisit to Europe. The judge had told us to be prepared to leave directly for the hotel after the court session.

Since I could not leave my car parked out in the open for the length of the trial, my good friend Jim Reid graciously offered to drive me to the south side entrance of the Los Angeles courthouse.

When I stepped from the car, the sidewalk was already full of luggage of various sizes—it gave the appearance of a Greyhound Bus depot. Other jurors, who had been screened but excused, had come to say good bye, and especially the spouses, relatives and friends of us jurors.

That day in court was dedicated to selecting six alternate jurors in the same manner as the regular panel was chosen—no one could detect who would be accepted of those already sitting next to the regular panel.

During the noon hour was the first time we were driven to lunch at the Biltmore Hotel, and escorted by bailiffs.

At four o'clock, the judge decided to adjourn court session, but a hand sign from the court clerk reminded him that the bailiffs had not been sworn in.

Two male and two female deputy sheriffs stepped in front of the wooden railing, and rigidly stood in line; and, immediately following, they raised their right hands as the court clerk gave them the following oath:

"You do solemnly swear that you will take charge of the jury and keep them together, that you will not speak to them yourself, nor allow anyone else to speak to them upon any subject connected with the case, except by by order of the Court, so help you God."

Somberly they all answered "I do."

These little ceremonies took place quite often, and they reflected the seriousness of the law. It also meant that from that point on, we, the jurors, were in the absolute custody of the bailiffs, and all necessary and proper communications which any of us would desire to address to others would have to be made through them.

Outside the Hall of Justice, newspaper and television cameras were excitedly taking pictures through the mesh-wire sliding gate from a distance, but to no avail.

We were then taken on a street route and when came at a bus stop corner, people who were waiting for the city bus transportation, looked at us as if we were prisoners; and those nearby the windows, where I was peering through the bars, were appalled at the word that I uttered to them—"Help!"

26

The jurors next to me laughed at my joke, but as I repeated it subsequently during the months we were sequestered, the laughter was caused not because of the word itself, but mainly because of the varied facial reactions of those who were asked for "help."

The Ambassador Hotel driveway had been closed temporarily and sheriff's guards were posted at the entrance. Television cameramen had somehow infiltrated and were waiting for the arrival of the bus in which we jurors were transported.

A crowd of sightseers were scattered, some with movie cameras, joining the news media photographers to snap pictures of us.

They held us inside the bus for about fifteen minutes. While waiting, from behind the bus driver, I observed a handful of photographers who seemed to be protesting or arguing with the sheriffs. The bailiffs would not allow them to get closer and take pictures of us inside the bus.

Finally, a hotel employee unlocked and opened a six-foot high wooden gate. The cameramen didn't give up. Unable to see above the top of the gate, they compromised by lifting their equipment above their heads and snapped pictures of us, while the bus was driven down into a tunnel underneath the hotel and out to the other side of the building.

We left the bus and were strolling along the walks and driveways when, still in the distance, other photographers were trying to take our pictures, but a bailiff ran and stopped them.

I understood that the newspapers were hungry for news and wanted to see our faces, and so forth, but having your picture in the newspaper as a juror in that type of trial..well, all you're doing is asking for trouble to be in the public eye, to be recognized, especially not knowing what repercussions might come out of it. I was tempted to be seen of course, because being an actor, having been in t.v. parts, small parts, nothing big, my ego would be a bit flattered. I want to be a celebrity, but being a celebrity might cost me a lot. So I had to come down, and come to my senses, and realize that I would never become an actor by being in a picture like that. So, safety was first.

We descended a flight of stairs and entered into what appeared to be the laundry-operating plants. After going through a number of doors, we finally exited on a floor someone called the casino floor; then we passed a small post office agency before we took the elevator up to the sixth floor—our new home.

As soon as we stepped out of the elevator, a bailiff sitting at a desk, logged in our arrival. The small area directly in front of the elevator was being temporarily used for the bailiff to sit and guard the jurors, and admit and screen visitors of the jurors.

The deputies ordered us to congregate in the south wing of the sixth floor. While everybody was seating themselves, a wellgroomed man with a crew haircut introduced himself as Captain Arden.

He then introduced the four bailiffs who had been sworn in court and were under his command: Deputy Albert Taylor, tall and sleep looking, senior bailiff; Deputy Otis Tull, particularly noticeable because of his eye glasses and thick moustache; the two female bailiffs were Miss Mollie Kane, tall and blonde, and Mrs. Colvig, pretty and well-coiffured.

Captain Arden welcomed us by inviting everyone to join him in a drink, with his compliments; some accepted, and others abstained.

He stated that the jurors would occupy the entire sixth floor, except the north wing, which belonged to Mr. Sammy Davis, Jr.

Then, as he stood up with a drink of scotch in his hand, he announced that our rooms would be distributed by a sort of lottery. The reason, he explained, was that some rooms had balconies and others didn't and he wanted to be fair to each and everyone of us. He also introduced the housekeeper of the hotel—she spoke a few words and extended her welcome on behalf of the hotel, and said to call upon her in case we needed anything.

Captain Arden proceeded by saying that there were no televisions in our rooms—no radios were allowed and telephone calls would be made only through the deputy-on-duty; that he would log the calls, and remind the person of the admonition given by the judge.

Before he finished, Captain Arden spoke of the type of entertainment that would be available to us. He pointed towards the adjacent room, and then at the one we were in and said: "These two rooms are to be used as recreation rooms. You are to use them when you become tired of being alone in your own room. Also, this is the only room where you will be able to watch television."

At this moment, he stopped and refilled his glass with liquor, Mollie added ice in his glass.

"Where was I," he said laughingly— Captain Arden, an ex-marine, was a good-looking guy, a young athlete—his broad smile revealed his white teeth, especially when he smoked a cigar.

He walked towards the center, almost like a model, showing his bright aqua-blue suit, and turning around, he looked at us and said, "Over here is a color television; you'll be allowed to watch any program except news, and that reminds me," he continued, "we'll get newspapers, but then again, they'll be censored as to eliminate anything concerning the Manson trial. You'll get magazines to read." He stopped for a moment and said "Does

28

anybody have any questions?"

"I do," said Mr. Paul White, a thin, slow-speaking man of about sixty years. "Yes, I do," repeated Mr. White.

"What kind of arrangements do you have for those of us who would like to attend church on Sunday?"

"I'm glad you brought that up, Mr. White," Captain Arden replied quickly. "How many Catholics? Raise your hands please."

Four of us raised our hands. There were four Protestants, and four who did not state their religious denomination.

"St. Basil's Cathedral, a Catholic church, is only two or three blocks from the hotel," said Mr. Payne, a gray-haired, handsome, medium-sized man. "We could go there."

"That'll be fine, what about the rest? I mean, the Protestants," inquired the Captain.

"Well, I atttend a Presbyterian Church," said the pious-looking Mr. White.

"It doesn't matter to me, I'm flexible," jovially said the red-headed lady, whose name she had told me was Mildred Osborne.

There were so many questions about little and insignificant details that Captain Arden, unable to answer them, suggested that one of the bailiffs would look into the precise schedule of masses and services and that it would be posted on a bulletin board for everyone, to see. Mollie Kane promptly volunteered to take care of that.

"Where's the bulletin board?" asked Mr. Scalise. "We don't know yet, but you can check with the bailiff sitting behind the desk in front of the elevator," Mollie answered loudly.

"And what about our rooms," still asked Mr. Scalise. "Why don't we settle down in our rooms and then we can continue," suggested Mr. Welch, but his voice was drowned out as someone asked repeatedly: "Captain Arden, Captain Arden"—we all directed our attention to a woman of about 60 years of age, but suddenly her question was interrupted when she tried to clear her throat—it sounded almost like a grating rattle.

The Captain waited and said, "Yes, Mrs. Madison?"

For a moment, she forgot what she was going to ask and openly she stated "Miss, not *Mrs.*, if you don't mind."

"Oh, I'm terribly sorry, Miss Madison," apologetically responded the young officer. Then, in a friendlier manner, he asked her again, "Do you have a question?"

"Yes," once more she cleared her throat and began to speak with a raspy voice. "I'd like to know about telephone calls and also the visiting hours."

"Surely, you'll be allowed to make one call per day," said the Captain, and then looking around the room, "and that phone call should be limited to a five-minute conversation. You will not be allowed to receive calls unless there's an emergency. Unfortunately, we do not have a telephone switchboard and we must control incoming and outgoing telephone calls. We don't want strangers to call you on the phone."

"Why?" someone asked. "Because the defense lawyers will do anything in their power to appeal for a mistrial in this case. You don't know half of what they may do to cause a mistrial. So needless to say, you are not, I repeat, you are not to talk nor discuss the case with your family or anyone else. No exceptions."

"Yes, Mrs. Hart?" asked the Captain, as he pointed to the attractive lady whom I had talked briefly with in the Courtroom.

"My husband is bringing some things this evening that I couldn't take along. Would he be allowed to come to my room?"

Two or three jurors, having similar questions, shouted out loud, making Captain Arden stand up and raise both arms to quiet them down.

"Hold it, folks. Wait ... a ... minute. I was just coming to that, folks." Then, addressing Mrs. Hart, continued, "visitors would only be allowed on Saturdays and Sundays. Spouses can, if they want, remain overnight on Saturday nights and must leave no later than ten o'clock P.M. on Sunday evening. The spouses, before coming up to the sixth floor, should check with the hotel clerk if they decide to stay overnight. The charge will be five dollars. No children will be permitted to remain overnight."

"What about those of who are not married? Are we also allowed visitors?" coarsely inquired Miss Madison.

"You mean overnight visitors, other than spouses?" challengingly asked the young officer.

"Well, since you put it that way—yes. After all, I have a gentleman friend of mine who's going to call on me."

"OLIVIA MADISON," teasingly said a shaggy red-haired young man by the name of Marvin Connolly. Again, the youngest member of the jury repeated, "OLIVIA MADISON," with the pretense of shock.

"I see no reason why not," said the Captain, "we don't care what anyone does in his room—as long as it doesn't interfere with the judge's admonition —you can have anyone in your room. Anything else?"

"Yes," I said, "I have a personal barber who comes to my home. Would he be permitted to come here and do the same?"

Captain Arden looked at the bailiffs as to ask their approval and then as he spoke to me, he rubbed his head and approvingly said, "Sure, why not. We all need a haircut once in a while." While everybody laughed, some took the opportunity to refill their glasses.

The meeting concluded abruptly without resolving many issues brought by the jurors. Obviously, the Captain could only answer generalities of the situation. He himself at various times had admitted he didn't know the answers to many of the questions. He explained that the hotel didn't expect the arrival of the jurors until a week later, and that we were to have been lodged downstairs in the cottages amidst the gardens, where we would have had more privacy. However, the hotel management had been unable to comply with our needs, due to anticipated reservations. Everything did happen for the best. Had we lived in the cottages down below, perhaps I wouldn't have been able to observe and see the many interesting incidents among the jurors. We would have been more apart, and more independent from each other. Who knows?

During the time we were sequestered at the Ambassador Hotel, we learned a great deal about how to live with others and with ourselves. We lived together long enough to learn about our psychological problems that confront all of us from time to time.

Little by little, I became more aware of the alienation of Mr. White, the puerile hostility of Ray Harris, the drinking weakness of Olivia Madison, the aloneness of Betty Clark, the dissatisfaction of Mr. Scalise, the husband-hunting safari of Mrs. Ruth Collingwood, the narrow-minded behavior of Martin Payne, the immaturity of Marvin Connolly, the naiveté of Daniel Jackson, the self-educated Mr. Welch, the sharp simpleness of George Kiefer, the many trips of Edith Rayburn, the insecurity of Violet Stokes, the popularity of Genaro Swanson, and the love affair of Mrs. Hart and Tom Brooks.

Among the bailiffs, I can also add the leadership of Mollie Kane; Albert Taylor, alternately brusque and charming; the coldness of Deputy Tull; the servility of Mrs. Colvig; the friendliness of Deputy Renkins; and the array of different deputies who stood on duty every evening and also on weekends. All somehow reacted different, some friendly, some brutally unfriendly, some who acted as though they were guarding the penitentiary, some even had the thought that we were prisoners, and the hotel was a sort of stockade.

Everyone participated in our everyday lives—they all contributed somehow to our morale. By their behavior, we responded accordingly. If they felt pretty bad, either because they had had a bad day at work, or because of a disagreement at home, they would reflect that feeling when they came on duty and, we would notice. The bailiffs had volunteered for the assignment,

31

and they signed their names on a roster—they made good money. Some even skipped parties over the weekend for the chance to make some extra dough. More of that later.

Deputy Taylor dumped all the room keys into a large cigar box. Nobody knew what the rooms looked like—what size or what color of carpeting. One by one, we picked up a key. Mollie had a list of the room numbers on a sheet of paper and as a juror would draw a key, she would write his or her name after the room number. We all filed out in search of our rooms.

I drew number 701, the only room above the sixth floor—actually, there is no seventh floor in the building. One has to climb a long flight of stairs next to the elevator in order to reach Room 701. At the top of the stairs, there is also a door leading to a penthouse, which is occupied by a middle-aged bachelor.

The room was decorated entirely in blue—carpets, draperies, bedspread, chairs—you name it. The furniture was French provincial style. I had taken one large valise with three suits, two pair of shoes, underwear, socks; also, a color portrait of my parents. Everything had been disposed of inside the drawers.

My shaving gear was all set in the bathroom. All of a sudden, I developed the urge to open the windows. To my dismay, I discovered that when I drew the draperies, they were made so it gave the appearance that the windows were larger than their actual size. The windows on both sides were not only small, but one had to stand on a chair to be able to see outside. The north view was the roof of the Embassy Room, the place where Senator Bobby Kennedy was shot to death by Sirhan Sirhan. The south view was a better one—the parking lot.

A funny feeling got hold of me. I thought to myself, "It's bad enough to spend six months away from home, locked up in a hotel room, but this is ridiculous, there's not even windows to see out. Is this going to be my new home?" It felt like I was in prison—condemned. Thrown in solitary. Abandoned away from everything. My mind wouldn't release me. I felt surrounded. I thought the walls were coming closer and closer. Without hesitation, faster than I could imagine, I packed everything almost as if I was rushing to board a departing train ... and ran down the stairs which ended right in front of the desk where the deputy guard was seated.

"Excuse me," I said. The guard was watching television.

"Yeah," he responded.

"I believe there are six additional rooms available for the alternate jurors. I'd like to change mine."

"What's your name," inquired the bailiff as he looked at the list of the twelve jurors.

"Zamora," I answered quickly.

"What's wrong with the room?" he questioned.

"I just don't like it. It looks like a cell, besides I get claustrophobia, there's no window. Would you help me?" As the deputy pulled out a drawer, I saw the box with the keys.

"Here," he said, offering me the box, "pick anyone you like, and if you want to check the room before moving in, it's all right with me."

"That won't be necessary, anything would be better than the one I have upstairs," I answered.

I picked the first one which was on top, key number 680. The room was located at the end of the north wing of the sixth floor. Boy, was I glad when I first opened the door and saw the layout of the room.

The motif was masculine. The gold carpet, although it wasn't new, enhanced the rich beige wallpaper. Even four original paintings, depicting scenes of Los Angeles, were laminated with shades of gold leaf. A marble-top coffee table with a huge lamp on it was surrounded by two, black leather, contemporary chairs.

The most interesting feature of the room was a three-foot high and one-foot wide, wall-to-wall counter beneath the windows. The simulated wood top was made of formica, and the front side was covered with a decorative woven grille sheet which concealed an old radiator.

Above the counter, two large windows were covered with thick black and silver draperies which also extended from wall to wall. The view from the windows reached as far as the eye could see. The ever-changing skyline of Los Angeles was captivating. Two tall buildings, which were being crected on the new Richfield Plaza, stood like giant black boxes on the horizon. Nearer to the hotel was a tall, steel skeleton of a structure through which one could see the City Hall of Los Angeles in the background.

Just below the window, I could appreciate the view of the garden grounds of the Ambassador Hotel called the East Garden. There is an octogonal-shaped fountain in the center, and symmetrical flower beds around it. The green lawn looked like a green velvet carpet, and the well-trimmed hedges on each side of the walkways leading toward the center made, as I found out later, a perfect setting for nuptial ceremonies.

Later, when visiting the other jurors' rooms, I discovered that my room had, in my estimation, the best decor; and in checking their bathrooms, I noticed that mine was ultra-modern in comparison to theirs. The only thing

I didn't like about my room was that it had two single beds. I had not slept on a narrow bed since I had served in the Army. However, I decided to accept the circumstances as they were, and make the best of it.

Again, I unpacked and went outside to see how the rest of my fellow jurors were doing. It was a sight. Standing on the threshold of my door, I observed two or three jurors carrying mattrresses on their backs from room to room. As I approached Olivia Madison's room, I heard her say that she didn't like her room at all. It had too much blue, and she was not fond of that color. Mr. Payne, across the hall, who didn't like his room either, exchanged with Olivia. But Olivia, after seeing the room of her next door neighbour, Mr. Welch, asked him to exchange. She told him her's was too big and cold-looking. Mr. Welch obliged.

"One more favor, Frank, if you don't mind," asked Olivia charmingly.

"Sure, anything, what is it?" said Mr. Welch patiently.

"Would you care to exchange bed mattresses? Mine is terribly soft." Then, as she sat to check Mr. Welch's bed asked "How's your mattress?" but was disappointed to find out that his was not hard enough.

"How about yours, Martin?" inquired Olivia of Mr. Payne, who was watching the scene next to me.

"You can have mine, I don't care," dryly responded the pleasant-looking juror.

Olivia found the new mattress was to her satisfaction. Both gentlemen, plus myself, helped exchange all the mattresses.

That night, Mr. Payne discovered he couldn't sleep well on the soft mattress and exchanged them the next day with Mr. Welch, who also disliked his. I helped them to carry the mattresses, and finally they seemed to be satisfied.

On the way back to my room, I stopped to see Mrs. Osborne, who told me she didn't like the gold-avocado combination of her room. It appeared to be dusty and dirty, and at night made her feel warm, even when the air-conditioner was on. She was happy to have a balcony but she would have liked to have another room, preferably painted blue.

Violet Stokes couldn't stand the noise produced by the plumbing pipes.

Mrs. Hart disliked her room. "It is too small and stingy," she told the bailiffs.

Mr. White made a comment about having a small room and no view.

Marvin Connolly jokingly remarked that his walk-in closet was larger than the room itself.

Mr. Scalise stated that he didn't like his bed.

Mrs. Clark didn't say anything about her room. However, the next day she moved to the room I had first occupied—room number 701. She claimed that rattling noises plus the sound of the elevator operating all night had kept her awake.

Mr. Swanson seemed to be the only satisfied juror.

The floor occupied by the jurors was guarded twenty-four hours daily by two deputies on eight-hour shifts.

One deputy, seated behind a desk on the south wing, logged in a three-ring binder the arrival and departure of anyone visiting the sixth floor. He also kept a record of phone calls made by the jurors on a hand-printed form with space for the jurors' names, room numbers, time and the name of the party called. A separate binder with rules and instructions of their duties was also available for the deputies on duty. Unfortunately, they never made use of it.

For reference purposes, I shall call the area above, "the little lobby." "The little lobby" was located in front of the elevator. We congregated there before going to court or meals, swimming or walks, church services or outings. Announcements and a schedule of events were posted on a wall mirror outside the elevator doors, which was used as a provisional bulletin board.

On the north wing, another deputy sat facing two elevators and a stairway. His duty was to see that no one went through the hallway. There was another stairway beyond the halfway mark, and closer to the north wing. However, because of its existence, after a week Deputy Taylor ordered that the north wing post be moved to the middle staircase. "That way" he said, "whoever is on duty can cover both entries." "And besides," he added, "the rooms at that end need no protection since they have been assigned to deputies", it was customary for some deputies to stay overnight, rather than drive a long distance home. A borrowed chair from a bailiff's room was placed in the hallway outside Mrs. Hart's room. Directly in front, a television set and a casual table with a lamp completed the ensemble of furniture for the bailiff-on-duty.

"What time are we going to supper?" asked Mr. Scalise to the bailiff-on-duty in the little lobby.

"I don't know, sir," replied the deputy.

"Aren't you eating tonight?" questioned the retired electrician.

"Sir, I've already eaten." Pause.

"Damn it! I'm starving. It's past seven o'clock!" suddenly erupted Mr. Scalise.

Because of his false teeth, his speech, and the words he spoke, sounded like a young child. Thinking perhaps that everyone had already eaten, Mr. Scalise really let the steam out of his system.

"You mean to tell me all have eaten? What about me? I'm accustomed to eating at four o'clock every day."

"Sir," responded the young-looking deputy, "I ate as soon as I came on duty. The country provides lunch bags for their bailiffs."

Then, so as to calm down the demanding juror, he added, "I'm sure you'll be going to eat pretty soon."

Mollie Kane, after witnessing the scene, went to Deputy Taylor's room. Shortly afterwards, the sleepy-eyed senior bailiff walked in and called "Chow time!" Deputies Kane and Tull shouted "Chow time!" simultaneously as they knocked on each juror's door.

We all met in "the little lobby" and boarded the elevator. We stepped out on the casino floor. The Casino Floor of the Ambassador Hotel is a small shopping complex. It lodges establishments for the traveler's needs such as a small post office agency, hair stylists' shops for men and women. It also houses a known bank branch, jewelry, lingerie, florist and apparel shops, a drug store, and an intimate entertainment nook called "Sammy's Place," named after Sammy Davis, Jr., who is talent co-ordinator for the Ambassador Hotel.

Next to "Sammy's Place" is the coffee shop, where we were to eat our weekday dinners during eight months.

The area designated for the jurors was located on the right side of the principal entrance of the hotel. It was an ideal spot for the bailiffs because it was away from the main dining-room area, where otherwise people would be within reach to talk to us and be aware of who we were, since the bailiffs wore uniforms. It was also an ideal spot for the jurors, because the glass windows, as well as the large door, gave access for us to view the red sunsets in the early evening hours. And, most of all, the parade of beautifully-dressed people, on their way to the Cocoanut Grove or to whatever function was being held in the hotel.

At first, the hostess had graciously arranged the tables together in banquet style with a "**RESERVED MANSON JURY**" sign.

"That sign has to go," demanded Mrs. Hart to Mollie. "It's bad enough to be locked up like monkeys, but to have a sign for everyone to know who we are—that's something else." The sign was never placed again. Mrs. Hart also suggested the tables be separated, and the bailiffs complied with her recommendation.

During the first weeks no one would seek a special seat or a table or choose a particular juror with whom to sit. No one knew precisely where he or she

36

was going to sit, and besides, there was such a need to know more about each other. I felt the more jurors I talked to, the more information I would receive. The more they revealed, the more they became known to me.

On Friday of the first week, we were taken to the Lautrec Dining Room at the hotel. That was the first time the jurors began to disclose their personal food dislikes. A trio furnished music for dining and dancing pleasure; the entertainment plus the food prices limited what we could ask on the menu. Mr. Scalise was the first to protest. He didn't like what the menu offered. He wanted a plain hamburger steak and would not settle for anything else. He argued with the waiter and later with the maitre d'—he lost. He ate nothing but an apple and a cup of coffee.

That was also the first night I discovered Mrs. Hart, who sat next to me, liked to drink C. C. Manhattans. Those who didn't drink, immediately wanted to know what the two C's stood for—"Canadian Club" she told them proudly.

That Friday night was the first time that I saw Mildred Osborne crying —she loved the music and felt that it would be a long time before we would be released from being sequestered. I invited her to dance, and that seemed to make her forget her over-sensitivity.

Mr. Welch displayed his dancing ability—he constantly asked Mrs. Colvig to dance. The 73-year old, retired sheriff proved that age is no limitation to enjoying one's self. He also danced with Violet Stokes, but as he told me later, only did it because she was the one who needed more exercise to reduce weight.

Having danced professionally, I opted to dance and show off a little. I invited Mollie, and she accepted, reluctantly, but only to apologize later for having refused, and for not having known that I was "such a good dancer".

The bailiffs awakened us at 6 A.M. and then led us to breakfast.

Being the first day, Deputy Taylor was not sure of the exact time for breakfast. However, we had to wait for him on account of oversleeping. Nobody paid attention, and instead we laughed and some even approved.

After breakfast, some wanted to return to their rooms and brush their teeth and see "Lucy"—a nickname for the bathroom call.

Others, like Mr. Payne and Marvin Connolly, would rather stay downstairs and wait for the others on the way to the sheriff's bus for the ride across town to the Hall of Justice.

The same type of transportation was provided at noon to take us back and forth for lunch, and at the end of court session, we'd be back at the hotel.

The routine was well-accepted and easy to live with—there was a lot of things we were learning about ourselves.

One might say we were developing a new set of customs, especially since we were among strangers. We joked in a shallow manner—we inquired about each other's family—likes and dislikes—hobbies—we discussed trips, vacations, and places we had visited—important people we had met—and we also made generalizations about domestic life. All simply to accommodate and settle our minds in the new surroundings. We accepted the routine and conducted ourselves as charming, likeable and interesting, making sure to avoid any conversation in regard to the Manson trial.

That first week at the hotel we did not go out, but remained on the sixth floor.

Our first day for receiving visitors after being sequestered was Saturday. Now I understand what a prisoner feels when he receives visitors, because that is the way I felt when I was first confined to quarters.

The clamor of new voices assured us of the existence of the outside world. The jurors took it upon themselves to go to other jurors' rooms and introduce the members of their families.

Children running in the hallway, and laughter and gaiety from friends who curiously visited their friend jurors.

Mr. Payne graciously introduced me to his charming wife, Della, and to his daughter, who was a nun, whose religious attitude denoted a strength in her belief when she spoke; and a surprisingly firm grip when she shook my hand.

My good friend Jim Reid arrived in the company of his mother, Mrs. Alyce Reid, who was visiting from Boston, Massachusetts. As if I didn't eat enough in the hotel, she kindly had baked a huge and delicious wine cake—one of my favorites. Jim brought me a bottle of Manhattans already mixed and a bottle of champagne as if to celebrate, but jokingly. I had remarked "Celebrate what? Being a prisoner?"

Our company was suddenly interrupted by another juror who wanted to introduce me to his family. Marvin Connolly, as he knocked on my door, said, "Oh! You have visitors—I am sorry, I didn't know."

"It's all right," I replied, "come in." Marvin came in followed by two young ladies, one of them I could easily detect was his sister. Anita—redheaded and with similar features to Marvin's. Also with him was his mother with the same outstanding characteristics, and another young lady, Spanish-looking, whom he introduced as his fiancée Maria, whom I later found out was New York-born, and of Greek ancestry.

Likewise, I introduced Jim and his mother and offered Marvin and his family a drink, but they apologetically declined.

On my way to the recreation room to get ice, Mr. Scalise dragged me to his room to meet his wife.

Before reaching "the little lobby," I encountered Mrs. Osborne, who happily introduced me to her husband, Grant.

When I reached my destination, Mr. Swanson called me to meet his wife, Sarah. Also Mr. Welch, who had a daughter with two children.

There was no ice—obviously everyone had used it for their guests.

"Mr. Zamora, do you have any guests today?" asked Deputy Mollie Kane.

"Yes, of course," I replied.

"Instead of having lunch down in the coffee shop, we will have a buffet-style luncheon served here, and your guests are invited."

"Thank you," I responded.

This sort of arrangement became quite common as the months passed simply because it would save money for the jurors for their guests' meals. The county gave allowances for jurors' meals but not guests.

" I want you to meet my wife," said Mr. White, "and my daughter, Lynn."

Immediately behind them, Olivia Madison, on her way to get some ice, introduced me to her boyfriend, Dr. Costello.

Jim Reid brought my Sony TC-630 tape recorder which proved to be enjoyable and popular among the jurors, especially since Mr. Reid, a disc jockey for many years, had recorded a two-hour tape especially dedicated to the jurors themselves.

As the months went by, I received more tapes of music only, especially put together by Jim and Mary Hyde—two engineers at Los Angeles radio station KPOL. Needless to say, the Sony tape recorder proved to be the best friend I had during the many hours that I spent in my room. There were at least thirty tapes, each two hours long, with the latest recordings and background music, some featured the voice of well-known KPOL disc jockeys —Bob Harris, Fred Vanderhurst, and George Crofford. I also received comedy tapes, and even the Broadway stage version of "Who's Afraid of Virginia Woolf."

When we jurors walked in court on July 17, 1970, everybody noticed that amongst the defense counsel was seated a large, partially bald-headed man. Mr. Reiner was not present.

Judge Older had no sooner gone through court formalities when he announced that Mr. Reiner had been replaced by Ronald Hughes as Leslie Van Houten's attorney.

39

What a contrast was visible by the substitution of Reiner by Hughes.
Whereas the former was impeccably dressed and well-groomed, the latter reflected an absence of self-cleanliness, not necessarily because of his being overweight, but mainly due to his long, unkept hair and bushy, yellowish beard, and—above all—the wrinkled and stained clothes he wore.

Quickly I glanced at the section where the prospective jurors were waiting to be called.

Donna, the woman who had predicted Mr. Reiner's dismissal to me, expressed with broad grin, a look of confidence, and as a sign of acknowledgement, I casually winked at her. Later, her name was called, and as she passed the jurors' box on her way to the judge's chambers, she crossed her fingers for luck. A few minutes afterwards, she came out and sat, not in the jury box, but on a chair nearby. She had not been accepted. Again, she was right.

We spent the rest of the week going to court as in a trance. We knew we were there for a purpose and yet, because of the formalities the law involves or rather because of the Judge mentioning that, "Since the trial was expected to be lengthy, six alternate jurors were to be selected. The alternate jurors would hear all the evidence and would be available to replace any jurors who might have to leave the case because of illness, disqualification, or other reasons."

Finally, on Tuesday, July 22, 1970, selected as alternate jurors were: Miss Edith Rayburn, a retired civil service employee; Mrs. Ruth Collingwood, a housewife; George Kiefer, Jr., a State Division of Highways' employee; Tom Brooks, an Army Corps of Engineers' employee; Daniel Jackson, a General Telephone Company installer; and Ray Harris, a Pacific Telephone Company maintenance man.

When the six alternate jurors joined us in the jury room, there were anxious faces and words of welcome passed from one juror to another.

"We're stuck together," we all muttered.

It seemed that we, all the jurors, waited for someone to talk in low tones about anything, perhaps about the length of time we would be sequestered or predicting the same. And yet perhaps, deep inside, we wanted to say to each other that the trial wouldn't take too long.

No one spoke about time. So we tried to find some bit of hope by just smiling and joking, but at the bottom of our hearts, we knew and dared not say aloud that we would spend a long time in that tiny jury room.

Judge Older had told us that the counsel would take two days to prepare their opening statements. We were to spend two days at the hotel. No visitors were allowed.

An equal amount of excitement and confusion was generated at the hotel with the arrival of the alternate jurors. Disappointments and usual complaints were in order as each one of them discovered something they didn't like or wanted to exchange in their rooms.

Speaking of exchanging—Daniel Jackson, without much convincing, allowed me to remove the two single beds of his room in exchange for two single beds in my room. The reason for the change was that my two beds had two independent headboards. His were attached by a large single headboard. The two beds latched together gave the appearance of being a king-size bed. The moving of the beds from room to room seemed to put poor Danny into a state of confusion. He didn't know what was going on. He simply stood by and let me do the work myself. I didn't mind; after all, it was for my benefit and comfort.

"How did you sleep?" I asked Danny the next morning while eating breakfast.

"Fine," he acknowledged. He asked, "What about you?" I laughed.

"What's so funny?" he inquired, annoyed.

"Unfortunately," I confessed, "I woke up two or three times during the night, struggling to get out of the middle crack formed by the two beds."

The thing that bugged me, as I recall the incident, was that while I disassembled, moved, and reassembled the beds, Danny didn't say very much. When Danny talked, I noticed he had a slight speech impediment—he lisped as he spoke. The combination of moving and lifting and talking at the same time made me very exhausted.

The trial began on the 24th of July, 1970. It was a Friday. I was somewhat excited and was wondering what kind of a trial it would be and what kind of evidence the prosecution had in store for us the jurors to deliberate when the time arrived, but before that, obviously, we had to wait for days, weeks, and even months.

The judge had told us that this case would take from three and one-half months to five months. We had accepted; we had said yes, and were willing to spend the necessary time to give these defendants a fair trial. We walked downstairs, one by one; we descended into the courtroom, walking to and sitting in our respective seats. The courtroom was full of people, among them the press, sketch artists, TV news reporters, writers, and also, international representatives of the press from all over the world. These people were seated on the right-hand side. On the other side, the left side, was the general public and, among them were perhaps, either friends or relatives of the victims or

41

defendants, as well as detectives and plainclothesmen. There was not one seat available—only standing room against the wall—I looked around and I observed the other jurors were just as speechless as I was. They were projecting their feelings to one another without saying a word or taking a look at each other...at that moment, for the first time, I felt their way of thinking in regard to mine was of equal degree of magnitude and excitement. I felt the empathy in our thoughts, and for that I was glad.

The defense attorneys, the prosecution attorneys, the court clerk, the court reporters, the deputy sheriffs in charge, as well as the guard deputies of the defendants, and the defendants themselves, we the jurors, all; all were anxious as to the outcome, but first we were waiting for the entrance of the judge. The court clerk asked each and everyone of the prosecution and defense attorneys if they were ready—they all answered affirmatively—then he dialed a number on the phone, waited and said, "Your Honor, we're ready." A couple of minutes later, an electrical signal with a soft buzzing sound alerted Deputy Sheriff Albert Taylor, who stood up and looking at everybody, shouted out loud: "Put newspapers away and cigarettes out, stand up please, and face the flag." At that precise moment, the judge entered from the very same door we had entered. The judge closed the door, and as he stood facing the flag, noticed that the defendants had remained seated. I didn't understand their behavior, nor know the reasons for refusing to stand up and face the flag.

"What are they trying to prove?" I questioned myself, "To show they disapporove of the ceremony involved around the flag, or to display disrespect for something that we abide by ... the symbol of respect for something we stand for? You can sit and clean your rear end with the flag, but it's what it represents that's the important thing. If we don't have those things within ourselves then what's the sense to have a flag?" I didn't understand the reason why and I tried not to find any answers. The prisoners sarcastically grinned at one another, and then looked up at their counsel for approval, and then at everybody, but to no avail. Everyone in the courtroom placed a hand on his chest as Deputy Taylor recited in a very monotonous voice, practically undecipheral, the Pledge of Allegiance to the flag:

"In the presence of the flag of the United States an emblematic of the Constitution and liberty and justice for all. The Superior Court of the State of California in and for the County of Los Angeles, Department 104, is now in session, Judge Charles H. Older, presiding. Please be seated, come to order, there will be no talking while court is in session."

After the judge sat down, all of us in the courtroom followed suit. He addressed Mr. Bugliosi and asked if the state was ready with its case.

The senior member of the prosecution team, attired in a dark-gray, conservative, business suit with complimentary vest, responded "Yes, your Honor."

As he said that, he faced the jurors. From behind a podium, which was positioned in front of the jury box, he took a glass of water, and after three swallows, he put the glass down.

Looking at the bench, he addressed the Court: "Your Honor," then glancing to his left said, "defense counsel," and back facing us, "ladies and gentlemen of the jury, I know that you have sat through an almost interminable length of time, and I apologize for all the repetition. By now, I'm sure you probably have some idea of what this is all about."

"That's not a proper opening statement," objected Mr. Kanarek, with pleading hands for emphasis. Judge Older overruled, and Mr. Bugliosi continued.

"I believe in making a short opening statement. However, I must warn you that the prosecution's summation at the end of the trial will last much longer."

Again Manson's lawyer protested by saying, "Your Honor, he cannot say that at this time."

"Overruled," said the judge again.

The prosecutor calmly glanced at Mr. Kanarek and in proper form resumed again.

"As you know, there are eight counts to the grand jury indictment in this case. The first seven are murder counts, the eighth count charges the crime of conspiracy to commit murder.

"Defendants Charles Manson, Susan Atkins, and Patricia Krenwinkel are charged in the same indictment with all seven murders, that is, the five Tate murders on August 9, 1969, and the murders of Mr. and Mrs. LaBianca on August 10, 1969. Each of these three defendants are also charged with eight counts of conspiracy to commit murder.

"Defendant Leslie Van Houten is not charged with the first five murder counts of the indictment—the five Tate murders. She is only charged with the murders of Mr. and Mrs. LaBianca in counts six and seven of the indictment.

"So, I would remind you that any evidence at this time, which pertains solely to the five Tate murders, should not be considered by you against Miss Van Houten for the simple reason that she is not charged with these murders."

"Your Honor, Mr. BUGliosi is being argumentative," objected Mr. Kanarek accusingly.

43

Some in the audience as well as the jurors laughed mildly for Mr. Kanarek deliberately had mispronounced the prosecutor's name. The trial had just begun, and already there were slanderous glances among the counsel for both sides; and now intimidating procedures—what's next?

One thing I couldn't understand was that, what the prosecutor had said a few minutes before, had been said over and over at the time they were selecting jurors. Why would Mr. Kanarek object to it as "argumentative"? The judge himself had said it when he introduced the case, and later the defense lawyer for Leslie Van Houten, Mr. Ira Reiner, had repeated it so many times. Not once did Mr. Kanarek protest—why now?

The judge tactfully overruled the objection but not before Mr. Bugliosi again turned to look at Mr. Kanarek, but that time with an attitude of discontentment, and after he took a sip of water from the glass he said with marked reason:

"I will get through these opening statements despite the discourtesy of defense counsel.

"In the early morning hours of August 9, 1969, Susan Atkins, Patricia Krenwinkel and Charles Watson murdered five human beings at the Roman Polanski residence, a secluded home at the top of a long, winding driveway, located at one-zero-zero-five-zero Cielo Drive, Los Angeles.

"Those five victims were: Sharon Marie Polanski, whose stage name was Sharon Tate; Abigail Folger; Voityk Frykowski; Jay Sebring; and Steven Parent.

"As I've indicated, the Tate murders took place in the early morning hours of August 9, 1969. Later that same day, in the late evening hours of August 9, 1969, another defendant, Leslie Van Houten, joined in the continuing conspiracy to commit murder.

"Pursuant to that conspiracy, in the early morning hours of August 10, 1969, these defendants murdered Rosemary and Leno LaBianca at their residence located at three-zero-one Waverly Drive, in the Los Feliz District area of Los Angeles."

Mr. Bugliosi paused here, and in a voice charged with emotion, said "The evidence at this trial will show that these seven incredible murders were perhaps the most bizarre, savage, nightmarish murders in the recorded annals of crime."

Lowering his voice, he continued, "I am, of course, excluding war time atrocities."

Then the prosecutor stopped briefly to look at each one of us and in a demanding way, he asked us: "What kind of a diabolical, satanic mind would contemplate or conceive of these mass murders? What kind of mind would want to have seven human beings brutally murdered?

"We expect the evidence at this trial to show that defendant Charles Manson owned that diabolical mind. Charles Manson, who, the evidence will show, at times has had the infinite humility, if you will, to call himself Jesus Christ.

"Charles Manson, ladies and gentlemen, is a frustrated singer-guitarist, a vagrant wanderer, pseudo-philosopher and a megalomaniac, who, coupled delusions of greatness with a thirst for power and intense obsession with violent death."

As Mr. Bugliosi was making those statements, I observed Charlie was rubbing his beard with his right hand and was smiling broadly with the three girl defendants.

"But most of all, the evidence will show him to be killer who cleverly masqueraded behind the common image of a hippie—that of being peace-loving. Besides Manson's passion for violent death and his extreme anti-establishment state of mind, the evidence of this trial will show that there was a further motive, which was almost as bizarre as the murders themselves.

"Charles Manson derived his apocalyptic views about a black-versus-white uprising from the Bible's Book of Revelations, and as an avid follower of the Beatles, thought they were speaking to him from across the sea through the lyrics of their songs. The evidence will show Manson's fanatical obsession with 'Helter Skelter', a term he got from the Beatles, and that he found complete support for his philosophies in the words sung by the Beatles.

"When the Beatles sang a song called 'Helter Skelter', Manson told his followers they were forecasting the rise of the black man against the whites —an event he predicted was at hand.

"The evidence will show that Charles Manson hated black people, but he also hated the white establishment, whom he called 'pigs'.

"The evidence will show that one of Charles Manson's principal motives for the Tate-LaBianca murders was to ignite 'Helter Skelter', in other words, start the black-white revolution by making it look like the black people had murdered the five Tate victims and Mr. and Mrs. Leno LaBianca.

"It was Manson's idea," Mr. Bugliosi continued, "that when racial conflict failed to develop, that he had said 'I'm going to have to show 'blackie' how to do it', hoping that this would cause the white community to turn against the black man, and ultimately, lead to a civil war. It was Manson's plan to blame the seven killings on black people, then hide with his 'family' in Death Valley to await victory by the blacks—Manson foresaw the black man winning."

Mr. Bugliosi stopped for a sip of water and continued with his opening statement.

"Manson, ladies and gentlemen, envisioned that black people, once they destroyed the white race and assumed power, would be unable to handle the reins of power because they were too inexperienced to lead.

"In Manson's mind, 'his family', especially his chosen followers, intended to escape from 'Helter Skelter' by going to the desert and living in the 'Bottomless Pit', a place Manson derived from Revelation 9, the last book of the New Testament and from which he found further support for his beliefs and philosophies.

"Manson," Mr. Bugliosi declared, "thought that his family and especially he would be the ultimate beneficiaries of the black-white civil war.

"I admit, ladies and gentlemen, that the motive was bizarre as the murders themselves, but we'll show evidence to support it, and to help you to understand why seven persons died. We'll bring several witnesses to testify about Manson's strange and bizarre philosophies. However, the principal witness of who committed the murders will be Mrs. Linda Kasabian, also indicted for the murders but expected to be granted immunity."

Mr. Bugliosi continued, raising his right hand with index finger extended as added emphasis, "Mrs. Kasabian will testify of her involvement as a driver in two murderous forays from the Spahn Movie Ranch in Chatsworth. She will testify that on the evening of August 8, Manson told her 'to get a knife, a change of clothing, and her driver's license,' and that he also told her 'to do eveything Tex Watson told her to do.'

"On Manson's orders, she accompanied Susan Atkins, Patricia Krenwinkel and Charles Watson, to the Tate home at 10050 Cielo Drive late in the evening of August 8 without being told what was planned. Although she didn't enter the Benedict Canyon home or commit any murders, she saw Tex Watson shoot Steven Parent in a car in the driveway and watched Watson and Patricia Krenwinkel kill Abigail Folger and Voityk Frykowski on the lawn. She did not actually see the murders of the beautiful, honey-blond Miss Tate or Jay Sebring, who died inside the house, but she did see Susan Atkins come out and say she had lost her knife inside.

"She will testify that on Watson's instructions, she threw the killers' knives and blood-spattered clothing over the side of a hill in Benedict Canyon.

"Her testimony will prove that when the group returned to the Spahn Ranch and reported what happened, Manson had told Watson and the others that they had been 'too messy' the night before and that he was going to show them how to do it.

"She will also testify that on the next evening, August 10, Charles Manson,

Tex Watson, Susan Atkins, Patricia Krenwinkel, Leslie Van Houten, and another family member named Steven Crogan, drove into the Los Angeles area on a mission of murder. The killers roamed about, initially looking for their victims at random.

"Linda Kasabian will testify that Charles Manson instructed her to drive to 3267 Waverly Drive in the Los Feliz District, a house he had visited a year before for drugs and LSD parties—she will testify that she was told to stop, park the car, and then Manson walked next door and went into the LaBianca house alone and returned several minutes later to tell the hands of victims had been tied up and then instructed Tex Watson, Patricia Krenwinkel, and Leslie Van Houten how they should be murdered, without causing 'panic' or 'fear'. He also told them to hitchhike back to the Spahn Ranch.

"We will also learn from Mrs. Kasabian's testimony that Manson instructed her to drive to a Sylmar gas station and directed her to deposit Mrs. LaBianca's wallet in the restroom.

"Mrs. Kasabian will testify that later that same night, Manson ordered her, Susan Atkins and Steve Crogan, to murder a man who Linda knew lived in a Venice apartment house, but that she deliberately prevented this murder by intentionally knocking on the wrong door."

Mr. Bugliosi once more stopped and relaxed to take a drink of water, and as he finished, he whetted his lips and at the same time, he pulled out a handkerchief and blotted his face. He then proceeded with his opening statement to the jury:

"Ladies and gentlemen, the evidence will prove that the overkill tactics of Manson's followers showed that they were willing participants in the killings. They committed these murders savagely, brutally—Voityk Frykowski received 51 stab wounds, was shot four times, and was struck on the head 13 times.

"Sharon Tate, ladies and gentlemen, who was 8 and 1/2 months pregnant at the time, was stabbed 16 times; Abigail Folger was stabbed 21 times; Jay Sebring was shot twice and received 6 stab wounds; Steven Parent was shot 4 times. Rosemary LaBianca was stabbed more than 40 times, and Leno LaBianca also died under 26 stab wounds. A knife and carving fork were left protruding from his body. Mr. LaBianca's flesh was carved with the word "WAR" and three "XXX's."

Mr. Bugliosi stated in a very fast pace "that the prosecution would show pictures and photographs depicting the word "PIG" which was printed in blood on the outside of the front door of the Tate residence."

He also mentioned "that further evidence will show that the words 'Death to Pigs,' 'Helter Skelter,' and 'Rise' were smeared in blood at the LaBianca home."

Looking at the three female defendants, I noticed at that moment that they were behaving in a disdainful sort of way and frequently, at intervals, had giggled and whispered among themselves. At times, they had tried to lean forward in an effort to say something to Charlie, but Patricia Krenwinkel's attorney, Mr. Paul Fitzgerald, gave them a disapproving look. I also noticed that Charlie, on the other side, had come to court today with a carved "X" on his forehead and was repeatedly scratching it—he was careful to use only his index finger and thumb of his right hand.

The Deputy District Attorney, briefly, for what seemed only a moment or so, glanced at his notes, and said: "We will present to you substantial physical evidence—which will include a .22-caliber longhorn revolver, the clothing worn by the killers, and the car used on the two nights in question which belonged to a Spahn ranch-hand." Then he continued by saying: "The three young women defendants will be linked by Linda Kasabian's testimony, but we will bring additional evidence in each of their cases.

"Susan Atkins, the testimony will show, that she told to three cellmates in Sybil Brand Institute: Virginia Graham, Ronnie Howard and Rosanne Walker, about her participation in the Tate-LaBianca murders.

"As for Patricia Krenwinkel, the people will offer evidence that her finger-prints were found at the Tate residence on the inside of a door in the master bedroom, and also, the fingerprints of Tex Watson.

"In Leslie Van Houten's case, the evidence will show that she told Diane Lake, another member of the family, of her involvement in the LaBianca murders."

Mr. Bugliosi then announced that "Mr. Paul J. Tate, father of Sharon Tate, would be one of the first witnesses scheduled to testify." Then he added: "He will be testifying for the limited purpose of providing formal identification of his daughter."

In closing his opening statement, the prosecutor said: "I have always subscribed to an old Chinese proverb which says, 'The palest ink is better than the best memory.' Consequently, I would suggest you write notes, the bailiff will provide you notebooks and Mr. Stovitz and I will ask your undivided attention, so you will be able to give the people of the State of California and these defendants the fair and impartial trial to which both of them are entitled."

Mr. Bugliosi, having concluded his opening statement, picked up his notes and returned to the counsel table.

The judge, looking at the clock, said: "The court will recess at this time."

Looking at us, he addressed, for the first time, the admonition that we would be hearing every time we left the courtroom: "Do not converse with anyone or form or express any opinion regarding the case until it is finally submitted to you," and then he finished by saying, "We will recess for twenty minutes."

The judge arose from the bench and left the courtroom. We then stood up, and as we waited for the bailiff to lead us out of the courtroom, I noticed that there was great excitement coming from the spectators' section, with some people rushing out, with attorneys on both sides in the case being detained by members of the press, on their way out.

The bailiff, after having given each one of us a notebook and pencil, led us upstairs, unlocked the door to the jury room, and then locked the door after us. And then began what was to be a long game of psychological warfare as to who could use the bathroom first, which later was to become commonly known as "Lucy." Initially, courtesy was the byword—ladies among ladies, and gentlemen among gentlemen—of course, the situation changed and we'll get into that aspect later. As a gentleman, I obliged, and let the others go ahead of me, in what seemed to be an endless line, and while waiting, my mind transported me back to the courtroom and I wondered what kind of instrument Manson had used to carve the "X" on his forehead. I was under the impression that prisoners are not allowed any sharp utensils, and for that reason, I had disregarded razor blades because that would give an inmate an opportunity to injure somebody else or himself. Since I couldn't come up with a reasonable conclusion as to what type of instrument he could have used, I decided to discard the matter entirely and focus my attention on my very real physical need at the moment. The line didn't seem to move fast enough—"My God, are they slow!" I thought to myself, but even before I had finished the thought, Deputy Taylor entered the jury room and shouted: "O.K., folks—time to go!" Oh well, c'est la vie!

Mr. Bugliosi said, out loud, "I call Mr. Paul Tate."

A well-dressed man, sporting a well-trimmed goatee and moustache, walked into the courtroom, led by one of the female deputy sheriffs, Miss Mollie Kane. They stopped in front of the witness stand. The court clerk, from behind a somewhat tall desk, raised his right hand and asked the witness: "Will you raise your right hand please and repeat after me: 'I do solemnly swear that the testimony I may give in the cause now pending before this court shall be the truth, the whole truth, and nothing but the truth, so help me God."

At this moment, as I observed this oath, I noticed that they got "rid of the Bible"—maybe I had seen too many movies in which they always placed the hand of the witness on a thick and heavy-looking bible and, as usual, the serious look of the court clerk and trembling hand of the person who is about to testify with a soured face, and even a lack of vitality in his speech as he repeats the words; but now in actuality, I discovered that an oath is not administered in real court of law the same way it is shown for dramatic effect in the movies.

Mollie Kane, all this time, stood next to the witness. The court clerk said: "Will you please be seated." Deputy Kane signaled the witness to the stand, and as he sat down, she adjusted the microphone to his voice level.

"Will you state your right name and spell it please for the court records," said the court clerk.

"Paul J. Tate, P-a-u-l J. T-a-t-e."

"What is your occupation, sir?" Mr. Bugliosi asked the witness.

"I'm a retired Lt. Colonel in the Army Intelligence."

"Were you the father of Miss Sharon Tate?"

"Yes, " he replied gravely.

While Mr. Bugliosi picked out some pictures from a stack of photographs he had on his desk, I noticed Mr. Tate glancing briefly at Charles Manson and the three female defendants, who appeared somber.

The prosecutor approached the witness stand with some photos and showed one to Mr. Tate, and asked him if that was his daughter, Sharon Tate, and he said that it was.

Then the attorney submitted the photo for identification and the Judge, marking on a pad, said: "So be it. P-1 for identification."

Mr. Bugliosi then wrote on back of the photo the identifying number and to avoid wasting time, submitted three more photographs for identification in the following manner:

"I have here, Your Honor, a photo of a male Caucasian, may I mark it P-2 for identification?" The Judge replied, "It will be so marked."

"I have here, Your Honor, a photo of a male and a female Caucasian; may I mark it P-3 for identification?" Again, the judge replied, "It will be so marked."

"I have here, Your Honor, a photo of a residence; may I mark it P-4 for identification?" And again, "It will be so marked," said the judge.

If the above seems repetitious or boring, bear in mind that by the end of the trial, we had heard the same language used to cover 297 exhibits entered by the prosecution, and 69 exhibits entered by the defense attorneys.

"I show you People's—2 (P-2) for identification—do you recognize this man?" asked Mr. Bugliosi to the witness.

"Yes, that's Jay Sebring" answered Mr. Tate.

"I show you a photo of two people—a man and a woman marked P-3 for identification. Do you recognize them?"

"Yes, that's Voityk Frykowski and Abigail Folger."

And then, finally, the prosecutor asked: "I show you P-4 for identification. Could you tell me what this photo shows?"

Mr. Tate, looking at the photo, soberly answered: "Yes, that's the house where my daughter lived."

Mr. Bugliosi returned to his desk, sat down and stated: "No more questions, Your Honor."

The judge then asked the defense counsel: "Do you have any questions of this witness, Mr. Fitzgerald?"

Half rising, looking at the ceiling, and at the same time adjusting his jacket, he replied, "I have no questions for this witness, Your Honor."

The judge then looked at Mr. Shin and asked him if he had any questions. "No, Your Honor," he replied.

Before the court had an opportunity to ask the two remaining defense attorneys whether they had any questions of the witness, Mr. Kanarek and Mr. Hughes had already stood up and stated: "No questions, Your Honor."

Judge Older then told the witness: "You may step down."

I had noticed that Mr. Tate was completely composed on the stand. On his way out, after he had been excused, I observed with surprise that he went to sit in the spectators' section and remained throughout the session.

Following the oath, the second witness to testify was a rather heavy-built man. He said his name was Wilfred Parent, a father of victim Steven Parent, who stated he worked as a construction superintendent. When Mr. Aaron Stovitz, on direct examination, asked him to identify a photo of his son with a girlfriend, Mr. Parent almost broke down. It was a sad scene. Mr. Bugliosi, suspecting the agony of the witness, promptly brought a glass of water to Mr. Stovitz, who, in turn, gave it to the witness.

Taking advantage of the delay, rapidly I took a look at the rest of the jurors and noticed the ladies had a moving, somber reaction. The defendants were listening scornfully. Manson had caught my eye at that moment as to challenge my searching look, but I didn't pay any attention to him, because I wanted to write down everything said in court.

After a pause to drink some water, Mr. Parent was asked to identify, from a photo, the car his son was driving the day he was murdered. The witness was steady for the remainder of his brief time on the stand. As before, there were no questions asked from the defense counsel.

51

Once finished with his testimony, Mr. Parent stayed in the courtroom for a while; later on, as I checked back, I noticed his eyes had become moist and reddish, maybe from crying he just couldn't take it and hurriedly left the courtroom before the session was over.

Sitting on a seat destined for witnesses before taking the oath was a light-colored woman. She was noticeable because of her nervousness. On the witness stand, she gave her name as Mrs. Winifred Chapman, and testified that she had been hired as a housekeeper at the Tate-Polanski residence since June 1968. Her duties were to cook for Miss Sharon Tate. This witness was extremely nervous, especially when Mr. Bugliosi asked her to tell the court and the jury the sequence of events from the time she last saw Sharon Tate to the time she discovered the bodies.

She was unable to explain herself, and Mr. Bugliosi, having experienced almost a similar situation a few minutes back, shrewdly asked again to bring a glass of water to the witness. She drank the whole glass at one time. I held myself from making a comment to my neighbour jurors. In a way it was funny, but I guess we all laugh at the incongruity of others, like when we laugh at seeing someone slip on a banana peel, even though we are sorry later.

Mrs. Chapman testified that on Wednesday, August 6, 1969, she had worked at the Tate residence—that day, she vacuumed the floor and wiped windows and doors. When asked by the prosecutor when she had last seen the victims, she answered as follows: Miss Abigail Folger left at 3:45 P.M., Mr. Voityk Frykowski left at 4:00 P.M., and she herself had left at 4:30 P.M. Thursday, she added, was her day off, and rather emotionally, she confided that Sharon Tate had wanted her to stay and sleep in the house that weekend, but that she had declined her offer. The witness, when she finished the last sentence, shrugged, tightened the lips, and momentarily closed her eyes, all at the same time.

The Friday morning on her way to work, Mrs. Chapman testified that she got off a city bus and then walked about two blocks up the hill. A neighbor recognized her and gave her a ride, but not quite to Sharon Tate's house. She walked through the gate, and as she passed by, noticed fallen wires on the ground. She said she didn't think anything of it nor of the white car near the entrance because there were always cars on the driveway.

Then, Mr. Bugliosi brought some photographs to her for identification purposes, such as an aerial photo of the Tate-Polanski residence and also a large blue-paint diagram-layout of same, which later the prosecutor used to establish locations of events pointed out by the testimony of witnesses involved in the Tate murders.

Mrs. Chapman, while continually looking at her handbag, placed next to her, kept opening and closing the zipper with her right hand—then, to control herself, she would utter words to herself in a low tone.

Mr. Bugliosi would sort of snap her out of her uneasiness by asking her questions which she would answer almost like forcing the words out of her mouth. She finally explained that after she had gone inside the house from the rear entrance, near the maid's quarters, she proceeded through the hallway leading to the living room.

She noticed both Miss Tate's bedroom at the right side and Miss Folger's at the left were unoccupied—but that when she reached the living room, she was petrified—she couldn't believe it—she saw Miss Tate's body in a pool of blood and then a man—his face covered with a towel and a white rope connecting their necks. She stared, speechless, and started to run as fast as she could—she stated that immediately on her way out, she began calling for help and that she saw other bodies lying on the lawn but didn't stop to check who they were.

Mrs. Chapman, while talking, kept rubbing her eyes and almost on the verge of crying, she continued saying that she went out to the neighbors, screaming with panic and fear and saying out loud: "Call the Police! There's blood and bodies all over the place—all over!"

Unable to control herself, she tried to take one more sip from the glass, but to her dismay, the glass was empty—she hadn't realized that she had drunk all the water. She looked rather disappointed.

Mr. Bugliosi also asked her how many parties were held during the time she had been working at the Tate residence. "Only one," she responded, "one large party held in the month of August." Her final testimony was the description of the premises and living arrangements. She identified a picture of the caretaker, Bill Garretson, who lived in the guest house, behind the Tate home. There were no more questions from Mr. Bugliosi.

Defense counsel, Mr. Fitzgerald, asked her about a loft platform which was shown on a picture—Exhibit P-4.

Mr. Shin declined to ask questions.

Mr. Ronald Hughes asked the witness if she had answered the phone when Mr. Roman Polanski called his wife from Rome. She responded affirmatively. He also wanted to know when Peter Sellers, the British movie actor, had called—she didn't know who he was. Mr. Hughes, after having introduced as evidence for the defense an empty black videotape box, asked the witness if she had seen it before—she shrugged her shoulders and answered: "I may have, but I don't remember."

There were no more questions. Mrs. Chapman was excused and admonished to return for further questioning the following Monday.

It was 3:00 P.M., and again, we took a 20-minute recess.

"Please give your attention!" exclaimed Mollie Kane as she entered the jury room with a piece of paper in her hand.

"There will be an outing this coming Sunday at the Los Angeles Arboretum. Anyone interested in going, please check your name out in the boxes 'Yes' and 'No' provided on this announcement."

"Can we take guests?" asked Olivia Madison.

"Yes," said Mollie.

"How many?" inquired Ray Harris.

"Two at the most," replied the tall blonde deputy.

"What about kids?" Tom Brooks questioned.

"No children allowed," Mollie stated emphatically.

"In that case, you can have two more guests on my account," Tom snapped at Ray, who had already complained about that factor.

"Sorry," said Mollie, and left the room.

When we returned and sat down in the courtroom, a young man was ready to take the witness stand. William Garretson, twenty years old, testified that he was presently living in Lancaster, Ohio, but had formerly lived in the guest cottage house, behind the main house, where Sharon Tate and the others were found slain.

His duties as a caretaker were to look after a bird and three dogs, among them, two poodles, the larger called Christopher. He mentioned that to his knowledge, the property where Sharon Tate lived was owned by his employer, Rudy Altobelli, who at the time the murders occurred, had left for Rome on business.

Garretson, through questions by Mr. Bugliosi, testified that on that day, August 8, 1969, a Friday, he got up at 1:00 P.M. In the evening, he hitchhiked and went down to Sunset Boulevard to purchase a TV dinner, Pepsi-cola, and some cigarettes. He returned approximately 10:00 P.M. He pushed a button on the right side to open the gate, and when he entered, he didn't see anyone on the premises nor did he notice any telephone wires on top of the gate or on the ground. Everything seemed to be in order, and that he heard no noise as he walked up a path behind the main house.

The prosecutor brought to the witness's attention a large drawing to assist him in pointing out the route he had followed.

Mr. Bugliosi proceeded then to ask him to relate the events following his arrival that evening.

54

Garretson continued by saying that he received a visitor around 11:45, just before midnight. Steven Parent arrived by himself and had brought a radio with him—a clock radio—and that he wanted to know if he (Garretson) would like to buy it or if he would prefer another one. The witness added then that the victim, Steven Parent, worked in an appliance place or somewhere which dealt with radios and stereos.

"Did you buy the radio from him?" asked the prosecutor.

"No," answered the shy-looking young man on the stand. Then he continued saying that his friend, before leaving, made a telephone call at about 12:00 midnight.

After Steven Parent left the guest house, he (Garretson) wrote a few letters and listened to the stereo. He stated that he didn't go to sleep. Later, he tried to make a phone call before dawn, but he couldn't because the line was dead or the phone was dead.

"Did this frighten you at all?" inquired Mr. Bugliosi.

"Yes," responded the witness. Garretson then explained that he fell asleep around dawn, that he didn't hear any gunshots or loud screams during the night. He also stated that the three dogs in his charge usually barked when someone approached the guest house, but not, to his knowledge, when someone approached the main house.

No more questions.

On cross-examination, the witness continued saying that Christopher, one of the dogs, started to bark and woke him up. He tried unsuccessfully to quiet the dog down, when all of a sudden, he looked up and there was a policeman outside in the patio pointing a rifle at him, near a picnic table.

Young Garretson tried to recall the scene, but somehow his words acquired a certain apathy of disgust: "I didn't know what to do. Then another policeman came and pointed another rifle, and then another one, and he was pointing a pistol, and he kicked in the door, and Christopher bit him on the leg."

Everyone in the courtroom, including Judge Older, roared with laughter. For a while, the laughter relieved the tension of the witness.

In a more relaxing manner, he went on to testify that the policemen dragged him onto the patio and threw him down on his stomach. Garretson then said that he asked them what was wrong. One of the cops answered, "Shut up, we'll show you."

Mr. Fitzgerald asked him: "What were you shown?"

The witness somberly responded: "Two bodies on the front lawn and one in the car." When William Garretson said the last sentence, his face became almost pale and serious. He was also excused and admonished to return for

55

questioning the following Monday.

Before the judge adjourned the day's session, he once more issued the usual admonition—not to discuss the case with anyone, either among ourselves or anyone else, until all the evidence had been submitted to us.

It had been a hectic and exciting day. The temperature outside was terribly hot. We dreaded the thought of getting inside the Los Angeles Sheriff department's jail bus.

Observing the inside structure of the bus, I reached the conclusion that if I were to draw a plan view of the transportation bus, I would show that it is divided by a welded mesh wire partition in two sections with a door on the center aisle.

Besides the driver, the deputies in charge of the jurors always sat in the front section of the bus, The front section also had, directly behind the driver, an enclosed compartment to accommodate six prisoners.

"Why that compartment?" I asked Mollie.

"That's to separate female prisoners," she replied, "from male prisoners who sit where you people are seated now."

"How many prisoners can you fit in this bus?" I inquired.

"Oh, about sixty," she answered.

"Folks, would you give me your attention please," said a rugged-looking deputy. "My name is Tracy and I'll be in charge of you for the weekend."

If he hadn't mentioned his name, I would have approached him and asked: "How come you left the movie industry to become a deputy, Mr. Tom Ewell?"

His build, nose, and even the voice sounded like the former 20th Century-Fox actor, except for the times when he tried to be funny. He didn't have it.

"There'll be no swimming this afternoon," he announced. "I know you're going to hate me, but there's a reason for it," he confided.

"We're taking you out to dinner. The reservations were made for 7:00 P.M., so, to be in time, we must leave at 6:30 P.M. from the hotel."

One of the jurors asked if we had to wear suit and tie, to which Deputy Tracy replied, "Absolutely."

The restaurant we were taken to was Nicolai's, and to our surprise, we were the only patrons with suit and tie. Oh well, that's one of the things we had to conform to while being sequestered. We did as we were told—regardless. The reason why this incident is mentioned is because of the high temperature that prevailed during the day.

The courtroom's ventilation was very poor and most of the jurors were rather uncomfortable. Then, riding on a bus with no air conditioning and continuing part of the evening all dressed up was more than one could bear in a day. However, the chummy and agreeable atmosphere among the jurors did overcome the uncomfortable disposition of being semiformally dressed.

As soon as we arrived back, some of the jurors asked for and were granted permission to take an after-dinner walk on the grounds of the hotel.

Luckily, that evening the California Beauty Pageant was being held at the East Garden of the Ambassador. It didn't take much convincing to persuade the two male deputies in charge to let us go by and watch the parade of beautiful contestants attired in bathing suits. However, we didn't stay long enough to rotate our eyes from left to right or to build our ego in awe at the array of exciting, young-looking girls. Mrs. Ruth Collingwood, one of the alternate lady jurors, complained that the cold evening air didn't agree with her and she wanted to return right away to her room.

Mildred Osborne attentively invited me to join her with other jurors to watch the show from her balcony, Unfortunately, a couple of palm trees obstructed part of the view down below, and for that reason alone, I joined Deborah Hart and Betty Clark at my next-door neighbor Edith Rayburn's balcony.

As when people watch television in their homes they play guessing games during the Academy Award presentation by previously selecting a star of their choice as an Oscar winner, so we also played the same game among ourselves as to which of the contestants would be picked as Miss California 1970. None of us won.

"That's not fair," jokingly shouted Deborah.

"Why not?" asked Edith Rayburn, somewhat puzzled.

"We couldn't see the faces," interjected Betty Clark.

"Yeah!" snapped Debbie, "we should have guessed the winner by her derrière and not by her face or figure."

"That's right," Betty added approvingly. "We should call this 'the Rear-end Show' instead of the California Beauty Pageant."

We laughed quite heartily.

However, the best laugh of the evening was when, at one time during the show, while staring intensely at the girls, I kept on saying; "I can't take this... especially in my delicate condition." Edith Rayburn, concerned, and unaware that my statement was meant as a joke, hurriedly left in search of someone to "help me." She returned quickly with another juror, Mr. Scalise.

"Can I help you?" the retired old man inquired innocently.

"No, you can't," I responded laughingly, and pointing down below, I added, "but you could bring me back one of those voluptuous girls—just one. Hurry!"

Mr. Scalise, unable to cope with the situation, evaded the subject by saying, " You go get her—I'm too old for that."

"But I can't," I pleaded, "not in my delicate condition."

Everybody laughed.

Edith Rayburn, needless to mention, was terribly embarrassed and asked everyone to leave, so she could retire for the evening.

That second weekend we spent at the hotel was more relaxing and, in a way, less confused. The faces of the spouses and relatives of the regular jurors whom I had previously met became familiar.

However, the alternate jurors had their families visiting them for the first time.

On my way to the recreation room to have breakfast, the door of George Kiefer, Jr., a fellow worker, was open. He had a full house of people to whom he graciously introduced me. His mother-in-law, his delightful wife, Betty, and their three children—handsome 19-year-old Dave who, according to his parents, had performed as "Little Ricky" in the "I Love Lucy" TV show when he was a baby; George, Jr., a split image of George, Sr.; and their younger child, Lisa.

The recreation room was filled with relatives, children, and friends. There were so many new faces that it was rather difficult to acknowledge whose juror's family they were.

Tom Brooks introduced me to his young-looking wife, Claudia, and their two children, Mike, 13 years old and a dead ringer of his father's looks, and Sharon, 9 years old.

Ray Harris's wife, Kathy, didn't leave his room, so it wasn't until a month or so after being sequestered that I met her.

Ruth Collingwood had previously spoken of her two adult children, but they didn't come to visit her. She explained later that her daughter had been working late and that her son had gone on a weekend trip with some friends.

Edith Rayburn and Daniel Jackson had no visitors.

Betty Clark, Martin Payne, Daniel Jackson, Marvin Connolly, Violet Stokes, and Tom Brooks with his wife and two children, plus myself, congregated in "The Little Lobby." We waited patiently for the ten o'clock hour so one of the bailiffs could take us to the swimming pool grounds.

The baliff assigned to escort the group was a charming deputy sheriff in his late fifties, who readily admitted to being a part-time actor, as were other sheriffs. His attractive, greyish, wavy hair and happy disposition made him look younger. We never saw him again. Some months later I discovered he and his boss, Captain Arden, had an exchange of words which caused termination of his chances to work overtime after court hours and on weekends.

It was a beautiful sunny morning. The jurors, during the week, after court sessions, had the preference to sit and relax behind the diving board area. Late in the afternoon, the only place around the pool with sunshine was that particular spot, thus why of the predilection.

However, when we arrived, there was already a girl lying on a chaise longue occupying part of the area. The clamor of our voices and comments didn't disturb her.

She lay still on her back with her eyes closed. I noticed that she was wearing an imitation-leather bikini that almost matched the color of her already-tanned complexion. The skin of her body appeared to be soft and tender. An orange towel fashioned like a turban covered her head. Her body looked so extraordinarily well proportioned. Her full breasts looked firm and undulated and her legs were beautifully shaped. For a moment, I felt like going nearby to see her face, her eyes, lips—then, in my most deepest and inner thoughts, I developed the urgency to touch and caress her and even...

"Wow," whispered Marvin Connolly behind me, "what a body." I didn't say anything.

"Hey, Babozo," said Marvin, patting my back, and with a different tone of voice.

"Yeah," I answered, surprised at what he had called me. "Where did you learn that word?" I inquired curiously.

"Never mind that, I'll tell you later, just look at that body," he insisted.

I nodded affirmatively and responded, "Yes, I saw her, and it's all real, too."

"You better believe it!" Marvin commented sharply as he sat on a chaise longue, still holding his eyes on the girl.

"Do you suppose we can go and talk to her?" I asked Marvin.

"Why not! I see no harm in it," he replied.

"But what about the admonition that..." I began saying, when, abruptly, he cut me off, and shrugging his shoulders, he repeated my question, "What about the admonition?"

"Well," I hesitated, "you know that we can't talk to people," but he quickly replied, "The judge didn't say we can't talk to people. The admonition refers only to..."

"I know what the admonition refers to," I intervened, "it refers only to the case, and I'm not interested in talking about that. Besides," I kept on saying, "she doesn't even know who I am, less yet that I am a juror on the Manson trial. Right?"

Marvin didn't say anything. He took one last puff on a cigarette, looked at me, and then searched for a place to dispose of it.

Without uttering a word, I pointed behind him to an empty ash tray on a small, round table which he took in his hand and, as he put the cigarette out, again stared at me and said, "What are you going to say?"

"Well, I can ask her for a match," I hesitantly replied, still watching his fingers mashing the cigarette.

"But you don't smoke!" he exclaimed and began to laugh, which sounded more like a cackling noise.

"Well, I'll think of something else... like, what's her name, and don't tell me she doesn't have a name," I snapped defensively.

"Of course, she has a name, but that's not the point."

"What's the point then?"

"Marvin Connolly... hey, Marvin, you have visitors," yelled Violet Stokes, already swimming in the pool.

Marvin and I glanced at the entrance gate to see who his visitors were. His mother and sister Anita were standing and waving at him while his fiancée Maria was coming toward us.

"Go ahead and talk to her," said Marvin, while waving back, and then, lowering his voice, he added, "Introduce me to her later." He left and walked away to meet Maria, who gladly kissed him.

In the background, Anita was waving at me. Graciously, I acknowledged her greeting by cupping my two hands in front of my mouth and softly yelled, "Hi, how are you?"

"Fine," she cried back.

"Hi, Bill," Maria said, and turned back leading Marvin by the hand to see his family.

A tall, friendly grey-haired deputy sheriff was standing at the girl's side. She was seated, pulling a cigarette out of a package, while he was waiting to light it for her. I still couldn't see her face. However, when she looked up and lifted her chin to accept the light, something stirred in my mind. Something made me wonder and search deep inside the storage of my thoughts.

"Where have I seen her?" I questioned myself, "Where?" Stupified, I sat on a nearby chaise longue and began rubbing my nose gently as to recollect a memory.

"Where?" I asked myself again, while unconsciously, my eyes fixed their attention in the crystalline water of the pool. I gazed intensely at the blue water.

Momentarily, away from everything and almost like being in another world, I visualized that interwoven strands of thoughts emanating out of my brain resembled those beams of solar rays cutting through the surface of the water.

"Where have I seen this girl before?" No answer.

My mind went on searching as deep as the lowest part of the pool in front of me. Suddenly, the morning sun dazzled me for a second. It was then when I noticed the silhouette of myself reflected on the water like a replica of Rodin's "The Thinker."

The reverie of my mind was brusquely awakened by the sound of splashing water.

Unable to remember and somewhat annoyed, I decided the best thing to do was to go in the water to "cool off" my mind, hoping perhaps the water would help to refresh my memory. With thoughts still on my mind, I plunged into the water by executing a jackknife, then, swam the length of the pool twice and rested upon the edge, still looking at the girl.

"Hi!" I said to the deputy as I approached him. The girl just stared at me.

"Hi!" he replied.

"I know we're not supposed to talk to strangers, but will you please tell the young lady that she reminds me of someone?"

The deputy laughed, and was about to relay my message when the girl coquettishly said, looking at the sheriff, "Tell the young man to whom you are speaking that he's wrong."

Then, defiantly, she turned around and, looking directly in my eyes, continued saying, "The young lady who I remind him of,,, it's me."

"In that case," I answered back, "would you tell the young lady in question that I'm very sorry, but if she'd be good enough to give me her name and phone number, I'd get in touch."

"Just a second!" disapprovingly snapped the deputy. "Mr. Zamora, I'm sorry, but you cannot talk with this lady."

"Why not?" I inquired, "She says she knows me, isn't that enough?"

"Perhaps, but not while I'm on duty," he replied firmly.

Resignedly, I answered, "I guess so," and went back to swim until I became totally exhausted. In fact, my overdiving and swimming activities caused me to finally fall upon a chaise longue and collapse in a long and restless sleep.

The sprinkling of water upon my face aroused me, and I opened my eyes to see Tom Brooks standing over me and hearing him say, "Hey Bill."

"Yeah," I answered half awakened.

"What did the deputy tell you?"

"Oh, nothing," I responded. "He just wouldn't allow me to talk to the girl."

"What a chicken shit," he exclaimed, half smiling.

I smiled back and picked up a book I had brought down with me to read— *Johnny Got his Gun,* by Dalton Trumbo.

The deputy had had the know-how and he was in uniform and all that, and the girl was very nice to look at. I didn't take it personally because in a sense talking to her was not permissable, so he was doing his duty, and of course he was invested with that duty.

That night, after dinner, we were told that a movie was going to be shown in the recreation room. Having previous experience in handling 16 millimeter sound projectors, I offered my services as projectionist to the bailiff in charge, since he openly confided that he had no knowledge of how to operate the machine. At my suggestion, we used the wall to project the movie instead of a small screen that had been provided. I also suggested to place the projector in the adjoining room to prevent the sound of the machine from interfering with the movie dialogue.

The audience participation was enthusiastic during the first reel; however, everyone left except Mr. Welch, George Kiefer, and Paul White and family.

The name of the movie was *Charade* with Cary Grant and Audrey Hepburn.

That Sunday, at one o'clock, some jurors and guests, plus jurors who had no visitors, were taken on an outing to the Los Angeles State and County Arboretum, located next to the Santa Anita Racetrack. The proximity of the outing made the bailiffs decide to return to the hotel for dinner.

Mrs. Chapman and young Garretson appeared on Monday morning, but their testimonies didn't add anything new.

The next witness was a rather handsome Mexican-looking man wearing a sportslike jacket. He stated his name was Frank Guerrero and briefly testified that he had been hired as a painter by Peter Shaw, a decorator. Furthermore, he testified that on Wednesday, August the sixth, he had gone to the Polanski residence to estimate the job which was a small back bedroom. On Thursday, August the seventh, he began to paint until 3:00 P.M. He worked all day Friday until 1:30 P.M. He was supposed to return the next Monday.

Mr. Bugliosi brought to him a photograph depicting the dining room of Sharon Tate and asked Guerrero if the screen window shown on the ground had been the same way when he left on Friday.

He replied, "No."

"No more questions."

Mr. Fitzgerald questioning: "Mr. Guerrero, did you meet any of the victims at the Tate house?"

"Yes," responded the painter, "except Jay Sebring, I knew of him because of the maid."

Mr. Shinn asked: "Where did you meet Voityk Frykowski?"

"In the back of the house—swimming."

"Dismissed."

"I worked five years as a gardener on the grounds of the Tate residence," testified the next witness—35-year-old dark-complected Tom Vargas. The senior prosecutor, Mr. Bugliosi, asked him what time he arrived at the premises and also when was the last time he saw any of the victims. Vargas stated that he arrived on Friday between 4:30 and 5:00 P.M.

Then he said, "Abigail Folger was leaving, she was driving a yellow convertible car." Then he saw Voityk Frykowski getting ready to leave by himself. Shortly after, Abigail left.

Later, he said he saw Mrs. Tate, Bill Garretson, and his (Vargas's) brother, Dave Martinez, also employed. He began working. He turned on the sprinklers, his duties were mainly watering and mowing the lawn.

"Did you see Mrs. Chapman?" asked Bugliosi.

"Yes," the witness said, "she left about 5:30. Later on, someone delivered two trunks, received a receipt, and signed it."

Then, because he knew Sharon was sleeping in the back room, he left the trunks outside. He saw Bill (Garretson) walking the dogs. He left the premises about 6:00 P.M.

The following witness was Dennis Hearst, a Bank of America employee, who also said he was going to college.

"He sounds like a smart aleck," one male neighbor juror said. Those who heard, acknowledged him with a smile of approval. The witness testified that he had gone to 10050 Cielo Drive at 7:00 P.M. to exchange a bicycle purchased by Abigail Folger.

"I drove in through the gate, pulled the bike out, and knocked on the door several times—nearly five minutes. Eventually, the door was answered by a man."

Mr. Bugliosi brought a photograph (P-2) of Jay Sebring, and Hearst identified him as the man who opened the door.

Sebring didn't sign the receipt, said the witness, nor did he see Abigail Folger or anyone.

Mr. Shin, on cross examination, asked the witness if Jay Sebring, at the time he opened the door, had anything in his hands.

"Yes, he had a green-colored bottle—like a 7-Up bottle."

"Was he drunk?"

"No, I didn't notice any influence of alcohol."

Hearst left the house at 7:20 and noticed everything was in order. He didn't return.

"No more questions."

It was nearly noon time. The tall and young-looking leader of the defense counsel, Mr. Paul Fitzgerald, stood up and asked the court if he and his colleagues could approach the bench to discuss some legal matters in connection with the next witness.

Judge Older decided to dismiss the jurors until 2:00 P.M. while he and counsel remained in court.

On the way to lunch, the transportation officer ordinarily would drive by the south and west entrances of the Hall of Justice building.

Occasionally, from the bus windows, we could see, exiting, the familiar faces of the press members and artists, as well as the spectators, also on their way to lunch.

However, one picture we became well acquinted with almost daily was a group of three or four girls kneeling on the sidewalk at the corner of Temple and Broadway Streets, in front of the Hall of Justice building. A crowd had gathered around them. The bus was halted at the intersection by a red light. The girls waved at us and, innocently, some of the jurors, including myself, waved back, not knowing whom they were. Shortly after, we learned from Miss Kolvig that those girls were members of the "family."

But what struck my attention was the headlines on a newstand: "Linda Kasabian's Day."

"Wow!" I said to Tom Brooks, who was seated behind me. "Did you read that?"

"Read what?" he inquired.

From the tone of his voice, I sensed he was trying to overlook my question. perhaps because of the judge's admonition. Somehow, I felt glad he didn't answer me. It taught me a lesson—it was the first and last time I would try to solicit conversation about the case to another juror or any other person.

It's not easy to avoid thinking about the case, especially at the beginning, when everything is presented at once. However, later, we jurors felt practically immune to speak about the case. No one wished to think about, let alone discuss the case, after a long day's session; a session which was filled with names, dates, exhibits, and a great deal of evidence to shock the most vacant mind.

Who would go home after a long day's work and talk about his or her

64

work? Would a typist go home and continue typing more? I'll bet she'd rather write free hand than type.

This type of philosophy could be applied to all clerics, professionals, and labor trades. There must be a reason why society has established an eight-hour working day with "coffee breaks" in between. Why is it that we go home? Why is it we have weekends off, or why is it we take vacations or holidays? Is it done with the intention of taking our everyday work routine with us or do we do such things to rest—relax—forget...ah ... that word, *forget*—that's what we tried to do—"to forget" until the time arrived to return and recycle our activities and customary duties again.

Linda Kasabian, star witness of the prosecution, could easily be described as a pretty-looking girl, who, under the artistry of a Hollywood movie studio make-up artist, could emerge as a beautiful young woman—slim, tawny haired, and petite.

When we entered the courtroom, Linda was already seated in front of the rail that separates the public and the court itself. She was flanked on both sides by two men, who were speaking to her in a low tone of voice. At first, I thought they were plainclothesmen, but I was wrong, they were her two attorneys, Gary Fleishman and Robert Goldman. Also amidst the group was Mollie Kane, who eventually led Linda to the witness stand.

Linda was wearing a brick-red dirndl skirt and a blue peasant blouse. Her almost blonde-looking hair was parted in the middle with two braids hanging over her shoulders.

Two bearded and long-haired young men walked into court and sat in two front-row seats. Their appearance was strikingly noticeable because of the white long shirts they wore, almost like Nehru-type jackets. Linda seemed bemused when the prosecutor asked the two men to leave. The two men were Robert Kasabian, estranged husband of Linda, and his friend, Charles Melton. Mr. Bugliosi explained that both men had been subpoenaed and thus could not listen to the proceedings.

Charles Manson's attorney, stocky Irving Kanarek, objected even before Gene Darrow, the court clerk, had finished reciting the customary oath.

Mr. Kanarek, desperately rushing his objection, stood up and shouted, "Object, Your Honor, on the grounds this witness is not competent and she's insane."

Immediately following in the same fashion, Mr. Bugliosi, moving from his table and into the middle of the courtroom, shouted: "Wait a minute, Your Honor, move to strike that and I ask the court to fine him in contempt of court for gross misconduct. This is unbelievable on Mr. Kanarek's part."

The judge, astonished as the rest of the jurors, calmly stated: "If you have anything to say Mr. Kanarek, come to the bench."

"Very well, Your Honor," replied Mr. Kanarek.

Then, at the suggestion of Mr. Bugliosi, the judge admonished us to disregard Mr. Kanarek's comments. While the counsel was at the bench, I could easily see that Mr. Fitzgerald was getting involved in what he was saying. His eyes and motion of hands revealed an agitated individual. I liked his demeanor, I wanted to hear what he had to say but obviously it was not possible. I said to myself, "That's a man to watch."

Meanwhile, Charlie and the female defendants sat staring at Linda from the very minute she was duly sworn. They tried to call her attention by making hand signals, but Linda just looked at them and wouldn't say anything. She appeared to be practically unaware of their gimmicks to catch her eye. The counsel returned to their tables.

Mr. Bugliosi, adjusting a microphone placed on the table, began the eagerly awaited testimony of Linda Kasabian, by asking her:

"How old are you, Linda?"

"I'm 21 years old."

"When and where were you born?"

"I was born on June 21, 1949, in Biddeford, Maine."

At that time, the prosecutor changed his line of questions and asked Mrs. Kasabian, "Linda, you realize that you are presently charged with seven counts of murder and one count of conspiracy to commit murder?"

"Yes," answered Linda.

Again, Mr. Kanarek stood up and objected as immaterial and asked Judge Older if he could approach the bench. Judge Older overruled the objection and wanted to proceed. Furiously, Mr. Kanarek then asked for a mistrial. Counsel and the judge had a conversation about the motion of a mistrial in which, ultimately, the court obliged and allowed the defense counsel to approach the bench so he could state, outside the presence of the jury, the grounds of his motion for a mistrial.

For the record, it is fair to say that Mr. Kanarek's reasons to object to every question the prosecutor asked was with the sole intention of making the witness feel confused, rattle her senses, upset the prosecution, and perhaps even irritate the patience of the judge. And the jurors? Well, we the jurors didn't appreciate it either, but we couldn't do anything but sit and listen like eighteen mindless individuals.

Throughout the proceedings, Linda Kasabian retained her composure and answered questions in a clear, calm voice, despite repeated interruptions by Attorney Kanarek, who was seeking to strike most of her testimony on various legal grounds.

He obstructed the sequence of events and every possible continuity of details during her testimony by constantly interrupting with objections.

The attorney representing the cult leader, Charles Manson, did object over two hundred times. A juror, George Kiefer, said to me during the recess: "Manson's attorney, Irving Kanarek, objected to the first 56 questions asked of Linda Kasabian, but was sustained on only two of them. How about that for a record?" I didn't comment, just smiled. I'm sure he was correct.

Linda was subjected to a strenuous questioning. She related every single passage of her life, including from the time she was a very young child up to the time of the bizarre happenings for which she was indicted. In between, she had been married first, then divorced her first husband, then married Robert Kasabian, divorced him, and then remarried him.

Finally, Mr. Bugliosi began questions that, to a juror, were important to write down for further use during the time of deliberation, such as when the prosecutor asked Linda Kasabian:

"Did you ever live at the Spahn movie ranch in Chatsworth, California?"

"Yes, I did," answered Linda, who afterward identified a photograph of "Gypsy" shown to her by the prosecutor as People's 28 for identification.

"Gypsy," whose real name is Katherine Shore, also known as *Kathy, Minime*, or *Minome,* according to Linda, was the one who told her of going to the Spahn Ranch.

"What did 'Gypsy' tell you that caused you to go out to the Spahn Ranch?" inquired Mr. Bugliosi.

"I told 'Gypsy' my husband rejected me, and then she invited me to go out to the Spahn Ranch...she said I would be welcome."

"What else did she tell you?"

Linda at that moment, trying to avoid listening to the giggling of the three female defendants, responded:

"She told me there was a beautiful man that we had all been waiting for... that he had been in jail a number of years."

Charlie smiled pleasantly at hearing that.

Then Linda testified she moved to Chatsworth Ranch July 4 of 1969, and that she met Charles Manson for the first time the next night, which would be July 5. Charlie was up and back of the ranch in a cluster of trees, and he was working a dune buggy.

Linda continued by saying that she had a conversation with Manson.

"What did he say to you?" asked the prosecutor.

"He asked me why I had come. I had told him that my husband had rejected me and that Gypsy had told me I was welcome here as part of the family."

Mr. Kanarek objected over and over about using the term "family" but was overruled by the judge.

"After you told Mr. Manson why you had come to the Spahn Ranch, did he do anything?"

"Yes, he felt my legs and seemed to think they were okay or whatever."

"Where did you stay that night?"

"In a cave up in back of the ranch."

"When was the next time you saw Mr. Manson?"

"The next night or maybe the next night...I am not sure."

"Where did you meet him?"

"Inside the cave."

"What took place up there?"

Mr. Kanarek objected over the last question and Linda's two attorneys stood up at the same time, objecting also, for the same question, and advised their client not to answer.

Mr. Bugliosi protested and asked the court to approach the bench.

During the several conferences between the prosecutors and the defense attorneys at the judge's bench, Linda patiently sat on the stand, sometimes quietly chatting with her two attorneys. The objection was sustained. A strike for Mr. Kanarek.

Rather than registering in this writing every single objection by the defense counsel and mainly those by Mr. Kanarek, I'll try to eliminate the repetitiousness of the proceedings and concentrate on the main issues of Linda Kasabian's testimony.

The following are some excerpts of her testimony in chronological order:

Q: The group was called a "family," Linda?

A: Yes.

Q: Did you become a member?

A: Yes, I did.

Q: You were a member of the "family"—what do you mean by that?

A: We lived together as one family, as a father ... and children.

Q: How many people were in the group you called a "family"?

A: I'd say maybe 20 stayed there all the time ... others would come and go.

Q: Were they mostly girls ... or boys?

A: Yes, mostly girls.

68

Q: Mostly young people?
A: Yes.
Q: Where did they sleep?
A: At the Spahn Ranch, some slept in the saloon, some slept in a shack behind the saloon...well, there were two shacks...and in the trailer...and one or two of the girls slept in George Spahn's house.
Q: Did you camp out?
A: Yes.
Q: Where was it that you camped out?
A: The first place we camped out was called the Waterfall.
Q: Where was that?
A: Near Devil's Canyon or in Devil's Canyon.
Q: And where was that?
A: One or one and one-half miles from the ranch...I'm not sure of the distance.
Q: When was it?
A: Maybe a week or a week and a half after I arrived.
Q: How long did you stay?
A: About five days to a week.
Q: Do you know who selected the campsite?
A: I don't know.
Q: What was taken, if anything, to the campsite?
A: A tent and sleeping bags, a few cooking utensils, a bag of brown rice, a few baby clothes for Bear and Tanya.
Q: Who is "Bear"?
A: Mary Brunner's baby, and Tanya is my daughter.
Q: That was all you took?
A: Yes.
Q: Was there any camouflage of the campsite?
A: No...I don't know.
Q: Were walkie-talkies used?
A: I don't know.
Q: Did Mr. Manson tell you anything there? (Again, her two attorneys advised Linda not to answer this question).
Q: When you went to the second campsite, when did you go there?
A: Possibly a week later...when I was at the ranch, I had no concept of time.
Q: You had no calendars?
A: No.

Q: One day just followed another?

A: Right.

Q: You didn't know a Tuesday from a Saturday?

A: No.

Q: How long after you went to the first camp did you go to the next?

A: About a week or a week and a half.

Q: Where was it located?

A: I'd say further up from the Waterfall, two or three miles...way into the woods.

Q: Where...?

A: Charlie found it.

Q: The second camp?

A: Right.

Q: What did you take to the second camp?

A: Everything. We took dune buggy parts, a dune buggy frame, some tools, a tent that could hold about ten people, some cooking utensils, a little bit of food, clothing.

Q: Was a walkie-talkie system set up?

A: Yes, there was.

Before the court adjourned for the day, Mr. Bugliosi submitted for identification, aerial photos of the ranch, depicting different spots and also photos of the other members of the "family"—"Brenda," "Mary Brunner," and "Snake."

Needless to say the end of the court session was welcome with signs of relief and contentment. We were all mentally exhausted and our fingers were worn out from writing down so many notes at a fast pace. Some of the jurors even claimed to begin to develop callousness at the tip of their fingers, where one usually holds a pen or a pencil.

As for this writer, while writing notes in such a fast manner, when a new page had to be flipped, the peculiar noise disturbed young Marvin Connolly, sitting in the front row of the jury box, perplexed perhaps at the speed and amount of material I was jotting down on my note pad.

We returned to the hotel.

A forceful pounding on the door stirred my senses. I was just ready to open the door when, again, a new knock indicated to me that it was coming from a different direction.

"Are you going swimming, Ramon?" yelled my next-door neighbor Mrs. Hart.

"Yes," I responded quickly, and questioned myself what moved her

70

to call me that.

"Okay, hurry up, I'll meet you in front of the elevator (the little lobby)."

Shortly after having been sequestered Mrs. Hart opted to call me Ramon for no apparent reason other than that she thought I looked more like Ramon than my true name, William. Ironically enough, in those days shortly before I was accepted as a juror one of my many ex-theatrical agents had thought that perhaps William or Bill wouldn't be sufficient to describe me physically, because I was contradictory of my physical appearance to what William refers. He thought that William would be very Anglo-Saxon. You would expect someone 6' 4", 6' 2". Zamora was a very beautiful name, he said, beautiful and very romantic. So you have a 6'2" who is a Zamora. They would expect a hunk of a man with beautiful looks, and really throw out that type of thing for women to Ahhhhh and so forth. I was far from what the name called for and so he said, "Would you please change that name? I want producers and directors and casting agents to know what to expect. The name is contradictory. It's deceiving."

So I went around asking for names and I didn't know what to do. I thought about everything. I went to people and asked what name. Someone suggested Mario or Tito, and I just couldn't—those two names Mario and Tito—just too diminutive. So I decided to take an uncle of mine's name—Ramon—and they thought it was beautiful, you know, Ramon Zamora. It's kind of euphonic and so forth so I let it go. But never did I tell anybody on the jury of this, and Debbie, for no reason whatsoever, called me Ramon, just out of the blue skies. Why...I don't know.

Mrs. Hart, an attractive, good-looking woman, wearing a fashionable one-piece black bathing suit with a short ruffle sewn at the bottom, was even more appealing to watch. However, that afternoon, I discovered that her ash-blonde hair was in fact a wig, and not her own. The wig fitted her so well that it even looked authentic and real, almost natural. I began to notice that whenever she went down to the pool area, she always wore a bathing cap. It wasn't until at the very end of having been sequestered that she revealed her real short and straight, light-brown hair, to the other jurors.

Talking with Mrs. Hart became quite a pleasure. I was attracted to her because of her quick wits, wonderful goodsense, perception, and general optimism.

It was fun to go swimming, if nothing else, to listen to the majority of the jurors sigh in unison. After swimming, everyone, exhausted, would rush to a chaise longue and collapse on their stomachs with arms hanging by their sides. They would fill their lungs with air and then exhale it with a sigh of

71

comfort. They repeated it over and over. The relief of being outdoors and relaxing for a few moments was indeed a superb way to overcome the lack of liberty and freedom.

Two prominent exemplars of that display of relief were Mrs. Hart and Mrs. Betty Clark. Their signs sounded like two women moaning and enjoying it, while being whipped.

Later, up in my room, preparing for dinner, I knocked on Deb's connecting room to offer her a Manhattan. Hesitantly, she barely opened the door.

"Here, have a drink," I said.

Surprised, she gladly accepted the cocktail, but most of all, wanted to know where I had acquired the bottle of "Manhattan already mixed."

"I don't know where Jim bought it," I answered, "but I'll phone tonight and tell him to get two bottles when he comes over the weekend, so you can have one."

"That'll be great!" she exclaimed, "I'll pay you for it. How much is it?"

"No, wait!" I protested, "wait until you get it—okay?"

She smiled and said "okay," and then, almost whispering, "Will you please raise the volume of your stereo tape so I can enjoy it?"

"Surely," I replied, "it'd be my pleasure."

Again she smiled while she thanked me and carefully closed and locked the door.

Deb's personality was a joy to share. Her constant companions at meal-time were, besides this juror, Genaro Swanson and Martin Payne. Both jurors catered her attentions and had similar family attachments in common, such as spouses and grown-up children. They understood each other and mingled very well, even though the two gentlemen didn't drink alcoholic beverages.

While at dinner, I began to choose jurors, those whose minds tuned in with mine; however, now and again, I would speak among all of them. Speaking with mutually minded people was a mighty tonic for my subconscious drives I had at the time.

Tom and Ray became very friendly immediately. We seemed to hit it right off. They seemed to be more talkative and receptive than the others. They would seek my company and even made sure we sat together on the bus, at lunch, and especially at dinner time.

We were allowed to order one cocktail at supper time, but by flattering the waitresses, the three of us would manipulate to be served an extra drink, free of charge. The service at the Ambassador was slow, so while waiting for dinner, we chatted and joked around. We made the best of the circums-

72

tances.

Conversation between men sometimes reaches limits where women are not allowed to be present. However, some close female friends of mine have assured me that a conversation among women, especailly when it comes to telling a sexy joke story, is even more shocking than that among men.

Well, Tom, Ray, and I indulged ourselves to talk "openly" in our conversations about women. One by one, we began screening the women among the jurors. We spoke in low voices so as not to be heard. Tom couldn't stand the "witch" as he referred to Edith Rayburn. In reference to Violet Stokes, they would say that her laughter sounded as if it was caused because she had something itchy between her legs. The jokes were interminable and, I might add—unprintable.

Ray thought Mrs. Osborne looked like an elephant and hated the dainty walk of hers. "Her big body and the delicate way she walks just don't match," he argued, when I defended her.

"You must admit she is big," Tom said suddenly.

"It's true," I acknowledged, "you just don't understand human nature. Don't you think it would be worse if she would walk heavily?"

"Well, she better not talk to me," Ray said positively.

"Oh, come on, let's not talk about her," protested Tom.

"Why don't we eat—the food is getting cold," I suggested.

"That's the best thing you've said all day!" Ray snapped at me.

"I agree," Tom said laughingly.

"I know it, I know it," I responded jokingly.

Deputy District Attorney Vincent T. Bugliosi, wearing a quietly cut blue suit with vest and a conservative, plain red-line tie, was busy at his table checking notes on a pile of yellow sheets.

The defense counsel were conferring with Charles Manson, and the three female defendants were speaking among themselves.

Everything seemed peaceful until Mr. Bugliosi began questioning Linda Kasabian for the second day. He questioned her about her life with Manson at the Spahn movie ranch.

Mr. Kanarek objected incessantly, but for the most part, was overruled by Judge Older.

"What happened between you and Mr. Manson that night in the cave?" asked Mr. Bugliosi.

"He made love to me," answered Linda Kasabian, "and we had a slight conversation."

"Can you tell us about that conversation?"

73

Linda stopped to think and then started to say: "I don't remember all of it...but he told me I had a father hangup and I said..." The prosecutor interrupted the witness in order to establish a fact by questioning her: "This is after you had sexual intercourse with him?"

"No," she responded, "I think it was before."

"Did he impress you when he said you had a father hangup?"

"Yes," said Linda and then added, "because nobody ever said that to me before. I have no father, and I hate my stepfather."

The witness appeared for the first time sort of moved by the question. The prosecutor didn't pursue any further questioning about her own father nor her stepfather, but about Manson's "family" recruiting tactics.

"Were there ever any male visitors at the ranch?"

"Yes."

"Did Charlie ever tell you to do anything with those visitors?"

"Yes." Linda looked at the three female defendants who were making hand signs at her. It didn't bother her nor did she pay attention, and continued, "He told us to make love to them and to try to get them to join the family. If they wouldn't, not to make love to them."

"I object... I make a motion for mistrial on the grounds that this testimony impugnes Mr. Manson's moral character and integrity!" shouted Mr. Kanarek. Judge Older denied the motion and asked Mr. Bugliosi to proceed.

The testimony then turned to a walkie-talkie warning system. Linda testified it was devised by Manson for alerting family members who were working at the back portion of the ranch. "They worked," she said, "on stolen dune buggies. They used a parachute over the dune buggy to camouflage it from helicopters."

She also testified that the "girls worked sort of like a guard tower with the walkie-talkie system, watching for passing trucks or if, you know, somebody came walking through, that would spot us."

The prosecutor attorney then wanted to know about other activities at the ranch.

He asked: "What did you girls do?"

"Anything and everything," replied Linda Kasabian.

"Like what?"

"Oh, help the men with dune buggy parts, take care of the cooking, sewing ...or other services for the men."

For a moment I thought Mr. Bugliosi intended to go deeper on "other services for the men" but he didn't.

Instead, he continued asking: "What type of work did the men do?"

"Mostly worked on the dune buggies."

"Did you ever see Mr. Manson do any physical work?"

"Very seldom," answered Linda.

I took a fast glance at Manson, who caught my eye as he was lifting his chin up to scratch it.

Linda Kasabian continued explaining that the family existed without any regular income.

Smilingly, the prosecutor asked her, "How did the family get their food?"

"We went on garbage runs...we used to go to the back of supermarkets, get the food they had thrown away, wash it up, and fix it."

Mr. Fitzgerald very seldom did protest; however, at this point he objected to the line of questioning, saying, "These people are not on trial for violation of the sanitation laws. Let's stay within the scope of this trial."

I, for one, grinned thinking that it was hilarious, but I noticed my neighbor jurors didn't approve of it. Judge Older overruled the objection.

Linda testified that the family ate "mostly vegetables...and never meat."

"Did Charlie ever say anything about what type of food you should eat?" inquired the prosecutor.

"Not really," said Linda while looking at her hands. "He used to be big on zu-zu's."

We jurors frowned and looked at one another. Some of us didn't know how to spell it and thanks to George Kiefer, who asked in open court for the spelling of the word, we found out.

Gladly, we heard Mr. Bugliosi ask "What are zu-zu's?"

"Candy and ice cream," Linda responded calmly.

"Linda, do you know what a sexual orgy is?"

"Yes, I do," said the witness.

Kanarek, like a rocket, stood up protesting: "I object, Your Honor, on grounds the questions by Mr. Bugliosi are prejudicial."

The prosecutor, well aware of Manson's attorney, corrected him: "The 'G' is silent, Sir. It is Bugliosi."

Mr. Kanarek apologized, but one could tell he had deliberately mispronounced the prosecutor's last name.

The judge waited and then simply stated: "Lets' proceed, gentlemen," and directing his attention to Mr. Bugliosi, "rephrase the question."

"There was a backhouse at the Spahn Ranch... it was called that?"

"Yes," Linda replied.

"About the middle of July in 1969, did a large number of guests and members of the family gather at the backhouse?"

"Yes, they did."

"About how many people were there?" asked the prosecutor.

"As many people as there were in the family and maybe three guests."

"Were these defendants present?"

"Yes," Linda said.

"What took place in the backhouse?"

Linda's attorneys asked and were granted permission to speak with their client as to advice her not to answer questions about her knowledge of what went on in the backhouse.

Mr. Bugliosi again asked the same question and Linda testified that "there was one particular girl. I don't remember her name. She was very young, maybe sixteen. She was very shy and very withdrawn. She was in the middle of the group and Charlie took her clothes off and started making love to her. She was pushing him away...and at one point, she bit him on the shoulder and he hit her in the face. And after that, she just fell back...then he told Bobby Beausoleil to make love to her and he told everybody to touch her and make love to her."

While Mr. Kanarek made a motion for mistrial, my neighbor jurors were asking among each other the spelling of "Beausoleil." Gladly, I told them and especially Olivia Madison, who didn't accept it, but apologized later. She was surprised at my French language knowledge.

Judge Older denied Mr. Kanarek's motion for a mistrial on grounds that Mrs. Kasabian's testimony was prejudicial. Mr. Bugliosi resumed.

"Did anyone who was present touch the girl before Charlie told them to do it?"

"No, I don't believe so," answered Linda, who at that point had maintained an extraordinary sense of composure. She kept her hands motionless and stared at the prosecutor unemotionally. Her voice was low and answered the questions without much hesitation. The audience in the courtroom was spellbound and speechless at the performance of the witness. Their minds were stirred by her testimony.

"After everyone touched the girl, then what happened?"

"Then he told everybody to make love to everybody."

Mr. Bugliosi insisted: "Then what happened?"

"Everybody made love to everybody."

"Could you define in more detail what you mean by that?"

Linda, without hesitation, explained: "Well, we all shed our clothes and we were on the floor and it didn't matter who was beside you—a man or a woman—you made love and touched each other and it was like we were all

76

one."

The audience was silent—only the sound of an electric fan was heard.

"Was everyone nude?"

"Yes."

"Was there sexual intercourse?" bluntly asked the prosecutor.

"Yes," answered Linda, "that is what I just said."

Mr. Bugliosi rustled among his notes and continued: "In your discussions with Charles Manson, did he ever say anything about right or wrong?"

"Yes...but everything was all right, there was no wrong."

"Did he ever say anything about 'sense'?"

"Yes, he did. He used to say 'no sense makes sense'."

"Did he ever say anything about how not to get caught?"

"He used to say 'you won't get caught if you don't get fought in your head'."

Mr. Fitzgerald objected on grounds of incoherency, but was overruled.

"Did he ever say anything on being willing to kill or be killed?"

"Yes, he used to say 'if you are willing to be killed, you should be willing to kill'."

"Did he say this many times, Linda?"

"I heard him say it once."

"One day in the woods at the Spahn Ranch, did Mr. Manson indicate to you that he was someone other than Charles Manson?"

"Yes, I remember he took me in his arms and said, 'Don't you know who I am?' and I said 'No, am I supposed to know,' and he didn't answer...he just sort of spun me around.

"Did Charles Manson ever talk to you about the Beatles?"

Mr. Kanarek, with a pencil in one hand, stood up to say, "I object, Your Honor, on the grounds of hearsay, conclusion, foundation," he corrected himself and using the pencil for emphasis, continued, "improper foundation as to who was present the time when it occurred."

Judge Older, as to help him, added, "Place?"

"Place, right. Thank you, Your Honor."

"Overruled," said the judge with infinite calmness. Everybody roared with laughter.

Linda answered: "Yes, there was a certain passage in one song where he said that he thought he heard—or did hear—the Beatles telling him, saying 'Charlie, send us a telegram'...he thought the Beatles were calling him."

Mr. Bugliosi's questions turned then to Charles Manson's attitude toward the Black Panthers, a Negro militant group.

Linda described that Manson told the girls to keep the three children and a boy out of sight, because the Black Panthers were watching and would kidnap their children and kill them. Linda slept on the roof one night to keep post as a guard.

"Did Manson ever explain why they were watching you?"

"He said they knew we were super aware, more than other white people, and they knew we knew about them and that they were eventually going to take over. His philosophy on the black people was that they wanted to do away with us because apparently they knew that we were going to save the white race or go out to the hole in the desert."

At this point, Mr. Kanarek and Mr. Fitzgerald asked to approach the bench, after they had objected to what Linda had said.

While the counsel were in conference at the judge's bench, I noticed Susan Atkins attracted the attention of Linda Kasabian. Susan, after having bit her fingernails, whispered, "You're killing us all."

Linda, without denying to have heard what the defendant had said, answered back, "You've already killed yourselves."

Mr. Bugliosi, after returning to his table, asked: "Did Mr. Manson mention the term 'Helter Skelter' to you?"

"Yes," answered Linda, and through a number of objections by Mr. Kanarek, she managed to explain what it meant.

"It is a revolution where black and whites will get together and kill each other and all nonblacks and brown people and even black people who do not go on black terms..."

Mr. Bugliosi snapped and asked her: "Did he say who was going to start 'Helter Skelter'?"

"Blackie," replied Linda immediately. "He used to say that Blackie was much more aware than Whitey and Super together...and Blackie was really together."

Mr. Bugliosi and Mr. Kanarek became involved in a slight argument. Judge Older, with severe authority, admonished both counsel "not to engage in colloquy."

Linda said she saw "Helter Skelter" written on a jug in the parachute room and on some door, but she couldn't remember where.

The testimony then moved into the events that led to the departure of the three female defendants, Tex Watson, and the witness herself, Linda Kasabian, who, allegedly under Manson's orders, went to the Tate estate, where the actress Sharon Tate and her four friends were murdered by knifing and shooting.

"Charlie," said Linda, "told us of getting white people together. He said that he was the only one to know how to get them together."

"Did you ever see or hear any member of the family disobey Charles Manson?"

"No," answered Linda, and then related an incident in which Mary Brunner, a family member, was reprimanding the children. "Charles prohibited her from doing it."

"Linda," said Mr. Bugliosi, "did Mr. Manson say anything about 'Helter Skelter' sometime during the day of August 8?"

"Yes, I believe that was the day he got back from Big Sur—he brought a girl with him—a girl called Stephanie. Then he told us about his trip, then he mentioned that people were really not together, that they were off in their minds, and that they just were not getting together. So he came out and said: "Now is the time for 'Helter Skelter'."

"What happened on that day, August 8, 1969, after dinner?" inquired the prosecutor.

"On August 8, the family ate together after sundown. Dinner time," continued Mrs. Kasabian, "was fun time, fun hour." Then she added seriously, "Maybe an hour after dinner...people were sitting around on rocks outside. I was on the porch and Charlie came up and told me off. I was standing closest to George Spahn's house. Then Charlie told me to get a change of clothes, a knife, and my driver's license."

Mr. Kanarek jumped up and objected, "Hearsay, and...may we approach the bench, Your Honor?"

At this particular point during the trial, I began to speculate in my mind the idea of writing a book about the trial itself. "Why not," I told myself, "after all *I am* a juror and what I think would be much more important and more true than any newspaperman out there in the audience."

The mind of a juror obviously reacts differently than that of the general public and press. A juror feels the impact of the testimony, then digests it, and after accepting that which is good, he discards that which is bad. There's no emotion nor bias against anything. The mind of the juror has, by law and moral certainty, to be sure of the evidence presented in court. Anyone writing a book about this murder case couldn't even touch the outside boundaries of a juror's mind. How can they? Is it possible that any of those press members and writers sitting out there in the audience, could say honestly "I heard everything during the Tate-LaBianca trial case and I believe the defendants are innocent or guilty?" Of course they can't. For reasons of being free they are capable to know more about everything...they ask questions about the defendants to counsel of both sides. They speak openly and exchange points of view, and are moved from what someone says. They have connections, they go places where events happen and are assisted by hundreds of phone calls at their offices and homes. They write everyday about it and are constantly on the alert to make any little detail appear sensational, appealing for the public. They live by the written word and it is their duty to sell it in order to survive and, along those lines, make themselves wanted as top newspaper writers with their ultimate goal of becoming famous novel authors.

"Me?" I questioned myself, "What chance do I have—I'm simply performing my civic duty." I don't have the training or the know-how formula to write a book. I wouldn't know how to start at the beginning. Then I thought that if I ever wrote a book, it probably would have to be interesting, catchy and appealing to the imagination of whomever decides to read it. A first glance at a book is considered half the interest to open it. The invitation to buy it would depend strictly on that very first page. What the author intends to say? Is it true or is it just fiction? Well, in my case, I continued thinking, everything is true, totally nonfiction. Obviously, the mere fact of sitting here on this juror seat No. 7 is not a lie. The testimony given by the present witness—it could be a lie, but then, her presence in this court room needs no proof. This trial has been covered extensively by every newspaper in the world as well as on radio and television.

My only reason for writing a book about the trial would be to let the world know what one feels being sequestered. There was no intention of me writing a book on someone else's misfortune. No, because a writer writes regardless. If you've got the feeling to write, you're going to write one thing or the other. Newspapers write good news and bad news. That's their job, so if they happen to report an accident, a fire, a drowning, that's their duty. It was a simple desire to let something out of me. I thought it would make me a better juror when the debating came. If someone brings something up I'll have something to fight it with. That doesn't mean I wanted to be contradictory for the sake of contradicting, but only for something I don't think is right, because morally I owe the victims, and not so much the victims as the defendants, the fairness of a trial, the fairness of the verdict. I don't want to condemn them because they had been there or because they were accused. I didn't want to accept it. I didn't want to believe it. I wanted them to know, to make sure, that I, as an individual, could put myself in their place, and not let circumstantial evidence make them appear guilty, but unfortunately, nothing came out in the trial that would indicate otherwise.

My intentions certainly wouldn't be to take advantage of the misfortunes of those defendants, but to expel right out of my chest what it feels being a juror in a trial of this magnitude—without any thoughts of capitalization.

"Why not?" I kept telling myself, "why not give it a try?"

At that very same moment, the counsel returned to their respective tables. Mr. Bugliosi started questioning Linda Kasabian once more.

"To the best of your recollection, what did you do then?"

"As soon as he told me to do these things, I went into George Spahn's house. I remember rummaging through a box for a change of clothes. I picked up a short denim skirt, and, I think it was, a lavendar knitted top."

"What color was the skirt?" rapidly asked the prosecutor.

"Navy blue...dark." responded Mrs. Kasabian.

"Then what happened?"

"I asked 'Squeaky' where my driver's license was, and she told me to look in a drawer... I believe I looked in all of the drawers. She told me to look in a box on the mantle and I think I told 'Brenda' to look for it. Then I went to the saloon because I remember seeing a knife there, and Larry was there in the front of the kitchen, and he gave me the knife, and Brenda gave me the the driver's license in Charlie's presence."

The prosecutor asked permission to approach the witness in order to identify two photographs. She recognized Charles "Tex" Watson (P-36) and "Squeaky," whose real name is Lynn Fromm (P-37)—both members of the "family."

"Then what happened after that?" resumed Mr. Bugliosi.

"Charlie told me to go with Tex and to do what he told me, and I got in the car and Sadie and Katie were already in the back seat, and Tex was standing by the driver's side."

Mr. Bugliosi stood up and walked behind defendants Susan Atkins and Patricia Krenwinkel, and pointing with both hands at the two defendants, asked, "Linda, when you say Sadie and Katie—are you referring to these two young ladies sitting here—Miss Susan Atkins and Miss Patricia Krenwinkel?"

"Yes," she answered.

Leslie Van Houten looked at Mr. Bugliosi and stuck her tongue out at him. He didn't notice it.

Linda was about to say something when the lawyer for the prosecution stopped her and said, "Now, let's slow down a little, Linda...you entered the car?"

"Yes."

"When you walked up to the car, where was Tex?"

81

"He was standing by the driver's side."

"Was he talking to anyone?"

Linda stopped to concentrate, and then, "'I think he was talking to Charlie."

"Then what happened?" asked Mr. Bugliosi, while writing on an 8-1/2 X 11 yellow sheet pad.

"He got into the car...and we started to drive away."

"Who's 'he'? Tex?"

"Yes, Tex," answered Linda.

"Was there a back seat in the car?"

"No, there wasn't...just the floor."

"But Sadie and Katie were there, behind the front seat?"

"Yes," Linda responded.

"Tex started to drive off the Spahn Ranch?"

"Yes."

"What happened at that time?"

"We got in the middle of the driveway and Charlie told us to stop. He stuck his head in and told us to leave a sign, and said, 'You girls know what I mean...something witchy.' "

Manson laughed softly at hearing Linda say that and later changed his facial expression.

"After Mr. Manson told you girls to leave a sign, what happened?"

"We drove off."

"Tex was driving?"

"Yes."

"At the time you drove off, did Manson see you off?"

"Yes, he did."

"Was he standing alone?"

"Yes."

"Did you observe the way Sadie was dressed?"

"She was dressed in dark clothing."

"Top and bottom?"

"Yes... sort of a baggy pants."

"Did she have any shoes on?"

"I don't think so.".

"What was Katie wearing?"

I noticed that Patricia Krenwinkel, for the first time, lifted her head up. She looked face to face at Linda, who, like before, ignored their consistent staring and proceeded to answer.

"She had the same dark tee shirt and levis."

82

The prosecutor asked the same questions about what Tex Watson wore the night in question and Linda testified that, "he was also in dark levis with a sort of turtleneck shirt...and he wore no shoes."

She also added that they all had taken an extra set of clothing with them, in addition to those each of them were wearing.

Judge Charles H. Older announced noon recess until 2:00 P.M. Before departing for lunch at the Hilton Hotel, all the jurors became involved in a guessing game. Everybody wondered what the middle initial "H" stood for in the judge's name. To make it exciting and utilize the idle time, they even bet one penny per person by submitting a name. Among names beginning with an "H" and which were selected: Horace, Herman, Herbert, Harry, Harold, Hector, Harvey, and a couple more which I can't remember. Violet Stokes collected the eighteen pennies and was to announce the winner after having found out herself through Deputy Taylor.

A few minutes later, we heard the familiar voice of Deputy Taylor. He walked in and said, "Okay Folks, let's go."

"I don't know what 'H' stands for," he replied when we all asked him. "I think that he just uses it for no apparent reason," he added.

"How can we find out?" inquired Violet Stokes.

"I don't know... wait a minute," said Deputy Taylor.

"Judge Older was a member of the 'Flying Tiger' Squadron. He was awarded many medals for having shot down enemy planes. There's a book with all the member's pictures and he's on it. Maybe there you can find it."

"Do you have the book?" asked Ray Harris.

"No," replied the sleepy-looking deputy.

"Where can we get it?" inquired two or three other jurors.

"I don't know," answered the tall, brusque sheriff.

That was the end of that game and I don't know who ended up with eighteen pennies.

Back in the courtroom.

"Linda," said Mr. Bugliosi, "as you drove off, did you know what you were going to do?"

"No, I did not know where we were going."

"Did you ask Tex, Sadie, or Katie what they were going to do that night?"

"No, I did not."

"Was there any reason that you did not ask them what they were going to do?"

"I was told right from the beginning not to ask questions."

"Who told you that?"

"Charlie did... they... they all did."

"You did not know what was going to happen?"

"Yes, I thought we were going to go on a creepy-crawling mission."

"What is a creepy-crawling mission?"

"A creepy-crawling mission is when you creep and crawl into people's houses and take things that originally belonged to you...because, in the beginning, it belonged to you."

Linda proceeded to relate one particular occasion in which Charlie was being fitted by some of the girls who had made him a long black cape. "He twirled the cape and covered his face and, in a low tone of voice, said something like 'Now, when I go creepy-crawling, people won't see me because they will think I am a bush or a tree.'"

Linda added that "all the girls laughed."

Oddly enough, now that we were in court, as I glanced at Charlie, he didn't find Linda's statement as funny as it appeared to the audience in the courtroom.

The judge admonished Mrs. Kasabian not to volunteer any information on her own or speculate on the question, unless a question had been put to her by the deputy district attorney.

The prosecutor shrewdly and deliberately asked questions so as not to skip any infinite detail of the continuity of events or of the state of mind of the witness. A very clever and ingenuous way—easy to follow and almost like answering questions I may have asked her myself had I been in charge of the interrogation.

He continued.

"Were there a gun and knives in the car?"

"Yes... three knives and one gun."

"Where was the gun?"

"The gun was in the glove compartment?"

"Where were the three knives?"

"On the front seat."

"Did you have any idea whatsoever that the knives and gun might be used to kill people?"

"No," responded Linda, appearing a little bit sad.

Mr. Bugliosi then asked Mrs. Kasabian to describe the knives.

"One," she said, "was a 'buck knife,'" which she had owned when she arrived at the ranch. One had a tape-wrapped handle and had been handed to her by Larry Jones, and the third knife resembled the second one. Linda identified her knife when the prosecutor showed it to her. For the record,

84

it was marked as P-39.

Mr. Bugliosi resumed by asking, "As you were driving, did Tex tell you what to do with the knives and the gun?"

"Yes, he did. He told me to wrap them in a piece of clothing which was my skirt, and if we got stopped or anything, to throw them out."

Linda also testified she had sharpened such knives while she stayed at the ranch and that she sharpened part of the top side of the blades as well as the bottom.

"Where did Tex drive the car to?"

"To a house on the top of a hill."

"How long did it take to get there?"

"I really don't know... maybe a half hour or an hour."

"What time did you arrive there?"

"Four or five hours after it became dark."

"Did Tex do all the driving?"

"On the way, yes."

"What happened when you arrived at the house?"

Linda, using her hand, replied, "Tex parked the car near a telephone pole... I don't know if he had wire cutters or what, but I saw the wires fall off after he climbed the pole."

"How many wires... two or..."

"There were a few."

"What happened then?"

"He got back into the car and drove down the hill and parked there."

"What happened at that point?"

"We got out of the car."

"The four of you?"

"Yes."

"Was Tex carrying anything at this time?"

"Tex was carrying some rope."

Again, the prosecutor, for purposes of identification, brought a white shiny rope and showing it to Linda said, "I have here a white—it appears to be nylon—rope, and I ask you if you have ever seen this rope?"

"It looks like the rope that Tex was carrying." The witness, unable to control herself, gasped for breath and slightly turned her eyes away from the blood-stained thick white rope.

The prosecutor continued.

"After you, all four of you, walked up the hill, what happened?"

"We climbed over the fence, and lights were coming towards us, and Tex

85

told us to get back and sit down."

Immediately following that, tears began to run down Linda's cheeks when Mr. Bugliosi showed her a .22-caliber Longhorn westernstyle pistol. The court room was tense and silent.

"Are you alright?" asked Judge Older. Linda didn't answer.

Judge Older added, "Are you able to go on Mrs. Kasabian?"

"Yes, I am," responded Linda, while sobbing and wiping her wetted eyes. Then, with resolute effort to keep her composure and fighting tears, she continued: "Then Tex jumped forward with a gun in his hand and struck his hand with the gun to the man's head, and the man said, 'Please don't hurt me, I won't do anything.'"

Linda cried and bent down, and among tears and sobs, she uttered, "And Tex shot him four times."

"Did you actually see Tex put the gun inside the car and shoot the man?"

"Yes, I saw clearly."

"How far away at the time?"

"Just a few feet."

"After Tex shot the man, did you see what happened then?"

"The man just slumped over and Tex put his hand into the car to turn off the ignition. He pushed the car a few feet."

"Your Honor, I have here a photograph of a male caucasian," said Mr. Bugliosi. "May I make it P-42 for identification?"

"It'll be so marked," said the judge.

The prosecutor, with words of warning, showed Linda the photograph. "Linda, do you recognize this man?"

With frowning face and tears, the witness managed to reply, "Yes, I do, that's the man Tex shot."

Linda continued saying that Watson then told her to go around the back of the house to see if there were any open doors or windows.

"Did you find any open doors or windows in the back of the house?"

"No," answered Linda, still holding back from crying, "I came around from the back and Tex was standing at a window, cutting the screen."

Then, following a tense and dramatic explanation, she said Watson instructed her to wait outside, to go back and wait at the car. She also mentioned that Tex may have told her to listen for sounds, but couldn't remember him saying it.

"I did," she testified, "and after a few minutes, I listened and I heard people screaming, saying, 'No, please, no.' " At that moment, Linda Kasabian cried out in the open. She tried to speak but couldn't. Her words were uttered between sobs... "It was just horrible... even my emotions cannot tell you how horrible it was."

Quickly, I glanced at the rest of the jurors. All of them appeared soberly serious. Some tried to show no emotion, especially when they discovered I was looking at them. Mrs. Osborne, Mrs. Collingwood, and Violet Stokes had moisted eyes, and among the male jurors, Mr. Welch seemed quite moved at the testimony of Linda Kasabian, who was wracked with sobs and tears as she continued saying,

"I heard a man scream out 'No, no,' then I just heard screams..." Linda sighed and looked around her and to the interrogator, "I don't have any words to describe how a scream is. I never heard it before. It was just unbelievably horrible—just terrible."

"Were these screams of men or women or both?"

"It sounded like both."

The prosecutor, almost like a tormentor, kept asking for details, such as, "Were the screams loud screams or soft screams or what?"

Linda, almost losing her serenity and with both hands on her ears, shouted, "Loud!...loud!" and resumed her emotional crying.

Mr. Bugliosi, to establish the frame of the coming testimony, asked the witness the duration of the screaming.

"Oh, it seemed like forever, almost infinite...I don't know...I don't know... I started to run towards the house." ..

"Why did you do that?" asked the prosecutor.

"Because I wanted to stop it, because I knew what they had done to this man, that they were killing these people."

"What happened after you ran towards the house?"

"There was a man who had just come out of the door and he had blood all over his face... we looked into each other's eyes for a minute, I don't know however long."

Mrs. Kasabian covered her mouth and looked upwards as she continued, "and I said, 'Oh, God, I am sorry. Please make it stop', and then he just fell to the ground into the bushes."

Mr. Bugliosi just stared at the witness, who, unable to control herself from crying, added, "and then Sadie came running out of the house, and I said, 'Sadie, please make it stop,' and she said, 'It's too late' and she also said that she left her knife inside and she couldn't find it.

"Then, while this was going on, the man had gotten up, and I saw Tex on top of him, hitting him on the head and stabbing him, and the man was struggling with him. Then I saw Katie with an upraised knife chasing a lady in a white gown, and I just turned and ran to the car down at the bottom of the hill." At this point, Linda broke down.

Mr. Bugliosi received a glass of water from Mr. Stovitz, who, attentively had foreseen the scene. Linda's voice began to tremble when she resumed her testimony, but she continued answering questions despite her shaken condition.

"How many times did Tex stab him?"

"I don't know. He just kept doing it and doing it...and doing it."

"When the man was screaming, do you know what he was screaming?"

"There were no words, it was beyond words, it was just screams...please?"

The courtroom was in absolute repose. No whispers were heard, nor did anyone cough for fear to miss a single word.

Mr. Kanarek, who usually bombarded every word that the witness uttered, was appallingly serene and didn't object.

Mr. Fitzgerald had a sad-looking face. Whereas he had chatted with Susan Atkins, this time he and the four defendants were totally somber and composed.

Judge Older adjourned the court session until the next day.

The newspaper men stampeded out to the phone booths outside in the corridor to report the latest issues of the Manson trial.

We jurors could only speculate as to what the newspapers would print in the headlines that evening. "They always print something else," said Ray, while waiting for the bus.

"Why is it that the main issues of importance are usually placed somewhere inside of the paper?"

"Why?" inquired Ruth Collingwood.

"Because 'no sense makes sense,'" Ray added jokingly.

Again, we went swimming, I tagged along with Mrs. Hart. Everybody except Mr. White and Mrs. Osborne had come down and we all were in good spirits.

Shortly after the arrival of the six alternate jurors, Debbie confided in me, while lounging around the swimming pool, that she felt the new jurors, for some reason, didn't fit in with the regular jurors. She expressed that Mrs. Ruth Collingwood and Edith Rayburn were a couple of hags. Ray and Danny too young and not with it. When I asked her about George, she hastily replied, "Oh, he gives me the creeps."

"What about Tom?" I asked.

She couldn't tell me at that moment because George was approaching to talk to us. She arose and dove into the pool.

George, unaware of what had been said, just approached me and made a remark, "Nice-looking chick that Mrs. Hart, ah?"

I didn't utter a word, just made a sound, "Aha."

George understood that I was unwilling to talk about Debbie, so, instead, we exchanged points of view in regards to the type of work we do—as we worked for the same company—boring, we both agreed, and decided to go swimming.

I swam back and forth, and looking at the high diving board made me feel like I should try it, to see what would happen. On my way up, near the third step, I didn't calculate the distance between steps, especially since I was climbing at a rather fast pace. I hit the shin or upper part of the instep —the pain was sharp. For a moment I couldn't even walk but I managed to descend slowly and sat at the edge of the pool. Debbie came to my side and half joking, exclaimed, "Pobrecito (Poor boy)." I forced a smile and began to massage the area the best I could, and the rest of the time I kept the foot submerged under water. Later, I tried once more. Tired and exhausted, I sat by Violet Stokes.

We had a brief, amiable chat, sort of an introduction as to what we thought of one another. That was my first conversation with Violet.

I discovered that Violet Stokes had become immediately absorbed in finding out the birthdays and wedding anniversaries of everyone. She gradually managed to obtain the desired dates and kept a record for herself. A day or two before the occasion, she would collect money to buy a card, have it signed, and then presented it to the person whose birthday it was. Those duties became paramount to her and she gave them her almost undivided attention to the point that she appeared to neglect the reason for which she was sequestered.

We spoke about nothing important, and in order to break the monotony, I was ready to go back in the pool. We all swam and felt extremely relieved of the pressures of the day in court. Violet complained that she didn't know how to dive. I, as a gentleman, offered to teach her. Debbie and Betty were nearby and also wanted me to teach them—graciously I obliged. So, for the next few days and weekends, they practiced my instructions. Debbie and especially Betty accomplished to learn a little, but poor Violet, that was something else. Her plump, almost round body would splash the surrounding area where she would dive—her swimming reminded me of a little puppy drowning in the water.

A few days later, a handsome-looking deputy sheriff, Ernie Post, joined the jurors to swim and he also tried to teach Violet and Olivia Madison how to dive, but the deputy, like myself, didn't succeed much as a teacher.

Olivia Madison was a sight to see—her diving would cause everybody to stop talking and concentrate on watching her dive. She would swim quite well but her diving ability was a classical example of jester diversion.

She would stand rigid near the edge of the pool, ready to dive, her head bowed to her chest and arms extended forward, then, without bending her knees, she would dive into the water with all the flexibility and grace of a log falling into a stream. She wouldn't use any impulse or momentum on her feet to spring from the ground—the results were almost indescribable —the whole body splashing into the water like a stiff board. Needless to say, I for one did look forward to seeing that natatorium display everytime.

Breakfast time was always pleasant. Everybody was quiet and silent. There were no comments and except for, "It's a beautiful day" or a simple, "Good morning," nothing important was spoken.

"I asked the female bailiff to take us up to our rooms, and she doesn't want to," said Edith Rayburn painfully.

"How come?" asked her closest card-playing companion, Ruth Collingwood.

"I don't know," replied Edith, while shrugging her shoulders.

"She's new, that's why, she doesn't know," stated Mr. White, finishing his full breakfast.

Mrs. Hart, seated at the next table, leaned back to our table and inquired as to why the bulky female bailiff wouldn't let the jurors go upstairs to see "Lucy." No one gave her an explanation. "I'll ask her", said Debbie. A few seconds later she returned with a defeated look.

Immediately after, at the bailiffs' table headed by Deputy Taylor, I noticed that the tall, large, mulatto-looking uniformed female bailiff leaped to her feet and dashed to the center aisle among the jurors, and announced, "There will be no one going upstairs. We have no time."

"Just a minute, M'am" I said loudly, "for your own information, it has been accepted among the bailiffs to take the jurors up to their rooms after having breakfast on court days and we have had ample time..."

"I have not been given orders to take anyone upstairs," said the bailiff.

"Perhaps you have not been informed as to what your duties are, M'am," I responded.

"Listen, young man!" she interjected.

Forcibly, I overcame her statement and said, "You listen! Just remember one thing, m'am, we are not prisoners, so, consequently, you cannot treat us as such. It takes only ten minutes to go upstairs and return. I am sure we will arrive at court on time."

The tall and almost giant female deputy sheriff gave me a dirty and somewhat sinister look. Senior Deputy Taylor was listening and aware, and looked at me harshly for the first time and then spoke to her. I was on the verge of apologizing publicly right then and there for my abruptness, however, her attitude prevented me from doing so.

Reluctantly, she escorted us upstairs.

All of the jurors looked at me as if I was a strange animal, but on the way to our rooms, the ladies thanked me for having stood up for them, especially Olivia Madison, who said "I have a lot of respect for you, Bill Zamora, what you did was commendable—you certainly are a gentleman—thank you."

I didn't do it for any of you in particular," I responded. "I did it simply because I cannot tolerate overbearance...as the strong stepping on the weak."

Charlie, for the first time since the trial began, wore a white long-sleeved shirt with appliqué embroidered flowers and fruits designs.

The three girl defendants also for the first time wore different hair styles. Rather than wearing their long hair loosely, they had braided it and had it resting on their shoulders.

The three female prisoners kept on staring also at the accused Linda Kasabian. Charlie tried to disturb her and hypnotize her in a sort of a way. The girls laughed at her and made her feel uncomfortable. At intervals, they broke out laughing but somehow it appeared to be a nervous laugh, not a true one, not from within. Mrs. Kasabian ignored and did not acknowledge them, even though she probably felt the tension or uneasiness of someone staring at her.

They also stared continually at the jurors with a defiant look. However, Manson would concentrate on looking steadily on one juror at a time until he felt he had managed to overpower this juror's senses of being in control.

Mrs. Hart proved to be his main target—perhaps due to her disposition in court or whatever.

Mr. White didn't allow himself to be overtaken and would exchange looks with Charlie through long periods of time without blinking an eye. Whenever this happened the jurors would whisper words of encouragement to the pious-looking Mr. White.

This juror—author was also subjected to the cult leader's attentions. The first time Charlie tried to hypnotize me I tried to keep up with him but fortunately I smiled accidentally, not knowing how to react, and that for some reason, discouraged him from continuing his game.

Mr. Bugliosi resumed questioning the witness, assisted by pictures and a

91

large blue-printed diagram of the Polanski residence. With a red-tip felt pen, Linda either circled or marked with an X the various spots where Tex and the defendants entered on their way to commit the crimes until the witness ran back down to the car.

Linda testified that she "was in a total state of shock" and that when Tex, Sadie, and Katie arrived, she had already started the car. Tex seemed really uptight because she had run back to the car, and then he told her to turn the car off and to push over so he could drive.

Mr. Kanarek had objected so many times that at one time Judge Older swiveled his chair and called the counsel to approach the bench. The judge, adjusting his black robe, bent over his desk and from the look of his face, he must have cited Mr. Kanarek for contempt of court.

Manson's lawyer, on the way back to his table, appeared annoyed. The serious look on his face made his cheeks puff up. For a few minutes, he didn't object and sat slumped with a pencil in his hand poking at his forehead.

"Did Katie and Sadie say anything as you were driving off from the residence?" asked Mr. Bugliosi.

"Yes," replied Mrs. Kasabian. "They complained about their heads, that the people were pulling their hair, and that their heads hurt... and Sadie even came out and said that when she was struggling with a big man, that he hit her in the head... and..."

Mr. Bugliosi, thinking that the witness had finished, interrupted and then asked Linda, "Did Katie say anything?"

"Yes, Katie also complained of her hand, that it hurt. She said when she stabbed, that there were bones in the way and she couldn't get the knife through all the way, and that it took too much energy or whatever, I don't know her exact words, but it hurt her hand."

"Are you finished?" asked the prosecutor candidly.

Linda nodded positively, but Mr. Bugliosi wanted her to answer with words, so the court reporter could record it.

"Did Katie say anything about one of the girls inside the house?"

"Yes, she did. She said that one of the girls was crying for her mother and for God."

Mr. Bugliosi then proceeded to inquire about their departure and stops on their way back to the Spahn movie ranch. Linda, in an at-ease manner, described step by step, that Tex, Katie, and Sadie changed their clothes stained with blood to the extra sets they had brought with them.

After having driven some blocks down the road, they stopped near a house with a hose in front of it. Tex parked the car a little below the house and then

92

told Sadie and Katie to wash the blood from their bodies. Then Linda heard voices of people coming out of the house. It sounded like the voice of a woman, an older woman.

"Then what happened?" inquired Mr. Bugliosi.

"I don't remember her exact words but she said, 'Who is there?' or 'Who is that, what are you doing,' and Tex said, 'We're getting a drink of water.'

"The woman got sort of hysterical and she said, 'My husband is a police-man—he is a deputy,' or something like that, and then her husband , a man with white hair, came out and he said, 'Is that your car?' and we said, 'No, we are walking,' and then we started walking to the car. The man followed us all the way to the car. We all four got into the car and the man came to the driver's seat and put his hand in the car to reach for the keys of the igni-tion, but Tex blocked him and grabbed his hand and drove off fast, so I thought the man's arm was going to go with him."

"What happened next?" asked the prosecutor while keeping notes and checking out those questions already asked.

"We drove for about ten or fifteen minutes, and then Tex stopped the car." Linda described how Tex handed her the bloody clothes and told her to dump them at the side of the road, a flat level road. She did so and then they drove off. While Tex was driving, he directed her to wipe the finger-prints from the knives, which she did with a rag, and then he told her to throw them out of the window while the car was in motion.

The first knife fell among the bushes, the second landed against the curb —it bounced off the ground and rested visibly in the middle of the road as they drove away. She did not recall throwing out the gun.

They drove some more and stopped at a gas station, where Tex ordered Katie and Sadie to go to the restroom, one at a time, and wash off. They drove back to the ranch, arriving approximately one hour after they had left the gas station. Charles Manson awaited them, he was standing by himself, in about the same spot when they had left.

When they got out of the car, Sadie mentioned that there was a spot of blood on the outside of the car which she had noticed when they were at the gas station. Then Charlie sent Sadie to the kitchen for a sponge and told her to remove the stains of blood. He also ordered Katie and Linda to check the entire car and wipe off any blood spots.

After that, Charlie told them to go into the bunkroom, which was called the "gun room" located at the end of the walk, near the corral. They did.

Clem, also known as Clem Tufts, and Brenda were inside. Mr. Bugliosi brought a photo of Clem to Linda for identification. It was recorded as

Mr. Kanarek interposed scores of objections. In an uninterrupting string of objections for questions, he almost matched the prosecutor.

Mr. Bugliosi's co-prosecutor, Mr. Stovitz, at one time, rose in open court and said, "Your Honor, may we ask Your Honor to ask counsel to make his objection and then allow the witness to continue? We are having great difficulty keeping the continuity of her testimony going with these constant objections."

(Damn it, my pencil broke down, but luckily, two neighbor jurors kindly helped me to reconstruct the ending of what Mr. Stovitz said.)

"I know the record reflects the objections because I have gone through the record, but I think the continuous interruption is made for one obvious purpose, to interrupt the witness's train of thought and also interrupt Mr. Bugliosi's train of thought."

I, for one, felt like standing up and applauding for what Mr. Stovitz had said. I know all the jurors felt the same way because they made remarks to the effect while we were recessing.

Despite the objections, however, Mr. Bugliosi strove at getting the witness's story into the record.

Linda testified that after a few minutes inside the gun room where Danny DeCarlo had a side bed, Charlie entered with Tex.

"Did Tex say anything after you were all in the bunkroom?" asked Mr. Bugliosi.

"Yes, he said, 'I am the devil here to do the devil's work.'"

Linda described the room as being small and that everybody was lying on the floor.

"Did Tex say anything else about the killings?"

"Yes," responded Linda, "he said that there was a lot of panic, and that it was real messy and bodies were lying all over the place, but they were all dead."

Then Linda said that Charlie asked them individually, "Do you have any remorse?" and Sadie answered "No" and Katie said "No" and then to herself to which she responded also "No" but that, in reality, she felt great remorse or fear of Manson. Charlie then told them to talk to no one and to go to sleep.

Linda said she was not positive as where she slept, but she remembers that she slept most of the day. Later that day, Sadie came and told her to come out and watch TV at the trailer, to watch the news. Linda mentioned that Tex, Katie, and Sadie did not mention any names when they left the Tate residence. She found out about the victims' names as they watched TV. She saw Katie and Sadie but she couldn't recall to have seen Tex around. That evening she had dinner with the whole family, all together.

"Was a girl called 'Snake' present?" asked Mr. Bugliosi.

"I can't be sure whether she was present or not," responded Linda. "Who else was present?"

Linda, looking at the defendants, replied, "Leslie was present, Sadie, Katie, Clem, Charlie... eventually, everybody was there. Some people went to the waterfall."

"What happened after dinner?"

"Charlie told me to get my driver's license and to get a change of clothes at the bunkroom."

"What did he say after he told you that?" inquired the prosecutor.

"He said that we were going out again tonight, that last night was too messy and he was going to show us how to do it, that we needed new weapons."

Linda, through Mr. Kanarek's objections, described the events of the second night.

She continued saying that she saw Tex enter with sort of two swords. Everybody left the house about the same time. They went to the car, the same car that belonged to John Swartz, a nonmember of the family. They all got inside. Linda sat between Clem at her right and Charlie in the driver's seat. The rest were seated in the back. She was given a leather thong which she put inside her jacket, Linda then said, "Charlie was wearing one around his neck, sort of wrapped around his neck—it looked like a hangman's noose.

Mr. Kanarek couldn't take Linda's description and, to his satisfaction, the judge sustained his objection. We were dismissed for lunch.

Again, we were taken to the Hilton Hotel. The waitresses were very congenial and quite efficient. The service was exceptionally fast and even Mr. Scalise was glad to be served his favorite dish on time.

Back in court.

The witness continued describing that Charlie and the rest of them got in the car and that she saw two knives that looked like swords. Linda said she had seen those two knives before in the ranch in the bunkroom and also saw them in the hands of others while playing or whatever.

Then she testified that before they left, Manson went after Bruce Davis to get money from him for gasoline. They drove off.

Manson was driving. She knew that the second night they were going to kill! She didn't want to go with them, she wanted to go to the waterfall, but Charlie had asked her and she was afraid to refuse him.

95

Then Linda said that Charlie told them that they were going to two different houses—one group will go to one house and the other to another house. They stopped for gas and cigarettes. Linda took over the wheel to drive. Charlie directed her to drive on the freeway. Linda couldn't remember exact details but she remembered a Fair Oaks sign where Charlie told her to get off—didn't know if it was right or left, etc. Charlie told her to stop approximately one-half mile after getting off at Fair Oaks. The witness said she didn't know the area, she guessed it was near Pasadena. Then she was told to stop in front of a house in a one-story residential area. Seemed caucasian area—no negroes, not mixed. A middle-class type of residence.

Charlie got out of the car and told her to drive around the block. When she returned, he was already waiting and got in the car. Linda said that they waited a few minutes to see a couple get in their car. Everybody was looking at the couple and Charlie wanted to go after the couple, but Mrs. Kasabian testified that Charlie said, "The man is too big."

While driving, Linda heard Charlie saying he had seen through windows and saw pictures of children on the walls, that he couldn't do it, but that they couldn't let children stop them, for the sake of children in the future.

They kept driving, until up a hill, where the houses seemed to be rich residential. They saw no people. The houses were modern, expensive-type. Charlie told Linda to stop and park in front of a big four-frame house, but decided that the houses were too close together.

The bizarre journey continued.

"After one hour or a little bit longer," Linda said, "I became sleepy."

They came to a church, pulled into the parking area, and parked. Charlie mentioned he was going into the church and talk to a minister, but came back saying that the building was dark and the doors were locked. They drove off and went into the freeway.

They got off at a residential area, around Sunset Boulevard, toward the ocean. Linda then said that Charlie directed her toward a dirt road which was very dark and that she saw what seemed to be the only house around, with a corral, and later was told to drive different ways, left and right. Eventually, they got back on Sunset Boulevard toward the ocean. She drove by Will Rogers State Park and beyond. Charlie instructed her to another street, rather hilly—difficult to drive because the brakes were in bad shape and Linda was afraid to have an accident.

They went back into the city—in a residential area—with foliage and vegetation. They were driving east when, after a few minutes, Charlie spotted a white sport Volvo car driven by a man. Manson ordered her to follow the car and to pull up beside the car at the next light and that he was going to kill the driver. The light changed to green and the car got away.

Charles Manson changed his mind to follow the car and Linda was told to drive to a particular place—a residential area. She mentioned that she had parked exactly at the same spot on one other occasion when she and her husband and friends were on their way down from Seattle, Washington, to New Mexico and they stopped off in Los Angeles, and this particular person knew Harold True, so they went to his house and had a party.

It was very late, very little traffic, around 2:00 A.M. She recognized the spot right away. Linda then asked Charles Manson, "Charlie, you are not going into that house, are you?"

"No", said Charlie, "I'm going next door."

"Then what happened," inquired Mr. Bugliosi.

"I saw Charlie put an object in his pants and then he got out of the car. He disappeared up the walkway, the driveway leading towards Harold's house and I couldn't see anymore—he just disappeared out of view."

The witness then testified that Manson returned to the car after several minutes, and that she remembered they all lit up cigarettes and that they smoked about three-quarters of a Pall Mall cigarette, however long that took.

When Manson returned, he called Leslie, Katie, and Tex and told them to get out of the car. Linda then said that she heard Charlie saying that there were a man and a woman upstairs and that he had tied their hands and that he had told them not to be afraid and that they were going to be alright, he wasn't going to hurt them.

"Did Manson give any instructions to Leslie, Katie, and Tex?" asked the prosecutor.

Linda, in a positive mood, responded slowly, "I am not positive, but it keeps ringing in my head that Charlie said, 'Don't let them know that you are going to kill them,' and then I think I heard him say not to cause fear and panic in these people. Then Charles Manson gave instructions to hitchhike back to the ranch after having finished the job, and Katie to go to the waterfall."

Tex, Leslie, and Katie left, each one was carrying a bundle of clothing. She saw no guns.

Eventually, Charles Manson got back into the car and proceeded to drive off. Charlie handed Linda a woman's wallet and instructed her to take the change and wipe the fingerprints from it and then to throw it out of the window.

"The reason," Linda testified, "is that Charlie wanted someone to pick

97

it up and eventually they would use the credit cards inside and be charged with the crime or whatever."

Linda didn't throw the wallet out of the window.

After fifteen or twenty minutes of driving, they got onto the freeway. She heard Manson say, "he wanted to show the white people." He stopped in front of a ladies' room at a gas station and told Linda to get rid of the wallet by placing it inside the toilet tank.

Court adjourned for the day and we returned to the hotel.

Deputy Taylor, assisted by Mollie Kane, had their heads filled with questions from the jurors about their necessities—laundry, cleaning, beauty shop and barbershop needs, banking, shopping, plus personal and individual demands.

Each juror was allowed seven dollars weekly for services of cleaners and laundry. A paper bag with a laundry check list provided by the hotel, was to be placed every Monday and Thursday morning outside one's room. The same valet who picked up the bags would deliver the laundry in a box and hang clothes from the cleaners inside the closet, two days later.

Johnny Mathis was performing nightly at the "Now Grove" of the Ambassador Hotel. Entertainers, while appearing at the formerly famous "Cocoanut Grove," stayed at the "Sammy Davis Suite" on the sixth floor—one room away from mine.

Mildred Osborne, Edith, and Ruth wanted and hoped the bailiffs would take the jurors some night. Mollie Kane flatly refused to hear any of it. She pondered upon the fact that performers sometimes used everyday news in their entertainment material and "one never knows," she stated, "they may mention the Manson trial and if the defense hears about it, they may use it as an issue to make a motion for a mistrial."

Because of a suggestion of mine, my barber was allowed to come to the hotel and exercise his craft among the jurors. I placed an announcement on the bulletin board asking those interested in having a haircut to sign it. All the male jurors rushed after dinner and waited for the barber to arrive at 8 o'clock.

George was the first to sign, and in the hall, he stopped someone dressed in white and inquired, "Excuse me, where are you going to cut our hair?"

"I beg your pardon," responded the man, out of bounds.

"Aren't you the barber?" asked George.

"No, I'm Johnny Mathis," said the well-known singer, while he laughed.

"Oh, I'm sorry," responded George, who continued toward the Little Lobby.

George later told me, candidly, that he didn't know who Johnny Mathis was. At first, I didn't want to believe him, but later, through my association with the chubby juror, I discovered that he meant it.

A day later, someone told me that Johnny Mathis had attempted to place an outside phone call but the operator refused to give him a connection, believing he was a juror. The entertainer had objected and referred to himself as being "Johnny Mathis" to which, it was said, the switchboard operator had exclaimed, "If you're Johnny Mathis, I'm Elizabeth Taylor!" Eventually, Mr. Mathis completed his phone call, much to the dismay of the operator.

Mr. Mathis's patience was strained further on Monday morning when the night-shift deputy on duty pounded vigorously on his door at 6:00A.M. to wake him. Again, he was mistaken for a juror.

I understand he opened his door but I wasn't informed of his reaction or his facial expression.

This incident happened twice to Mr. Mathis, which prompted Deputy Tull to place a sign on the Sammy Davis Suite to avoid future embarrassment to other entertainers who would reside there while performing.

Gradually, I became friendlier with the jurors. At first, some would limit themselves to their rooms. Others, except for a short visit to the recreation room or a casual walk, kept pretty much to themselves. Little by little, we would joke and tell each other fun stories.

Everybody was pulling mild jokes on everyone. No one felt insulted. One time, on the way to my room, I walked behind Violet Stokes without her knowledge. Her room door was wide open and she entered without stopping, going directly to the bathroom. Instinctively, I walked in and tiptoed to the bed where I laid down, placing my hands behind my neck and crossing my legs. I waited, nonchalantly. She strolled out of the bathroom, still unaware of my presence, walked past the bed to a dresser and turned, startled, after hearing my "exaggerated" snore. This type of prank brought the jurors together.

The next morning, Thursday, July 30th, Mrs. Kasabian continued her testimony.

Linda, through questions by the prosecuting Attorney, Vincent Bugliosi, testified that Charlie had told her to keep the change and leave the credit cards in the wallet. Manson told her to leave the wallet in the restroom, so a black woman could find it.

Then she was told to drive off to the freeway. She drove a long, long way. She recalled having seen oil wells, and after one hour of driving, they ended up at a beach, a beach not close to a city.

Charlie told Linda to stop and park the car two blocks from the beach. They all got out of the car and started walking toward the beach. Charlie told Clem and Sadie to stay a little bit behind him and Linda. The witness then described that she and Charlie walked hand in hand on the beach and that it was sort of nice, it felt good.

They just talked and she gave him some peanuts and Charlie, in return, made her forget about everything. She told him she was pregnant. They started to walk back. They arrived at a side street, a corner, and a police car came by and stopped to ask them what they were doing and Charlie told them that they were just taking a walk. Then Linda added that Charlie said something like, "Don't you know who I am?" or "Don't you remember my name?" as if the policemen were supposed to know him. They just said no. It was a friendly conversation. It just lasted for a minute and then they walked back to the car hand in hand. Sadie and Clem were already in the car.

Manson repeatedly had told his attorney to let the witness answer the question. However, at that particular moment, I saw Charles Manson hit Mr. Kanarek shoulder to shoulder. Mr. Kanarek, short and bulky, didn't even move and pretended as if nothing had happened.

"When you told Mr. Manson that you were pregnant," asked Mr. Bugliosi, "were you pregnant by him?". .

Linda replied, "No" and the prosecutor inquired: "What is the next thing that happened?"

"Again, I took over driving. We drove down the hill and got back the same way we had come in, and Charlie asked us if we knew any people at the beach. We all said 'No.' Then he looked at me and said 'What about that man you and Sandy met? Isn't he a Piggy?' I said, 'Yes, he's an actor.' And he asked me if the man would let him in. And I said, 'Yes' . And then he asked me if the man would let my friends in, Sadie and Clem. And I said 'Yes' and he said, 'Okay, I want you to kill him,' and he gave me a small pocket knife. And at this point, I said, 'Charlie, I am not you. I cannot kill anybody,' and I don't know what happened at that moment, but I was very much afraid. And then Charlie started to tell me how to go about doing it and I remember having a knife in my hand and I asked him 'With this?' and he said 'Yes,' and he showed me how to do it."

Linda, raising her right index finger and motioning across her throat, demonstrated how Manson showed her how to kill the man.

Then she continued saying: "He said, 'as soon as you enter the house, as soon as you see the man, slit his throat right away' and he told Clem to shoot him. And then he also said that if anything went wrong, you know, not to do it."

With Mr. Bugliosi inquiring, Linda told that she met the man while hitchhiking with another member of the family, a girl named Sandra Good. The man had taken them to his apartment. Both girls were allowed to take a shower and then the man gave them something to eat. Linda admitted quite openly having had sexual intercourse with him.

Mr. Bugliosi submitted, for identification, photos of the man who picked up Linda and Sandra and also of his apartment building.

Linda continued saying that Manson asked her to show him the apartment where the man lived. She took him there. Sadie and Clem stayed behind. Linda and Charlie went inside and upstairs. She led him to the wrong floor and pointed at a door, a different door than that belonging to the man's apartment. They walked downstairs to the car and Charlie gave Clem a gun.

"Did Manson say anything?" inquired Mr. Bugliosi.

"Yes, at this point, he said something...he said that if anything went wrong, you know, just hang it up, don't do it; and, of course, to hitchhike back to the ranch and for Sadie to go to the waterfall. And then he drove off."

"Before he drove off," asked the prosecutor, "did Mr. Manson tell Sadie and Clem anything?"

"Yes," replied Linda.

"What did he tell them?"

"While I knocked on the door, for them to wait around the corner until I entered, and then to ask the man if they could come in."

Reconstructing the scene under severe questioning by Mr. Bugliosi, Linda explained that she, Clem, and Sadie went inside the apartment house.

"And I knocked on the door, which I knew wasn't the door, and a man said, 'Who is it?' and I said 'Linda.' And he sort of opened the door and peeked around the corner and I just said, 'Oh, excuse me, wrong door,' and that was it."

"Linda, why did you knock on the wrong door?"

"Because I didn't want to kill anybody."

The witness continued saying that on their way downstairs, Sadie went to the bathroom and after, the three of them walked along the beach. Clem waited to get rid of the gun, but couldn't do it because there were too many people.

Linda remembered to have heard Clem and Sadie sing the Beatle song about piggies and forks and knives, and eating your bacon. They kept walking and Clem finally found a place, near a sand dune, where he stashed the gun. Then they hitchhiked toward Malibu.

101

They got a ride by a man, to a house near the beach at Topanga Canyon Boulevard. The house had a platform—like a front porch—with large windows. There were a few trees. She had been there the day before. They knocked on the door and a girl answered it. Linda explained that when they entered she sniffed pot. They joined the man living there and the girl to smoke some pot. They sang some Beatle songs. Then they hitchhiked toward the San Fernando Valley—back to the Spahn Ranch.

They got a ride from a sort of "straight-looking guy." Linda and Clem got off at Santa Susana and walked to the Spahn Ranch. Sadie continued riding with the man, maybe to the waterfall as Charlie had instructed her.

Linda said that when she and Clem arrived at the ranch, everybody was sleeping.

Then, unexpectedly, Mr. Bugliosi asked the witness: "Do you know what LSD is?"

"Yes," responded Linda and added that since 1965, she had taken it approximately fifty times.

The deputy district attorney wanted to know if the witness had intentions to leave the Spahn Ranch. Linda testified that she wanted to leave and that on the morning after the second night, she packed a few things, including a sleeping bag with some of her daughter Tanya's clothes, and hid it by the road.

"Why did you plant the sleeping bag by the road?"

"I had to hide it," replied Mrs. Kasabian, "He wouldn't let me walk out of there knowing that I had seen what I'd seen."

Linda then said she was taking care of the "elks," a word the family used when they referred to children. When Charles Manson wanted her to go to town and visit Sandy, Mary Brunner, and Bobby Beausoleil who were in jail, she did not see Sandy and Mary because they were in court. She couldn't see Bobby, because her ID was no good. Charlie told her to go the next day.

Practically everybody was at the waterfall. She had pizza for dinner. Everybody slept on sleeping bags or on the ground. Linda continued saying that she got up rather early and drove a VW to get to the ranch.

She didn't tell Charlie of her leaving because she was afraid to tell him. For her trip, she wore a green dress, put some makeup on, and wore her hair behind the ears. John Hanna loaned her his car and gave her two dollars and a Shell credit card, the same he had given her the day before. She wanted to escape and although she spoke with Hanna and had seen Bruce Davis, she didn't tell them that she was going to escape. She drove off in a Volvo car. She stopped where she had hid the sleeping bag.

Mr. Bugliosi asked Linda why she left her fifteen-month-old daughter, Tanya, at the waterfall.

Linda, without any significance, replied, "Tanya was with Brenda...and the whole family at the waterfall. There was no way I could go down there and get her without them asking questions."

"But, weren't you afraid for her sake?" inquired the prosecutor.

"I knew I had to leave, and something within myself told me she would be alright. I was confident I could make it back and pick her up."

Linda continued saying that she picked up two young hitchhikers and told them about her plans of escaping and decided to go with them to New Mexico.

The next day, the car broke down near Albuquerque.

She wrote a letter to the family and explained. Then she hitchhiked to Taos, New Mexico, hoping to find her husband, Bob Kasabian, and then to a place called Ojo Sarco, where she found him. But her husband couldn't help her because he had another woman with him.

She stayed for a few days at John Sage's, a friend of her's, whom she testified as being the founder of the Zen Buddhist macrobiotics retreat in Taos.

Linda said she told John Sage that she had left Tanya with the people who killed Sharon Tate.

A week after, Sage loaned her money to buy a round-trip plane ticket to Los Angeles and gave her one hundred dollars to hire a lawyer to help her to get her child back.

In Los Angeles, Linda called the Malibu police station to investigate about her daughter Tanya. They referred her to a social worker, who, at the time, discovered someone was posing as Tanya's mother. Linda got hold of a lawyer, Paul Rosenberg, whom, after three weeks, managed to reunite Linda with her daughter.

Linda returned to Taos, New Mexico. She made phone calls to get more money, but to no avail. Then John Sage gave her one hundred dollars to return to Los Angeles to cover expenses of lawyer and transportation in order to retrieve Tanya.

After one more trip back to Taos, she stayed for a few days. Her husband, Bob, was still "on a trip" with his girlfriend called Susan.

So, she decided to hitchhike to Miami, Florida, to see her father. Her father put her up in a place. She felt relieved, was pregnant, and had Tanya with her. It felt almost like a vacation.

Linda continued saying that she made some phone calls to her mother, whom had been separated about twelve or fourteen years from her father. While in Miami, she read newspapers and watched television about the Sharon

Tate case, but that she had no courage to call the police, nor the relatives of the victims. She wanted to see her mother, so her father paid for her to go home. Her brother waited for her in Boston. Eventually, she surrendered to the police after having read in a Bostonian newspaper that she was wanted in connection with the Tate murders.

Her mother called the police and managed to have them send an ordinary car to the house, rather than the conventional police car. That way, the neighbors were nor aware that Linda Kasabian was being arrested at the beginning of December 1969.

Finally, Linda testified that she had given birth to her child, Angel, while she was in custody.

Mr. Bugliosi, setting aside the yellow pad containing his notes and pick-up his wristwatch, which he usually placed in front of him, said: "No further questions. The defense may inquire."

The judge noticed that it was 2:50 P.M. and called for a recess of twenty minutes.

We jurors didn't know which of the defense counsel would start cross-examining the witness. Surely, we expected the boisterous Mr. Kanarek to be the first, however, we soon found out through one of the bailiffs that Mr. Paul Fitzgerald was indeed the first lawyer of the defense to attempt to discredit Linda Kasabian's testimony.

After we walked in and sat down in our respective chairs, I noticed that the courtroom reminded me of a bullring. The judge was the trumpetist who announces the start of the bullfight. We the jurors were the referees. Mr. Fitzgerald, the matador, waiting for the bull to come out. Linda, the bull (on her way to the witness stand). Mr. Bugliosi and Mr. Stovitz, the picadors (men on horses who usually poke the bull to infuriate him so he can give a better performance). The rest of the defense counsel—considered them bullfighters. The defendants were the incoming bulls and the press was the general public, hungry for entertainment and bloody news.

As in any bullring, they have ushers and a cashier. I considered the bailiffs ushers and the court clerk the cashier.

The only difference was that the bull in this case was a passive but strong bull—a bull unafraid to the rigors of the game. Mr. Fitzgerald, dressed in a blue suit with an unusually colorful embroidered patch over the upper left side pocket, looked, in my imagination, like a matador with a "suit of lights." He was ready to fight.

I, as a regular juror, had many questions for Mrs. Kasabian, but obviously couldn't exercise that prerogative and hoped, along with the rest of the jurors to have those questions asked by any of the defense counsel and discard them from my mind.

Mrs. Kasabian was in a most peaceful attitude. She didn't appear nervous or worried about what those four counsel would ask her. She had admitted openly that she had taken drugs and that her sexual life had been free and easy. She knew she was accused and charged of seven counts of murder and one of conspiracy to commit murder, and yet she still maintained a certain degree of stability.

Unbelievable.

She knew the four counsel were there to defend their clients for their lives. She expected them to have her torn to pieces, in front of everybody, to make her appear as a liar and even make her say that it was not true what she saw happening in those two fateful nights. Her testimony had planted the seeds of guilt in the four defendants. She had given precise details as to every move they had made during the time she eyewitnessed those bizarre murders.

We jurors knew about what the defendants had done those two nights and we even learned, according to her testimony, that Manson's fantasy known as "Helter Skelter" was the crux of the motive behind the Tate-La Bianca slayings. We knew of Manson's directorial tasks.

Linda Kasabian was so composed and sure of herself that at one time, for the first time, she managed to smile delicately. She smiled at no one in particular. I just couldn't believe anyone could be so at ease and composed as Linda Kasabian.

Mr. Fitzgerald, on the other hand, has appeared more subtle and direct while objecting. He only objected when it had been necessary. We jurors felt sympathy and sided with Mr. Fitzgerald's behavior in court. We respected him and listened more carefully to what he had to say. Maybe the reason was that while Mr. Kanarek objected most of the time, just for the sake of interrupting the proceedings, Mr. Fitzgerald relied on substantially important objections. Mr. Aaron Stovitz, I believe, had honorably mentioned about

Mr. Kanarek's poor courtroom tactics. We mentally agreed wholeheartedly.

Mr. Fitzgerald, from the beginning, went right into the question of Linda's drug use.

"Do you recall when you first ingested LSD?"

"Yes, it was in Boston, it was Christmas Eve of '65."

"And is there some way to describe the experiences that you would experience each time you ingested the LSD?"

Linda, without hesitating, answered right away, "I would call it a reali-

105

zation."

Mr. Fitzgerald proceeded to ask questions in regard to the acquisition of LSD.

Linda expertly responded that LSD comes in capsules of different sizes and also comes in tablets of different colors and is measured by micrograms.

"Did it appear to you that when you took LSD, it affected your normal thought process?"

"No, not really," answered Linda.

Mr. Fitzgerald wanted to know, "How long does it usually take when one ingests LSD for it to take effect?"

Linda replied that the reaction depends on the acid, the surroundings, the type, and the quality.

"It also depends on the dosage, is that right?" asked Mr. Fitzgerald.

"Yes."

"Have you taken LSD in different dosages?"

"I never knew the exact dosage, no."

"Was there some reason you never knew the exact dosage?"

"Well, the dosage was not usually inscribed on the capsule or tablet, so I don't know."

"Wow!" I told myself, "I couldn't answer that fast and straightforward."

Mr. Fitzgerald, trying to get even with Linda, asked her, "Now, how were you able to arrive at the approximate figure of fifty LSD experiences?"

"Because I can usually remember the exact trips."

The defense counsel then asked the witness about other drugs she used.

"You have also ingested peyote, have you not?"

"Yes, I have," Linda answered, and then, through questions and answers, she explained that peyote is a form of cactus and it looks like a button, and that it grows in southern Texas. It gives hallucinations, but they are different, not vivid in nature. She couldn't describe the results. She had no words.

"But you have taken peyote. Is that right?" insisted Mr. Fitzgerald.

"Well, my sole purpose for taking it was for realization, God realization."

"That was to discover God?"

"Yes."

"Were you successful in your endeavor?" inquired the tall lawyer.

Linda, responding very calmly, said: "I realized you don't have to take peyote or LSD to discover God."

While explaining her use of drugs, Linda stated that she had never taken an overdose of LSD, so she couldn't say if it is possible to lose control of one's mental faculties under those circumstances. But she admitted that while

106

taking LSD, sometimes, she would see things moving that were actually stationary. She rejected the thought to have seen God under LSD, but at the same time, she said that under delusions, she believed that she could see God through acid, the acid told her it was God.

Then Mr. Fitzgerald asked her, "What is an acid trip?"

Linda replied, "An acid trip is a LSD trip. What I have been doing the last fifty times."

Mr. Fitzgerald asked Linda a rather complicated question, such as, "Let's say, on Monday you ingested some LSD, and you see and experience something. Correct?"

"Okay, yes," said Linda.

"On Wednesday, you are not ingesting any LSD."

At this moment, the witness frowned her face and uttered words that sounded as, "Uh—er—huh?"

The lawyer for the defense continued.

"And you are seeing and hearing things, but the things you see and hear on Wednesday are as real as the things you heard and saw on Monday?"

Linda practically without any amount of reflection, quickly responded, "Usually the things I saw and heard on Monday were in my own head, and they were not real. But the things on Wednesday, when I was not under the drug, were real, were stationary."

Mrs. Kasabian readily admitted, under Mr. Fitzgerald's questioning, that she also had taken methydrine hydrochloride, commonly known as "speed," and psilocybin, a drug which she said was a "derivative from mushrooms."

She testified that she had taken speed for two or three months. The effects, she said, "were pure electric energy, not natural," and psychologically, it affected her very little. She couldn't sleep. She experimented with it while in San Francisco. She also admitted taking merealine and was questioned about STP and belladonna, which she did not take.

Mr. Fitzgerald went on to the subject of witchcraft and Mrs. Kasabian again answered his queries with forthrightness.

"You referred during your direct testimony to the hanging of little items from trees near you campsite in Devil's Canyon during the month of July 1969."

"Yes, that is correct."

"Little pieces of string, little pieces of wire, little pieces of paper?"

"Yes."

"And those things had a purpose?"

107

"Yes. So that we could find our way to the campsite."

Mr. Fitzgerald had kept walking behind the three female defendants with crossed arms and at intervals, he looked at the ceiling as to concentrate.

"Weren't those also witchy things?"

"Yes, that's what they were called."

"Do you know why they were called witchy things?"

"No, not particularly."

At that moment, Mr. Fitzgerald stopped and, projecting his voice directly at the witness, said, "Didn't you feel that you were a witch during the month of July 1969?"

Linda conventionally smiled at the question and responded, "I was made to feel I was a witch," and added, "yes."

Mr. Fitzgerald seriously inquired, "Did you or did you not refer to yourself as a witch?"

"While I was there, yes, and at one point, once when I left, I referred to myself as a witch."

Linda went on saying that she called herself "Yana, the Witch" because when she first entered the ranch, Gypsy told her that they all assumed different names and she was told by everyone that she was a witch. The name just came to her so she assumed that name.

Mrs. Kasabian rarely allowed herself to smile. However, Mr. Fitzgerald's questions about her having been a witch made her smile more often and added more fuse of indignation to the defense counsel.

"Do you profess to have magical powers?"

"No, I don't."

"Do you feel you were a witch?"

"I think I tried to make myself believe I was a witch."

"Did you act like a witch?"

"No, I acted like myself."

Now, get hold of the following answer, which immediately after Linda answered, I personally burst out laughing only to have a few reprimanding faces of disapproval among the jurors. I didn't care.

The defense counsel asked, "Were you a good witch or a bad witch?"

Linda, while smiling, replied, "I was a good witch, at the time I was referring to myself as a witch."

Mr. Fitzgerald barely glanced at the jury box and didn't seem to mind my laughing, however, when he asked the following questions of the witness, his face became hard and forward.

"Didn't you attempt to practice the art of witchcraft?"

"No, I don't even know what witchcraft is. I don't know rituals."

The defense counsel, his body still and slightly raising his voice, inquired, "Well, was this whole thing about calling yourself a witch just a joke?"

Linda cautiously responded, "I don't know. When I came into the ranch, they told me I was a witch and that they were witches, so they made believe that I was a witch, too."

As a final question about witchcraft, Mr. Fitzgerald, while pacing back and forth, asked Mrs. Kasabian:

"You never saw anybody at the Spahn Ranch do anything a real witch would do, did you?"

Linda never answered that question. Mr. Aaron H. Stovitz, the co-prosecutor, sagged in his chair, threw a pencil he was holding on the table, raised his arms in disbelief, and interjected in a loud voice, "What would a real witch do, Your Honor?"

Mr. Stovitz's question provoked an outburst of laughter in the courtroom. Even Judge Older laughed pleasantly.

The defense counsel proceeded to ask questions about the use of the word "family" and what did one have to do, if anything, to become a member of the "family."

Linda replied that she considered them a "family" while she was at the ranch and added that she didn't know if there was any special thing one had to do in order to become a member of the "family."

Mr. Fitzgerald attempted unsuccessfully to make the witness admit that the term "family" was a word of her own use. He then switched his interrogation to the subject of "making love at the ranch."

Linda testified that she was never forced in any fashion to participate in lovemaking. She admitted that she made love with more than one person. Without much concern or emotion, Mrs. Kasabian said at one time, "Well, I remember I made love with Leslie and Tex, the three of us together."

Right away I glanced at Leslie and she seemed surprised but underneath her facade, she smiled and accepted it.

Linda continued, "And then Snake made love to me, and then Clem was there and he made love to me. That is all I recall."

The defense counsel asked, "I take it, during the period of time you were making love to them, you were unaware of what other persons were making love with whom?"

"Sometimes I looked up, you know, but...."

Mr. Fitzgerald, "And was this a pleasant experience for you?"

"Well, it was a different experience."

109

"Did you enjoy it?"

"Yeah, I gues I did. I will have to say I did."

The courtroom jammed with spectators murmured softly and even tittered out of shock or enjoyment. We jurors just sat there like statues, with no feelings for one way or another. But rest assured that thoughts crossed the minds of more than one of the jurors that the pretty young girl in pigtails on the witness stand, as well as the defendants and the rest of the family members, had quite a thing going on at the ranch. In fact, Marvin Connolly, Ray Harris, and this juror, while waiting in the jury room for the bailiff to lock the courtroom and take us back to the hotel, had a brief conversation.

Ray mentioned, "You know that Spahn Ranch must be 'the place' to spend a wild time."

"Yeah," said Marvin jokingly, "I'm ready to go this weekend."

"I'm ready to go NOW!" snapped Ray, and then asked me, "What about you?"

"Well," I replied reflectively, "remember that if you go, you must give and share with more than one person at the same time, regardless of sex."

"Oh no! Not me!" Ray cried defensively.

"Gee," Marvin said pensively, while rubbing his walrus moustache, "I didn't think of that."

"Obviously, you didn't," I stated, and in a mock eerie voice, I added, "well, I guess you two gentlemen ARE NOT going to the ranch this weekend for that wild time."

"You bastard," Ray said in a friendly manner, and the three of us burst out laughing.

Ray was kind of a noisy fellow. He wants to be the he-man type of thing. I don't like this. You don't have to be a big strong guy to be virile. He's kind of bow-legged, puffy hair. Charming guy, but he was always talking of his conquests with women and all that, like the thing was the axis of one's life. I love sex like anybody else. When I go to bed to have sex I enjoy it, but I'm not going to control my life because of this fact.

Later on television (after the trial) I said that Manson actually represented the image of what man would like to be, to have all those women do his commands and do what he pleased. After all, man would like to have as many conquests as he possibly can. This includes bisexuals and homosexuals or whatever...the ultimate in conquests.

Manson had the gift of gab. He knew how to go about it. He was able to make these people feel wanted, make them feel beautiful. Let's face it, he made these people feel ten feet tall and he, himself, wasn't even six feet tall.

On Friday, July 31st, as we walked in the courtroom, I noticed that Linda Kasabian was dressed in a new outfit. Still in pigtails, she was wearing an orange Mexican-style skirt with a white, greentrimmed embroidered peasant blouse.

Exactly at 9:44 A.M. the court session began. I also noticed that when Judge Older entered the courtroom, he didn't bang his gavel, in fact he never used one, even when there were agitated statements among the counsel or voices in the audience. He just addressed the counsel.

Mr. Fitzgerald resumed questioning the witness.

Linda, through a detailed synopsis, gave an account of her past. She explained that, at an early age, she felt like a little blind girl in the forest and felt innocent. Then left home at the age of sixteen and married a young man named Robert Peaslee with whom she traveled all over the United States and divorced, and later married Robert Kasabian in September 1967. She spent the interim years in a series of hippie communes at Miami Beach, Greenwich Village, Venice, and the Haight-Ashbury district of San Francisco.

She lived in several communes with her second husband, including groups called "The American Psychedelic Circus" in Boston, and "The Sons and Daughters of Mother Earth," near Taos, New Mexico. The two of them returned to California, and the day she broke up with her husband she went to the Spahn Ranch with her baby, Tanya.

I suppose we jurors had to evaluate the type of life Mrs. Kasabian lived before she was called upon to go along on the Tate-La Bianca murder rampages. We had to listen and learn of her whereabouts in order to establish the amount of veracity we should give to her testimony. Mr. Fitzgerald obviously was trying to convey to us that her drug-oriented background along with her present state of mind, should leave our minds confused, and her testimony would be of a less impact.

However, the more Mr. Fitzgerald demanded of her private sexual llfe, the less Linda Kasabian seemed to be disturbed. Her answers were forthright and to the point. No hesitation. Her calm attitude was enough to make any counsel feel exasperated and even drive him insane. Such was her well-controlled behavior on the witness stand.

Mr. Fitzgerald continued his cross-examination and asked Mrs. Kasabian intimate questions, such as, "Who did you sleep with in the cove, if anybody, on July 6th?"

"Let me see. I'm not sure if it was that night or the night before. I slept with Charlie that night."

111

"Did you sleep with anybody on the 7th?"

"I don't know. I can't go back there and remember exactly—you know, dates and who."

The defense counsel wanted to know if she had slept with, if anyone, on the 8th, the 9th, the 10th etc.

Linda finally responded, "No," and then as to relieve the counsel from asking her the same line of questions, she said, "eventually, I slept with all the men except Larry. So I don't know the dates."

"What sort of activity did you engage in during the day of July 5th?"

Linda stated that she had to explain first the night of July 4th, in which she met Tex Watson, who took her into a dark shed and made love to her, which was an experience that she never had before.

"You had never had sexual intercourse before?" asked Mr. Fitzgerald.

"No. I am saying that the experience I had in making love with Tex was a total experience, it was different."

"How was it different?" asked the defense counsel.

"That my hands were clenched when it was all over and I had absolutely no will power to open my own hands, and I was very much afraid—I didn't understand it."

Linda continued saying that later she questioned Gypsy about what happened and she told Linda "that it was her ego that was dying."

Linda was slightly interrupted when, instigatingly, Charles Manson whispered out loud to Mr. Fitzgerald, "Ask her about the five thousand dollars."

Mr. Bugliosi indignantly stood up and objected to Judge Older.

After the interruption, the counsel approached the bench and we were dismissed for morning recess.

A picture which caused many laughs in the jury room during recesses was to watch Mr. Scalise sitting in a chair with his feet propped up on the table. Inevitably, he would fall asleep there and display all the typical ingredients of the early silent movies—he snored loudly with his mouth open, his teeth would rattle.

Ray would deliberately hit his book on any object within his vicinity to disturb Mr. Scalise. It was funny to look at the old man sleeping, but the jurors did not appreciate Ray's antagonistic behavior.

Mr. Fitzgerald resumed his interrogation.

Linda stated that she had a conversation with Tex Watson in which she told him that she was on her way to South America with her husband and his friend, Charles Melton, who had inherited some money. She added that

112

them and some other people were going to South America by boat and sail around the world. Linda then said that as soon as she had mentioned money, Tex "started going on this trip" and telling her that it wasn't her money, that it was everybody's money and it was just there to take, and that there was no right or wrong. It was just theirs. Mrs. Kasabian testified that Tex told her "but there's no wrong" and that he just kept going on and on. Then she said, "And I accepted the fact that there was no danger in doing it, and that was about the conversation."

However intricate and meticulous in the questioning which Mr. Fitzgerald imposed upon the witness, he didn't succeed in establishing whether Linda stole the five thousand dollars or not. He did manage to find out that, in the absence of her husband, she had taken a bottle of acid (pills) out of their trailer.

Mr. Fitzgerald switched to a new pattern of questions in regard to Charles Manson's behavior and philosophy.

Linda Kasabian stated that Manson made love to her four times and that while Charlie made love to her, he would talk of his beliefs. Linda mentioned that although she disagreed with his philosophy in some respects, she couldn't tell him so, because she had always been told, "Never ask why." The girls used to always tell her, "We never question Charlie. We know that what he is doing is right."

"Were you afraid?" asked Mr. Fitzgerald.

"Yes," responded Linda.

"What were you afraid of?"

"I was just afraid, He is a heavy dude—man."

Everybody in the courtroom laughed.

Manson and the three female defendants joined the laughter.

After everybody quieted down, Mr. Fitzgerald, looking up at the ceiling and crossing his arms, a characteristic gesture of his, asked Linda, "What is a heavy dude?"

"A dude is a man. Heavy. He just had something, you know, that could hold you. He was a heavy weight, you know, he is just heavy. Period."

Mr. Fitzgerald, looking straight at the witness, asked her, "Did you love Charlie?"

Linda rubbed her forehead and looking at Charles Manson said in a quiet voice, "Yes, I did. To be truthful I felt...I felt that he was the Messiah come again, you know, the second coming of Christ."

Checking Charlie's face, I noticed that not once did he dare look at Linda. He ignored her and occupied himself with a pencil and a drawing book. Sadie,

113

Katie, and Leslie, taking a hint from him, also didn't pay attention.

Linda then said that she loved Charlie because when she first met him, he generated love and truth—she believed practically everything Charles Manson told her, but questioned some of the things he said.

Mr. Fitzgerald asking, "I believe on your direct examination, you said, 'no sense makes sense,' what do you mean by that?"

"I don't know. That's what Charlie told me."

Before the session was adjourned, the defense counsel asked, rapidly, of terms which the witness had heard while at the Spahn Ranch.

Linda said that the term *Karma* is "what you have to do to pay for it." Blacks have been under the white—like picking up garbage left behind by the whites, and that *karma* is coming. That is, it is going to be the reverse —whites are going to pick up the garbage left behind by the blacks. The *karma* is, somehow, already happening and the blacks are going to start "Helter Skelter."

Linda stated that she couldn't relate exactly as to how, what, or who told her what. She learned the philosophy partly from Charlie and partly from the girls.

When Mr. Fitzgerald questioned the witness about the prosecutor's promise of immunity in return, she replied, "It is just a piece of paper. As far as I'm concerned, I am doing what I feel I must do."

Then, somberly, Linda added, "From the moment it happened, I knew that I would be the one to tell the truth; I knew I would be the one to tell it, and I never had immunity in my mind. I never knew this was going to happen. This is something that to me I look upon as a miracle. I just know I have to do this, whether it's immunity or not, it doesn't matter.

"I want to tell it as it was...it is my own conscience."

"Are you testifying because you are afraid of the death penalty?"

"I don't believe anyone dies from the death penalty."

"Your are testifying to save your own life?"

"No, because I stated once before I could give my life if none of this happened... it is not a matter of saving my life. It is just a matter of telling the truth."

"Amazingly serene," said Mrs. Osborne, seated in front of me, while leaning over and covering her face with a note book.

"Indeed," I replied, trying to disguise my voice as not to be noticed.

Of course, Mildred referred to Linda's composure, which showed no affect or emotion in the tone of her voice.

"Shh!" exclaimed Olivia Madison. Mildred and I just smiled.

Court adjourned.

It had been a long and informative week. We all needed a rest and looked forward to going out for dinner. Friday was the only day of the week that the bailiffs would make reservations and take us out to dinner. The Friday evening outing had become a sort of adventure in cuisine. The bailiffs wouldn't tell us where they would take us and it developed into a sort of guessing game. They wouldn't give hints. However, the route the bus driver followed usually gave us a clue and that way, we would name the restaurant before reaching its location.

Tom, Ray, and I, after having our complimentary cocktail with dinner, would chip in with me in buying a bottle of wine. We sat together most of the time.

The dinner talk was gay and animated, ranging from the Vietnam war to Marlon Brando's newest picture, from the growing need of things left at home to the latest political intrigue in Washington.

"Hey, Bill!" said Tom, "come on down to my room and have a drink."

"What's up?" I inquired.

"Drink—what else?" snapped Ray.

"No, really, why don't you come?" Tom frowned impatiently.

"Okay, I'll be there," I responded, and then asked, "What time?"

"Oh, about ten or fifteen minutes after we get home... I mean the hotel," he corrected himself, and we both laughed.

"We better start thinking of the hotel as our new home," I said. "It'll be a long time—I don't know but I just have that feeling."

"Oh, cut it out," said Tom as he looked at me seriously for a moment and went on.

"I'm glad you're part of this jury."

"Why?" I asked.

Tom looked over at me steadily for a moment or two. Then he looked at the rest of the jurors who were seated next to our table and leaned forward a little.

"No kidding, Bill," he said slowly. "I'm glad a guy like you is part of this jury because you're interesting to talk to, and like you said, it's going to take months before the end is over, and by far, you seem the friendliest guy. Keep it up."

"You're putting me on," I said, "but thanks anyway."

Tom's invitation was indeed charming and sincere. During the week after court session, Olivia, Tom, and I would always go to the recreation room and run into each other in front of the refrigerator. We were all after ice cubes for a drink before dinner.

Olivia's favorite drink was a Manhatten, later she changed to martinis, which was Tom's favorite drink. At noon, while at lunch, everybody collected olives left out of club sandwiches and gave them to Tom. Such was his popularity as a drinker of martinis.

I liked Tom. He appeared to be a dedicated father to his children and a devoted husband to his wife. On weekends, regardless how late he went to sleep, he would always get up and go out and swim with his two children. His wife stayed in bed and wouldn't come out until they had breakfast in the recreation room. The weekend was dedicated entirely to his family and for that I respected and was glad to have Tom as a friend.

On the bus, returning to the hotel, Tom confided to me that his wife had brought him some engineering magazines, and if I would be interested in reading them.

"Thanks, but no thanks," I responded, "I have enough given material in court to keep me busy."

Tom would read those magazines during recesses and times when we were just waiting in the jury room for some unexplained reason.

On my way to Tom's room, my nextdoor neighbor, Mrs. Deborah Hart, stopped me and suggested to join her and other jurors to play a game of Password.

The Password game turned out to be disastrous. No one seemed to know or care about the rules. I was the loser because my partner, Violet Stokes, misunderstood the meaning of the word on account of my pronounciation. Everybody laughed at the way I pronounced the word after a couple of rounds. I felt irritated and walked out of the recreation room and into the little lobby.

A few minutes later, Debbie came over and apologized.

Ray, standing on the threshold of his room door, called me and offered me a beer. Tom had brought a tin metal putt and a couple of golf clubs to Ray's room. Debbie joined us at my suggestion and the four of us had a grand time at practicing golf putting.

Genaro Swanson, aware of the laughter, also joined us and practiced. He declined an offer to drink and left a short while after, to his nextdoor room.

That was the first time Mrs. Hart had given herself to be friendly and open in conversation to Tom and Ray. It also led to the four of us practicing golf everyday after court on the hotel grounds. Tom, Ray, and Debbie would bring their drinks, individually, hidden under a towel and place them near a tree.

As a joke, Tom and Ray would aim at one another's glasses and nearly succeeded.

Eventually, Ray acquired his own golf club and Mr. Hart provided his wife, Debbie, with one.

Again, on Saturday, at 10:00 A.M. we were taken around the pool. I wanted to see the beautiful girl in the bikini again. She was there.

"There's your chance," said Marvin, "go and talk to her."

I ignored him and kept walking. However, deep inside of me, my mind was no longer trying to discern with the eye of a detective as where had I met or seen this girl. I wanted to talk to her. Know more about her. "Jesus," I thought to myself, "it's been so long since I've spoken to a girl, a beautiful girl like ... Christ, I don't even know her name."

"What are you going to tell her?" insisted my redheaded friend juror. Again, ignoring Marvin's question, I accelerated my walking pace so I could lie down on the chaise longue next to her's..

She laid still on her back, with her eyes closed, facing the sun. Deliberately I stood next to her and began removing my shirt, trying to capture her attention. She didn't react, nor even open her eyes. I knew she was not sleeping because when I first glimpsed her presence, she was shufflling the pages of a magazine, which at that moment lie on the cement besides the chaise longue. I took the longest time possible to remove both my shirt and matching Bermuda pants. No reaction. Then I applied Coppertone suntan oil on my body and made the most clumsy unnecessary noises. Still she didn't acknowledge my presence. I glanced at her thin and appealing waistline—further down, her almost perfect navel formed a tiny hole. I shivered out of pleasure.

"Damn it!" I told myself, "You want to play games? Okay, you've asked for it." Without hesitation, I dove in the pool, came out instantly, and went back to my chaise longue, wet and dripping.

Without mercy or thinking of the consequences, I shook my hair, with both hands, on top of her body. The sprinkling of drops of water didn't bother her one bit. Amazed, I sat on the chaise longue, still staring at her, when finally I noticed she opened one eye. She sat up and searched around. Seeing no one around within a radius of ten feet, she addressed me in an "as a matter of fact" attitude.

"Be more careful the next time, will you?" She laid back again and added, "I don't like to be awakened with water, got it?" She closed her eyes.

"You were not asleep," I said, without apologizing.

"Yes, I was," she responded defensively, without opening her eyes.

"If you sleep like that," I answered, "then you can sleep through anything." Then, half jokingly, I exclaimed, "No one sleeps through that sound!"

117

No response.

"Gee, I'm sorry," I said. "I must confess that it was intentional but... but..." She opened her beautiful brown eyes and stared at me as she sat up and smiled.

I looked at her full breasts and somewhat dazed continued saying, "but what's a man suppose to do when..." Somehow, the words didn't seem to come out. I felt like I was under a spell.

"When what?" she interjected gently.

"Listen," I said, trying to be nonchalant, "I know we met someplace before. Somehow I can't remember where."

"Have you ever had the feeling that you know somebody?" she asked me, and then added, "when in reality, you don't?"

"Sometimes" I replied, "but in this case, I'm positive that we met before."

"You're right, I was just teasing you," she said in a more relaxed manner. "We met at a party in Santa Monica."

"What's your name?" I asked her.

"Laura... Laura Castro," she said, "now do you remember?"

"Go on, tell me more about yourself," I insisted.

"Well, we met at a party in Santa Monica and you were with a girl... a girl I believe from Colombia, I don't know for sure."

Laura pronounced the words with an accent, an accent I couldn't detect. It was not Spanish or French. It sounded like a combination of both.

"I was with a Brazilian fellow, who..." Her face became serious for a moment. She picked up her hand bag and pulled out a package of cigarettes and matches. I grabbed her matches from her hand and helped her light the cigarette. Just before she bent to reach for the light, she looked up at me and smiled. "Now, do you remember where we met?"

"I've been to only one party in Santa Monica," I replied. "That was about three or four years ago and if you had been there, I must have seen you... wait a minute..."

Surprised, I looked closely at Laura and cried, "Your hair! That's it...it's your hair. You didn't have it that long."

Laura laughed heartily and conceded that all her life she had long hair but that on that occasion, she had it cut short.

Laura's hair reached above her waist line and was strikingly beautiful —a shiny black color.

Suddenly, while speaking to Laura, I discovered that the two female bailiffs hadn't said anything about my talking with her. However, at one point during our conversation, I explained to Laura the reason for my being at the Ambassador Hotel. I warned her of the regulations and, oddly enough, she confided to me that she had not read nor cared to know anything about the Manson trial. That suited me fine!

Other jurors received visitors in the pool grounds. At lunch time I invited Laura to join me for lunch. Laura stated she preferred sunbathing rather than eating.

"What about tonight?" I eagerly inquired. "Would you like to come to visit me? Or perhaps you'd care to see a movie at the recreation room?"

"What are they showing?" she wanted to know.

"*The Pad and How to Use it*, a Universal Picture," I responded. "They say it's a funny, good picture."

"Sad, that's what it is!" she snapped up argumentatively. "I saw it and didn't like it. I didn't care for the ending."

"Well, just come over tonight—we don't have to see the movie." I said, trying to convince her, but suddenly Laura cut me off.

"No thanks—I've a date tonight."

"I see," I said, while holding from showing my disappointment. Silence.

Laura sensed my change of attitude and smilingly exclaimed: "C'mon, it's nothing like that! My uncle came from Brazil last night and he's taking me out to dinner tonight. I promised him and besides, we have to talk."

Again, I noticed Laura became suddenly serious, almost sad. Somehow, it became obvious that Laura was a very sensitive girl—of changeable moods. I wanted to ask her if there was anything wrong, or perhaps if she cared to talk about whatever bothered her. Then I thought that it was only my imagination—that it was a fabrication of my mind. I discarded those thoughts momentarily.

I stared at Laura intensely and we both smiled.

"What picture would you like to see next Saturday night?" I asked, taking for granted she would accept my invitation.

"I don't care," she answered.

"I have a Universal catalog with all their pictures."

"How about a musical?" Laura said.

"Sure," I responded, while thinking of one musical film... *Thoroughly Modern Millie?*"

"I saw it."

"Well, there's only one more," I said, "the Universal Studios don't produce many musical films."

"Which one is it?" Laura asked impatiently.

"Flower Drum Song."

"That'll be great! I haven't seen it," said Laura.

"Time to go, Mr. Zamora!" shouted one of the female deputies.

"Okay, I'll see you next Saturday," Laura said.

I wanted to stay and talk with her more.

A few minutes before all the jurors were to go upstairs to get ready for lunch, I approached and tried unsuccessfully to persuade the two female bailiffs for one of them to remain and keep custody of Mrs. Betty Clark and Mr. Payne, who also wanted to stay and enjoy the outdoor environment a little longer. However, one of the female deputies informed me that the senior bailiff had told her by phone that "he wanted everybody upstairs whether they wanted to go to lunch or not."

Reluctantly, Mr. Payne, Mrs. Clark, and myself joined the rest of the jurors. "All week long inside," I said to Mrs. Clark, "and we can't even stay outdoors."

Betty folded her arms in an annoying manner and, as to be heard, she responded, "No such luck!"

One of the complimentary assets which I enjoyed while being sequestered at the Ambassador Hotel was the use of my 400 Sony tape recorder.

Interestingly enough, I had placed it center, on the wall-to-wall counter beneath the windows. The two powerful speakers set at each end of the counter and diagonally, slightly facing the middle of the room, produced a true stereophonic sound. The music provided me with wondrous and countless hours of pure relaxed joy. The music was my companion whenever I wanted to be alone and, on more than one occasion, sufficed me with the necessary mood to either write or make love.

I shall always be grateful to musical strings and piano concertos, for they endeavored me to awake my literary spirit and raise my sexual romantic passions.

Many times, some of the jurors came knocking at my door. They wanted to sit and listen to my music. They were always welcome.

Debbie, my next door neighbor, had previously asked me if it would be alright to plug in a connection with a speaker into my tape recorder so she could also enjoy the music at the same time. Upon my approval, her husband brought the equipment but the plug didn't fit the outlet of the Sony. However, through some electrical device I managed, at the expense of eliminating the sound of one of my own speakers, to pipe the music directly into her room. The connecting wires hung outside from my bathroom to her room.

Mr. and Mrs. Hart thanked me a lot. They both told me they loved the type of music I played and warned me not to be concerned about keeping them

120

awake in case I wanted to play music in the late hours of the evening. They guaranteed me they always went to sleep with soft background music. Mine, according to them, was better than perfect. I was glad for them.

Little I knew what it would cost me to become a Samaritan. Mrs. Osborne, the nextdoor neighbor to Mrs. Hart, and Miss Edith Rayburn on the other side of my room, both wanted me to also provide them with music. Although they had no wires or speakers, just the same, they wanted me to connect their rooms with some music.

The weekend outing again was to an unknown place; however, for security purposes, they did not disclose our destination.

The week before, Mollie had announced, in advance, the place we were going and also the time of departure. This time, she did not want to divulge any particulars about the outing.

Ray Harris became terribly upset and made Mollie aware of it. He contended that he had to know ahead of time so his wife could hire a babysitter for his two children or else he would have to take them along. Tom was on his side.

Mollie, unable to cope with their protests, finally explained that "last week, she got hell' from Captain Arden. The fancy written announcement she had conceived the week before was against the young captain's way of thinking. "An announcement like that," Mollie told us, "could fall in the hands of the press... and that's why he (Captain Arden) is against any announcement ahead of time."

Then Tom suggested to Mollie to let the jurors know verbally as where we were to be taken on Sunday without a written announcement.

Mollie refused and stated that anyone of us could tell one of our guests the place of destination and that they, in turn, might possibly inadvertently tell someone else.

"Before you know it," Mollie added, "the press would be there taking pictures... and the defense counsel could use any little excuse for a mistrial. We cannot risk or take a chance. Understand?"

"No sense makes sense!" shouted Ray.

Some of the jurors chuckled.

Tom and Ray did not go.

"Marineland of the Pacific" was the place and had been visited by some of the jurors before. The bailiffs allowed the management to have our pictures taken while feeding the sea whale killers, only on the condition that such photographs would not be released for public use until the trial was over.

However, Oskar Stokes, Violet's husband, an avid amateur photographer, became quite astute and took snapshots of only the jurors. Oskar would constantly hunt for us and, needless to say, it was annoying for some of the jurors. Mrs. Betty Clark wouldn't allow him to take her picture, nor would Olivia Madison or I.

Olivia, during dinner, would have her share of martinis. Her demeanor and table manners would gradually change and diminish as she would drink many martinis.

One day she blew her top when she discovered a "candid" snapshot of her's taken by Violet's husband. The picture depicted Olivia eating a mouthful of ice cream sundae. It showed her mouth curled up, hair out of place, and the look in her eyes was retarded and sleepy. It showed Olivia a little less than intoxicated. For obvious reasons, Olivia couldn't tolerate the nearby presence of Violet Stokes's husband.

It became clear to the jurors that Oskar's purpose to take so many snapshots of the jurors was more than just a hobby.

"I wouldn't want to have more than one picture of the jurors," stated Betty in the presence of others.

"Thanks!" I teasingly exclaimed.

"No, really. Do you think Violet's husband wants those pictures for nothing?"

"He has something else in mind," said Olivia.

"You bet your sweet life he has!" stated Mildred.

"You mean he's going to sell those pictures after the trial?" I inquired, pretending not to have thought about it.

"Right!" shouted Olivia.

"He'd better not come near me," said Betty, as a matter of resolution.

"Neither I!" said Mildred and Olivia in unison.

"Count me too!" said this writer.

We also discussed why the bailiffs would allow someone like Oskar, a nonjuror, to take pictures of us. No one came up with an answer; however, we all came to an agreement that Violet had become an "apple girl" and that she could get the moon if she asked for it from the bailiffs.

For dinner, we went to the 'Princess Louise,' a unique shipboard restaurant anchored permanently in the Port of Los Angeles. The restaurant had a commanding view of the main channel of Los Angeles Harbor. However, we jurors were restricted from going anywhere on the ship. The food which was served was mandatory, that is, we couldn't order anything on the menu. Everybody was served well-done roast prime rib of beef, au jus, except the bailiffs, who had a choice of asking how they wanted it cooked.

122

Most people to whom I have spoken thought that we jurors of the Manson trial were always taken to the best places and that we had no limit as what to order on the menu. Nothing could be further from the truth. The five dollar dinner allowance in a restaurant such as the Princess Louise didn't give us much choice as what to ask for on the menu.

I have eaten before at such restaurants and it is quite different. You sit alone, you wait, and eat what you want; of course, that means more money, but psychologically speaking, you do receive better service.

We jurors had already begun to be annoyed with one another. The fact of being thrown together in a room, away from people and faces in general, only added discomfort among the jurors themselves and friction between jurors and bailiffs.

Another issue of importance was that the waiters and waitresses would pass the word to other customers as to who we were. Curious people would go out of their way just to take a glance at us. It made us feel like dummies or robots, rather than human beings.

I remember one time, when the bailiff, wearing civilian clothes, had escorted three or four of us to 'Lucy'. The cabins converted into restrooms at the Princess Louise are small. The bailiff waited outside. A man approached me inside and quite excitedly, addressed me:

"Do you know that the jurors of the Manson trial are dining here tonight?"

"Really?" I acted astonished.

"Yeah, man," he said with assurance.

"What do they look like?" I inquired in a bewildered manner.

"I don't know," he replied reflexibly, "but I'll find out."

He exited, and those jurors who were inside with me, burst out laughing.

On Monday morning, we didn't go to court immediately. We waited two long hours before we walked in the courtroom at exactly 10:55 A.M.

Mr. Fitzgerald again lost another round of questions when Linda insisted that she would "tell the truth" about the murders even if she did not have immunity, saying, "I want to tell it as it was... it is my own conscience."

"Are you testifying because you are afraid of the death penalty?"

"I don't believe anyone dies from the death penalty."

"You are testifying to save your own life?"

"No, because I stated once before, I could give my life if none of this happened... it is not a matter of saving my life. It is just a matter of telling the truth."

Linda Kasabian answered Mr. Fitzgerald's increasingly aggresive questions quietly, almost without emphasis.

"Did you scream, attempt to hide, run away, or call the police the night

123

five persons were killed at the Tate residence in Benedict Canyon?" the attorney asked.

"No," she responded.

"Did you do any of those things as you ran from the estate grounds, past homes, and back to a car parked at the bottom of the hill?"

"No," she replied.

Mr. Fitzgerald also questioned Mrs. Kasabian's credibility by suggesting that it was she who had suggested to some people that "they go the house of Harold True and kill some people."

"I certainly did not," the witness replied.

Pursuing the same line of questions, Mr. Fitzgerald asked if she was the one who suggested an actor in Venice as a possible victim. Linda indicated that she had not, until Manson had asked her about the man.

After her account of the two nights of murder, Mr. Fitzgerald repeated essentially the same questions about her actions at a service station at the ranch the day after Leno La Bianca and his wife, Rosemary, were killed.

The defense counsel asked Linda if she had said anything about the murders the day she visited the Hall of Justice after the La Biancas were killed, or when she talked to officers at the Malibu Sheriff's Station about her child, Tanya, or when she went before a court weeks later to get the child back. In each instance she replied, "No."

"You weren't afraid to call the police because of the fear something could happen to your child, were you?" Mr. Fitzgerald asked.

"Yes," she replied, "to both of us."

"You abandoned your child to the very people you profess to be afraid of, right?"

"Yes, I had to," Linda responded, "because something inside of me told me that Tanya would be safe."

In a fast pace, Mr. Fitzgerald asked Mrs. Kasabian questions about her reaction to seeing Steven Parent shot to death by Charles Watson, known as "Tex" Watson.

"Did you scream?" inquired the lawyer.

"I screamed inside," replied Linda.

"Did you do anything to stop Tex?"

"No."

"Did you run?"

"No."

"Did you try to hide?"

"No."

124

"After you heard screams in the house, did you attempt to run?"

"Yes, towards the house."

"And then what did you do?"

Linda kept up with the tempo. Mr. Fitzgerald asked her questions, and she answered them quickly.

"I just ran, I had to climb up over an embankment and over the fence, and then laid down on the ground for a few minutes to get myself together."

Mr. Fitzgerald proceeded inquiring.

"Did you, Mrs. Kasabian, question Tex Watson about why the murders were committed?"

"No," Linda answered and then continued saying: "but, I said, 'Wow! You killed these people for money.' "

Then the witness testified that Watson showed her some money he said was taken from the victims.

Mr. Fitzgerald asked about the second night.

"Did you attempt to ask not to go?"

"I did it with my eyes, but not with my voice."

"Did you act like you were sick or pretend to faint or cry?"

"You couldn't cry at the ranch," Linda said. "I said no with my eyes and my heart, but not with my voice."

Mr. Fitzgerald, in a last attempt, continued cross-examining Mrs. Kasabian and asked about the murders and how she could, if she had wanted, have reported them to the police, but did not.

To close his interrogation, Mr. Fitzgerald asked Linda if she was helping a writer for *Life* magazine to prepare a book about her life. Mrs. Kasabian admitted this, but denied that the prospect of a twenty-five percent share in the profits was influencing her testimony.

"Why then are you doing it?" Mr. Fitzgerald asked. "To be famous, and secure money for yourself? Isn't that right?" he asked.

Linda, as before, with placid attitude, but sincerely, replied, "I don't care. I don't care if I am famous or not. It doesn't matter."

Then, raising her head and looking at the jammed courtroom, she added, "Actually, the purpose for the book is so that younger people can relate to me and see that this road I went down is not the way and they will go another way. That is my purpose."

I guessed Mr. Fitzgerald encountered a Chinese wall in Linda Kasabian. According to the way he conducted his cross-examination, he only asked questions about Linda herself, her life, and very little about "the murders."

On the other hand Linda Kasabian's serenity was by far too real for anyone to question. Her answers were sincere and to the point. She left no trace of doubt in our minds that she was telling the truth. To my knowledge the witness was linked in one way or another with the Sharon Tate-La Bianca killings and that made her already famous. It didn't influence me that she was writing a book and would get twenty-five percent of the profits. Of course I almost thought it would be a natural thing. After all she was a personality involved in this crime and people would like to know what was going on in her mind. It didn't affect me one way or the other because it's a natural thing to do now. Everybody writes a book and if you're not capable someone else will. Her reason why was obvious, an opportunity. She was there saying all these things. Why shouldn't she say them to someone else, a writer who could embellish them. I have read the book *In Cold Blood*, and Truman Capote went over in jail and got the guys to talk about it and they were killers. But he brought them out as human beings. I didn't see the accused as killers. I got to know them as people. People with feelings. Because after all you see them day, day, day, after day. It's not like you are just hearing about them or seeing a glimpse or a picture, and I believed her.

Linda Kasabian was brutally honest. She really didn't have ways to portray something that she wasn't. She went out of her way to expose herself in every single detail of her sexual life. How much more intimate can you get? When you expose yourself you are drunk with truth, I mean what is left? She went to bed with anything, she did everything in bed, men, women, everything else. She spoke at such length about all those things, being married, the narcotics and so forth, so it was nothing, so when this came in, well, it's just one more thing that she was involved in. And had it not been for her we would never have known about these murders.

She said, "I am not like you (Manson) I cannot kill." She said that to him two or three times in her testimony. "I'm not like you, Charlie, I cannot kill." I believed her. But I, as a juror, wanted to know why she, having been an accomplice the night of those slayings, could get away with it. We had been told by her testimony that she did not participate but only eyewitnessed the crimes. Why is it then that Mr. Fitzgerald skipped the issues involved around the crimes and dwelled upon other matters which only prolonged the length of the trial? Or was it perhaps that Mr. Fitzgerald thought of the jurors as a group of ding-a-lings, with no minds of their own? And, he perhaps tried to frustrate the jurors by evading the issue?

I am sorry to say that Mr. Fitzgerald failed on behalf of his client. Not once, during his cross-examination, did he try to bring the innocence or lack of participation of Patricia Krenwinkel in the crimes for which she allegedly

126

was indicted. However, the trial still was in its diaper state and Mr. Fitzgerald may have had something in mind. We'll see. The judge adjourned the morning session for lunch.

The temperature outside was hot. TV cameramen tried desperately from a long distance to take pictures of the jurors but the bus blocked their view. "What happened?" asked Edith Rayburn. "Who knows?" replied someone.

Inside the bus, the windows were whitened with Bon Ami. Deputy Taylor and Mollie were carefully concerned about where we sat and ordered us to sit farther back—away from the front of the bus. The bailiffs prohibited the jurors to open any windows and also told us not to look outside.

"Please," emphasized Mollie. We didn't understand, even though they tried to explain to us that they were only doing what they were told to do. The driver followed a different route to the place where we were taken to lunch. The newsstand outside the Hilton Hotel was covered with a white sheet and the sheriffs led us to the dining room through the kitchen to avoid newsmen and cameramen, rather than through the front entrance. We noticed the press was not around.

Lunch at the Hilton had become a habit. Everybody sat more or less in the same place. Tom, Ray, and I would ordinarily sit at the same table. Mrs. Ruth Collingwood and her close friend, Edith, would also sit together; however, Ruth would follow Ray. Ruth, for some unknown reason, acted uncomfortable in my presence and to a certain extent I resented it. We would avoid each other but at lunch, ironically, we would end up at the same table, facing each other.

Tom and Ray knew of my feelings. Ray especially would say remarks to the effect of making the situation more intolerable. Ray was beginning to respond almost like a child; the more I told him not to make statements about my friendship with Ruth, the more he would do so. He caused me more than once to become embarrassed. It was not very ethical on his part, especially at meal time.

On the other hand, Ray would continually refer to Mildred Osborne as "the elephant." He knew that Mildred befriended me and sensed my liking for her. He enjoyed hearing me defend Mildred. I, like an idiot, fell in his trap more than once.

However, that morning in the jury room, while we were waiting to be taken down to the courtroom, Ray displayed no sign of decency in front of the other jurors. Ray Harris deliberately made every type of noise in order to keep awake those who wanted to take a nap. Those who read books or knit were equally disturbed.

Now, while we were eating, he continued his savorless jokes. I ignored them for a good length of time. He continued and finally again brought the uneasy state of my relationship with Ruth in the open.

I ignored him up until he asked me, "Why do you hate Ruth?"

Ruth and I looked at one another intensely. Obviously, from the look on her face, I gathered she believed I had told Ray something in regard to his question.

"I don't hate Ruth or anybody else," I replied, still looking at Ruth's face. Then, turning to Ray, I added, "but quite the contrary, you seem to have the infinite capacity to maintain in your small head a hate for Mildred Osborne. Why?"

"Me?" said Ray, as if what I was saying was the first time he ever heard it.

"Yes, you," I said seriously. "Do you realize that ever since we have sat together, your favorite speaking subjects have been Mildred and Ruth? You must dream of them every night. Well, I tell you, you can go on talking about them, but just leave me out of the conversation. Understand?"

Ray didn't answer.

"I'm glad you spoke that way," said Ruth, somewhat relieved. "For a while I thought you really didn't like me."

"To tell you the truth," I replied, "I'm not crazy about you any more than you are about me. However, we must comport ourselves like decent people and not like enemies."

"You're right," Ruth said, "I'm glad we're talking."

"We will from now on," I responded. We both smiled and rose to go back to court.

Mr. Dave Shin, representing Susan Atkins, was the second defense counsel to cross-examine Mrs. Kasabian. Amazing but true was the fact that Mr. Shin did a "catastrophic job of poor representation" in behalf of his client. His Korean accent and weak vocal chords could have been overlooked had he conducted an interesting and challenging cross-examination.

Mr. Shin, for what appeared to be an hour, interrogated Linda about her pretrial conversations with Mr. Bugliosi, Mr. Stovitz, and other personnel involved in the murder trial. I, as a juror, couldn't see the importance. It didn't make sense to hear Mr. Shin asking questions of some unrelated area of the subject, while his client, Susan Atkins, was being tried for committing murder.

I took a look at the other jurors and noticed that neither one of them were taking notes. There was no need. Court was adjourned.

The next day, a funny thing happened to Mr. Ronald Hughes on his way to court.

It had become noticeable among the jurors, bailiffs, and, presumably, amidst members of the press, that Mr. Hughes had been wearing the same suit since he replaced Mr. Ira Reiner. Leslie Van Houten's new lawyer wore the same suit—a one-time light-gray striped suit which, because of over use, had gradually acquired a tan, almost yellowish shade.

At the beginning of the morning session, Mr. Hughes walked in court and as he reached for some documents at the far end of his table, the seams of his jacket gave way.

At that precise moment, Deputy Taylor announced to the counsel that Judge Older wanted them in his private chambers. Mr. Hughes went coatless.

The bearded, balding lawyer came out almost immediately, walked to the railing separating the court from the audience and said, "I'm told by the Judge I must wear a jacket this morning. Does anyone have a jacket?"

Everybody gasped with surprise when a young man volunteered to loan him his jacket. Mr. Hughes' large frame didn't fit into the coat. It was too small. Still another brave man gallantly allowed Mr. Hughes to wear his jacket. It fit rather tightly but just the same, the attorney returned to the in-chamber conference with the judge.

Mr. Shin continued his cross-examination.

The sharply dressed lawyer of Korean ancestry would also repeat an identical question previously asked by Mr. Bugliosi or Mr. Fitzgerald. The witness answered the same way as before. It was like a "repeat performance." He didn't ask any questions of his own but only brought out the testimony already established in the records of the court reporter again. It made me wonder if he had paid attention while Mr. Fitzgerald was questioning the same witness. We jurors had made comments at various times of his "short siestas." Once more, I have to use the same term as before —Mr. Shin "failed" on behalf of his client. He showed no preparation nor animation in his cross-examination.

Mr. Shin was also intrigued with a subject which had little, if any, pertinency to Linda's testimony, as when he asked her, "Do you believe in Santa Claus?"

And again, the sharp sense of humor of co-prosecutor Aaron Stovitz caused laughter in the courtroom, when he asked out loud, "Then or now, Counsel?"

Mr. Shin's last question was in regard to a $ 25,000 reward.

"I never heard of any reward," answered Linda.

No more questions.

Judge Older addressed Charles Manson's attorney and said, "You may cross-examine, Mr. Kanarek."

What a contrast. Whereas Mr. Shin skipped most of the main issues during his cross-examination, Mr. Kanarek did exactly the opposite. He dwelled upon a particular aspect of her previous testimony until he wore it thin.

After asking one or two questions, he would come back to the same question. Mr. Kanarek's tactics were beyond belief. He was notable for allowing no continuity in his questions. Sometimes he got hung up by merely repeating himself or just establishing a conversation with Linda in which she ultimately would concede and say, "I don't understand," meaning she didn't understand the unnecessary verbosity of the defense counsel.

Other times, Mr. Kanarek would prolong his way of thinking that he couldn't even reframe his own question.

Mr. Kanarek questioning Linda, "You don't understand what?"

The witness, somewhat puzzled, "Didn't I answer the question the way I am supposed to answer it?"

Mr. Kanarek, establishing conversation, "Well, has anyone told you that you are supposed to answer questions in a certain manner?"

"No, but I thought I answered your question, but you kept asking."

"Well, my question is..." Mr. Kanarek couldn't remember so he asked the court, "May that question be read back, Your Honor?"

"Which question, Counsel?" said Mr. Stovitz.

George, seated at my right, couldn't control himself and laughed aloud. The rest of the jurors just tittered.

Judge Older, quite moved but without showing it, said, "Reframe the question, Mr. Kanarek. It's been a long while since we've gone by it."

"Very well, Your Honor," said Mr. Kanarek, and again, he would get involved in a phraseology which, as the days went by, became familiar to our ears and I may add, it was monotonous and terribly tiresome.

He would say: "Well, did you, in fact, say that?" And, as to be helpful, he would add, "Well, would you reflect upon that for a moment and tell us whether, in fact, you did state (whatever)... Did you, in fact, say that?"

That was Mr. Kanarek's way to ask questions.

Unquestionably true, he managed to upset the witnesses at times and objections from both the prosecution and the other defense counsel. What about the jurors? He nearly put us to sleep. We fought not only the lack of any air ventilation in the courtroom, but also the tedious and endless questioning of Mr. Kanarek which lasted eight agonizing and boring days. Day after

130

day, he would carry a shipload of law books under his left arm while hauling a heavy dilapidated overnight bag with his right hand. Mr. Kanarek's cargo appeared to give one the strong impression that he was fully prepared and that he was going to explode the minds of the witnesses and discredit their testimonies. With the enormous bundle of books and transcripts, Mr. Kanarek made one wonder that he was "digging in" through that material in the most minute detail and then bringing into court the secret that would split the case wide open.

Undoubtedly, every one of the defense counsel did their best to their ability to come out intelligently and clearly. However, Mr. Kanarek's fault was his overbearance with words which didn't answer questions we jurors wanted to hear. The redundancy of his questions was also a handicap which enabled us jurors and, I presume, the rest of those present, to feel exasperated and quite truthfully "fed up."

It was a relief when noon recess arrived.

We were taken for lunch at the Biltmore Hotel.

Most of the jurors had the "special," which consisted of beef tacos, fried rice, and beans. The chef de cuisine obviously was not well aware of the true flavor Mexican dishes are made of and his recipe was mainly to satisfy tourists and not Southern California residents.

Ray and Tom didn't sit with me, nor the rest of the time we were sequestered. We kept at a distance only during meals, but would chat and even visit occasionally in each other's rooms at the hotel.

We returned to court and the counsel asked Judge Older to approach the bench. Mr. Fitzgerald wanted to discuss some legal matters. They were all assimilated facing the judge, some even had their elbows on the bench. I was particularly intrigued at the court reporter, who, while operating his machine, would bend sideways to be able to hear what was being said. Somehow, the bending of his head reminded me of the illustration of the dog on the "His Master's Voice" RCA record label.

I chuckled at what I was seeing when suddenly, Mr. Aaron Stovitz moved towards the center of the court, and cried out, "Your Honor! Your Honor! Mr. Manson just held up the *Times* edition and showed it to the jury!"

Mr. Stovitz's body blocked my view of Manson—it happened so quickly that, personally, I was in the midst of confusion. There were so many things to see at one time. However, I saw court bailiff Albert Taylor rush and grab a newspaper from Manson's hands, and fold it up. Charlie ducked, thinking perhaps that the deputy was going to hit him on the head, and grinned when he found out otherwise.

Some members of the press and other spectators stood up to get a better view of what was going on. The counsel spread out. Manson stilled grinned with gusto. The three female defendants approved of him and joined in laughter.

"Remain seated!" said Deputy Tull.

Judge Older, for what appeared to be the first time, spoke with a tone of anger. "Will counsel approach the bench?"

The courtroom was tense. Everybody had their eyes trained at the bench. The faces of the counsel were individually attentive to what Judge Older was telling them. Mr. Bugliosi walked out of the group, received a newspaper from Deputy Taylor and gave it to his partner, Mr. Stovitz, who subsequently handed it to the court. Someone then called Bailiff Taylor to approach the bench.

From the look on Deputy Taylor's face, we jurors could easily deduce that Judge Older was reprimanding or somewhat questioning him as how the newspaper got into Manson's hands. Deputy Taylor usually sat in front of a desk with a six-file drawer cabinet at his left. On top of the cabinet usually rested a pile of law books and, occasionally, empty coffee cups and news-papers. The cabinet was situated directly behind where Charles Manson was seated. The tall deputy, while speaking to the judge, pointed at the file cabinet, from where Manson had reached out his hand to seize a copy of the newspaper and displayed it for us to see. Thus, why of the deduction.

Judge Older picked up some notes, stood up brusquely and in an unusually hard tone of voice, announced, "This court is now in recess," and rushed out of the courtroom. A couple of jurors were already on their feet when the counsel began to file behind the judge and into his private chambers.

There was no question that some of the defense counsel had brought the newspaper into court, and now Judge Older was to find out who was res-ponsible.

True, it may not have been the counsel's intention to make it available to Charles Manson, but a lawyer on this case would have to be more careful. We jurors were told that the defense counsel would do anything to delay or complicate the trial, that they would also hunt for any little reason and use it as an excuse for a mistrial. Did they? We will never know.

The law specifies that no one is guilty unless proven beyond a reasonable doubt, and yet, the lawyers of the defense research every code of law to prove and make their clients appear innocent even when they know the accused are guilty.

The thing I questioned myself was that, suppose they are granted a mistrial for any reason—doesn't that mean their clients still have to go through another trial? How many times can these lawyers ask and be granted such objections?

"What's going to happen next?" George Kiefer asked me.

"I'm in the same boat as you are," I replied, as we both stood up to go upstairs in the jury room.

"I bet you," George continued saying in a low voice, "that's why they shielded the bus windows at noon when we went out to lunch."

"Maybe you're right," I whispered back, and then added, "to prevent us jurors from being exposed to outside information."

We waited in the jury room the rest of the afternoon.

The jurors tried to keep themselves busy. Betty and, especially Mildred, pulled out their knitting bags and utilized their time. Mr. Scalise slept considerably, and Danny trailed him pretty closely. Mr. Welch occupied himself with a book of crossword puzzles. Edith and Ruth occasionally broke out in a friendly argument while playing canasta games. George, Marvin, Martin, and Violet were set to put together a large round jigsaw puzzle. Mr. White displayed his interest on the trial by meticulously transferring his 6" X 9" court notes onto an 8.5" X 11" pad.

Genaro, between talks with Debbie, enjoyed himself by reading a novel of western flavor—*Barquero*. Tom divided his time by reading an engineer's magazine and, at intervals, chatting with Ray, Debbie, and myself. Ray made sure his presence was observed by continually pounding on the table with his notebook, but especially by going out near the front door and making his voice sound like Deputy Taylor's, "Okay, folks, time to go!" His imitation was remarkable.

Oh yet, I forgot to mention Olivia Madison. Well, she did what she had done previously. She kept fixing her hair and, of course, visited "Lucy" frequently.

We jurors suffered the consequences for what Manson did. The bailiffs, by order of Judge Older, had whitened the windows of the bus, chosen a special route to and from the Ambassador Hotel to avoid newstands, and made certain we did not have access to radios, television, and telephones.

Mr. Scalise protested vigorously when he was told he couldn't speak personally with his wife. Telephone calls were made by way of writing a message which the bailiff on duty would read to the person he was instructed to call.

Mr. Scalise wouldn't accept the ruling. He went to see Deputy Taylor and both had a heated conversation in the little lobby.

"I must talk to my wife," demanded Mr. Scalise.

"I'm sorry, but no one can phone tonight," said the senior bailiff.

" I tell you... my wife is waiting for my call," insisted the retired electrician, and then added, rather concerned, "if she doesn't hear from me tonight... she'll go crazy."

"I have to make a business call," demanded Olivia Madison.

"I understand what you're going through," said Deputy Taylor. He shook his head wearily, "try to see my position... I'm only following instructions."

"Don't give me that stuff!" Mr. Scalise cried exasperatedly, "YOU are the one who gives the orders. Baloney."

"I'm not going to stay here and listen to...." Deputy Taylor reflexed his thoughts for a moment and said, "The Judge said no phone calls tonight, and that means everybody."

The lofty sheriff returned to his room and slammed the door.

"You wait until you hear what I'm telling you!" shouted Mr. Scalise. The color left his cheeks and his mouth tightened—he looked dumbfounded.

"I'm not surprised at anything," said Olivia, staring at Mr. Scalise, who, meanwhile, had sat down at the top of the stairs, and began with his usual habit in fiddling with his retractable tape measure.

"Right you are to say so," he observed.

"Just think nothing of it," Olivia retorted.

Mr. Scalise stood up, then, taking his leave, walked up the hall and shouted, "I've had it!" and went inside his room.

Next in line to have his phone message related was Tom Brooks. Deputy Mollie Kane was at that moment assisting the jurors. Everyone who was in the little lobby could hear what Mollie read on the phone. The blonde female bailiff hung up and announced, "Claudia (Tom's wife) told me to pass on to you that she understands now why jurors must be sequestered."

"Big deal!" exclaimed Olivia, critically.

Mollie stared at her to show careful incredulity—surprise. But it was Martin Paine who wilted under the remark, he touched his mouth with the back of his hand and shook his head.

"I don't mind being sequestered," stated Olivia, "but what I do resent is being treated not as a human being, but strictly as a prisoner without rights."

Mollie volunteered to help Olivia with her business call, but the annoyed-looking juror turned down the offer and returned to her room.

Everybody started to hate the situation. The whole thing. All of it. Some began to complain among the others, others displayed a certain amount of artificiality and shallowness in their conversations. Some started getting sick and tired of what had become of them. They felt they were living a boring life based on phony values. A few accepted and remained calm.

134

Later in the evening, Mr. Scalise came over to my room and talked about how "ridiculous" it was to be sequestered. He complained that his wife was all alone in the house, that she was not well and needed him. He himself had an ailment of the eyes, and was not happy with the set up at the hotel. He didn't know if he could take it much longer.

"You'll get over it," I said, and we bid good night.

The next morning we waited in the jury room.

Outside of the presence of the jury, Mr. Fitzgerald moved to strike the entire jury on the grounds that panel members might have been prejudiced by seeing the headline on the newspaper held by Manson. Mr. Kanarek argued in support of the motion.

Judge Older denied the motion but agreed to pull the jurors individually to the witness stand and ask them if they had seen and read the headline on the newspaper.

We jurors kept apart from each other. Nothing was spoken, nor did anyone say anything or mention the incident. However, I noticed that Mr. Scalise had placed a bottle of tablets on the table and asked to be reminded as when to take them.

Betty Clark, with crossed arms and cigarette in hand, stood by the window staring at the Federal Building across the street. Ruth and Edith played cards. Debbie and Genaro sat together and smoked. Olivia, also smoking, spent time visiting "Lucy." Tom and Ray both had placed their feet on a table, and were discussing the possibilities of going out to bowl. George, Marvin and Martin Paine were locating pieces on the jigsaw puzzle. Danny, rocking on the chair with one hand under his chin, had his eyes closed. Violet began reading *The Love Machine*. Mr. Welch asked for words to complete his crossword puzzle. This juror was observing everybody behind Mildred, who was knitting.

So, one by one, we descended into the courtroom. They began by calling Juror Number One, Mrs. Mildred Osborne. When she returned, some wanted to ask her questions but she simply went to see "Lucy."

The next juror, Betty Clark, also didn't make any comments.

By the time Juror Number Three, Marvin Connolly, was down, Larry shouted out loud, "Okay, folks! This is the time to tell the judge all your grievances—I sure will!" Nobody made any comment and just waited for his turn.

"Okay, Bill," said Deputy Taylor, "it's your turn." I buttoned up my jacket and followed him into the courtroom. The room was packed with people. The court clerk asked me to raise my right hand and repeat after

135

him:

"I do solemnly swear that the testimony I may give in the cause now pending before this court shall be the truth, the whole truth and nothing but the truth, so help me God."

I had heard that oath many times, I knew the words by heart, but for some reason, this time, the words couldn't come out. I must have been nervous and now that I recall, there's no question about it, I was petrified with fear in not knowing what was coming up. I hadn't the slightest idea what it was all about.

"Would you please be seated, sir," said the court clerk. It felt somewhat funny sitting on the witness stand, watching all those people staring at me. Their eyes watched every move I made. Then I assisted the bailiff to adjust the familiar microphone to my level voice and, for a second, I smiled out of fear or whatever.

"Would you state your name and spell it, please, for the court records," said the court clerk solemnly.

"William M. Zamora, Z-A-M-O-R-A."

"Mr. Zamora," said Judge Older, "do you know why I brought you down here?"

"No, Your Honor," I responded.

Then he continued, "Mr. Manson had a newspaper in his hands, were you able to read the headlines?"

"No, sir, I didn't."

"But you did have an opportunity to see the newspaper, didn't you?"

"Yes, Sir," I tried not to volunteer any information for fear of not being able to express myself clearly and especially because of my English pronunciations. However, to clarify my positive response, I offered an explanation and stated, "I noticed that Deputy Taylor grabbed a newspaper from Mr. Manson's hand."

Judge Older, sensing my position, gave me a benevolent look and said, "Had you the opportunity to read the headline, would that affect your ability to weigh impartially the evidence on this case?"

"No, sir," I responded.

"Mr. Zamora, I'm going to ask you the same question I asked the other jurors, Do you swear on your oath as a juror," Judge Older turned firm, "that you can and will act impartially and fairly in the matters submitted to you and that you can and will base your verdict solely on the evidence presented in this trial and in accordance with the court's instructions?"

"Yes, I do," I answered.

"Thank you, Mr. Zamora," said the judge.

"Don't mention it," I replied, and laughter came from the courtroom.

When the rest of the jurors came back, no one asked anyone why we had gone downstairs. I personally at the time didn't know what the headline read and could only speculate but without really caring to know or finding out about it.

However, at the end of the guilty phase, I overheard a conversation between George Kiefer and Daniel Jackson.

"I told the judge," George stated, "that I didn't vote for Nixon in the first place," to which Danny replied that he had mentioned in court, "I think it ought to sell a lot of newspapers."

Both alternate jurors agreed that their responses to Judge Older's questions prompted rounds of laughter. Nevertheless, George observed, "It wasn't meant to be funny. I don't understand why they laughed."

Deputy Taylor escorted us downstairs. The courtroom was crowded and every eye was following us jurors. As soon as Judge Older sat behind his desk, the three female defendants rose together and said in sing-song unison: "Your Honor, President Nixon says we're guilty. Why go on with the trial?"

I frowned upon what the accused were saying. I didn't know what they meant.

"Sit down, ladies," Judge Older ordered sternly.

A couple of days later, I discovered by accident what the headline on the newspaper read which caused the incident and furor in court.

Inside the Hall of Justice building, the corridor leading up to the coroner's receiving room, there was always a line of hearses, sometimes with corpses inside of them, and near the exit, two large-wheel rubbish receptacles. The jurors would always walk away from the hearses and garbage containers, as they permeated a strong detesting smell. However, this particular day, an incoming vehicle made the jurors step aside next to the wall except me, who opted to walk along the hearses when, lo and behold, on top of all the garbage, a Los Angeles Times newspaper copy was widely exposed with its heavy black printed words, "MANSON GUILTY, NIXON DECLARES."

I understood from that moment on the speculation the headline stirred among the counsel and Judge Older himself. The Nixon headline had everything and the newspapers, quite understandably, played it for all it was worth.

Newspaper readers, weary of reading about the Vietnam war, devoured everything that was within the case. Public opinion and that of President Nixon's, could not have influenced the jurors' minds. Mr. Nixon and everybody else could have stated before the trial began that Charles Manson was guilty and it wouldn't have affected us jurors at all. We eighteen selected jurors were the only ones facing the evidence day after day, and twelve of us would eventually balance the verdict of guilty or not guilty, regardless of Mr. Nixon's or anyone else's opinion.

Unfortunately, neither the counsel nor the judge gave enough credit to the jurors who had, under oath, given their word of honor that they would render an honest and fair verdict upon the evidence presented in court.

The course of the trial, interrupted by events surrounding President Nixon's remark, resumed with Mr. Kanarek's cross-examination of Linda Kasabian.

Mr. Kanarek advanced his examination slowly and went over the same grounds repeatedly in questioning the witness about her use of drugs in 1969 during about a month when she lived with Charles Manson and his family at the ranch in Chatsworth.

The same as Mr. Shin, Mr. Kanarek dwelt on Mrs. Kasabian's admitted use of LSD "about fifty times."

Mr. Kanarek, standing in the middle of the courtroom, began asking the witness to describe each LSD trip.

Oddly enough, Linda observed, "Yes, I can remember each time I took LSD."

"You must be kidding," I thought to myself. "Anyone being able to describe the number of times that he or she eats or drinks something for a whole year must have quite a recollective memory." I didn't believe Linda Kasabian, and the shrewdness of Mr. Kanarek showed when he asked her to relate details around each of the fifty times she took LSD.

Linda testified that during her first trip of LSD in Boston, she just sat and listened to music. Her second LSD trip was in New York in the company of a guy who told her about the Haight-Ashbury district in San Francisco, California. They also talked about love. Her third LSD trip, she couldn't think or remember. Mr. Kanarek suggested if that many trips of LSD had left any scars on her memory.

Linda denied it and added that she had not kept a score card as to how many trips she had taken. Touché! for Mr. Kanarek.

"How would I know?" said Linda, "I meet someone and then decide to take LSD."

Linda continued her testimony about LSD and said that while she was pregnant with Tanya, she only had two or three LSD trips. She stopped because she was told that it was dangerous for the child which was to be born.

She observed that having a companion during a LSD trip makes one know the person better. She stated that she has had sexual relationships during

138

LSD trips.

Linda mentioned that she was given medication the first day at the ranch. She took one LSD trip while Charlie went to Big Sur and explained that it was a weak trip and that Sadie gave it to her. Linda was not sure what type it was, but suggested it could have been mescaline—not quite so intense—but mellow.

"It's a fair statement," said Mr. Kanarek, "that you don't remember anything that happened at the Tate home because of those fifty LSD trips?"

"No," replied Linda, "it's not a fair statement."

Mr. Kanarek continued with the same line of questions.

"Mrs. Kasabian, on the night, on the second night that you left the Spahn Ranch, did you know that you had participated with three other people who, all together, you and the three other people together, had killed five people?"

"No," answered the witness.

"Directing your attention, Mrs. Kasabian, to the second night and your state of mind, your thinking as you left the Spahn Ranch on the second night. Did you know that what you and three other people had done the night before caused the killing of five people?"

Linda responded that she didn't understand the question and that she didn't know the answer.

Mr. Kanarek daringly suggested, "You mean you don't know what answer Mr. Bugliosi wants you to give?"

Immediately, Mr. Bugliosi stood on his feet and protested out loud, "Your Honor, I object to this. These are unbelieavably outrageous remarks!"

I, personally, as a juror, didn't approve of such antagonistic remarks. Surely, that was a very poor courtroom tactic and Mr. Kanarek only proved to be less than admired and respected as a professional lawyer.

We jurors wanted to hear facts exposed through a series of intelligent questions and not be witnesses to slanderous and dubious accusations. Was Mr. Kanarek's purpose to indulge us jurors to believe him? Was he trying to disqualify, in open court, the integrity of Mr. Vincent T. Bugliosi as an honest deputy district attorney? He didn't succeed. Mr. Kanarek succeeded, however, when he irked the patience of the counsel, judge, and the jurors at the expense of his client, Charles Manson, who repeatedly elbowed him.

Court adjourned for the day.

At dinner time, I noticed that for the last four days, Mr. Scalise didn't join the rest of the jurors. He remained in his room. He visited me every night. One night he came to my room and chatted with me, he spoke about his "show dog" and worried that his wife didn't know how to clip the hair on the dog's ears. He wanted to bring five thousand slides of his prize-winning dog from home to show the jurors. He complained and complained and complained...z-z-z-z-z-z . When I woke up, he had left the room.

As I expected the next day in court at the start of the morning session, Judge Older announced in open court that Mr. Scalise had asked to be dismissed because of a stomach ailment. He was replaced by alternate juror Ray Harris. Ray was selected by lot from the six alternates.

The trial contined.

Mr. Kanarek maintained a strong pressure on the witness. He wouldn't overlook any little answer without dissecting every word. We jurors were somehow tired and felt the same fatigue and strain the witness was undergoing.

Indeed, Mr. Kanarek showed a remarkable sense of intelligent approach during his interrogation; however, the length and redundancy of his questions made Mr. Kanarek's performance appear boring and tedious.

The witness, on the other hand, gradually began showing fatigue and her answers declined in tempo and sharpness. Judge Older, at two different times, asked if she wanted a rest, but Mrs. Kasabian always regained her composure, refused suggested court delays, and continued her testimony.

Mr. Kanarek then returned to his table and selected two 8 X 10 color photographs and asked the court permission to approach the witness. Judge Older granted permission and Mr. Kanarek then showed Linda a color picture of a victim. We jurors couldn't see the picture but from the explanation given by Manson's attorney, we knew it was the picture of Steven Parent. The picture as we jurors saw it at a later date during the deliberation, depicted young Parent slumped over in the front seat of his Rambler automobile after being shot twice in the left arm, once in the chest, and once in the face by Tex Watson.

"Do you recognize this man?" asked Mr. Kanarek.

Linda partially saw the picture and turned her head away. While sobbing, Linda said that it was the man in the car who Tex shot four times in the driveway of the Polanski residence.

Mr. Kanarek kept pointing the picture at the witness but his sadistic intentions of shoving the photo in front of her face were defeated when the court ordered him to return to his table and to conduct his cross-examination from there.

However, Mr. Kanarek asked permission again to approach the witness and Judge Older granted it.

With two pictures, Mr. Kanarek walked in front of the jury box and "accidentally" dropped the folder containing two photographs.

Mr. Stovitz rushed promptly and bent down to pick up the pictures. It was too late, some of the jurors, including myself, had already caught a glimpse of the gruesome photographs.

Humbly, Mr. Kanarek apologized to the court for the incident and then showed Mrs. Kasabian a picture of the body of Voityck Frykowski, lying on the lawn outside of the Tate residence. The victim, stabbed fifty-one times, shot twice in the chest, his head severaly bashed in as a result of blows received by the butt of a gun, and his face, totally covered with blood except for his staring, protruding eyes, was shocking to one's sense.

"Do you recognize this man?" asked Mr. Kanarek.

"Oh God," Linda gasped, turning her head and crying.

Recovering her composure a little, she looked from the witness stand to the defense table and mouthed to the defendants: "How could you do that?"

I glanced at the three girl defendants and they didn't seem to be moved by the question.

Mr. Kanarek, as to prevent the witness from looking at the accused, inquired, "Do you know the man shown on this picture?"

"It's the man I saw at the door," Linda answered.

Mr. Kanarek pressed upon the witness to hold the picture in her hands but Mrs. Kasabian refused.

"She has already looked at it, Your Honor!" shouted Mr. Bugliosi. "Is there any necessity for him to continue flashing it in front of her face?"

Mr. Kanarek, facing Mr. Bugliosi and then the court, grinned with pleasure while he said, "Your Honor, it seems like I am the one that is always the villain."

Linda Kasabian's crying was interrupted when Judge Older asked her if she had seen the photograph well enough to identify the victim.

"He was the man I saw at the door," she replied.

The judge addressed Mr. Kanarek: "Alright, you may return."

Reluctantly, Mr. Kanarek returned to his table. He just stood up facing Linda who was crying quite openly.

The jurors kept shifting their eyes from the witness to the defense counsel. Nothing was said for a few seconds. Eventually, Mr. Kanarek moved to the center of the courtroom, behind the counsel of the prosecution and, with a disdain, almost sarcastic attitude, inquired: "Why are you crying now, Mrs. Kasabian?"

With a paper tissue, Linda rubbed her eyes gently and replied, "Because I can't believe it. It is just... I don't know."

141

Mr. Kanarek, in a typical pose of his, opened his legs and crossed his arms while holding a folder in one hand, he asked: "You can't believe what, Mrs. Kasabian?"

Linda, recuperating, responded "that they could do that."

"That they could do that?"

"Yes."

"I see," said Mr. Kanarek. He walked two steps toward the witness, and added "not that you could do that, but that they could do that."

"I know I didn't do that!"

"You were in a state of shock, weren't you?" said Mr. Kanarek, still advancing one more step.

"That's right."

Attempting to show Linda's complicity, Mr. Kanarek asked her: "How do you know you didn't if you were in a state of shock?"

Linda rubbed her eyes gently with the tissue, looked at Mr. Kanarek with assurance, and responded:

"I do not have that kind of thing in me to do such an animalistic thing," and then, her voice raising, "I just know I didn't do it, Mr. Kanarek."

"But your state of shock might have made you forget whether you entered the Tate house. Is that right?"

"I know I didn't go into the house," Linda replied and added "the shock didn't affect my memory."

The defense counsel then asked her to identify a photo of the body of Abigail Folger.

Linda glanced at the picture, then kept her eyes on Mr. Kanarek's face as the lawyer held the picture in front of her and urged her to take it in her hands.

"She doesn't have to take it," said Judge Charles H. Older, "she can see it."

Mr. Kanarek continued asking questions about the night at the Tate residence and once more he asked Linda to identify a large color photograph of the body of Sharon Tate.

The photograph depicted the late actress dressed in see-through tops and bottoms. Pictorially speaking, the picture was shocking. The almost nude body of Sharon, lying on her left side, showed her eight and one-half months pregnant and sixteen stab wounds, with a white rope around her neck, and in a lake of blood.

With both hands, Linda covered her face and gasped, "Oh God, Oh God," and began to sob.

The courtroom was absolutely serene. I glanced at the other jurors and all

142

appeared motionless. Linda turned away from the picture and cried.

Ronald Goldman, Mrs. Kasabian's attorney, and Deputy Tull led her weeping from the witness stand.

Judge Older recessed court so Linda could regain her composure but she did not return to the witness stand for the rest of the day.

After waiting in the jury room, the jurors went down to court simply to hear the judge's usual admonition. We were dismissed until next Monday.

The weekend recesses always reflected the fanfare and good spirits among the jurors. Families and friends were excluded from joining us for dinner on Friday nights and for that reason, we referred to the evening of the last working day of the week as "Jurors' Night."

Debbie loved Mexican hot food and became quite excited when she heard that we were going to Casa Vega, a Mexican restaurant located in the San Fernando Valley. Everybody ordered South-of-the-Border food, except for Danny who preferred New York steak.

Saturday morning, at the pool, was a disappointment. I waited and kept looking constantly at the entrance for the Brazilian girl to enter. Nothing. Laura didn't show up.

Marvin and Martin invited me to join them for a paddle tennis game but I declined their offer and sat by the entrance. I skipped luncheon. Instead, I went outside and stood near the fire escape window, checking down below if Laura had arrived. No sign of her.

I looked at my watch and it was half past twelve, and I grew impatient. I paced up and down the area, turning at the end of the balcony, then back again, like a sentry on guard duty. I was making up my mind or trying to, on whether to return to my room or to wait longer, when I heard what sounded like someone calling my name. I went inside to investigate. Approaching the little lobby, I saw someone bending over to pick up an object. At my sound, she straightended up, a little startled. It was Laura.

At the sight of her, so unexpectedly, for I had thought she wouldn't come, I became so excited I could hardly breathe. My hopes soared.

"Mr. Zamora, you have a visitor," said the heavy-looking sheriff.

"You bet your sweet pee pee!" I responded gladly. He didn't hear me or didn't care because he was watching television.

"Hi, how are you?" said Laura, and smiled.

I greeted her back, a little nervously I realized, for my voice trembled oddly, like a fool I thought.

"Come to my room," I suggested selfishly, glad she and I would be alone.

"Oh, I have to return to the car, my uncle is waiting," she answered readily

143

"and he'll be disappointed if I'm late." Then, as to console me, she added, "You don't know Brazilian uncles."

No, I did not know, but I nodded.

"My uncle treats me as if I was his own daughter," she continued "and can't trust me out of his sight."

"Won't take but a minute," I said and held her hand. We began to walk towards my room. The narrowness of the hall prompted me to lead in front of Laura. When we were approaching my room, she slowed her steps, then brought herself to a stand still.

"Listen, Bill," Laura said, "I just thought of something. Instead of going in your room now for a while, why don't I come up and spend more time with you tonight? My uncle will be leaving this afternoon for the weekend visiting my aunt in San Jose, and we can have more time to ourselves."

I did not hesitate to think. I did not have to. It was too good to be true. I believed Laura. My heart raced like a wild animal's after a mile-long chase.

I said, "Yes" with enthusiasm and led her back to the elevator.

Laura left and in my excitement I forgot to ask her at what time she would be returning.

"You have a beautiful wife," observed Sheriff Gonzales.

"She's just a friend of mine," I answered.

"Why did she leave so soon?" asked the Mexican-descent Deputy inquisitively.

"She'll be back this evening."

"Good for you," he said.

"You bet your... thanks," I replied and left to go back to my room.

One may say that my behavior was like a high school student. However, the fact of having been sequestered for so long and unable to attain a man's intimate desires made me behave somewhat younger than my true years. I didn't care. Laura had said she was coming later and that was my only thought for the rest of the day.

I spent the whole afternoon playing paddle tennis with Marvin and Martin. At first, Marvin didn't seem to have coordination or speed. Every day after court session, when the jurors were taken down to the swimming pool area, Marvin would be the first to grab the paddle racket and ran to wait in the courtyard for a challenger. The redheaded juror practiced and practiced until he developed a good sneaky technique which made him along with Danny top competitors. The two young men, both of few words, didn't appreciate my defeating them.

I was surprised and glad to see Martin play paddle tennis so well. The

144

some sixty-year-old mortician possessor of a trim physique and looking good for his advanced age, took his defeats charmingly. Lack of harmony eventually developed between them which made me withdraw from participating in future games. More of this later. The food of the coffee shop at the Ambassador Hotel tasted even better that evening—Perhaps because of the mood I was in.

After dinner, I offered my services gladly as projectionist. The movie was shown in the recreation room, which consisted of two rooms. The large one, which had a big window overlooking the pool and grounds down below and the city in the background, was used to seat the audience. The small room was used for playing cards and housed two refrigerators for the jurors to store perishable foods of their own. Bathroom facilities were located next to it. Upon my suggestion, the projector was placed on top of an ironing board as no table was available in the small room.

I delayed starting the film until Laura arrived.

Laura was beautifully dressed in brown and white colors. Her long black hair fell over her shoulders and made her look like a kind of goddess, I thought. At the recreation room, I proudly introduced her to everyone.

All the jurors present and their relations, as well as Senior Bailiff Tracy and his assistant, Deputy Gonzales, approved of her looks and they congratulated me on my good taste.

I sat Laura in the back of the room, knelt, and asked her, "Would you like something to drink?"

"Like what?" she responded.

"I have Scotch, if you wish."

"Yes, that'll be fine."

I started to rise when Laura whispered, "Bill..."

"Yes?"

"I'm sorry, but..." Laura said, lowering her voice, "I drove my uncle to the airport and didn't have time to stop and eat something."

"Would you like me to make a sandwich?"

"Oh, that would be great," Laura smiled and added seriously, "You don't mind, do you?"

"Oh yes, I do," I replied teasingly as I rose.

I was fixing drinks for Laura and me when Deputy Tracy walked in and asked if he could have one also. How could I refuse—he was in charge for the weekend. Gladly, I gave him a stiff drink. Later, after the end of the first reel, he came back for more and on the third time, when he took another drink, he jokingly offered to buy me a bottle. Tracy, that was his first name, seemed out of pain and acted as if I was the best friend he ever had.

After setting up each reel, I would sit on the floor next to Laura, holding her hands.

Laura was enjoying *The Flower Drum Song* when suddenly, Deputy Gonzales opened the door from the hall. He closed it immediately so the light and the voices of those in the little lobby wouldn't disturb those watching the movie. Deputy Gonzales's silhouette stopped and looked around searching for someone. He stood right in front and signaled me to follow him.

I had no idea what he wanted me for. I rose and walked outside into the hall and waited while he carefully closed the door behind him.

"Tracy wants to speak to you," Gonzales said and pointed at the door of the room where Deputy Taylor usually slept during the week.

"Can't he wait until the movie is over?" I exclaimed.

"It's important Bill,"replied Deputy Gonzales, in Spanish, and again he opened the door where Tracy, smoking a long cigar, and Evelyn, another deputy, were standing up, waiting for me.

"What is this all about?" I inquired and smiled at them. However, their firm reaction indicated to me something was out of order.

"Zamora," Tracy began saying, "how long do you know that chick?"

I didn't like the term he used nor the tone of his voice in which he spoke. Deputy Tracy sensed my feelings and apologized before I even mentioned it, "Oh, I'm sorry," he said as he puffed his cigar.

"What I mean," he continued saying, "is that if you met this girl at the hotel, you can't have her visiting you.

"It is against the rules."

"I thought you knew her," Evelyn spoke, "you two were talking at the pool last week and no one told me that... I wouldn't have let you talk to her if..."

Tracy coughed and after he cleared his throat, he brought it out in the open why he had sent for me.

"I want you to tell that girl to leave. You don't know her."

The three deputies stared at me intensely, waiting for my reply. I hated their guts and at that moment, felt like going to my room, pack everything, and leave.

"To hell with it!" I thought to myself.

My eyes must have looked stormy. I wanted to reply but couldn't. My hands were shaking and wet with perspiration.

"Why did you have to wait until now?" I finally said with a deep voice to control my anger.

Then, turning to Gonzales, "Why didn't you tell me this afternoon she couldn't visit this evening. Why?"

"We didn't find out until a few minutes ago," interjected the Tom Ewell look-alike sheriff. Something in his face stopped him and he didn't say why she had to leave.

"What did you find out?" I inquired firmly.

"Bill, there are regulations that we have to abide by and..." Tracy hesitated in his words and looked to the other deputies as for support, and sat on the bed.

"Look," I said, still controlling my anger, "I came here because you wanted to talk with me. Now you tell me what the reason is that Laura has to leave."

"Zamora," said Deputy Gonzales, "you don't know that girl personally and bes..."

"Who says I don't know her?" I snapped up furiously and looked at the bailiffs.

"I met Laura three years ago—isn't that long enough for anyone to visit someone as a friend? I don't make the habit of inviting strangers to my room, you know!"

"Maybe you don't know her that well," said Evelyn, "we have to protect you and make sure no one speaks to you about the case."

"Protect me from what? She doesn't care about the trial... she doesn't even..."

"You don't know Kanarek or Fitzgerald...they're fast."

"Yes, man," said Gonzales, nodding his head.

Tracy had already laid on the bed and was smoking his cigar. He seemed to enjoy watching the rings of smoke he produced. His relaxation upset me.

"Let's get this over!" I said, raising my hands and moving one step towards Tracy. I stared at him and said: "Tracy..."

"Yeah," he said rather weakly. Things seemed to be closing in on him.

"You wanted to see me... now, let's get this business straightened out once and for all."

Then, moving one step closer, I added, "Why does Laura have to leave? You know the reason and I'd like to know it."

I wanted a definite answer, but I had no idea I'd be told that one of the jurors was responsible.

"Yes, Bill," said Tracy, "a juror came over and told us. I'm going to write a letter to the judge and tell him everything. We can't take chances, especially when the juror revealed that you met this girl down at the pool."

When Tracy mentioned the pool, I felt my head swimming, and the veins in my neck ached with a mixture of pain and hate. Yet, I kept seeing Tracy's face through misty eyes as if what he had said din't affect me. Then, casually, I asked which one of the jurors had made the statement, knowing full well in advance the name of the juror wouldn't be disclosed to me. Tracy asked me again to tell Laura to leave the sixth floor.

"You don't expect me to tell her out there in front of everybody, do you?" I asked sarcastically.

"Oh no, you can tell her after the movie is over," Tracy answered.

"After the movie is over and in *my* room!" I snapped determinedly.

"Okay, but it has to be before midnight, before the night shift takes over."

I walked out of the room and Deputy Gonzales followed me. "I'm sorry, Hermano (brother), said the husky Mexican deputy as he placed a hand on my shoulder.

"Forget it," I said, with despise and shook his hand off. "I don't need your sympathy," and went back to sit next to my guest.

Laura searched my hand and whispered, "Everything okay?"

"I'll tell you later," I responded. We both smiled and squeezed our hands. While pretending to be interested in the movie, I sensed Laura knew something had happened. She kept staring at me with her beautiful brown eyes, begging me to tell her. I felt uncomfortable and rose. Laura followed me to the small room and once more wanted to know if she had caused me any trouble for being there. I reassured her that there was no trouble—just a misunderstanding.

"I don't care to see the rest of the movie, do you?" Laura asked me. I didn't answer.

I was thinking how to begin to tell her to leave, when unexpectedly, she took my hand and said, "Let's go to your room."

We exchanged looks for a second, smiled, and, hand in hand, left the room.

"Excuse us," I said as Laura and I walked through the little lobby where Martin was seated on the stairs going up to Shirley's room, and Marvin and Danny were spread on the floor watching a baseball game on television. They stared at us.

From the corner of my eye, I caught Marvin's face, who blinked at me as a sign of approval.

We climbed the stairs and then into the narrow hall that had a floral red carpet on it. The walls were painted black with old-fashioned electrical devices on each side, streaming light as we walked by. We could hear voices chattering inside the rooms. I opened the door with my key and said, "Come on in."

"Your room is beautiful," said Laura as she sat down and looked around.

"For the time being, it's okay," I said.

"Are the other jurors' rooms the same as yours?"

"No," I replied, "however, those jurors who have seen this room, claim that I have the best. Oh well, who cares. Do you want a drink?"

"Yes, the same please," she said and got up.

"You certainly have an elegant room," Laura said admiringly and walked towards the window.

"Oh, Bill, isn't the view wonderful?"

"It sure is," I murmured behind her and offered the drink.

"Look at those two tall buildings—what buildings are they?"

"The Richfield Plaza," I responded. "The equivalent of Los Angeles to New York's Rockefeller Center."

I came closer to her.

Laura turned around excitedly saying, "Is that right?" We were face to face and very close. Everything was still. Our eyes met and held momentarily, and gradually lowered at one another's lips.

"I just read it some place..." we kissed softly, "but don't quote me," I added and then we kissed again, soft and gentle.

Laura walked back to the chair, sat down and rather flirtatiously said, "I know why they called you. You want me to tell you?"

"I'm not so sure you know, but go right ahead."

"In the first place, they called you to tell you that you didn't know me and to get rid of me. Is that right?" Laura said with assurance.

"And, in the second place?" I retorted, covering my astonishment and sitting down.

"I was coming to it," she snapped back while taking a sip from her drink. "They also told you that *I am* a spy! Am I right or not?"

Unable to say anything adequately, I laughed loudly. Laura didn't think it was funny. She gulped her drink in one setting and stood up facing me, with both hands on her waist.

"Well, aren't you going to throw me out?"

Laura's brown eyes were sparkling and shiny. The effect of the drinks had made her aggressive.

"They told you that, didn't they?" she demanded to know.

"Yes," I answered. "In the first place you guessed correctly, but in the second place, you're a little bit off."

"But why, Bill? I'm no spy. I don't care to know anything about what you see or hear in court. I came here because I wanted to see you and have

149

a good time—I don't know—perhaps I'd better go..."

Laura began to leave when suddenly, there was a knock on the door.

"Please don't leave now," I whispered to Laura, "stay a little longer." I pointed at a chair for her to sit down and then peered through the door. It was Jim Reid.

My friend, noticing I had company, wanted to leave right away. However, I needed his moral support. Jim had previously met Laura a week before and his presence, I felt, would make Laura change her mood. Jim could stay a while I thought, then leave after so Laura and I could talk about more important and intimate things. It worked. After he joined us for a drink, Jim left.

Laura and I spoke quite openly about topics of current nature. In the course of our conversation, I was happy to discover Laura and I had much in common intellectually and that, besides her striking beauty, she possessed a remarkable degree of intelligence. She was equally interested in many of the things that meant most to me.

Without her knowledge, I disapproved intensely the amount she drank and the excessiveness of her smoking. However, the important thing was that for the first time since I had been sequestered, I felt fulfilled and complete in Laura's company.

A heavy pounding on the door disturbed us. It was Deputy Gonzales reminding me that it was almost one o'clock A.M.

"Just two more minutes," I said.

We had to say goodbye before she left my room.

When I held her hands, Laura stepped back in a manner shy yet eager and then threw her arms around my neck. Her arms were astonishingly warm and her embrace sensually crushing. We kissed. Her lips were delicate and tender.

While holding Laura in my arms, I felt a strange and pleasant warmth stealing over her. It was rather like a feeling of unity and protection, too. I placed my hand caressingly over her long black hair, and felt its softness as I stroked it gently. With her eyes closed, Laura lifted her head backwards and seemed to love it. The yellow light on the ceiling gleamed on her tawny skin, making it appear even more golden. Laura opened her eyes and looking up, smiling, she murmured, "I wish I didn't have to go..."

"You'll be coming back," I responded, and kissed her on the forehead. "I promise..."

Hand in hand, we went down to the elevator where I kissed her goodnight and when I returned to my room and retired I laid awake in the darkness for a long time.

I stretched tiredly and put my hands behind my head in the way I had a hundred times before. I sensed the serenity of the night. Then I became restless. My thoughts were filled with Laura. I began remembering the smoothness of her skin, the earnestness of her beautiful brown eyes, her sensual long black hair, the crushing of her arms...and the tenderness of her lips. I quivered with pleasure and... sighed with desire... and drifted off to sleep.

On Sunday, we were taken on a private boat tour of the Port of Los Angeles. It was a very comprehensive tour which covered a personal narrative description of the harbor and its history to date, which has become the largest man-made harbor in the world. We were shown places ordinarily prohibited to the public and we also viewed the resting place of the S.S. *Queen Mary.* Everybody enjoyed the trip except for me. I was still furious inside and determined to find out who had protested Laura's visiting me. Mollie had been informed of my dilemna and, earlier, on the way to church, she had insisted on my accompanying the group. She attempted to cheer me up, but to no avail.

Throughout the excursion, I stood next to Deputy Gonzales who had expressed understanding toward my situation. I kept asking him to tell me who had said it, but Gonzales wouldn't name the juror and felt it would be unethical to do otherwise.

For dinner, the bailiffs took us for dinner to the famous Ports O' Call Village, where cobblestoned streets front quaint shops designed after an early California town, and feature exotic merchandise.

Before leaving the restaurant, Deputy Gonzales finally hinted it was a male juror who was planning to write the judge; however, the dark-complected Mexican deputy still refused to mention his name.

Unable to learn the name, I began to check out each male juror by the process of elimination.

The one whom I'd blamed more was Mr. White. His conservative attitude and manners made him appear to be the only juror capable enough to write the judge about Laura. For several days, I tried to avoid him. I didn't have the courage to face him for fear that I'd say something and also because my accusations might have proven to be erroneous. I was not sure if he was responsible for preventing Laura from visiting me.

My suspicions about Mr. White declined considerably a few days later. One evening after dinner, we were escorted for a walk. Debbie and Betty walked side by side. They walked fast. I was trailing behind them and I could hear the murmur of their voices. It was not my intention to listen, but as I came nearer, I overheard a brief conversation between them.

"I can't stand him, he's worse than a woman!" said Betty.

"The thing I don't like about him is that he can't talk without touching me," Debbie remarked as she broke a small branch from a nearby bush.

"Yeah," agreed Betty, "when we are inside the elevator, he's always rubbing his body next to mine and he's even pinched me several times with his filthy hands."

"He did that once to me!" Debbie snapped, "And I kicked him—that's what I did!" Debbie said, slapping the branch against other bushes as emphasis, and then added, "Who would believe a man like him would act like that?"

I must admit that it was difficult to believe what I overheard, especially since the pious-looking Mr. White, in no way, gave any indication of being "free with his hands."

On Monday, Mr. Kanarek resumed his cross-examination and again repeated questions which the witness had already answered.

I, as a juror, was jotting notes down as fast as possible. I wrote incomplete sentences, using only key words and leaving empty spaces between them. I memorized by associating ideas.

Late at night in my room I would fill in the missing words by memory and then type the complete sentences. However, during the last two days of Manson's lawyer's interrogation, his questions became somewhat confusing and almost irrational, causing my memory to research deeper. Mr. Kanarek's marathon performance reflected lack of comprehension in the manner he presented his questions.

One such question was, "Mrs. Kasabian, were your ideas of time the same before you started taking drugs as they were after you started taking drugs, but before the date of your arrest?"

Linda reflexed for what seemed to be a long time before answering. Quickly, I noticed that the jurors' faces as well as Linda's appeared puzzled and thought the question was incoherent.

"You have so many words," replied the witness. "I'm not following you," and then added flatly, "I don't understand the question."

"Who can?" I told myself and chuckled.

The lawyers for the prosecution appeared bored and tired, and didn't bother to object at that moment.

Judge Older, however, somewhat annoyed and rightly so, called the counsel to approach the bench.

Mr. Kanarek returned to ask questions of no importance or significance for the jurors to write down.

Court adjourned.

Following the daily court sessions and shortly after arriving at the hotel, Deputy Taylor would go downstairs to pick up the jurors' mail.

At an earlier date, he had announced, "By instructions of Judge Older, you are not allowed to read any incoming letters containing issues pertaining to the Manson trial case."

Mildred Osborne, Olivia Madison, and Edith Rayburn were the only jurors who asked questions regarding their mail. They lived alone and were concerned because they had no one at home who could bring their mail to the hotel. They didn't know what to do.

Deputy Taylor suggested for them to change their home mailing address to the hotel. "However," he said, "I'm going to check each letter you receive before handing it over to you."

"I don't like anyone to read my mail," Edith Rayburn stated indignantly.

"I didn't say I was going to read the letters!" snapped Deputy Taylor defensively.

"Then what?" Edith wanted to know.

The deputy's voice was overlapped by another question.

"How about business letters?" asked Olivia Madison before she cleared her throat.

"No problem," replied the bailiff.

"And bank statements?" observed Mildred.

"The same," said the sheriff.

"What about love letters?" Ray Harris asked jokingly.

Some jurors chuckled. Deputy Taylor's grin ceased when Edith inquired seriously, "You mean, you're going to read our personal letters? I don't like that!"

Deputy Taylor, with great effort, explained to Edith and the other jurors that before handing over a letter, he would inquire if the juror had any knowledge as to who the letter was from.

"Letters from spouses and relations are alright," he said, "but..." he continued, "if the juror doesn't know the name or can't remember it, or maybe he can't recognize the handwriting, then I would ask the juror to let me read the letter in his presence."

"What if anyone refuses?" Edith inquired challengingly.

"Then we'd send it back," retorted the bailiff.

"Suppose it doesn't have a return address? Then what?" still inquired Edith.

"We'll keep the letter until the trial is over and then give it to the juror."

"What if it were something important? How would I know? An emergency for example?" Edith protested defiantly.

"If an emergency arises, we'll discuss it then, okay?" answered the tired bailiff.

Deputy Taylor found himself in hell and high water and did his best to answer question after question.

"Gee," I whispered to Debbie and Betty, "I wouldn't want his job !"

"Neither would I," observed Debbie.

"A thankless job—that's what it is," Betty remarked.

Only five jurors received mail that day. Mildred received a friendship card signed by some girls she supervised at work. Olivia received bad news from a neighbor—Olivia's house had been robbed a week ago.

Martin Paine was sent a thick envelope containing nearly twenty or thirty small cards with handwritten thoughts by young nuns—friends of his daughter, also a nun. Mr. Paine graciously passed the cards among the jurors to read since the messages were also addressed to them.

Marvin glanced quickly at his letter and, annoyed, went to his room.

Deputy Taylor was relieved with pleasure when he read the New York return address on Edith's letter.

"Charles Rayburn...," her brother—not a stranger.

That evening at the coffee shop, some of the jurors started choosing who they wanted to sit with. Debbie wanted me to follow her, but her table was already occupied by her constant companions—Genaro, Martin, Betty, and Violet.

Edith and Ruth always sat together.

Mildred and George would pair on the same table.

Tom, Ray, and I would occupy a booth.

The rest of the jurors were "floating jurors." They would sit wherever a seat was available. Their company was not necessarily regarded as *personae non-grata*, except perhaps for the reason that they didn't add salt and pepper to their conversations. They would simply listen and wouldn't chatter or "gossip" about the other jurors. They wouldn't commit themselves. They were accepted but not hunted for their company.

Mildred Osborne and Edith stood up excitedly to see Sammy Davis Jr. arriving in a small foreign car and, later on, Walter Winchell, the retired columnist and looking pale as a white tub, stepping out of a large limousine. The ex-radio commentator was robed with a heavy overcoat. He looked sick.

154

"I'm sorry to see him looking so bad," Mildred commented.

"My God, he's old...what do you expect?" someone said.

When the meal was finished, Marvin said, "Bill, could you come to my room with me a minute? I have something I want to show you."

"Sure," I responded, "what do you have? Dirty pictures?"

He didn't answer—just grinned.

I followed Marvin out of the restaurant and into the elevator.

As soon as he opened the door, Marvin offered me a drink but I declined. My host's room was painted in light blue and the usual hotel decor was altered by the presence of an oil painting depicting a girl in a bikini suit.

"But she has clothes on!" I observed jokingly.

Marvin had pulled out the top middle drawer of a triple dresser and was busy looking for something. He didn't answer.

"Who painted it?" I asked nonchalantly.

"I did," he replied, "it's one of those paintings by the numbers' system —you know."

"Is that right?" I said, while picking up the painting to see it closely.

"Maria bought it for me. Do you like it?" Marvin asked.

"Yes, I do," I responded conventionally.

"I don't," he stated coldly.

He handed over a letter and asked me to read it.

"Who is it from?" I inquired.

"My boss," said Marvin, "the foreman of the company where I work."

The letter addressed to Mr. Connolly and dated August 7, 1970, read in part:

"It has come to my attention that our accounting department is in need of a statement of your daily expenses. As you are aware, our contract limits our employees to be paid while serving jury duty for a maximum of twenty working days. However, in your case, you have been paid regularly since May 11, 1970.

"It is my duty to inform you that we must have in our files, as soon as possible, a complete record of your daily expenses, signed by someone responsible. The total amount of expenses will be deducted from your salary.

"Please be advised that contrary to the above could cause cancellation of your salary and may incur termination of your employee status."

This was the second letter of such nature Marvin had received and he was pretty upset. He stated that he had spoken to Deputy Taylor who, in turn, had explained the situation to the judge. The redheaded juror then showed me a copy of a letter Judge Older had written to the president of his company,

155

asking for support and understanding. Among other things, His Honor mentioned in the letter that Mr. Connolly, as a citizen, was needed at the time, and that having one of his employees serving as a juror should be regarded by the president himself and the company he presided over, as one patriotic gesture for justice.

"Could you help me?" asked the youngest juror of the panel.

"What can I do to help you?"

"I want you to help me write a letter to the judge so he can talk to my boss," Marvin said. He immediately brought a draft of a letter to my attention which he had already begun to write.

"On second thought," I said, "I'll take that drink."

Marvin poured and served two Scotch drinks.

I interpolated certain words between the sentences of his draft letter and then showed it to him for approval.

Marvin didn't like the changes nor the "big words" I had inserted. He decided to send the letter as he had originally written it.

Marvin's approach indulged me to discard him also as a possible suspect about preventing Laura from visiting me.

"I haven't seen Maria. How is she?" I asked, "Has she found a job yet?"

"No, she's not working. She's still looking."

Unexpectedly, Marvin disclosed that he was rather disturbed at Maria. He confided that he had met her about a year before and had become engaged to be married three months afterward. However, she had no transportation and since he had been sequestered, Maria was using his foreign-made car. He didn't mind.

Maria, an ex-New Yorker, wasn't familiar with the city of Los Angeles, but was helpful to his mother who didn't know how to drive, but who knew the area.

"Two days ago," Marvin began saying, "Maria had a minor accident and scratched my car badly. I don't mind that as much, as having her come over to see me and not mentioning anything about it."

"Maybe she was afraid," I said unknowingly.

"No, something is wrong!" he observed and gulped his drink down all at once.

I felt from his reaction that the subject was uncomfortable and too personal for him to discuss so I didn't pursue the matter any further, and returned to my room.

On Tuesday morning, Linda, led by Mr. Kanarek, explained her reasons for having taken LSD. She testified that one of the reasons she took LSD was to extend her mind.

The purpose, she said, was to expand her powers of thinking which she was not able to acquire without LSD.

"Why did you take LSD?" Mr. Kanarek asked.

"I took LSD to discover God and self-realization—to find myself and where I'm going."

"What did you come to realize about God's realization?"

"That He is... He is the Supreme Being. He is the Creator of the Universe. I had a little knowledge of God when I was a young girl."

Linda then added that when she was at the ranch, she more or less forgot about God.

"At what point?" inquired Mr. Kanarek.

"Possibly before I got to the ranch."

"Can you tell us possibly when?"

"I don't know... before I came to the ranch, I was searching for God."

"After you went to the ranch seeking for self-realization and God—when did this search end?"

"I don't know."

"Why did you take LSD after you left the ranch?"

"Because... I like it."

Mr. Kanarek's questioning then moved from the Spahn movie ranch to the Tate residence, to the La Bianca home, to New Mexico and over the same ground again and again apparently without obvious pattern.

At one point, the defense counsel asked Mrs. Kasabian about the night she had been at the Los Feliz district residence of Mr. Leno and Mrs. Rosemary La Bianca, and showed her a picture of the body of Mr. La Bianca.

For the record, as far as this juror-writer was concerned, the photo in question was the most abominable of all the photos submitted for evidence.

The picture depicted the victim lying on his back in a pool of blood, his head covered with a white material which was tied around his neck with an electrical wire. A large kitchen knife was jammed vertically into his throat and a carving fork was stuck in his stomach and the word "WAR" was also written on his stomach. It was bizarre and shocking!

"Oh-hh-h... Oh God!" Linda screamed. She bent over slightly and then she stared hard at the defendants. They didn't react.

Mr. Kanarek brought another picture and held it in front of the witness's eyes and asked her to identify the leather thong that bound Leno La Bianca's hands. The colors of the picture were so vivid that the hands appeared wrinkled and the blood dried and spotty.

157

Linda testified that those thongs were similar to the ones Charlie had told her to carry on the second night, but she wasn't positive.

Mr. Kanarek then attempted to ask the witness whether she was afraid when she left the ranch.

Mr. Bugliosi stood up and protested, "I object on the grounds that the story has gone into *ad nauseum*."

Judge Older sustained the objection.

Still, Mr. Kanarek wanted to know whether she had taken drugs since leaving the Spahn ranch two days after the seven killings last summer.

Mr. Bugliosi, obviously losing his patience, arose and objected that the question had been asked and answered a week ago.

"Sustained," said the judge.

In the afternoon, abstaining from questions about drugs, Mr. Kanarek switched to exploring more of Linda's past sexual life.

He inquired, "Did you tell Gypsy that you wanted to go to a place where you could get as many men as you wanted?"

"No," replied Linda, and smiled.

Did you tell Gypsy that your husband didn't satisfy you sexually?"

"No."

"Did you tell Gypsy that you wanted to leave because of your husband's inadequacies?"

"Yes."

"Then, because of that, you asked Gypsy that you wanted to live at the ranch. Is that right.?"

"No. She invited me."

Mr. Kanarek formulated different approaches to the same questions and received basically the same answers.

The judge adjourned the session for the day.

Ray and Tom were extra friendly with me for they were aware that Laura had been forced to leave. In the past, they had invited me for drinks in their rooms, so, likewise, I invited them both for drinks this evening, but Tom was delayed because he was talking with his wife on the phone. Ray and I chatted for a while.

The curly-haired telephone maintenance man wanted to help me and we became involved in the same detective game of discovering who had informed the bailiffs he planned to write the judge about my inviting Laura up to my room. Ray immediately disqualified Tom from blame, and then—himself. I thoroughly agreed. There was no question in my mind. They were my close companions.

We thought next of George.

"George couldn't have done it," Ray told me. "He works at the same place as you and besides, he likes you."

"What about Frank Welch?" I asked.

"Oh no—he's not the type. He doesn't care anyway," Ray answered.

"Now, let's see," Ray continued, "Marvin and Danny?... no... they wouldn't do that."

"There are only three jurors left," I stated. "Genaro, Mr. White, and Martin Payne."

"Forget about Genaro," snapped Ray, "I heard him say that he was sorry you couldn't have Laura up here."

I didn't say anything, just stared at Ray sipping his Old Fashioned drink.

"Well," he finally observed, "we have Paul and Martin left."

"I don't believe Martin would say anything like that..." I said, "...so... that leaves Paul White. Do you think Paul said it?"

"I'm not so sure," Ray answered, "maybe...however, I'm inclined to think Martin said it."

"Why?" I inquired.

"Because I don't trust him—he's a bastard!" Ray exclaimed and then continued, "Martin is always talking with the deputies and he kisses their asses. Yeah, I'm sure he said it! Mark my words—it was Martin!"

"It's hard for me to believe that Martin would do that," I said. "We attend church together and... but why?"

"I don't know why he said it, and I doubt he could write a letter. His vocabulary is poor and besides, I don't trust him."

Ray surprised me. I didn't know he felt that way about Martin Paine.

"Still, you're not sure he is responsible," I stated. There was a knock on the door. It was Tom.

Ray never did answer my question and the conversation was directed at urging the majority of the jurors to participate in going bowling. Mollie had told Ray and Tom that if there were not enough interested jurors, she couldn't obtain authorization from Captain Arden who would ask the Judge's approval.

Before they departed, Tom asked Ray and I if we could join him at his room for "one more drink." Ray accepted but I took a raincheck. I wanted to watch TV.

I left my room with them. As Ray passed by Debbie's room, he knocked soundly on her door and invited her. My nextdoor neighbor graciously joined them.

On Wednesday, the defense counsel proceeded and oddly enough followed in continuity (or were my notes wrong?) the sequence of events to establish that Linda was a thief.

"Mrs. Kasabian, are you familiar with the expression 'Ripoff'?"

"Yes."

"What does that mean?"

"To steal," responded Linda.

"Mrs. Kasabian, have you ever been convicted of a felony?" asked Manson's lawyer.

"A felony?" retorted Linda. "I'm not sure what a felony is."

Mr. Kanarek smiled and rubbing his hair, tried again, "Well, have you ever been convicted for the possession of narcotics?"

"Yes."

"And did you go in the truck?"

"Yes."

"Did you take anything?"

"Yes, I took some money and a knife."

"How much money did you take?"

"About five thousand dollars."

"You knew that money belonged to Mr. Melton, didn't you?"

"Yes."

"Did you ask Mr. Manson to hide you in the hills because you were afraid that your husband and Mr. Melton might find you?"

"I guess so."

"Why?"

"I'm not so sure."

"To whom did you give that money?"

"I gave it to Leslie."

"Didn't you give it to Tex?"

"I'm not sure... I remember Leslie was there when I gave it to either Tex or Leslie."

Mr. Kanarek then wanted to know how many times Linda had spoken to Charles Manson.

She related, "When I met him, he asked me why I had come and I answered him 'because my husband didn't want me.' The next time it was in the cave —he tried to make love to me. Then at the waterfall, he asked me what I thought of him. I thought he was beautiful. I guess I told him so.

"The occasion when he tried on the cloak—he said (Manson) 'now, when I go creepy-crawling, they're going to think I'm a tree or a shadow.' "

160

Linda remarked that everybody laughed.

"Now, would you tell us what other conversations you had with Mr. Manson," inquired Mr. Kanarek.

"I remember one time... I remember him having a sword in his hand... that he could cut himself and have the power to heal himself."

"Do you have another conversation?"

"Another time, when he told me about Tanya."

"Have you already told us about all the conversations between you and Mr. Manson?"

"No."

"Then, will you tell us now?"

"I can't think of anything right now."

"Well, the time is right now!" Kanarek said.

Linda didn't answer, just smiled.

She tried to recollect her memory, but couldn't relate any more occasions when she had spoken to the hippie cult leader.

Mr. Kanarek continued his interrogation. He wanted to speak personally with Linda Kasabian outside the courtroom but she had avoided him.

In open court, Mr. Kanarek pressed the issue in the following typical exchange:

"Why don't you want to talk to me?"

"Because I was told you couldn't be trusted," Linda replied.

A broad grin spread across Mr. Kanarek's face, and laughter in the courtroom broke his next question.

Manson's attorney walked toward the witness and said in a stage whisper that could be heard throughout the court room, "Thank you, Mrs. Kasabian."

Then he turned to Judge Older and declared, "Your Honor, I have no further questions at this time."

Suddenly, there was a considerable amount of excitement among the spectators, counsel, and jurors, as well.

Mr. Kanarek walked to his seat and sat down. Manson said something to him but the short-bully attorney didn't acknowledge him. He entire figure looked relaxed, yet somehow tense.

It had been eight and one half days since Mr. Kanarek had begun his lengthy cross-examination. For a while, it felt like it had been a way of life. We jurors expressed our delight and were happy to know the trial was progressing. To remember the time and date when Mr. Kanarek completed questioning Linda Kasabian, Ray and Genaro jubilantly circled the day on a calendar hanging in the jury room and wrote within:

"Kanarek finished exactly at 11:28 A.M., Wednesday, August 12, 1970. AMEN!"

Mr. Ronald Hughes, representing Leslie Van Houten, was next and the last of the defense counsel to ask questions. The bearded, balding defense attorney appeared impatient as he addressed the court.

"Your Honor, I make a motion that this witness be submitted to a psychiatric examination."

"The motion is denied," Judge Older said. "Let's continue."

The counsel sat down and then began his cross-examination at eleven forty-seven A.M., by reading from a list of typed questions. From my seat, I observed the pages were lined sheets of paper—very unconventional.

Mr. Hughes' first question was, "How do you feel love is?"

"Well, there's different kinds of love," Linda said. "There's a personal sort of love—earthly love, and universal love."

"How do you feel about the defendants in this case now?" inquired the shaggy-novice lawyer.

"Well, I feel compassion for them. I wish they would be up here and do what I'm doing—tell the truth."

One of the funny aspects was the performance rendered by Mr. Hughes. Apart from his sloppy appearance and physical demeanor, he displayed lack of voice control while asking questions. Sometimes his interrogation would begin at a low tone of voice and then would gradually build to a crescendo—almost shouting. Then, slowly, he would descend into a whisper. It was difficult to listen and follow his questions. Many times, he tried to use the microphone but Judge Older has ordered Deputy Taylor to remove it from his table. Mr. Hughes had more than enough vocal volume.

Mr. Hughes was also subject to criticism from his fellow defense counsel, the prosecutors, the judge, and even the jurors—for the repetitive pattern of his cross-examination.

His questions, lacking comprehension and bearing no importance in the trial, prompted occasional laughs from everybody, including Charlie, the female defendants, Linda Kasabian, the counsel, and even we jurors. His manner of questioning evoked laughter, especially when he asked:

"At first, you thought Mr. Manson was Jesus Christ, you were a witch —and now, Mr. Manson is the Devil—are you now an Angel?"

Before Linda had an opportunity to reply, the judge stopped her and said:

"Just a moment, Mrs. Kasabian." Then, addressing the heavy-looking attorney, added, "Ask your next question Mr. Hughes."

"Do you feel Mr. Manson is the Devil?"

"A devillike man... yes," Linda replied.

The sparkling good sense of humor of Mr. Stovitz was again present by his effervescent objection to one of Mr. Hughes' complicated questions. Mr. Hughes asking:

"Now, Mrs. Kasabian, let's take a stituation. Suppose 'A' talks with 'B', 'B' goes and tells 'C' what his interpretation of 'A's' conversation was with him. Now, 'C' turns around and tells someone else what 'B' thought or said about the conversation between 'A' and 'B'. Is it not a fact that what 'C' heard was only what 'B' told him?"

(Watch it—here it comes.)

"I object to the question. It's improper algebra."

There was laughter throughout the courtroom.

"Sustained," Judge Older said, also enjoying the co-prosecutor's remark. Mr. Hughes continued.

"Now, directing your testimony—I believe it is proper to characterize that you referred to the defendants as 'them' and to yourself as 'me'. At one time you considered yourself as part of this family—what do you consider yourself now?"

For the first time since he had finished his cross-examination, Mr. Kanarek stood up and, highly disturbed, exclaimed:

"Objection, Your Honor, on the grounds that there is no showing of any family. It is assuming facts not in evidence. It is a matter of sheer and absolute lifting by the bootstraps. I also object on the grounds that it is calling for a conclusion, hearsay..."

The defense counsel, for a moment, appeared as if he was going to continue enumerating more objective issues; however, he caught Judge Older smiling at him and decided to stop.

The judge sustained his objection and Mr. Kanarek not only smiled back but also thanked His Honor. I tittered at seeing such a display of ethics.

"Mrs. Kasabian?" asked Mr. Hughes, "do you cry with remorse for the mutilated children of Biafra?"

"I object as being immaterial," said Mr. Stovitz.

Judge Older sustained the prosecution's objection, and then called for noon recess.

"Let's celebrate!" Genaro announced in the jury room.

"Celebrate what?" asked Ruth.

"Kanarek's departure. What else?" chanted Ray happily.

"Okay, folks—let's go!" Deputy Taylor yelled as he opened the door of the jury room.

"Hold it a minute, Al!" snapped Mollie at the senior bailiff and walked in. Mollie Kane wanted to make an announcement.

"Listen everybody," said the hard-looking blonde sheriff. "I have good news. Judge Older has given his approval for you to go bowling once a week."

"Where are we going to bowl?" Violet Stokes inquired.

"As of now, we don't know which bowling alley," responded Mollie, "I called about ten different places and they all seemed to be booked for leagues."

"But when do we start?" Danny Jackson asked.

"Maybe next Tuesday or Wednesday," Mollie replied. "I'll let you know as soon as I phone a few more places and find out if they will accept us.". .

Then, rather hastily, she checked the time on her wristwatch and added, "Okay, let's go. We'll be late."

Instead of the Hilton—the usual lunch hour habitat—the bailiffs drove to Chinatown. Some jurors cheered and welcomed the change of food. However, Ruth Collingwood didn't eat because she didn't like Chinese food. She wanted something else.

Ruth's ire became noticeable especially when she saw that Deputy Taylor, who abhorred Chinese food also, was being served a succulent New York steak plate. The widow wanted the same but was not permitted. Ruth, who always spoke about her deceased husband, blew her top to the surprise of all the jurors. She was pretty upset and just kept staring at the senior bailiff eating his appetizing-looking steak.

Another incident that occurred at the same time and worth mentioning was that, the tables at the restaurant—in a room of our own—were arranged in banquet style. We sat close to each other, something the jurors had avoided long ago for reasons previously mentioned.

The Louis XVI-style chairs didn't help any in the comfort or the morale of the jurors. How's that again? What do chairs have to do with the morale of the jurors? Indirectly, yes! Explanation: Before the food was served, Ray, seated and finding himself with no elbow room, slid his chair back and discovered accidentally that by doing so, the chair produced a hollow-cracking noise against the linoleum floor. It was a rather disturbing and painful sound to one's ears. Violet, seated next to Ray, laughed in doing the same. Tom gave it a try with his chair. Next were Debbie and Frank, and then Marvin, George, Danny, and even this juror, followed suit. It was fun that first day. However, at later dates some jurors felt irritable at the sound of the chairs cracking.

We returned up to the ninth floor of the Hall of Justice and then down to the courtroom on the eighth floor.

Mr. Hughes resumed his cross-examination.

Waving a plastic bag filled with a greenish leafy substance similar to marijuana, he approached Linda Kasabian and asked her to describe the bag's contents. The bearded lawyer was attempting to illustrate his questioning about the use of various drugs.

"It's a green, meaty substance..." Linda said. "It looks like really-refined marijuana with a lot of stems."

"Hey, Bill," George said, signaling me to bend over toward his side—I did. Placing his notebook below the eyes, he whispered, "Bullshit, that's what it is in that bag. I bet you."

Mildred Osborne, sitting in front of me, couldn't help from overhearing, and chuckled.

Mr. Hughes had opened the plastic bag and then waved the substance under Linda's nose.

"Smell it," he said. "Does it smell like marijuana?"

"NO," the witness answered and wrinkled her nose, "I believe it's catnip."

The defense attorney proceeded then to ask questions regarding Mrs. Kasabian's use of drugs in an attempt to show drugs had altered her thinking.

Mr. Hughes questioning:

"Have you taken Morning Glory seeds?"

"Yes."

"Have you taken 'magic' mushrooms?"

"Yes."

"Have you taken hashish?"

"Yes."

"Have you taken psycilodin?"

"Yes."

"Have you taken emil nitrate?"

"Yes."

"Have you taken mescalene?"

"Yes."

Mr. Stovitz, after an hour of listening to such questions about drugs and requiring professional answers, objected:

"Your Honor," he said, "this type of questioning called for the testimony by a 'drug expert.'"

"I submit that she's an expert in drugs!" shouted Mr. Hughes...

The remark caused Linda to laugh.

165

Linda subsequently answered "No" when she was asked if she had taken: Asmador, tolatche, cocaine, opium, freon, nutmeg, Romilar (cough syrup), demarol, Dramamene or "cyclone."

Mr. Hughes's fellow defense counsel joined the prosecution to object to his long line of questioning which appeared to have no connection with the case itself.

I, as a juror, could find no reason why Mr. Hughes asked questions such as: "Mrs. Kasabian, do you have a tattoo on your body?"

"Yes, I do," she said.

The lawyer did not pursue the question.

Also, questions as to whether she had smoked or not in the courtroom in the presence of the jury. They were "ridiculous" questions and rightly so, they were objected and subsequently sustained, respectively by Mr. Bugliosi and the court.

Mr. Hughes closed his cross-examination by asking:

"When Mr. Manson was a devillike man, you loved him then?"

"Yes."

"Do you love him now?"

"Yes."

"Do you love the girls now?"

"Sure, I love everybody."

"You don't love Mr. Kanarek, who you feel is dishonest—do you?"

Linda turned around to look at Manson's lawyer and replied:

"Sure, I love him."

During the final phase of Mr. Hughes' cross-examination, I was surprised to hear him requesting that the jury members be allowed to question Linda Kasabian.

Judge Older denied the unusual request and then ordered co-prosecutor Mr. Aaron H. Stovitz to begin redirect examination of the witness.

No more questions.

At this point, an interesting observation came to my mind. Not once since he had begun his cross-examination had Mr. Hughes attempted or implied he was representing Leslie Van Houten. He concentrated on asking questions pertaining to the "family" as a single group and ignored, completely, the tall, slender and attractive alleged murderess he was representing.

Some jurors, including myself, didn't know that the law allows the counsel to have more than one round of questioning.

Mr. Aaron Stovitz, wearing a tan, light summer suit, conducted the redirect examination of the witness.

Mr. Stovitz's style was sharp and fast. His court presence was that of an experienced lawyer. He spoke firmly and his questions were well calculated. However, Mr. Stovitz lacked the finesse and savoir faire Mr. Bugliosi displayed.

Whereas Mr. Stovitz appeared physically stronger, Mr. Bugliosi's eloquent, shy, almost humble manners, made him appear sincere and much more strong.

Mr. Stovitz's redirect examination was brief and his questions were, in the opinion of this ex-juror-writer, of prime importance. He asked questions to clarify several points in her testimony.

Mr. Stovitz asking:

"Now, you stated that you did not particularly understand the phrase 'penalty of perjury,' but you knew what perjury is. Is that right?"

"Yes," answered Linda.

"And if you testify falsely under oath, there are certain penalties attached to it."

"Yes."

Mr. Stovitz turned around and walked back to his chair and sat down.

He continued: "Now, has anyone ever told you what the specific penalty for perjury in an ordinary case is?"

"No."

"Has anyone ever told you what the penalty for perjury in a capital case is?"

"Yes."

"Do you have a state of mind as to what the penalty for perjury in a capital case is?"

"Yes."

"What is that penalty?"

"The death penalty."

It was interesting to observe that Mr. Kanarek and Mr. Fitzgerald were at this point arguing among themselves.

Mr. Kanarek objected to every single question and would not even allow Mr. Stovitz to finish the question without him objecting.

Obviously, Mr. Kanarek's purpose was to obstruct the proceedings. Mr. Fitzgerald knew it and had signaled his fellow counsel to cease or calm down, but to no avail.

On the other hand, there was a certain amount of difficulty for we jurors to follow the continuity of the questions and answers. Very likely, that was Mr. Kanarek's intention and to a point he succeeded, but not to the advantage of the defense as it proved to be at the end of the trial.

Mr. Kanarek objected to almost all of Mr. Stovitz's attempts at clarification with Mrs. Kasabian. The barrage of objections seemed to alternately anger and amuse Charlie, as he urged his lawyer to stop speaking out, even though Judge Older was sustaining at least half of the questions.

Following prosecutor Mr. Aaron H. Stovitz, the defense counsel took up the same task and to the surprise of everyone, their recross-examinations were brief.

Linda Kasabian testified, under recross-examination by Mr. Fitzgerald, that she had made no agreement with the prosecutors about the custody of her son, Angel.

She added that she had signed only Angel's birth certificate and an agreement assigning temporary custody to her mother.

Questioned by Mr. Shin, Linda said she tried yoga exercises while in jail "to still my mind" and also reaching for what she referred to as "God awareness."

"I did it so that I would be together, so that I wouldn't be nervous," she said, "because I had never sat up on a witness stand and voiced myself to a lot of people before."

"Would you describe your yoga experiences?" asked Mr. Shin.

"Haven't you ever sat down and closed your eyes and meditated?" said Linda. "That is what it is. I try to clear my mind of all thoughts and concentrate on the third eye—a center behind your eyes. I don't have the words for it beyond that."

Mr. Kanarek questioned Linda if she had taken drugs while being in prison. The witness replied "no" and that she had exercised yoga instead.

Manson's attorney then questioned Linda how she felt being a "free woman" (Superior Court Judge Charles H. Older granted immunity from prosecution by dismissing seven counts of murder and one count of conspiracy to commit murder against Linda Kasabian).

"I don't feel like a free woman, but technically I am," said the witness. "I am under protective custody so I am not free to do as I please."

"But there is no force that can force the protective custody on you... you are free to come and go?" continued Mr. Kanarek.

"I guess so. I don't know. I have not tried it," replied Linda.

Mr. Kanarek, who could easily be cast as the double of the fine actor, Akim Tamiroff, was suddenly interrupted by the unexpected appearance in the court room of a young serviceman, wearing a Purple Heart and several other combat decorations.

The uniformed Marine corporal made an attempt to interrupt the proceedings of the trial but Judge Older ordered him out of the courtroom.

The craggy features of Mr. Kanarek accentuated his discontent as he tried to object the judge's orders.

Deputies Taylor and Tull escorted the intruder by forcing him out of the court room.

Judge Older admonished the jurors to disregard such incident as part of the trial from our minds, and then the usual admonition at the end of the court session.

The four-day long weekend brought more exasperation among the jurors. The outing on Sunday was cancelled and on Monday, Labor Day, guests were permitted. On Wednesday, a picnic was planned and preparations got underway the day before. Unfortunately, no one had the spirit nor the desire to go because relatives and friends were not allowed to join the jurors. They dreaded the thought of spending an entire day with each other. Some wanted to remain at the hotel but were refused.

Ruth was not feeling well, but just the same they forced her to go. She became sick.

None of the male jurors volunteered to accompany the bailiffs to go shopping. I offered my services without anticipating that I would be carrying the entire load by myself.

The location for the picnic was a delightful park situated in the mountains between Palmdale and Los Angeles. The place was closed for the season and that gave us the opportunity to roam at random—individually without escort.

The mood of friendship among the jurors was in such a state of mind that no one wanted to unload and set up the goods. Mr. White however was most gracious and took charge of the fire and cooking of hamburgers and hot dogs. We all spread out and wanted no part of each other.

The mountains were whispering—the air was fresh. It was a pleasure just to breathe... and overhead it was all bright blue, a place to relax... a reason to smile... mind refreshed.

Betty was the first to make the move of independence and started to walk away from the group.

"Where are you going?" I asked Betty casually.

"You see that peak? She stopped and pointed at a series of mountains in the distance.

"Yeah," I answered.

"Well, the peak in the background is mine!" and jogging away, she shouted, "I don't want anyone near me!"

The character and demeanor of some jurors was very coy.

We were provided with blankets. Ruth and Debbie, in no time, took one

169

and laid under a tree, and began to play canasta.

Genaro, Violet, Martin, George, and Mollie Kane set the croquet game and the latter became a casualty when, instead of hitting the wooden ball, hit her ankle. That put Mollie out of circulation for the next week or so.

The large swimming pool was so inviting that, without hesitation, I put my trunks on and dove into the water.

Tom, Ray, and Debbie walked around the pool and seemed to enjoy the surroundings. Shortly after, Ray and Marvin joined me at the pool and Tom and Debbie were left alone. They walked slowly and at one time they sat under a tree where they drank three or four beers. They had discovered each other. Nothing was thought about it but their sudden togetherness brought a question to my mind. Tom went wherever Ray did, but not this time. Why? On the other hand, Debbie had changed considerably in her manners and behavior whenever she was around Tom. I could not tell anything at the time, but the fact of being a man, made me suspect that perhaps in due time, something would develop, but I discarded the thought because I trusted Tom and Debbie as being "happily married" to two different dedicated spouses. They both appeared intelligent and aware of their responsibilities and positions at the time.

Marvin and I swam and tried to call everyone's attention as we splashed into the water from the water slide. Tom and Debbie, and later Violet, joined us. We had a great time, even more so when three strange young girls unexpectedly started to paddle on foam rubber rafts. Ray, Marvin, and I dashed towards them and made the best of the situation. However, the immediate presence of a female baillff, Evelyn, made the conversation rather corny and silly. We couldn't make out.

Chow time was called and Paul White was diligently making sure everybody had enough. His courteous approach made some of the jurors uncomfortable. The pious-looking juror, unable to participate in any physical sport, opted for making himself available, only to discover that whenever he sat down, the jurors would quickly disappear. Tom, Ray, Violet, and Debbie would not allow anyone to sit with them. They had monopolized a picnic table and when Paul asked them if he could join them, they simply refused him in a joking manner, though the implication was obviously positive. I felt embarrassed for him. Betty Clark couldn't bear his presence nor would not allow anyone near her. She wanted to be left alone and was determined to enjoy the peaceful surroundings without bothering to comply with rules of etiquette.

Frank Welch, provided with a large hat, brought along a book of crossword puzzles to keep himself occupied. His delicate condition made him stay in the shade for fear of getting sunburned.

Danny and the chubby bus driver, Sam, played baseball.

Deputy Taylor, a tall man—six foot four—with rather sharp features, joined me where I was seated. He seemed to be friendlier and receptive. We spoke about his job and the years he had been in the Sheriff's Department. He spoke of Judge Charles H. Older having been an Ace Flying Tiger in the Air Force. He didn't know what the middle "H" of the Judge's name stood for. Marvin, Danny, Ray, and Tom eventually gathered around to join the conversation. I glanced at Debbie and called her to join the group but she refused. Debbie told me later she didn't care for the slow-moving sheriff.

The differences of ages and preferences among the jurors made Mollie Kane work twice as hard to please everyone.

Ruth became sick on the way back to the hotel. She remained in her room. After recuperating, she felt terribly unhappy because no one cared for her.

The truth was that the lady widow juror had tried to find some male juror to befriend her. Her only friend and companion was Edith Rayburn, who, like Ruth, was unmarried. Both kept themselves company by taking turns in each other's room to play canasta. However, the length of the trial and lack of friendship had gotten hold of Ruth. The canasta games had become an issue of discussion between she and Edith.

At a later date one evening, they invited Marvin and I to play with them. We gladly accepted. Our ability to play canasta was an item of disagreement. They lost most of the time and on one occasion, Ruth became disturbed at Edith for the way she played. They had heated words and that was the end of their playing sessions and friendship. They avoided each other and looked somewhere else for conversation and companionship.

Ruth had two grown-up children —a young man and a daughter. For the first two months, Ruth would constantly talk about her two children. Like a mother, she would only speak highly about them. However, on weekends her "beloved children" wouldn't show or telephone her. It was sad. The lady juror always gave an alibi for the absence of her children. No one had ever met them. Ruth clung to the memories of her husband and she didn't speak two sentences without remarking that "her husband this and her husband that." It was very noticeable and for that reason, some jurors avoided sitting at the same table where she sat. They were afraid she would bring up her consistent subject—her husband who has been dead for the last twelve years.

"She has no right to insult me," Edith told me shortly after they disassociated.

"You mean you are not talking to each other?" I said.

"Not at the moment," replied Edith, and then added, "if she wants to talk to me, it's all right, but she better not expect me to speak first."

"Why?" I inquired casually.

"Because she hasn't earned the right to be *my* friend, that's why."

Edith and Ruth became estranged for the remainder of the trial.

We returned to court.

The twenty-one-year-old blonde witness, Linda Kasabian, was pressed for her views of Charles Manson by defense attorney Mr. Ronald Hughes.

"Do you feel that God has sent you to tell who Charles Manson really is?" the bearded, balding lawyer asked.

"That's what I feel in my heart," she replied and then continued, "I'm not really sure."

Mr. Hughes then wanted to know whether her mission was to tell the world that Charles Manson was the devil.

"Objection, as immaterial," said Deputy District Attorney Bugliosi.

Simultaneously, the witness replied, "He's a false prophet."

Linda then, in a series of statements, confirmed once again that she had stopped believing that the bearded, long-haired defendant was Jesus Christ when she looked into the eyes of one of the victims, Voityk Frykowski, as he staggered out of the house covered with blood.

Linda went on to say that she had a vision which she subsequently described as "insight." Describing her reaction, she said:

"All of a sudden, I saw within myself what Charles Manson was doing and that he was leading myself into self-destruction."

Mr. Hughes then asked:

"Did that vision tell you what Mr. Manson was?"

"Yes," she said, "I felt that he was the devil."

The defense attorney then asked the witness if she had ever heard Manson order any of his followers to kill them.

Linda said that she had on the second night when Manson had told her to drive to the Los Feliz district.

In response to the question she testified:

"I'm not positive, but I thought I heard him say, 'don't let them know you're going to kill them.'"

"Why are you not positive, Mrs. Kasabian?" inquired the bearded attorney.

"I don't know. I don't know if I want to believe it... something in my own

172

mind said that's what I heard, but I'm not positive."

Prompted by Mr. Hughes's questions, Linda admitted that Charles Manson had never told her he was either Jesus Christ or the devil.

"Would you have believed Mr. Manson if he said he was Jesus Christ?" the attorney asked.

"I believed him and he didn't even tell me," Linda said.

Mr. Hughes switched his line of questions to a subject he had already covered quite extensively—questions about her practice of yoga and drugs.

The bushy attorney encountered a wall of the prosecution's objections that his questions were "irrevelant."

Mr. Hughes' voice became louder as he met objection after objection.

Judge Older sustained thirteen to fifteen consecutive objections and twice cautioned the defense attorney to lower his voice.

Judge Charles H. Older, uncharacteristically, to control his outrageous indignation at Leslie Van Houten's lawyer, stated:

"Let the records show that you have asked a number of questions in almost a yelling voice."

The heavy-looking attorney didn't say anything and continued:

"Why did you name your son Angel?"

"Irrevelant," objected Mr. Bugliosi.

"Sustained," said the Court.

Mr. Hughes was asking Linda Kasabian about her beliefs in reincarnation and extra-sensory perception when Judge Older ordered him to end his recross-examination.

He did—reluctantly.

The judge obviously felt that Mr. Hughes had exhausted all reasonable questions of importance in his recross-examination.

Linda Kasabian's days of testimony were compressed into a sharply contrasting picture when the prosecution opened redirected examination and the defense got another opportunity to cross examine.

Going over the transcript of her testimony, Mr. Bugliosi asked Linda "what she had meant to say." The prosecutor wondered what she thought when she said she was an emissary of God.

"I feel that I'm doing the Will of God," she said, and looking at the four defendants, she added, "I feel that they did wrong and I did wrong and being up here is my repentance... I think that's the Will of God."

Then the witness insisted upon questions by Mr. Bugliosi that she had not been prompted by the prosecution in her testimony and that she had only told the truth.

No more questions.

"You told lies to authorities in California to save your child, didn't you?" asked defense attorney Paul Fitzgerald.

"Yes," Linda admitted.

"You would lie to save yourself, wouldn't you?" asked the defense counsel again.

Linda replied that she thought more of her children than herself.

Naming several members of the "family" who lived at the Spahn Ranch, including Charles Manson, Mr. Fitzgerald wanted to know if it was not possible that any one of them might be the father of Angel, her second child, a boy.

Linda openly admitted that it was possible. However, the petite blonde witness said she was convinced that her five-month-old baby was the son of her husband, Robert Kasabian.

In response to Mr. Fitgerald's questioning, Linda testified:

"I saw my husband in my child's face when it was born. That gave me justification for believing he was the father."

"You would lie any day of the week to save your children, wouldn't you?" Mr. Fitzgerald asked again.

"I have in the past," answered Linda, matter-of-factly.

The mod-dressed lawyer, representing Patricia Krenwinkel, not satisfied with his examination, proceeded to ask Linda about the known and established orgy that she had previously testified under Mr. Bugliosi's direct examination.

Mr. Fitgerald, reading from one of the many transcripts inquired:

"Were you asked these questions and did you give these answers:

"Question: In addition to hugging and kissing that took place at the orgy, did any other type of sexual activity take place?

"Answer: Yes.

"Question: You had sexual intercourse with Tex and Clem?"

"Answer: No intercourse with Tex—with Clem I did, yes.

"Question: But you did have some type of sexual activity with Tex also.

"Answer: Yes."

"Did you give those answers to those questions?"

"Yes," said Linda, "but I think they're jumbled around."

"Would you like to explain that?" said Mr. Fitzgerald, as he looked up at the ceiling and folded his arms—a typical mannerism which displayed he was thinking ahead to a line of questions in order to establish a vital and stronger issue.

"Yes," responded the witness.

174

"Please do," said Mr. Fitzgerald and walked behind where Manson and his lawyer were seated.

"There was hugging and kissing between Tex and I, but there was intercourse between Clem and I," explained Linda.

"And what sort of sexual activity did you engage in with Snake?" (Diane Lake, an ex-family member).

"Hugging and kissing," answered Linda.

The courtroom was in complete repose. There was a great amount of interest among the audience and the press were meticulously jotting down every statement.

I noticed some jurors were carefully glued to their seats and didn't make an attempt to make any noise with their feet or chairs. To do so would have denoted their uncomfortable state of mind on account of the intimate questions the defense counsel was asking.

Likewise, the defendants were listening with interest and even the court reporter, who usually didn't react, appeared to be especially attentive as not to miss any word.

The defense counsel continued.

"There was no other form of sexual activity that took place between you and any other participant. Is that correct?"

"Yes."

"With the exception of sexual intercourse with them?"

"Right."

"There was no form of oral sexual activity, is that correct?"

When Mr. Fitzgerald asked the above question, the reaction among the jurors was like if they hadn't heard it. It was a reaction of shifting chairs. From the corner of my eye, I observed that everybody was awaiting the answer from the witness.

No response. Linda frowned and didn't reply.

Mr. Fitzgerald raised his voice and enunciated a variation of the same question:

"You did not orally copulate the penis of any male person present, is that correct?"

The pressure of the state of mind of the jurors, including this juror, was of enormous embarrassment. Everybody was afraid to breathe for fear of being noticed.

Mr. Bugliosi and Mr. Stovitz stood up at the same time to object. The latter ceded Mr. Bugliosi to speak out:

"I object on the grounds of undue harassment and embarrassment, Your

175

Honor," said the prosecutor. "There is a section of the Evidence Code to that effect."

Surprisingly, Judge Older overruled the objection and instructed the witness to answer the question.

"What was the question?" asked Linda Kasabian.

("Wow!" I told myself, "it's bad enough to sit here and listen but how can one be seated still?")

The jurors were just swallowing their own saliva for fear of displaying any emotion. I was doing the same. Mr. Fitzgerald repeated the question and again he sounded solemn and precise:

"You did not orally copulate the penis of any male person present, is that correct?"

Linda frowned upon the question and candidly retorted:

"What does that mean?"

I looked at Mr. Fitzgerald's face and for a moment he didn't say anything. After a pause, he inquired:

"Mrs. Kasabian, are you familiar with oral-genital relations?"

"Objection, Your Honor!" shouted Mr. Bugliosi.

Judge Older changed his mind and sustained the objection.

It was clear that Linda Kasabian's cool and remarkable control had indeed caught Mr. Fitzgerald in a dead-end street.

The veteran lawyer, unable to rephrase the question without causing further embarassment to himself and everybody, hesitated and opted for changing the subject.

I was appalled to discover that Mr. Fitzgerald's shrewdness had once more been defeated by the serenity of the State's star witness. He proceeded to nowhere.

Under questioning by Mr. Dave Shin, lawyer for defendant Susan Atkins, Linda Kasabian, who was wearing her hair shoulder length instead of her usual pigtails, testified that she received "vibes" from Charles Manson and admitted she had tried to communicate whith the three women defendants by "vibrations" to tell them to "tear away their false faces and step into the light."

Mr. Shin asked Linda what she meant by that.

The witness explained that she meant "the little game faces they wear into court—the invisible masks—people put on faces. When you look at someone and try to hide, you make all sorts of faces and try to hide yourself."

She also testified that she had experienced "vibrations" while in jail waiting to testify in the trial.

Mr. Kanarek followed and he inquired:

"What information have you received through vibrations from the universe?"

"That to be here now, testifying, is the Will of God!" Linda replied.

"Did you send out vibrations in order to receive this information?" the attorney asked.

"Yes, I did," said the diminutive Mrs. Kasabian.

"Would you state what are the vibrations that you sent out?" continued Mr. Kanarek.

"It is sort of like when you get down on your knees and you pray and then you wait for an answer," she replied.

Mr. Kanarek's questions were interrupted with repeated objections, which were sustained.

The lawyer requested at several times for a conference at the bench. Judge Older repeatedly denied it and admonished the attorney to get on with his questioning. Mr. Kanarek objected that his client was being denied due process of law and a fair trial.

"Let's proceed or the questioning will be terminated!" exclaimed Judge Older, somewhat disturbed.

"I can't ask any questions," Manson's lawyer finally said.

"Then sit down," the judge said with authority.

Mr. Kanarek sat down, still protesting.

The fourth defense attorney, Mr. Ronald Hughes, encountered nearly a score of successful prosecution objections in getting Linda Kasabian to answer three or four questions.

His last question was:

"Are you willing to be examined by a psychiatrist?"

"Oh, Your Honor," imposed Mr. Bugliosi. "Ridiculous!"

Judge Older sustained the objection and dismissed the witness. Linda Kasabian sighed deeply and her eyes glistened with contentment when she resumed her seat beside her attorney. A few minutes later, she walked out of the courtroom—a "free woman."

It was a relief to see Linda Kasabian step down from the witness stand. We jurors had listened to her answering the same questions over and over.

The last three days of her testimony were tedious and boring. I noticed that none of the jurors were taking notes in their books, except for me, who was occupied jotting important points at random.

Following the main witness for the prosecution, an array of witnesses were introduced by Mr. Bugliosi.

Timothy Ireland, under questioning, testified that on the day nine of August

177

1969, at about one or one thirty A.M., he heard a man screaming, "Oh God, no! Please don't! Don't, don't, don't! Please don't!"

He stated that "at the time, he was at the Westlake School for Girls."

Using a large diagram (P-98) the witness marked with a red pencil the location of the school—on a winding road nearby the Tate residence.

Very likely, the screams the witness heard were those of Voityk Frykowski at the time Linda said she saw a man staggering out of the house and his face covered with blood.

Mr. Fitzgerald attempted to prevent the witness from revealing what he heard, objecting on the grounds it was "hearsay" but Mr. Kanarek opposed the objection—startling everybody.

"May I request counsel," quipped Deputy District Attorney Aaron Stovitz, addressing Mr. Kanarek, "not to assist the prosecution."

"Oh, but I think Mr. Kanarek's joinder should be put in the records for history," added Mr. Bugliosi smilingly.

The girls' school counselor added that he spoke to a camp supervisor after he heard the screams, then got into his car and drove around the area to try to determine what was happening.

"I didn't see anything," he said.

He was dismissed.

Mr. Rudolf Weber's testimony was of significant value and paralleled that of Linda Kasabian's.

The robust, white-haired witness gave an account of what he saw the night of the Tate murders.

He related that he lived down the hill from the Tate residence. Speaking with a foreign accent, he said that about one A.M., he got out of bed in his pajamas, thinking something was wrong with the plumbing. He checked it and found out that it was alright.

"So I went out and saw four people, three young women and one man," the witness said.

"Did you do anything?" asked Mr. Bugliosi.

"So," I said, "what the hell do you think you're doing?"

Mr. Weber stated then that the man responded, "We're just taking a drink of water," and that the man had a sort of pleasant attitude.

"What happened next," inquired the prosecutor.

"My wife got excited and said 'you have the nerve and if you don't leave now... my husband is a sheriff and we're going to make a report.' Then they started walking down the street where there was an unfamiliar car parked in the middle of the street. They got in and I noticed the license plate was GYY

178

435. I walked towards the car and extended my hand as if I was to take the ignition key. They had already turned the key on and then they sped right away."

"Was there anything else?" asked Mr. Bugliosi.

"There were no spoken words, except those in front of the house."

Oddly enough, the defense counsel chose not to cross examine the white-haired gentleman, especially when the witness had recalled the license plate —the same license number of the yellow 1959 Ford which was borrowed without permission from the owner, John H. Swartz, a ranch hand at the Spahn movie ranch in Chatsworth and which was used during the forays on the eighth, ninth and tenth of August 1969.

Obviously, the defense counsel felt unable to find proofs to contradict the testimony of Mr. Weber and, by simple arithmetic, allowed we jurors to believe that Linda Kasabian had spoken the truth when she testified that Tex had ordered them to wash the blood from their bodies. Mr. Weber verified also her comment that he reached into the car to grab the car keys, as they prepared to leave.

Mrs. Winifred Chapman repeated essentially the same testimony. Due to her highly nervous behavior, she was excused.

The next witness was Jim Asen, a neighbor living two houses from the Tate residence. He saw Mrs. Chapman running toward the next house and then she came to his home. Mrs. Chapman was in hysterics and asked for help. The young man called the police.

Mollie Kane finally told us that tonight—Tuesday night—we were to go bowling, the preparation for which had required several weeks of waiting. The jurors were full of excitement and eager to participate in the indoor sport.

Mr. Paul White, physically handicapped, remained at the hotel, to study his trial notes and to read a gift book he had just received from his wife.

Dinner was scheduled at five thirty P.M. instead of seven and immediately after, we parted in the usual means of transportation—a jail bus. We didn't care. We were dressed casually and the knowledge of going out at night gave everybody a feeling of freedom and relaxation. Laughter and contentment prevailed among the jurors. Mollie Kane and Kathy Colvig wore pantaloon ensembles and they looked very appealing. Their personalities and behavior changed considerably that evening. They were more friendly and, as one juror put it, "they looked more human."

The bowling alley on Pico Boulevard was located at a far distance, which we all felt was to our advantage. More time away from the hotel. Four adjacent lanes had been reserved by Mollie. I noticed Betty, Tom, and myself were the only jurors carrying their own bowling bags.

Betty, who had befriended me recently, remarked that her friend Debbie had sided with Tom and Ray in one lane. I was surprised to discover that Mrs. Clark had also noticed the closeness of Tom and Debbie. Marvin joined Betty and I in the next lane. Martin, Violet, and George assembled in the following, and in the last, was Danny with Olivia and the two bailiffs, Mollie and Sam—the chubby transportation officer.

Some jurors didn't want to participate for different reasons.

Mildred confessed she was a diabetic and her doctor had advised her against it. She was happy to watch us bowl while knitting a long coat in time for Christmas. Mr. Welch, Edith, and Ruth flatly declared themselves incompetent and too old. Genaro refused because his wife wouldn't want him to play without her. He kept score for Debbie, Tom, and Ray.

A few minutes later, the delightful bar hostess, a plump woman in her forties, came over and took our orders. I bought a round for the group I was playing with. Betty had a plain ginger ale and Marvin and I had a beer. Marvin apologized for not having any money, due to the delay in receiving his pay check.

"Don't worry," I told him, "just make sure you hit the pins."

In a little while, the balls began to roll down the lanes, hitting the pins with a crackling noise. I observed that in the first group, the drinks began to disappear as quickly as they came. Genaro was not having much to say, but was watching Tom and Debbie, who were talking freely. They restricted their conversation to necessities of nonsense, concerned with what they were doing, and neither had yet called the other by name. Ray set out to be a funny man and he was an asset to his group.

Betty proved to be an excellent bowler. Despite the slim appearance of her body, she displayed skill and good physical throws. Marvin and Danny were a disappointment—their abilities in the bowling alley were not half as good as in the paddle tennis court.

Tom had a tremendous swing but after releasing the ball, his delivery was not coordinated. Ray, very much as myself, was a mediocre bowler, and it was the same for Martin and George. Violet and Debbie had fun and enthusiasm.

Olivia, as in swimming, found a teacher in Sam, the chubby bus driver. She lofted the ball, which appeared to be heavier than her own person. The amount of her drinking, combined with the effort involved, discouraged the juror after a second attempt.

Mollie Kane—tall, tough-looking bailiff—confided in me that she was afraid to throw the ball with all her strength. To say the least, Mollie had the strongest throw I've ever seen. I warned her not to do it for fear of her breaking the machine.

We left the bowling alley shortly before a regular league was to begin. The spirits were high among those who had plenty to drink.

Debbie and Tom, who usually sat in the last row, and Ray insisted to have the bus stopped at a liquor store to purchase some beer. Their wishes were granted. What followed after, inside the bus, established a routine which some jurors learned to dislike intensely. The three of them, after finishing their beers, would roll the empty cans or bottles toward the front of the bus. Mrs. Colvig or some other bailiff on duty, would return them. It was a joke that lasted the rest of the time we were sequestered. However, the first night riding in the jail bus was an experience never to be forgotten. The laughter and applause, combined with the screams, yells and rattling sound of beer cans rolling down the aisle floor, plus pounding, stomping and kicking against the seats, produced an atmosphere of insanity. People outside in the street, who watched the black and white bus pass by undoubtedly must have thought that a riot among prisoners was taking place inside. Such was the behavior of the jurors seated at the rear—namely, Tom, Ray, Debbie, and Violet. Genaro and Martin chaperoned the group with loud laughs of approval. The noise was so disturbing that one could not hear what the next person was trying to say.

Their behavior was beyond belief, they deliberately made themselves obnoxious so as to upset the rest of the elderly jurors. I didn't know their reasons or suspected why they would go out of their way to make themselves appear repugnant.

I had noticed before, especially in the jury room, that Debbie, Tom and Ray, together with Violet, would put on a great act of childish activities, joking and laughing at the minute any one of them would move. They also had boastful talks or secretive whisperings, glancing at each other from time to time and making sure that they were being watched.

Deb, Tom, Ray, and Violet formed "the clique" and managed to finally sit together. They stimulated each other and they liked to be near each other. The night we went out bowling, they took an open initiative in their relationships to make known to the rest of the jurors that they were united as a group. Discordance existed among some jurors and I didn't know why.

Before we stepped out of the bus, Mollie announced that a meeting was to take place immediately in the recreation room.

The meeting was presided over by Deputy Michael Pappas, a darkcomplected officer, who preferred to be called "Mike." The deputy sheriff started to say that some grievances had come to his attention and then he expressed his desire to help in any way possible to alleviate them. Mollie Kane moved forward and handed him a piece of white paper containing a list of new changes regarding jurors' activities after court sessions.

Mike read the items to be discussed for approval, such as, itinerary of church services on Sundays, grocery shopping trips once a week at a nearby Thrifty's, an assigned day for the barber to come to the hotel, and ladies' appointments for shampoo and hair styling at the Casino floor. By popular demand, dinner time was scheduled at six o'clock daily at the coffee shop of the hotel. Dinner on Fridays remained the same since we usually were taken to different restaurants. Visitors' privileges was a shakey subject to discuss but the item which stirred quite an argument was the "walk after dinner."

It had been customary, shortly after dinner, to have one or two bailiffs escort any juror who wanted to go for a walk on the grounds of the hotel. The argument was on account of the speed in which such walks were conducted.

I had not attended any walks for the pleasure of watching television. Also, swimming and paddle tennis were enough exercise for me. However, there were others whose only outlet for exercising was to walk and they wanted to maintain that privilege. The variety of ages among the jurors made them differ how fast or how slowly they wished to walk.

"The walks are going to be done at a normal pace," said Mike.

"That's a good idea," agreed Mr. Welch, the eldest juror.

Edith and Ruth mumbled among themselves and seemed also pleased.

"What about those who like to walk fast?" inquired Debbie.

"Yeah, like me!" snapped Ray who, like myself, had not gone for a walk.

"The walk will be fast enough for everybody," replied Mike, trying to accommodate.

"Well, I am not going to crawl, I like to walk fast and I need the exercise," Debbie announced openly.

"But there are some of who who cannot walk faster—like Paul and I," observed Mr. Welch.

"I don't care if you can't walk," said Ray. "Does that mean I have to walk slow?"

"Let's hear from everybody," stated Mike, and then, directing his attention to Mildred, he asked her: "Mrs. Osborne, what's your opinion?"

"Well, I for one like to walk slow and enjoy my walk—I can't walk fast,

182

especially after having eaten dinner. I'm not trying to say we should 'crawl' like someone said, but surely not racing either."

"Well, it so happens I like to race!" shouted Debbie positively.

Mr. White tried to say something but his voice was downed among other voices. I hated to think myself in the spot Mike was.

Debbie, for one, had shouted continuously, and at that point, had removed her shoes and sat on the floor in a yoga position with a tall can of beer, sipping its contents between questions and answers.

Mollie Kane made an announcement which only brought antagonistic remarks. She said: "Since the majority of the jurors are unable to walk fast, it's only fair we should conduct the walk in a fashionable normal pace."

Debbie and Ray sided together and protested. The rest retaliated, and for a moment there was confusion and the meeting went out of order.

"Wait a minute folks!" exclaimed Mike, as he stood up, "hold your voices down!"

Still, some were speaking, but stopped when they heard the bailiff in charge shout, "QUIET!......Please!"

There was silence for a moment.

"Let's hear from Bill," resumed Mike, after he saw I had raised my hand.

"Well," I began to say, "I have a suggestion that hopefully might solve the problem. Why not have two walks? A fast walk and a slow walk? That way, no one would be left out and everybody would be happy."

"We don't have the manpower to spare," stated Mollie.

"Okay," I replied, "have the same bailiff take two walks or else send another officer after the first group returns."

"It can't be done," Mollie retorted, "the majority rules and that's the way it is going to be."

"And who's the majority?" asked Ray, knowing well in advance who they were.

"Paul, Frank, Ruth, Edith...Mildred," replied Mollie, "they can't walk fast for medical reasons."

The bailiff, assuming a mediator's attitude, continued saying, "You people go down swimming, play paddle tennis daily, and go bowling once a week. What else do you want? Now you want to take away the only means of exercise for these people. It's not fair!"

"Well, I'm not going to crawl," Debbie stated defiantly, "and I have to have a walk."

Suddenly, the meeting turned into a personal feud between Debbie and Sheriff Pappas. If seemed that Debbie's husband had been inadvertently stopped a month or so before and the guard on duty wouldn't allow him to walk in to visit his wife. The visitor had arrived late on a Friday night—one o'clock in the morning. To comply with regulations that visitors were allowed only on Saturdays and Sundays, Mr. and Mrs. Hart felt that 12:01 A.M. on Saturday was considered the beginning of the weekend. Before giving authorization to let Mr. Hart go through, Mike, who at the time was in bed asleep, told the officer on duty to make sure the visitor had proper identification.

Debbie had not forgotten the incident and made her feelings known about it. Mike defended himself by stating that he had not seen the man nor had he ever met her husband. He offered his apologies.

Mrs. Hart openly stated her views and in a moment of anger, called the officer a "creep" and said that she didn't like him.

"I don't like you either," said Ray seriously.

Mrs. Hart, her voice full of smirk remarks, could be heard through the recreation room. Her hatred and contempt for the deputy made her lose all restraint.

I didn't believe what was being said and taking a quick glance, I noticed most of the jurors were stupified, speechless. The rage Debbie displayed was far from the usual well-mannered lady. She was a completely different person.

"Well, if you people don't like me, I can't help it," Mike said, half smiling, so as to cover his feelings. "But as long as I'm in charge, you'll do as I tell you." Then, changing his mood, the part-time actor-officer added, "I'm a fair guy, if you play ball with me, you can get away with anything. At the moment, there will be escorted walks after dinner but in a normal pace fashion. I don't intend to have my people running or chasing after anybody or walking fast."

There was silence for a second until Mr. White broke the spell and commented, "I think Bill has a good point, if we...."

"Oh, shut up Paul!" yelled Debbie, as she grabbed her shoes in one hand and the can of beer in the other. She stood up.

"May we leave?" asked Edith. "This no longer is a meeting. I don't have to sit here and listen to all this screaming."

Edith, followed by Ruth, left the room.

"Is there any more questions?" inquired Mike as he looked around. No one said anything. Mike and Debbie exchanged glances. Their eyes remained fixed on each other for a moment, hatred seeping from both directions.

"Too bad our fun got loused up," she commented, leaning forward slightly to make it plain that her comment was directed at Mike.

184

Debbie finally turned and motioned to Violet by saying, "Let's get the hell out of here," as she led her out of the recreation room.

Witness Number Twelve was John Harold Swartz, Jr., a truck driver working at the Spahn Ranch. A nonmember of the family, the ranch hand testified that Manson and the girls used his car and especially one time without his permission. He stated that he usually went to bed between nine and ten P.M. He heard the sound of his car's engine started up. He got up and saw his automobile driven off the ranch. He identified the car through a photograph and also the "pink" slip. He also testified that on August 16, 1969, he was arrested on account of auto theft, and released later. In December 1969, he said that he noticed the license had been removed from his 1962 Ford to a 1959 Ford. He had not given permission to anybody to do so. He stated that Charlie and Tex helped him at the ranch with the horses.

Jerry De Rosa, a police officer, testified that he received a radio call from communications and arrived at the Polanski residence approximately 9.05 A.M. on Saturday. He was met by Mrs. Chapman and Mr. Asen. Mrs. Chapman informed him about the bodies and blood all over, etc. The officer identified photos depicting fallen telephone wires on the premises.

Then he said that he walked towards a white Rambler, saw a dead body. The doors were closed and windows too, except the driver's seat window. Another officer arrived. Both walked to the garage and then the room above. No one in there. They proceeded towards the front of the Tate house— noticed two bodies laying on the grass, both appeared to be dead. Two other officers arrived and gave them support by waiting outside. They walked into the living room and discovered two bodies and also noticed the word "Pig" written with blood on the front door. Also observed suitcases blocking the driveway, and a pair of glasses. Then he walked towards the two bodies —a female and a male—dead bodies, entered the master bedroom, exited the house and then went to the guest house, where he saw a male caucasian sitting in the living room (William Garretson), placed him under arrest, and took the prisoner to the West Los Angeles Police Station.

William Whisenhunt, a police officer, testified that when he arrived at the Tate residence, officer De Rosa told him of the bodies. He entered through a window because he saw blood in the front entrance door and suspected someone might have been inside. Noticed three bedrooms, observed that the front window was partially opened, and that it had a horizontal slash on the screen.

Then he proceeded from the hallway to the pool area towards the guest house. As he approached the caretaker's house, he heard a voice from inside

185

which said, "Be quiet." As he opened the door, a dog attacked him and bit him. (Laughter in the court room.) He observed there was a stereo on the premises and was set on volume 4.

Robert E. Burbridges, a police officer, testified that he noticed outdoor floodlights and some Christmas lights outside the garage. He stated that he also found some pieces of wood shaped like a gun's grip.

Raymond Kilgrow, telephone company repairman, testified that he thought the telephone wires had been pulled aside four different connections. Two going to the Tate residence and two to the caretaker's.

Michael J. McGann, sergeant, Los Angeles Police investigator, stated that he arrived at one thirty P.M. He inspected the entire premises and found no ransacking, neither in the caretaker's house or in the garage to his recollection. No drawers were opened or anything like that.

He added that he found a purse owned by Abigail Folger on a sofa—it had nine dollars and sixty-four cents (eight dollar bills and one dollar, and sixty-four cents in change). Voityk Frykowski had two dollars and forty-four cents on him. Jay C. Sebring—eighty dollars (four twenty-dollar bills). In Sharon Tate's bedroom were eighteen dollars (one ten dollar, one five dollar, and three dollar bills). Steve Parent had, in his pocket, nine dollars (one five dollar and four dollar bills); also, a wrist watch, clock radio and miscellaneous.

Officer McGann described that he found approximately one half full of a sac, equal to 76.9 grams, of marihuana in the living room in a cabinet in the west wall of the Tate living room. Thirty grams of marihuana and ten capsules of MDA were found on a night stand east of the bed occupied by Voityk Frykowski and Abigail Folger. Cocaine (one gram) in Jay Sebring's car. He also found additional marihuana in two different locations in the car: 2.9 grams loose in the case and 3.4 grams in a film can and two-inch butts of marihuana. No shell cases from gun shots were recovered. He found a knife on top of an overstuffed sofa, just behind the seat cushion in the living room.

John Finken, investigator for the Coroner's Office, testified that he cut the ropes that Sharon Tate and Jay Sebring were connected with and removed the property.

Dr. Thomas T. Noguchi, coroner for the County of Los Angeles, provided an accurate description of the collective 102 stab wounds inflicted upon the victims in the first night.

Dr. David A. Katsuyama, Dr. Noguchi's assistant, took the stand at a later date to give an account of the sixty-seven wounds suffered collectively by the victims Leno La Bianca and his wife, Rosemary La Bianca.

Mr. Bugliosi asked Dr. Noguchi to please explain to the jurors what an autopsy is:

"An autopsy," the oriental-descent witness said, "is the medical procedure to determine the cause of death." Then he went on to describe each of the wounds in detail.

The four defendants sat somberly and listened with a rather combined mood of interest and curiosity, while Dr. Noguchi testified on the grizzly details.

Describing the wounds with the aid of an almost life-size drawing of each victim, the neatly dressed Dr. Noguchi said that, "Miss Tate was stabbed eight times in the back, four times in the chest, and one time each in the abdomen, right thigh, and both arms.

"The cause of her death," he continued, "was due to the five multiple stab wounds in the chest and back, which penetrated the heart, lungs and liver, causing massive internal hemorrhages. Each of those five wounds could have been individually fatal," Dr. Noguchi testified.

According to the coroner, Sharon Tate was eight months pregnant. He said that the male fetus in her womb was unharmed and could only have lived fifteen or twenty minutes after the mother's death. In addition to the sixteen wounds, she suffered two superficial cuts on her left arm, plus rope burns on her face and neck.

Dr. Noguchi could not speculate but it was his opinion that the rope burns were consistent with hanging and then he explained, though not clearly, that the beautiful actress and the hair stylist, Jay Sebring, were possibly hanged with the same rope around their necks, or merely used to hold both victims during the stabbing.

Dr. Noguchi, with a Japanese-accentuated speech, spoke comprehensively in total attention of the courtroom.

He observed that:

"I believe, based on wound findings in the left side of the cheek and the way the rope was tied at the scene and placed over the beam of the living room, I would form the opinion that Miss Sharon Tate had been suspended for not too long a period, but perhaps a partial suspension for a short time... I believe the suspension was caused during the agonal stage—the dying process."

"Jay Sebring's cause of death," Dr. Noguchi continued, "was due to multiple stab wounds. He received a total of seven wounds." Three fatal wounds and one gun shot wound, which the witness considered to be fatal.

"Abigail Folger's cause of death was a stab wound in the aorta, which

187

was penetrated by a sharp strong instrument. She received a total of twenty-eight wounds—five or six of them fatal—all penetrating.

"Voityk Frykowski's cause of death," the coroner testified, "was the result of receiving fifty-one multiple stab wounds—seven fatal wounds. Thirteen lacerations which, collectively, may have been fatal. Two gunshot wounds: one in the left back which was fatal in itself—the second was found in the left thigh.

"Steven Parent's cause of death," according to Dr. Noguchi's testimony, was caused by multiple gunshot wounds in the chest. He received a total of seven wounds, four fatal and one defense wound in the left arm, possibly caused with a sharp instrument.

Under cross-examination, Defense Attorney Paul Fitzgerald asked Dr. Noguchi whether suggestions by police officers might have influenced his opinion of the type of weapon used to inflict the 102 stab wounds on the victims at the Tate estate.

The coroner replied that he thought he influenced authorities more than he has been influenced by them.

"Are you capable of making mistakes?" asked Mr. Fitzgerald.

Smiling broadly, Dr. Noguchi replied, "Omissions perhaps, no major mistakes."

The length of Dr. Noguchi's testimony made the defendants tired and weary. Charles Manson sat almost immobile in his swivel chair, head down, his long hair covering his face.

On the way to court this morning, Edith Rayburn fainted for lack of oxygen in the elevator. At the time it happened, some jurors held her from falling down and then laid her outside in the middle of the corridor on the Casino floor.

Everybody stood around looking down at Edith. Having been a medic while in the army, I urged everybody to move away to let her breathe. Then I asked someone to open the door leading up to the swimming pool area. Ruth was sure it was a heart attack.

After a few minutes, a doctor came over and took the juror's pulse. He diagnosed that there was nothing serious—no heart attack—just a mild suffocation perhaps due to the number of people riding the elevator.

Edith recuperated and the jurors made their entrance into court on time.

Debbie was another casualty the same morning. Her right foot was bandaged, and she was wearing sneakers and carrying her regular shoes in one hand.

"What happened?" I asked.

"Oh, nothing," she responded and smiled, "just a little pain in my big toe. I twisted it."

I didn't believe her. Debbie confessed the next day the reason for her sore foot. It seemed that for the last three days, Mildred Osborne, her next-door neighbor, had been pestering Debbie about keeping the door between their rooms opened so she could also enjoy the music being played in her room piped in from my tape recorder. Debbie refused and was pretty uptight with the female redheaded juror.

At the time it happened, she said she was talking to Violet, Ray, Tom, and Genaro.

Mrs. Hart was telling them that the next time Mildred asked her the same thing, she would get her... At that time, Debbie demonstrated—she rose and kicked her foot in the air.

"Unfortunately," Debbie added, "I kicked an upholstered chair... I had no shoes and... *wow*! Did it hurt!"

"Bad girl!" I observed jokingly.

"It was worth it," she remarked and laughed.

We walked down to court.

As before, Charles Manson and the three girl defendants failed to stand up for Judge Older's entrance and bailiff Taylor's statement which marked the opening of each day's session.

Later, during the day, Charles Manson protested and interrupted Mr. Kanarek's cross-examination. He outbursted against his own lawyer, apparently upset because of his attorney's questions.

Charles stood up and said, "Your Honor, this man is not doing what I ask him, not even by a small margin. He's your attorney—not my attorney."

Judge Older attempted to cut him off, by saying, "Mr. Manson, you are to keep quiet."

Deputy Taylor moved behind Charlie and made him sit down.

Charlie continued, "I would like to dismiss this man and get another attorney."

"Think about what you have said," Judge Older replied, and then allowed Mr. Kanarek to continue his interrogation of Dr. Noguchi.

Charles Manson was joined by Mr. Fitzgerald, who was disturbed by the line of questions, since he considered it potentially damaging to his client, defendant Patricia Krenwinkel.

According to Linda Kasabian's testimony, Mr. Kanarek obviously aimed to have Dr. Noguchi say that Abigail Folger had been pursued by Miss Krenwinkel with an upraised knife, on the lawn of the Tate home, and would

189

have survived her wounds had Mrs. Kasabian called for immediate medical attention. The coroner declined to give such an opinion.

Ken Baggot, a newsreel cameraman for ABC, was the next witness who testified that he discovered the clothing near the Tate residence which the defendants wore the night of the Tate killings. The clothes were brought in large plastic bags and were submitted for evidence.

Deputy Sheriff Helen A. Tebbe testified that while on duty at the Sybil Brand Institution for Women, she took the accused Susan Atkins to have her hair washed and set. The witness stated that, with the defendant's own hair brush, she picked up hairs on it, put them in an envelope and turned it in to her lieutenant supervisor.

Mr. Joseph Granados, an investigator for the Los Angeles Police Department and an expert in classifying blood tests, was led by co-prosecutor Vincent T. Bugliosi through a series of questions that revealed the blood types of the five victims at the actress' rambling ranch-style house.

The witness testified that the blood on the front door used to scrawl the word "PIG" was Type O with an M subgrouping. Sharon Tate was the only victim with that blood classification. According to the investigator, there was a barefoot print in blood of the actress' type on the front porch. He theorized that the attackers presumably got blood on their feet in the interior of the house where Sharon Tate's body was sprawled in front of a living room couch. He also stated that the bloody towel used to write the word on the front door was found in the living room between the bodies of the actress and Jay C. Sebring.

Chemist Joseph Granados's monotonous voice was dragging and hard to understand. Wearing a wrinkled blue suit, he pulled out a lab test report and read it aloud.

Juror Number Nine, Mr. White, who wrote most of the trial procedures, asked the court to have the witness repeat certain statements about his report. That gave me time to prepare a chart like this:

Victim's Name	Blood Type	Subgroup
Steven Parent	B	MN
Voityk Frykowski	B	MN
Abigail Folger	B	MN
Jay Sebring	O	MN
Sharon Tate	O	M

Mr. Bugliosi asked the expert if he had tested for blood findings on the sports' knife found on the couch in the living room. Granados answered that he had and his test was negative.

Then he said that he found a trail of blood down a hallway, past the back bedroom, and out onto a path near the swimming pool at the side of the house.

Through questions by Mr. Bugliosi, the witness said he was not sure but it was his opinion that that was Abigail Folger's path as she fled her assailants before finally collapsing on the front lawn. He also mentioned that he tested blood spots and smears found at twenty nine places and that the two knives he found in the house measured as follows:

A pocket-type sports' knife (P-39) with a blade of three and three-sixteenth inches, and the other was a steak knife with a longer blade, which through lab tests revealed the blood to be that of an animal.

The jury had heard descriptions of how the murders had been committed, but it was Granados who introduced the jurors to the first material evidence. He produced a large sketch drawn by himself. The sketch depicted the body of Sharon Tate next to a couch and Sebring's body, his head towards Sharon's head and feet away. The bodies were at right angles. A rope connected around their heads, which later had been cut by the Coroner's Office, and the rest of the rope was hanging from a raft on the ceiling.

Quite a bizarre sketch to look at.

The witness testified that he conducted tests for blood on rope as well as on the clothing found by the ABC cameraman. He found blood-type Positive O in a black velour sweater shirt, and Linda Kasabian had testified that Tex Watson wore a similar shirt on the first night. He found negative reaction to human precipitation in most of the clothing. His final testimony focused on fingerprints evidence found at the Tate home.

Frank Struthers, Jr., stepson of Leno La Bianca and son of Mrs. La Bianca, gave testimony about how he came home from a Lake Isabella vacation to find his mother and stepfather murdered.

Asked by Mr. Aaron H. Stovitz to describe the situation, the youth said, "My sister Susan's boyfriend, Joe Dorgan, and I went through the kitchen and into the living room and we saw Leno crouching there."

"Did he appear to have been armed or hurt in any way?" the prosecutor asked.

"We didn't stay long enough to see, but when we left, we knew something was wrong," the teenager calmly replied.

The witness continued saying that he and his companion ran to a neighbor's house to call the police, who went into the La Bianca home and discovered the bloody body of Mrs. La Bianca in a bedroom and also that of her husband in the living room.

The young witness identified a wallet belonging to his mother. It was the same wallet that prosecution witness Linda Kasabian earlier testified was the one Charles Manson instructed her to hide in the restroom of a Sylmar service station following the slayings of the La Bianca couple.

Frank Struthers was composed throughout his time on the stand. He was neatly dressed and well groomed. His voice seemed to waver only when he was asked if he recognised a watch shown him by the Deputy District Attorney, Mr. Stovitz.

"I'd seen my mother wear it many times," he replied.

The defense didn't ask any questions and young Struthers was followed to the stand by Mrs. Ruth Sivick, who owned a dress shop with the victim, Mrs. La Bianca.

Mrs. Sivick dressed sharply. She said she had visited the La Bianca home about six P.M. the night of the slayings to feed two of the couple's three dogs. The witness, with a trembling voice, said that Mrs. La Bianca had telephoned her on Saturday morning to say they would be away that weekend and requested her to take care of the pets.

Mrs. Sivick identified photographs of the La Bianca home, saying everything was in order at the time she was there. She mentioned there were missing words smeared on the refrigerator and on an oil painting in the living room. The photographs, taken after the murders, showed "Helter Skelter" painted on the refrigerator door. The word "Rise" was painted on the painting.

Mr. Stovitz showed her a carving fork and knife plus a bread knife, but she could not definitely identify them as belonging to her friend.

John Fokianos, a neighborhood news vendor, knew Mr. and Mrs. La Bianca for about two years as a customer. He said the couple talked briefly with him about the "Tate" event— the big news in the *Los Angeles Times,* but that they had bought the *Herald Examiner.*

The witness said that the victims talked about nothing unusual except that they were a little tired from the trip and that he saw them heading east on Franklin Avenue, pulling a trailer.

Police Officer William Rodriguez of the Hollywood Division testified that on Sunday, August 9, 1969, he went to 3301 Waverly Drive accompanied by another officer. He arrived at eight thirty-five P.M. He noticed the front door was closed, but unlocked and no damage to it. He entered and walked into the living room. He discovered a male body lying by the couch—he observed the stomach was cut and had lacerations. He went outside to the radio car to have an ambulance to back him up. Sergeant Cline arrived, and officer Rodriguez said he remained on the premises about two-and-one-half hours.

Sergeant Edmond Cline, police officer, advised by Officer Rodriguez, testified that he also saw the male body in the living room. Then he went to the bedroom at his right that, at first glance, he observed what appeared to be the dead body of a female. He went out to the ambulance and then returned inside. He observed when the male nurse checked the pulse on the wrist of the woman, she was pronounced dead. Going through the home, he observed various writings on the wall and on the refrigerator, which appeared dried. He remained on the premises about one-and-one-half hours.

Sergeant Danny Galindo, a police officer assigned to the Homicide Division for about twenty years, testified that he went to the La Bianca home at one A.M. and talked to various officers. He stayed there for about ten or twelve hours, inspected the grounds in and outside the house, and looked for weapons or any evidence in connection with the crime. He sustained that no weapons were found. No bloody clothes were located. The pillow was removed from the face of Leno La Bianca and he saw the head of the victim inside of a pillow case, knotted around the neck with an electrical wire connected to a massive lamp. He observed that in the abdominal area, there were kitchen utensils protruding above the navel, like a fork—a knife. The word "WAR" was written on the stomach of Mr. La Bianca.

Other similar utensils were found in the kitchen. As someone turned the body of the victim, Sgt. Galindo said he noticed that the hands of Leno La Bianca were tied with leather thongs. Then he clipped the electrical cord from the base of the lamp. The deceased was wearing pajamas—fully dressed —the buttons slightly undone. Mrs. La Bianca was wearing a bathrobe. No struggle appeared to have taken place. The witness stated that Mrs. La Bianca's head was also wrapped with an electrical cord attached to a lamp which had been dragged off its stand. Then he added that her head was also slipped into a pillowcase. Her hands were free—one hand was underneath her and the other was up. Looking around, he saw no signs of ransacking. Still, he found coil collections, diamonds, jewelry of expensive quality, a gun collection, expensive camera equipment, a high-priced stop watch, and other costly items which were undisturbed,—indicating to his professional knowledge that robbery was not a motive for the killings of the La Biancas. All the drawers were in place, the closets in his opinion were intact. No breakage of any sort. No damage on doors in the rear. He found a lady's purse lying on a cabinet in the kitchen. The purse was opened. There was no lady's wallet inside. He looked into all the closets and, finally, found in the car parked in the driveway of the residence—in the glove compartment—a wallet with the usual contents: driver's license, credit cards, about $ 200 worth of uncirculated nickles, and a bunch of keys.

Sergeant Gary L. Brody, police officer, testified that he saw the body of Leno La Bianca at the morgue and that he witnessed the pillowcase being removed from the victim's head and subsequently he saw a knife stuck in the victim's throat.

Dr. David M. Katsuyama, deputy coroner, testified about the autopsy he performed on Mr. and Mrs. La Bianca. Using enough large diagrams, Dr. Katsuyama told how many stab wounds had been thrust in the victims' bodies.

The medical examiner, speaking loudly and fast and in a very broken English, declared that the cause of death of Leno La Bianca was due to multiple stab wounds in the neck and abdomen, causing massive hemorrhage. He also said that he cut the electrical cord around the neck and then removed the pillowcase from the head.

In detailing the wounds suffered by the market-chain executive, Dr. Katsuyama said that six of the twelve stab wounds would have been fatal, individually. There were a total of 26 wounds, and he described the knife found in Mr. La Bianca's neck as having a blade four and seven-eighths inches in length, one-sixteenth of an inch in thickness, and a varying width of thirteen-sixteenths to three-eighths of an inch.

In response to questions by Mr. Bugliosi, Dr. Katsuyama testified that the word "WAR" was scratched into the victim's skin over an area stretching from the ribcage to the belly button.

The next day Dr. Katsuyama, questioned by Mr. Bugliosi, testified that Rosemary La Bianca bled to death after she was stabbed 41 times.

"Any one of eight stab wounds the victim received would have killed her," said the small medical examiner while adjusting his thick spectacles. He also said that cuts from a dull-edged object such as a screwdriver or one of the points on the electric plug were also found on her back.

The size of the knife, according to the deputy coroner, was a knife with a double-edged blade at least five and one-half inches long, about one-inch wide, and from one-sixteenth to five-sixteenth of an inch thick.

Dr. Katsuyama said that fourteen of the stab wounds on the lower back —all in her hips—were post morium, because the wounds lacked the color which ordinarily appears around the tissues. The blood, if any, was lighter and is usually dark if the person is still alive.

Deputy District Attorney Bugliosi recalled Chemist Joseph Granados to the stand. The shabby-looking witness, still wearing the same wrinkled blue suit, testified that he had conducted a microscopic examination and blood test on hairs found on a pair of denim pants from the bundle of clothing found by the ABC cameraman and compared them with the hairs taken from Susan Atkin's hair brush at the Sybil Brand Institute.

The chemist discovered that both samples of hair appeared to be the same in many factors.

"The hairs were matched," he said, "and microscopically they are identical side by side, the characteristics are the same in color, length, and size inside the medula, and also the internal structure appears to be the same."

In a surprise move, the defendant Susan Atkins stood up and in a loud, painful voice, asked Judge Older, "Your Honor, if you don't get me out of here, I will scream and yell," the prisoner leaned over the table and holding her stomach with one hand, began sobbing.

"It hurts too much," she said, "let me out of the courtroom... if you don't I'll....." Her words were drowned in tears as she complained of a severe pain. Mollie Kane and another female bailiff removed her from the court.

The witness continued testifying and gave an enormous account of all the tests he had conducted at the Tate and La Bianca residences. Mr. Fitzgerald, Mr. Shin, and Mr. Hughes were glad to receive negative answers from Police Chemist Granados in regards to questions about comparison of their client's hair, with the clothing allegedly discarded by the slayers with hair on them.

On cross-examination by Mr. Shin, the witness said he could chemically prove the samples matched only in blood type.

"In other words, you are just guessing that the hairs may be similar. Is that right?" asked Mr. Shin.

"Yes," admitted the chemist.

Susan Atkins's health problem forced Judge Older to adjourn the court session two hours early.

Tuesday and Wednesday we didn't go to court. However, we were taken to the Hall of Justice and waited and waited. We did nothing but wait.

Our lives had become reduced to one dreary word—"Wait." We found ourselves maneuvered into those two adjourned small rooms, and from the dirty windows we contemplated the bustling City of Los Angeles below. We were forced to mark time, and to justify our existence while we waited, watched, and hoped for something to happen.

We wished the bailiff would come and tell us to go down in court so we could perform what we were supposed to do—to sit in court and listen to the evidence and not to sit in the jury room and be forced to listen to the noise and childish behavior of Ray, Tom, and Debbie, and the stupid cackle of Violet.

While sitting and doing nothing in the jury room I could not help thinking that our talents were dulled by routine and corroded by anxiety and as we waited they grew increasingly worthless and our incentive was hopelessly eaten away little by little.

Without my consent I became a shrewd, perceptive, critic of my fellow jurors. I was able to analyze and judge their characters as the months passed by. I noticed their hidden flaws and gradually I weighed their motives and even predicted some of their actions.

Besides swimming and paddle tennis after court sessions, bowling on Tuesday nights and a choice of taking a walk on the hotel grounds or watching television after dinner—there was not much to do. During the day, there was so much reading that I already had absorbed readily about fifteen novels, plus magazines and articles from different sources. I became naturally indecisive and restless as what to do with the precious time and energy I had on my hands. So, to justify an old belief and desire of mine which had always resulted in feverish bursts of planning and excitement, I decided to follow a course of action and do it—to write a book—a book about the jurors of the Manson trial!

The next day when I announced it in the jury room, maybe without realizing it myself, there was erected an invisible but quite tall impenetrable wall between myself and the rest of the jurors. Almost instantly they avoided me. Those who eagerly sought my company at the dinner tables kept away from me and would, almost like a miracle, sit together. They refrained from talking about themselves in my presence and even less about their backgrounds, families, or inward struggles. As a consequence, they did not make it easy for me, though in part, I had already become aware of their dreams, hopes, cares, and fears. Eventually, the jurors detached themselves from the thought that I was invading their privacy and tried to ignore the fact by being distant and aloof in their conversations. In the course of time, I frequently indicated to them that what I would write would be strictly the truth, there would be no lies and what anything anybody did or said would help me more.

"The only thing I regret that I won't be able to write," I told them, "is that there is no romance among any one of us."

They laughed when I said it without suspecting that later on, a real romance bloomed between a female regular juror and a male alternate juror.

At the beginning, Debbie told me that she felt that the new alternate jurors didn't fit with the regular jurors and for that reason she apparently ignored them. But gradually, in my company and that of the other jurors, I noticed that she began to talk to them, especily to Tom and Ray who had been sitting with me.

Deputy Taylor came to the jury room and announced that the delay was because the defendant, Susan Atkins, was ill.

When we returned to court, the female defendant appeared to be still in pain and sat all day with her head buried in her arms on the counsel table. However, she sat upright after Judge Older called an at-bench conference. Nobody paid attention and the trial continued.

Jerome A. Boen, officer investigator of the Los Angeles Police Department, testified that single latent prints were found at the Tate's home matching those of defendant Patricia Krenwinkel and also Charles (Tex) Watson.

The witness testified under questioning by prosecutor Bugliosi that Patricia Krenwinkel's left little fingerprint was lifted from a door leading from Sharon Tate's bedroom to the pool area in the rear of the house. According to Officer Boen, the other print matched with Tex Watson's right ring finger and was found six to eight inches above the door knob of the front door.

The witness added that no fingerprints were found at the La Bianca home nor where there should have been—on the handle of a fork sticking from Leno La Bianca's abdomen.

Frank S. Escalante, a police officer, testified briefly that on April 23, 1969, he rolled fingerprints on Charles Denton Watson in the Valley Service Division jail. He was booked on a misdemeanor.

Jack E. Swan, a civilian fingerprint specialist working for the Police Department, took the stand to tell that he rolled the fingerprints of Patricia Krenwinkel upon her return from Mobile, Alabama.

Sergeant Harold J. Dolan, fingerprint impressions expert, testified that he prepared two large boards containing large photo copies of the fingerprints of Patricia Krenwinkel and Tex Watson.

On the direct examination by Mr. Bugliosi, the witness, using the boards, explained that ten points of similarity are standard and generally accepted as conclusive proof in comparing fingerprints. He went on to say that he found eighteen points on the latent print found at the Tate home in comparison of an exemplar belonging to Tex Watson. He also conducted the scientific comparison in regards to Patricia Krenwinkel, and according to his opinion, the latent print which contained eighteen points and that of the exemplar of the defendant, were the same.

No fingerprints were traced or made readable at the La Bianca home. It was his opinion that the slayers removed the fingerprints.

Steven Weiss, an eleven-year-old boy, testified about finding the western-style .22 caliber-type gun that allegedly was used to shoot three of the victims at the Tate estate.

The young boy said he found the gun on September 1, 1969, as he was fixing the sprinkler on the hill behind his home. The young fellow explained that the grip was in the same condition as when he found it, except with dust scattered all over the gun and that he was being very careful with the pistol as to preserve it for fingerprinting evidence.

He had brought it to his backyard and placed it on a table and called his father. Under cross-examination by Defense Attorney Paul Fitzgerald, the witness testified that when he first picked up the gun, he did so from the barrel.

"Why?" asked Mr. Fitzgerald.

"Because, that way," he said, "I would not touch the grip as not to remove fingerprint marks."

"How did your father handle it?" inquired the defense counsel.

"With both hands—all over the gun," the boy replied.

The handsome youngster, who seemed so small in the large witness chair, brought a burst of laughter from the jury, who looked at him with sympathy, and others in the packed courtroom.

The young witness said that his father turned over the gun the day it was found but that apparently the police did not connect the gun with the Tate case until he himself talked to them on the phone again sometime in December.

"Who told you to call them?" inquired Mr. Fitzgerald.

"I heard on the radio that detectives were looking for such a gun and I thought of calling to inform them that I was the one who had found a gun more than three months earlier."

Mike F. Watson, a Los Angeles police officer assigned to Van Nuys Station, testified that he received a radio car call and went to 3627 Longview Valley Road in the San Fernando Valley.

The officer said that Steven Weiss, in the presence of his father, handed him a .22 caliber gun. The witness stated that he took seven empty cartridges and two live shells from the long-barreled revolver and that the wood paneling of the right side was missing.

Robert L. Calkins, office investigator for the Sharon Tate case, declared that the first time he saw the gun was on December 16, 1969. He testified that he had mailed out approximately three hundred announcements to various police agencies throughout California and out of the state in regards to locating the gun. He stated that he received inquiries later on. He wrote confidential letters in order to locater the murder weapon, and his division contacted various persons who had purchased .22 caliber weapons. The investigators went over to look at these guns without informing the owners that they were working on the Sharon Tate murder case.

The witness testified also that he made hundreds of phone calls, wrote letters, etc., all in the presence of his partner, Sergeant McGann, and under the guidance of his supervisor. The witness stated that before they found the alleged murder weapon, the investigators had searched the Hollywood Hills approximately ten times but not in the area behind the Weiss home. He finally mentioned that at that time the Tate case had priority in the Investigation Section of the Los Angeles Police Department.

Sergeant Dudley D. Barney, assisting on the investigation of the Tate murder, testified that while covering the case he discovered the fragments of bullets in the White Rambler (license MPK) parked outside of the Polanski residence in Cielo Drive.

William J. Lee, sergeant, police firearms expert, testified on the results of ballistics tests run on the .22 caliber gun. The witness said that of the four bullets and several bullet fragments found in the victims or near their bodies, only the one discovered in Jay Sebring's body was definitely fired by the weapon.

Under questions by Mr. Bugliosi, he stated the others could have been fired from the pistol but that there were insufficient markings on the death bullets to make a definite determination.

The well-spoken ballistics expert said that it was his opinion the three pieces of wood, side by side, appeared to belong to the right hand grip of the gun (P-40).

The next day, we arrived at the Hall of Justice and waited in the jury room until past ten o'clock. When we sat in the jury box, I immediately noticed that one of the prosecutors, Mr. Aaron H. Stovitz, was missing. Seated next to Mr. Bugliosi were two other gentlemen who stared at the jurors as we walked in the courtroom.

"What happened? Where's Mr. Stovitz?" Mildred asked.

"Who knows," I replied, tightening my teeth as not to be noticed.

Deputy Taylor ordered everybody to stand up as Judge Older walked in. His Honor stopped and faced the flag until Bailiff Taylor had finished the daily ceremony.

The judge, adjusting the black robe around his collar neck, announced in a surprised statement that Mr. Aaron H. Stovitz had been replaced as co-prosecutor in the trial. His Honor didn't state any reason why the deputy

199

district attorney had been removed, and simply proceeded to introduce his successors: Mr. Ronald Musich and Mr. Stephen Kay.

Of the two lawyers, Mr. Kay seemed to be the youngest. His tall and slim body frame gave an indication as if he had just stepped down from a high school building. However, the glasses he wore gave him that studious and knowledgeable look that most young men have when they are given big opportunities.

Mr. Musich appeared cool and composed. As the trial progressed, neither Mr. Musich nor Mr. Kay conducted a redirect examination of the witnesses. Both assisted Mr. Bugliosi in the extremely important murder trial. There was no question that the dismissal of the competent, sometimes volatile Mr. Stovitz, was a missing figure.

Mr. Bugliosi took the burden alone and it became apparent that he had to put in more working hours. At times he looked tired, perhaps due to the strain and enormous responsibility that the trial involved. Mr. Bugliosi displaced enough capacity to handle the case alone, but the tension imposed made him lose his temper a couple of times. He retaliated more often to Mr. Kanarek's objections and it was a relief to see the serene prosecutor alive and powerful. I, for one, was wondering if Mr Bugliosi had the guts, or if he was going to let the defense counsel get away with the constant interruptions and say nothing.

Mr. Bugliosi stood on his own admirably and in all fairness, he proved to be an exemplar of a conscientious dedicated lawyer. He pulled no tricks, nor tried to gain the jurors' sympathy. He simply performed his profession. His tactics were no more than to establish the truth from the witness through calculated and intelligent questions.

The following witness to the stand was Edward C. Lomax, a sporting goods salesman who formerly worked as marketing manager for High Standard, the firm that manufactured the gun allegedly used at the Polanski residence. He testified that he examined the three pieces of wood and discovered they were made of walnut wood, and that to his knowledge, they belonged to a gun such as the one found by the young boy. He stated the weapon was a nine-shot, nine-and-one-half-inch barrel, same as People's 40. He recognized it because the longhorn revolver often called the "Buntline Special" was modeled after the revolvers designed by Ned Buntline for Wyatt Earp.

Thomas J. Walleman, who gave his occupation as an optical technician from "time to time" said he lived for about three years at the Spahn Ranch. He testified that in the summer of 1969, about a month before the Tate slayings, he received a phone call late at night from a woman. He turned the call over to Mr. Manson who later told him, after hanging up, that the caller was "going to come out and do the whole ranch in."

The witness rather disjointedly related that Charlie told him they were going to see someone. They got into John Swartz's 1959 Ford car—Walleman added that Manson left for a while and returned with a pistol and placed it on the seat between the two of them. The witness testified that he put the gun on his belt and they drove to Franklin Avenue in Hollywood. Manson asked him for the gun and went to the apartment of the caller.

When shown the murder weapon by Mr. Bugliosi, the witness replied, "It looked something like that but I can't be sure... it was a long one like that."

The testimony of Walleman was constantly interrupted by Mr. Kanarek and Mr. Fitzgerald, whose objections were sustained most of the time. The reason why Charles Manson went inside of the apartment was not disclosed, because Mr. Bugliosi was stopped short in his questioning before the witness could relate what happened after he and Manson arrived at the Hollywood apartment house.

Due to technicalities, most of the courtroom proceedings during this day were conducted out of our presence.

While waiting in the jury room of Department 102, the "clique" opted to go all the way to express their contempt among the rest of the jurors. Tom, Ray, and Debbie brought with them their golf putters to practice in the jury room. Not satisfied with hitting the ball against a wall, they decided to use a large tin paper basket instead. The noise produced at intervals sent everybody on their feet and eventually out of the room. No one dared to protest, including this juror-writer, who for lack of courage simply withdrew from the scene and followed Betty, Thelma, and Olivia who had already established themselves in the smaller room. Mr. Welch walked in shortly after and stationed himself near the window to continue reading Volume No. 4 of his *Encyclopedia Brittanica*. Marvin and Danny brought their own chairs and joined those of us who wanted peace and quiet. It helped, but not enough. The "clique" sensed the reason of our departure and to display their resentment they continued making louder remarks accompanied by constant bursts of laughter.

Olivia Madison, who had been pacing the floor could not take it any longer and took upon herself to shut the door off just as a golf ball rolled into the room. Mr. Welch welcomed Olivia's initiative and acting instinctively he took the ball and hid it behind a paper basket. He returned to his seat and assumed a position as being completely absorbed in reading the book. He

201

waited. The rest of us just stared at each other approvingly.

One full minute had not gone by when the cracking sound of another golf ball hitting the door made us aware that the "clique" was retaliating. Nothing was said. Suddenly the door was opened wide. It was Ray who slammed the door against the wall as he entered. Debbie and Tom both holding golf putters in their hands walked in and searched for the missing ball. The rest of us pretended to be unaware of what they were looking for. No one offered any indication as where they could look for the golf ball.

It almost felt like two adult teams were playing "Hide and Seek."

"Here," said Debbie, "this will do." She grabbed the metal paper basket and placed it in the center.

Ray discovered where the ball was and as he picked it up, he shouted, "I got it! I got it!" and then added, "Okay, Violet, it is your turn now... hit it."

Violet Stokes, a short plump, young woman appeared in the threshold of the door and giggled. She noticed our stern faces and without much concern she turned around and disappeared.

Through the facial expressions of Mr. Welch, Thelma, and Marvin, I deduced that Mrs. Stokes was going to hit the ball against the metal paper basket. Effectively, the ball rolled in but didn't hit the container. Ray's turn was next. He bounced the ball on the floor and went out of the room. The bow-legged juror hit the receptacle hard enough to produce the type of hollow noise we were running away from. Debbie and Tom were next and they also hit the target, causing a tumult of yells and boisterous laughter among the foursome. They left the room and again Olivia shut the door.

"Golf is an outdoor sport," declared Frank Welch, "It shouldn't be played inside... they're acting like kids."

"Not only that," observed Thelma, "the way they hit that ball somebody might get hurt."

"Why don't we hide the ball for good the next time they hit it this way?" suggested Frank.

"That wouldn't stop them," said Betty.

"Why?" someone inquired.

"Because they have more balls than you can think of."

The double meaningful remark made some of the jurors chuckle and it helped to break the spell of annoyance we were going through. We laughed ...stopped and laughed.. and laughed again.

We attempted to imitate the "clique's" manner of laughing and even forced ourselves to continue laughing until the bailiff came in to inform us we were going down to the courtroom. The "clique" frowned upon our laughter and dared not ask why we laughed and laughed. They didn't like it, and for a while through our laughter, they received a mild treatment of what they had been giving to the rest of the jurors.

Danny De Carlo, a gunsmith by profession and an ex-member of the family, testified that he met Charlie at the Spahn Ranch in 1969. He stated that he went there to repair a motorcycle and remained on Manson's invitation until late August of that year.

De Carlo, a dark-haired and hippie-looking young man in his twenties, was a most colorful witness. He brought much needed relief for laughter among the long line of police, scientific and ballistics' expert witnesses. Wearing an olive T-shirt, blue jeans and boots, he answered questions in regard to the type of life the family led at the ranch.

The witness, a former member of a motorcycle club called the "Straight Satans," said he was asked by Manson if he liked to move in and live at the ranch.

De Carlo explained:

"Charlie opened the door for me and told me I was welcome—he said I could have everything I wanted."

"Did he say anything about the girls?" inquired Mr. Bugliosi.

"He said the girls didn't belong to anybody," responded De Carlo, "and if I wanted to make love to them, I could."

"What happened next?" asked the prosecutor.

The witness twirled his moustache and grinned as he answered Mr. Bugliosi's question, "I moved in the first day I was at the ranch."

Everybody in the courtroom laughed.

Danny De Carlo named nearly all the members of the family. At that time, the witness revealed there were about five men and thirteen girls living in the western-style buildings of the Chatsworth Ranch.

"How did Tex Watson appear to you?" asked Mr. Bugliosi.

"He was... happy-go-lucky... like a puppy dog," said the ex-Navy gunner's mate. "I liked Tex, he was quiet."

The witness then stated that the group called themselves "the family," a communal group in which everything belonged to everybody and in relation to the girls' roles, as directed by Manson, was to take care of the men.

"The means of support," observed the witness, "was through selling pop bottles and the broads panhandled and collected food from the backs of markets on garbage runs."

"How did the girls feel about Manson?" asked Mr. Bugliosi.

203

"They worshipped him," replied Danny De Carlo, "and at various times, they told me that he knew all and saw all."

"Did you ever hear Manson tell the girls to walk around in the nude?"

"Yes," answered the witness, "they took their clothes off anyway."

"You liked that, didn't you Danny?" asked the prosecutor.

De Carlo, seated with folded arms and a leg placed on top of the rail, replied earthly, "Yeah, I dug it."

The general laughter, plus the noise produced from Danny's boots against the stand, prompted the court reporter to look up expecting to hear the answer repeated.

"I *liked* it," said Danny, leaning over the stand and adding to the amusement of Judge Older and the rest of the spectators in the courtroom.

"Did you ever hear Mr. Manson give any instructions to the girls, including these defendants, with respect to sex?" inquired Mr. Bugliosi.

The prosecutor encountered a score of objections while trying to prove that Charles Manson was the leader of the family. De Carlo answered questions about Manson's philosophy, his feelings about blacks and whites, and his theory about "Helter Skelter."

Under questioning by Mr. Bugliosi, De Carlo testified Manson would give orders when to eat and that he would do all the talking at dinner time. In regard to conversations referring about blacks and whites, the witness stated that Manson didn't like black people.

"What did he say about black and white people?" the prosecutor wanted to know.

"He didn't like the idea of black people fooling around with white girls," replied Danny. "He was dead set against that."

"Did he say anything else?"

"Well, he wanted the white people against the black people."

Before the witness could explain what he meant by that, Mr. Kanarek objected vigorously about Manson's "supposed distrust and dislike" for black people.

Judge Older firmly told him to stop interrupting and admonished the defense counsel for the last time. Since Mr. Kanarek continued objecting, the court called the counsel to the bench. Mr. Kanarek, obviously cited for contempt of court, sat down and quieted down long enough to have the witness explain that Manson was trying to get whites against the blacks, and vice versa.

"When the blacks and whites were finally against each other," observed Danny De Carlo, "we'd just sit up on the top of a mountain and watch them shoot each other."

204

"How's this going to happen?" asked Mr. Bugliosi.

"Yes, we all were going to watch."

"Who is We?" inquired the prosecutor.

"The family, all of us, with binoculars."

"What did he say about the Black Panthers?"

"He said the Black Panthers would eventually overcome the police."

"Did he say anything else?"

"Yes... they were going to come to the Spahn Ranch and shoot all of us."

Danny De Carlo continued his testimony and stated the women were posted as guards. He also said Manson played the guitar, sang only songs of his own, and that Charlie used the term "Helter Skelter" in his songs. Manson liked to listen to the Beatles' two-record white album in which the song "Helter Skelter" was recorded. "Manson told him that the Beatles were aware."

Under questioning by the prosecution, the witness explained Manson's use of the word "Pigs."

"Who were the Pigs, besides the police?" Mr. Bugliosi asked.

"The white-collar workers. People who work from eight to five daily."

I noticed there was no reaction from the jurors.

Judge Older adjourned the court session at four o'clock, admonished the jurors and announced that due to the "California Convention of Judges," he would recess the trial for the first three days of the week, including Labor Day, Tuesday, and Admission Day.

The unexpected lengthy holiday recess created an atmosphere of unhappy feelings on some of the jurors.

"I'm sure the convention is more important than the trial," Betty White said sarcastically in the jury room.

"How can they do this to us?" asked Mildred impatiently.

"Doesn't he know we have a home?" Betty asked to herself.

"He doesn't care, that's all there is...." the slim-looking juror opened a package of "Kool" and lit a cigarette. She walked towards the window, and blowing forcibly, the smoke against the glass, whispered audibly, "Bastards."

Betty caught my eye, and as to cover up, she let out a single burst of laughter —a mannerism which she followed during other similar occasions.

The outing on Sunday was cancelled and instead we were taken to Disneyland on the following day. No guests were allowed and that in itself brought some unhappy remarks, especially from the "clique." They wanted to spend the day by the pool but because of lack of manpower to escort those who wanted to stay at the hotel, were forced to join the rest of the jurors. Actually, the main reason they objected to going was on account of Deputy Michael

Pappas who was in charge of the excursion. They resented his presence.

The multi-million dollar amusement park had less visitors than on the weekend and proved to be an enjoyable experience. Two lovely young ladies, acting as hostesses, led us through a comprehensive tour which was highlighted with a succulent luncheon at a local restaurant featuring an accordion player and a violinist.

Frank Welch and Marvin shared a table with me. Frank wanted to dance as soon as he heard the music.

Mr. Welch was not a man to bore anyone—he was a self-taught successful man. His youthful attitude made him popular and he rather dance than eat. He rose and suggested Marvin and I join him in asking the hostesses to dance. We declined. He danced with both hostesses and then with Ruth Collingwood who turned out to be a fine polka dancer.

When I noticed that Frank had asked Debbie to dance and she had refused him flatly, I couldn't help thinking what she had told me some weeks before. Debbie had expressed how much she detested the "old man Welch's" insistence of asking her to dance. She wished Frank stopped dancing—period. It bored her.

I knew Marvin liked Mr. Welch. I wanted to share my little secret and for that reason I motioned him to observe the reaction on Debbie's face and her company. Marvin couldn't believe it and for lack of words, he simply stated, "I don't understand it, at least Frank doesn't try to bother anyone."

Frank Welch who has always been happy and friendly, suddenly became a hermit. The seventy-four-year-old retired sheriff locked himself in his room and skipped dinners. He refrained from watching television in the recreation room. He spoke very little and acted differently. I didn't know the reason of Frank's seclusion until Marvin himself, rather worried and concerned, admitted to me that he had made the senseless mistake to disclose to Frank what Debbie had said. That day, Frank was taken ill to the doctor. He had complained of having heart trouble. Marvin felt responsible.

"I shouldn't have told him," he said. "I feel guilty."

"Oh, come on," I exclaimed, "don't be ridiculous. If anyone should feel guilty, it should be me. Look at it this way. If I hadn't told you, you wouldn't have been able to tell him anything in the first place. Right? Consequently, I feel equally responsible as you do. Don't worry, Frank will be alright. You'll see."

Indeed, Frank Welch recuperated and once again became the happy individual he was before. However, till the end of the trial, he never spoke directly to Debbie nor did he ask her again to dance. Frank and Debbie sat together in the courtroom and yet they never spoke to each other. Frank kept away from the "clique" and even from Violet who, for lack of dancers, had become his dancing partner.

During the trip to Disneyland, Mike Pappas and I got along well on account of our mutual interest in movies. He encouraged me to write a book and to tell everything that was going on among the jurors. Unlike Olivia Madison, a retired drama critic who had told me that she couldn't see anything of interest to write about the jurors, Mike saw the potential material the jurors themselves were providing with their own idiosyncrasies. Mike was right. There were plenty scenes of human interest between the jurors themselves, and the attitude of bailiffs was also predominantly important.

One example was Mike himself who didn't get along with Mollie. It seemed Mike had tried to get the tough blonde female bailiff in bed, but to no avail. His jokes didn't register with Mollie and quite often she would hit him or punch him hard on the shoulder. Mollie's hands were big and strong and to say the least, she was feared because of her strength. There was no question that Mollie had the right kind of job.

Deputy Taylor on the other hand got along beautifully with Mollie. Because of their close relationship, Ray and George mentioned the possibility of an existing affair between the two bailiffs. They based their suspicions on the fact that Mollie spent a great deal of time in Deputy Taylor's chambers.

Also noticeable was the fact that some sheriffs didn't care nor get along with Deputy Taylor. Many heated arguments were overheard inside his room and even in the hall. One such occasion was the time he had words with a female deputy by the name of Elsie. In due time, I shall explain the incident which involved some jurors.

"If they produce a movie from your book," said Deputy Pappas eagerly, "you better make sure they choose me to play myself in it."

"Who do you think should play my part?" I inquired.

"Oh... perhaps Richardo Montalban or Fernando Lamas," Mike replied.

"But why not me?" I answered objectively.

"Because you have an accent... and besides, you look too young."

We both smiled. Oddly enough, Mike's statement was a typical Hollywood producer's reaction and it wouldn't surprise me if either of the two afore-mentioned gentlemen actors would be strong candidates to portray Juror William M. Zamora on the screen. We'll see.

On September 17, 1970 at 9:45 A.M., we walked in the courtroom and after a few minutes, Judge Older called the counsel to join him in his private chambers for further discussions. Looking in front of me, I noticed Betty had written

207

on a full page of her note book: 'BASTARDS.' She didn't show it to anyone but to Mildred and I. Marvin, seated at her left, caught a glimpse of the writing and then stared at me with a look of disbelief. His eyes protruding wide open caused me to pretend as if I didn't know what he meant. The counsel came out at 9:55 A.M. and the trial continued.

According to Danny De Carlo, Charles Manson told him he would rather shoot people than birds. The witness related an incident where Charlie objected to his shooting of a bird at the Spahn Ranch.

Asked by Mr. Bugliosi what his job with the family was, the witness replied, "I took care of the guns."

He then listed the guns kept at the ranch as five rifles, two shotguns, a submachine gun, and a .22 revolver gun.

De Carlo described the pistol as a western-style "Buntline Special."

Mr. Bugliosi brought to his attention the gun allegedly used in the crimes for identification, and the witness stated, "Yeah, its similar to it."

Then he added that he had seen Manson carry and fire the long-barreled revolver at the ranch.

"What did Mr. Manson say with respect to the .22-caliber revolver?" Mr. Bugliosi asked.

"Well," De Carlo said, "he traded my truck for it."

The witness went on to say he last saw the gun in the early days of August 1969, when it disappeared from the bunkhouse.

Asked if he had seen the buck knife (P-39) at the ranch, he answered, "Yeah."

He also said he had seen the girls wearing black T-shirts and that he had gone with Charles Manson to purchase about 153 feet of three-strand nylon white rope at a Santa Monica Boulevard war surplus store.

"Does it appear to be the same type of rope that Mr. Manson bought?" Mr. Bugliosi asked, showing De Carlo the blood-stained rope.

"Yeah," the witness replied.

Mr. Bugliosi showed De Carlo a leather thong and asked whether he had ever seen Manson wear one similar to it. The witness said he had.

The prosecutor switched his interrogation to Manson's beliefs, and De Carlo answered mostly in monosyllables, saying simply, "Yeah."

Mr. Bugliosi inquiring.

"Did you ever hear Mr. Manson call himself something?"

"Yeah."

"What?"

"Devil."

"What did he say about the devil, Danny?"

"That the devil will eventually be the leader."

"Did Manson say anything about the devil being on the loose?"

"Yeah."

"What did he say?"

"That he was the devil."

Mr. Bugliosi continued asking questions in regard to Charles Manson and the witness testified that he heard the hippie cult leader saying he wanted to make a movie.

De Carlo finally said that he was arrested at the ranch on August 16, 1969, during a raid by the Sheriff's Department.

Questions about his sexual relationship were mostly overruled. However, he disclosed having had sexual intercourse twice with Linda Kasabian.

On cross-examination by Mr. Fitzgerald, the tatooed witness admitted that he was heavy beer drinker.

"Were you drunk ninety-nine percent of the time you were at the Spahn Ranch?" the lawyer asked.

"Yeah," the witness replied, "I was feeling good drunk, not passed out."

Elaborating on his admission, the short witness (about five feet, five inches) brought laughter when he observed, "I was feeling good. I didn't pass out on the ground."

Then, reflexibly and rather comically, added, "I did go out to lunch a couple times... I guess... but usually I was just feeling good."

Mr. Fitzgerald, through questions, managed to have the witness admit that he once heard Manson say he loved black people and that he could not recall the cult leader saying that he hated black people. The defense counsel, in an unexpected move, brought a startling question to the witness, "Is it not true that you hate blacks and not Mr. Manson?"

Danny De Carlo, looking at Manson, cool and unmoved by the question, answered as a matter of fact, "We think about the same about that."

Under Mr. Fitzgerald's questioning, the witness described the bunkhouse where he lived at the ranch. Amusingly, he told of breaking the tuning knob on his radio so that some family members could not switch from jazz music— which he liked—to rock and roll music—which they favored.

De Carlo, when asked by Patricia Krenwinkel's attorney about how persons became members of the family, replied, "I'm not sure," and then added, "there were no membership cards given out, so I don't really know who was member or not."

An unexpected rustle among the spectators and whispered comments drew my attention to the entrance door.

209

Two deputy sheriffs escorted a tall, lanky and pale-looking man—a handsome man—wearing a dark blue blazer and gabardine gray slacks, and sporting handcuffs. The sheriffs walked the prisoner to the front of the rail, where he stood staring vacantly at the ceiling.

His cheekbones were prominently defined and his eyes looked like the the eyes of an insane person—strong, steady, and wide open. The sharply dressed inmate, with well-barbered brown hair, appeared to have lost a considerable amount of weight. The expensive-looking clothes he wore didn't fit him.

"Would you state your name, please," said the court clerk, "and spell it for the court records."

The prisoner remained silent. The court clerk, having asked twice the same question, turned helplessly to Judge Older who, in turn, addressed the man, "Your name, Sir?"

No answer. The judge did not press the man to give his name even though he finally showed a sign of life as he merely smiled when the three female defendants waved at him.

The judge directed the defense counsel to proceed.

"Do you recognize this man as 'Tex Watson'?" asked Mr. Fitzgerald to the witness on the stand.

"Yeah," De Carlo simply replied.

Before being removed from the courtroom, Watson stared briefly at Manson and he seemed oblivious of his presence.

Under Mr. Shin's cross-examination, Danny De Carlo testified that no one had approached him in regards to a $ 25,000 reward.

"Did the police approach you?" asked Susan Atkins's lawyer.

"Yes," answered the witness.

"What police officer?"

"The one sitting behind you."

Mr. Shin moved away and pointed at a man seated behind him, "Mr. Gutierrez?"

"Yeah."

"What did you say when they told you about a $ 25,000 reward?" asked the Korean descent attorney.

"I told them to shove it," replied the diminutive witness.

Mr. Kanarek inquired about De Carlo's passion for guns.

Manson's counsel interrogating:

"Mr. De Carlo, you said you love guns. Would you tell us what kind of love is that?"

"Well..." said De Carlo, as he dusted off his boot, "I love guns more than I love my old lady."

A strong laughter from the spectators.

Mr. Kanarek joined in the amusement and pursued with the same topic. "By your 'old lady,' Mr. De Carlo, do I take it you mean your wife?"

"Yeah," answered the witness.

"Is it a fair statement to say that you love guns more than you love people?"

De Carlo for a moment changed his facial expression, and replied, "I didn't say that. I said that I loved them better than I loved my old lady." Again, everybody laughed.

Mr. Kanarek, unable to get an adequate and satisfactory response from De Carlo, changed his line of questions to that of his drinking habits.

"Now, you told us you were smashed the night before you were arrested. Is that right, Mr. De Carlo?"

"Well, I was feeling pretty good... drinking... laughing... having a good time... grabbing asses."

A tremendous roar of laughter flooded the court room.

"What do you mean by 'grabbing asses,'?" insisted Mr. Kanarek.

"Well, having a good time... GRABBING ASSES!"

Mr. Kanarek, still unable to receive an answer of his liking, opted to change his interrogation again, and brought a transcript to the witness. Mr. Kanarek made De Carlo read certain questions and answers which he had made under the prosecution's direct examination.

Following the admittance by the witness, Mr. Kanarek accused Mr. Bugliosi of coaching the answers to Danny De Carlo.

The senior prosecutor leaped out of his chair and exclaimed, "That was a ridiculous and inflammatory remark, Your Honor."

Then, adjusting his vent, added solemnly, "What does that have to do with the price of tea in China?"

Mr. Kanarek, stumbling for appropriate words, asked the judge to swear him in so he could testify himself about some remarks the prosecutor had made at him at the counsel table.

Mr. Kanarek's request arose the ire of Mr. Bugliosi and incited him to say, "Your conduct is grounds for disbarment."

The atmosphere between counsels which was already appallingly hostile, prompted Judge Older to interfere:

"Alright, Gentlemen," interjected His Honor, "that'll be enough."

Mr. Ronald Hughes, holding a pencil in his hand, rose and asked for a mistrial because of the conduct of both attorneys in front of the jury.

Judge Older, having reached the end of his patience, pointed with his finger at Leslie Van Houten's lawyer, and with a severe tone of voice, told him, "We don't need to hear from you. Sit down, Sir."

Mr. Hughes obliged as the judge instructed the jury to disregard from their minds the entire incident and exchange of words between counsel.

The trial continued.

According to Danny De Carlo, under Mr. Kanarek's cross-examination, Manosn prohibited him to drink but he didn't obey him.

"Did you get wine at the ranch?" asked Mr. Kanarek.

"Yeah, but one of the girls dumped it on me, behind the ranch. I was mad."

"Since you've been in Los Angeles, have you had anything to drink?" asked the stocky-looking lawyer.

"Irrevelant," objected Mr. Bugliosi.

"Sustained," stated Judge Older.

Mr. Kanarek, in a series of questions, asked the witness if Linda Kasabian had taken, in his presence, white pills while he was at the Spahn Ranch.

De Carlo replied twice, that he didn't know.

Then the attorney switched his questions in regard to the sexual activities of the ex-member of the family. Mr. Kanarek failed to make De Carlo say that he was somewhat jealous of the attention some of the girls gave to Manson. Pursuing the matter, Mr. Kanarek asked, "Did any one of the girls ever put you down?"

"Never," replied the witness, twisting his moustache violently.

"I had the time of my life. I got along fantastically with them," and he confidently, pointed at the three girl defendants, and said, "Ask them."

Under Mr. Kanarek's questioning, the short-moustached motorcyclist named those girls with whom he had sex at the ranch. At one point, De Carlo emphasized, "Of all the girls at the ranch, 'Ouisch', also known as Ruth Morehouse (family name Ouisch), was by far the best lay."

When Mr. Kanarek asked if he had sexual relations with Gypsy, Danny De Carlo replied, "Yes," and then with a grin on his face, added, "Although Gypsy got mad at me when I made love to her with my boots on."

Judge Older joined the roar of laughter in the crowded courtroom.

"Is it a fair statement to say that you really don't remember anything... except on matters of sex?" asked Mr. Kanarek and bent his back forward to hear the reply.

Danny De Carlo, brushing his moustache with his fingers, allowed himself enough time to breathe heavily and then answered the way he preferred most,

212

"Yeee... ah."

The answer drew loud laughter, especially from the jurors whose proximity to the witness stand made them aware of the sound of pleasure De Carlo made as he responded to the question.

Finally, Mr. Kanarek wanted to know where the witness was staying while in Los Angeles.

The defense counsel also questioned De Carlo about having a police officer with him at all times, near to him, allowing him not to drink.

"In fact," said Mr. Kanarek, "the police officer sleeps in the same room you do. Is that right?"

"Yeah!" shouted Mr. Bugliosi, somewhat imitating the witness, "Under the same sheet."

More laughter.

Sergeant William Lee was recalled to the witness stand to testify that 15 of 45 empty cartridges he found in a gully at the Spahn Ranch matched up with the firing marks made by the .22-caliber gun used to shoot three of the five victims at the Tate home.

Mrs. Eleanor Lalay, manager of the Beach House Apartments, testified briefly that from July 22, 1969, through March 1970, she had a tenant in Apartment Number 501 by the name of Salorilim Nader. She said that he was an actor and had left Europe sometime in March.

Mrs. Ruby Pearl, stable manager of the George Spahn Ranch, declared she had worked for twenty years in that capacity. She said that George Spahn was eighty-three years old and lives at the ranch and that owner had lost his sight a few years back. She described the activities of the ranch. One—which is to rent the ranch to motion picture companies—and another—to rent houses. The red-haired witness testified that she first met Charles Manson in the summer of 1968, when he came to the ranch on a long school bus with some boys and girls. They remained.

They were given free living quarters in exchange for services. The girls were to do office work, cook, etc., and the men had the trucks to maintain. She described Tex Watson as a good mechanic, who worked on trucks and dune buggies. She heard Manson tell some of the people to do something with the school bus.

"A few months later, they transformed the bus real pretty," said the hoarse-voiced witness.

"They removed the seats, put plywood on the floor, a sink at the front, a hot water heater on the top. Manson told Paul Watkins and Tex to do those things and they got busy and did it. The girls had to do the painting."

213

She stated that the group called themselves "the family."

Later, the group was told to fix the saloon into a concert hall. They did it from top to bottom. "Just beautiful," said Mrs. Pearl.

Then she explained that the family at first lived one-half mile from the ranch but they thought the distance was too far for walking and decided to move in the western-style saloon near the entrance.

Mr. Bugliosi then got down to link Manson to several key items of evidence through the testimony of Mrs. Pearl.

Wearing a scarf of flower-colored pattern, the witness testified she saw a gun at the ranch similar to the .22-caliber western-style the prosecutor showed her. She also identified the stained rope and said that Manson brought a rope to the ranch that looked just like the one the deputy district attorney showed her. Mr. Bugliosi also attempted to link evidence with the murders, as when he took to the witness stand, the plastic bags containing the dusty, stained dark clothes. Mrs. Pearl examined them and said she had seen them on a boiling pot, where they were being dyed by "Squeaky" (Lynn Fromne).

Finally, Mr. Bugliosi brought the leather thongs with which Leno La Bianca's hands were tied and asked the witness if she had seen them.

"Manson wore them all the time around his neck," said the witness, avoiding to look at the defendant.

Under cross-examination by the defense, the witness explained that she recalled having seen the gun in 1968 in Randy Starr's trailer, and when asked why she remembered it, she replied, "Because the gun had a long barrel... very unusual. I have never seen any gun of that type."

In regards to the rope, she said, "Charlie brought a rope exactly like that to the ranch around July 1969 and showed it to George (Spahn) who wanted to buy it."

In respect to black T-shirts, she stated, "They all wore them and Randy Starr (deceased) and I found this one." (Referring to P-258, a black T-shirt).

David Brian Hannum, a cowboy at the ranch, testified about having been arrested on August 13, 1969. He said Linda Kasabian borrowed his 1961 Volvo from him on August 12, 1969.

The witness stated that Linda didn't return it and instead, she wrote him a note indicating his car was in New Mexico. The young cowhand related that he received the note two weeks later from Susan Atkins. She gave him a piece of torn letter—with no envelope. The condition of the letter was allegedly torn. He recovered his car personally at a Shell gas station a month and a half later.

When asked by Mr. Bugliosi, "Did Manson ever ask you to join the family?"

The four defense counsel leaped from their seats and unanimously objected the question.

Mr. Fitzgerald protested by saying that, "it was beyond the scope of these proceedings."

Mr. Kanarek and Mr. Shin joined him.

"Establish your foundation Mr. Bugliosi," said Judge Older, rubbing his right ear—a habit His Honor displayed whenever he had to speak. Mr. Bugliosi stated that in order to establish his foundation, he would have to approach the bench. His request was granted and after resuming his direct examination, he asked, "You didn't join the family of Mr. Manson, did you?"

"No, I didn't."

The typically attired cowboy witness told then of Manson's criticizing him for killing a rattlesnake.

"What did he say?" asked Mr. Bugliosi.

"Charlie asked me how I would feel if he chopped off my neck like I had to the snake," testified the blond-freckled witness, and then, rather apprehensively, looking at Manson for a few seconds, he continued saying, "He said it was better to kill people than animals."

Ralph Marshall, police officer for the City of San Fernando, testified that on August 16, 1969, around five P.M., he booked Sandra Good and Mary Brunner—two family members.

Samuel Olmstead, a sheriff deputy stationed at Malibu, testified that he went to the Spahn Ranch on July 28, 1969.

The witness said he stopped at Santa Susana and Topanga Canyon intersection about a mile from the ranch, and that he saw the defendant Charles Manson sitting on his dune buggy.

Manson told him that he was watching for Black Panthers whom were going to attack his family. He gave his name as Charles Summers. Charlie asked the witness and his companion if he could lead them to the ranch, otherwise, they might have been liable to have some shooting. When they arrived, the witness said he saw Manson run inside a building and that he came out immediately after, followed by nearly eleven other people.

The witness then related a conversation he had with Manson in regard to the Black Panthers.

"The defendant," the witness said "wanted to join forces with the police to wipe the negro community out."

The brusque-looking cop then gave a near precise account of Manson's comment to him.

"You cops should get smart and join up with us. Those guys (Black Panthers) are out to kill both you and us. I know you hate them as much as we do.... we should keep them from stopping us by stopping them first."

George Grap, a real estate salesman, formerly a deputy sheriff, testified that he also had seen Charles Manson hiding in the bushes at the same intersection and that he told the officers he was a "lookout against Black Panthers."

The ex-sheriff said that he had an independent conversation in which the defendant declared, "We got into a hassle with the motherfuckers and we put one of them in the hospital."

The talkative witness said that Manson mentioned that one of the Black Panthers had offended one of the girls of the family.

Barbara Hoyt, an ex-member of the family, testified that she lived at the Spahn Ranch from April through September of 1969. The witness, wearing a tangerine-colored minidress, described the habits and doings of the family. She said they had their meals at the back house and that Manson ordinarily talked during dinner time about "Helter Skelters."

Questioned by Mr. Bugliosi about Manson's "Helter Skelter" discussions with the family, Miss Hoyt answered, "Charlie said 'Helter Skelter' was coming down fast... he said the blacks would rise up against whites and everyone would die but us, 'the family'."

The brown long-haired witness added that she heard Manson say, "I'd like to show the blacks how to do it."

The witness stated then that she learned about the Tate murders on the day following the slayings. In a barely audible voice, she testified that she heard over television about the Tate killings at Johnny's (John Swartz) trailer.

"Sadie (Susan Atkins) came into the trailer where I was watching TV at the ranch and asked me to turn the channel to news. She then called Tex and Katie."

The tall teenager (eighteen years old), who wore black-rimmed and thick-lensed eyeglasses, continued saying, "After watching the news they left and I remained in the trailer. Before that, they usually didn't watch the news."

The witness then related that shortly after, Manson had ordered those under eighteen years of age to go to the "Wike Shop," a place they designated for children. The witness said she talked with Susan Atkins through a field telephone.

Susan wanted her to bring three sets of dark clothes, and to bring them in front of the ranch—the kitchen area. Miss Hoyt observed that when she arrived to the area, Manson told her that they had already left. Jim Flynn was present and she returned to the back house.

The prosecutor then asked the witness some questions that implicated Leslie

Van Houten.

Barbara Hoyt in her own words explained that a day or so early in the afternoon, after the television incident in the trailer, she was with Snake (Diane Lake), Leslie Van Houten, and the babies.

Four men came to the ranch. The witness explained that Leslie told her one of the men had given her a ride from Griffith Park and she didn't want to be seen, so she covered herself with a white sheet. Leslie didn't come out of the sheets until the man left after waiting about fifteen minutes in the 'back house.'

"Eventually," the witness continued saying, "I left for the desert area in Indio with Tex and the rest of the family. Charlie joined us a week after being released from jail."

Then she went on to say that they stayed at Lotus Mine, Parker Ranch, and Myers Ranch.

"Charlie told us to move from one place to another—the most a couple of days," the tall dark-haired witness testified.

Miss Hoyt then brought testimony that showed Manson's leadership. The witness observed that when they were at the Myers Ranch, Manson told Tex Watson to go down to the bottom of a wash and fix the dune buggy.

"Tex," said the teenage witness, "left a couple of minutes later to go fix it."

Another time, she said she saw Manson slap Lucy (a family member) twice on the face and that Tex didn't say anything. She never heard Tex say anything to Charles Manson.

Miss Hoyt said they slept on the ground. One night, Manson, unable to sleep, told them angrily to get up—that they should not go to sleep until all of them slept together.

In a rather embarrassing situation, Mr. Bugliosi asked the attractive witness to tell about the time Manson forced her to perform a sex act on Juan Flynn, a male member of the family.

Mr. Bugliosi inquiring, "What did Mr. Manson ask you to do with Juan Flynn?"

Miss Hoyt appeared almost petrified when she heard the question. She looked down at her minidress and pulled down her skirt so as not to reveal her upper thighs. She squinted her eyes and moistened her lips and wanted to say something but she didn't.

"Barbara, would you rather not answer?" Mr. Bugliosi asked patiently.

A flash of steam accompanied Mr. Kanarek's objection.

The witness, jurors and the rest of the audience tittered and took the opportunity to take a good breath to relieve the embarrassment. The three girl

217

defendants, giggling, seemed to enjoy the scene.

"Reframe your question," Judge Older said.

Mr. Bugliosi, for lack of proper words, repeated the question the same as before, but with more understanding which prompted the witness to make an effort to answer after a slight pause, "You mean... that oral... what do you call it?"

"Oral copulation."

"Yes," responded the witness, staring out over the courtroom.

"Did you want to do it?"

"No," answered Barbara, somewhat relieved of the pressure she had undergone.

Under questioning by Mr. Bugliosi, the former member of the Charles Manson family then testified about overhearing a conversation between Susan Atkins and a teenage member of the family, Ruth Morehouse (Ouisch).

Before the testimony was given, Judge Older instructed the jurors to consider the conversation as evidence only against Miss Atkins and not against the three other defendants.

The witness, rather shakily, described the incident.

"Sadie and Ouisch were talking in the kitchen about the Tate murders and I was in the bedroom of the ranch house."

"What did you hear?" asked Mr. Bugliosi.

"Sadie said that Sharon Tate came out and said, 'What's going on here?' Then Sadie said she told her to 'Shut up, woman,' then she said that Sharon Tate was the last to die because she (Sadie) wanted to see the others die first."

Before the morning court session began, we were informed by Deputy Taylor that one of the defense counsel, Mr. Ronald Hughes, had called the judge to inform him he would be late a few minutes on account of a minor auto accident he was involved in. The trial was delayed briefly.

Using a diagram of the Myers ranch house, defense attorney Paul Fitzgerald made Barbara Hoyt show that she was in a bedroom at one end of the house when she supposedly overheard Susan Atkins talking to Ruth Morehouse in the kitchen at the other end of the structure.

The witness estimated that she was about fifteen to eighteen feet from where Sadie was at the time. Mr. Fitzgerald claimed that the distance was actually more than thirty feet.

Under Mr. Shin's cross-examination, the witness was questioned about her ability to overhear the conversation.

At one point, Susan Atkins' lawyer tried to discredit Miss Hoyt's version of the conversation by saying, "Your memory of that particular day was foggy, is that right?"

"That's not so," Barbara replied.

Under cross-examination by Manson's attorney, the witness readily admitted that she was nearsighted and couldn't see very well without her thick-lensed glasses.

Mr. Kanarek had the witness remove her glasses and while examining them, he walked behind Mr. Bugliosi, a distance of about fifteen feet. Standing behind the counsel table, Mr. Kanarek asked the witness how many fingers he was raising. She could not do so.

The defense counsel, walking with a raised hand, approached the witness within two feet and even continued getting closer.

Suddenly, rather defensively, Miss Hoyt brushed the attorney's hand aside before she could tell him the number of fingers he was extending.

The defense counsel kept asking the witness questions regarding the condition of her eyes until Judge Older stopped him and told him, "Your questions are not fair, Mr. Kanarek."

As Barbara Hoyt sat on the witness stand without her glasses, I noticed that she appeared to be a good-looking girl, although her manners were a little childish.

Subsequently, the lawyer represting Charles Manson conducted an experiment that seemed to prove Barbara Hoyt's distance estimate was in error, but at the same time, he inadquately showed that the witness could hear well at a long distance.

Mr. Kanarek, wearing a kelly green suit with trousers extending two inches below the ankles, asked permission of the judge to go beyond the dividing rail.

"Step outside," remarked Mr. Fitzgerald and everybody laughed.

The counsel walked into the audience section of the court room to get Miss Hoyt to estimate how far she was from Miss Atkins at the time of the conversation. Mr. Kanarek, standing in the middle of the aisle, began to lower his voice. The witness stopped him at a distance of approximately forty feet. When the stocky attorney noted that it was much farther than that she had stated before—a distance of fifteen to eighteen feet—Barbara said, "Well, I can hear you perfectly well and Sadie was talking much louder than you are."

Due to the lengthy cross-examination of Mr. Kanarek, Mr. Fitzgerald, as well as Mr. Shin, joined the prosecutor, Mr. Bugliosi, to interpose objections.

Mr. Fitzgerald objected at one point that the questions of his fellow defense

219

counsel were immaterial, irrevelant and a waste of undue time to which Mr. Kanarek retorted that the statements of the witness just couldn't be accepted without finding out the state of mind in which she was at the time.

Judge Older interceded and replied, "I didn't ask you for an argument," and then overruled the objection by Mr. Fitzgerald.

Mr. Kanarek's final question to the teenager was, "Is it a fair statement, Miss Hoyt, to say you have been in a mental institution during the past two years?"

"Within the last two weeks," replied the witness without hesitation.

Under redirect examination by Mr. Bugliosi, the tall teenage girl was allowed to clarify that she had been treated for a drug overdose at Queen's Hospital in Honolulu. She explained that it was a regular hospital—not a mental hospital—but that she had been in the psychiatric ward.

Many guests joined the jurors on the Sunday outing to the Pomona County Fair. The excursion was a complete fiasco due to the limited time we were allowed on the grounds. It would have required an entire day for one to be able to see the hundreds of exhibits and demonstrations.

The jurors mingling among thousands of visitors and walking about the displays at different paces and directions made it difficult and wearisome for the bailiffs. It was practically impossible for the deputies to escort the jurors and keep them in a group.

Also, the various opinions suggested by jurors and guests as well, made the whole affair confusing. A great deal of time was spent trying to decide where to go. Some wanted to see the cattle and horses. Others wanted to see plants and flowers. Still, others wanted to ride a monorail, which was not included in the tour.

Luckily, everybody wanted to take a close look at a display of a moon rock brought back by Astronaut Armstrong in Apollo 11.

Betty Clark would automatically sign "yes" on the outing list as soon as she would find out that the members of the clique were remaining at the hotel.

"Are you going?" I would often ask her.

"I wouldn't miss the chance for the world," she replied.

"Why?"

"Because that's the only way to have peace and quiet," Betty observed.

Violet was the only one of the clique who would go; however, on the Sunday trips, she never spoke nor carried on as openly as when she was with the clique. Her husband was very serious and hardly spoke to any of the jurors. Violet followed suit and her personality was entirely different in the presence of her husband.

The outing on Sundays was a relief and it is fair to say that both the "clique" and the rest of the jurors were glad to be away from each other for a few hours.

Donald Dunlap, deputy sheriff, testified in direct examination that he participated in the raid of August 16, 1969, at the Spahn Ranch. The witness said the first time he saw Charles Manson at the ranch was underneath a building—hiding.

Under Mr. Fitzgerald's questioning, the officer explained how he got hold of the prisoner.

"How did you do it?" asked the defense counsel.

"I recovered him," replied the deputy.

"Didn't you pull him from the hair?"

"Yes."

"Is that what you call—recover?"

"Yes," answered the short, tough officer, causing a few laughs.

Mr. Kanarek wanted to know through the witness how many officers participated in the raid and how many helicopters. The sheriff replied that there were about forty officers involved and one helicopter. The defense counsel then introduced as evidence, some thirty snapshots taken at random during the raid.

The blonde-complected witness, after finishing his testimony, stepped down and walked arrogantly like he had springs on the heels of his shoes.

Juan Flynn, originally from Panama, testified that he had lived two and a half years at the Spahn Ranch, and that he had been six years in this country since he left his native land.

Flynn, a tall blonde with curly hair, also identified the various items used in the slayings at the Tate home.

The witness, pointing at the rope placed on the prosecutor's table, said he recognized it because he liked it when he first saw it, about two months before the raid by the Sheriff's Department. He described it as being made of three strands of nylon and that it was made different from what cowboys ordinarily use. At the time he stated he wanted a piece of it as well as George Spahn.

Mr. Bugliosi then brought the gun asked Juan Flynn if he had seen the revolver.

"Yes, I saw him (Manson) with it several times. On one occasion, he fired it in my direction when I was walking with a girl on the other side of the creek at the ranch..."

The rugged, tall-looking Juan Flynn stood up in the witness stand to demonstrate what Manson had done. The witness appeared like a giant while waving his arms and projecting in a loud, strong voice, he added, "Manson followed us and fired a couple of shots... to scare us or something. I don't know what he had in mind."

Judge Older allowed the testimony into the record for the purpose of identifying the defendant with the gun, but His Honor admonished us jurors to disregard the comments about the shooting incident.

Under questioning by Mr. Bugliosi, the colorful, curly-haired witness related that in June 1969, he participated in a conversation in which Charles Manson, Bruce Davis, and Clen Tufts (Steve Crogan) were present. The discussion took place at dusk on the boardwalk in front of the Spahn Ranch.

The witness observed he heard Charles Manson saying, "I want to show the whites how to kill the motherfucking Negroes and the pigs... anything that supports the establishment.

According to the witness, Manson began to use the term "Helter Skelter" when the Beatles' two-white record album came out.

While the counsel approached the judge's bench, the witness, very relaxed, leaned on Judge Older's table on one elbow, then quickly would change position and played his fingers on the bench as if he had a drum on his lap.

The witness continued saying that Manson told the family that, "this was the beginning of the Karma."

Juan Flynn, wearing striped pants and sandals, slouched on the witness stand, moved his legs constantly, and pounded on the bench as he explained what "Karma" was.

"You know... when the black people were going to take over."

Testifying in a marked accent, the Panamanian-born witness said that about a week before the raid, he saw some people in the late evening hours —around eight P.M. He stated he was inside John Swartz's trailer when he heard Susan Atkins say, "We're going to get those motherfucking pigs." Then he said he looked out and saw, from the window, seven people driving off in a 1959 Ford.

Under questioning by the prosecutor, Juan Flynn named the passengers: "Sadie (Susan Atkins), Patty(Patricia Krenwinkel), Leslie, the one with the pretty face..."—Leslie Van Houten smiled broadly at the witness—"Tex Watson, Linda Kasabian, Clem Tufts and Charlie in the driver's seat."

Court adjourned.

The next day when Juan Flynn walked in, I noticed he had his hair totally curled up—evidently he had washed it and it appeared as if he had a curly wig on. Somehow his hair looked like Michelangelo's David. Some of the female jurors commented on the fact that men and not women are born with

222

curly hair.

"Why, it isn't fair," Betty Clark said.

My laughter was cut short when Betty looked at me with wide open eyes and observed, "You, too, have curly hair."

"*She* has curly hair," I said, referring to Mildred.

"Yeah, but mine is a wig," admitted the redhaired lady.

"Anyway, you have beautiful hair," I said, trying to discard the subject, "Why wear a wig?"

"You know women, we like to change," retorted Mildred.

"I guess so," I replied, unable to make my point.

"Shhh... shhh..." whispered Ruth, as the judge walked into the courtroom.

Mr. Bugliosi continued his direct examination and brought some pictures to the witness for identification.

Juan Flynn, a Vietnam veteran, testified that a couple of days after the Tate-La Bianca murders, he had a conversation with Charles Manson in the kitchen. The witness explained that he wanted something to eat. He walked in and threw down some haystack he had with him and sat down.

Susan Atkins, Snake (Diane Lake) and other girls were in the kitchen with Charles Manson. The witness said that he noticed Charlie brush his shoulder horizontally and soon afterwards, the girls left the room.

"Then Charlie," said Juan Flynn, "grabbed me by the hair and pulled a knife at my throat and said, 'You son-of-a-bitch, don't you know I am the one behind all these killings?' At first, I thought he was only boasting, but then Charlie gave me the knife and said, 'Go ahead, kill me if you want to,' but I refused to take the knife," the witness said, "and I brushed him aside and told him, 'I don't want to kill you.'"

The curly-haired witness added that Manson, rather pleased, answered, "If you feel like that, why don't you go to the waterfall and make love to my girls?"

Juan Flynn, somewhat excited, in a boisterous manner, stated that he responded to Manson:

"If I go there, ninety-nine percent of the chances are, that I will catch syphillis and gonorrhea, and you will be the first I'll come to see."

A little bit relaxed, the witness volunteered, "The girls were beautiful but......"

"That will be enough, Mr. Flynn," said the judge and asked counsel to approach the bench.

I noticed at that moment Charles Manson and the three female defendants

223

were staring intrinsically at the witness. There seemed to be a type of quietness, not the usual still, calm silence—but different. The spectators were busily observing the witness, who, after having removed his leather sandals, began doing "bending exercises." Judge Older and counsel turned around to see, and amused, joined the laughter in the crowded courtroom.

The muscular witness appeared restless at times. He smiled occasionally at the female defendants. Between questions, he occupied himself by getting hold of the microphone and swinging it to and from. At intervals, he would search inside his pants' pockets, pull out a book of matches and play with them for a while until he would snap out a single match and insert it between his teeth.

Under Mr. Bugliosi's interrogation, Juan Flynn gave examples as when Charles Manson had made members of the family participate in sexual activities.

The witness, an ex-heavyweight boxer, stated that the leader of the family had forced Barbara Hoyt, in the presence of others, to perform what the witness referred to, for lack of better words, as, "Mr. Manson made the girls suck my dick all day long—you know, or eat each other's in the hills."

Equally brutal and naked, Mr. Flynn displayed, openly, one mannerism of his, which we jurors tried to overlook but that somehow became distracting, that of the witness' "constant gestures of scratching his loins," without regard nor respect to those present.

Mr. Bugliosi continued leading the witness through his testimony.

Flynn declared he had told the authorities out in Shoshone (a desert town in Inyo County) about Manson's boast in the kitchen at the Spahn Ranch. Juan further stated that the officer who had interviewed him had taped the conversation.

The Panama-born witness also told to the prosecutor about a nighttime incident in the desert where Charles Manson tried to sneak up on him with a knife.

The witness observed, "One night I couldn't sleep. I heard something and got up and saw Mr. Manson tiptoeing around... when I went outside—naked—it was pretty hot you know—he started shaking and said 'hello' meekly. Then he called one of his coolies, Clem Tufts (Steve Crogan), and we talked."

The witness added that he was armed at the time.

Mr. Kanarek objected as hearsay, irrelevant, and no foundation. He was overruled.

Still, the attorney objected and wanted to approach the bench and state further objections on behalf of his client.

Charles Manson tugged his lawyer's coat and sarcastically said, "You're overruled, sit down."

Under cross-examination, Mr. Fitzgerald asked the witness if he worked for Charles Manson while at the Spahn Ranch.

"I didn't work for Mr. Manson," replied the tall, husky witness.

"You didn't like him, did you?" asked Mr. Fitzgerald.

"I want to say that I didn't like him nor dislike him—I just kept my own values," answered the witness.

Juan Flynn testified he didn't believe everything Charles Manson said but that he went along. The unshaved witness stated he had slept next to the defendant but took his precautions and that when he became afraid, he left.

He denied that he got paid $ 4500 dollars for a published book about his life story while at the ranch. He said the money was taken by Paul Watkins and Brooks Poston, two ex-family members.

Up until this time, the defendants had kept calm and quiet, except for occasional remarks which caused brief exchanges with the judge.

However, Charles Manson began to speak out more and more and even tried to sing a song. The judge, holding his temper and disturbed by the lyrics, "The old gray mare ain't what she used to be......She is a judge now..." ordered the defendant to stop. Deputies Taylor and Tull moved and placed themselves behind the prisoner.

"Stop from what?" replied the hippie cult leader. Manson, smiling, looked at the jury, then addressing the court, added, "Why don't you stop doing what you are doing? You are a woman!"

"Alright," said Judge Older, "remove Mr. Manson."

Deputy Taylor escorted the inmate who, without offering any resistance, was locked up in a cellroom situated at the right side of the judge's bench. A small, mesh wire window on the door allowed Charles Manson to hear the proceedings of the trial.

Manson was allowed to return a short while later. Just as he was to sit down, he addressed the spectators' section and said, "I'd like everyone to know I am not represented in this trial. I do not have an attorney. I am not allowed to speak for myself."

Again, Judge Older ordered him escorted out of the courtroom by the bailiffs.

The three young women co-defendants were shortly banned from the courtroom after they stood up and shouted to the judge:

"The judge is a woman!... the judge is a woman!"

They also refused to quiet down and Judge Older calmly told them: "The record will reflect that the defendants may return at any time they wish to comply with the court rules."

Deputy Taylor, aided by Deputy Tull, wired a small loudspeaker in a jury room where the three female defendants were to follow the proceedings until they promised not to disrupt the trial.

As the defendants were led out the door, Leslie Van Houten told the judge, "The judge is a joke."

Susan Atkins chided the judge by saying:

"Your wife's in the front row, telling you what to do."

Immediately, some jurors tried to locate Mrs. Older, but no one was sure since no one had seen her.

Deputy Taylor later verified that indeed the judge's wife had been in the courtroom, but not in the front row.

Under Mr. Shin's questioning, Juan Flynn admitted that when he came back from Indio County, an officer approached him and asked him if he was willing to testify, but that he didn't, because he was afraid for his life.

When Charles Manson's attorney assumed his turn to cross-examine the witness, needless to say, he spent a great deal of time.

The stocky lawyer defiantly and deliberately exhausted the patience of the prosecutor, fellow defense counsel, Judge Older, defendants, and the witness. God only knows how the audience felt. Last, but not least, the patience and perserverance of us jurors were beginning to wear out.

It had been twelve weeks since we've been sequestered and have been away from our homes and friends. We jurors all wanted the trial to end as quickly as possible. Mr. Kanarek didn't help!

The excitement caused by the implication of Mr. Kanarek's questions produced a theatrical courtroom event, worthy of being filmed.

One such implication occurred when the Akim Tamiroff-like attorney told the witness, Juan Flynn, "You only answer those questions that the prosecutor has told you to answer."

Upon hearing the slanderous remark, the counsel for the prosecution leaped from his table and angrily told Mr. Kanarek to shut up! Unable to control himself, Mr. Bugliosi, still shouting, declared, "Mr. Kanarek has, continuously, from the beginning of this trial, been accusing me!"

His Honor, pointing at the prosecutor, warned him he would not tolerate anymore colloquy between counsel and asked them to approach the bench.

Mr. Bugliosi stood up immediately and eagerly responded:

"I'd be glad to, Your Honor."

On his way to the bench, he made known—loud and clear, "I'm not going to take it anymore," then simultaneously, he raised his chin as he brushed his neck briskly with a hand and added, "I'm fed up to here."

While waiting for the trial to be resumed, two lady jurors were excited trying to locate Sal Mineo among the spectators. Mildred was somewhat annoyed because she couldn't see him. Olivia asked me to point the ex-child actor out to her.

"What is he wearing?" Olivia wanted to know.

"He's seated on the last row," I said. "You can't miss him... he's wearing dark glasses, sport shirt and..."

"Yes, I see him!" observed Olivia. "He's wearing something around his neck... oh no... it can't be!"

"What is it?" asked Mildred, still unable to see the actor.

"It's a leather thong—that's what it is," Olivia whispered to Mildred.

The coincidence of having heard and seen evidence about "leather thongs" made Sal Mineo's attire appear less than what the lady jurors expected. They were disappointed. The dark-complected actor visited the courtroom a couple more times at a later date.

The next morning, we had to wait about an hour before the trial resumed. The defendants, who had been absent, were seated in their respective chairs as we jurors walked in the courtroom. We all waited.

"Hail, Caesar!" chanted the three female defendants in unison as soon as the judge entered for the formal opening of the day's proceedings. The three female defendants stood with their right arms extended in a Hitler-type salute.

Manson, who had been leafing through a trial transcript, immediately followed suit. He stood up as if the chanting had been his cue and joined in by saying, "Your Honor, may I suggest that the court continue to try itself, as it has been doing a very poor job of showing the public any justice. You've only shown your force and power."

"Mr. Manson," said Judge Older camly, "I order you to sit down, Sir."

Challengingly, Manson started to sing, "That old black magic has me in its spell..."

"Remain quiet during the proceedings so that we can continue the trial," the judge countered.

Manson ignored the court and continued singing, "That old black magic that you keep so well."

"You are now disrupting this trial."

"Those icy fingers... the same old witchcraft..." Manson tried to hit a high note but his voice was drowned by the stern command of Judge Older.

"I order you once again to sit down Sir, and stop this!"

"I'd like to go back to my room and relax," humbly replied Charles Manson and faked a yawn. "You can handle your own matters."

"Sit down, Sir," Judge Older ordered.

The prisoner obeyed.

Still, audibly, he continued speaking, almost to himself.

"All my life, I find it hard not to do what I'm told, because all my life I've done what I have been told."

"Let's proceed," said His Honor, but Manson obviously hadn't finished yet.

"Now, Your Honor, if you would allow me to maintain a voice, I could bring to you the thought that I have done what I'm told."

"I order you to stop, Sir," said Judge Older firmly.

"You have been ordering me forever," Manson said and raising his voice, added, "All my life you have ordered me. You have ordered me to cease to live. You bring me in here and you charge me with murder and you say I have rights and you hold up rights in front of me but you give me none."

"For the last time, I order you to stop or you'll be removed from this courtroom," Judge Older warned him. "Let's proceed."

Manson looked at the jury, then the judge and finally to those in the audience and solemnly exclaimed, "You are going ahead. But are you going ahead to look at yourselves. Look at all of you. Where are you going? You're going to destruction, that's where you're going. You will end up being judged. That's what you are going to do. All of you—everyone of you! It's your judgment day, not mine. I've already judged me."

Judge Older, unable to control Manson, ordered him removed from the court with admonishment that he could return provided he consented to be quiet.

"Have a good day," Manson said as Deputy Taylor led him to the cell room facing the audience.

Judge Older also warned the three female defendants but didn't display much patience for them. No one could blame him.

They chanted, "Who are you judging? Follow your own reflection, the guilt you find is yours."

Then separately, one said, "Who are you on judgment day?"

Another, "Look at yourselves men, you're a machine."

The defendants were removed and they also mimicked their leader and said, "Have a nice day," to the judge on their way to jury room of Department 104.

Mr. Kanarek continued cross-examining Juan Flynn.

He asked the witness if having been in Vietnam and having killed people had affected his mind. Juan reflexed for a while and replied that since he came back he had to cope with a "new world."

"What do you mean by 'cope with a new world?' " asked the defense counsel.

Juan Flynn didn't reply. For the first time, the witness sat still. He looked intensely at the floor. Wrinkles formed above his brows as he concentrated. His lips recessed backwards. Slowly, he raised his head and stared above those seated in the courtroom. He didn't move nor blink. His face appeared serious—hard. The muscles of his jaw released their rigidness, allowing his vocal chords to form words for his answer....

"Yes... it affected me. In Vietnam, everybody wears green fatigues... there's nothing but green jungles... green makeup... in general, it is a green hell of a world! When I came on a plane back to the States—I noticed the lights... city lights. ...People dressed in different colors... also the blonde hairs. In Vietnam, I saw nothing but green, black and green clothes... a green HELL OF A WORLD!"

Silence filled the courtroom.

Mr. Kanarek, standing near the dividing rail, didn't interrupt the witness. Only the sound of the electric fans blowing air was heard. The hot temperature in the room added impact to the dramatic testimony of the witness. Juan Flynn's face was moist and tears were in his eyes. The big, husky witness appeared small and sad.

His views of Vietnam sounded almost like an actor reciting a powerful soliloquy—his timing was perfect, his hands remained still, his body motionless, and even his speech carried no foreign accent.

Gradually lowering his face, the witness fixed his eyes on the floor and continued, "You know, all here is different, people are different, they dress differently and act differently...."

Juan raised his eyes and turned around to see some of the jurors. With emotional feeling, he added, "I...I rather not talk to you about this..."

The witness, trembling, bowed his head and took a large breath to relieve himself.

Silence.

Mr. Kanarek hadn't moved, just listened attentively in the middle of the courtroom. The attorney's body seemed erected, rigid, almost like a statue. He stared at the witness, and then exchanged looks with His Honor. Judge Older looked up at a clock facing him across the courtroom.

229

He repeated the usual admonition and dismissed the jurors for lunch until two o'clock.

A funny thing happened to me on the way to the Hilton... as I sat down on the front seat inside the bus, my zipper came apart, I couldn't zipper it down or up... it was partly zippered but somehow the middle of it came open. Luckily, I had my jacket on and was able to cover myself from the incoming jurors as they were passing inside to their seats. Seated in front of me was Mrs. Colvig, a female bailiff who made it impossible for me to work out the stupid zipper before I descended in front of the Hilton Hotel.

Somehow I managed to walk up the electric escalator, walk up on the second lobby and into the restaurant. Once seated, the fly came out—nude, opened —and once more tried effortlessly to fix it. However, things became worse as I manipulated it one way and another. The end of the zipper broke loose and I immediately covered my lap with a blue napkin and appeared to be safe enough for the time. But how would I get up in front of all those people? Shall I ask the bailiff to take me to the rest room and perhaps it can be fixed there? Then I thought I had better wait to have the waitress take my order and then ask the bailiff but I noticed he hadn't ordered yet. What to do? Oh hell, just wait and pretend like nothing has happened.

In the meantime, while the conversation of the jurors was silly and boring, I decided to keep myself occupied by reading the book, *Tell Me That You Love Me Junie Moon*.

The bickering and griping at the table was unbearable. This time they were complaining about the food—the food that was charged to guests on the weekend. My mind was uptight, the bowl of soup I ordered—cream of chicken—was too salty and much too much. The waitress was concerned and out of courtesy I told her that I was just not hungry. Then she brought me a cup of fresh fruits and I ate it all. It was good although my lip was sore. I had cold blisters which were bothering me and the remedy I had applied the night before didn't do one bit of good. Well, the lunch was over and as I walked out, immediately put my suit jacket in front of me.

The transportation officer made a comment about me having bowled 232 the night before. He was keeping score and noticed that somehow, I had come out rather good.

He said, "There goes the two hundred thirty two man."

We walked together as the rest followed us. I tried to smile but my thoughts were set on covering my front so no one would notice my uncomfortable appearance. The day was warm and the smog out in the street was thick as an Arab's eyebrow. I took a look at the background of the city—couldn't

230

see a thing.

Got inside the bus and was glad for the moment.

On the way to the Hall of Justice, I thought of sewing the fly with a needle that the lady jurors had kept in a file cabinet on the top drawer, where there were some safety pins and rolls of thread. I pictured myself going through the drawer and with a nonchalent way, would pick up needle and thread and go into the men's room and get to work on those miserable slacks—those slacks which had given me the same trouble before.

Then I thought of giving them to one of my brothers. Let's see, which of my brothers? Ricardo probably—he needed them more than anyone. But then I thought of Nachito or Benito. Oh well, there'll be plenty of time to think about whom I shall give these slacks or better say—the suit.

We arrived at the Hall of Justice. We didn't go in the parking lot nor through the gate as we usually did. Instead, we parked on the one-way street behind the main entrance of the building.

I got out, covered myself again with the jacket, and as we walked in the parking lot towards the electric gate, I noticed one sheriff in a prone position with gun in hand and resting on the right side of a police car pointing towards somewhere—the wall or was it a window? He was prepared to shoot. I couldn't tell, there was a little commotion. They stopped us and the sheriff guard in charge of the gate called the female bailiff, Kathy Colvig, who was escorting us. I tried to listen to what he was telling her but obviously he didn't want me to hear. I asked Kathy and she didn't answer me. They pushed us aside behind the main building. As we moved, everybody wanted to know what was happening—no one knew. Then I heard someone say that there was a shooting taking place, but couldn't see anything. I decided to find out and stubbornly I approached Kathy again and said, "What's going on?"

"Oh, it's just a drill," she said.

"A drill?"

"Yes."

Then Ruth, one of the female jurors who was next to me, told me something but I couldn't hear, so she said, "I'll tell you later, but rest assured, that was no drill. She thinks we are stupid enough to believe such a thing. A drill? Bah!"

"I agree with you," I answered.

A few minutes later, we walked through the gate and once more we passed the alley which had become so familiar to us. The odor of leftover foods, the smell of dead bodies inside the hearses, and the familiar faces of the prisoners busy cleaning the pavement or unloading trucks with the boxes containing perhaps the food for the next two weeks. We all arrived inside an elevator—not the one the prisoners carried garbage in, but the one with the fat attendant, a colored, fat sheriff that when he breathed, he expanded his belly and always seemed to be in a world of his own. Nothing bothered him and he simply looked at us almost like we were not there.

We reached the jury room. I waited to be the last one to enter because I didn't want to be seen. Suddenly I realized that I hadn't checked the file cabinet. Filled with frustration, I couldn't open it. Mildred quite simply showed me how and to my dismay, there were no needles or thread nor any safety pins. Disappointed I went out and saw there was no one waiting so I rushed and opened the door of the bathroom.

There was someone inside. I waited and still with my jacket in front of me, stood outside. I probably looked silly, but luckily no one was aware, not even Mr. Paine as he came out. I went inside, didn't remove my pants as there was no need. Simply sat down and began to work out the zipper—no hope. Then I remembered and noticed that some time ago I had sewn the bottom part of the zipper so as the zipper wouldn't get off the string of beads which conform a zipper. I had no shears or anything to cut the threads and then began to put the head zipper into the channels. Satisfied, I walked out. No one had noticed the length of time I had spent in the restroom nor had anyone tried to get in. Although it had been customary to just close the door, unlocked, this time I had locked it.

Deputy Taylor came at 1:45 to say that we were going down an hour later than usual.

"Good," I told myself, "I'll sleep a little."

But there was so much laughter from the "clique"—two of them decided this time to sing songs from a book that belonged to Tom Brooks.

They were obviously following the musical notes but the results were atrocious. Genaro Swanson tried to reach high notes unsuccessfully and his hoarse laugh would, at intervals, burst out. His laugh was not an ordinary laugh— when Genaro laughed, he commanded the attention of anybody. He laughed not with the subtleness of pleasantry but the uproarious type—it denoted either a lack of education as when you hear someone vulgar and despicable, or as when you hear a financier laugh with a sense of security and self-assurance —laughing without giving a damn who hears it or what anybody says.

You could almost say, that if you didn't see Genaro laughing, one could picture him fat, big, and tall with a cigar in his mouth and boisterous as if he was sitting on a hot pan; however, he was neither big or tall, nor did he smoke cigars. He was short and chubby although stern. He wore eyeglasses—powerful ones—almost like lenses because he was nearsighted. He smoked nonfilter cigarettes and when he finished each one, he made sure he got the full value of it—he smoked them to the last milimeter. His right hand's three fingers, thumb, index, and heart were yellowish from so much tobacco use.

One of the many times, going down in the elevator of the hotel to the coffee shop, I stood next to him. He spoke to me directly in my face; well, I almost went into shock from the strong smell of tobacco coming from his mouth. He said something but it was secondary in my mind—I was only paying attention to the strong and repulsive odor of cigarettes emanating from his breath. He laughed then—a shouting laughter and concluded with a hideous coughing. Luckily, the elevator had reached the Casino floor and I was able to breathe outside in the hall where there was a pleasant draft of early morning fresh air.

"Boy, it's enough to make anyone sick," said Betty surprisingly, a heavy smoker herself.

Now, we are in the jury room and the laughter is constant and idiotic. They're overdoing it. Somehow Miss Texas (Debbie) is going along with the singing, she's the leader of the clique. Her voice is drowned out most of the time by the laughter of Genaro. She also stopped and laughed half the time to correlate with the laughter of her singing partners. Practically everything that they said or did caused Debbie to laugh.

Miss Texas was a rather attractive woman—she was born in Texas, that's why I called her Debbie Texas. She wore a wig which was between salt and pepper color or dirty blonde with specks of ash tones. She had, to my knowledge, two wigs of the same style and one which, according to her—"she was breaking in"—meaning the wig was too tight to wear. Deb-Texas had a habit of which she was not aware, she kept tucking in her natural hair at the back of her neck, using fingers from both hands. By doing so, the wig was stained and dead looking at the edges.

Miss Texas practically indulged her friends to follow her where she sat. If someone occupied a chair where it would separate one juror member of the clique, she managed somehow to make that juror move closer to the clique or manipulated an exchange with an outsider. That way, they all sat together, drank together, laughed together, and ate together. In doing so, they all spent the time together, that's why one of the "outsiders", Marvin to be exact, baptized that group "The Clique"—appropriate and self-explanatory. Also, that brought the attention of the bailiffs, especially Kathy Colvig, a female bailiff, who befriended the clique.

After the first time we went out to bowl, the elderly jurors remained at the hotel.

233

The bowling had become a night out for drinking beer. The main reason had been switched to play one or two games and then move on to the bar—especially Tom, Ray and Deb, escorted by Mrs. Colvig. The rest of us just hung around and waited for them to finish their drinking and dancing. On the bus, returning to the hotel—Wow! The same thing over and over.

In the courtroom...

The four defense counsel made much of the fact that the witness was on the stand with the purpose to become a "celebrity" and further his show business career by lying about Mr. Manson.

However, it was under Mr. Kanarek's questioning that the motion-picture extra and stunt man denied it solemnly by announcing, "I am not here to pompous myself."

"Now, Mr. Flynn," asked Mr. Kanarek, "is it a fair statement to say that you want to advance your movie career on account of Mr. Manson?"

"Well, I tell you right now," responded the witness loudly, "that's the kind of publicity I wouldn't want!"

"But you want to become a famous actor, right?"

The witness paused for what seemed a long time and replied, "Yes."

"And you are using this case to do it.... right?"

Flynn stood up quickly and pointing accusedly at the attorney, exclaimed, "You big.... CATFISH, YOU!"

The audience roared with contentment. Surprisingly, the judge didn't admonish nor say anything to the witness for his outburst.

To support Juan Flynn's testimony about Manson allegedly intimidating the witness with a knife against his throat and admitting that "he was behind all those killings," Mr. Bugliosi shrewdly brought forward immediately another witness.

David Steuber, a California Highway Patrol investigator, who testified that Juan Flynn had told him nine months ago, the same conversation in the presence of Paul Watkins, Brooks Poston, and Paul Crocket.

The officer, who had a tremendous resemblance to Mery Griffin's ex-sidekick buddy Arthur Threacher, played a tape recording of his conversation with Flynn.

Judge Older admonished the jurors before we listened to the tape to consider it only as the veracity of Juan Flynn's testimony and not against Charles Manson.

Court adjourned.

Again, the following day, Deputy Taylor came to the jury room to announce that it would be "a little while" before going down to the courtroom. We waited two hours.

The defendants had been brought back to court. The next witness was Sergeant Paul Whiteley, a detective working for the Los Angeles Police Department, who testified that he booked Bobby Beausoleil at 3:45 A.M. on August 7, 1969 (another family member who was found guilty of first-degree murder and sentenced to die for the killing of musician Gary Hinman).

The defense counsel declared in unison they had no questions, except Mr. Kanarek who wanted to remind the judge about his continuous objection of the irrelevancy on the presence of the witness.

At that point, Charles Manson started pounding on the table with a yellow pencil he had in his hand. Judge Older, observing, didn't say anything and proceeded to dismiss the witness.

"Can I interrogate the witness?" asked Charles Manson, surprisingly, as he rose. Judge Older denied him the strange request and the prisoner retorted indignantly, "You are killing me. Your court is killing me. Do you think I'm going to sit down here and just watch you killing me?"

"Mr. Manson," said the judge, "you are going to be quiet or I will have you removed from court like the other day, if you don't behave."

Manson didn't stop. Instead, he kept pounding furiously with the pencil and said something like, "I'm going to do something about this."

Immediately, Deputy Taylor stood up and moved slowly towards the inmate. I noticed the press, my fellow jurors and everybody were avidly trailing the colloquy between the defendants and the court.

Judge Older curtly asked the accused, "What are you going to do?"

Manson mumbled something but stopped when His Honor addressed Mr. Bugliosi, "Call your next witness."

"I'm going to cut you down!" shouted Charles Manson.

At the same time, he leaped over the table in front of him and proceeded on top towards the judge's bench. Deputy Taylor, nearby, scrambled over the table and quickly grabbed the prisoner. Somehow Manson managed to release himself and when he was about to jump on the floor towards the judge, he exclaimed, "In the name of Christian justice, I'm going to cut off your head!"

Deputy Ernie Post (the young bailiff who tried to teach Olivia how to swim) ran over from behind Deputy Taylor and spectacularly slid over the table and got hold of Manson's leg. Both men stumbled to the floor with Sheriff Post topling on Manson. The courtroom broke into an arena of excitement. Everyone stood up. More deputies rushed over through the audience, pushing aside some spectators standing in the aisle, as they hurdled over the railing in the middle of the courtroom.

For a moment I thought that some of those in the courtroom might come forward and aid the cult leader—causing a riot of some sort, but the extreme caution of the deputies stopped anybody from tresspassing the dividing railing. The jurors felt safe and at ease.

This was one of the pragmatic demonstrations of Manson. I guess he was bored or something. He loved the stage and the attention. But this was just part of the parade of little gimicks, like the change of hairdo or shaving his beard and posing all the time for the artists to draw. He posed for me once too.

But his behavior in court did not get into the deliberations. This is how much we gave them the benefit of the doubt. Because their behavior in court had nothing to do with the killings themselves. There were seven people killed. Somebody killed them. Now they can get up and say, "I didn't kill, I didn't kill, I didn't kill." I don't care if they say it ten thousand times, the thing of it is to get up and prove it, substantiate it. I'm sure the defense counsels wanted to do just that but they couldn't. They didn't know where to start, poor guys. And you can not sway twelve jurors who are not dumb and just go and say let them go free, they are innocent and so forth.

Manson, meanwhile, was being toned down by Deputy Post with the assistance of Deputy Taylor and another sheriff. The three officers led Manson out of the courtroom with his hands twisted behind his back.

After the prisoner had been wrestled into submission, Judge Older, amazingly calm, declared, "The record will show that Mr. Manson came over the counsel table in the direction of the bench and was subdued by the bailiffs, and I order him removed from the courtroom."

Immediately followlng the disruptive conduct of the hippie cult leader, the three women defendants burst out chanting something that the court was unable to describe to the court reporter for the record.

Judge Older, still magnificently calm, ordered Mollie Kane and another fe - male bailiff to remove the three defendants.

All in all, the incident happened so quickly. Exciting? Yes... but hard to believe that Manson, unarmed, and of such short height could dominate physically the strength and alertness of the deputies.

The trial resumed and Mr. Bugliosi called several police detectives to discuss their investigation of the slayings. ..

Manuel F. Gutierrez, a sergeant with the Los Angeles Police Department, simply testified for the record what he had observed Manson and the three girls do in court.

The Spanish-looking witness said that he had seen Manson make some gestures at Mrs. Kasabian. He saw an "X" on Manson's forehead and that the girl defendants did the same the following day. Mr. Bugliosi wanted to set clear, Manson's leadership, in the jurors' minds.

Albert J. LaValle, also a sergeant of the Police Department, testified that he drew the large plan of the Tate residence (P-98) from an aerial photo. The large drawing was being used to mark locations of events and people.

Jack Holt, a deputy sheriff of Los Angeles County, testified that he was the only custodian of some documents previously introduced as evidence.

DeWayne Wolfer, a Los Angeles Police officer and an expert in firearms, testified that he went to the Sharon Tate residence with Sergeant David Butler to detect different sounds that could be heard within the surroundings. The witness explained that he and his partner conducted a series of pistol tests with a sound level machine. They had a walkie-talkie radio communication to determine the signal as to when the weapons were fired with the stereo machine on and without it. The tests showed that the sound-measuring equipment didn't show any reading when the gun was fired in the living room of the Sharon Tate home while the stereo was being played in the guest house at the rear.

The qualified technical witness talked calmly, objectively, as technical men do and concluded by saying that it was his opinion that William Garretson probably did not hear the gunfire during the rampage because he had his stereo phonograph tuned to a high level.

Jerold Friedman, a Hollywood resident, testified that he received a phone call at 11:45 P.M. from his friend Steven Parent. The witness said that the victim sounded excited about being in a big Star's place. He stated that Steven, whom he had known for two or three months, wanted to visit him but that he told him it was too late.

Mr. Bugliosi called, in succession, some witnesses who, directly or indirectly, participated in some routine legal technicality, such as:

Mrs. Gloria Hardaway, a senior clerk at Sybil Brand Institute, who brought a document to court which was identified as the release papers she prepared for Sandra Pew (Sandra Good).

Mrs. Rachel Burgess, a Los Angeles deputy sheriff, who, on September 23, 1969, prepared the release papers for Mary Theresa Brunner at 8:30 P.M.

Mr. Bugliosi also recalled to the witness stand:

Sergeant Michael McGann, who testified that the bloody clothes believed to have been worn by the murderers were found below Benedict Canyon Road, thrown over an embankment one and eight-tenths miles from the

Tate estate. According to the witness, it was another one and eight-tenths miles to where the western-style revolver was found.

Sheriff Deputy William Gleason testified that he was in charge of the multiple arrests on August 16, 1969, at the Spahn Ranch. The witness stated that there were twenty-seven adults and five or six children arrested. Most of them were sleeping in the saloon. Two trailers were located; in one slept Susan Atkins, Leslie Van Houten, and in the other, John Swartz slept alone. Juan Flynn, Mary Brunner, Danny De Carlo and John Reinhart were arrested in the room called "the gun room." All were charged with grand auto theft.

Under cross-examination by Defense Attorney Mr. Fitzgerald, the officer said that one hundred two deputies—ten percent carrying weapons—twenty-five vehicles, and two helicopters were used during the operation which began at two A.M. from the Malibu Station and arrived at the Spahn Ranch at four A.M. From four A.M. till six A.M., different squads arrived from the hills—hiking and hiding in different fashions. Personal property was seized at the location. The prisoners were released two or three days later without charges.

Virginia Kathleen Graham (Castro) admitted she was on parole for committing petty theft and forgery. The attractive, well-dressed woman testified that she met Susan Atkins on October 20, 1969, at the Sybil Brand Institute for Women. She described the surroundings.

Under Mr. Bugliosi's interrogation, the well-spoken witness testified that she and the defendant were assigned to Dormitory 8000, a large room with some sixty beds.

"Everybody would laugh at her," the witness said, "because of her name —Sadie Glutz."

"Did she say anything to you?" inquired the prosecutor.

"Yes," replied the talkative Mrs. Graham.

"Sadie came into my bed area and sat down and we started to talk about many things. I advised her not to talk too much, and even told her about what had happened before to someone and who did get into trouble."

The witness went on to relate that Susan Atkins, at times, raised her voice and somehow became excited as she was telling about the murders at the Tate residence.

"She was almost on the verge of re-creating the incident," observed Mrs. Graham.

"Sadie told me she felt no remorse and that she felt at peace with herself."

"What did she mention about the murders?" asked Mr. Bugliosi.

"Sadie said that when she went to one bedroom, she saw Abigail Folger reading in bed. Then she went to other parts of the house and saw Sharon

238

Tate dressed in a type of bikini, sitting on the bed with pillows behind her back. Jay Sebring was sitting on the bed and both were engrossed in a conversation. They didn't see her. Then Sadie told me that she went back to the living room."

"Did she tell you what happened next?" asked Mr. Bugliosi.

"Yes," replied the witness.

"Sadie said that there in the living room was where she stabbed a man about five times (Voityk Frykowski). The man, bleeding, went outside in front of the house and yelled, 'Help... help...'"

The witness, imitating Susan Atkins's tone of voice, quoted the defendant, saying, "And would you believe there was no one around to hear him?"

"What did she say about Sharon Tate?" Mr. Bugliosi wanted to know.

"She said that Sharon Tate was the last one to die," answered Mrs. Graham, and then added that Susan Atkins had also said, 'I had Sharon Tate's hand behind her back. She was crying and saying, "Please don't kill me.... all I want is to have my baby."'

The witness then said that she heard her cellmate say, ' But I told her, "Shut up, bitch, I have no pity for you." She kept begging me to spare her, but I stabbed her about four or five times.'

Mrs. Graham told Mr. Bugliosi that she had knowledge of the $ 25,000 reward, and had not received any money for it nor were her intentions to sell her life story rights.

Mr. Fitzgerald skipped his right to cross-examine the witness.

Mr. Shin slowly managed to ask Mrs. Graham if she was a lesbian.

"That's new to me," replied the witness. "I'm not."

Judge Older adjourned the court session and told us about Monday, October 12th being a holiday. In spite of having been dismissed earlier than usual, we had to wait a long while before Deputy Taylor escorted us down to the bus. All the jurors were annoyed and made many unhappy comments in regard to it.

"Surprise!" amusingly said Mr. Welch.

The jail-bus windows were all covered with a white substance—it looked like Bon Ami—the glass windows were opaque. We couldn't see. On the way to the hotel, everybody displayed, in one way or another, their discontentment. Some were even furiously upset and disappointed.

Mrs. Collingwood, sitting behind me, had something to say.

"Here we are," she said, "two and a half days isolated in two small rooms, seventeen different people, upset and feeling edgy for lack of activity—lack of movement—lack of being able to do what we were chosen for. But no

—how long can we go on waiting? Now this...what's next?"

"I feel the same as you do," observed Edith. "There's no reason in the world why we had to wait so long to go down in the courtroom. What do you think, Bill?" Mrs. Rayburn then asked.

"Maybe it's due to some newspaper headline," I retorted, "something we shouldn't see and may misinterpret."

"You're talking like you have been brainwashed," Edith said accusingly.

"Listen you two," interjected Ruth, "we've already been locked up three months, and don't think for a moment they're going to jeopardize the case now. It's been too expensive and too risky to let us see anything or anybody."

"She's right," I declared.

At that moment, Deputy Tull stood up and announced, "Ordinarily, we would allow you to see outside; however, under the circumstances, we are forced to follow our supervisor's orders. I'm sorry for the inconvenience."

No one replied.

Everytime the bus driver changed gears, the vehicle jerked recklessly. Edith, Ruth, and Betty didn't appreciate the "chauffer's" lack of skill. Mildred was even more aware. On a different day, the same officer, while driving, had made sudden stop causing the redheaded juror to brace her feet against the front seat to prevent herself from being thrown forward. She was disturbed to discover the heel of one of her shoes was broken beyond repair. At the time, Mildred was knitting and Mollie advised her not to do so in the future, otherwise she might stab herself accidentally with one of the large knitting needles.

The transportation officer was tall, well built, about thirty-five years old, crew-cut hair with an oval face, chinless, and hard serious. He had driven the bus about eight to ten times.

Basically, he was a good driver but his arrogant personality emerged as one approached him. None of the jurors dared to even look at him for fear of being ignored.

He attempted to beat me physically. It all began when the defendants had been removed from the courtroom.

We jurors of Department 104 were transferred to whatever jury rooms were available.

We liked the jury room of Department 102. The two rooms were situated in the northeast corner of the Hall of Justice. It had better ventilation and for all purposes, was much more spacious for us to walk. The enormous corner room had two large tables which were used eventually to play ping pong. Three boxes of paper tissue, placed horizontally and attached with scotch tape, sufficed the net. The outside view from the eighth floor was more interesting and picturesque. The smaller room near the entrance, which housed some six metal lockers, was used twice daily by the bailiffs to change their civilian clothes from their uniforms, and vice versa.

The enclosed surroundings of the jury room led Ray to feel depressed. He felt somewhat rejected if his jokes didn't get across the table and that generated a puerile hostility which he only used in front of the jurors.

He would pound heavily on the table with his notebook—walk to the bathroom, flush the toilet, and slam the door just for the sake of it—or continuously hit a golf ball against a metal paper basket with a golf club. Other times, he would imitate the voice of Deputy Taylor and yell out loud, "Okay, folks—time to go!" which made everyone rush out, only to discover it was a false call.

Deb, Tom, and Violet would also participate and aid by patronizing with their approving laughs and roars.

Very few jurors were not irritated by their childish behavior; however, one by one, the rest of the jurors began to disperse and look elsewhere for peace and quiet. Some took refuge by taking their own chair and sitting in the smaller room. Others would rather stand and wait away from the noise by the entrance door, and others would walk as to reject from their minds any sign of anger.

That was what happened. The more dislike the jurors showed, the more excessive noise would come from them. Any disturbance that would annoy them, it would surely take a prominent place in their activities. Somehow, all the jurors managed to control themselves through the day, despite their emotional upsets.

I must admit, that day my mind was pretty uptight. I had a splitting headache. My association with Ray and Tom was still on good terms. We spoke to each other but their lack of consideration and respect for the elder jurors had made me indirectly step out of their company. They sensed my feelings.

Upon arriving at the hotel, I was the first to leave the bus and the first to get inside the elevator and also the first to step out in the hall towards my room. I shut the door and leaned against it. I needed a certain amount of solitude. I wanted to be alone and pull myself together.

It had been customary of Ray to pound heavily on my door followed by the rest of the clique. That day was no exception. Someone knocked and quickly I opened the door and expectedly caught Ray ready to knock once more. He smiled and walked away.

"Are you satisfied?" I asked him indignantly.

Ray looked back over his shoulder and continued smiling. I felt my face frozen with anger. A burning lump in my throat made me feel I would never be able to speak again.

"I want you to stop knocking on my door," I said as an ultimatum. "I warn you."

Ray didn't say anything. Some jurors had stopped and watched my actions, approving of them. Ray knew with deep conviction that he would never do it again.

Furiously, I slammed the door against curious eyes. Again, another knock on the door. No sooner I opened the door that the arrogant tall bus driver walked into my room and with his right hand grabbed my left shoulder forcibly.

"If you slam that door again, I..." he said with glaring eyes.

"Get your hands off me!" I shouted and at the same instant, jerked myself free from his grip. He advanced towards me. I noticed his fists forming.

"Get the hell out of my room," I yelled and took refuge behind a chair.

A flash of intuition told me to be ready to use the chair to defend myself in the event the deputy tried to hit me. The Nazi-looking sheriff realized my intentions. Behind the intruder I looked across the heads of the jurors standing in the door. They were watching with disbelief. Some jurors had a worried look in their eyes. I was frightened and shaking. The officer, his nostrils flaring with hatred, placed his hand to his gun holster and moved forward. I stiffened.

"What's the matter," Deputy Tull said suddenly as he made his way through the jurors. Boy, was I glad to see him. Sheriff Tull, senior bailiff for the weekend, glanced around and understood the situation.

He asked again, "What's wrong Mr. Zamora?"

"Mr. Tull, I want you to tell this man to get the hell out of my room," I said, with dubious authority and then added, "I'm going to write a letter to the judge and tell him everything. This is outrageous."

Both officers stood silent and motionless.

"Leave Mr. Zamora alone," said Mr. Tull and took the officer by the arm, leading him out. The bus driver said something inaudibly and reluctantly left my room.

"Don't pay attention, Mr. Zamora," Deputy Tull said apologetically.

"Like hell, I will!" I protested. "He was aiming for his gun and if you hadn't arrived in time, I don't know what would have happened."

"He has no experience in dealings with people," observed Mr. Tull.

"That's no excuse. I'm not a criminal He barged into my room without

242

my permission. He has no right. Tell him to stay away from me."

"I'm sorry for the incident," Mr. Tull said, and closed the door carefully.

Frustratedly, I turned on my stereo and walked towards the window. The Los Angeles sky was darkened by gray clouds. Idly, I stood looking down below at the East Gardens. The green grass was specked with brown spots. Autumn was here. Suddenly, I gasped and felt lonely. I thought of Laura.

"Tomorrow's Saturday," I told myself. "Maybe I'll see her."

Back in court. . . .

Ronni Howard, whose true name is Veronica Hughes, stated that she had been convicted for extortion in 1955, of forgery in 1962, and had used a long list of aliases.

Miss Howard, obviously once an appealing looking woman and now although still attractive in some ways, her puffy face reflected a hard past.

Under questioning by Mr. Bugliosi, Miss Howard testified that Susan Atkins told her about taking part in the five slayings at the Tate residence on August 9, 1969. She related the conversation took place in November of 1969 while both were inmates in Dormitory No. 8000 at the Sybil Brand Institute for women.

The long raven-haired witness said that she and the defendant whose bed was next to hers were discussing about what had shocked them more than anything else. The witness observed the conversation went something like this:

Miss Atkins: "I know something that would blow your mind off."

Miss Howard: "Nothing could blow my mind off."

Miss Atkins: "Oh yeah? Did you hear about the Tate murders?"

The witness then related that the defendant began telling her about how she stabbed Sharon Tate.

"Susan Atkins went to one of the bedrooms and saw Abigail Folger, then went to another bedroom and saw a man sitting on the bed where Sharon Tate was lying down. They were all brought to the living room."

Referring to the actress, Susan Atkins told the witness, "She couldn't believe what was happening."

According to Miss Howard, the defendant admitted that Sharon Tate pleaded for the life of her baby but Susan Atkins told her "Shut up, you bitch, I have no mercy for you," and began to stab her in the chest.

"What did she say?" asked Mr. Bugliosi.

"Well," replied Miss Howard, "she said that 'when you stab a person, it's just like having a climax. The more you do it, the better you like it.'"

"What else did she tell you?" insisted the deputy district attorney.

243

"Sadie wanted to open up Sharon Tate's stomach to get the baby, but that she didn't."

The large-breasted witness added, "Sadie said that when she killed people, she felt thrilled and that everything in life is a sexual intercourse—in and out. In and out goes the knife."

The accused murderess was brought into the courtroom briefly so Miss Howard, a girl with sensual lips and alluring hazel eyes, could identify her.

"Yes, that's Sadie," said the witness.

Miss Atkins, with both hands in her pockets, smiled and then averted her eyes without speaking.

Under cross-examination by Miss Atkins's attorney, Mr. Dave Shin, the witness conceded she knew of a $ 25,000 reward offered by English actor Peter Sellers and other movie-star friends of Sharon Tate.

"I feel I deserve it," the witness said.

Miss Howard claimed she was the first person to relate Susan Atkins's conversations about the Tate murders to the authorities, giving the police their first "big break" in the case.

Asked if she had made sexual advances to Susan Atkins while in prison, Miss Howard smiled and said, "Of course not."

"Why do you smile?" asked Mr. Shin.

"Because of the question," responded the witness.

Mr. Shin then wanted to know if she had been to Sharon Tate's residence before the incident which occurred in August 1969. The witness answered, "Yes—I did go with a gentleman." The gentleman's name was not disclosed.

Mr. Shin proceeded with a number of questions in regard to a letter which Miss Howard received from the defendant. Susan Atkins didn't sign the letter but the witness recognized the handwriting as that belonging to Miss Atkins.

No more questions.

Again, the counsel approached the bench and shortly after, the judge dismissed the jurors for lunch.

That was Wednesday morning. In the afternoon, and the next day, we remained in the jury room. On Friday, we still hadn't been called to go downstairs. The jurors were restless.

"Just how long are we suppose to wait?" asked Edith impatiently. "For the last two weeks, we hardly have gone down to the courtroom. We've been enclosed in these two small rooms. How much longer will it last?"

"Seventeen people, seventeen different minds, seventeen different faces, seventeen different opinions as how one feels being locked up," stated Betty

244

annoyingly, and went on, "We've been taken away from our families. Our everyday routines have been warped and some destroyed. It'll be a long time before we get back in the swing of things."

I noticed that everybody was expressing their feelings openly. One by one, they stated their points and some added something to what others had already started to say.

"Just think this is a trip or a vacation," suggested Frank, trying to make the jurors feel at ease.

"But this is like going on a trip without necessarily enjoying it," Ruth said. "At least when one goes on a vacation trip, one gets to choose the place one wants to go."

"And when you want to go back home, you go," Mildred interjected.

"And the type of transportation you take is your pleasure," said Betty, "and not that lousy dirty jail bus."

Edith, Mildred, and Betty were busy knitting. Danny pretended to be sleeping, and occasionally opened one eye to see who was talking at the time. He didn't offer any comment. Marvin looked stupefied and didn't speak a word. Olivia, upon returning from "Lucy," had missed part of the chatting, but she also expressed her views soon enough.

"It's been three months already since we left our homes—three long, solid, tedious months which have been taken from our lives. Only to prove our way of life to those in our society that seventeen people—seventeen good, honest established citizens have foregone their everyday obligations, their relatives and dear ones, their children, their spouses, their parents, their pets —to perform their civic duty. WELL... civic duty is fine and even exciting at the beginning, but when civic duty trespasses the boundaries of our given time—when our freedom of doing what we ordinarily do is suddenly taken for three, four or five months, then it's not civic duty—it's a depravation of our rights and our senses."

Betty, who had stopped her knitting to smoke a cigarette, walked towards the window and observed, "We are nothing but seventeen mindless individuals."

The thin-looking juror, for a moment, seemed to get stuck with the number "seventeen" as she continued saying, "We're seventeen robots who are told to go here and there. We are seventeen people who are treated by the sheriffs not as mister so-and-so or misses so-and-so, but as a number. We're simply a number denoting a digit." Betty added sarcastically, "We seventeen jurors shouldn't have feelings nor ask any questions. The bailiffs wouldn't want that. We shouldn't suggest anything and never.. never expect to be pleased as a human being. We're thrown together whether we like it or not."

For a while, the conversation was directed against the bailiffs but it was Betty who thought that the one responsible for us being sequestered was Judge Older himself.

"The bailiffs are only following orders and are not to be blamed," she said.

"I'm not going to hold my tongue anymore!" Ruth said indignantly.

"It's embarrassing. Why should I give up the privacy of my home and love of my children for this? Who do they think they are? Gods??? I'm going to write a letter to the judge and tell him everything, including names, you'll see."

Whether or not Ruth Collingwood followed her intentions was never verified. However, she proved to be a sort of lookout for herself and rarely committed herself to exchange her feelings openly. Ruth appeared bitter and cold among the jurors, especially after she and Edith Rayburn broke up their friendship.

In the courtroom. . . .

Gregg Jacobson was a powerful and intelligent witness. Dressed in neat mod fashion and with a thick moustache, the witness said he worked in music record production. He testified he was closely acquainted with Charles Manson from May of 1968 until a few weeks after the five slayings on August 9, 1969, at the Tate residence.

Jacobson's important testimony focused entirely on Manson's philosophy of life and death and his belief that a black versus white revolution was imminent.

The witness, a tall handsome young man, observed that he became friendly with the hippie cult leader and when they spoke alone, they got into a "pretty good" conversation about right and wrong.

"What did he say?" Mr. Bugliosi wanted to know.

"He said that there was no right or wrong, and that there was nothing wrong with killing—it was all in man's mind," stated the witness.

"Did he elaborate on wrong?" asked the prosecutor.

"Manson said that he personally could do no wrong. There wasn't good or bad."

"Did he say anything about death?" asked Mr. Bugliosi.

"He said he didn't believe in it. He said he had died long time ago. It was just a physical change that took place at the end—the essence of life went on and on... Death is a concept of man. It doesn't exist."

"Did he say death was beautiful?"

"Yes," replied Jacobson, "Charlie said that when he experienced death, it was beautiful!"

The witness stated that Manson had told him that there was no wrong in killing a human being. If someone was killed, his life would go on. There was no wrong to kill.

"What did he say about time?" asked Mr. Bugliosi, while checking out his line of questions on a yellow pad.

"It doesn't exist," answered Jacobson. "It's also a concept of man. Man invented it."

"What about pain?"

"Exists in the head only."

The witness went on to give an example of what the defendant had told him:

"Manson being in the desert, with no clothes or anything, would overcome cold and heat for a long period of time."

In a line of questions and answers, the witness explained, "Manson didn't want to do anything with the establishment. Everything was coming to an end—the Karma was turning. Manson called himself Jesus Christ and other times the devil. He spoke about the relation between whites and blacks."

According to the witness, Charles Manson wanted to start the "Helter Skelter," a name the hippie cult leader applied to the supposed upcoming racial revolution.

Gregg Jacobson, although fashionably attired, wore no socks. He testified that Manson derived that name for the race war from the title of a Beatles song and their songs, particularly, "Blackbeard" and "Revolution 9" which were frequently discussed by the defendant in connection with his revolution theory.

The witness added, "Manson felt the Beatles were singing directly to him through the lyrics of their songs, and he believed the written word in the Bible was reflected in what the Beatles were doing. Charlie thought the Beatles' song 'Revolution 9' related directly to Revelation 9 in the Bible and he also believed the Beatles were the four angels mentioned in the Book of Revelation."

Under questioning by Mr. Bugliosi, the interesting witness explained that Revelation 9 in the Bible makes reference to a "bottomless pit" in the desert as a refuge for the chosen few who will survie Armageddon, the last battle between blacks and whites.

Through his testimony, Gregg Jacobson stated that Manson's plan to move to the desert from his quarters at the Spahn ranch was also in line with this biblical reference.

"Did he say how the 'Helter Skelter' was going to begin?" asked Mr. Bu-

247

gliosi.

"Yes," responded the witness. "The blacks were going to rift up—dismember—the white people. There was going to be an open confrontation. The blacks would win. It was their turn. It was their Karma. Action and reaction."

"Did Manson say what he intended to do while this was happening?" inquired Mr. Bugliosi.

"Yes, he and the family were going to the desert and descend with a rope into a bottomless pit—habitable in the desert."

"Did he tell you whether or not the blacks were going to be able to handle the reins of power?"

"Ultimately not. They were going to come back and be what they are. Eventually, in essence, the blacks would come back to Mr. Manson."

Mr. Bugliosi introduced, as exhibit P-266, a two-record white album. Jacobson explained that Charles Manson, upon hearing the record at his home, went out and got himself a record player.

"Charlie listened to the records being played over and over again. All the songs were played but especially "Blackbeard", "Revolution 9", "Sexy Sadie" and, of course, "Helter Skelter"", testified the witness.

"Manson could quote from these songs," said Jacobson.

Mr. Bugliosi then asked the witness to describe what messages Manson interpreted from the lyrics of the Beatles songs. According to the witness, the defendant explained what the Beatles tried to convey to him.

"'Helter Skelter' was the Armageddon, the last battle between blacks and whites. It was coming down.

"The word 'bottom' meant the 'bottom of the pit'.

"'Blackbeard' were the Black Panthers, 'they're going to rise up!'

"'Piggies' were the 'White Establishment'.

"'Revolution 9' had no discernible lyrics except for the line 9, 9, 9...

"'Sexy Sadie' was presumably the reason Susan Atkins was called that."

Gregg Jacobson testified that Charles Manson changed his philosophy as he got to know him better.

"One day he told me he wanted firearms," said the well-spoken witness.

"Did he give you any reasons?" inquired the prosecutor.

"Yes, one of them was the 'Helter Skelter' were coming. He needed them for protection."

Mr. Bugliosi then asked Jacobson when he had last seen the defendant.

The witness explained Charles Manson came over to visit him at different hours of the day.

"Sometimes he came alone, sometimes with other people."

248

The witness couldn't substantiate as to the exact times when the shaggy hippie leader visited him. However, he remembered that he saw Charles Manson on August 9, 1969. He testified that he saw the change that the defendant had gone through. Describing the occasion, Jacobson said, "The last time he came by my place in Beverly Glen, I can only compare him with a cat that has been caged and suddenly is freed. Like a bobcat. Almost like a militant... rebel. You could see it in his face, his eyes, his hair was on end. It was almost as if electricity was pouring out of him. He had a wild look."

The witness admitted having visited the Spahn ranch about one hundred times within a period of one and a half years. He went on to say, "The group called themselves 'the family.' I heard the girls being referred to as witches. The role of the girls, if any, were to cook, to take care of things, to have men come over—because he (Manson) needed the power. The functions of the girls were also to have children to serve the men. On and off, Charlie approached me to join him. I did not join the family. I always felt a distance. The longest I ever stayed with the family was about two or three days."

When asked to describe the demeanor of Charles Manson, Jacobson observed, "He was like a puppy, always wagging his tail—full of life— very likeable."

"Did you see him change?" asked the prosecutor.

"Yes, after August (1969) he became quiet—lack of spark."

Describing the relationship between members of the family, the witness explained that Charles Manson maintained that one could either be on his side or against.

Asked about his present job as producer of musical records, Jacobson believed that Manson had musical talent. The witness stated that he had worked for Terry Melcher, son of well-known actress Doris Day. Jacobson spoke to Melcher about Charles Manson and even tried to talk the son of the actress-singer into giving Manson a recording contract, and make a film documentary about the defendant. They thought it was a good idea to convey, in film, Charles Manson's message of love and peace.

Jacobson said that he and Melcher went to the Spahn ranch twice to audition the hippie cult leader.

"As tactfully as possible, I tried to tell Charlie 'there was no interest. ' "

The witness proceeded by saying that Manson called him after the failure to arrange the recording contract and asked him if Terry Melcher had a green telescope on the porch of his Malibu beach house.

The witness said, "I told him, 'Yes, he did.' Manson then said, 'Well, he doesn't now.'"

Jacobson then added, "I think the sole purpose in calling me was to let me know that he knew where Terry lived."

"Do you have anything against Mr. Manson?" asked Mr. Bugliosi.

"No," replied the witness.

"Do you dislike him?" insisted the prosecutor.

"No," responded Jacobson.

Under cross-examination by Mr. Fitzgerald, the witness stated that at the time he was employed by Terry Melcher, he had the title of vice president. The answer made the counsel smile doubtfully. The leader of the defense counsel asked questions about music production work of the witness and his business relationship between him and Charles Manson.

"Charlie was sincere in his philosopy," observed Jacobson. "He was an intuitive song writer. He communicated best with music. His subjects were multi-faceted. He was unique, strong—a dramatic package (as an entertainer). I always took Charles Manson seriously and had great respect for him."

Mr. Kanarek followed the same suit of questions. It was a long and confusing set of questions and answers that didn't get anywhere. Finally, the stocky lawyer switched his interrogation to that of the "bottomless pit."

Manson's attorney attempted to get the witness to concede that the cult leader, "was joking when he talked about the rope to go down to the center of the earth."

"I didn't say earth," replied the witness, hard faced.

According to Jacobson, Charles Manson decided to send out "his girls to work in topless bars so they could make enough money to buy a particularly expensive rope to lower 'the family' down into the bottomless pit."

This line of cross-examining evoked laughter from the crowded courtroom, including Judge Older. We were dismissed until the following Monday, October 19, 1970.

The judge, before starting the proceedings, asked the defense counsel if they had talked with the defendants in regards to returning to the courtroom and conducting themselves in a proper manner.

Mr. Fitzgerald, in a rather jovial mood, asked and was granted permission to approach the bench to discuss the matter. Meanwhile, I noticed Jacobson walking towards the witness stand. He was wearing faded levis with a red maroon sweater underneath a grey-brown plaid sports jacket. As soon as he sat down, he removed his shoes and, again, he was wearing no socks.

Looking at the audience, I noticed a young man seated in front of the newsmen's section. He was dressed in a blue suit and wore glasses. He gave the impression of being a recently graduated university student. I wondered if that day was his first assignment. He was extremely attentive and rigidly aware of the proceedings.

Carl George, a CBS TV newscaster, smiled at us and winked an eye. Some of the other reports also smiled.

Mr. Kanarek resumed his cross-examination. He asked Jacobson if he considered himself a hippie. The witness replied that he had heard the word but couldn't refer to it because he didn't know what it meant.

Mr. Kanarek, at the moment, was having a hell of a time trying to hold some books in his hand and the mike which Judge Older had ordered him to use because of the unusual disturbing noise the air conditioning was making.

After a lengthy interrogation that lasted all day long, Mr. Kanarek asked questions in regards as to why Jacobson went to the Spahn ranch. Manson's lawyer sustained that the witness was just trying to get sexual favors from the girls living at the ranch.

"Never," answered Jacobson.

On Tuesday morning, Judge Older announced, "The hours of court session have been changed as follows:

"Morning session will begin at 9:00 A.M., instead of 9:45 A.M., until twelve noon. The afternoon session will begin at 1:30 P.M. instead of 2:00 P.M. until 4:30, instead of 4:15 P.M. There will be fifteen-minute recesses during the morning and the afternoon."

Needless to mention it, the jurors were unanimously happy to know of the change. We wanted the trial to end soon so we could go home.

Upon resuming his interrogation, Mr. Kanarek succeeded in having Jacobson admit that he was under the influence of narcotics when he talked with Charles Manson.

When asked by Mr. Hughes if he considered "Charles Manson an interesting and intelligent individual," Jacobson replied, "Completely."

No more questions.

Shahrokh Hatami, born in Iran and personal photographer of Sharon Tate, identified a picture of Charles Manson as resembling a man he saw at the actress' home about five months before she and four others were killed at the rented estate.

Hatami testified he visited Sharon Tate twice a week because of a TV documentary show. He filmed the blonde movie star as she packed for a trip to Italy. Sharon left a day or two after he filmed her. Roman Polanski, the the actress' movie-director husband was gone to Rio De Janeiro to attend a film festival.

251

Under Mr. Bugliosi's questioning, the witness, a close friend of Miss Tate, stated, "I saw from the window that someone had entered the front yard of the residence... he was hesitant, not very sure where he was going, and somehow, at the same time, walking very aggressively. He walked in without knocking."

The witness, with shoulder-length graying hair, was an oddly interesting character. He spoke in a very heavy foreign accent and his physique was rather "bully." His predominant features were his dark, oily skin, large nose, square jaw and heavy-bearded face.

"I came out and asked what he wanted. He mentioned a name unfamiliar to me," the witness testified, "and I angrily told him this is the Polanski residence. I directed him to take the back alley to see the owner in the back house."

Mr. Bugliosi tried to have the witness demonstrate the same manner and inflation of voice he had used at the time he spoke to the man. Hatami did so, but didn't seem to get angry.

He described the man as thin, about thirty to thirty-two years old, with long dark brown or nearly black hair and a stubble of a beard.

Hatami continued saying, "I had the impression the man was 'upset' as he walked away on a path because the man didn't say anything like 'I'm sorry.' He just walked to the back alley.

Mr. Kanarek objected and asked Judge Older to strike down from the record the last statement.

His Honor sustained the objection.

"What happened next?" inquired Mr. Bugliosi.

"Sharon came out for about four or five seconds," answered the witness.

"Could the man see Sharon?" asked the prosecutor.

"He could have easily seen her," answered Hatami, who went on saying that the honey-blonde actress didn't say anything to the man nor did the man say anything to Sharon Tate.

Mr. Bugliosi stated then he didn't have anymore questions at the moment, but later, Judge Older interrupted the prosecutor and said, "Do you have any more questions which the jurors shouldn't hear?"

"Yes, Your Honor," replied the deputy district attorney.

"Alright, I'll ask the bailiff to remove the jury and take them upstairs," added the judge.

The jurors mumbled among themselves as soon as they were led out of the courtroom.

"We're nothing but seventeen mindless idiots," said Betty, while sitting with her legs propped up on the chaise longue—her favorite position.

Mr. Welch, seated by the window overlooking the Pasadena Freeway North, asked Olivia who was reading a magazine, "Did you bring your dictionary?"

"No, I forgot it," replied the juror.

"What word are you trying to find?" I asked.

"Facts," answered Mr. Welch.

"Facts?" I repeated.

"Yes, facts—that's what they're trying to do. They (lawyers) are trying to find out some facts for us to consider later."

"Yes," Betty said sarcastically.

"They're rehearsing the scene."

I laughed.

"She's right, they're rehearsing the scene," interjected Mr. Welch. "You know, the last scene."

Then, directing his attention to me, he added, "What do they call it when a play has been rehearsed and then they have the last scene—you know, the last night? What do they call it Bill?"

"You mean the dress rehearsal," I said.

"That's right, the dress rehearsal. That's what they're doing downstairs. They are dress rehearsing so we could see the final scene."

"Well, let's hope they give a good performance," said Betty, almost to herself, as she knitted a pair of moccasin slipper.

"They must be sifting what they want us to hear," added Olivia.

Olivia, since I disclosed that I was writing notes about the jurors as well as about the case, had ceased to offer any comments and avoided to give any information of herself. She was afraid I would publicize her intimate private life. She avoided me.

While sitting in the smallest of the two jury rooms, I couldn't help to notice each one of the jurors. Gradually, I studied each juror individually and the mere fact Olivia rejected my company, I opted to describe her first in my notes.

Olivia was slow in her reflexes, slow in her manners. One would say she was about sixty years old. She had a very light, dry skin complexion. She had dyed blonde hair but wore a small wig piece which covered part of her forehead, in sort of bangs. To attach both her hair and wig, she used a bow with a pin underneath. She wore bows of different colors, according to what color dress she wore. The pinkish makeup of her face was unevenly distributed, especially around her wrinkles and eyes. Because she didn't apply talcum powder to her face thoroughly, she left uncovered spots which appeared

253

as slick, shiny areas and it gave her the appearance as if she had been perspiring. Her eye shadow was also badly applied. She used black eye shadow which seemed too dark for her white complexion. Again, because she spread it at random, she left ugly looking little black spots, suggesting as if she had blackheads around her eyes. She used black derma pencil above her natural eyebrow line. Her thin-looking lips were covered with a vivid red-colored lipstick, which she constantly kept applying.

Olivia was a difficult person to get to know and she never tried or offered conversation. In some instances, she spoke brilliantly.

We returned to court at 4:00 P.M. Mr. Fitzgerald and Mr. Kanarek passed their rights to interrogate the witness. However, Mr. Kanarek asked the judge to write off the entire testimony of Shahrokh Hatami because it was irrelevant and had no connection with Mr. Manson. His objection was denied.

Twice, Judge Older told Mr. Kanarek that he had the opportunity to cross examine the witness.

Why didn't he? Why Mr. Fitzgerald and especially Mr. Kanarek, representing Charles Manson, didn't ask questions was beyond my comprehension. Obviously, they couldn't deny the fact that the witness was telling the truth.

Under cross-examination, Mr. Hughes, bushy-bearded and long-haired himself, asked Hatami, "Are you a hippie?"

The witness, with dirty-looking long hair and wearing a wrinkled suit, which he probably used for special occasions only, replied, "No Sir, I am not, sorry."

The answer brought a good laugh for obvious reasons.

On Wednesday morning, everybody commented about the new look of my hair. The night before, the barber discussed with me the possibilities of changing the style of my hair. Upon his recommendation, I combed my hair differently, but it lasted only one day. I just couldn't take it. I felt conscious and embarrassed. The mirror reflected a different me. I didn't like it! Funny? Sure I felt funny. My face had a different shape. My forehead was covered with bangs and my ears hidden under curls. Yuk! I looked ridiculous. Happily, the next day I went to court with the "old" look of the natural way of combing my hair.

Witness No. 66 was Rudolph Altobelli, who stated he was a personal manager for actors and actresses. He owned the estate where Sharon Tate lived at the time she was slain. He said he knew Terry Melcher, a former tenant of the same premises. He rented the house to Roman Polanski for for $ 1200 a month in February, 1969. He met Charles Manson at Danny

254

Wilson's home, a member of the Beach Boys musical group, on Sunset Boulevard in the summer of 1969. Gregg Jacobson was present and two or three girls. They were listening to a tape that Charles Manson had recorded.

On direct examination by Mr. Bugliosi, the witness testified that at approximately 8:00 or 9:00 A.M. he was taking a shower when he heard one of his dogs—Christopher—bark. He went to the door and he saw Charles Manson, who introduced himself. Mr. Kanarek objected as hearsay but was overruled. The witness continued his testimony by stating that the defendant was alone, had entered and already passed the screen door.

Altobelli, a sharp-looking dressed man, observed that before the accused finished introducing himself, he remembered him. The witness then said he asked Charles Manson if he had gone to the front house and the latter responded, "Yes." He told the defendant that he didn't like anyone to disturb his tenants and that he was busy getting ready to leave the country.

"Where?" said the witness Charles Manson asked him.

"Rome," Altobelli said he answered, "I have two clients that are making a film there."

Charles Manson then proceeded to say he was making a film himself, to which the witness said he replied, "Yes, I know you're talented," and then excused himself.

Mr. Bugliosi asked the court to have Charles Manson brought into the courtroom to be identified. Surprisingly, the defendant came out without a beard, but still with long hair. The prisoner was smiling and in a way he did look rather handsome. The hippie cult leader had tried to disguise himself, thus why he shaved off his beard. Charles Manson remained silent and expressionless as Altobelli pointed him out as the same man who had talked to him.

Mr. Fitzgerald again declined his right to ask questions of the witness.

Mr. Shin wanted to know the circumstances as to when the witness met Charles Manson at Danny Wilson's.

Mr. Altobelli, as he rubbed his hair, replied that because he was a personal manager, he checked up and down—everybody—especially those with talent.

"Where down?" inquired Mr. Shin.

"I don't know," answered the witness.

"Did you look into his eyes?"

"I don't look into anybody's eyes. I think it's rude."

"Well, you said that you checked Mr. Manson up and down when you first met him. Is that right?" asked Mr. Shin again.

"Yes, I noticed he has a gap in his front teeth. I like to look into people's teeth."

On cross-examination by Mr. Kanarek, Altobelli played with the stocky attorney like a cat with a mouse. At one point, Altobelli hurled question after question at the defense lawyer. Spectators and reporters sat there enthralled at the spectacle. It wasn't often that we jurors saw that sort of a witness.

Mr. Kanarek began asking questions to the witness as why Mr. Altobelli didn't want Mr. Kanarek to go to the residence where Sharon Tate lived and check the premises. Immediately, the witness erupted in a calm and composed manner and responded that that wasn't what he had told him.

Before the jurors could write down the dialogue of questions and answers, there was a speedy, almost shouting exchange of statements between defense counsel and the witness.

It seemed, according to the witness, Mr. Kanarek had phoned him and wanted to visit the house. The owner of the estate would allow no one into the house unless provided with a court order. Mr. Kanarek, upset with the answer, had told Altobelli, "We'll take care of you. We'll hold the entire trial in your house. You wait and see."

Things became excited in the courtroom. Mr. Kanarek and Mr. Altobelli held the most heated conversation between counsel and witness since the beginning of the trial.

Progressively, the argument reached a high point and Mr. Bugliosi objected as being argumentative and emotional on the part of Kanarek. The defense counsel admitted he was a bit emotional due to the false accusation from the witness. Then it became almost personal.

Manson's attorney stated that Altobelli really didn't have respect or regard for the law. The witness, overpowering the defense counsel, denied emphatically and in a loud voice exclaimed, "I didn't say that. What I said was: 'The law would be a circus whenever Mr. Kanarek would be present'."

Practically all the jurors responded with a hearty laugh of approval and were joined by the general audience and reporters. Judge Older smiled subtly.

Unconsciously at that moment, I had been observing Mr. Fitzgerald's face. He was looking and listening to Mr. Kanarek. His look was of disbelief, as if he would be saying to himself, "You, jackass—you're too much, man! Just too much! Boy, they must have scraped the bottom of the American Bar Association to get you up here."

Upset with a feeling of patience and tolerance, Mr. Fitzgerald turned around and unexpectedly caught my look. He knew I had been staring at him— watching him. He couldn't help but smile at me. He felt and knew I was reading his thoughts. Mr. Fitzgerald sensed that his feelings had been revealed

256

and exposed because of the dislike he showed toward the preposterous and ridiculous performance of his partner. The tall defense counsel also sensed he couldn't do anything, but sit and wait. That's why when he caught my eye he read my feelings. We both knew—we both sensed as if we had something in common in regard to Mr. Kanarek's line of questions. We couldn't help but smile, with good inner satisfaction.

Mr. Fitzgerald abruptly changed his attitude and looked down at a piece of paper in front of him. In one or two minutes later, again in unity, we both raised our heads and looked at one another. No smiles, no extra presensory look, just a look as if we were saying, "It's alright, we know him, don't we?"

Mr. Kanarek continued his cross-examination and asked the witness about the whereabouts of Robert Conrad, a man who happened to answer the phone at Mr. Altobelli's home on a Sunday noon.

Lunch hour arrived and we were dismissed.

In the afternoon, Mr. Kanarek continued his interrogation and wanted to know how many people were at a party given by Mr. and Mrs. Polanski and if there were many wearing long hair.

"Yes. Women," replied Altobelli, causing laughter.

Looking at the audience, I noticed Sal Mineo was seated in the rear. He was wearing a white turtleneck sweater.

"I mean men with long hair," explained Mr. Kanarek.

"Roman Polanski has long hair down to his shoulders," said the witness and smiled.

"Why do you smile?" inquired the stocky lawyer.

"Because I see Mr. Hughes's hair—is long," replied Altobelli.

The courtroom crowd roared with laughter. One of the reporters looked at Mr. Hughes back and acted disgusted as if she could smell the bearded attorney's hair.

All the questions asked by Leslie Van Houten's lawyer were objected and sustained. Twice in a row, Judge Older had to ask Mr. Hughes to sit down if he didn't have any more questions but the shabby attorney asked Altobelli, "Did Jay Sebring ever whip you?"

"That will be all, Mr. Hughes. Your examination is over."

Mr. Hughes objected but nevertheless, Mr. Bugliosi started his brief redirect examination which consisted to verify if the man called Robert Conrad was the known actor by the same name.

"No, he is a different person," responded the witness and was dismissed."

Charles David Koenig, a Standard Oil Company employee, testified about finding the wallet of murder victim, Rosemary La Bianca, on December 10,

1969.

The tall, blonde witness, speaking nervously, said he found the wallet hidden in a toilet bowl at a Sylmar gas station where he worked.

Court adjourned at 4:30 P.M.

That night was bowling night, and boy! Finally a romance broke down between two jurors. You guessed it. Tom Brooks and Debbie Hart.

Betty and I bowled on the same lane. The clique would only play two games and then moved on to the bar escorted by Kathy Colvig. Between drinks and laughter, Ray would dance with Violet and especially with the attractive deputy Colvig, whose husband was also a deputy sheriff working for the County Sheriff's Department.

Tom and Debbie would only dance with each other. The way they clung to each other was enough to make one wonder they were attracted to one another. Nothing had been thought about it. However, that evening, they were closer than they had been before. On the way back to the hotel, there was no singing, no comments, no noise. The clique was quiet. I couldn't understand their silence. Curiously, I turned my head to see the jurors seated behind me.

Back at the rear of the bus, I caught the silohuettes of Tom and Debbie kissing—he caressing her hands, her face; she doing likewise. They were unresponsive to my watching. Then, startled, they discovered that I had turned back to watch them.

They stopped. They sat in silence and looked outside as the street lights crept inside the bus and shadows flashed upon their faces. Debbie was not having much to say, but watching Tom, liking him in spite of herself. They resumed their necking. They kissed and kissed some more.

In a little while, the bus arrived at the hotel. Yet, there were other sessions in the bus.

Soon afterward, Genaro Swanson had a visitor. It was Debbie. She would walk into his room and talk for a few minutes. Tom occupied a room next to Genaro's and across from Ray's. But it was difficult to determine whether it was Genaro she had gone to visit, or Tom.

Debbie was quickly assimilated into their group. Tom and Ray both enjoyed drinking beer—life at the hotel was not boring—they enjoyed talking together. After that, Debbie came often to Ray's room with Tom joining them later. This series of drinking meetings led eventually to a closer relationship among them, which gradually changed their behavior through the end of the trial.

Debbie changed considerably and I was astonished and shocked when I discovered that, in reality, she was having an affair with Tom.

Her change perhaps didn't seem obvious to others as it seemed to me. She appeared more attractive, more radiant, more coquettish, which invariably produced a new outlook in her life. She probably displayed qualities of happiness which she never knew she possessed. She used her entire charm and desired to live it up!

Nevertheless, she was quite capable of becoming unfaithful and never inferred in the presence of her husband on the weekends, the slightest pang of remorse. So as not to impoverish her relationship with her husband, she would remain in her room the entire weekend—outside the door she would hang the sign Do not Disturb provided by the hotel and, written on a piece of paper, she would indicate to the maid, not to bother making up the bed, just leave towels outside the door.

She managed to succeed in making her husband happy and content and every weekend, he would stay overnight. In the morning he would go to the recreation room, wearing his bath robe, where we had breakfast served. He would fill two plates with scrambled eggs, sausages and potatoes, coffee, and sometimes, sweet rolls. She wouldn't even return the dishes—she would leave them outside as not to be seen and give her husband the impression of harmony in their life.

Tom appeared to be humble and helpless, but frequently, he was demanding and aggressive in his conversation. He avoided making decisions or testing his ability because he was afraid of being unmasked. He didn't want the rest of the jurors to know what was really inside him because he thought it was very different from what he was presenting to the jurors. As a result, he became selfish and overly concerned with himself. In some ways, Tom's behavior was the same as Debbie's. His wife Claudia would arrive early Saturday morning and feed breakfast to their two children. Tom remained in his room while Claudia would bring him breakfast in bed.

Betty Clark couldn't believe it. The slim-looking juror avoided expressing her views openly because she knew of my taking notes for a book. However, one night, as we were escorted for a walk, Betty exclaimed, "It's sickening. How dumb can their spouses be. Both serving Tom and Debbie in bed. Hmph. . . . if they only knew what's going on during the week. Oh well, I guess they will be the last ones to find out."

During lunch hours at the Hilton, Deb and Tom finally managed to sit together. They made the issue a laughing matter as to disguise their intent. They would sit next to each other and during the meal, he would occasionally clasp her wrists and she would look at him radiantly and beautifully. For a

259

moment, they would just stare at each other, no words or sounds would come from their mouths. Gradually, they would break the spell and with unutterable joy, they would smile into each other's eyes and resume their meal.

I had been thinking about Laura. She had not come to the pool, and when I phoned her, she was never home. I didn't see Laura that weekend.

On Sunday morning, Betty, George and others, including myself, were ready to go to the pool. After a while, we were told there were no bailiffs available to escort us. Betty and George, attired in sports clothes, opted to pace back and forth the entire length of the hall. The rest of the jurors annoyedly locked themselves in their rooms.

I decided to transcribe my handwritten trial notes into typing format. Betty and George asked me to please leave the door open so they could listen to my tape music. Eventually, they stopped by my door and informed me that they couldn't see why the jurors weren't allowed to go downstairs.

They pointed out three deputies who had been stationed outside my door and chatted for almost three hours.

The two jurors relieved themselves of their frustrations as they expressed their gripes. Other jurors had, at various occasions, mentioned the lack of cordiality and friendship between bailiffs and jurors.

"Bastards," Betty said angrily.

"Hey, Bill," uttered George, "why don't you write a letter to Judge Older? You're pretty good at that sort of thing."

I didn't say anything, just smiled. Deep inside I was also burning with anger.

"I'm not going to write anything," observed Betty. "One of these nights, I'll be walking out of here—straight home!"

"How?" I inquired.

"It's easy," responded Betty, "just walk down the stairs. The bailiffs are too busy watching television."

"Nobody sees you," interjected George, and added, "It's true, Bill."

Betty and George left my room. So I sat down and wrote a letter to the judge using the Ambassador Hotel's stationery.

The Honorable Charles H. Older
Superior Court No. 104
Los Angeles, California
Sir:

I'm writing this letter reluctantly, against my own wishes, but because of the attitude and behavior of some bailiffs I'm obliged to inform you, hoping something could be done to remediate the situation.

Although I'm solely expressing my feelings you can be assured that all the jurors feel just as indignant as I do.

I know your time is valuable and needless to say you are a very busy man, on the other hand you know we the jurors because having being sequestered, have lots of time to think about things of little importance, things which ordinarily wouldn't occupy one tenth of a second of our minds had we the freedom to roam around our own homes and to do as we please. But we are not at home—we know that and we accept it. We also know that we can't expect to have as much choice of doing things, things as we do them outside in our own free environment. But when these little things are taken away from us simply because of attitude of bailiffs in charge of us, and which in no way affects nor breaks the rules of what you have admonished us, then these little things become very important, especially when these little things are 'very few'.

Please advise me if we are wrong... but we would like to know... isn't the duty of these bailiffs to see that we the jurors are kept in a maximum of cordiality among bailiffs and ourselves? Isn't the duty of the bailiffs to see that we make the best out of the surroundings especially due to the length of time we have and will spend away from our homes and dear ones? Are these bailiffs here with the purpose of guarding us day and night? Are they? Because if they do, they are doing it in a very unguarded manner... like many times they are sound asleep at night, while on duty. Do they suppose to sleep while on duty? It is known fact among jurors that anybody can walk anytime at night or shall I repeat what two jurors stated? They said: 'Anyone of us could get killed and the bailiffs would be the last ones to know.'

Or like the times a weekend bailiff is performing his duties with smell of alcohol in his or her breath... is that a proper and correct manner to conduct his duties as a law enforcement officer? What kind of respect can one display to a Deputy Sheriff who's responsible under your oath to supervise as a bailiff under such circumstances? I'm sure you would feel as repugnant as we do if one of the counsels presents himself under the same condition in court, especially if they go to your private chambers as a couple bailiffs have come to my room. What would you think, Your Honor?

Now, we are allowed one telephone call per day. That's fine. No complaint about it... but if one makes a phone call and one can't hear nor can't be heard at the other end, all because the bailiff is watching TV with the sound of it blasting out loud, well that is something else. It is bad enough to wait until 'commercial time' to have him dial the desired number but to have to scream, to shout loud on the phone because the noise around us, coming from the

TV set is too loud. Result, no one can hear during the conversation on the telephone. One doesn't dare to ask anyone of these guards to tone down the volume, that would be practically impossible. Would you tell me... are these bailiffs being paid to come to the hotel to watch TV?...to watch their favorite TV programs and telecast events? Because that's all they do. No one cares if they do or not watch TV, provided they attend their duties first.

Other times, we have to wait until they have finished watching the end of a TV program to take us down to the pool area. Usually this does happen when we come from court every day. 10 or 15 minutes are precious for us, considering that if we don't go on time the sun is gone. It happens every day... 4 or 6 jurors all dressed in swimming and gym attires waiting and even begging to be taken down in front of the elevator, only to have one of us finally drag the bailiff away from the TV set; when she finally does it, you can be sure her face is far from happy.

We realize that there is shortness of manpower but today, the excuse was beyond my tolerance and patience. Today, Sunday, it was a very beautiful day, sunny and pleasant... a perfect day to go out... well there were at least 3 jurors plus myself who wanted to go down to the pool... it was exactly 10:25 A.M. We wanted to go out and breathe all the air we could get in our lungs, just as long as we could be outside for a little while. Did we? You guess it, no, we didn't. We were told that lunch hour was at noon and that there was not enough time. Now for your information, the pool is just outside the elevator, a very short distance, even shorter than going down to the coffee shop. One hour and one half of sunshine on the weekend is worth a lot to us, since we can't even see the sun from the jail bus opaque windows on weekdays, less enjoy it. Is that asking too much? The truth why we weren't taken down was because the bailiffs (3 of them) were having a nice, interesting chat, they couldn't be bothered. I watched them closely, they were talking outside of my room all the time until 2:30 P.M. You figure it out why. I can't.

We don't expect to be treated like children nor like flowers but certainly not like seventeen mindless prisoners. We are serving as jurors and we regard it as the most important civil function we have to perform but when the boundaries of our essential needs are taken away from us, when we are deprived of our simple way of living, without breaking nor evading orders from you, Your Honor, then is time someone should speak up, is time someone should say what is going on. No one gets anywhere suffering silently and in dignity.

Quoting from the juror's creed I shall close this letter by saying: 'As a juror

I understand the importance of my function and I will perform it.'

Very truly yours,
William M. Zamora
Juror No. 7

I hesitated to mail the letter. Then I showed it to Mildred, Betty and George at separate times. They approved and encouraged me to send it. I did.
Back in court.

Due to the new schedule of court sessions, the courtroom was practically empty. Gradually, the newspaper reporters began filling the seats.

Mollie Kane, who ushered the public to their seats, told us that if the members of the press arrived in court fifteen minutes later than when the session begins, then they lose their seats to somebody else.

After having approached the bench, Mr. Fitzgerald began assembling the accused's chairs. Judge Older called Deputies Taylor and Tull and told them to bring down the defendants.

Charlie walked in clean shaven and carried an electric shaver in his hands. Manson said, "Good Morning" to Judge Older but received no reply. Charlie's clean face made him look younger. The receding hairline on his forehead gave the indication of being an intelligent man; however, the long hair tied in a pony tail fashion made him appear to be a pirate bucaneer.

Rose Anne Walker, a former cellmate of Susan Atkins at Sybil Brand Institute, testified about conversations she had with the defendant about the Tate-LaBianca murders while both were inmates.

Mrs. Walker, a young overweight-looking woman, indicated she and the defendant were listening to a broadcast of the Tate-LaBianca murders on the radio when Sadie made a comment, "That ain't the way it went down."

While constantly kicking with her feet the inarticulate witness went on to say that Susan Atkins made another comment as when the police were looking for a person whose glasses were found at the Tate residence. According to the witness, Susan Atkins said, "Just because the glasses were there doesn't mean that that person was there."

Harold True, a graduate student at California State College, Los Angeles, testified that he lived at 3267 Waverly Drive.

The hippie bald-headed witness said he had met Charles Manson in March of 1967 at his residence in Topanga Canyon. True stated that Manson and members of his "family" visited him several times when he lived at 3267 Waverly Drive, next door to the house where the La Biancas were slain.

Under questioning by Mr. Bugliosi, True said he thought the house next door was vacant at the time he lived on Waverly Drive, and that the La Biancas moved there after he had left for Ethiopia on a tour of service with the Peace Corps.

According to True, Linda Kasabian and her husband had visited him at that address before she joined the Manson "family" in July of 1969.

Terry Melcher, record producer, son of actress Doris Day, walked into the courtroom through the same door Judge Older and the jurors entered.

The collar-length dark-blond hair witness testified that he met Charles Manson at the house of Dennis Wilson, drummer for the Beach Boys musical group.

On direct examination by Mr. Bugliosi, Melcher explained that on one occasion—September 1968—while visiting at Danny Wilson's house, he heard Charles Manson's tape recorded singing in the background. That same day, the witness said he was driven by Wilson to his home at 10050 Cielo Drive, the estate where Sharon Tate and four others were later killed.

"That day," Melcher stated, "Charlie was in the back seat of the car, humming and playing his guitar." The witness added that Manson and Wilson didn't enter the house.

Terry Melcher, a six footer and wearing a tieless beige gabardine sport suit appeared bored and restless. The bushy moustached witness said that Gregg Jacobson spoke to him quite often about Charles Manson's musical talent and even asked him about one hundred times to go to the ranch to audition the defendant.

Mr. Bugliosi, under great strain, finally succeeded in getting comprehensive answers from the witness-son of Doris Day.

Melcher described his impressions when he went twice to the Spahn Ranch in Chatsworth in May 1969 to hear Manson play a guitar and sing.

He observed that the people at the ranch were mostly girls and some guys. They all went to the stream bed in an orderly fashion—single file—maybe because of the narrow path and at approximately equal distances from each other. They descended to the bottom of the stream by using a rope. Charles Manson sat on a big rock and sang about ten songs. Everybody sat around the hippie cult leader and listened to his songs which were mostly spoken with guitar music in the background. The "family" would sing along and laughed as Charlie would say some joke.

"That was the audition," the witness said. "It lasted two hours. I was not impressed with the songs. I was mostly impressed with the scene—by Charlie's strength and obvious leadership he had over those people. Those people surviving under such conditions—in tents. You know."

Asked by Mr. Bugliosi if he considered Charles Manson a good singer, Melcher answered, "I was not impressed with his singing. I classified him as an average singer." Then, looking out into the spectators, Melcher added, "I've been producing records for a long time, so I know what's good."

The witness went on to say that before he left the ranch, he spoke with the defendant about generalities of the record business. Upon his departure, he gave Charles Manson everything he had in his pocket—about fifty dollars, hoping it was not construed as payment for services.

A few days later, Terry Melcher said he went back with Michael Deasy, a guitar player who owned a mobile trailer to record Charles Manson's singing at the stream bed while seated on the rock.

According to the witness, "The performance the second time was identical except that the first time it appeared spontaneous. The second seemed... pretty rehearsed."

The final question of Mr. Bugliosi was in regards to a telescope the son of the movie star owned at the time he was living at Malibu Beach.

"It disappeared in July 1969," replied the witness. "I know for sure because I had a gathering on July 4 of that year. I never did get it back."

On cross-examination by Defense Attorney Mr. Fitzgerald, Terry Melcher repeated in different words that he was impressed with the unity and strength of the group he found at Spahn ranch.

"They seemed to have a lot of freedom," he said.

"They seemed to be living by their own rules, their own laws. They seemed to be a principality within Los Angeles County."

Upon concluding his interrogation, Mr. Shin wanted to know whether the witness and Manson parted as friends.

"That's what I thought," replied Melcher as he looked at the defendant.

Mr. Kanarek stood up and announced, "Since Mr. Melcher says he still considers himself a friend of Mr. Manson, there's no reason to cross-examine."

Judge Older immediately faced the jurors and admonished us to disregard Mr. Kanarek's statement. Then, severely addressing Manson's attorney, warned him again from making such remarks and concluded by saying, "Your statement made before the jury was totally inappropriate and you know it."

We were dismissed for lunch.

While at the Hilton, the topic of conversation was Terry Melcher.

"All I can say is that he may be the son of Doris Day, whom personally I admire and like through her singing, movies and TV shows," said Ruth

Collingwood, an avid moviegoer, "but this fellow, this son of hers, surely reflects an arrogant, uneducated man."

Edith, an ex-English teacher, interjected and said, "He may be a producer or call it what you please, but surely he doesn't talk intelligently nor appears to be smart."

"Oh, he got the job because of his mother," added Ruth.

"Wait a minute," I interrupted.

The two lady jurors stared at me.

"Smart he is," I continued, "anyone going steady with Candice Bergen can't be that dumb." They smiled, agreeing with me.

That afternoon, back in court...

Stephanie Scham, an eighteen-year-old girl, testified that she met Charles Manson at a gas station. She was with a friend and the cultist asked her if she wanted to go up to Big Sur. She said yes and left her male friend. They spent about three days at Big Sur, returned, and stayed one day at the Spahn ranch. She became a member of the family.

During her testimony, Miss Scham never ceased from smiling. Charlie refused to look at her. She smiled only at the three female defendants.

Mr. Bugliosi, under a rain of objections, managed to ask the witness if Charlie ever discussed "killing."

"Yes," replied the witness, and mentioned the names of those who were present at the time she heard the conversation. Judge Older told us to disregard the last answer.

Miss Scham testified that in August and September of 1969, she spoke with Manson about being homesick. During the September conversation which took place in the desert, she mentioned that Charlie noticed that she wanted to go home so he hit her a couple of times with the butt of a rifle and knocked her down.

Charlie tightened his teeth with anger and stared at the witness intrinsically. He began making signs at her like carrying a baby in his arms. Miss Scham shrugged her shoulders and frowned to let the defendant know she didn't understand what his gesture meant. Nor we, the jurors.

We returned to the hotel.

As soon as the jurors stepped out of the elevator, those heading to their rooms, made some remarks about the changes in the corridor. Before closing my room door, I noticed the TV set placed outside Debbie's room was gone. The bailiff was reading a book.

"Bill," whispered George, "your letter got some results. Both TV sets have been removed."

I walked towards the little lobby and effectively, the other TV set was also gone. The whole atmosphere seemed quieter. I was astonished and somehow felt sorry for the bailiffs on duty. However, when I realized that they were being paid to protect us and not to watch TV, I no longer felt guilty.

Except for those jurors whom I had shown the letter, no one else knew. The other jurors wondered but dared not to ask why of the disappearance of the TV sets. Everybody however was content in being able to make phone calls without having to scream. The only juror that appeared unhappy with the change was Martin Paine, who befriended every deputy on duty.

That same evenlng, Deputy Taylor knocked on my door to tell me that Captain Arden was on the phone. I trembled, not knowing what to expect. Deputy Taylor led me to his room and left the room.

Captain Arden told me Judge Older had given him my letter and then said he (Arden) would come to the hotel to discuss the grievances mentioned in the letter. He thanked me for writing the letter and hung up.

Deputy Taylor was waiting outside and gave me a serious look. The corners of his lips were tightened. He wondered what it was, the reason for Captain Arden calling me, and behind his expression, his mind was in a whirl and he felt a sense of curiosity.

I was too tired to worry about it, so I headed back to my room. I needed a certain amount of solitude, locked the door and drifted off to sleep.

Back in court...

A number of less important witnesses paraded through the stand to testify minor points of interest to the trial.

Janet Marie Owens, butch-looking and an ex-inmate who met Susan Atkins at Sybil Brand Institute, identified a letter she received from the defendant on December 18, 1969, at a long Beach address.

Lila Koelker, a sheriff deputy of Los Angeles County, assigned as housing officer of Cell Blocks No. 4000 and No. 5000 at Sybil Brand Institute, described the procedure of outgoing mail at the prison.

"Isn't that silly," said Manson, looking up at Judge Older as the latter was stating the testimony should be considered only against Susan Atkins.

Carolyn Alley, lieutenant sheriff deputy at Sybil Brand Institute, testified that she was aware of letters written by Susan Atkins. The witness stated that signs are posted regarding regulations about letters being censored and if there is an indication of criminal activity, they bring it to the attention of the investigation agency in charge of such jurisdiction of someone interested.

John Wm. McKeller, Sr., police sergeant in the City of Mobile, Alabama, testified he placed Patricia Krenwinkel under arrest in December 1969, in the city of Mobile.

Speaking in a very southern accent, the witness said that he and another officer saw a car pass by with a white female who was wearing a hat. He observed the female cover her face on both sides. They followed and stopped the car at the intersection of Higgans and Buck Hill Road.

Patricia Krenwinkel gave her name as Mary Montgomery but he recognized her as the subject the police were looking for and placed her under arrest.

We were dismissed for lunch.

Seated opposite me at the same table was Mildred Osborne. Since I wasn't too hungry, I opted to observe and write about her.

Mildred was always attired elegantly, blossomed out in resplendent colors, and every detail was considered carefully in her fashionable way of dressing. She would gaze at exemplars and copied them to fit her needs.

Her ensembles would consist of matching outfits with corresponding color of shoes, earrings and dress pins—she knew how to combine patterns and colors. She was constantly studying new knitting stitches and peered at magazines to copy the latest fashionable sweaters, shawls and even long-knit coats —she would ceaselessly knit until she ran out of yarn. She looked upon this as her only diversion and she worked hard at it. She developed and practiced small crafty devices and chatty gambits to gain recognition among the jurors, like being extremely polite. She dressed well—she spoke kindly—she walked swiftly like a feather; in fact, Mildred brought feminine relief to the starved jurors, even though she was on the heavy side. Later, she reduced considerably.

Of her personal life, little was known about Mildred. Although married, she seemed to have a bad relationship with her husband. Her supervising position surely reflected an intelligent woman and that might have accounted for her differences with her spouse. Mildred's unemployed husband was no challenge for her and it reflected whenever they sat together or joined in Sunday outings.

The natural redhaired juror befriended George Kiefer and his wife. One time, George confided me she was to obtain a divorce as soon as the trial was over. He also mentioned that Mildred had told him her husband didn't approve of the seven wigs she owned.

Mildred, to the last minute of the time we were sequestered, rendered to her credit the honor to conduct herself like an educated person.

Brooks Poston, an ex-member of the family and presently residing in the desert town of Shoshone with another former family member, Paul Watkins, testified basically the issues of Manson's philosophy.

Poston, a thin, long-haired blonde, staring wide-eyed, said he met the cult leader in the summer of 1968 at the home of Dennis Wilson.

Under questioning by Mr. Bugliosi, the witness candidly explained how he joined the family.

Poston, by his own admission, said, "I didn't know very much. I just left home and I asked Charlie if I could join him. Charlie then asked me if I could make love to a girl in front of twenty-five people."

Poston, like other past witnesses, described the way the family lived at the ranch. But most important of all, the witness strongly believed and was convinced that Charles Manson was Jesus Christ.

Under questioning by Mr. Bugliosi, the witness stated, "Charlie said that the Karma was coming—that it was the turn of the white to become slaves of the negro. He said the black was going to arise and cover the white—like night covers the day. After blackie had the world, he'd see he didn't want it because it was too much responsibility and he'd give it over to Charlie."

Poston, talking as if he was in front of a group of alcoholic anonymous members, appeared somwhat relieved of disclosing what he knew and felt about Charles Manson.

He continued saying that Manson spoke to the family and told them, "Shit was coming. That Helter Skelters were coming down—that they were going to the desert and go down—that the pigs needed a good whacking."

Asked by Mr. Fitzgerald, Poston said that Manson told him of being convinced the Beatles were speaking to him directly via their songs. He stated that the cultist thought he heard the words, "block that Nixon," on a Beatle song entitled "Revolution 9."

Avoiding to see the defendant, Poston added, "Charlie related this to Revelation 9 in the Bible. There are no lyrics in that song but that is what Charlie thought he heard in the part of the record where you heard machine guns and the oinking of pigs."

Under Mr. Kanarek's cross-examination, Poston testified, "Charlie told me to die. He was trying to convince me to die. Charlie told me 'You are a lifetime behind, you will have to give it up.'"

Then startling, the witness, a pathetic thin-looking young man, added, "And then Charlie ordered me to lay down and die, but I couldn't figure how to do it."

Still hard to believe, the witness said that over a several-months' period, he stopped as much as possible all physical activities—like eating, drinking water, and so forth.

Mr. Kanarek, following his customary line of questions, asked the witness to enumerate the times Charles Manson had asked him to die.

Painfully slow, Poston took long pauses to relate the occasions. Manson's attorney managed the witness to concede that he was never physically threatened with death by the cult leader. Mr. Kanarek argued that his client was talking about the death of Poston's ego and not the death of his body.

When asked by the stocky lawyer what death meant to him, Poston replied, "I believe in two kinds of death—death of an ego and carnal death. Death of an ego is when one gets off the big white horse, when one stops being pompous, and carnal death, which I have seen...like when my father died...that is physical death."

For a moment, the witness spoke as if he had come to life. He spoke with more authority and answered the questions faster.

"Were you aware when Mr. Manson spoke to you?" asked Mr. Kanarek.

"At the time he spoke to me, I tried to do what he told me to do—I gave myself mentally to Charlie."

Unexpectedly, Manson spoke out loud and said, "Did I ever tell you to do anything? I told you to do what YOU wanted to do."

"Why did you come to testify?" asked Mr. Kanarek again.

"Because my mind told me so," answered the witness.

"You haven't any mind to do anything!" the hippie leader spoke up as he rose from his chair.

"That will be enough Mr. Manson," Judge Older interjected, and then by the suggestion of Mr. Bugliosi, His Honor admonished the jurors to disregard the comments.

Paul Watkins, twenty years old, 5′5″ tall and weighing 125 pounds, testified he met Charles Manson in the spring time of 1968. The hippie-young looking witness said he was hitchhiking from Big Sur when Brenda (a family member) gave him a ride and asked if he wanted to go to the ranch and see Charlie. Watkins acceded and became a member of the family.

Under direct examination by Mr. Bugliosi, Watkins stated that Charlie asked him 'to recruit girls to come to the ranch' but that the defendant scared them off because he looked like the devil.

"What did he say?" inquired the prosecutor.

"He told me to go out and get girls without touching them and bring them to the ranch, but I didn't do it too much because I was sort of busy with the girls at the ranch."

Following testimony of how each member met the hippie cult leader, the witness excitedly related issues pertaining to Manson's philosophy.

Helter Skelter, taken from a Beatle's song, signified the Karma was coming.

Watkins explained Manson's theory in a rather different manner, maybe because he had a close association with the defendant.

According to the witness, "the whitey daughters were going to live in San Francisco—then the blackies, unable to satisfy their frustrations, would turn against the establishment. There would be atrocious crimes from Watts into Bel Air, Beverly Hills, up into the rich districts, and make the establishment upset, who in turn, would go shooting all blacks—but only blacks from the ghetto when underneath they were the real killers. The blacks would come up and say 'look what you're doing to my people.' Whites and blacks would fight against each other. The blacks would win and be on top. Then Charlie and his family would go underneath to a bottomless pit. Eventually, the blacks wouldn't be able to hold the reins and the whites would come back again and we would be happy ever after."

"Did you take it seriously?" asked Mr. Bugliosi.

"Yes, indeed," quickly replied the handsome young witness.

"Did Manson appear serious about it?" proceeded the prosecutor.

"Yes," again answered Watkins, and continued saying what Manson had said on one occasion, "The Romans killed the Christians. Today the Romans call themselves Christians, when really, the true Christians had died two thousand years ago with Jesus Christ. Now the Romans are pigs."

Watkins, seated restlessly in the witness stand, testified that Manson had told him he had died on the cross and he was experiencing it all over again he could feel the spear as it went inside his stomach he could feel the nails. Manson told him he was the Christ that died two thousand years ago and that his mission was to complete the Karma of the world.

"He spoke frequently about death," said Watkins, "usually on acid trips at the Spahn ranch and Barker ranch. He was always talking about death —Death is Charles's trip."

Dramatically and absorbingly shocking, the witness related an occasion when Charlie tried to strangle him while taking acid. It seemed that Manson, while being on top of Watkins, was hardening his fingers on the young man's throat until he was going out of air.

The witness observed, "I had given up. Then I heard Charlie say, 'I'm going to kill you.' I couldn't talk, so mentally with my eyes, I resigned to die. Charlie jumped up, smiled and said, 'then if you are willing to die... then you don't have to die,' and then he said, 'let's go and make love.'"

"Did you know Charles Watson?" asked Mr. Bugliosi.

"Oh yes, he was a dumb old country boy. I liked him."

Under cross-examination, Mr. Fitzgerald asked the witness, "Do you know that Charles Watson is a college graduate?"

"Yes, I did. He mentioned that he was a star in college," replied Watkins.

"And you call that dumb?"

"Well, he acted dumb."

Watkins was wearing blue bell-botton slacks, the flair at the bottom pleated in the middle with a grey background. Very unusual. His long sleeve, blue-white stripped shirt had solid white fabric on the collar and cuffs.

Mr. Kanarek, like previous cross-examinations, didn't miss a single opportunity to ask questions which, in reality, didn't add very much to the significance of the real reason why the witness was testifying. Mr. Kanarek wanted the witness to describe the colors and shades he saw while under the influence of LSD.

"No, I won't tell you. It's the most ridiculous questions I've ever heard," said Watkins. "I've taken about 150 to 200 trips and you want me to tell you all the things that I saw and thought. No I won't ."

On redirect examination, Mr. Bugliosi asked, "What did you have to do to become a member of the family?"

"You had to give everything that you own to Charlie."

The witness then said that everybody in the family was willing to do anything for Charlie. Watkins referred to the occasion when Charlie told Sadie to go to Rio de Janeiro and bring back with her one-half of a cocoanut. She started to go out when Charlie stopped her and said, "You don't have to go."

Frank Fowles, district attorney of Inyo County, identified some photos of Myers' and Barker's ranches and their surroundings. According to the witness, the series of photos were taken in his presence and to his knowledge, they depicted a fairly good description of what the locales really looked like.

He described the road leading to Myers Ranch as one of the toughest roads.

"In fact," he said, "it's hardly a road—narrow and inaccessible—one practically has to build it as one drives on. I myself get off and on the vehicle when I go on the road, at certain areas, and let the driver proceed, who to my judgment, has to be a good driver. No ordinary car could take the beating—it would have to be another jeep or a dune buggy."

He also inspected a black-painted school bus where he discovered a massive amount of clothing.

Under cross-examination by Mr. Shin, the witness stated he conducted an experiment at the Myers ranch. He remained in the bedroom while some people were in the kitchen to see if he could hear voices. He also heard water running from the faucet which Mrs. Myers had turned on. The test lasted about fifteen seconds. It was his personal opinion that he could hear the voices in a normal pace and manner.

James Pursell, State Highway Patrol officer, testified that on October 10, 1969, he and his partner proceeded to Barker's ranch. They were joined by two other officers. One of the latter, with the assistance of binoculars, pointed out a dark object in the hillside. It appeared like a hole, at times to be covered —not natural. They saw a figure stretched out, looking around, and then disappeared into the hole. The witness said he ultimately went to the hole which was about 100 or 150 yards from the Myers ranch. He observed a mattress, a sleeping bag, a field telephone, and communication wires leading on top of a ridge about 100 feet further up. He could see good from the hole and even better from the top of the ridge.

Officer Pursell removed three subjects from the hole. One of them was defendant Patricia Krenwinkel, Snake (Diane Lake), and the other he couldn't remember her name.

The defense counsel didn't ask any questions.

After having a recess, Mr. Bugliosi asked the court to have one of the court reporters read out loud from the witness stand three letters which defendant Susan Atkins allegedly had written. It was stipulated that the reading was done for the benefit of the jury.

Exhibits 8, 9, and 11 were expressly submitted as evidence against Susan Atkins. All three letters were written to former cellmates who had been with her at Sybil Brand Institute for Women.

One of the letters, sent to Ronni Howard, contained the passage:

"I can see your side of this clearly. Nor am I mad at you. I am hurt. In a way only I can understand. I blame no one but myself for ever saying anything to anybody about it.

"In the word 'kill' the only thing that dies is the ego. All ego must die anyway, it is written. Yes, it could have been your house or my father's house also. In killing someone physically, you are only releasing the soul. Life has no boundaries and death is only an illusion.

"When I heard you were the informer, I wanted to slit your throat. But then I snapped I was the informer and it was my throat I wanted to cut."

A second letter, mailed to Jo Stevenson in Fisher Lake, Michigan, said:

"Well, because of my big mouth, they just indicted me."

The third letter was sent to Kit Fletcher, a butch-looking woman in Long Beach, and read in part:

"Why did I do it, and why did I open my big mouth to a cellmate? I did what I did because I did it... now I want to save my soul... this body which I don't care."

Judge Older, after conferring with counsel at the bench, addressed the jurors and told them that due to minor technical issues, they were to be taken out of the courtroom.

The first one to complain was Betty. She looked so upset that she didn't allow anyone to talk to her. I sensed her feelings and stayed away. Later, she herself asked me if I was going out to bowl.

"Of course," I responded, "it's one of the few chances we have to go out. Are you going?" I asked her.

"Certainly," she replied before inhaling on a cigarette. "I wouldn't miss it for the world." She exhaled and added, "I just thought of a game while bowling at the same time. You want to join me?"

"What game?" I wanted to know.

"I'll tell you tonight at the bowling alley."

I walked to dinner with George and Danny joined us at the same table. George mentioned that he had heard Deputy Taylor tell the deputies on duty that there was not going to be any televisions on while telephone calls were made. I pretended as if I didn't know anything. Then I expressed how pleasant it was in such a way as to let them know I was the one responsible.

There were no words. George smiled and winking at me, got the message. Danny, although he listened, didn't pay attention or didn't care even when George lifted his glass of water to toast with me for the decision made by Deputy Taylor.

George didn't go bowling. He complained of a bad leg ligament. Danny walked up to the bus with me and to my surprise, he sat behind my seat. While the vehicle was in motion, he leaned over towards me holding himself on the back of my seat and talked during the entire ride. It was the longest time he'd spent talking with me.

He spoke of things about himself—he was enthused and excited. I, on the other hand, became interested and receptive to whatever he had to say—I wanted to hear and absorb what he had to tell me.

"More for my book," I told myself.

Danny's mind at the time was not on boxing—his favorite subject—nor football. Danny wanted to talk about his whole family—father, mother and brother, and the events around them.

Danny began pouring out his story. It seems since early childhood, Danny was a very unhappy boy. He grew up in an environment which had hardened his love and respect for his father. Danny resented his father and couldn't understand it. He wanted to love his father as most boys love their fathers.

One Christmas, when he was a boy, he'd received a pair of boxing gloves from his dad. His father would play and box with him. Sometimes, Danny would cry because his daddy would hit him too hard and with tears in his eyes, he would return the punches to his dad's legs with all his strength and pain swelling up inside him. He would cry even more.

Danny's mother was a housewife and kept an immaculate spotless home. Her children were always clean. She was a good mother.

Danny's only brother, although older than he, has the same light complexion and likeness. One could easily detect them as being brothers.

Danny's resentment towards his father developed when he and his brother heard their parents constantly arguing. His parents would insult each other in their own bedroom away from the presence of the children. Then, for two or three days afterwards, Danny's father would disappear. Finally, he would return, drunk, and sleep all day. When Danny and his brother arrived from school, their father would just be getting up from bed. He would pour himself a drink. He wouldn't eat or be bothered by Danny's insistence to help him put the boxing gloves on and play with him. His father would yell and brush him aside.

For a moment, I turned around to see Dan Jackson. I noticed his large blue eyes were hard. He had wavy blonde hair. He smiled uneasily and continued saying that his father was a drunkard. He himself didn't drink nor smoke. He hated his father, as a child, and now—as a man.

"Why?" I asked him hesitantly.

"Because he was no good to my mother and to... nobody."

I wanted to ask my fellow juror more questions. I was grateful he had volunteered to tell me about his father. He spoke faster than I could comprehend. Danny, with a somber look on his face and hunting for words, disclosed that his father had wanted a baby girl when he was born—thus why the resentment had blossomed.

"Where's your father now?" I asked. "Is he living at home?"

"Hell, no!" he responded bitterly.

"He left my mother when I was a kid. She divorced him and raised my brother and I."

Danny's eyes were steady and his speech impediment became accentuated with hatred when he said, "My father never sent money for anything."

Then, almost like visualizing the image of the man he was speaking about, added, "He never even came to see us. My mother had worked all those years. She sacrificed everything for my brother and I."

I had met Danny's mother. She had visited him about once a month in the company of a man whom I suspected to be Danny's father.

"Oh no," he said amusingly, "he's my mother's boyfriend. She deserves to have fun. My brother is married and I am twenty-six. She fulfilled her duty as a mother. Now she can enjoy herself."

"Where's your father?" I wanted to know.

"He's in San Francisco," he replied and smilingly added, "Sick."

"Is that the way you feel about him?"

"Wouldn't you? After what he did to my mother and..." Danny stopped and instead asked me again, "Wouldn't you?"

"My parents have been married fifty years," I answered. "They had sixteen children. Eight of us are still living and we're a very close family."

Danny didn't say anything. The bus had arrived at the bowling alley.

"Bill," he said, as we readied to bowl, "does your father drink?"

"My father doesn't drink nor smoke," I replied.

"You're lucky," Danny responded, and placed himself to throw the ball in the lane for practice.

It crossed my mind when I had observed him practice boxing in the gym, that the punching bag he was pounding represented his father's face—he would hit harder and harder as to vent his anger and frustrations stemming from his childhood.

My thoughts of Danny were interrupted when Betty came to my side and whispered, "Okay, Bill, here's the game. Instead of referring to the pins as numbers, let's give them a name. Judge Older would be pin No. 1—he's responsible for us being sequestered for this long period of time—make sure you hit him every time.

"Pin No. 2 will be Kanarek—he could stop asking stupid questions—he's responsible for delaying the trial. HI....T HIM!"

"Who's No. 3?" I inquired.

"Bugliosi," Betty replied, and noticing my surprised look, she added promptly, "Oh yes, he's as much to blame as the others. Bastards!"

Eventually, Betty and I assigned names to each of the remaining pins.

Pin No. 4 became Deputy Taylor at my suggestion. The senior bailiff had been after me since the mailing of the letter.

Pin No. 5 was Mr. Fitzgerald. No. 6—Mr. Shin. No. 7—Mr. Hughes. No. 8—Deputy Mollie Kane. No. 9—Sheriff Tull. And No. 10 was left out and open so we could pick up any person secretly—like a juror or whomever.

The game acquired more excitement and somehow, visualizing the pins were people, made us relieve our frustrations. We couldn't talk to those people, but, by golly, no one couldn't stop us from playing the game of pin faces. Childish? Perhaps. But what a satisfaction one feels when one releases one's thoughts through games of faces. Try it. Betty and I felt much better after having bowled.

Thursday and Friday, we didn't go to court and that made most of the jurors terribly upset.

On Friday night, Olivia, Mildred, Betty, George, and myself wanted to stay in the hotel rather than going out to dinner. Mollie, for some strange reason, approached those of us who appeared to be annoyed and in an extremely persuasive manner, induced them to join the group for dinner.

I couldn't understand it. It had been customary to leave those at the hotel who desired so. Reluctantly, I accepted her persuasion and dressed in a mod fashion.

Casually, we all walked to the bus when lo and behold, to my surprise, sitting on my seat was Laura. I didn't know why she was there.

Looking around, I observed that each of the other jurors had also been caught by surprise with their guests sitting in their seats.

"What's the occasion?" George jubilantly shouted.

"Today is the fortieth wedding anniversary of Mr. and Mrs. Paine," responded Deputy Mollie Kane, who had organized the event.

"Where's my wife?" George asked again.

"I'm sorry," replied the blonde-looking sheriff, "she couldn't come over as she wasn't feeling well, but she told me to tell you she'll see you tomorrow."

George's jovial mood changed considerably. He felt lonesome.

Marvin's mother and sister were waiting for him. Edith's surprise guest was a lady friend. Later, Edith confided in me she wished Mollie had arranged to have someone else instead of the lady in question, whom she felt didn't know her very well. The retired teacher seemed rather disturbed and unhappy.

Mildred's guest was her estranged husband. She was also unhappy. According to the redheaded juror, everybody knew in advance about the surprise anniversary party, except her. She wanted to dress more elegantly.

Betty quietly sat with her husband. Ruth had no guests. Like some mothers would do, she covered the absence of her two grownup children by stating they were busy.

Genaro, sitting next to his delightful wife, and the Paines, across the aisle, exchanged points of married life.

Mr. Welch chatted with his tall, good-looking daughter. Danny's guests were his mother and her boyfriend. Olivia was occupied telling her doctor friend about the next Sunday outing. She wanted him to join her, but he was unable to commit himself because of his unpredictable busy schedule.

Violet and her husband sat quietly. At the rear of the bus, Debbie, Tom, and Ray sat with their respective spouses.

Upon entering Little Joe's, an Italian restaurant where Mollie had made reservations for the occasion, a most interesting and funny scene took place. Everyone had found seats except Debbie, Tom, and Ray, who wanted to sit together with their mates. There was room for one couple at Mildred's table but none of the three jurors would accept her invitation. Debbie, in the company of her husband, couldn't make others switch places.

Mollie, on the other hand, was desperately trying to make everyone happy. None of the jurors wanted to move and give room to the above-mentioned couples. Eventually, Debbie put her foot down and told Mollie she and her husband would wait in the bus rather than be seated where the deputy had told them. Ray followed suit. Tom, however, accepted and reluctantly sat at Mildred's table. Soon after, Ray and his wife sat with Mr. and Mrs. White. Both couples seemed terribly upset. Mr. and Mrs. Hart remained standing. Mollie, feeling the tension among the jurors, finally managed to get a table for the three couples, away from the rest of the escorted jurors, whereas Debbie took it upon herself to reunite the three couples.

On account of this incident, the relationship between Mollie and the members of the clique became cold and distant. Mollie was trying to do her duty and did her best to show no partiality. The clique turned to Deputy Taylor and from then on, they practically kissed his rear end to obtain little favors. The clique shrewdly made themselves available to call on the senior bailiff at all times. Whereas it had been customary to knock on Sheriff Taylor's door, the clique simply would walk in. They had first hand information as to the forthcoming events over the other jurors, and the over friendliness with the brusque deputy reflected their behavior as if they had been vested with special privileges.

Mollie, on the other hand, wouldn't allow them to do as they pleased and thus, the clique resented her. She was not persuaded easily and on more than one occasion, they had open confrontations because of her decisions. Mollie had their number!

Each table received a pitcher of house wine, compliments of Captain Arden. The handsome officer went about to greet each juror and his guest. Betty turned her back to ignore the salutation.

Everybody toasted the happy couple, and they responded cordially.

On the way back to the hotel, I held hands tightly with Laura and, needless to say, I was an extremely happy man. The bus ride didn't bother me and my thoughts were full of the pleasure of Laura's company.

At the hotel, Marvin, his mother and sister came to my room for a nightcap. I turned on my tape recorder with soft background music, which prompted Marvin to sense my desire to be alone with Laura. They left shortly after. I was pleased.

"At last....alone with you," I exclaimed as soon as I closed the door.

Laura said nothing but she began to look feverishly at the bottles of my impromptu bar table and casually asked me to fix her a double drink of Scotch.

"Of course," I said. Laura stood up and went to the window overlooking the bejeweled city.

"You're looking great, Laura," I said, trying to get things started.

"That's so," she said, without turning to look at me.

I pretended not to catch her meaning, but deep inside I knew how much difficulty it was costing me to say things like that. She seemed aloof...nonchalant.

I put her drink on the wall-to-wall counter beneath the windows. She grabbed the glass and rushingly gulped three swallows in succession.

"What's the rush?" I said, half jokingly.

"What a beautiful outfit you're wearing," she said, avoiding my question.

Without responding, I took Laura's hand in mine and led her back where she had been seated. She immediately lit a cigarette. Looking at her, I noticed she had a beautiful breast... well molded, round and firm. Her long, dark, straight hair covering half her face was shiny. I knelt in front of her.

I buried my head in her lap, my hands holding her waistline caressed the soft material ... my fingers, like caterpillars, worked their way up.

"Stop it, Bill," she urged, but with little conviction. Her protests didn't sound convincing.

Without uttering a word and still kneeling before her, I kept staring at her lips....her eyes.... again, her inviting lips.

Unable to control myself, I lunged my head between her warm breasts and passionately kissed them. I must have acted ravagedly. Laura stopped me momentarily and carefully placing my face in her hands, pulled my chin up to kiss me softly and warm. Encouraged, I searched for a more intimate kiss, but stopped when I noticed Laura had tears in her eyes.

"What's wrong, honey?" I said. Laura cried more.

"Anything wrong?" I asked once again.

The beautiful Brazilian girl, making a valiant effort, tried to speak but the words wouldn't form.

"I'm sorry, Bill," Laura said, "it's just that... I.... I had.... wanted to see you... but..."

Laura stood up and rushing back to the window, picked up her glass and

279

emptied its contents.

"I wanted to see you, and I find it is just what I thought it would be. I've got to get out of here before..."

Laura started to leave, when unexpectedly I grabbed her in my arms and said, "Wait a minute. You're not leaving just now. Why?" I snapped.

"Alright," Laura said, releasing herself, "give me another drink and I will tell you."

"Tell me WHAT?" I demanded to know.

"What I've been trying to do... to KILL myself—that's what," Laura replied sobbingly and sat down on the bed. She leaned over, held her head in her hands and wept compulsively. Laura cried hysterically.

Repeatedly, she kept on saying: "I don't know what to do. I'd wish to......"

My mind had been filled with my own problems, but I had learned long before that when one cannot find the solution to one's own problems, the best thing one can do is to look for someone with a greater problem and help him find its solution.

I switched my thoughts to a conversation of my friend's predicament. So I suggested to Laura to tell me all about herself. I knew that she was in no mood to make love or.... it was exactly one A.M.

Laura painfully told me she had left her native country two years before because of her love for a married man. It seemed she had clandestinely carried on an affair with him, despite her parents advice. The man had told her he wouldn't divorce his wife and to discourage her romance, he wouldn't even see her. Laura, broken-hearted, departed for the U.S.A. She wrote but never received an answer from her former lover. She felt lonely and filled with bad memories. She despised her parents and the only relative whom she cared for was an uncle, her mother's brother.

Laura wanted to commit suicide. We discussed the issue to great lengths.

I tried to give Loura some advice but she wouldn't accept or hear of it. She felt no one could help her. Laura was considerably shaken by the fact of having told me her story. Her face was tear stained and she kept clutching her handkerchief with her small hands. She was a pathetically pale and unhappy figure.

I studied her for a moment.

"Laura," I said, "if you want some friendly advice, I think you had better give some thought to your family and especially to yourself. You are living in the past. Why don't you come up with the day you live by... there will be a day when you'll be...."

With a wave of her hand, Laura cut me off.

280

"Please, Bill... Don't lecture me. I'm only too well aware of what is in store for me."

She stood up and walked to the window overlooking the East Garden down below, then she continued, "But I'm confused, I guess. I'm lonely and though my work is pleasant.." she said, being careful to keep her back to me for fear that her facial expression would not convince me of what her words conveyed. I guess she knew, only too well, that she wasn't convincing herself.

"You know something, I tried to commit suicide once," I admitted solemnly, "but now, I couldn't do it. I think I'd have a hell of a problem just thinking of it." I smiled at Laura as she turned back to me.

"That's where the problem lies," she observed seriously, "I keep thinking of doing it."

She threw herself back down on the chair, picking up her drink again. She sipped at its rim and found it good to her taste.

"But once you have tried it and failed, then you attempt it once more, hoping it will be the last time," Laura said, squeezing her glass.

"Not me," I responded quickly.

If I had been that fellow she had fallen in love with she probably would have done it. But I was an innocent passerby, I suppose because she confessed to me that she could have fallen in love with me had it not been for this guy before. But as long as this guy was alive or whatever it would always be like a shadow behind her when we kissed. Besides I didn't want to pursue the relationship after the trial was over because I personally don't like a woman who drinks. I'm not a drinker or smoker and she smoked and drank so I said "fine" right there. When I go with a girl and she smokes, that's ten points less—so now she has ninety points. She drinks? that's another ten points—that's eighty, and then if she doesn't dance that's ten points—seventy. Anything below fifty—forget it.

We fell silent for a moment, each devoting our full attention to each other. Our eyes searched each other's thoughts. The music being played on my tape recorded at that very instant was "Laura." What a perfect timing.

"Let's dance," I said.

She didn't reply—just rose.

We moved closer to each other. And then, standing face to face, leaning magnetically towards each other, we let our hands touch and kissed gently.

Laura's features were fine, but what attracted my immediate attention were her brown eyes and voluptous mouth. She sensed my desire and moved away from me.

I approached her and stared at her. She lowered her eyes and nervously opened and closed her hands. I bent over her face and sliding my hand over her shoulders, I pressed my lips against hers. She remained motionless for an instant, then she squeezed me in the vise of her arms... the warmth and the movement of her mouth made me tremble. Shivers ran up and down my spine.

Again, we kissed. But that time, our lips opened, our tongues touched and searched... we felt almost hesitant and anxious as if we both wanted to enter a depth beyond ourselves. We stopped. Our faces were close. As if by a signal, we smiled. Then our faces grew serious as something stirred into embarrassment. With firmness, we pressed our bodies against one another. My arms tightened around her slim waistline. I felt a shuddering feeling inside of me.

Carefully, I began to undo Laura's blouse and slowly slipped my hand inside, cupping one of her soft mounded breasts. Laura moaned deliciously and her lips parted even wider as our tongues searched and coaxed each other. Laura released herself momentarily and offering me her glass, asked, "Can I have another drink?" Laura paused, waiting for my answer.

"Oh, come on," I protested and while wrapping my arms around her, I kissed her hard and passionately, pushing her towards the bed.

Laura rose quickly to her feet. Carrying her empty glass, she started towards the bathroom, stopped in the doorway, glanced at her watch, and said, "I'll have to get going pretty soon," and disappeared into the bathroom.

I didn't want Laura to leave. I wanted her and I was determined to have her. When she returned from the bathroom, I offered her the drink she wanted in order to have her remain a little longer.

"Sure, I'll fix you another drink."

"I forgot. That's right," she observed amusingly, as she walked into the living room.

"You must be exhausted. Conscientious, honest jurors need their sleep. You have to have some rest."

I merely smiled. "We didn't go to court today," I admitted.

"Why don't you stay here tonight? Anyway, it's already two A.M." Then, turning my head to look at the bed, I added, "I only have one large bed, but if you wish, I could separate it in half—there's two single beds attached together and besides, I could use some sleep myself."

"Sleep?" Laura replied, half smiling.

"Well.... in time," I smiled back.

Laura's brown eyes snapped open and she lifted her head.

"Why?" she asked seriously.

"For a thousand reasons."

"Be more specific."

"You're a very lovely girl," I responded, "and besides, I want you."

Laura dropped her head. "What do you mean?"

"You know very well what I mean... I like you..."

The words were scarcely out of my mouth when slowly, Laura seized my arms and crushed me close to her. Her lips suggested me to kiss her.

"Oh Laura," I uttered helplessly, and we kissed.

Soon the lights were out and all was quiet and Laura, the beautiful Brazilian girl, was in bed beside me. I grabbed her and squeezed the breath out of her. She kissed me then and her lips were sweet and soft. Laura and I grasped each other so tightly and full of excitement. After a while, we consummated our love.....my heart pounded furiously with happiness. A relief descended upon me such as I had never known for a long time.

We lay still a moment, basking in each other's arms magnetically. This was what I had waited for so long... so long...

"It's late, Bill... I have to leave," Laura whispered.

We kissed good night.

"Thanks more than I can say, Bill," Laura said.

That was all so astonishing. It was hard for me to accept her thanks because I was the one who should have thanked her.

I closed her brown eyes with a kiss and with great effort, I murmured, "Laura, it is very strange, but I never felt like this before. I don't quite know what I feel, but it's very much like what I had always imagined happiness to be."

"I feel the same," Laura answered, "in many ways."

We walked towards the elevator holding hands. I dreaded the thought of her departure but it was inevitable.

"Good night, darling," Laura whispered, and kissed me.

Then she was gone. I drew a long breath and went back to my room. I laid long in the dark and the pillows still smelled of Laura's perfume.... I sighed with pleasure and fell asleep.

The next day, my perceptions proved to be quick—my nature amiable and willing. I felt strong and alive. For the first time since I had been sequestered, I felt camly sure of myself—complete. I greeted everyone with new assurance and authority, yet in a detached manner. I no longer felt like a prisoner at the Ambassador Hotel.

"I have a lover," I told myself. The corners of my mouth turned up now in a constant secret smile. I would have someone to visit me weekly... and make love. The bitter days were over. Yes, I had Laura and.... I was happy.

Marvin, Danny, and Martin invited me to join them in a couple of paddle tennis games. My enthusiasm was such that my opponents didn't win one single game. I'd discovered that nothing could bother me. With a contented inward smile, I thanked my playmates after the exalted crescendo of the games and jumped in the pool. I was on Cloud Nine.

At noon, I phoned Laura but there was no answer. I tried again and again, but with no luck. Laura didn't answer. I worried. There was only one girl whom I felt I could desire: Laura.

I had known her so long, but even so, I didn't know how she felt about our recent love affair. I had allowed my imagination to soar above the clouds. Maybe Laura wouldn't want to discuss my love for her and was trying to avoid me; otherwise, why wouldn't she answer the phone? I knew Laura had loved someone, but I didn't care. I thought our love affair could help her become free of past memories. I wanted to be part of Laura and would do my best to comprehend her complexes and the reasons behind some of them. In time, I thought she would love me—accept me. I would try to find out as much as possible about her childhood and that would give me more insight in order to help her more so. At that moment, the only thing that bothered me was that Laura didn't answer the phone. Where was she?

Laura never did call.

When I returned to my room, after a harrowing afternoon, I sat down and wrote a letter to Laura. I declared my feelings and invited her to visit me as soon as possible.

"Show time!" shouted one of the bailiffs outside.

"Just a minute," I replied. I went in the bathroom and washed my hands, pressed a cool damp cloth to my forehead, and then looked at myself in the mirror. My eyes reflected defeated thoughts my brain had conceived. I felt uncertain. So I decided to move closer to the mirror, and see what I would see.

The second time, I was determined to see only positive thoughts through the mirrors of my mind: my eyes. That time I felt I would break through. No luck.

Frustrated, I went out and joined the rest of the jurors for dinner. I was bored through my own fault. Halfway through dinner, Deputy Tull accompanied by Deputy Gonzales, went hurriedly upstairs, to console a lady juror who was crying.

"It's Mildred," someone said assumingly. We wondered why.

Later, in the recreation room, as I was preparing the projector to show films, Deputy Gonzales, in the presence of only two jurors, mentioned that it was Violet crying because of a marital rift. He went to her room with Deputy Tull to pacify things. Deputy Tull was still controlling the situation.

"That man is too old for her," said Bailiff Gonzales.

"That's true," interjected Frank Welch. "I stopped asking Violet to dance because she told me her husband is jealous."

"But you're 74 years old!" George remarked incredulously as he laughed. "He shouldn't be worried."

"Oh yeah?" Frank snapped joyously, "Violet's husband is almost as old as I am!" We all laughed.

The week before, the projector was being repaired, so that evening we had a double feature. George and Frank sat through the showing of *The Thrill of it All* with Doris Day and James Garner plus *Trouble with Women* with Ray Milland and Teresa Wright. I had seen both pictures.

Deputy Gonzales kept leaving and returning at intervals. During his short visits, he would tell me about Violet's alleged rift with her husband.

Through observations during the past months, I had discovered that Violet and her husband Oskar had been married five years or less. Their marriage was an unsuitable one, the difference of years made him appear old enough to be her father. That in essence was obvious whenever the spouses and guests were allowed to join the jurors at luncheon or dinner on weekends.

Violet and Oskar would go to dinner and even if they hadn't seen each other for a week or more, after a few comments, they'd spend an hour or an hour and a half in the restaurant without saying much to each other. They failed to enjoy the deep and personal contact married people share. They conveyed a void rather than a closeness in their relationship.

It was sad to watch Violet and her husband at those times. Ordinarily, she would always laugh and giggle constantly, but in the presence of her husband, she behaved altogether differently. Because of the lack of conversation between them, she would notice and observe elsewhere, and listen to what everybody did and said, in a restrained manner. She would even laugh at some joke or remark made by a juror in the adjacent booths.

Oskar very seldom spoke nor offered any conversation and while he sat with his young wife, he reminded me of someone sitting alone, eating in an isolated farm or in a remote weather station or in a lighthouse surrounded by water.

I didn't know how rejected Violet felt, but I couldn't help think that that man—her husband—perhaps ten or fifteen minutes before dinner, if he had for all natural purposes engaged in sexual enjoyment with his wife and that even immediately following the love that Violet had just made to him, wouldn't that make him more receptive? More amorous? More talkative?

Then I thought that perhaps he behaved differently when they were alone, though I doubted it in my mind.

Oskar's handshake emanated cold unfriendliness. A handshake without "salt and pepper." A handshake of a man who could not be trusted. Maybe that was one of the reasons he only spoke briefly at times and it only happened when someone would sort of force him to answer without offering or volunteering any information, nor would he make comments about anything.

Oskar was the least popular and least liked of all jurors' spouses.

The most important news I acquired that evening was from Deputy Gonzales. The chubby but sternly built Mexican-descent sheriff charmingly inquired if I had seen Laura lately. Then, as he had done before, apologized for having gone to my room and asking Laura to leave. It had been some while ago. However, this time he disclosed the name of the juror who had caused the departure of my girlfriend.

I listened to Gonzales almost with suspended breath and felt a surge of annoyance, almost of hate for the juror. When my discomfort was brushed aside and obliterated by an unconscious laugh, I thanked Deputy Gonzales and went to my room.

I laid in bed and felt like beating the pillows with my clinched fists.

"How could he?" I told myself.

It was Tom Brooks who had caused me all that distress. Then I began to put two and two together. Ray Harris had premeditatedly tried to make me believe it was some other juror.

I was hurt and bewildered at what I considered to be a double cross. I was resentful and a bit puzzled at the attitude of Tom. He kept on coming to my room with wine and kept insisting for me to go to his room for drinking.

In the back of his mind, there was undoubtedly the hope that I would be able to accept his invitations and so he insisted stubbornly that I go into his room and drink with him.

Back in court....

For over a week, we waited in the jury room. Our moods were antisocial and none of the bailiffs would even give us a hint as why we hadn't gone to court. We were restless. Some of the jurors had speculated this waiting was due to the next witness, Bobby Beausoleil, convicted killer of jazz musician Gary Hinman. Another rumor was that Gypsy, a member of the family, allegedly the next witness, had been declared insane causing the delay in the trial proceedings. The rumors proved to be false.

We finally descended into court. Seated on a chair, prior to taking the witness stand, was a young girl of light complexion. Her oval face denoted a sensitive expression when she smiled.

Shortly after, the counsel came out of Judge Older's chambers. Mr. Kanarek was the last one. He carried his old scratched briefcase, plenty books, and notes. A pathetic display of undone homework.

Charlie was released from the adjacent cell room and attracted attention because he had a new short haircut.

The witness, who gave her name as being Diane Lake, testified under direct examination, that Charles Manson had "talked many times in the summer of 1969 about killing people."

"Did he ever say why he wanted to kill people?" asked Mr. Bugliosi.

The auburn-haired witness answered, "We had to be willing to kill pigs to help black people start the revolution—Helter Skelter."

"Did he ever say who was going to start this revolution?" asked the prosecutor.

"Charlie said, 'I'm going to start the revolution,' " Diane replied.

Mr. Bugliosi then linked her testimony towards Leslie Van Houten, pertaining to the murder raid on the La Bianca residence.

The pudgy-faced young girl explained that she saw Leslie Van Houten arriving at 7:00 A.M. on one morning. Miss Van Houten was accompanied by three men who arrived fifteen minutes later. Miss Lake added that she overheard Leslie saying, "Don't let that man see me because he gave me a ride from Griffith Park."

Miss Van Houten hid underneath the sheets of a bed. The man stayed about three minutes. Leslie came out from the sheets about two minutes after the man left.

Miss Lake then said she saw Miss Van Houten burn "a rope... and her own clothes," when she returned to the Spahn Movie Ranch. The defendant then gave her "some Canadian nickles" and other coins.

On another occasion, the seventeen-year-old witness testified that she was with the defendants at the desert—at Willow Springs. They had a conversation outside the house in the late afternoon. According to Miss Lake, Leslie Van Houten had told her that she had stabbed someone already—dead—and that she had wiped off fingerprints even in places where the knife wasn't touched. Leslie then took some food, ate it, and took something to drink.

Mr. Bugliosi wanted to know if the defendant had mentioned how she felt at the time.

The witness responded, "Leslie said that at first, she didn't want to do it, but later it was fun."

Miss Lake also stated that Leslie described that there was a boat outside the house and that she hitchhiked back to the ranch.

Under questioning by Mr. Bugliosi, the witness also testified that Patricia Krenwinkel had told her at Willow Springs in the desert that "she dragged Abigail Folger from the living room."

Under cross-examination by Mr. Fitzgerald, Miss Lake denied she had been ill under mental disorder and that the reason she had been committed to Patton State Hospital, was for therapy. Mr. Fitzgerald dwelled heavily on the fact the witness had lied before the Grand Jury. He didn't try to discredit her testimony about his client, Patricia Krenwinke.

Mr. Kanarek devoted his interrogation to the witness' past sexual life before and after she met Charles Manson. He was overruled.

We were dismissed for lunch.

In the afternoon, Manson's lawyer, upon arriving late, apologized to the court, counselors, defendants and the jury for being late.

Sneakily, I bent over between Mildred and Betty and imitating Judge Older, I whispered, "May the record reflect that this is about the tenth time Mr. Kanarek apologizes for being late." Those around me tittered.

Upon resuming his questioning, Mr. Kanarek confined himself to finding out how many hours the witness had talked with either Sergeant Gutierrez or Mr. Bugliosi, and how many times she had taken LSD.

All the jurors felt sleepy. The process was slow and most everybody was yawning. It had been customary for us jurors to carry wet paper towels and apply them to our eyes or wrists to keep awake.

Finally, when Mr. Kanarek finished his line of endless irrelevant questions. Mr. Hughes asked the court to approach the bench before beginning his interrogation. While the counsel was in session with the judge, the defendants addressed Diane Lake, but she ignored them. Susan Atkins looked at the witness with daggered eyes.

Counsel returned to their seats.

Mr. Hughes stood up and with pencil in hand, stated, "On account of Your Honor's ruling, I will not ask any questions of the witness."

Charlie furiously shouted out loud, "Go home! Go home! You're a lawyer! If you are not going to ask any questions—go home... go home!"

Judge Older admonished the defendant and Mr. Bugliosi began his redirect examination.

The prosecutor asked some questions that helped clarify what the defense counsel had asked.

288

Mr. Bugliosi also asked Diane to answer questions in regard to the time she had gone to his office and what he had told her about the perjury she had committed before the Grand Jury.

Mr. Fitzgerald and Mr. Kanarek protested but Judge Older overruled their objections.

Charlie spoke out loud again, and said, "One of these days, *you're* going to be overruled MISTER !"

"Mr. Manson, I admonish you, Sir," answered the court. "More outbursts and I'll have you removed from the courtroom."

Charlie, still yelling, replied, "You're going to be overruled."

Judge Older ordered the prisoner to be taken out. Deputies Taylor and Tull escorted Charlie whom, on his way out, addressed the judge and said sarcastically, "I leave you with your flunkies, and if it was just you and me, it would be different."

Diane Lake, relieved of the presence of Charlie, stated under questioning that on one occasion, Charlie slapped her face, causing bleeding and split her lips badly.

Miss Lake conceded, "When I was about twenty minutes into an LSD trip, Charlie got up and slugged me in the mouth... right after that, I thought I saw a red feather across the moon."

The petite witness added, "Charlie hit me with a chair leg and kicked and whipped me with a cord. He said, 'I'm going to kill you Snake, I'm going to kill you.' "

"Snake" was the nickname given Miss Lake when she was a member of the hippie cult.

She concluded stating that Charlie had told her not to say anything to any authorities and she lied to Sergeant Gutierrez and on the Grand Jury for reasons of being afraid—afraid to be killed by members of the family.

Finally, Mr. Bugliosi asked the witness how she felt about coming down and testifying.

Diane Lake responded, "I feel relieved because I'm telling the truth."

The entire testimony of Diane Lake was lengthy. Whereas Mr. Bugliosi took briefly eleven minutes, the defense counsel spent day after day. Eight days to be exact.

During Mr. Shin's cross-examination, the jurors fought to keep awake. The way he went about asking questions was absolutely impossible to follow and understand. It was unbelievably fastidious, and hard to comprehend, that the trial could go on and on.

Diane Lake's testimony was a treacherous slow paced interrogation.

Dr. Blake Skrdla, a psychiatrist appointed by the court to study Diane Lake's file, testified that to his knowledge, Diane had the capacity for recalling conversations. It was the doctor's belief that LSD has less damage than alcohol and that there was no evidence that brain damage had been demonstrated by LSD. He found no evidence of psychosis in the case of Diane Lake. He discovered the young girl was neither mentally disordered nor mentally ill and that she had high normal or high intelligence.

Dr. Harold C. Deering, another doctor who was appointed to examine Diane Lake, testified that according to his tests, he evaluated Diane Lake as being able to recall conversations. It was his opinion that she was capable to recollect, distinguish visions which are there but cannot be seen. The witness stated that she was schizophrenic neither before nor when he examined her.

On cross-examination, the defense counsel tried to prove that Diane Lake still had residuals of LSD and consequently her testimony was not valid. The professional witnesses did not concur with this theory.

Upon dismissing Dr. Deering, the 84th witness of the Manson trial, the prosecutor asked the court to have Patricia Krenwinkel produce samples of her handwriting, using the phrases scrawled in blood at the La Bianca murder scene.

The defendant refused to act in accordance with the order, whereas Judge Older told her, "If you fail to comply, the prosecution may argue to the jury that your failure to comply is circumstantial evidence of consciousness of guilt."

Mr. Bugliosi made a notation and after a short period of time, he stood up as he had done eighty-four times before, to call his next witness and anticipating our guesses, he announced, "Your Honor, the people of the State of California rest their case."

"Wow!" whispered some jurors with joy. The prosecutor then asked the court to consider the exhibits submitted as evidence. The judge asked the counsel to approach the bench.

We jurors couldn't believe it. We were happy that the trial was nearing the end. It was exactly 3:35 P.M. and though we still had an hour, we were dismissed until the following Monday.

Back at the Ambassador Hotel.

Upon arrival, some jurors wanted to cash their checks. Marvin Connolly never missed an opportunity to join those jurors going to the bank. His only interest was to chat with the bank clerk, a petite oriental girl who responded happily to his weekly visits or whenever.

Friday night, and again everybody was trying to guess where we were going for dinner, especially when Mollie had emphasized the place required evening clothes.

The reservations had been made at the Circus Room, located at the top of the Sheraton-Universal Hotel. None of the jurors except this author had been there before. Everybody was pleased with the locale.

The clique sat together as usual. Mrs. Hart was beautifully dressed in a black sheath dress which was a perfect match for the stunning diamondlike necklace and earrings set she wore.

Every juror was well dressed and the surroundings brought gaiety and a festive mood.

Before dinner, I ordered a large bottle of imported wine and shared it with those at my table—Betty, Edith, Ruth, Frank, Marvin, and Danny.

A musical trio began to play so I rose and went directly to Debbie and asked her to dance. She was enthralled in a conversation with Tom and dryly declined my invitation by responding that her companion juror had already asked her. They didn't get up to dance.

Frank and I danced with most of the lady jurors and the female bailiffs, Kathy Kolvig and Mollie Kane.

Tom and Debbie walked hand in hand to see the view from the window, disregarding what any of the jurors thought. They were standing at the edge of a large window. In the distance, the city lights could be seen—sparkling. They embraced each other sideways. Looking at the beautiful and fantastic panorama of the San Fernando Valley below, they stood there for a long time.

"I believe we have a romance among the jurors," said my dancing partner, Ruth.

"Who?" I inquired.

Ruth laughed and jokingly said, "You and I," and we burst out laughing.

"Look at them," Ruth added.

Tom and Debbie stood there watching the view, oblivious to the presence of others. They stood there, side by side, until it was almost time to return to the hotel.

Everybody speculated as to what was going on between Tom and Debbie. The two of them were together, away from everyone else, yet each juror was so busy speculating with thoughts that for a moment, the couple might have just as well confessed to all the jurors that they were in love.

Tom and Debbie knew they were certain to be a topic of conversation between the jurors. They also knew that no one would have the guts to tell them openly about their affair. They treated each other with the wary respect skilled fencers give to opponents who are equally adept.

291

During the next weeks, they saw each other frequently in Tom's room, but there was always something about them that made it impossible for the jurors to go beyond a certain point of gossip.

For a time, Tom, a large man with an innocent boyish face, tried to pretend. Debbie became cold and passive in my presence as to make others think otherwise.

Their affair did not remain concealed long from the rest of the jurors.

The absence of Tom and Deb at the clique table made the rest appear somewhat lost without their leader. They all seemed quiet and composed. Ray ignored everybody and stood facing the wall for 45 minutes.

Miss Kolvig, who had befriended the group, helped to break their silence by asking Ray to dance.

Violet, an avid dancer, felt ignored, but Martin eventually felt compelled to invite her to dance.

Genaro was left alone at the table. This scene was to be repeated at later various occasions which prompted the charming juror to be the first to disassociate from the clique. He was the first casualty. His decision made him friendlier and more receptive to the other jurors, although he maintained a certain amount of contact with the clique.

Genaro Swanson, an outgoing man with a jovial personality, eluded gossip and maintained an easy going friendship with everyone of the jurors. During the first two weeks at the hotel, he had joined those going to the swimming-pool area, then abruptly decided against it. He became part of the clique and, upon discovering the romance of Tom and Deb, avoided their relationship.

He stayed in his room teaching himself how to play the guitar. To break the monotony of being indoors, he divided his time by reading novels of western flavor or by solving jigsaw puzzles on a card table in his room which was visible from the little lobby since he always kept his door open.

Genaro, to everybody's surprise, joined Mildred, Betty, and Edith in the difficult handiwork of knitting.

The Sunday outing was a tour of the U.S.S. *Denver* anchored at her home-port in Long Beach. The Navy personnel on duty patiently answered questions while leading the jurors throughout the amphibious boat. They served lunch at the captain's table and after, a movie was shown starring Raquel Welch. Wow!

Back in court.

On Monday, due to some technical matters which had to be taken care of outside the presence of the jury, Judge Older dismissed us and then said to return after two or three days.

On Thursday morning, every juror with pad and pencil in hand, was ready to jot down notes from the first defense witness. As we waited, I noticed there was no one seated on the witness stand.

"Your Honor," Mr. Fitzgerald spoke as he rose, "subject to our later entering exhibits, the defense rests its case at this time."

The surprise move brought gasps of incredulity from spectators in the crowded courtroom. Everyone was startled. The jurors reacted without showing any visible signs of emotion, though deep inside, they were thrilled to see the trial ending as the defense attorneys followed quickly with the stunning step of resting their case without calling a single witness to the stand. The jurors watched intently.

Particia Krenwinkel, following her lawyer, stood up and addressed the court saying, "I wish to testify at this time."

Co-defendant Susan Atkins jumped up and made the same request.

The excitement was overwhelming. Mr. Bugliosi, at that point, requested a conference with the defense attorneys at the judge's bench.

"This should be in the presence of the jury!" shouted Susan Atkins immediately, standing next to Patricia Krenwinkel.

As the attorneys approached the bench, Miss Atkins continued speaking, "We should be allowed to take part in the same conference because it is our defense."

Two female bailiffs, who had been assigned permanently to escort the female defendants, blocked the girls' way as they appeared to attempt to follow the lawyers to the bench.

Shortly after talking at the bench, Judge Older recessed the court and asked the attorneys and defendants to come to his chamber for further talks.

Upon returning to court, Judge Older again announced that the trial would recess for a few days to allow the prosecution and defense attorneys to prepare their suggestions for instructions to the jury.

Back at the hotel.

The dark days in the month of November brought sad feelings among the female jurors. They wanted to spend Thanksgiving Day at home with their relatives or friends.

Debbie and Violet had become quite sensitive and would allow no one to even mention spending the Christmas holidays at the hotel. They lofted a campaign of accepting no one's opinions and optimistically, they expected to be home for Christmas.

Thanksgiving dinner was a sad occasion. Again, Mollie suggested a place nearby her home. The maitre d' at the Queen's Arms Restaurant, with good intentions, had arranged a private room for the jurors. The jurors wanted to dine among the crowd, see other people's faces and enjoy the traditional holiday.

Instead, they were thrown together in a small room, causing disharmony for the mere reason of too much togetherness. The moods and sour faces of the jurors brought a note of exasperation for the bailiffs in charge, who themselves had become victims of the circumstances, and wanted to be at home with their families.

On Saturday, Michael Pappas, the senior bailiff for the weekend, arranged immediately after dinner an escorted outing to a nearby movie house to go see *Hello Dolly*.

Everyone, except the clique, jumped up with pleasure at the opportunity of being able to leave the hotel. I was ready to join those going when an unexpected phone call of a friend informed me she was coming to visit me. There was nothing I could do but stay and wait for her at the recreation room while watching television dressed in levis.

Kathy Nosko, a delightful and charming redheaded woman, employed by the same company I work for, arrived about one and a half hours later. Kathy noticed my casual attire and made a comment about the rainy weather. It was pouring outside.

"Let's go to my room," I said and led the way.

Kathy followed me without saying a word. As soon as I opened the door, I noticed the lights in the room were out. I closed it quickly for fear of having made the mistake of opening the wrong door.

I checked the number outside and it was my room—Number 680.

"It can't be," I said to my guest, "I always leave the lights on." Kathy didn't respond.

Again, I opened the door. It was dark when suddenly, the closet door squeaked and as it opened slowly, its automatic light switch clicked on. A huge odd shadow emerged. I screamed with panic for I didn't know what it was and turned around.

The lights went on and a chorus chanted, "Happy birthday to you... happy birthday to you... happy birthday dear Bill... happy birthday to you!"

I couldn't believe it. Kathy and my good friends, Joe and Barbara Thibodeau, had combined their efforts to surprise me. They did, and how!

The "large shadow" turned out to be Chuck Burton. The six-foot, four-inch tall, 200-pound, friendly fellow worker, using his raincoat as a cloak, scared the pants off me with his simulated vampire silhouette.

The surprise birthday party turned out to be a successful event and despite the weather conditions, twelve out of eighteen invited guests showed up.

Unfortunately, at eleven o'clock, Michael Pappas and his assistant came over and announced that my neighbor had complained of the noise. Mike didn't say which of my neighbors had gone to tell him she couldn't sleep, but urged the party to continue across from my room. I was upset and for a moment, I blamed Debbie; however, it was Edith who had complained.

There was so much food to be eaten that the bailiffs on night guard duty helped themselves to a good portion. My guests left at the second warning of Mike. It was beyond my comprehension to believe that on a Saturday night and under the circumstances, I was not allowed to have guests.

Edith, an elderly lady, had protested and needless to say she would have made a scandal had I opposed her. The thing I couldn't understand was that, previously, at my invitation, Betty, Ruth and Edith herself had come to my room to eat a delicious meatloaf that Mrs. Reid, my tenant's mother, had baked at my request. During the entire length of the trial, the jurors were never served meatloaf.

I resented Edith and tried to ignore her because of the incident.

Characteristically speaking, Edith was taken by the clique as a scatter-brain. She would talk and talk and talk. All the while, the clique would make signs of fun behind her back. Edith didn't care and would insist on talk-king. Eventually, the clique gave up and accepted her without much respect, but Edith, a Seventh Day Adventist, was a lady of considerable sensitivity that stood her ground, fighting solitude and the memory of her everloving fiancé.

The eldest of the female jurors was from New York but had moved to California some years back. She had never been married although in her early years, she was engaged to a young man who died a day or two before the wedding took place. Edith cried when she spoke of the circumstances around the passing of her future bridegroom but never disclosed the details.

Because of her conversations, Edith gave the indication she was still a virgin.

One Sunday morning, Edith received a large group of retired church-going friends. The talkative juror asked me to loan her some chairs, and to save walking distance, I opened the door connecting our rooms to deliver the chairs promptly. The look on the faces of Edith and her guests was something else.

Later, Edith openly disclosed the incident among the jurors, adding that some of her female visitors had made a strong issue of the fact we had a common door and advised her to lock the door on her side. Edith was startled and followed their advice.

For a while, the jurors made a joke of it, especially when Edith unwittingly mentioned she walked in her sleep.

"Can you see yourself, lying on your bed," asked Debbie, "and then, Edith dressed in a nightgown, walking through the door?"

"Yeah..." George added laughingly, "and Edith saying with opened arms, 'Bill, Bill, where are you?'"

"That's a $ 64,000 question," I responded, meaning Edith was sixty-four years old and much too old to satisfy my sexual appetite. I must admit, I dreaded the thought.

The alternate juror relieved her frustrations by describing her extended trip to the Orient and took pride to explain the customs and habits of the Japanese people. She handled the chopsticks quite well whenever we were taken to Chinese restaurants and took it upon herself to teach those around her their use.

She was an avid card player, enjoyed television, and spoke with an English accent. She knitted about twenty pairs of moccasins and sent one pair to Judge Older for Christmas.

Another week had gone by. The Sunday outing was to Solvang, a Danish town located two or three hours north of Los Angeles. I didn't go because the weather had been hot and riding in the county jail bus was like riding in an oven. Later, during the colder months, the draft of air passing through the windows made everybody shiver, even with the bus heater working. Transported prisoners had ripped the rubber at the edges of the windows.

On Monday, we were taken to the Hall of Justice but never went down to the courtroom. The jurors kept themselves occupied. For reasons unknown, we were kept in a different jury room; the jury room of Department 105 was very spacious and had plenty of chairs.

Betty and I, by coincidence, both pulled chairs towards the window for warmth from the cold air generating throughout the room, and realizing she was always cold, I ceded the place to her.

Everybody made the usual comments or made remarks of little importance, if nothing else, to make the time pass.

Edith argued as to why we had come so early since Judge Older had told us to be in court at 10:00 A.M. Edith spoke as fast as she knitted a pair of green and white moccasins.

Olivia traveled back and forth to see "Lucy."

At the same time, Violet was laughing nonstop; she laughed for no reason at all. Her laugh sounded more like a giggle since it was not sustained, and did not sound sincere.

George, seated next to me, swiveled his chair and looking out the window, made a remark as to be heard by only those around him.

"Its funny, isn't it? She tells everybody to shut up, but she never shuts up herself."

Betty, without looking at George, caught the remark and exclaimed: "No such luck!"

I chuckled and then continued observing my fellow jurors.

By accident, or mere coincidence, at that moment, no one was speaking, but the squeaking of the chairs at varying sounds throughout the room was ceremonious. Hardly anyone could move without making an acute noise.

This discovery gave a good opportunity especially to Ray to execute the screeching of his chair in all directions as to find the most distracting and hideous noise. Oddly enough, Ray smartly stated, as he enjoyed the process, that the squeaking sounded as if someone was playing a symphony.

"Symphonies don't sound this way," Ruth argued. "You may say that this is the way the instruments sound when the musicians are tuning them."

Ray ignored Ruth and continued swinging his chair all ways. Eventually, he gave up his playing since no one paid him any attention.

It had been a hectic day. We had been waiting in the jury room without having gone down to the courtroom. The fact of having been inside and not having accomplished a darn thing during the day made everybody edgy.

The clique took this opportunity to take advantage to annoy those jurors who were concerned for not having put in a full day's work. They had gone out especially to make more noise than usual. There was a definitely divided feeling among the two groups. You may say there were those who had accepted to be sequestered with the sole intention of performing their civil duty, and those who had accepted under false pretenses to be sequestered for fun and game purposes.

The temperature had been hot and smoggy inside the bus, where we had been prohibited from opening the white opaque windows, causing us to feel irritable and sleepy.

At the Ambassador Hotel, as we walked in the hallway on the way up to our rooms, I felt apprehensive because I knew, in advance, that the fan installed in the ceiling of the elevator for some reason circulated hot air instead of cool air, which only added to our unhappy frame of mind.

We walked into the elevator and casually, everybody followed those whom they wanted to stand next to. The already established elevator game was to press all the floor buttons and then, once we were on the sixth floor, quickly press the buttons before the doors opened so the elevator would return to the first floor again.

That, in itself, had been hilarious at the beginning, but on this day, no one was in the mood for such unwanted childish pranks, including the bailiff himself, who was not in a receptive mood. Deputy Taylor had accepted it from the very beginning and would even chuckle, but deep inside, one could tell that he did not like it. He tolerated it by ignoring and overlooking the game.

As I had seen before, I noticed Ray's arm, without Violet's knowledge, reaching at waist level behind and around her, for the elevator buttons.

Once we had reached the sixth floor, the elevator began to descend again. Since I was standing near the board, Deputy Taylor annoyingly addressed me, "Come on, Bill."

I didn't answer.

The elevator, having reached the first floor, Ray once again, in the same manner, pressed the buttons and right afterwards, shoved Violet against me, but this time I retaliated by pushing her back to Ray, which she didn't appreciate. She didn't mind Ray's actions but she resented mine. Besides accusing me of pushing her, she insinuated that I was responsible for the delay in reaching the sixth floor. After she called me a few indecent names, all my wrath burst forth, and I damned her with an adjective that was hotter than the elevator.

As the weeks passed by, Violet and I avoided each other.

One evening, I entered the recreation room to read the newspaper, There was no one around. Shortly after, Violet came in and we both looked at each other. Nothing was said. Silence. When she sat opposite me, I leaped up from the couch and walked recklessly, heading back to my room, but something within my mind took hold of itself.

I had noticed that when Violet had sat down, she was challenging my emotional stability as to how well I could stand being next to her or whatever. I returned and faced her with a shadow of a smile.

Violet had become the darling of the bailiffs. She would do anything for them and get everything she wanted in return. Where other female jurors had failed, Violet had succeeded in managing the bailiffs to take her "to see Lucy" at anytime she wanted during the Friday evening meals at the restaurants.

She was always going in and out of the bailiffs' rooms and even while the transportation bus was in motion, she wouldn't wait until the end of the ride to talk with them. Instead, she would walk from the back of the bus to the front where the sheriff would sit just to tell him something.

The bailiffs had repeatedly told us from the very beginning that while the bus was in motion, to remain seated and to stand up to exit only when the bus had come to a complete stop. The reason, they said, was because we could get hurt and besides the County of Los Angeles would be held liable if some tragedy occurred and they, the sheriffs, would be reprimanded or lose their jobs and that, they emphasized, would be the last thing on earth they would want to happen.

I remember one day, Violet was returning to her seat when Marvin Connolly scooted forward on his seat and leaned towards me, placing a hand on my right shoulder. I gave an involuntary jerk as to find out what it was.

"Hey, Bill," he said. I leaned back, still looking forward while Marvin whispered in my ear, "Look at her, with that body and the way she walks, she reminds me of a piggy pork with a feather up her ass."

For the record, the name I had called Violet on the elevator was "Piggy." No, I didn't repeat the rest. Later on, she was baptized with the name "Giggles" for obvious reasons.

On December 2, 1970, there was a great deal of excitement at the hotel due to the arrival of South Vietnam Vice President Nguyen Cao Ky, who was winding up his United States visit in Los Angeles. The jurors resented his visit as it limited their freedom and activities at the hotel.

He arrived at the Ambassador from San Francisco around 10:00 A.M. We were confined on the sixth floor and instead of going down to the coffee shop for lunch, they brought the food to the recreation room as not to interfere with the mob of people the police and security agencies were expecting.

There were 1000 demonstrators outside, and to be on the safe side, the deputy in charge cancelled any outings whatsoever.

That morning rained heavily and it was a dark and cold-looking day. The corridor had been quite busy and it looked and sounded like a busy sidewalk.

Betty and George were constantly walking from one end to the other. They were exercising, trying to keep their muscles active from the lack of movement.

Approximately 50 Los Angeles police officers guarded the exterior of the hotel and an undisclosed number of Secret Service and Federal Bureau of Investigation Agents were inside. In fact, on our own floor at the end, next to the balcony, across from Sammy Davis Jr.'s suite, there was a suite destined for the sole purpose of an observation point for detectives and plainclothesmen to watch and see any abnormality.

According to the newspaper, President Nixon invited Vice President Nguyen Cao Ky to tour the United States. Ky, speaking to 1000 persons at the World

Affairs Council luncheon in the Ambassador Hotel's "Now Grove," declared that communist guerillas "directed by Peking" would interfere by war and subversion with the democratic progress of his neighboring countries. According to one of the guards at the hotel, his speech was called, "The Way to Peace in Vietnam" and he told me that while Ky spoke, there were at least 150 antiwar demonstrators marching on Wilshire Boulevard. Two yards from the hotel entrance, he also said they carried a Viet Cong flag as well as signs critical of Ky's visit. The jurors were glad to see him leave.

The entire week, we rose every morning at the usual time and were ready to leave for court, and at about 11:00, some deputy would knock on our doors to inform us we were to remain at the hotel. We didn't know what was going on. The bailiffs had gone out of their way to make sure the jurors were kept away from any incoming news. We wondered what was happening.

Finally, one day, Bailiff Taylor and Deputy Kane told the jurors that Judge Older was coming to the hotel to announce some important news. The speculations as to why the judge himself would come to see us in person relieved the monotony of bickering and distress that had prevailed during the week.

The jurors congregated in the recreation room a few minutes before the arrival of the magistrate. Frank Welch, Paul White, and Olivia Madison wanted everybody to stand up as His Honor entered, but received no support. Betty was especially against it. She and the rest felt that there was no reason for it.

Judge Older, accompanied by a court reporter, was ten minutes late and when he entered, only three jurors rose. Frank offered a jokeful salutation by asking the advocate if he had gone to Las Vegas to gamble.

His Honor smiled and then got to the object of his visit. He informed us that Mr. Ronald Hughes, defense lawyer for Leslie Van Houten, had been missing and that his absence would cause several days' delay in the trial.

It seemed the balding, 250-pound counsel had driven to a high rugged timberland camping area in Las Padres National Forest near Sespe Hot Springs and had been stormbound because of last weekend's heavy rainfall conditions. Judge Older added that as the weather cleared, he had dispatched two helicopters and several ground crews to search through the mountainous area for the attorney. It was his hope Mr. Hughes would be located soon.

Judge Older ended by saying that he, the prosecution, and the defense attorneys had been working closely in his chambers on the instructions to the jury.

"What about Christmas?" asked George unhappily. "If we are still sequestered, can we have a pass to go home?"

Every juror waited for His Honor to respond.

Judge Older smiled and without committing himself, stated he was unable to answer but that he had been thinking about it.

George, still unhappy with the answer, poured himself out and complained briefly about the existing schedule of activities at the hotel, and the manner in which the bailiffs handled it. Too many bosses.

Deputy Taylor and Mollie, standing behind the judge, tensed up and smilingly one of them moved forward and prevented the juror from proceeding. They offered to "make amends for the benefit of each juror."

Judge Older's departure turned the meeting into an open forum of protests. Betty left immediately for her room. Olivia wanted to attend to some personal business. Debbie and Violet wanted more details for Christmas. Ruth wanted to go home because her son had been drafted into the Army. Marvin feared he would be fired from his job. The rest of us were just plain fed up with the delay of going to court.

Unfortunately, the results of the meeting put George at the top of the black list of Deputy Taylor, with this author juror trailing a strong second place, especially since the senior bailiff knew I had written a letter to the judge.

The following day, posted in the little lobby, I read:

JURORS' WEEKDAY SCHEDULE

MONDAY	Drugstore	Those jurors desiring to make purchases at the drugstore will be taken to Thrifty Drugs immediately after dinner. (Purchases on days not designated for drugstore may be made by the bailiff when convenient.)
TUESDAY	Special Activities	Personal laundry, TV, etc. Occasionally special planned activity.
WEDNESDAY	Bowling	Every Wednesday will be Bowling Night at the Western Bowl. Dinner will be eaten early enough so that we can be at the bowling alley by 7:00 P.M. We will leave the hotel coffee shop and board the bus directly. Jurors should bring sweaters, etc. to dinner with them. Any juror not desiring to either bowl or watch will be returned to the jury floor and will remain on the floor. Lack of continued interest may

		cause cancellation of this activity.
THURSDAY	Drugstore and Beauty Salon	Jurors desiring to make purchases will be taken to Thrifty Drugs immediately after dinner.
		Lady jurors desiring to have hair done must make an appointment no later than Monday of the same week. Ladies have a choice of either the Magic Mirror salon or the Ambassador salon. All ladies must attend the same salon on the same night.
FRIDAY	Dinner Out	Arrangements to have dinner out at various restaurants will be made each week.
WALKS		Jurors will be escorted on walks in the evening in one group only. The walk will be taken at a pace reasonable to accommodate all jurors.

ANY JUROR WHO DOES NOT DESIRE TO PARTICIPATE IN ANY ACTIVITIES PLANNED FOR THE JURY PANEL WILL BE ALLOWED TO REMAIN AT THE HOTEL. HOWEVER, DUE TO PERSONNEL LIMITATIONS, THOSE JURORS NOT PARTICIPATING WILL BE TAKEN TO THE DINING ROOM *ONLY*. NO OTHER ACTIVITIES OFF THE FLOOR CAN BE HANDLED.

Any juror who has a request, or idea, to present for the entertainment of the jury should advise Deputy Taylor or Deputy Tull, who will take the matter up as to feasibility and approval. Jurors are requested NOT to ask other deputies for approval or recommendations.

The following days were long and hopeless. The jurors, for lack of activity, assembled in groups to divert themselves in their favorite pastime or hobby.

During the day, Marvin, Danny, Martin, and I played paddle tennis. The daily practice made Marvin a tough contender especially since he had given up smoking. Danny, between games, exercised skip rope ceaselessly around the pool to the admiration of everyone. Many tried to jump with the rope but none were able to equal the skill and ability of the featherweight pugilist.

Genaro practiced guitar and his neighbor Tom Brooks, who practiced banjo, joined him for a duet.

Paul White had been given an illustrated book about binding or fastening ropes and was fascinated with the art of entwining knots.

George kept himself busy building a model airplane.

Mildred had sent for her sewing machine and started making her own clothes.

Frank had one of his daughters bring an exercycle to his room.

Ray had received a bottle cutter from his wife and devoted his time converting empty wine and beer bottles into artistic drinking glasses. George also had one.

Debbie and Violet spent most of their time returning visits to one another.

Betty knitted on and off in the recreation room.

Edith, Ruth, and Olivia spent most of their time in their rooms.

Day after day we waited anxiously to return to court.

One night, I stayed late to watch television; the recreation room was stuffy. I reached the switch light and turned it off. The light reflection coming from the window gave the room a penumbra effect—enough to see.

I could not only see the hallway which after passing "The Little Lobby," at the end was Genaro Swanson's room, but also was able to enjoy a rather cool breeze coming from the corridor.

"Good!" I told myself.

I had placed, under my head, a large seat cushion from one of the chairs. In fact, I was so comfy that my mind was engulfed entirely on the movie being shown at the time, *Strangers When We Meet,* starring Kim Novak and Kirk Douglas.

All of a sudden, I heard the familiar sound of a door knob being released after opening a door and, to my surprise, I noticed Deb coming out of Tom's room, barefooted and wearing a short terry cloth robe which she ordinarily wore down at the pool. They kissed good night ardently and Deb, after seeing no one around, tiptoed back to her room.

I glanced at my watch and it was 2:20 in the morning. I didn't want to believe it. Maybe my dirty mind was telling me to think of it, but unfortunately, the less I tried to think of it, the more I thought of it. Then I began to speculate and I trembled when I thought what might be the direful consequences if their spouses at home would ever find out. But quite obviously, they didn't think of the repercussions that could overcome because they continued seeing, visiting, and acting as if the world around them was not aware or didn't exist. Perhaps a better way to express it would be to quote what one juror said in regard to their relationship:

"Tom and Debbie are insulting our intelligence by thinking that all of us don't know what's going on between the two of them."

The routine of eating three times daily at the coffee shop, especially without going to court, urged me to bring something to keep me occupied, like reading a book or writing notes about the jurors.

Worried looks were exchanged across the tables as jurors considered the possibility of having some of their private problems exposed to the outside world after being sequestered.

All the jurors had been informed by myself of my intentions to write a book about the jurors themselves. Tom Brooks and Mrs. Hart felt I was aware of their romance. But I speak with an accent and consequently you might deduce, "He can't speak English without an accent—less to write a book." I guess this would be sufficient logic. They weren't serious enough to consider me a writer—a gossiper perhaps. They thought I was capable of just opening my mouth and telling all, but not of putting it down in black and white, and consequently they didn't pretend to conceal their love affair.

Everytime Mr. Paine would order his meals, for some reason, the waitresses would serve him last or else they would serve his plate to some other juror whom perhaps had ordered the same, but not necessarily the same vegetables. Other times, even if a juror had not ordered some salad or soup, some juror would grab it and that would cause the waitress an extra trip to the kitchen while the juror who had ordered would wait and watch unhappily while the others ate.

With all this diversification of attitudes and the accumulation of small dissatisfactions at dinner time, did sooner or later, spoil our mood and jarred our self-esteem.

Martin had complained but nothing would change his opinion or attitude. He disliked the food and the inefficient service of the employees.

He took to criticize the dinners at the Ambassador Hotel, with other jurors present. But what made some of the female jurors object, was his constant repetition of the word "balls," which he would say as the most outspoken dissatisfied client and which, eventually, was bound to have an effect on those jurors resigning to sit in his company.

On one occasion, I was sitting in the company of Betty and Edith. In a jokeful manner, I tried to imitate Mr. Paine by saying "balls".

Edith looked at me and disgustedly warned me, "Don't say that word in front of me!"

"Why?" I asked. "Martin says it all the time..."

"I don't care if he says it!" Edith snapped angrily at me. "To me it is a dirty, ugly word and if you want to know, I can't stand that man. He has no manners."

Betty agreed thoroughly.

Again, Judge Older went to the hotel to inform the jurors that since Mr. Hughes had failed to appear, he had appointed Mr. Maxwell Keith to defend Leslie Van Houten. The judge added that he had given the new lawyer ample time to properly prepare himself. He further informed us that we were to remain at the hotel until notified to appear in court.

To everyone's disappointment, His Honor announced the jurors would not go home for Christmas but that they could meet with their families at the hotel. It was as if a bomb had exploded. No one wanted to volunteer, in any way, to make the holidays a happy occasion.

Our daily shopping habits had changed and had become more impersonal. A few of us did manage to be taken into large department stores to make our purchases during the holidays. Grocery shopping was handled by a female deputy sheriff.

We felt like cogs in a wheel—even our morality and religion seemed to have strayed. Every juror had different attitudes.

While carrying on her affair with Tom, Debbie appeared calm, complacent and smiling in front of the jurors, even though we all wanted to go home.

And there was Danny's disturbing habit of pretending to be asleep anywhere at any time at the dinner table during conversations that didn't interest him, even during times he would ride an elevator. Danny developed this habit only after he got to know most of the jurors. Danny's impatience and periods of deep depression and self-doubt often made him ill mannered and short tempered.

Marvin Connolly had been distant and unfriendly towards me. I didn't know why. His fiancée had not been visiting him; however, on one Sunday afternoon while visiting the Los Angeles Municipal Museum in the company of his fiancée Maria, he appeared more receptive but speechless. Maria, at one point, followed me leaving the redheaded juror. I felt uncomfortable and soon after, we returned to Marvin's company.

The next day at the pool, Marvin confided to me he had broken his engagement to Maria because of irreconcilable points of view. For one thing, the juror intensely disliked Maria's lateness in getting ready whenever they had a date and most of all, because she had lied about the accident involving his car.

Marvin observed that Maria cried upon his telling her the bad news and wanted another chance.

"I felt this was coming so I decided to call the whole thing off," Marvin admitted.

Then he added, "Hey Bill, don't tell anyone about my breaking up with Maria. Okay?"

"Is that an admonition?" I uttered half smilingly.

"Yeah," Marvin replied, and smiled back.

The same day, Ruth and Edith joined Marvin and I for lunch. The topic of conversation was Debbie and Tom. Marvin felt uncomfortable and didn't believe the rumors.

"Of course we, as jurors, should have more respect, especially to each other," Ruth said indignantly.

"It's a shame... a shame," interrupted Edith briskly. "How can they do this to their families?"

"Don't turn around just now," Ruth continued, "but when you have a chance, look at them. They are sitting so close to each other that they are playing kneezies."

I had observed all along what was happening but was determined to keep my mouth shut and find out if the other jurors were capable of noticing that Tom and Debbie were not concerned with the looks of the jurors. Obviously, the jurors couldn't disregard their "togetherness" by just ignoring it, but no one ever told them that it was known among the jurors of their affair. We withheld our opinions from telling them they lacked decent respect for the other jurors and for their families as well.

"You're right," Edith said, "I saw them—Oh well, I'm not going to be bothered about it. They deserve each other."

Marvin Connolly hadn't said a word. He just kept on listening, somewhat disgusted with the gossip at the table, but after a glance, he exclaimed, "Unbelievable!"

Later, Marvin, Danny, and the rest of the jurors used the same expression at every given opportunity as a joke.

The long recess of waiting at the hotel made some jurors become friendlier to one another in separate groups.

Betty, though still friendly with Debbie, was the second juror who became another casualty of the clique.

Betty Clark was quiet but self-possessed. She was dignified and poised. She did not care much for parties and never danced during the nine and a half months of sequestration. She preferred being by herself—away in a quiet corner, knitting or just standing with a cigarette in her hand looking out of the window.

Betty preferred simple dinners with her husband in her room or very few old friends. She was not in any sense of the word, gregarious. The thin-looking juror had strong opinions. If she did not like somebody she wouldn't tolerate pretention—she either would say something to the effect or walk

306

away, or better still, ignore that person as if he didn't exist.

Betty told me that her life had been secluded and full of hardships. Her father had been an alcoholic and after years of quarrelling with her mother, had abandoned the family. On several occasions, her father had beaten her sister and even her mother. Betty loathed the thought of those years—she detested the fact that her mother had sacrificed herself in order to give her only two children an honest, decent upbringing.

Betty began to work for a living at a very early age. She helped her mother with the domestic duties of the house and through limited savings she attended school, graduated, and married happily.

When Betty first met her husband, it was a sort of mutual admiration. They both had the same likes and dislikes. They enjoyed immensely hiking and hardly a weekend went by without them making a visit to their cabin in the mountains, which they purchased for themselves as a tenth wedding anniversary gift.

Betty had, like her mother, two children but unfortunately one died at birth. The other son, Steve Jr., grew up to be an example of a studious young man. He has become a scientist and due to his high degree of intelligence, a scholarship has been awarded to further his scientific researches.

Betty felt proud of her son's success and it was her opinion that her son is the reflection of what she would like to have been had she a better childhood. Her husband on the other hand, couldn't be any happier. He had, as he put it, "a perfect marriage." He worked along with Betty for the right decision in how to educate Steve Jr. at home. They invested upon their son, love and care and especially taught him the respect and courtesy towards others. The juror's husband felt contented and rather proud and when it came to food, he couldn't find a better qualified *chef de cuisine* than Betty. Her knowledge of dishes ranged from 300 to 1000 recipes. She's the possessor of a large number of cook books, plus hundreds of idle recipes taken from magazines and food sections in the newspapers.

She became an outspoken juror gradually. Her remarks were derived from the foul playing caused by some of the jurors. She would hear somebody say something and automatically she would make a remark.

As friendly as I was to Betty, she never confided me what she disclosed to George.

It seemed that night after night, while Betty was asleep, she was awakened by voices coming through the opening of the air shaft. The voices were those of Tom and his guest Debbie, who, late at night, were involved in a passionate dialogue of love compliments. The giggling and moaning that usually followed irritated Betty, and to quiet down the sound of the voices, she covered the ventilator with one of her pillows. The trick worked certain nights except those when the protagonists were more emotionally involved in their love affair.

One night, according to George, Betty heard Tom's voice saying, "Why are you taking your clothes off?" to which Debbie's voice replied, "It's hot here..."

George couldn't remember the exact words but then added that Betty, upon hearing an exchange of filthy words, let all her rage burst forth by shouting in the vent so as to be heard. The lovers stopped and from then on, they were more cautious about raising their voices.

Betty and Debbie, for the remainder of being sequestered, avoided each other for obvious reasons.

As to find out how the jurors felt about Tom and Debbie's affair, I conducted an indirect conversation with those jurors who were receptive to the subject.

One time, I was talking to Genero Swanson's wife about the subject of Debbie's affair in the recreation room. Genaro came in and she felt that her private opinion may have inadvertently slipped out, so she hurriedly changed the subject. She never once mentioned Debbie's and Tom's names during the rest of our conversation for fear Genaro would find out. He refrained amazingly well from common gossip among the jurors.

Paul White's self-control was remarkable. He never commented upon the course of the affair.

Frank Welch's jovial personality made him popular. Although he eluded gossip, he admitted he was aware of the affair and urged me to write everything about it.

Marvin Connolly didn't respond upon asking him indirectly about the affair, so I dropped the subject.

Danny Jackson and I got involved in an argument. Frank had stated that Danny would make a good lawyer whereas I contradicted him openly. Danny didn't like it and started to ask me why.

I responded, "You don't like to debate—instead, you prefer boxing. Lawyers have to debate. Debating requires your mind, your speech and your personality."

Inadvertently I had mentioned "speech," knowing beforehand that Danny had a slight speech impediment.

To even the score, Danny answered, "Everybody who comes into this country after three months learns to speak English better than you."

Danny was right. I had been accused of not wanting to lose my accent, but never before like he had put it.

He never seemed to forgive me for daring to defy him. He was utterly disappointed for he had wanted to win the argument.

Martin was narrow in his experiences with social groups. Many of his brief conversations about generalizations were hastily made. He only recognized what he discovered, not at testing out what he believed he saw.

Mollie Kane arranged a Sunday outing to the San Bernardino resort area, just north of the famous Rim of the World Drive.

The excursion turned out to be a successful event on account of bailiff Michael Pappas, who was in charge —Deputy Mike's liberal ideas brought a relief of freedom.

Upon entering the jail bus equipped with sanitary facilities, Mike handed me a pocketful of money and instructed me to distribute it among the jurors —three dollars per juror.

"The money," Mike announced, "is for your lunch. We didn't make reservations, so you can eat anywhere you want at Big Bear Village."

"You mean we're going to be on our own?" asked Frank happily.

"Yes," Mike responded.

The jurors were thrilled and couldn't wait to arrive at the planned destination so they could roam around freely.

Upon arrival, we were given about three hours to return where the bus had been parked.

Betty immediately took off with her husband and wanted no part of any juror's company for the length of time given.

Edith, with three dollars in hand, acting like a child given a piece of candy, didn't know where to start as she stepped off the bus.

Olivia was uncertain where to go.

Marvin, in the company of his friend Tony, seemed unable to make their minds up as where to head. Tony graciously asked me to join him and Marvin for a beer.

The three hours passed by quickly and upon returning to the bus, Mike wanted to tell me something privately.

"You have to put this in your book," he stated as he laughed.

"What is it?" I inquired curiously.

"You should have seen some of the female jurors. They didn't know where to go. They were lost." Mike laughed more. "Ruth and Edith—but especially Ruth couldn't find a rest room so she had to go inside the bus. Luckily I was around; otherwise, she would have peed in her pants!" Mike laughed heartily. "You have to put that down in your book!" Mike emphasized again.

309

"Now you understand what being sequestered does to a person," I said seriously.

"I can see all you people will have to readjust yourselves back to normal living," Mike answered.

"You bet your sweet peepee!" I snapped immediately.

On the way back to the hotel, we picked up a bag full of pine cones which later Mildred decorated with red and green spray paint for Christmas.

The waiting at the hotel brought Debbie and Tom closer every day. They were happy in each other's company. If he hadn't been for Tom, Debbie would have gone crazy. How much loneliness would she have had to accept. Her husband Irving very likely would not have gone on a trip around the world if she hadn't encouraged him.

I noticed how she would bring Tom beer cans and towels and sat on the bench to watch him play paddle tennis. Between ball returns, he would glance at her and their eyes would meet, expressing much more than words could say. One could tell that she would look at his lips with enticed desire, but they could not kiss her back.

The childish attitude of Tom's wife, Claudia, changed considerably to that of a mature adult when she sensed that Tom was paying too much attention to Mrs. Hart.

Where she had been friendly and happy with all the jurors, she became apart and distant.

At the beginning of Tom's sequestration, she had brought some twenty books for the jurors to read. Now, during the holidays, Claudia took it upon herself to show the jurors how to make Christmas bell decorations using old Christmas cards in the recreation room.

While she was explaining, she would look over and notice that her husband was not around which made her suspicious and aware. Two or three times, she went to her husband's room to find him drinking beer with another juror —Mrs. Hart. This scene had been repeated whenever she had wondered where her husband was, so as a precautionary measure, she explained to the jurors working on the decorations that she only had enough time to instruct them once through. She returned and stayed at her husband's room.

Debbie didn't want to accept the reality of spending the holiday season sequestered at the hotel. However, as the months went by and as the weeks progressed one after the other, she began to see the fact that day by day we had to spend the holidays away from our homes. Debbie was the first who came to say how much she hated it because she had already planned a trip around the world with her family. Working for Trans-World Airlines gave her an opportunity which ordinarily wouldn't be possible, especially since she would only pay the minimum fee as all employees of airlines do.

Of course, things developed differently from what she had planned. The affair between she and Tom made her stop complaining about not going home for Christmas. She no longer bothered to say that being locked up in the hotel was horrible and sad, lonely and restless. The same thing happened with Tom —from the beginning he kept from going to the Sunday outings and gradually, he stayed out from any activities except on Fridays, when the jurors went out to some restaurant—then he was really expansive and jolly, but only with the clique. He always sat next to Debbie and played kneesies. Their behavior was so open to each other that there was no question in the jurors' minds that they were carrying on an affair—a torch for each other—they only had eyes for each other and they even began to act without bothering to look around for who was watching them. They couldn't care less.

Aware of Debbie's husband taking a trip around the world and realizing she would be alone at the hotel, Claudia urged Tom, who usually remained at the hotel, to attend the Sunday outing to Paradise Cove Beach,— a movie and television location area on the Pacific Ocean.

The drive was a long one along the busy winding highway that lead eventually to the beach.

Claudia and Tom, carrying a guitar, sat at the rear of the bus. They didn't speak to any of the jurors and upon arrival they walked away from everyone, sank in the sand, and played the guitar. The jurors sensed the watchful, jealous eyes of Mrs. Brooks on her husband.

The excursion provided an excellent opportunity to the jurors to walk by themselves along the beach or to go deep-sea fishing for half a day, escorted by a female deputy who purportedly had written an informative book about deep-sea fishing. The majority took advantage of the expertness of the bailiff's instructions and, needless to say, the outing was so enjoyable that by popular vote among the jurors, they were taken back the following Sunday.

Upon returning from the fishing boat, I noticed Tom and his wife had moved closer to where the bus was parked. Their attitude appeared as if they had been feuding. Their faces were hard and silent. When the jurors went by their side, Tom relaxed his face for a moment to look up at the jurors, but Mrs. Brooks turned her back and shouted something at her husband. Tom remained silent—his eyes searching over the roaring ocean and his body hunched over the guitar.

The clique, in a very shrewd movement, had managed to brainwash deputy Taylor to have them taken to Sammy's Place—a cozy saloon—for drinks and dancing with live musicians.

The clique, with a plastic container, ordinarily would accompany bailiff Taylor and deputy Colvig to get some ice. They would return after two or three hours.

On one occasion, upon returning to the sixth floor, the escorted jurors who had gone for a walk were attracted to the loud music coming from Sammy's Place.

Betty Clark, out of curiosity, peeked inside and instinctively called me to join her. Right in the middle of the floor, dancing cheek-to-cheek were Debbie and Tom, and beside them were Ray and deputy Kathy Colvig equally engrossed in each other. They didn't see us.

"I was wondering why it took so many people to get one bucket full of ice," Betty said sarcastically, and then added, "now that explains it—why they always return talking loud and happily."

"Do they bring any ice upstairs?" I asked Betty.

"I doubt it," she replied jokingly and further observed, "by the way those couples were holding each other, I'm sure the ice would have melted."

Meanwhile, the clique patronized deputy Taylor with all sorts of practical jokes, including a taped version of a bugle call reverie. They would play it for him in the morning. Deputy Taylor was noted for being a heavy sleeper.

Another joke introduced by the clique—"Who's Got the Chicken?"—involved the stealthy placement of a rubber fowl under pillows and other unlikely spots.

Monday, the twenty-first of December, was a day to remember because it was the day we returned to court. We had been waiting at the hotel since November twentieth—almost a month. Two of the jurors during the month had changed somewhat—physically. Genaro Swanson had added a thin-looking moustache. However, all eyes were on me when I first appeared in the court room because I had a full-grown beard and trimmed moustache.

The defendants screened the jurors as each took his seat. Charlie smilingly winked at me and made a gesture of approval at the appearance of my beard. The newsmen were taking notes and the artists were busy drawing the panel jury.

As soon as the proceeding started, Judge Older introduced to us Mr. Maxwell Keith, the newly appointed lawyer to represent defendant Leslie Van Houten. Mr. Keith, nearly sixty years of age, stood up and looked to the jurors with a mixed smiling-and-somber look.

Miss Van Houten immediately leaped to her feet and protested having Mr. Keith as her lawyer. Judge Older denied her request and ordered her to sit down. The slim-looking inmate refused to obey the judge and as she was ejected, she shouted to him, "I won't fight you!" Then, as an afterthought, she sarcastically remarked, "Yes, I will fight you—but not now!"

Miss Krenwinkel rose and shouted some undiscernible phrases and promptly was removed. As she was being led out, the defendant shouted at Judge Older, "Why don't you just kill us now?"

Susan Atkins followed suit and on her way out shouted, "Anyway! Who's got the chicken?" The Los Angeles *Examiner* sunday issue had covered an entire page dedicated to the Tate-La Bianca case jurors being sequestered at Christmas time and they had mentioned the above established game among the jurors.

Manson was next. Deputies Taylor and Tull escorted him out after he had stood up with folded arms and addressed the audience, "Are you actually serious? You can't be serious. Your whole Constitution is based on the right of a man to defend himself."

The prosecutor stated his argument by explaining that he would open first, then the defense would speak, and then he would close his summation.

Mr. Bugliosi began his open argument calmly and, aided by a large board, he read a blowup of a printed page that read:

CRIMINAL HOMICIDE

I. MURDER: The unlawful killing of a human being with malice afore-thought.
Malice may either be expressed or implied.
1. Expressed: Intent to kill.
2. Implied: Killing results from an act by the defendant involving a high degree of probability, it will result in death, and the defendant acts with wanton disregard for human life.

A. *First-degree Murder*
(1) Killing by poison, lying in wait or torture; *OR*
(2) Willful, deliberate and premeditated killing; *OR*
(3) Killing in the perpetration or attempted perpetration of arson, rape, robbery, burglary, mayhem or 288 P.C.

B. *Second-degree Murder*
The unlawful killing of a human being with malice, aforethought, but *without* premeditation.

II. VOLUNTARY MANSLAUGHTER:

The unlawful killing of a human being without malice aforethought. (Killing upon a suddèn quarrel or in the heat of passion where there is *considerable* provocation.)

During the process, Mr. Bugliosi explained once more what conspiracy meant and recalled the example he had given us about A, B, and C. Then he mentioned that very frequently he would refer to transcripts, but only for the highlights of the witnesses' testimonies.

Mr. Bugliosi continued with the elaborated argument, listing the main issues from the different witnesses, not necessarily as they came to testify in court, but in order of the antecedents, as they happened in the court, of the Family's history up until the realization of the crimes committed.

Mr. Bugliosi conveyed issues in his narration that Charlie Manson was the leader of the family—that he made everyone do as he wanted, as he pleased. No one slept until he went to sleep, and the same with eating and sexual intercourse, and the ultimate of his bettings—to kill to commit murder.

The prosecutor then observed that the defense would state out loud that Mr. Manson forced no one to do anything—that everyone was free to come and go.

"Of course," said Mr. Bugliosi, "that's not the issue in this trial," and added, "Charles Manson was the mastermind who sent his robots out on missions of murder."

Mr. Bugliosi, wearing a dark gray suit with vest and conservative dotted-blue tie, raised his voice to bring color and vividness to his speech. His voice had great range and his timing was that of an actor reading a line.

Charles Manson was brought back into court after the last recess.

The prosecutor climaxed his first day's argument by showing the jurors before and after photos of the five badly butchered victims at the Tate residence. Mr. Bugliosi, carrying the five colored photographs, approached the jury box and solemnly stated as he pointed at one picture, "This is what Sharon Tate looked like in real life... a beautiful creature."

The people in the audience, unable to see the photograph, showed their eagerness by bending forward and sideways but to no avail.

"Here is the ghastly horrifying way she looked after Sadie, Katie and Tex savagely murdered her," commented Mr. Bugliosi as he showed a picture that revealed the naked body of the pregnant actress lying in a pool of blood.

Charles Manson, the only defendant in the courtroom at the time, interrupted the prosecutor at that point, by saying:

"And in color, too! That should influence them."

After Mr. Bugliosi had shown the photographs, he stated:

"It was not enough for Charlie that his robots had just viciously butchered five people. Even while the blood was still trickling from the victims' bodies, he wanted to know from these robots if they had any remorse."

As he concluded, Mr. Bugliosi looked sideways for a moment to see Charlie, who was rubbing his devilishly trimmed beard and smiling.

"After all, there was no need for remorse... you should let birds live—yes, and rattlesnakes, yes—but no human beings, according to Charlie... a real considerate guy."

The next day all the defendants were in court. They were dressed not as prisoners but with rather fashionable dresses, especially the tall, slim Leslie Van Houten, who looked chic in a beaded, fitted dress with long sleeves. Charlie was wearing a shiny, gray coat. Somehow, it looked like a cross between a Flamenco jacket and a Confederate soldier's jacket with a vertical array of buttons on each side. Charlie looked very striking, especially with the newly trimmed beard.

Again, Leslie Van Houten asked—politely—the Judge something which we could not hear because of the sounds of the chairs and voices in the background.

The following colloquy took place:

"What is it Miss Van Houten?" asked Judge Older.

"Your Honor, I would like to make a motion," said the defendant.

"Your lawyer can make it for you."

"But Your Honor, I want my own lawyer—not this man whom I don't know."

"If you don't sit down, I'll have you taken out of the court room," replied Judge Older firmly.

Leslie Van Houten became boisterous and unintelligible. She was removed by order of the Court and again she stopped in front of the Judge's bench and said:

"I'll take care of you, you'll see."

Mr. Bugliosi continued his argument without paying attention, but about two minutes after, Patricia Krenwindel stood up and did almost the same as Leslie Van Houten. She was also removed and said somewhat the same remarks to the Judge on her way out.

Mr. Bugliosi, by order of Judge Older, kept on looking at his notes so as to continue the delivery of his argument, but instantly, Susan Atkins got up and shouted:

"We're nothing but prisoners!"

The Court, without any hesitation, ordered her to be removed. Susan, as she passed by in front of Mr. Bugliosi, snatched some of his yellow page notes so as to throw them on the floor. The female deputy escorting the prisoner caught the defendant's hand and locked her arm behind her back. At the same time, with his other hand, Mr. Bugliosi tried to stop Susan and shouted, "You little bitch!"

The prisoner laughed loudly as she was being dragged from the court room.

The handsome prosecutor spent a great deal of time recapping the testimony of major prosecution witnesses to stress the main evidence in the motive.

"Charles Manson, and he alone, had a bizarre motive," said Mr. Bugliosi, "a simple bizarre motive: Murder. It was not money obviously, no personal property was taken from the premises nor from the victims. The residences were not ransacked, drawers were not opened—at the La Bianca home, there were expensive collections of coins, guns and also a large amount of money."

Mr. Bugliosi emphasized his point by repeating what Susan Atkins had said to Virginia Graham that "when they went to the Tate residence, everybody was going to be killed—not robbed."

"Otherwise," he continued, "why was Frykowski stabbed thirteen times and not twice? Rosemary La Bianca was stabbed forty-one times. They could have been robbed, with no need to kill in both nights. In view that hardly anything was taken from the residences, the mission on both nights was clear and simple: *Murder.* Why were these murders committed? It appears there were three motives: Manson's hatred for human beings, passion, and lust for violence—anyone having these vile desires must be savage. Death is Charles' trip."

Mr. Bugliosi allowed himself a brief pause to take a sip from a glass of water. He continued, "Another motive was Manson's anti-establishment, his hate for the established citizen—but the principle motive was Manson's Helter Skelter mania, that was his religion. Charles Manson's twisted mind was to start a war between black and white men. Imagine the inevitable barbarianism which ended by such bizarre crimes. Ladies and gentlemen, the evidence came from the witness stand."

Mr. Bugliosi pointed at the witness stand, pounded mildly on the podium, and added, "He told Linda Kasabian 'now is the time to show blackie how to do it'."

The prosecutor then went on to enumerate different examples of how Helter Skelter philosophy was promulgated over and over to the members of the family, such as signs written at the ranch and using the same words at the residences where the crimes were committed. Mr. Bugliosi then submitted strong arguments linking the co-defendants of Manson.

"The fact that Tex Watson was present, which was proved because of his fingerprints, is enough circumstantial evidence against his co-conspirators, the three female defendants. No two fingerprints are identical. Patricia Krenwinkel's fingerprints and Susan Atkins' hair tests from Sergeant Granado and her confessions to other inmates at Sybil Brand Institute.

"Linda Kasabian gave evidence to what Charles Manson told Leslie Van Houten. Linda Kasabian proves beyond any doubt that Charles Manson's motive was to kill and the weapons which were used were obtained by him. The rope, several witnesses proved, was the same rope bought and carried on Charlie's dune buggy. It was proven also that he had been at the Tate residence and that he had been hostilely received by Mr. Hatami. Further evidence occurs with the leather thongs which he no longer had on his neck while at the beach and, of course, Charlie's own confession to Juan Flynn two or three days after he saw them leave from the ranch. Ladies and gentlemen, his confessions made afterward without Linda Kasabian's testimony are sufficient to find them guilty of first-degree murder."

Mr. Bugliosi brought excitement to his powerful argument when he reviewed Linda Kasabian's testimony.

The prosecutor called the petite Mrs. Kasabian the "Star Witness" of the prosecution.

"Her story of the Tate-La Bianca killings was not budged one iota in the twenty-five thousand pages of cross-examination. The defense attorneys will concentrate on portraying Mrs. Kasabian as living a drug-oriented, sexually promiscuous life. So what?" the prosecutor asked.

"What does that have to do with the fact that Linda was with these defendants on two nights of murder? Although she is not an angel, she is not cut from the same cloth as the defendants."

Then, Mr. Bugliosi, as to cover the guilt participation of Leslie Van Houten in the La Bianca murders, read from a transcript her conversation with Diane Lake.

The sharp-looking prosecutor quoted the young woman as saying, "Miss Van Houten told her she didn't want to stab the person at first, but finally did and found that she enjoyed it."

"We have another sweetheart to join Susan Atkins," Mr. Bugliosi said. "They love stabbing people!"

Mr. Bugliosi stressed that the prosecution had proven beyond a doubt that Linda Kasabian was along that night because she left Rosemary La Bianca's wallet in a Sylmar service station where it was later found.

"To fool the La Biancas, ladies and gentlemen, Charles Manson wore the same mask he has here in court—that of a peace-loving man."

Mr. Bugliosi then quoted from Linda Kasabian's testimony that when Manson came back to the car that night, he told "Tex," "Katie," and Miss Van Houten that he had tied up a couple inside and instructed the trio not to panic them. The prosecutor said that the La Biancas had no reason to know that they were being prepared in a soft voice and with a soft manner—for horrible deaths.

He added:

"Both had pillow cases over their heads. Electrical cords were wrapped around their necks and Leno La Bianca's hands had been bound with a leather thong."

The deputy district attorney then suggested: "The La Biancas still could have walked, or might have called the police or locked the door if they had not believed with assurance everything would be all right."

"This man," said Mr. Bugliosi sarcastically as he pointed at Manson, "has to be one of the most considerate men in the world. They should erect a a monument to him at the United Nations. He wouldn't harm a flea. The only problem is that he thinks it's grand to murder human beings. He does believe in murdering human beings!"

Again, Mr. Bugliosi took a pause to take a sip from a glass of water and then added:

"On the night the La Biancas were killed, Manson and his followers conducted a random search for murder victims from Pasadena to Sunset Boulevard to the beach.

"On that evening, no one in this community of seven million persons was safe from Manson's unsatiable lust for death, blood, and murder!"

The prosecution lawyer concluded by saying that Patricia Krenwinkel was guilty of seven counts of murder, Susan Atkins for five counts, Leslie Van Houten for two, and that since Charles Manson *was not* one of the actual killers and Susan Atkins *was not* at the La Bianca estate—*still*—they were all guilty—by joint responsibility rule.

"Ladies and gentlemen, Charles Manson masterminded these seven slayings by sending out his zombies on missions of murder. Manson preached love and practiced cold-blooded murder. There's only *one* verdict, and that is the verdict of guilt by first-degree murder!"

Back at the hotel, I was taking a shower when Mollie knocked on my door. Luckily, I was already drying so I went to the door with a towel around my waist.

"Could you be ready at ten-thirty for a meeting in the recreation room?" she inquired.

"Okay. Oh! By the way," I began asking her, "who's holding the meeting?"

"Alb and I," she responded.

"Fine. I'll be there."

As I closed the door, it dawned on me that twice before Mollie had knocked on my door and twice I had appeared with a towel draped around my waist.

Amusingly, I reopened the door to find her knocking on Edith's door. I mentioned the coincidence to her and she answered: "My timing is good! Isn't it?"

"Yeah! Watch it the next time—I may not be able to put anything on when you approach my door again."

We both laughed and I closed my door.

Unfortunately, that day I had a terrible pain on my left side near my waist. Perhaps it was due to having slept in the crack between the two single beds which formed the king size bed. I vaguely recalled sleeping on that side. Because of the sore back, I was a restless sleeper. I usually awakened every hour during the night. Hotel beds rarely accommodate me comfortably. I joined the meeting.

"We can't take chances to take you out of the hotel," Mollie observed, "so, for Christmas Day, we have reserved two rooms downstairs. The Embassy Room and the Gold Room."

"Is the Embassy Room where Bobby Kennedy was shot?" inquired Olivia Madison to Mollie.

"Yes," interjected Ruth quickly, "that's the room."

George wanted to know what kind of arrangements had been provided for children. Mollie replied that the Gold Room was for those jurors who had children only.

"That suits me fine," whispered Betty. "I couldn't take Tom's children."

Mollie announced that guests were allowed.

The preparations had been started. Mollie ordered a Christmas tree which was placed in the recreation room. No one wanted to help with the tree decorations except Violet, Mildred, and this juror writer.

Martin Paine and I worked on and off to make ornaments as Mrs. Brooks had shown us and hung them on strings.

The Los Angeles *Examiner* sunday issue carried a whole page relating to the world the jurors of the Manson trial—how they were busy and happily preparing for the holidays while being sequestered.

319

Mollie appeared in a photo holding one of the ornaments. Every juror had a good laugh when they read the exaggerated information in the article, which was far from the truth. None of the jurors were happy.

Every juror, except Danny and I, had some sort of display outside on the door. Both Danny and I wanted no part of any holiday activity. The "clique" hung a huge snowman poster on Danny's door.

I personally didn't feel like the rest because being sequestered meant I was not going to San Francisco to spend Christmas with my family. No one had dropped in to see me during the Christmas holidays. I was sad and lonely. Laura had not visited nor called me. She was never home when I called her. My letters were never answered. I didn't know why she had kept away. I wondered why.

Debbie's three teen-age children had come to decorate her door to surprise her. Mr. Hart, before leaving on his trip around the world, had brought his wife a beautiful tree but Debbie had sent him back to return it for a small, blue, frosted tree.

"How can she do that to him?" said Betty. "Debbie should be glad to have any tree. She has the nerve to demand from her husband after what she's doing to him. Ough!"

George, walking at her side, and I, trailing behind them for lack of space around the pool, stared at the thin-looking juror and listened attentively.

Betty and George felt that Debbie was playing with fire and that, at the end, she would get burned. The two jurors agreed they couldn't do that to their own spouses.

To add to the confusion, Mollie departed for Colorado to join her mother and sister for the holidays. The absence of the tough-looking but likeable female bailiff was felt among some jurors, especially at the time of Christmas Day reception, when everything seemed to be out of order. The bailiffs who substituted for those who worked normal hours treated the jurors like real prisoners.

George had a light altercation with a chubby transportation officer when he was told he couldn't go to the next room to join his daughter.

George and the bailiff had cutting words. George's temper raised considerably. Jokingly, I intervened as to avoid any fight, but the freckle-faced deputy seriously stressed, "I can take both of you!"

I pulled George, who followed me reluctantly, away. The alternate juror swore he would do something to go back home because he was fed up with the length of time the trial had taken and he couldn't take it any longer.

One night, shortly before Christmas, I was called to the little lobby for an

320

outside telephone call.

"Hello, Bill," said a mellow deep voice. I recognized it.

"Jim Reid," I said, "I told you not to call me—the bailiffs don't like it."

"Bill, it's important."

For a second, my friend's voice hesitated and then continued:

"Laura's uncle is here and wants to speak to you...."

"What happened?" I asked him.

"He'll tell you... here...."

My heart contracted. Perhaps Laura had become pregnant.

"Hello, Mr. Zamora?... You don't know me. I'm the uncle of Laura."

The seriousness of the man's voice overlapped his heavy foreign accent.

"Yes," I answered, hoping he would speed up and say what he had to tell me. The suspense was killing me.

"Mr. Zamora... I don't know what to say... I...." over the wire, I heard the man give an inarticulate cry and then a sound like the dangling receiver of the phone had been dropped. My eardrums ached.

Again, I heard Jim's voice saying, "Bill...."

"Would you please tell me what's going on there?" I said, beginning to feel exasperated.

"Bill... Laura's dead...." Jim stated flatly.

Silence.

"My God!" I exclaimed. For a second, it was all I could say.

This was all so shocking. I grasped for words and for an instant it was hard for me to concentrate any longer.

With an effort, I uttered, "how did it happen?"

"In an accident... an automobile accident...." Laura's uncle had told Jim what had happened.

It seemed Laura had gone up to San Jose to see some relatives. Upon returning to Los Angeles, accompanied by her uncle, Laura was driving along side a huge truck which made her nervous. She slowed down and tried to pull over on the shoulder when, unexpectedly, another car behind, hit her automobile. The severe impact caused Laura to lose control of the wheel, and the car plunged into an embankment. Her uncle suffered minor injuries. Laura died a few hours later.

"Is there anything I can do?" I asked miserably to Laura's uncle when he returned to the phone.

"Nothing...." he replied, and then added, "Thanks, Mr. Zamora, for having been so wonderful to Laura. If it hadn't been for you, she would have... done away with herself. Thanks again... Perhaps this way is better... have a

321

good night's rest and tomorrow when you think of Laura..." I heard the man cry, "...please...pray for her soul..."

"I'm sorry, Sir," I said with trembling lips and then, "good night..." and slowly hung the receiver on the phone.

Upon returning to my room, I felt my eyes moist and nostrils dilated. I knew with deep conviction that I would never see Laura again. When I reached my room and slammed the door against the curious eyes of some of the jurors, I turned on the tape recorder and played the music loudly. I threw myself on the bed and gave way to a tortured sob. The rest of the week dragged into an eternity.

Christmas Eve was a sad occasion. Every juror locked himself in his own room until the reception.

Betty remained in her room with her husband. Edith had some six guests, members of her church, and they left early.

Ruth was very happy because her daughter had come to visit her and shrewdly invited Marvin and Danny, who had no visitors, to her table. Ruth had confided openly to some jurors that the two young jurors would be a good "catch" for her daughter. Ruth was especially fond of Danny and wanted her daughter to meet him.

Genaro and Mildred stayed a short while with their spouses. Paul White's wife, Sylvia, was bedded down with a cold but their two teen-age children, Paul, Jr. and Lynn, arrived to keep him company. It was at Paul's invitation that I join him and his family.

Lynn's sweet beauty was that of a Madonna. Her brother, a young rascal, asked me to get a vodka and Seven Up from the bartender so his father would not find out.

Olivia Madison had bought herself a colorful jersey pantsuit and had spent two hours in the beauty parlor. The retired drama writer was expecting company and had asked me to help her entertain her guests, whom she claimed were young people of the "jet set" generation.

Olivia's company consisted of three young and attractive couples. They all appeared bored. Olivia came over to my table and asked me again to please join her guests for a while. Olivia had taken advantage of the open-bar facilities and was feeling no pain. She could be joked out of anything but her weakness for drinking.

Dr. Little, Olivia's boyfriend, didn't show up at the party and sent his two daughters instead with their respective boyfriends. The other couple was visiting from Texas and, to my surprise, I discovered they were brother and sister—Vito and Dena. Both were most charming and pleasant to talk with.

322

Dena was an especially appealing and enchanting girl. Her deep blue eyes, ash blonde hair, and radiant complexion caught my attention immediately. All of a sudden, the party began to come to life.

Dena's beautiful and sensitive smile brought relief to my sadness. Her youthful attitude masqueraded her deep concern with the complexities of this world. Dena brought, with her presence, a whole set of new values to my life. I suddenly realized my entire behavior had been depressed on account of Laura's death. Fortunately, none of the jurors suspected, for I did not want their sympathy. Dena's forwardness was indeed that of the new generation: bold, clear, and to the point. She openly expressed her desire to see me after the trial was over and wanted to know if I was "going steady" with anyone.

"No woman has visited me for the last month or so," I confided.

"But you are involved with someone, aren't you?" Dena inquired suggestively.

"What is this?" I protested. "A questioning?"

"When I want something, I usually get it," replied Dena as she got up and asked her brother to dance and then, rather coquettishly, exclaimed "like dancing?" Vito didn't know what she was saying as he had been busy talking with the others.

Upon her return, the dazzling young-looking girl sat next to me and unexpectedly declared, "If I'm going to see you again, I want to know where I stand. Are you going with anybody?"

She was serious.

I just looked at Dena and didn't say anything. Her frankness astonished me. I couldn't believe it.

Unaware to my thoughts, I smiled tenderly. Dena's eyes stared at me, waiting for my reply. Unconsciously, under the table, I placed my hand over hers and squeezing them warmly I responded, "No one."

For a moment, Dena and I just looked at each other like no one around existed. We both smiled with contentment. Our spell was interrupted when Vito announced he had to get up early to catch a plane to Forth Worth.

The three young couples departed. Dena promised to write me soon. She did.

In the meantime, I noticed that Marvin, and especially Danny, had been drinking more than usual. Danny's hair was ruffled.

George, Martin, Frank, Ruth and her daughter, Marvin, Danny, and I decided to go to midnight mass. At the last minute, Olivia wanted to join the group. She was unable to stand up, much less walk. She asked George to help her by holding onto his arm.

As soon as we returned to the hotel, George excitedly entered my room and wanted to tell me that Olivia had upset him.

It seemed that on the way to church, Olivia tripped at least a half a dozen times on the four blocks' walk and if it hadn't been for her holding onto George's arm, she would have fallen flat on her face on the street.

"Anyway," George said, "I was thinking maybe the fresh air would do her some good, maybe I could help her out. She was... you know... happy all this time and you know, she was fun to be with... she wasn't nasty or anything. We went inside the church and it was packed. So, we went downstairs to a good-sized chapel.

"The mass started and the priest read the letter from Saint Paul to Titus and Olivia said, in a real high-toned voice that everybody turned around to hear her, "Oh, I just love Paul."

"Yes... yes," I whispered, "take it easy. So do I."

"The services continued and the priest talked about forgiving other people and turning the other cheek, and then mentioned some people have a problem with drinking. I doubt if Olivia heard the word 'drink' but that seemed to trigger her mouth and she started to get nasty."

I smiled, and George continued.

"When they started the communion, I got up to go to communion. She stood up and said in a loud voice: "Oh, where are you going?"

"I'm going to communion."

"Well, I want to go, too."

"No. You can't. You have to stay here. I'll be right back."

"Okay," Olivia finally said.

George then explained that he was unable to control the intoxicated juror and asked Mable, the female deputy in charge at the time and wife of the Sergeant Chief of all the deputies, to sit next to Olivia to control her.

"Olivia would not be consoled and began to get really obnoxious, aggressive, arrogant... and kind of nasty."

"On the way out of church," George continued, "the mass on the main auditorium had not finished and the people trying to exit were being blocked by those standing outside the church.

"Everybody waited on three landings and Olivia was really wound up tight," George said, and then imitating Olivia, added "her mouth was going 'yakky, yakky... chacki, chacki'.. and it was obvious to everybody that she was drunk and that she could barely stand up. I still offered her my arm, but she refused me."

Again George imitated Olivia's voice and continued: "*'No*! I'm not going to take any arm.... You're just another shitty Catholic,' and she said it very loud—loud enough for everybody standing on the three landings to turn around and stare at her."

"At this stage of the game, I walked off and left the whole group. *Forget it!* I don't want to be with that old bag that she can't control herself that much."

"You're upset," I said, "since you walked in..."

"You damn right! Because I feel that was too much!"

George finally calmed down and after a while, we talked about the other jurors. George confided to me an incident between him and Ruth, which only proved that jurors under sequestered circumstances would do anything to fight loneliness.

Ruth's room was located diagonally across from George's and both visited each other occasionally. One time, at Ruth's room, she suggested intimate relations and even placed her hand on George's leg. After he told Ruth he couldn't do it because he loved his wife, George fled immediately back to his room. George admitted the incident to his wife. Three months later, George's wife announced that she was pregnant but it only proved to be a false alarm.

Back in court, Mr. Fitzgerald, looking very pale and speaking in a soft voice, began his final argument by reading word-by-word the first part of the Grand Jury Indictments. The defense lawyer emphasized his delivery by looking straight at the jurors, but not necessarily individually. Then he continued by just enunciating the names of the victims. Then, he finally read the indictment of conspiracy.

The tall-looking attorney had only a few written notes and made almost no use of the trial transcripts. He raised the question of murder and stated, "Little has been spoken about murder and less about conspiracy. The trial could have taken less time than it has. I apologize for the length of the trial and I feel sympathy and empathy for you."

He moved to the center of the court room and added, "Charles Manson and these defendants cannot be tried for their behavior as hippies—even if they were right-wing hippies. I have confidence that you will have the courage to declare the verdict of conviction." Mr. Fitzgerald promptly excused himself and smiling, half embarrassed, corrected himself, "I mean, the verdict of innocence."

Slowly, the defense counsel approached the jury box and eloquently stated, "You cannot reach a verdict by speculating. You have to be certain—not just partly—of any evidence. You have to be morally certain. You have to be sure beyond any reasonable doubt. Use your common sense, analyze these witnesses. You, ladies and gentlemen, have more experience than me. Use your intelligence. Don't be beguiled. You said that you could acquit a defendant even if the defendant didn't take the witness stand. I believed you, and still believe you."

Mr. Fitzgerald walked back nearly to his seat and, staring at the ceiling, observed, "You are going to be instructed by the court that the defendants relied on the state of evidence presented in court, and that they can choose to remain silent by their own case. If we were to rebutt every murder, we would be here until 1974. The question is that you should be careful, that you should not be influenced by photographs of evidence, some of which are gruesome... horrible. You'll see seventy-four different photos of dead bodies."

The defense counsel paused and, raising his voice, asked, "Is that necessary? Some are in color. Seventeen of stab wounds and gunshot wounds.

"You listened to some terrible descriptions of the same – it is hard not be moved or influenced. When we hear about killings, we are terrified, we don't like it. All we can think of are vengeance and retribution.

"These photos, if you please, are not pleasant. Any photos of Viet Nam or an accident are not pleasant. In California Civil Court, photos are not admissible because they only seek repulsion. You'd be shown these photos at the very time when you have to deliberate, whether they did it or not! It is only the tendency to seek reaction. Try, please, not be influenced by photographs."

The senior defense counsel took a brief pause and added, "Now, in addition to what you said when you were selected, you promised that the fact they are accused of multiple murders, you were not going to be influenced or moved. You said you would be able to judge them innocently."

Upon returning from lunch, Mr. Fitzgerald spoke of the definitions of premeditated and deliberate—the roots and significance of such words. Then, linking his argument to that of Mr. Bugliosi's, he stated, "We are not talking about first-degree murder. The prosecutor had said, mindless—robots—zombies, and those who followed all orders explicitly cannot commit first degree murder. They are not capable to think. They follow orders only, they're incapacitated. Where, where is the evidence of agreement between Charles Manson and Patricia Krenwinkel? Between Susan Atkins and Charles Manson? Between Leslie Van Houten and Charles Manson? There was none."

Following those questions, Mr. Fitzgerald retaliated the statements against the evidence submitted by witnesses Ireland and Garretson. According to the defense counsel, they could hear from three-quarters of a mile. Mr. Fitzgerald continued:

"There's evidence of plenty of drugs on the Tate premises. Why didn't Charles Manson send men instead of girls—some girls, the barrister tells us—to look at Voytick Frykowski and Abigail Folger. They were big, tall people. Also, why didn't Charles Manson sent a machine gun or a bigger weapon? Also, why didn't they run away—maybe to Mexico? No! They stayed right here at the Spahn Ranch. They stayed twenty-nine days. Did they try to remove the license plate of the car? No!"

Mr. Fitzgerald leaned on the podium and loudly asked us, "To really think of why—what—how—when. Real simple words—nothing profound, nothing legalistic—yet, simple ordinary words."

Mr. Fitzgerald's argument was lengthy and interesting and when he spoke about Linda Kasabian, he stated, "Linda Kasabian's performance as a witness was a model of contentment, suave-spoken, presentable—a model of decor. She appeared to be intelligent, courteous, reserved—in total, a great facade of a performance in front of the jurors. I was moved and even questioned myself that I would have to be a Perry Mason to break her down and make her confess that she was lying."

Mr. Fitzgerald, in his powerful delivery, scathingly attacked the testimony of Linda Kasabian. The senior defense counsel stated in his final argument, "Ladies and gentlemen, Linda Kasabian claimed she did not know their mission that night... and she put on a good facade while she testified, leading you to believe she was sweet and somewhat misguided, with very little human experience. Linda Kasabian conveyed the image of being some sort of new American Puritan, when in reality, she is a sophisticated young woman who knows her way around. She has been married twice. Has two children. Has hitchhiked across the country seven times. Has lived in eleven to twenty communes. Has taken drugs since she was sixteen and has had sexual liaisons too numerous for any of us to count. Would you gamble your life savings on her testimony?" asked the attorney. "If you wouldn't, then you can't gamble my client's life on her testimony."

Mr. Fitzgerald, in a change of pace, mentioned that he would wrap up his argument. All of a sudden, he turned somber, rhetorical, and softly spoken.

"Without any authority from my client or the other defendants," Mr. Fitzgerald said, "I would like to sincerely and honestly apologize for their conduct and behavior."

He walked two steps toward the center and admitted:

"I ask you to blame me and not my client, Patricia Krenwinkel, for refusing to supply exemplars of her handwriting. I apologize to the court and the jurors especially for perhaps having asked questions to all witnesses, questions which might have offended you."

Mr. Fitzgerald, softly speaking, turned his argument into a powerful and vivid speech. His face was filled with sorrow and almost to the verge of tears. Enunciating word by word, he became almost childlike, innocent, humble, timid. Retreating his body momentarily, he looked into our eyes. His eyes slowly becoming redder, his throat having difficulty to articulate or mouthing words—words to convey, to reach our compassion, our sorrowfulness.

"I implore you. I beg you. Have the courage to acquit these defendants. I beg you to make every conceivable effort to divorce the incredible character assassination from the cold, hard facts."

The handsome, baby-faced counsel thanked the jurors again. When he finished his argument, he turned around and as he reached for his chair and sat down, he pulled a handkerchief and gently wiped his eyes. The silence was disturbed only by the sound of the fans.

I looked at the audience. They had their eyes clawed in all the jurors, anxious to see their reactions. The press and television newsmen wanted to take note of the reactions displayed by any juror. The jurors sat still and none released their emotions.

At that moment, as I looked at each juror, I wondered about the final verdict. Would the jurors vote guilty or not guilty? Or perhaps, we would wind up in a hung jury. I trembled for a split second and tried to jot down more notes.

As I looked again, the defense lawyers—all of them—appeared petrified. None of them said anything. Mr. Fitzgerald had buried his head into his hands—he remained in that position for a few minutes. Suddenly, he lifted his head and looked toward the judge's bench. He stared in that direction but as if there was nothing to see—a blank wall. One could shake one's hand in front of his face and he would not have blinked or seen a thing. The tall, handsome attorney appeared almost as if he had run a long distance without stopping. He looked tired, exhausted, and beaten. There was silence in the court room. Even the Judge seemed appalled. Serenity flooded among spectators, jurors, and counselors. Judge Older proceeded and asked Mr. Shin to start his final argument.

The neatly dressed and soft-spoken Mr. Shin stood up and walked directly to the center. The Oriental attorney carried with him a large handwritten chart which read "Presumption Of Innocence." The small but well-built lawyer explained the nature of such a statement. Then, pulling out two sheets of paper from a manila envelope, he showed them to the jurors. On one sheet, the name Roni Howard was printed, and on the other, Virginia Graham.

"These two witnesses have been accepted as true eligible witnesses," said the attorney of Susan Atkins meekly, "but their behavior and fast conduct against the law made them questionable." The lawyer mocked their testimony and immediately linked them with the twenty-five-thousand-dollar reward.

Mr. Shin pulled another sheet with the name Danny DeCarlo at the top. As he held the sheet in front of the jury, I noticed there were about four items which marked the past police record of DeCarlo; his different kinds of arrests and convictions. The defense counsel again reminded us that the witness was liable for the twenty-five-thousand-dollar reward, and made a point of the fact that DeCarlo had never held a job in his life.

Sarcastically, Mr. Shin asked the jury, as he moved towards them, "How would you like to have him as your son-in-law or your brother-in-law?"

The other defense counsel and some jurors laughed. I didn't feel it was a reason for laughing—for me, it was not funny at all.

The proceedings under Mr. Shin were very slow—almost to the point of stillness. He made some attempt to indulge the jurors to take notes and suggested them to use the method of elimination in reaching their verdict.

"By the time you get to the jury room, I know you all will be curious to see the pictures of the victims. I know, because I was curious to see them myself. I ask you not to see them. Weigh only the evidence without looking at such material, which undoubtedly, will move you and make you go the wrong way. Base your judgment on the evidence and not in pictures."

Mr. Shin moved back towards the center of the room and began speaking about the testimony of Linda Kasabian.

"The time when Linda Kasabian cried on the witness stand—let's see, almost for three minutes she cried. Don't let that compel you and make you change your verdict. Who knows? She might have cried because she was on trial and possibly afraid to be condemned to the gas chamber."

With a little smile, Mr. Shin added sarcastically, "Sure! If I was afraid of the gas chamber, I'd also cry. I'd cry for a whole year!"

Mr. Fitzgerald, who had gotten up to get a glass of water, burst into a laugh, followed by Mr. Kanarek. Mr. Keith simply ran his hand over his hair while looking at the jurors, who remained motionless.

The petite lawyer, in order to make a point, unfolded a short story of his.

"When I was thirteen years old, I wanted a harmonica, but I couldn't afford it. So I went to a five-and-ten cents store and as I was admiring it, I just put it inside my sleeve. I felt guilty. When I walked out, no one followed me but, inside, I thought that everybody was following me. I arrived home and hid the harmonica under the mattress. My father noticed my behavior. At school, the following Monday, I felt as if somebody was going to tell the police. I was

329

unhappy and guilty, but fortunately, my father gave me some money and I took it to the store that day. Right afterwards, I felt the day was sunny, the birds sang everywhere—I was happy. That's the way these defendants feel right now."

Mr. Shin attempted to bring forth his final argument but with little conviction, and ended it by asking for a Not Guilty Verdict.

Mr. Kanarek, in his final argument, didn't waste any time to remind the jurors of what Mr. Fitzgerald had told us, "You are going to live for the rest of your lives with this verdict. We must consider that this case, due to the extreme publicity generated by the press, was given more than it should have received. The law enforcement is to be blamed."

Immediately, Mr. Bugliosi arose and protested, and Judge Older sustained his objection.

Mr. Kanarek continued by telling the jurors about how good and comfortable the Ambassador Hotel was, but that it must have been a "jail for them."

"Imagine what Mr. Manson has been living in. In a dungeon... a dungeon," he repeated.

"Since we are going to discuss this case..." he added, and passed the first color picture of Sharon Tate.

I noticed some of the jurors didn't want to see them and quickly passed them to the next juror without looking at them.

Mr. Kanarek proceeded to show some other photos and the same thing happened again. The majority refused to see them or even look at them.

I found myself holding some while looking at another, when all of a sudden I was pressured to pass them all. Everybody was watching us and naturally they noticed I was taking longer than anyone else. By conscience, I had to see them. Yes—one by one.

"I can see this is going to be a rough deliberation," I told myself. "A tough meeting of jurors." Then I thought, "Wow! I didn't think it was going to be this tight."

Obviously, some jurors were afraid of even seeing those photos. To my belief, I thought they ought to see them—see what the lawyers had been talking about the past months.

"What will it be?" I said to myself and added pensively, "Please God, give me the strength to be able to reach an honest and fair decision on this coming deliberation."

The second day of Mr. Kanarek's final argument, he started saying, "You should get to the inner reaction of true evidence."

Then he surprised everyone by adding, "Take for instance, Mr. Welch. Mr. Welch has been retired from the Los Angeles County Sheriff's Office since..."

Judge Older had no sooner heard the juror's name when he called the defense counsel to approach the bench with the rest of counsel from both sides.

Mr. Welch meanwhile, astonishingly said to Marvin, half smiling, "When I heard my name, it woke me up."

Of course, the eldest of the jurors was simply joking as no one could sleep, especially Mr. Welch, who was juror 3 and sat in the front row. Judge Older maintained a watchful eye on the jurors.

Mr. Kanarek's argument after two days, hadn't started to use any of his notes, of which he had plenty—a thick stack of written yellow pages, court transcripts, and some other folders.

Like Mr. Shin, Mr. Kanarek brought to the jurors' attention a huge white board and with a black-tip pencil, he drew a horizontal line which he referred to as the neutral line. Then he drew another line close and parallel to the first one but which cut the previous one (neutral line) at midpoint. He called the second line the civil line. Then he drew a third line in a diagonal fashion from left to right, passing through the intersection of the first two lines. The diagonal line he called the criminal line.

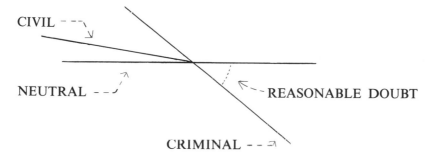

Upon explaining the meaning of the chart, Mr. Kanarek declared that the area between the neutral and criminal lines comprehended the state of reasonable doubt.

After spending about a quarter of an hour, the stocky lawyer established his trend of thought and introduced the false verdict that Linda Kasabian testified during her long testimony on the witness stand. He argued, "Linda Kasabian cannot be accepted as a reliable witness. A witness who has been charged with seven counts of murder and one of conspiracy. She's an instrument programmed by the prosecution. Linda Kasabian lied and consequently her testimony is not valid and, concurrently, the evidence supplied by other witnesses could not corroborate—simply, because she was not telling the truth."

The jurors always tittered with sarcasm whenever Mr. Kanarek made use of the personal pronoun "us". He addressed the jurors as if he was one of them. Unfortunately, none of us jurors could stand up and let him know that he was not a juror. Mr. Kanarek's job was to try to get us on his side and I supposed that was the best way he knew how.

Charles Manson's lawyer presented at great length Linda Kasabian's life, including "her candid attitude in court which in no way reflects her true identity. The fact of her sexual relationships with members of the family and her affair with John Sage and how she obtained money from him, left him, and defrauded him—perhaps from sexual favors."

Apart from attacking Linda Kasabian's conduct, Mr. Kanarek also brought to the jurors' attention something he had done all through the trial: charging the witnesses of being an instrument and being programmed by the prosecution.

He repeatedly mentioned that the Assistant District Attorney, Mr. Vincent Bugliosi, had casually and in a friendly way, used her name, Linda, in open court and that probably she called him Vincent in his office.

Mr. Kanarek insisted that we should use that liaison of friendship as an example of the training, rehearsing, and programming that took place and developed among officers of the law and especially between Mr. Bugliosi and Linda Kasabian.

"Surely, we, counsels for the defense, could have done the same thing," he said, "had we the opportunity to speak with her, but she refused—she denied us, and Mr. Bugliosi took the opportunity of talking to her. Why?"

Mr. Kanarek, while using the court transcripts, endlessly quoted every answer and question and even the objections made by Judge Older.

The short and fat lawyer, beyond the scope of limitation, prolonged his final argument by reading over and over and then analyzing, word by word. The final argument of Mr. Kanarek reflected a total lack of preparation.

He went as far as to read the mistakes from the transcripts made by court reporters and with a silly looking smile, apologized to the jurors without having their revisions recorded.

After two days of his boring and tedious delivery, the court room was practically empty, except for a half-dozen dozing reporters here and there. Others, sagging on their seats, appeared bored. At intervals, they would rise and leave the room and then return to follow the same pattern.

Mr. Kanarek repeated himself to the point that his fellow counsel were also tired looking and sleepy.

Upon entering the third full day of his closing argument, Mr. Kanarek's main target still was Linda Kasabian. He stated, "Linda Kasabian is the Mr. Magoo of this trial. She is like that cartoon character who leaves all the havoc in his wake but comes out unscathed. Mrs. Kasabian was along when those events took place, not because of anything Mr. Manson did, but because she was an intimate of Mr. Watson's."

For a change of argument, Mr. Kanarek labeled as "illogical and preposterous" prosecutor Mr. Bugliosi's theory that Manson master-minded the murders to trigger a black versus white race.

Mr. Kanarek shouted, "If this was to start a black-white war, why did it stop on the second night?" questioned the stocky attorney. "Why wasn't there a third, fourth, and fifth night if that was what was supposed to take place?"

Then, excitedly, added:

"If that theory were true, why didn't they try to make it obvious that Negroes committed the crimes... like leaving a picture of Cassius Clay or maybe Martin Luther King?"

Mr. Kanarek, working his way through more than 1,900 pages of transcript, described the Tate-LaBianca trial as a "political trial" and claimed that Charles Manson was innocent.

Speaking of his client, he said, "Mr. Manson has become a symbol of one of the confrontations going on in this country today. Mr. Manson scratched an 'X' on his forehead as a form of free speech... as a symbol of his protest at the way he is being treated."

The next day we were kept in the jury room due to some conference in the Judge's Chambers. While waiting, I wrote these notes:

December 31, 1970, 9:50 A.M. Now that we're seated, the mood among us jurors seems rather low and depressed, mostly, I would guess, tired and fatigued. Today is the last day of the year. We're glad its all over. When we talk about 1970, we will remember it as the most unhappy year of our lives.

We have already spent over five months listening to the evidence and have taken notes to use as reference when we enter the deliberation stage. However, the primary factor we're concerned about now is the duration we've been sequestered and, of an even more sensitive nature, the behavior of one-third of the jurors who have completely become obedient servants of the bailiffs in charge.

These jurors (the clique) have exceeded the normal attitude and behavior one would ordinarily expect from an everyday ordinary respectable citizen. Deborah Hart, Ray Harris, Tom Brooks, Violet Stokes and Martin Paine have even gone so far as to deliver—daily—large dishes of banana splits to the bailiffs on duty after their dinner hour. Needless to say, the results have been more than rewarding.

Not only have they received 'special' favors from the deputies but have succeeded in causing these bailiffs to turn against others who have simply acted accordingly to their environments.

Many a time on Wednesday night before going to bowl, someone other than the clique has asked Deputy Taylor loudly—for everyone to hear—the possibilities of going to see a movie in the neighborhood theatre, and incredible as it may seem, the bailiff has literally shouted 'NO!' emphatically enough to discourage anyone from asking again. The two-thirds of the jurors could only watch and see the one-third go bowling and even though one-half of the people were required to justify bus transportation, these four or five 'special' jurors received their request for bowling due to the fact they were on the 'right side' of the bailiffs.

Other nights after dinner, the 'special' jurors and the bailiffs would drink together and the jurors would cater to the bailiff on his free time. Indeed a very successful maneuver on their parts.

Anytime one would pass the bailiff's room, the 'special' jurors could be overheard laughing at the most silly, idiotic or stupid statements the bailiff would utter.

The latest event in their favor resulted in a special trip for Ray Harris and Debbie Hart to Compton, a Community far away from Los Angeles, so that Ray's new bowling ball—a Christmas gift from his wife—could be measured and punched for holes. This happened after our arrival at the hotel and they didn't even stop for dinner.

When we had finished dinner, George and I went to my room for relaxation and socializing. Later on, George returned to his room and I was in the midst of searching for some notes when I overheard voices in the quiet hallway. Curiously, I peered outside and observed Mrs. Colvig and another bailiff returning with Debbie and Ray. Mrs. Colvig and Ray were cozily walking together.

Mrs. Colvig was startled at my sudden appearance and to remove her uneasiness, I looked the other way and pretended not to notice the situation. They were returning from Compton.

As you may notice, it took two bailiffs to accompany these two jurors, while the rest of the jurors—fifteen to be exact—were under the jurisdiction of only two bailiffs, Albert Taylor and Claudette, an attractive Negro female deputy.

That particular evening, we were unable to indulge in our evening stroll as

334

Taylor had to remain on the floor and Claudette, who disliked walking, found many excuses to avoid the issue.

Later on, Edith revealed to me that she was upset about the special outing. As a result, Taylor found himself inquiring to Edith why she was angry at him.

The lady alternate juror blurted out and revealed the special outing taken by Ray and Debbie, accompanied by Mrs. Colvig and the other deputy, whose absence from the hotel had eliminated her chances to take a walk. She felt one deputy would have been sufficient.

Needless to say, Taylor was astonished and speechless. There was no possible explanation he could offer to satisfy the irritability of the pointed juror nor justify the situation. He finally retreated to his room.

We entered the court room without any further incident.

During his final argument, Mr. Kanarek constantly talked about the prosecution's main witness, Linda Kasabian. Everything he stated and contradicted was based solely on her testimony. He would begin with a specific issue and then, automatically, he would change in midstream. It was apparent he had not prepared his final argument. Mr. Kanarek, in all honesty, constantly dragged the presentation of his rebuttal argument to the point of stillness.

The jurors, in all their efforts, vainly tried to follow his words and trend of thought, but his statements neither followed through nor concluded any particular issue. He skipped from one issue to another without any continuity. One thing we, the jurors, noticed was that during Mr. Kanarek's rebuttal, he didn't debate the issues and evidence brought out by the prosecution, but only attacked the prosecutor himself and his office on the grounds that it was a personal vindication against the defendants by the prosecution.

The slow process of the rebuttal was surprisingly interrupted when a woman accompanied by a tall man, entered the court room. The woman walked fast and stopped right in front of the dividing rail and yelled: "I came here to defend my brother!"

The intruder uttered another sentence but it was drowned out because of the commotion and excitement in the room. The young-looking woman, who was wearing a white suit with very little makeup and with her hair out of place, was defiantly escorted out by one of the bailiffs.

Quietness prevailed for a moment in the room. The jurors gazed at the scene attentively and, in unison, switched their heads towards Judge Older who, at the time, called another bailiff to the bench followed by the court reporter. Mr. Fitzgerald wanted to approach the bench as well as Mr. Kanarek, but their wishes were denied. The Judge admonished the jurors to disregard what the woman had said and told them that the woman had nothing to do

335

with the case.

At first I thought it was Charles Manson's sister, but someone else mentioned that perhaps it was Charles Watson's sister. Still, another said and even wrote it down on a piece of paper and handed it to me. The paper read: "She was one of Mr. Kanarek's girlfriends."

Mr. Kanarek continued his argument and surprisingly announced, "I am trying to speak no longer than necessary. Last night I reviewed the transcripts and cut out great chunks of what I was going to say in an effort to make it shorter for you."

He didn't keep his promise. Time passed by and indeed Mr. Kanarek absorbed it, but he failed to impress us. He didn't pull any smart tricks to which we could interrogate one another, or to place some degree of doubt in our minds about the evidence presented.

Mr. Kanarek wound up his final argument after seven long days. The attorney representing the hippie cult leader asked and pleaded the verdict of Not Guilty for his client, Charles Manson.

Back at the hotel, it was New Years' Eve and there was no place to go. The jurors had to remain on the sixth floor of the Ambassador Hotel. What a drag!

Deputy Taylor, accompanied by Mrs. Colvig, pushing a shopping cart full of bottles of champagne, knocked on every juror's door to hand them a bottle.

Nothing could make us happy except to go someplace and celebrate the New Year fashionably. A few jurors had their relatives visiting them for a while. George and his wife and Mildred and her estranged husband joined me and, while dancing to my stereo-taped music, we drank four bottles of champagne. Genaro, a teetotaler himself, graciously offered me his bottle.

Connie Stevens, who was appearing nightly at the Cocoanut Grove, held a party after the show at the Sammy Davis Suite. The versatile and pretty actress chatted for a while with some jurors—Marvin, Danny, and, later, Mildred, George and myself.

Upon my asking, Miss Stevens gave Danny a New Year's kiss but only after George gave the slim, shy juror a good push. There was no need for anyone to push me when the delightful chanteuse kissed me. Danny became an ardent fan of Miss Connie Stevens.

Two days later, by Miss Stevens' invitation, the jurors were taken to see her perform and she was great. The show was a highlight for some of the jurors who disclosed having never been nor seen a show at the world-famous Cocoanut Grove.

On the night of her last performance, Miss Stevens was presented with a rubber chicken as a souvenir with signatures of only the Clique. The presentation was made by Debbie in the recreation room and I must say that Mrs. Hart's voice sounded like that of a child.

Betty Clark confided to me later that she couldn't believe her eyes. She had heard Debbie scream and yell in the same room at Mike Pappas, and now, like a little shy girl, she was portraying an innocent role, altogether different. Her love affair with Tom was well accepted by the jurors. No one bothered to comment any longer about it. Betty also told me she had refused to accept the bottle of champagne from Deputy Taylor on New Years' Eve.

Accompanied by Mike Pappas and Mollie Kane, the jurors (except the clique) were taken to Palm Springs. On our arrival, cameramen were allowed to take films of the jurors on the condition that such films would be released on television only after the trial was over.

The outing was a complete delight. Mr. and Mrs. John Conte, owners of the El Mirador Hotel, were more than charming hosts and thanks to their attention, the jurors relaxed over the weekend with a ride up the Palm Springs Aerial Tramway. Mrs. Conte personally escorted the jurors to show them the KMIR Channel 36 NBC Studios, which she owns, located on the beautiful grounds of the El Mirador Hotel of Spanish architecture.

Once again, we were in court. Mr. Maxwell Keith, representing Leslie Van Houten, stood up and after addressing the counsel, Judge Older and the jurors, stated that Leslie Van Houten was not guilty of the charges against her.

"I consider myself an interloper," said Mr. Keith, and then explained that he had a few handicaps including the fact that he had never met the late Mr. Hughes.

In a low-keyed but solemn voice, the veteranlike attorney stated, "Ladies and Gentlemen of the jury, I will talk briefly. I will confine my argument with two main chapters. I beg you to please help me because only you know about the demeanor and behavior of the witnesses.

"I remind you to check especially the character of Linda Kasabian through her every abuse and sexual promiscuity. I found from records that she had been a sort of sinister person. She has been charged with different accounts of fraud, theft... you name it.

"Her testimony of being a little girl in the forest was far from her true identity. I didn't see her on the witness stand but if she gave in impression of being a little girl lost in the forest, it was a fraud, a facade, a false front, an insult to you, ladies and gentlemen. She was wily and willfully lying all because of the immunity. And, further, I think that brings into play probably the strongest human drive that there is: self-preservation. I don't think I have to tell you what involves self-preservation which can turn people into liars."

337

Mr. Keith, armed with eloquent words and strong gestures, at intervals, paused to convey his thoughts in the right direction. He kept talking about Linda Kasabian.

"Ladies and Gentlemen, judging from Linda Kasabian's character as I found it to be from these records, she has ample capacity to deceive. She was driven by the strongest human drive as I told you—self-preservation."

Mr. Keith stopped and staring at the jurors intrinsically, pointed to one of the defense counsel.

"I'm going to repeat as Mr. Fitzgerald said: if you find that the credibility of the witness is not for you to believe, I urge you to acquit Leslie Van Houten. If you think she falsely characterized herself, I urge you to overlook her entire testimony."

Mr. Keith then moved to argue against Diane Lake's testimony.

"Without Diane Lake, the prosecution has no clue, no testimony from anybody. It has to be corroborated and the only one would have be from Diane Lake. Who's she?" Mr. Keith questioned sarcastically.

"She's the one that has been an accomplice to many faults. She's a drug addict. She has been committed as you know, not as a physical patient, but as a mental case. We know she didn't tell the truth when she was on oath before the Grand Jury. Worst of all, she was told by Sergeant Gutierrez she better come out with some answers or else. She was sixteen years old and even if you believe the testimony of this little girl, it is the prosecution who's on the spot. Any admission by one confession ought to be judged by us with caution because such admission may damage the person who's on trial, when we can't even remember one day from the day before and within more reason, how come a little girl can give testimony with a drug-abuse background and having been committed for the mentally ill? To me, and I trust, to you ladies and gentlemen, the conversation based on her testimony is dispensable... its frightful."

Mr. Keith, in an unprecedented manner, blasted: "Don't do it!"

For a moment, the defense attorney composed himself and with a matter-of-fact attitude, continued, "Now, we're going to talk about the robot theory. The prosecutor in this case has repeatedly referred to the female defendants and Mr. Watson as robots and zombies and on one occasion, he referred to them as mindless individuals—mind you—mindless individuals.

"I can tell you that this theory was advanced by Mr. Bugliosi. It is impossible for any one of us to believe—that the only way he is going to make us believe—that they committed these murders is by saying that someone told them to do so.

"Certainly, there must be something to it."

Mr. Keith suggested that Mr. Bugliosi has propounded the "robot" theory for a reason.

"He's a very brilliant man—Mr. Bugliosi," the defense attorney said. "He always has something in his mind. He has a purpose."

Mr. Keith then proposed the prosecution's purpose was to convince the jury that his client Watson, Sadie, and Patty were "totally dominated" by some other person.

"Otherwise," he argued, "it's impossible to accept that they went on to kill people they never saw or heard of before. It's kind of like a horror show. Isn't it? I do suggest, after hearing all the evidence, that they didn't have the know how and capacity of doing such things—such horrible murders. It's not the first time in history of such instances of domination. Rasputin, for example, comes to my mind."

Mr. Keith then added that if the jurors consider drug use, mental condition, and mind control of the defendants, they couldn't be found guilty of anything.

"This is his [Bugliosi's] argument. It's his baby," said Mr. Keith. "If you believe this theory, you must acquit these defendants."

Mr. Keith, in order to explain the charge of conspiracy against the defendants, stated:

"I shall give you a very personal illustration. Suppose Mr. Bugliosi has been planning, for months, the murder of Mr. Kanarek but along the way he can't execute it, then I come in and Mr. Bugliosi tells me 'Hey Max, I'm having trouble with Kanarek. I want you to kill him.' Now, Mr. Bugliosi is guilty of first-degree murder but I, although I killed Mr. Kanarek, am not guilty of first-degree murder, because it was only in an emotional state of mind.

"Don't do it!" Mr. Keith repeatedly shouted. "Maintain your own individuality—your own integrity don't give up your opinions—your findings. Set Leslie Van Houten free. Thank you."

After a short recess, the prosecutor began his rebuttal.

Mr. Bugliosi, speaking in a forward and strong manner and without hesitation, stated the procedure in which he would conduct his closing final argument.

Eloquently and well defined, Mr. Bugliosi gave the indication of having been prepared. He started by saying:

"Even if the late Clarence Darrow was alive, he wouldn't be able to save these defendants from being guilty."

The prosecutor went on to use the analogy between an "octopus" and Manson.

"An octopus," he said, "has no teeth, no claws to defend himself but he has

339

a bag which distributes a black liquid and it becomes dark around him which protects him from his enemy. That's the way Manson is. He uses his family to portray his murderous desires. These defendants are guilty as sin but the defense, also like an octupus, has attempted to escape in a cloud of ink. I intend to penetrate that screen and clear up the waters. Because of that, I will take a little longer than I expected."

Mr. Bugliosi limited his argument mostly to a comprehensive point-by-point rebuttal of the defense arguments.

First, the prosecutor retaliated ably more than a dozen factual errors that Mr. Fitzgerald had made in his closing argument. The deputy district attorney, in a confident and hard-hitting manner, told the jurors:

"Mr. Fitzgerald misstated the evidence so many times that at first I couldn't believe it. I thought he was intentionally deceiving you. But I've tried six jury cases with him and he's an ethical attorney. I can only conclude he wasn't listening to the evidence and didn't take the time to check the transcripts."

In a single reference to Susan Atkin's attorney, the prosecutor said, "I want to apologize on behalf of Mr. Shin. He's told you that one of the prosecution's witnesses [Ronni Howard] had eighteen aliases and he was sure none of you had more than five. I'm sure you don't have any, and I apologize for him."

Describing Mr. Keith's final argument on behalf of his client, the prosecutor called it masterful, ingenuious and rather interesting, considering he was dealing with a hopeless situation.

Immediately after, Mr. Bugliosi went on to discuss Linda Kasabian's admitted heavy use of LSD when Mr. Kanarek jumped up and said: "Can we include marijuana, too?"

"Sit down Mr. Kanarek, you are interrupting again," Judge Older said, who had cautioned the stocky attorney about eight times in the first twenty minutes of the prosecutor's summation.

Mr. Kanarek's aggressive court room tactics frequently aroused the ire of the jurors and even his fellow counsel.

Mr. Bugliosi's patience reached the top and finally defended himself in the open.

The well-attired attorney displayed himself to be a master at spotlighting the previous insults stated by Mr. Kanarek. The prosecutor retaliated at that moment with such techniques and finesse that it made the entire audience and especially the jurors attentive and aware that Mr. Kanarek had it coming.

The salt-and-pepper curly haired Mr. Kanarek sat with a pencil in his hands and would smile contemptuously.

Mr. Bugliosi made the most of his remarks in response to earlier accusations by Mr. Kanarek.

"I will not take these false accusations from the gutter," said Mr. Bugliosi annoyingly, and then added, "to hear Mr. Kanarek tell it, the Los Angeles Police Department and the District Attorney's Office took the prosecution's witnesses in some back room... got them together, gave them scripts to follow and programmed and trained these witnesses and framed his client, Charles Manson, is a most vicious insult."

The prosecutor continued aiming a verbal fusilade at Mr. Kanarek, who previously had labeled the trial as a circus.

Mr. Bugliosi said, "We all know a circus has a clown and it wouldn't take more than one guess as to who the Pagliacci of this trial has been. However, it is not true, this trial has not been a circus at all whatsoever. This trial has been conducted with dignity by Judge Charles Older. There's no disputing that fact."

From then on, the prosecutor delivered a stampede of retaliations directed to Charles Manson's lawyer.

He accused Mr. Kanarek of misstating and manufacturing evidence to fit Irving's "Alice in Wonderland" version, sprinkled with wishful thinking, and asked, "Am I suffering from an intellectual hernia or is Irving Kanarek?"

Mr. Bugliosi, with an eloquent, timely and almost perfect choice of words, certainly denoted a disturbed sense of emotion as he counter attacked the past accusations of Mr. Kanarek.

The court room was simply electrified by the powerful speaker and the eyes of the spectators, reporters and jurors were blinkless. There was "action in court."

The extravaganza of words, one by one, indulged everybody to sit tight, motionless and made them unaware of what the next person was doing. Everyone's eyes were set on the center of the court room.

The highlight of the prosecutor's counter attack statements was when he came in defense of the body of the District Attorney's Office. He defended it to the hilt.

He stated:

"The integrity and dignity bestowed upon a lawyer to work not only for the truth but for the pride of being part of this great land of ours. Throughout the world, they know, here in the United States of America, the truth in our courts prevail and we are not to be insulted or accused especially in cases of death such as these."

Mr. Kanarek stood up and furiously moved for a mistrial on grounds that he was the target of a personal attack, but Judge Older denied the motion

341

after suggesting to Mr. Bugliosi that he use some restraint.

Mr. Bugliosi obliged and moved on to prove that the finger prints found at the Polanski residence were those of the defendant in question, Patricia Krenwinkel.

"The Los Angeles Police Department," he said, "needs only ten points to make a case and seventeen points is simply sufficient to have Miss Krenwinkel found guilty of murder in corroboration with Linda Kasabian's testimony. Linda testified that she saw Patricia Krenwinkel drag Abigail Folger from the bedroom.

"Mr. Fitzgerald claims," the prosecutor continued, "that maybe Patricia Krenwinkel was at the Tate residence on Wednesday or Thursday, and that's why maybe her fingerprints were found there, or that maybe she went visiting and maybe swam in the pool."

Mr. Bugliosi, in a fast smart set of words, retaliated by adding, "Why didn't Paul Fitzgerald bring anyone to testify that Patricia Krenwinkel had visited the Tate residence? Why? Because there was no such visit. The only time she went there was the night of the murders and she swam, but not in the swimming pool, but in a river of blood.

"Ladies and gentlemen, she even went as far as to the bedroom. What was she doing there? Linda Kasabian told us she had seen Patricia Krenwinkel chasing Abigail Folger. Linda Kasabian gave in this court, a brutal, frank testimony of the truth. She gave true answers to all questions. She even went as far as to offer voluntary information."

Mr. Bugliosi, assisted by transcripts, read a few passages and continued:

"Linda Kasabian offered information of her past life which the defense counsel would have no way to know. She testified about her drug habits, her police record and sexual promiscuities. She even told us that she had made love to another woman. She was frank and repulsively truthful. She left nothing."

Mr. Bugliosi continued and argued:

"Mr. Kanarek told us that Linda Kasabian wasn't the all-American girl. Of course, she's not. We never told you so, but her testimony was an open door to the world to know of those horrendous crimes."

At another point in his summation, Mr. Bugliosi defended Linda Kasabian's testimony and stated, "She couldn't lie. She did say *only* the truth and had no reason to lie. She, being a member of the family, went along with the crazy ideas of Charles Manson although she later found out that he was no good. She testified she thought he was the Messiah, the Jesus Christ—that he emanated good and love. So you can see she didn't fabricate her testimony to obtain immunity. She wasn't like Charles Manson—a killer, a master cold-blooded killer.

"Charles Manson is a vicious, diabolical murderer who gave the order that caused seven human beings to wind up in the cold earth."

At that moment, Charlie evoked a burst of laughter when he made a growling sound like that of a roar of a lion. Everybody laughed, including the defense and a couple of jurors.

Mr. Bugliosi continued and spoke about Linda Kasabian's immunity. He said, "Why shouldn't she want the immunity? Why would she want to spend the rest of her life in prison? That immunity was like icing on the cake to Linda. It is obvious that her testimony was in keeping with human experiences. Why would she keep it a secret? She had to relate what she knew. Even assuming that she testified for an immunity, Linda Kasabian testified the truth and the counsel should have that in consideration."

Mr. Bugliosi, approaching the jury box, questioned, "Ask yourselves in the jury room: Why would Linda Kasabian testify against those defendants? Why would she lie? There's no reason for it. She wouldn't pick up these defendants out of the blue sky. Why?"

After having covered every single issue meticuously pertaining to the two nights the murders took place, the prosecutor discussed the doctrine of circumstantial evidence and dealt with the arguments of the defense attorneys.

Mr. Bugliosi argued, "The defense has tried to create the impression that the prosecution's case in the seven killings was based solely on circumstantial evidence.

"It was based," he declared, "on both the direct testimony of Linda Kasabian, a witness to three of the murders, and such circumstantial evidence as fingerprints found in the Tate house and the gun used in the murders."

Following a lengthy series of statements made by the scores of witnesses, the prosecutor linked the defendants to prove they participated in the killings by charging:

"Tex Watson was co-conspirator of those murders. He killed Voityck Frykowski, Jay Sebring, and of course, he left the exemplar of his fingerprint. He also killed the La Biancas.

"Patricia Krenwinkel—(1) Linda Kasabian testified she observed the defendant operating the knife and that she complained because the knife penetrated a bone as she stabbed the victim.

"(2) Her fingerprints in the bedroom, seventeen prints; that fact alone is enough to convict her.

"(3) Confession to Diane Lake that she dragged Abigail Folger from the

343

bedroom."

The prosecutor then enumerated reasons as to why Patricia Krenwinkel was also guilty of killing the La Biancas.

He counted, "(1) Linda Kasabian testified that she went with Patricia Krenwinkel to the house.

"(2) Juan Flynn testified that he saw a group leaving the ranch the night of the La Bianca murders—Patricia Krenwinkel was one of them.

"(3) Refusal to print the words, showing a consciousness of guilt on her part. She would have been only too happy to do it had she been innocent.

"(4) The fact that the Tate murders are very similar to those of the La Biancas and, finally, her apprehension in Alabama."

Mr. Bugliosi followed the same procedure with the next defendant, "Susan Atkins—(1) Linda Kasabian testified that she was there on the night of the murders—even saw her running—so we know she was one of the killers.

"(2) Susan Atkins confessed to three people: Ronni Howard, Virginia Graham, and Rosanne Walker.

"To Rosanne Walker, her incrimination of the glasses left at the Tate Residence (glasses found at the murder scene were unidentified). She told Rosanne, 'that ain't the way it went down,' meaning that's not the way it happened.

"(3) Also, many other things that Sharon Tate was wearing. One doesn't know these little details.

"(4) Her letter to Kit Fletcher. Her own confession in her own words, 'Why did I do it? Why I opened my big mouth to that cellmate? I did what I did and that's it.'

"(5) Clothes found on People's 53 had the same hair as that of Susan Atkins —same medula circumference, color, and length.

"(6) Barbara Hoyt testified that Susan Atkins told her she wanted three sets of clothing.

"(7) The day after the Tate murders, Barbara Hoyt was watching television. Susan Atkins walked in and who did she call in? Charles Watson and Patricia Krenwinkel. She knew that they had killed the victims brutally and as the announcer spoke, they laughed. Five people butchered to death. Immediately after showing the news, they left.

"On the night of the La Bianca murders, Susan Atkins was guilty," the prosecutor continued, "because (1) Linda Kasabian testified that she was with her the entire evening.

"Since we know—I repeat—*since we know* that Susan Atkins was at the house of the La Biancas because of (2), Juan Flynn's testimony of Susan Atkins leaving the Spahn Ranch the same night of the killings.

"(3) What Susan Atkins told Juan Flynn: 'We're going to get these fucks. On the night of the La Bianca murders, Susan Atkins was willing and eager to murder the La Biancas. There is no reason not to believe it.

"(4) The similarity between the Tate and the La Bianca murders.

"(5) Although she never confessed, she certainly implicated herself by saying that she wasn't in the second house, and that in itself proves she was involved surely in the Tate house and which connects her with the La Bianca murders."

Mr. Bugliosi paused for a moment to rearrange his notes and proceeded to prove Leslie Van Houten was guilty of first-degree murder.

"Leslie Van Houten—(1), Linda Kasabian testified that Leslie Van Houten was dropped at the La Bianca residence.

"(2) Juan Flynn saw them leave in a car on the night of the murders. Leslie Van Houten was one of them.

"(3) Diane Lake and Barbara Hoyt both gave testimony indicating that the incident in the backhouse took place after the La Biancas murders which incidentally, without going into much interference, occurred around two and four A.M.

"(4) Of course, Leslie Van Houten confessed to Diane Lake, but it couldn't be more obvious that she was referring to the La Bianca murders. Take this into consideration, Leslie Van Houten said that she stabbed the victim.

"(5) Leslie Van Houten said that the person whom she stabbed was already dead, and don't put it past the fact that she sat and ate watermelon. We're talking about savages—not human beings.

"(6) She told Diane Lake she wiped the blood and fingerprints and Sergeant Gutierrez testified that there were no fingerprints found on the fork or the knife.

"(7) Diane said she wasn't sure but that Leslie Van Houten told her about a boat outside the La Bianca residence, although it could be possible that it had been in the newspapers. But, remember this, she said that she remembered some description of the boat.

"Diane testified that the murders took place in the Griffith Park area and we know that's the area where the La Bianca murders occurred, and also about her hitchhiking to the Spahn Ranch. There's no evidence that there was any reason about making up this story.

"There's no question that Leslie confessed to Diane Lake about the murders at the La Bianca house."

Mr. Bugliosi took a long sip of water, readjusted his vest and continued his detailed summary of evidence against each of the defendants.

As the prosecution launched the evidentiary summary on the hippie cult leader, Mr. Bugliosi told the jurors:

"Charles Manson. Who is Charles Manson? The evidence shows that there is only one. A vicious coldblooded murderer.

"Manson is like a chameleon—changes with the background—has a different mask to everyone. To put it bluntly, Charlie is a phony and a con man, but he is polished and sophisticated in the practice of his trade. Kind and soft. But he slipped and that was his mistake.

"He surely is not going to display his true face that commanded the brutal killings at the Tate house on August 8th and he is not going to show the face he wore when he ordered the horrible murders at the La Bianca residence.

"He will not show you the face when he almost shocked Paul Watkins to death. He will not show the face when he put a knife to Juan Flynn. He will not show you the real face as when he hit Stephanie Schram with a rifle butt and he will not show you the face when he slapped the mouth of poor Diane Lake.

"Of course, he will not show you that face because he has a different mask —a different face for the world to know he is innocent. But, behind that sweet innocent face is the face of a sadistic diabolical murderer who sent his robots to commit murders. *Murders* ladies and gentlemen. However, we have stripped away the veneer and layers of deception and what we see is the face of an incredibly vicious coldblooded murderer."

Mr. Bugliosi enumerated the important issues to prove Charles Manson was guilty.

"(1) Linda Kasabian was with Charles Manson both nights. She saw his conduct, she saw him sending his robots to portray those murders, and also the second night, and since we know—*we know*—ladies and gentlemen, because Linda Kasabian was telling the truth."

Mr. Bugliosi, holding the blood-stained rope, said:

"(2) The rope. Danny De Carlo testified that he went to buy this rope with Charles Manson and he identified this same rope which was tied to Jay Sebring's and Sharon Tate's necks.

"Ruby Pearl also testified that the rope is the same. She saw it at the Spahn Ranch.

"Juan Flynn also said that he even used it and that Manson used it and kept it in the dune buggy.

"This is not a regular type of rope and all these witnesses felt that the rope is the very same and described it and it is just too close to that rope used in the Sharon Tate case."

The prosecutor, holding the gun previously entered as evidence, said,

"(3) The revolver. Well, it apparently belonged to Charles Manson. Juan Flynn and Danny De Carlo testified that they saw Charles Manson fire the same gun. De Carlo even drew a sketch and it came out to be exactly as People's 40. Danny also testified that not only did Charles Manson fire this gun, but also carried it around the Spahn Ranch in a holster. Also, Manson carried a sword knife in the dune buggy along with the rope on the front seat. He also testified Charles Manson ordered his robots to assassinate.

"(4) Barbara Hoyt testified that she heard Charles Manson calling the defendants obviously the night of the murder.

"(5) Johnny Swartz testified that Manson came over to him and borrowed his 1959 car—the same time the two particular nights.

"(6) One week before August 16, Juan Flynn saw Manson driving off in Swartz's car and then what he told Juan Flynn.

"(7) The leather thongs used on Leno La Bianca. Just as circumstantial evidence. Charles Manson uses the same type around his neck.

"(8) Sergeant Gutierrez testified that Charles Manson attempted to intimidate Linda Kasabian here in court by using movements with his hands.

"(9) Diane Lake said that Charles Manson told her to tell nothing to the authorities.

"(10) During the raid, Charles Manson was hiding under the building. Why?

"(11) Jacobson's testimony that he observed the dramatic change of Charles Manson. He said that Charlie was 'like an animal in a cage.'

"(12) Charles Manson's confession to Juan Flynn: 'You son-of-a-bitch! Don't you know that I'm the one who's doing all these killings?'

"(13) Los Angeles County has over seven million people. Out of one million homes, Charles Manson just happened to go to these two homes, and the probabilities again prove that he knew these houses.

"(14) The philosophy of Charles Manson is definitely interwoven with the motive of these killings. Legally speaking, motive is never a burden for the prosecution to prove guilt, only guilt beyond the reasonable doubt."

Mr. Bugliosi, discussing at length the philosopy of Charles Manson, said, "Since these murders were of a bizarre nature, likewise, Charles Manson is a bizarre maniac. 'Helter Skelter seemed to be the main topic with Charlie,' his lieutenant testified—close friend Paul Watkins. Manson's philosophy gave ammunition power to his bizarre desires.

"Jacobson, Poston, and Watkins testified that in a way he was a megalomaniac. With thirst for power and constant obsession for violence and death he decided to show the whitey how to do it.

"In February 1969, Charles Manson spoke of atrocious murders to Poston and that is precisely what he ordered his zombies to do in August 1969. He even told them to write the words 'Death to Pigs.'

"Manson told Watkins that he was going into the rich people and commit those murders, even when Watkins knew, and believed then Charles Manson was God, he didn't want to be around, so he left.

"Diane Lake testified that Manson told her: 'I'm going to start this revolution.'

"These seven murders were committed in the same precise manner in which Charles Manson had told Paul, Juan, and Diane. Seven precious human beings were savagely murdered by his robots. Helter Skelter—Revelation 9—Revolution—Pigs—Crazy? Sure it is! It just happens to be the principal motive for these murders.

"An equally bizarre motive and what could be more bizarre than to write —with the victims' blood—the words Helter Skelter.

"The defense contends that it is not true that Charles Manson was trying to use the black people for his murders. But, how come about the credit cards? And the wallet? Which was placed in the gas station in Sylmar? So some black woman would pick it up!

"The fact that this area is predominantly white is irrelevant. The only thing we're concerned about is that Charles Manson is on trial and that he told Linda Kasabian he would hope a black woman would find it and so blackmail the black people. So the black people would be accused of such atrocious crimes and the police authorities would automatically believe that blacks committed these crimes.

"But mind you, it is actually obvious that Charles Manson's state of mind was not rational and that his method was irrational.

"Ladies and Gentlemen, we're dealing with a man who tried to make the black people appear as the ones who commited the murders. Since we're dealing with the unusual, bizarre and incredible murder, we should consider that Charles Manson is likewise.

"He was familiar with not only Revelation 9 but also about the Apocalypse —the last destructive battle to take place on the face of this earth.

"So, in view of the nature of these brutal, bizarre murders there is no question as to the motive of them. It shouldn't even be considered.

" 'Death to Pigs'—'War' on Leno La Bianca's stomach—'Helter Skelter' and 'Rise,' which are associated with murder.

The prosecutor, speeding up his speech manner, solemnly proclaimed, "It is the people's contention that only the defendant and only him alone could have left the writing of these words. In our old, good, fashionable judgement, when have we heard of a crime with the word 'Pig' written with the blood of the victims?

" 'War' is less likely to be found on the scene of a murder. It certainly refers to conflict where thousands are killed in war. It does not associate with two people in their home.

" 'Rise' and 'Helter Skelter' have absolutely nothing to do with murder, except to Charles Manson. What in the world do they have to do with these crimes? It has to do with Charles Manson's bizarre mind. It was no other than Charles Manson's obsession in his unique, significant way—it was part of his religion.

"The same words were found at the Spahn Ranch. When they printed those words, they left their identification for the world to see.

"Throw all the evidence out the window, all of Linda Kasabian's testimony, but no reasonable human being can be responsible for these murders but Charles Manson.

"He was not only the leader but the instructor, teacher, and philosopher of death who preached to the defendants accused at this trial. They left their fingerprints of their master at the scene."

Mr. Bugliosi was briefly interrupted when a curvacious blonde stood up behind the rail and yelled, "I have proof that key prosecution witnesses were coerced, bribed, and threatened."

Judge Older immediately had her removed from the court room by Deputies Kane and Tull.

We returned to the hotel.

There was concern among some of the jurors who would be the foreman of the panel jury. Mildred, Olivia, George and Frank congregated in my room. Betty also joined the group.

"There's no one qualified except you," said Olivia openly, "I've been watching you closely and I liked the way you expressed yourself to Kathy Colvig."

A couple days before, coming out of the elevator, Olivia had expressed her discontentment because the clique was favored with special treatments. Mrs. Colvig denied Olivia's charges, but I, in the company of another juror, displayed our similar resentment. Thus, Olivia felt my outspoken attitude would qualify me as foreman of the jury.

"The clique would want Martin," added Olivia, "and he does not have the vocabulary nor the know how."

"I'll vote for Bill," Frank said flatly. "He'll make a good foreman."

"You have forgotten Paul," interrupted Mildred.

"Oh, not him!" snapped Betty, "he couldn't control the meeting."

"Let's count how many votes the 'clique' has," suggested George.

"Debbie, Violet, Ray, Genaro, and Martin himself... and also Marvin," stated Betty.

"Marvin?" Olivia asked increduously, who had befriended the curly red-haired juror.

"Of course," Betty replied quickly. "He's for Martin all the way."

"We're divided," Mildred said, who wanted to be the foreman herself, but knew that none of the jurors wanted a female foreman.

"What do you say?" asked Frank. "Do you accept my vote?"

"Sure I do, thanks," I replied while looking at Betty who I felt knew I wanted to be the foreman. "But let us pull for the best and not be moved by personal feelings."

"You can have my vote, too," Olivia uttered.

"And mine too," Mildred snapped.

I waited for Betty to announce my support. I knew she didn't want Martin to be the foreman but at the same time, she wouldn't back me. Why? I never knew.

I slept restlessly that night. In my mind, optimistically, I weighted the possibilities of becoming foreman. I won't deny I enjoyed the process and the ultimate thought of being one.

The responsibilities attracted me and needless to say I would have been flattered had the jurors entrusted me as their leader. Trailing behind those thoughts were other thoughts which eventually discouraged me and made me decide not to seek the nomination. For one thing I felt the news media would publish my picture and might inadvertantly publish my home address. I didn't want that type of publicity. And the foreman is target No. 1. The counts of the indictment were signed only by the foreman. He did represent the rest of us, but only one signature. My pride was hurt but I said to myself "There are times in life when you have to face reality and pay the consequences."

The following night, I approached the same people who had come to my room and confided to them that I was not interested in becoming the foreman. I was afraid of the outside consequences once the trial was over and besides, my parents by letter had begged me to decline.

It was Friday, January 16, 1971, and we were back in court.

Mr. Bugliosi, looking pale and fighting a severe cold, stood up and with poise and dignity, launched his final plea to the jurors. The courtroom was filled to capacity. No one talked. Everybody listened to the exciting and turbulent speech of the prosecutor.

Mr. Bugliosi continued talking about Charles Manson's culpability. He argued, "When Charles Manson encountered Mr. Hatami at the Tate house. Manson knew that the people who lived there were of excellent means. So, indirectly, he ordered the massive murders at the former residence of Terry Melcher, who later, at the findings of these murders, practically paralyzed with fear, as reflected in his answers when he stated in this court that he thought that Manson was his friend.

"The La Biancas, victims of the second night, also of easy circumstances and members of the establishment, were 'Pigs' as Charles Manson refers to them. He didn't pick up people from skid row. *No*, Charles Manson hated the establishment, the luxurious plush type of living. The Tate residence was a good example of that.

"There was also his hate, lust, and passion for human death. Charles Manson knows how horrible death is—that is why he is fighting for his life. He knows that death is the ultimate punishment there is."

The prosecutor then analyzed Charles Manson's definition of love.

"As you know, Charles Manson reversed the definition of the word 'love.' It is the opposite of what a word means—like peculiar is odd, different. Charles Manson used the word 'love' as 'death'. His hatred for human beings, his insatiable passion for death—*death*. His whole life was cut off because of death. The times he told different people to die... die... die... that there was nothing wrong to die... that everybody has to die in one way or another, in order to love you must be willing to kill.

"So, day to day, month to month, he was talking about murder—death. His preoccupation with revolution as Poston said, 'Death is Charlie's trip!' "

Upon hearing this blasting remark, Manson yelled into the court room to Mr. Fitzgerald, "Paul, he should have been a preacher!"

Mr. Bugliosi smiled slightly and continued, "It took someone with a morbid, lust passion, and with precise ingredients of hatred to order these murders. The Tate and La Bianca murders are synonymous. And the most powerful block of evidence in the trial against Charles Manson!

"He is the total combination of the family, directing them in everything they did and surely corroborates the testimony of Linda Kasabian."

Mr. Bugliosi's final words were florid and filled with spice. He continued:

"No one even remotely testified that anyone other than Charles Manson was the one who gave the orders. Linda Kasabian corroborates with a certain amount of evidence, but most important, we have a massive bulk of evidence which proves beyond the reasonable doubt who committed these horren-

351

dous bizarre murders.

"The defense may be hoping for a miracle, but this case was not based on a Perry Mason script and Erle Stanley Gardner was not there to help Paul Fitzgerald, Irving Kanarek, Dave Shin, or Maxwell Keith."

Holding a glass of water in one hand and punctuating his comments with the other, Mr. Bugliosi added, "There's not one speck of evidence that these defendants didn't commit these bizarre murders. And these witnesses had the courage to come and testify for a moral obligation. They came to tell the truth.

"The chemistry of the truth is to emerge for fresh air. People like Juan Flynn are terrified for their lives at the hands of Charles Manson's family. To think that Juan Flynn has nothing to gain by it is simply inconceivable.

"Charles Manson is a man who had the infinite audacity to consider himself to be Jesus Christ, that he had the power to give life, to mastermind the brains of these robots—his family. He thought he had concomitant rights to kill.

"And on the hot summer evening of August 8, 1969, Manson sent out from the first hell at Spahn Ranch, three heartless blood-thirsty robots—Tex Watson, Susan Atkins and Patricia Krenwinkel, and unfortunately one human being, a little hippie girl—Linda Kasabian—who was to come and defy him. Because of that, you are able to hear the story of slaughter.

"To think that Roman Planski, movie-director husband of Sharon Tate, couldn't have conceived of a more monstrous, macabre, savage and thirst-bizarre murder for a plot of a movie.

"What resulted in those two nights was perhaps the most inhuman horror-filled hour of savage murder and human slaughter in the recorded annals of crime. As the helpless victims begged and screamed out into the night for their lives, their life blood gushed out of their bodies, forming rivers of gore.

"If they could have, I'm sure Tex Watson, Susan Atkins and Patricia Krenwinkel would gladly have swam in the river of human blood and with gorgiastic ecstacy on their faces.

"Susan Atkins, the vampiress, actually tasted Sharon Tate's blood. She and the other defendants carried Charles Manson's merciless orders to the hilt. These defendants wanted their day in court—well, they had it. They wanted a fair trial with twelve fair jurors—well, they had it and that is all they deserve.

"As sure as night follows day, as sure as I am standing here, these people are guilty of murder. Now, you folks are the judges of this long trial. I ask you to come back from the jury room with a verdict of guilty."

Mr. Bugliosi reached an emotional climax when he read the names of the victims out loud. The names we had heard since July 1970 seemed somehow new as Mr. Bugliosi spoke them, pausing after each as the sound faded in the silent court room.

"Sharon Tate... Abigail Folger... Jay Sebring... Voityck Frykowski... Steven Parent... Leno La Bianca... and Rosemary La Bianca."

The prosecutor stepped aside the podium and dramatically stated, "They are not here with us now in the court room. But, from their graves they cry out for justice. Justice can only be served in this case by coming back in the court room with a verdict of guilty."

Not a sound in the air was audible—not a movement—and not even a cough from a cold was heard.

Mr. Bugliosi, with erect posture, moved defiantly towards the jury box and again exclaimed loudly:

"Ladies and gentlemen! They demand justice! The people of the State of California demand justice! The plaintiff of this case demands justice!"

Then, dabbing at his mouth and forehead with a folded white handkerchief, he quietly complimented us jurors on our patience and attention and urged us not to let the People of California down.

He concluded by saying, "Thank you."

About a minute after the prosecutor had ended his summation, Charles Manson yelled into the court room to Defense Attorney Mr. Fitzgerald:

"Paul! He *should* have been a preacher!"

Mr. Fitzgerald smiled, as well as Mr. Bugliosi, but the latter made no response to the hippie cult leader's remark. Most of the jurors ignored Manson's statement.

Judge Older called for a twenty-minute recess.

The jurors were excited. They exited immediately, escorted by Deputy Taylor. No one spoke about the upcoming deliberation except for idle comments such as, "it's about time" or "I never thought I would see this day arrive" or better still, someone said, "we're finally going home." Regardless of what anyone said, everybody seemed to be satisfied.

As soon as we returned to court, Judge Older began reading the instructions to the jurors (each instruction was on a separate sheet):

1

Ladies and gentlemen of the Jury:

It is my duty to instruct you in the law that applies to this case and you must follow the law as I state it to you.

As jurors it is your exclusive duty to decide all questions of fact submitted to you and for that purpose to determine the effect and value of the evidence.

353

In performing this duty you must not be influenced by pity for any defendant or by passion or prejudice against him. You must not be biased against any defendant because he has been arrested for this offense, or because a charge has been filed against him, or because he has been brought to trial. None of these facts is evidence of his guilt and you must not infer or speculate from any or all of them that he is more likely to be guilty than innocent.

In determining whether any defendant is guilty or not guilty, you must be governed solely by the evidence received in this trial and the law as stated to you by the court. You must not be governed by mere sentiment, conjecture, sympathy, passion, prejudice, public opinion or public feeling. Both the people and the defendants have a right to expect that you will conscientiously consider and weigh the evidence and apply the law of the case, and that you will reach a just verdict regardless of what the consequences of such verdict may be.

2

If the court has repeated any rule, direction or idea, or stated the same in varying ways, no emphasis was intended and you must not draw any inference therefrom. You are not to single out any certain sentence or any individual point or instruction and ignore the others. You are to consider all the instructions as a whole and are to regard each in the light of all the others.

The order in which the instructions are given has no significance as to their relative importance.

3

You must not consider as evidence any statement of counsel made during the trial; however, if counsel for the parties have stipulated to any fact, or any fact has been admitted by counsel, you will regard that fact as being conclusively proved as to the party or parties making the stipulation or admission.

A 'stipulation' is an agreement between attorneys as to matters relating to the trial.

As to any question to which an objection was sustained, you must not speculate as to what the answer might have been or as to the reason for the objection.

You must never speculate to be true any insinuation suggested by a question asked a witness. A question is not evidence and may be considered only as it supplies meaning to the answer.

You must not consider for any purpose any offer of evidence that was rejected, or any evidence that was stricken out by the court; such matter is to be treated as though you had never heard of it.

The masculine form as used in these instructions applies equally to a female person.

The word 'defendant' as used in these instructions, applies equally to each defendant in this case except as you may be otherwise instructed.

The testimony of a witness, a writing, a material object, or anything presented to the senses offered to prove the existence or nonexistence of a fact is either direct or circumstantial evidence. Direct evidence means evidence that directly proves a fact, without an inference, and which in itself, if true, conclusively establishes the fact.

Circumstantial evidence means evidence that proves a fact from which an inference of the existence of another fact may be drawn.

An inference is a deduction of fact that may logically and reasonably be drawn from another fact or group of facts established by the evidence.

It is not necessary that facts be proved by direct evidence. They may be proved also by circumstantial evidence or by a combination of direct evidence and circumstantial evidence. Both direct evidence and circumstantial evidence are acceptable as a means of proof. Neither is entitled to any greater weight than the other.

7

You are not permitted to find a defendant guilty or any crime charged against him based on circumstantial evidence unless the proved circumstances are not only consistent with the theory that that defendant is guilty of the crime, but cannot be reconciled with any other rational conclusion, and each fact which is essential to complete a set of circumstances necessary to establish that defendant's guilt has been proved beyond a reasonable doubt.

Also, if the evidence as to any particular count is susceptible of two reasonable interpretations, one which points to a defendant's guilt and the other to his innocence, it is your duty to adopt to that interpretation which points to his innocence, and reject the other which points to his guilt.

You will notice that the second paragraph of these instructions applies only when both of the interpretations appear to you to be reasonable. If, on the other hand, one of the interpretations 7a appears to you reasonable and the other to be unreasonable, it would be your duty to adopt the reasonable interpretation and to reject the unreasonable interpretation.

8

Evidence that a witness attempted to suppress evidence against himself in any manner, such as the intimidation of a witness may be considered by you as a circumstance tending to show a consciousness of guilt of a particular defendant that attempted to suppress said evidence. However, such evidence is not sufficient in itself to prove guilt and its weight and significance, if any, are matters for your consideration.

9

It is permissible to prove that the defendant Patricia Krenwinkel was ordered by the court to make certain handwriting exemplars during the trial and that she failed to make such exemplars. Defendant Patricia Krenwinkel stated to the court that her refusal to make such exemplars was based upon the advice of her attorney. The court advised her in open court outside the jury's presence that she had no legal right to refuse, that she had an absolute right to make such exemplars notwithstanding her attorney's advice to the contrary, and that the failure to make such exemplars might be the subject of argument to the jury by the prosecution and instruction to the jury by the court. The fact that she failed to comply with the order to make such exemplars is not sufficient standing alone and by itself to establish the guilt of Patricia Krenwinkel, but it is a fact which if proven may be considered by you in the light of all other proven facts in deciding the question of guilt or innocence in accordance with all the court's instructions to you. Whether or not such conduct shows consciousness of guilt and the significance to be attached to such a circumstance are matters for your determination. You are not to consider such circumstance in connection with any defendant other than Patricia Krenwinkel.

10

Evidence has been admitted as against one or more of the defendants, but denied admission as against the others.

At the time this evidence was admitted, you were admonished that it could not be considered by you as against the other defendants.

You are again instructed that you must not consider such evidence as against the other defendants.

Your verdict as to each defendant must be rendered as if he were being tried separately.

11

Certain evidence was admitted for a limited purpose.

At the time this evidence was admitted you were admonished that it could not be considered by you for any purpose other than the limited purpose for which it was admitted.

You are again instructed that you must not consider such evidence for any purpose except the limited purpose for which it was admitted.

12

The Court has previously admonished you to consider the tape-recorded statement of Juan Flynn, introduced through the testimony of Officer Dave Steuber, for a limited purpose only.

You are now instructed to disregard that previous instruction.

13

Juan Flynn, a witness in this case, has testified about an incident that allegedly took place prior to his testifying here in court in which he received two notes: Note No. 1 began 'How many changes does it take to make one big change...' and Note No. 2 began 'This is an indictment on your life because it is coming down, and when in course of human events....'

At the time this alleged incident was testified to, you were admonished that it was to be considered by you only in determining the state of mind of the witness Juan Flynn if you determine that such an incident took place.

You are instructed that you may not consider this evidence for any other purpose.

14

Linda Kasabian, a witness in this case, has testified to a statement allegedly made by 'Gypsy,' also known as Catherine Shore, about the character and personality of Charles Manson as well as life in the family.

You are hereby instructed that you may consider such evidence only in determining the state of mind of Linda Kasabian at the time 'Gypsy' allegedly made such statement and for no other purpose.

15

Linda Kasabian, a witness in this case, has testified to statements made by her to two young hitchhikers on or about August 12–15, 1969. This evidence has been received for the sole purpose of determining, if necessary, the state of mind of witness Linda Kasabian at the time the statements were made.

357

16

Neither side is required to call as witnesses all persons who may have been present at any of the events disclosed by the evidence or who may appear to have some knowledge of these events, or to produce all objects or documents mentioned or suggested by the evidence.

17

Every person who testifies under oath is a witness. You are the sole and exclusive judges of the credibility of the witness who have testified in this case.

In determining the credibility of a witness you may consider any matter that has a tendency in reason to prove or disprove the truthfulness of his testimony, including but not limited to the following:

His demeanor while testifying and the manner in which he testifies; the character of his testimony; the extent of his capacity to perceive any matter about which he testifies; his character for honesty or veracity or their opposites; the existence or nonexistence of a bias, interest, or other motive; a statement previously made by him that is consistent with his testimony; a statement made by him that is inconsistent with any part of his testimony; the existence or nonexistence of any fact testified to by him; his attitude toward the action in which he testifies or toward the giving of testimony; his admission of untruthfulness; his prior conviction of a felony.

18

A witness willfully false in one material part of his testimony is to be distrusted in others. You may reject the whole testimony of a witness who willfully has testified falsely as to a material point, unless, from all the evidence, you shall believe the probability of truth favors his testimony in other particulars.

However, discrepancies in a witness' testimony or between his testimony and that of others, if there were any, do not necessarily mean that the witness should be discredited. Failure of recollection is a common experience; and innocent misrecollection is not uncommon. It is a fact, also, that two persons witnessing an incident or a transaction often will see or hear it differently. Whether a discrepancy pertains to a fact of importance or only to a trivial detail should be considered in weighing its significance.

19

You are not bound to decide in conformity with the testimony of a number of witnesses, which does not produce conviction in your mind, as against the testimony of a lesser number or other evidence, which appeals to your mind with more convincing force. This does not mean that you are at liberty to disregard the testimony of the greater number of witnesses merely from caprice or prejudice, or from a desire to favor one side as against the other. It does mean that you are not to decide an issue by the simple process of counting the number of witnesses who have testified on the opposing sides. It means that the final test is not in the relative number of witnesses, but in the relative convincing force of the evidence.

20

The fact that a witness had been convicted of a felony, if such be a fact, may be considered by you only for the purpose of determining the credibility of that witness. The fact of such a conviction does not necessarily destroy or impair the witness' credibility. It is one of the circumstances that you may take into consideration in weighing the testimony of such a witness.

21

Motive is not an element of the crimes charged and need not be shown. However, you may consider motive or lack of motive as a circumstance in this case. Presence of motive may tend to establish guilt. Absence of motive may tend to establish innocence. You will therefore give its presence or absence, as the case may be, the weight to which you find it to be entitled.

22

A statement made by a defendant other than at his trial may be either an admission or a confession.

An admission is a statement by a defendant, which by itself is not sufficient to warrant an inference of guilt, but which tends to prove guilt when considered with the rest of the evidence.

A confession is a statement by a defendant which discloses his intentional participation in the criminal act for which he is on trial and which discloses his guilt of that crime.

You are the exclusive judges as to whether an admission or a confession was made by any defendant and if the statement is true in whole or in part. If you should find that such statement is entirely untrue, you must reject it. If you find it is true in part, you may consider that part which you find to be true.

Evidence of an oral admission or an oral confession of a defendant ought to be viewed with caution.

23

No person may be convicted of a criminal offense unless there is some proof of each element of the crime independent of any confession or admission made by him outside of this trial.

The identity of the person who is alleged to have committed a crime is not an element of the crime. Such identity may be established by an admission or confession.

24

A person is qualified to testify as an expert if he has special knowledge, skill, experience, training, or education sufficient to qualify him as an expert on the subject to which his testimony relates.

Duly qualified experts may give their opinions on questions in controversy at a trial. To assist you in deciding such questions, you may consider the opinion with the reasons given for it, if any by the expert who gives the opinion. You may also consider the qualifications and credibility of the expert. In resolving any conflict that may exist in the testimony of expert witnesses, you should weigh the opinion of one expert against that of another. In doing this, you should consider the relative qualifications and credibility of the expert witnesses, as well as the reasons for each opinion and the facts and other matters upon which it was based. You are not bound to accept an expert opinion as conclusive, but should give to it the weight to which you find it to be entitled. You may disregard any such opinion if you find it to be unreasonable.

25

In determining the weight to be given to an opinion expressed by any witness who did not testify as an expert witness, you should consider his credibility, the extent of his opportunity to perceive the matters upon which his opinion is based and the reasons, if any, given for it. You are not required to accept such an opinion but should give it the weight, if any, to which you find it entitled.

26

In examining an expert witness, counsel may propound to him a type of question known in the law as a hypothetical question. By such a question the witness is asked to assume to be true a hypothetical state of facts, and to give an opinion based on that assumption.

In permitting such a question, the court does not rule, and does not necessarily find that all the assumed facts have been proved. It only determines that those assumed facts are within the probable or possible range of the evidence. It is for you, the jury, to find from all the evidence whether or not the facts assumed in a hypothetical question have been proved, and if you should find that any assumption in such a question has not been proved, you are to determine the effect of that failure of proof on the value and weight of the expert opinion based on the assumption.

27

A defendant in a criminal action is presumed to be innocent until the contrary is proved, and in case of a reasonable doubt whether his guilt is satisfactorily shown, he is entitled to an acquittal. This presumption places upon the State the burden of proving him guilty beyond a reasonable doubt. Reasonable doubt is defined as follows: It is not a mere possible doubt; because everything relating to human affairs, and depending on moral evidence, is open to some possible or imaginary doubt. It is that state of the case which, after the entire comparison and consideration of all the evidence, leaves the minds of the jurors in that condition that they cannot say they feel an abiding conviction, to a moral certainty, of the truth of the charge.

28

Evidence that on some former occasion a witness made a statement or statements that were consistent or inconsistent with his testimony in this trial may be considered by you as evidence of the truth of the facts as stated by the witness on such former occasion. However, you are not bound to accept such statement or statements to be truthful in whole or in part, but you should give to them the weight to which you find them to be entitled.

29

It is a constitutional right of a defendant in a criminal trial that he may not be compelled to testify. Thus, the decision as to whether he should testify is left to the defendant, acting with the advice and assistance of his attorney. You must not draw any inference of guilt from the fact that he does not testify, nor should this fact be discussed by you or enter into your deliberations in any way.

30

In deciding whether or not to testify, the defendant may choose to relay on the state of the evidence and upon the failure, if any, of the People to prove every essential element of the charge against him, and no lack of testimony on defendant's part will supply a failure of proof by the People so as to support by itself a finding against him on any such essential element.

31

All persons concerned in the commission of a crime who either directly and actively commit the act constituting the offense or who knowingly and with criminal intent aid and abet in its commission or, whether present or not, who advises and encourages its commission, are regarded by the law as principals in the crime thus committed and are equally guilty thereof.

32

A person aids and abets the commission of a crime if he knowingly and with criminal intent aids, promotes, encourages, or instigates by act or advice, or by act and advice, the commission of such crime.

33

A conviction cannot be had upon the testimony of an accomplice unless it is corroborated by such other evidence as shall tend to connect the defendant with the commission of the offense.

34

Corroborated evidence is evidence of some act or fact related to the offense which, if believed, by itself and without any aid, interpretation, or direction from the testimony of the accomplice, tends to connect the defendant with the commission of the offense charged.

However, it is not necessary that the corroborative evidence be sufficient in itself to establish every element of the offense charged, or that it corroborates every fact to which the accomplice testifies. The evidence required to corroborate the testimony of an accomplice is sufficient if it tends to connect the defendant with the commission of the crime in such a way as may reasonable satisfy the jury that the witness who must be corroborated is telling the truth. It is not necessary that the evidence used to corroborate the testimony of an accomplice prove independently that the defendant is guilty of the offense.

34a

Evidence corroborating the testimony of an accomplice need not connect the defendant with the commission of the offense beyond a reasonable doubt.

In determining whether an accomplice has been corroborated, you must first assume the testimony of the accomplice has been removed from the case. You must then determine whether there is any remaining evidence which tends to connect the defendant with the commission of the offense.

If there is not such independent evidence which tends to connect the defendant with the commission of the offense, the testimony of the accomplice is not corroborated.

If there is such independent evidence which you believe, then the testimony of the accomplice is corroborated.

35

If the crimes of murder or conspiracy to commit murder, the commission of which is charged against the defendants, were committed by anyone, the witness Linda Kasabian was an accomplice as a matter of law and her testimony is subject to the rule requiring corroboration.

36

The testimony of an accomplice ought to be viewed with distrust. This does not mean that you may arbitrarily disregard such testimony, but you should give to it the weight to which you find it to be entitled after examining it with care and caution and in the light of all the evidence in the case.

37

You are instructed that evidence sufficient to corroborate the testimony of an accomplice may be slight and entitled to little consideration when standing alone. The evidence is sufficient even though slight if it tends to connect the defendant with the commission of the crime.

38

You are instructed that the evidence required to corroborate the testimony of an accomplice may be either circumstantial or direct.

39

Murder is the unlawful killing of a human being, with malice and aforethought.

40

Malice may be either express or implied. Malice is express when there is manifested an intention unlawfully to kill a human being.

Malice is implied when the killing results from an act involving a high degree of probability that it will result in death, which act is done for a base, anti-social purpose and with a wanton disregard for human life or when the killing is a direct casual result of the perpetration or the attempt to perpetrate a felony inherently dangerous to human life.

The mental state constituting malice aforethought does not necessarily require any ill will or hatred of the person killed.

Aforethought does not imply deliberation or the lapse of considerate time. It only means that the required mental state must precede rather than follow the act.

41

All murder which is perpetrated by any kind of willful, deliberate and premeditated killing with malice aforethought is murder of the first degree.

The word "deliberate" means formed or arrived at or determined upon as a result of careful thought and weighing of considerations for and against the proposed course of action. The word "premeditated" means considered beforehand.

If you find that the killing was preceded and accompanied by a clear, deliberate intent on the part of the defendant to kill, which was the result of deliberation and premeditation, so that it must have been formed upon preexisting reflection and not under a sudden heat of passion or other condition precluding the idea of deliberation, it is murder of the first degree.

The word "deliberate" means formed or arrived at or determined upon as a result of careful thought and weighing of considerations for and against the proposed course of action. The word "premeditated" means considered beforehand.

If you find that the killing was preceded and accompanied by a clear, deliberate intent on the part of the defendant to kill, which was the result of deliberation and premeditation, so that it must have been formed upon preexisting reflection and not under a sudden heat of passion or other condition precluding the idea of deliberation, it is murder of the first degree.

The law does not undertake to measure in units of time the length of the period during which the thought must be pondered before it can ripen into an intent to kill which is truly deliberate and deliberated and premeditated. The time will vary with different individuals and under varying circumstances. The true test is not the duration of time, but rather the extent of the reflection.

41a

A cold, calculated judgement and decision may be arrived at in a short period of time, but a mere unconsidered and rash impulse, even though it includes an intent to kill, is not such deliberation and premeditation as will fix an unlawful killing as murder of the first degree. To constitute a deliberated and premeditated killing, the slayer must weigh and consider the question of killing and the reasons for and against such a choice and, having in mind the consequences, he decides to and does kill.

42

The unlawful killing of a human being, whether intentional, unintentional or accidental, which occurs as a result of the commission of or attempt to commit the crime of burglary or robbery, and where there was in the mind of the perpetrator the specific intent to commit such crime or crimes, is murder of the first degree.

The specific intent to commit burglary or robbery and the commission or attempt to commit such crime or crimes must be proved beyond a reasonable doubt.

43

Every person who enters any house with the specific intent to steal, take and carry away the personal property of another of any value with the specific intent to deprive the owner permanently of his property is guilty of burglary.

The essence of a burglary is entering such place with such specific intent, and the crime of burglary is complete as soon as the entry is made, regardless of whether the intent thereafter is carried out.

44

Robbery is the taking of personal property of any value in the possession of another, from his person or immediate presence, and against his will, accomplished by means of force or fear and with the specific intent permanently to deprive the owner of his property.

45

If a human being is killed by any one of several persons engaged in the perpetration of, or attempt to perpetrate, the crime of burglary or robbery, all persons who either directly and actively commit the act constituting such crime or who knowingly and with criminal intent aid and abet in its commission or, whether present or not, who advise and encourage its commission, are guilty of murder of the first degree, whether the killing is intentional, unintentional, or accidental.

46

Under the court's instructions to you, a finding that any defendant is guilty of murder in the first degree as to Counts 1-7, inclusive, must be based upon either a willful, deliberate, and premeditated killing with malice aforethought, or a killing which occurred as the result of the commission or attempt to commit the crime of burglary or robbery, as these types of murder are defined elsewhere in these instructions. The jury must be unanimous as to the degree of murder if you find any defendant guilty of murder. The jury need not be unanimous as to which of those two types of murder a finding of murder in the first degree is based upon.

47

Murder of the second degree is the unlawful killing of a human being with malice aforethought when there is manifested an intention unlawfully a human being but the evidence is insufficient to establish deliberation and premeditation.

48

In the crimes charged in Counts 1-7, inclusive, of the indictment, there must exist a union or joint operation of act or conduct and a certain specific intent.

In the crime of murder, there must exist in the mind of the perpetrator the requisite specific intent for each type of murder as set forth in the definitions of those offenses elsewhere in these instructions, and unless such intent so exists that crime is not committed.

49

The specific intent with which an act is done may be manifested by the circumstances surrounding its commission. But you may not find a defendant guilty of a willful, deliberate, premeditated murder of the first degree unless the proved circumstances not only are consistent with the hypothesis that he had the specific intent to kill a human being with malice aforethought, which was the result of deliberation and premeditation as those terms are defined elsewhere in these instructions, but are irreconcilable with any other rational conclusion.

Also, if the evidence as to such specific intent is susceptible of two reasonable interpretations, one of which points to the existence thereof and the other to the absence thereof, you must adopt that interpretation which points to its absence. If, on the other hand, one interpretation of the evidence as to such specific intent appears to you to be unreasonable and the other

interpretation to be unreasonable, it would be your duty to accept the reasonable interpretation and to reject the unreasonable.

50

The specific intent with which an act is done may be manifested by the circumstances surrounding its commission. But you may not find any defendant guilty of any of the offenses charged in Counts 1 through 7, inclusive, based upon the unlawful killing of a human being occurring as a result of the commission or attempt to commit the crime of burglary or robbery, as distinguished from willful, deliberate, and premeditated murder of the first degree or unpremeditated murder of the second degree, as those types of murder are defined elsewhere in these instructions, unless the proved circumstances not only are consistent with the hypothesis that he had the specific intent to steal, take, and carry away the personal property of another of any value with the specific intent to deprive the owner permanently of his property, but are irreconcilable with any other rational conclusion.

51

The specific intent with which an act is done may be manifested by the circumstances surrounding its commission. But you may not find a defendant guilty of murder in the second degree unless the proved circumstances not only are consistent with the hypothesis that he had the specific intent to kill a human being with malice aforethought but are irreconcilable with any other rational conclusion.

Also, if the evidence as to such specific intent is susceptible of two reasonable interpretations, one of which points to the existence thereof and the other to the absence thereof, you must adopt that interpretation which points to its absence. If, on the other hand, one interpretation of the evidence as to such specific intent appears to you to be reasonable and the other interpretation to be unreasonable, it would be your duty to accept the reasonable interpretation and to reject the unreasonable.

52

Murder is classified into two degrees, and if you should find any defendant guilty of murder, it will be your duty to determine and state in your verdict whether you find the murder to be of the first or second degree.

53

If you are convinced beyond a reasonable doubt that the crime of murder has been committed by a defendant, but you have a reasonable doubt whether such murder was of the first or of the second degree, you must give to such defendant the benefit of the doubt and return a verdict fixing the murder as of the second degree.

54

Before you may return a verdict in this case, you must agree unanimously not only as to whether any defendant is guilty or not guilty, but also, if you should find him guilty of an unlawful killing, you must agree unanimously as to whether he is guilty of murder of the first degree or murder of the second degree.

55

The intent with which an act is done is shown by the circumstances attending the act, the manner in which it is done, the means used, and soundness of mind and discretion of the person committing the act.

For the purposes of the case on trial, you must assume that each of the defendants was of sound mind at the time of his alleged conduct which, it is charged, constituted the crimes described in the indictment.

56

A conspiracy is an agreement between two or more persons to commit any crime, and with the specific intent to commit such crime, followed by an overt act committed in this state by one or more of the parties for the purpose of accomplishing the object of the agreement. Conspiracy is a crime.

In order to find a defendant guilty of conspiracy, in addition to proof of the unlawful agreement, there must be proof of the commission of at least one of the overt acts alleged in the indictments. It is not necessary to the guilt of any particular defendant that he himself committed the overt act, if he was one of the conspirators when such an act was committed.

The term "overt act" means any step taken or act committed by one or more of the conspirators which goes beyond mere planning or agreement to commit a public offense and which step or act is done in furtherance of the accomplishment of the object of the conspiracy.

56a

To be an "overt act", the step taken or act committed need not, in and of itself, constitute the crime or even an attempt to commit the crime, which is the ultimate object of the conspiracy. Nor is it required that such step or act, in and of itself, be a criminal or an unlawful act.

57

Each member of a criminal conspiracy is liable for each act and bound by each declaration of every other member of the conspiracy if said act or said declaration is in furtherance of the object of the conspiracy.

The act of one conspirator pursuant to or in furtherance of the common design of the conspiracy is the act of all conspirators. Every conspirator is legally responsible for an act of a co-conspirator that follows as one of the probable and natural consequences of the object of the conspiracy even though it was not intended as a part of the original plan and even though he was not present at the time of the commission of such act.

58

It is not necessary in proving a conspiracy to show a meeting of the alleged conspirators or the making of an express or formal agreement. The formation and existence of a conspiracy may be inferred from all circumstances tending to show the common intent and may be proved in the same way as any other fact may be proved, either by direct testimony of the fact or by circumstantial evidence, or by both direct and circumstantial evidence.

59

Evidence that a person was in the company of or associated with one or more other persons alleged or proved to have been members of a conspiracy is not, in itself, sufficient to prove that such person was a member of the alleged conspiracy.

60

No act or declaration of a conspirator that is an independent product of his own mind and is outside the common design and not a furtherance of that design is binding upon his co-conspirators, and they are not criminally liable for any such act.

61

Where a conspirator commits an act which is neither in furtherance of the object of the conspiracy nor the natural and probable consequence of an attempt to attain that object, he alone is responsible for and is bound by that act, and no responsibility therefor attaches to any of his confederates.

62

The act or declaration of a person who is not a member of a conspiracy is not binding upon the members of the conspiracy, if any, even though it is an act which tended to promote the object of the alleged conspiracy.

63

Evidence of the commission of an act which furthered the purpose of an alleged conspiracy is not, in itself, sufficient to prove that the person committing the act was a member of such a conspiracy.

64

Every person who joins a criminal conspiracy after its formation and who adopts its purposes and objects, is liable for and bound by the acts and declarations of other members of the conspiracy done and made during the time that he is a member and in pursuance and furtherance of the conspiracy.

A person who joins a conspiracy after its formation is not liable or bound by the acts of the co-conspirators or for any crime committed by the co-conspirators before such person joins and becomes a member of the conspiracy.

Evidence of any acts or declarations of other conspirators prior to the time such person becomes a member of the conspiracy may be considered by you in determining the nature, objectives and purposes of the conspiracy, but for no other purpose.

65

Any member of a conspiracy may withdraw from and cease to be a party to the conspiracy, but his liability for the acts of his co-conspirators continues until he effectively withdraws from the conspiracy.

In order to effectively withdraw from a conspiracy, there must be an affirmative and bona fide rejection or repudiation to the other conspirators of whom he has knowledge.

If a member of a conspiracy has effectively withdrawn from the conspiracy he is not thereafter liable for any act of the co-conspirators committed subsequent to his withdrawal from the conspiracy, but he is not relieved of responsibility for the acts of his co-conspirators committed while he was a member.

66

In Count 8, the defendants are charged with conspiracy to commit murder

370

in violation of Sections 182.1 and 187, Penal Code of California, a felony, as follows:

That on or about the 8th through the 10th day of August, 1969 at and in the County of Los Angeles, State of California, Charles Manson, Charles Watson, Patricia Krenwinkel, Susan Atkins, Linda Kasabian, and Leslie Sankston (whose true name is Leslie Van Houten), the said defendants, did willfully, unlawfully, feloniously and knowingly conspire, combine, confederate and agree together to commit the crime of murder, violation of Section 187, Penal Code of California, a felony.

It is alleged that the following were overt acts which were committed in this state by one or more of the defendants for the purpose of furthering the object of the conspiracy:

OVERT ACT NO. 1

That on or about August 8, 1969, the said defendants, Charles Watson, Patricia Krenwinkel, Susan Atkins and Linda Kasabian did travel to the vicinity of 10050 Cielo Drive in the City and County of Los Angeles.

66a

OVERT ACT NO. 2

That on or about August 8, 1969, the defendants, Charles Watson, Patricia Krenwinkel, and Susan Atkins did enter the residence at 10050 Cielo Drive, City and County of Los Angeles.

OVERT ACT NO. 3

That on or about August 10, 1969, the defendants, Charles Manson, Charles Watson, Patricia Krenwinkel, Susan Atkins, Linda Kasabian, and Leslie Sankston (whose true name is Leslie Van Houten) did travel to the vicinity of 3301 Waverly Drive, City and County of Los Angeles.

OVERT ACT NO. 4

That on or about August 10, 1969, the defendants, Charles Manson, Charles Watson, Patricia Krenwinkel, and Leslie Sankston (whose true name is Leslie Van Houten) did enter the residence at 3301 Waverly Drive, City and County of Los Angeles.

66b

The defendants are also charged with the commission of the following public offenses:

371

COUNT 1

That on or about the 9th day of August, 1969 at and in the County of Los Angeles, State of California, the said defendants, Charles Manson, Charles Watson, Patricia Krenwinkel, Susan Atkins, and Linda Kasabian did willfully, unlawfully, feloniously and with malice aforethought murder Abigail Anne Folger, a human being.

COUNT 2

That on or about the 9th of August, 1969, at and in the County of Los Angeles, State of California, the said defendants, Charles Manson, Charles Watson, Patricia Krenwinkel, Susan Atkins and Linda Kasabian did willfully, unlawfully, feloniously and with malice aforethought murder Voityck Frykowski, a human being.

66c
COUNT 3

That on or about the 9th day of August, 1969, at and in the County of Los Angeles, State of California, the said defendants, Charles Manson, Charles Watson, Patricia Krenwinkel, Susan Atkins, and Linda Kasabian did willfully, unlawfully, feloniously and with malice aforethought murder Steven Earl Parent, a human being.

COUNT 4

That on or about the 9th day of August, 1969, at and in the County of Los Angeles, State of California, the said defendants, Charles Manson, Charles Watson, Patricia Krenwinkel, Susan Atkins, and Linda Kasabian did willfully, unlawfully, feloniously and with malice aforethought murder Sharon Marie Polanski, a human being.

66d
COUNT 5

That on or about the 9th day of August, 1969, at and in the County of Los Angeles, State of California, the said defendants, Charles Manson, Charles Watson, Patricia Krenwinkel, Susan Atkins, and Linda Kasabian did willfully, unlawfully, feloniously and with malice aforethought murder Thomas John Sebring, a human being.

COUNT 6

That on or about the 10th day of August, 1969, at and in the County of Los

Angeles, State of California, the said defendants, Charles Manson, Charles Watson, Patricia Krenwinkel, Leslie Sankston (whose true name is Leslie Van Houten), Linda Kasabian, and Susan Atkins did willfully, unlawfully, feloniously and with malice aforethought murder Leno A. La Bianca, a human being.

66e

COUNT 7

That on or about the 10th day of August, 1969, at and in the County of Los Angeles, State of California, the said defendants, Charles Manson, Charles Watson, Patricia Krenwinkel, Leslie Sankston (whose true name is Leslie Van Houten), Linda Kasabian, and Susan Atkins did willfully, unlawfully, feloniously and with malice aforethought murder Rosemary La Bianca, a human being.

67

In the crime charged in Count 8 of the indictment, there must exist a union or joint operation of act or conduct and a certain specific intent.

In the crime of conspiring to commit murder, there must exist in the mind of the perpetrator the specific intent to commit murder of the first degree by means of a willful, deliberate and premeditated killing with malice aforethought, as a type of murder is defined elsewhere in these instructions, and unless such intent so exists that crime is not committed.

68

The specific intent with which an act is done may be manifested by the circumstances surrounding its commission. But you may not find any defendant guilty of the offense of conspiracy to commit murder charged in Count 8 unless the proof of circumstances not only are consistent with the hypothesis that he had the specific intent to commit murder of the first degree by means of a willful, deliberate and premeditated killing with malice aforethought, as that type of murder is defined elsewhere in these instructions, but are irreconcilable with any other rational conclusion.

Also, if the evidence as to such specific intent is susceptible of two reasonable interpretations, one of which points to the existence thereof and the other to the absence thereof, you must adopt that interpretation which points to its absence.

If, on the other hand, one interpretation of the evidence as such specific intent appears to you to be reasonable and the other interpretation to be un-

373

reasonable, it would be your duty to accept the reasonable interpretation and to reject the unreasonable.

69

The intent with which an act is done is shown by the circumstances attending the act, the manner in which it is done, the means used, and the soundness of mind and discretion of the person committing the act.

For the purposes of the case on trial, you must assume that each defendant was of sound mind at the time of his alleged conduct which, it is charged, constituted the crime described in the indictment.

70

In this case, you must decide separately whether each of the several defendants is guilty or not guilty of each of the offenses charged against him. If you cannot agree upon verdicts as to all the defendants, but do agree upon a verdict as to one or more of them, you must render a verdict as to the one or more upon which you agree.

71

Each count charges a separate and distinct offense. You must decide each count separately on the evidence and the law applicable to it, uninfluenced by your decision as to any other count. Each defendant may be convicted or acquitted on any or all of the offenses charged against him. Your finding as to each defendant charged on each count must be stated in a separate verdict.

72

As to Count 8 of the indictment each defendant in this case is individually entitled to, and must receive, your determination whether he was a member of the alleged conspiracy. As to each defendant you must determine whether he was a conspirator by deciding whether he willfully, intentionally and knowingly joined with any other or others in the alleged conspiracy.

73

I have not intended by anything I have said or done, or by any questions that I may have asked, to intimate or suggest what you should find to be the facts on any questions submitted to you, or that I believe or disbelieve any witness.

If anything I have done or said has seemed to so indicate, you will disregard it and form your own opinion.

74

You have been instructed as to all the rules of law that may be necessary for you to reach a verdict. Whether some of the instructions will apply will depend upon your determination of the facts. You will disregard any instruction which applies to a state of facts which you determine does not exist. You must not conclude from the fact that an instruction has been given that the court is expressing any opinion as to the facts.

75

Both the People and the defendants are entitled to the individual opinion of each juror. It is the duty of each of you to consider the evidence for the purpose of arriving at a verdict if you can do so. Each of you must decide the case for yourself, but should do so only after a discussion of the evidence and instructions with the other jurors.

You should not hesitate to change an opinion if you are convinced it is erroneous. However, you should not be influenced to decide any question in a particular way because a majority of the jurors, or any of them, favor such a decision.

76

The attitude and conduct of jurors at the beginning of their deliberations are matters of considerable importance. It is rarely productive or good for a juror at the outset to make an emphatic expression of his opinion on the case or to state how he intends to vote. When one does that at the beginning, his sense of pride may be aroused, and he may hesitate to change his position even if shown that it is wrong. Remember that you are not partisans or advocates in this matter, but are judges.

In your deliberations the subject of penalty or punishment is not to be discussed or considered by you. If you return a verdict of guilty or murder in the first degree as to any particular count or a verdict of guilty of conspiracy to commit murder as alleged in Count 8, then the matter of penalty or punishment as to those counts will be considered and determined in a separate proceeding. If you return a verdict of guilty of murder in the second degree, as to any count, the matter of penalty or punishment as to that count will be determined in the manner provided by law.

You shall now retire and select one of your members to act as foreman, who will preside over your deliberations. In order to reach a verdict, all twelve jurors must agree to the decision. As soon as all of you have agreed upon a verdict, you shall have dated and signed by your foreman and then shall return with it to this room.

As soon as Judge Older finished reading the instructions to the jury, Deputies Taylor, Tull, Kane and Kolvig and the Chief Deputy Sergeant stood up rigidly inside the rail and were given the following oath:

Do you solemnly swear that you will take charge of the jury and keep them together; that you will not speak to them yourselves, nor allow anyone else to speak to them, on any subject connected with the case except by order of the court; and when they have agreed upon a verdict, you will return them to the court, So Help You, God?

"I do," they all responded and immediately the jurors were conducted by Bailiff Taylor out of the court room. The hussle and excitement in the court room was palpitating. The artists and newsmen were busy jotting down their observations. The spectators' eyes were trained on the jurors.

Deputy Taylor's first issue of order was to separate the panel jury and the alternate jurors. The panel jury was kept waiting for about twenty minutes until Deputy Taylor and the court clerk carried the exhibits to the jury room of Department 104, which was Judge Older's Department.

While we waited, nothing was said and for a while it seemed that everyone was avoiding each other. Eventually, I suggested that we could use the time to nominate someone for foreman, but there was no cooperation. Everyone was dispersed around the room except for Debbie and Ray, who kept whispering to one another.

Finally, Deputy Taylor came in and led us to our own jury room which had been occupied by the three female defendants. The jury room was filled with some two hundred sixty-three exhibits submitted by the prosecution plus one hundred five exhibits entered by the defense.

At first the general feeling was of curiosity; there were so many charts and photos to see in front of us. We couldn't start looking at them nor discuss them without first electing one of us to be foreman.

Since no one seemed to initiate the nominations, I suggested that we all should write a juror's name on a piece of paper and that the two jurors who received the most votes should be entered in a final vote. Everyone agreed. I read the names out loud while Violet, at my suggestion, wrote them down.

The following were given one vote each: Mildred, Ray, Paul, and Genaro.

I received two. Martin and Frank acquired three votes each and were the two contenders.

After the first count between Martin and Frank, both received six. Frank gladly conceded before a second vote was cast. Thus, Martin Paine was elected foreman.

The photos were handed out, one by one. The charts were set against the walls; and such items as the knife, gun, rope, etc., were placed on top of the table for everyone to examine.

On account of starting late in the day, the initial session lasted only one hour and ten minutes. We didn't discuss anything in depth and just looked at the exhibits. However, we talked and agreed we should start deliberation the next day, which was Saturday. Some, like Betty, wanted to work on Sunday also so we could get it over with. She was overruled.

We returned to the hotel. Television cameramen and news photographers and reporters were eagerly waiting outside to snap our pictures to no avail.

Under orders from Superior Court Judge Malcom Lucas (Presiding Jurist of the Criminal Court), a police motor escort was provided for the jury bus as it went to and from the hotel during the deliberations. It made the jurors feel important.

No visitors or telephone calls were allowed during this time; however, that Friday night we were taken out to dinner across the street from the hotel to a brand new restaurant in the Equitable Insurance Building. Back at the hotel, after dinner, I stayed up late reading my notes and checking important items which I had questioned. The clique also went to bed late.

Outside in the hall, Debbie, Tom, and Ray, with beer cans in their hands, were running and laughing as a result of having placed a tape recording of "Reveille" under Deputy Taylor's bed set to go off at four A.M. He slept through it. Part of their fun was stopped when Deputy Tull caught them trying to short-sheet his bed, and forbade them to hang on the walls.

We returned to court. Dressed in casual attire, we arrived to deliberate on Saturday. Martin Paine, the foreman, asked the jurors to remain silent for a minute and pray for guidance. We all bowed our heads and shortly after idle discussions, we got underway.

After an hour's discussion to which the foreman contributed very little, someone mentioned that I should start talking. There was marked evidence that the foreman had trouble in explaining himself and that he lacked preparation in using his notes.

I replied that the foreman should open the deliberations. Martin looked rather disturbed and suggested he wanted everybody to speak informally.

377

His voice was strained for words and as he spoke, he gave me a stern look of discomfort.

Martin Paine embarked upon an easy lofty position in which he gradually ignored my suggestions and declined to make specific statements about his position.

The clique's members, Debbie, Ray, Violet, and even Martin resented my attitude and made me aware of it. It was not my intention to cause any hard feelings. I was simply trying to make the foreman lead us in a pattern of discussions. It was obvious that he was unable to do so.

Stubbornly I refused to set a plan for discussing the issues and sat motionless to listen to the others.

Ray and Marvin were constantly bringing up points that were not coordinated. Genaro would follow them with Debbie and Violet trailing behind.

At noon, we didn't leave the ninth floor. The bailiffs brought box lunches for us.

Upon returning to deliberate, the jurors were restless because of my silence.

Finally, Genaro and Marvin accused me of not contributing to the discussion.

"When my turn comes, I'll have something to say," I replied.

Ray, Marvin, and Genaro, as well as Debbie and Violet, together with Martin, excitedly responded with questions to me. It was obvious the jurors had no leadership and for the sake of dignity, I opted to begin the deliberation by asking a question, "Do you all believe the testimony of Linda Kasabian?"

There were some ayes and some who avoided comment.

"It's not quite clear for me the fact that while these crimes were being committed that Bill Garretson as well as the neighbors couldn't hear the screams for help from the victims. Was Linda Kasabian perhaps lying?" I asked.

A torrential stream of answers flowed from everybody. However, it was Ray who, through a large aerial view of the Tate grounds, demonstrated that it would be impossible for anyone to be able to hear anyone calling for help because of the topographical location of the Tate residence. There are mountains on both the north and west sides of the house. Besides, if the wind were blowing in the wrong direction, it might have been impossible for the neighbors to hear.

Following that simple question, we all agreed that Linda Kasabian was telling the truth.

However, to verify our belief we asked, in writing, for an after-dark visit to the Tate residence and the La Bianca home. Judge Older denied our request in open court without explanation. We continued deliberation.

"Linda Kasabian's testimony was pertly and convincingly delivered," Frank Welch offered and concluded by saying, "there's no need to visit these two houses."

"Yes," Paul White added, "all the lurid details stood up under vigorous cross-examination by Mr. Fitzgerald and Mr. Kanarek."

Marvin and Ray agreed and expressed themselves by stating that Linda Kasabian had told everything explicitly, even things pertaining to her private life which, in essence, she needn't have.

When my turn came to express an opinion, I said, "It is impossible not to believe Linda Kasabian. When she told the sequence of events under the command of Manson and guidance of Watson, the defense was unable to change a word in her testimony while conducting the cross-examination. Linda Kasabian told the truth on the witness stand as she saw the crimes happen and she answered every question freely—but changed nothing."

Every juror spoke and declared his point of view. Unanimously, the jurors agreed to accept the testimony given by Linda Kasabian.

For lack of leadership and acting as foreman, I introduced a suggestion which was accepted immediately.

With typed notes in hand, I began, "We all have listened to every detail and have taken notes during the trial. However, except for the killings committed, we actually don't know how they were committed. I mean the procedure and who killed who."

Then, picking up my notes, I continued, "I have here a brief summary of what I believe may have happened those two nights. It's based on what was said in court and I would like to start relating the events of the first night."

"That's a good idea," Frank Welch uttered.

"Also," I went on, "I would like you to help me in the sequence of events."

"You start," Ray said, pointing at me, "and if anyone feels like adding something, let him say it for the benefit of establishing the sequence."

"That's a good point," said Olivia. "I for one, if I don't agree with Bill, will say so."

"By all means, please do," I responded in the middle of murmuring statements.

At first, I began relating how possibly the events could have happened. Later, the jurors, one at a time, continued adding statements and verifications of evidence presented in Court.

We followed, step by step, from the very beginning, when Manson told Watson and Patricia Krenwinkel, Susan Atkins, Leslie Van Houten, and Linda Kasabian to go kill everyone living at the Tate residence.

379

With the assistance of photographs and drawings, we put the alleged killers at the scene of the crime. The car—the place where they parked—and where they walked up to the Tate residence. The cutting of telephone wires—how they hid when they saw the headlights of a car. How Tex Watson shot and killed young Parent. The removal of the screen door. When Tex ordered Linda Kasabian to stay behind and watch for noises.

The actual happenings inside the Tate house we deduced were as follows:

Patricia Krenwinkel and Tex Watson walked through the back door and that's where they left their fingerprints. Susan Atkins entered but left no identifying marks. Voityck Frykowski was asleep on a couch in the living room. Abigail Folger was reading and Sharon Tate was conversing with Jay Sebring in her bedroom; she was laying down and he was seated at the edge of the bed.

Tex Watson ordered Patricia Krenwinkel and Susan Atkins to bring all the victims to the living room. Susan Atkins brought in the actress and her companion. Patricia Krenwinkel followed behind Abigail Folger. Voityck Frykowski was awakened. There was panic. The victims were told they were going to be killed.

Frykowski offered all he had in his pockets but was pushed down and told to shut up. Sharon Tate began to cry. Abigail Folger perhaps moved over to console her friend but was stopped. The alleged killers likely took it upon themselves to take charge of each of the victims. In the middle of the excitement, Jay Sebring likely tried to escape but was shot in the back by Watson.

According to our discussion, Sebring was the first victim inside to die. From then on, there was chaos among the victims. Upon hearing the gunshot and seeing one of their friends shot to death, everybody ran to save his own life.

Patricia Krenwinkel, with a knife in her hand, ran after Abigail Folger. Sharon Tate was held by Tex Watson. Frykowski, half asleep, was stabbed by Susan Atkins but somehow he managed to pull the hair of his attacker, whereas Watson came to her defense and shot him and hit him repeatedly on the head with the butt of the gun. Obviously, the butt broke and that accounted for three pieces of wood found at the scene of the crime. The pieces fitted perfectly with the gun which, according to testimonies of Juan Flynn, De Carlo, and others, belonged to Charles Manson.

Meanwhile, Miss Folger, in a white gown, screaming and yelling for help after being stabbed, eventually ran outside the house but Patricia Krenwinkel caught up with her and although the coffee heiress fought valiantly for her life, the invader consummated her intent and killed her. Miss Folger's mutilated body was found in the grass (shown on a picture).

Susan Atkins lost her knife and went outside to get another from Linda Kasabian. She didn't have any. The knife Susan Atkins had lost belonged to Linda Kasabian.

Susan went back inside and got hold of the eight-and-a-half-month pregnant Sharon Tate. Immediately after, Voityck, fighting back the fusilade of blows from Watson's pistol, ran out the front door and saw Linda Kasabian. He asked her for help. Linda Kasabian couldn't do anything but watch Tex hit the victim over and over again. Linda Kasabian, crying, ran down the hill and fearfully waited for her companions to return. Frykowski fell dead on the lawn.

Inside, Sharon Tate had asked to be spared and begged for the life of her child. Susan Atkins, upon Sharon's request, replied: "Shut up, you bitch! I have no mercy for you!"

And while Tex held the honey blonde actress, Susan Atkins stabbed her over and over in the chest. Possibly, while still alive, Sharon Tate and Jay Sebring were connected with a white rope and hung by their necks from a loft over the living room.

The final scene of the crime was completed when the alleged killers, by order of Manson, scrawled in blood the word "pig" on the front door to make it appear that the assailants were blacks.

The jurors couldn't determine whether Patricia Krenwinkel was responsible for the writing of the word "pig", but it was their decision that either one of them could have written it.

Precisely in order, and point by point, we followed the testimony of each witness, such as Mr. Webber's. The witness in question not only recognized the defendants but gave an accurate description of the car's license plate. Then, Linda Kasabian threw the bundle of clothes and the gun along the road, and two witnesses stated finding of same. Along with the testimony of Barbara Hoyt when the alleged killers were watching television, there was too much coincidence for the jurors not to believe the witnesses.

Prior to establishing the patter of events on the second night, we also brought into discussion the fact that Charles Manson knew ahead of time the premises of the Tate residence.

Mr. Hatami, Greg Jacobson, Rudolph Altobelli, and Terry Melcher testified they had seen Charles Manson on the premises and they couldn't possibly all be lying. Again, it was too much coincidence for the jurors not to believe the witnesses.

The deliberation continued by describing the events of the second night.

We all agreed that likely it went like this:

Manson, in the company of Susan Atkins, Leslie Van Houten, Patricia Krenwinkel, and Tex Watson, with Clem Tufts and Linda Kasabian driving the same car, left the Spahn ranch and went to the La Bianca home.

Manson ordered Leslie Van Houten, Patricia Krenwinkel, and Tex Watson to go inside the house and told them "not to cause panic" to the victims and then hitchhike their way back to the ranch. Manson left with the rest and handed Linda Kasabian a wallet to dispose of later at a Sylmar gas station ladies' room so a black woman would find it.

The deliberation became agitated and quite heated.

Everybody accepted Leslie Van Houten to be guilty except Marvin Connolly. He believed strongly she was guilty of second-degree murder.

For a while, we were involved with repeated arguments. Genaro surprisingly changed his mind and turned to favor Marvin's theory at the end of the second day. Ray, Debbie and Violet were hesitant to follow suit. However, their feelings or beliefs were not closely stated. They just felt Leslie Van Houten was not guilty as the others.

"They are guilty as a dollar bill!" shouted Frank Welch.

Immediately Marvin retaliated at the retired sheriff and in an adamant manner, uttered, among other things, "You're like a child. You don't know what you're talking about."

Frank felt deeply offended. Holding himself from exploding, he opted to give Marvin a piece of his mind and quite seriously stated, "You don't have any manners. I have as much right as you do to express an opinion."

Frank, somewhat resentful, added:

"You should have more respect for your elders. I am seventy-four years old and you certainly have no right to speak to me that way."

Marvin didn't respond at the moment but surely felt embarrassed.

Ray covered the gap of silence by taking Marvin's side and then added cutting remarks towards me.

The jurors were almost on the verge of dividing their feelings when suddenly I decided to take the initiative to calm down the situation.

"There's no reason why we should insult each other. We're all adults and should behave accordingly. If anyone has a personal gripe against someone, I beg you to bury it outside of this room. We have been given the highest privilege given to any man. That of sitting in judgment of the fate of another man. We must weigh the facts carefully and above all apply the common sense which we would exercise in our everyday affairs in this jury room with us.

"We have a common cause, a common duty to determine whether these defendants are guilty or not. Again, I beg you to overlook your personal feelings of hatred and let us work together. We need each other. You're all intelligent people and I have the confidence you'll do your best. I know I will. Thank you."

"I feel better already," Frank said, as he patted my shoulder in approval. "Bill is absolutely right." I bowed to him as a sign of thanks.

From then on, the deliberation took a smooth course of discussions.

To reassure ourselves about some evidence presented in court, we sent two other requests to Judge Older. It was our intention to read the letters Susan Atkins had written to three former cellmates in the jury room and discuss them.

His Honor denied our request but allowed instead the court reporter to read them in open court. Susan Atkin's confessions appeared to justify her involvement with the Tate slayings.

The second request was to hear the Beatles' record album. The lamentable condition of the worn-out records plus the antiquated equipment on which they were played, proved only to be a lengthy boring eighty-three minutes of listening. In spite of the monotonous tune, the jurors were able to pick up some of the words such as Helter Skelter, Revolution, etc. The Beatle's album and the Bible provided support to link Charles Manson's philosophy about a race war between blacks and whites.

Marvin still wasn't convinced Leslie Van Houten was guilty of first-degree murder. No one had brought arguments to convince him. Paul White led a very comprehensive challenge. He based his arguments on Instruction 45 but Marvin counter-attacked that there was no evidence presented in court of robbery. He firmly stated he would not be convinced of that.

Two more days had gone by and we still were discussing the culpability of Leslie Van Houten. The jurors were studying their notes at night trying to locate a point on which to argue the next day, but none were successful. We were stuck.

Olivia Madison had tried to convince her friend Marvin and frantically observed, "If we can't convince you, then *you* convince us."

Marvin, holding Instruction 47, read it aloud and stressed that there was insufficient deliberation and premeditation on the part of Leslie Van Houten to make her guilty of first-degree murder.

During coffee breaks, the jurors strolled along the halls. Frank approached me and whisperingly said:

"I know you can come up with something that would convince Marv and reassure the others."

"I'll try," I responded. "I have a plan that may work."

As soon as we returned to deliberation, Ray and Marvin counterattacked each other but basically it was the same issues they had brought to light.

Marvin Connolly did not dispute the contention that Leslie Van Houten had knifed Mrs. Rosemary La Bianca to death. But he claimed that the stabbing had been a case of second-degree murder, that Leslie had gone there but not with a premeditated thought to kill anybody, and he emphasized his argument by saying that Tex Watson and Patricia Krenwinkel had been involved more seriously at the time the fatal killings took place. He finished by saying she should be guilty of second-degree murder.

Throughout the deliberation we all, at one time or another, had referred frequently that Leslie must have known beforehand why the three of them had gone inside the La Bianca home.

I didn't say anything for a good amount of time. The other jurors had noticed my silence. There was a reason for it. I wanted to listen and grasp what was said.

Basically, we all felt the same about Leslie's participation except for three people—Genaro, Debbie, and Violet. They seemed convinced but were unsure of themselves. We had been discussing the same things over and over and didn't seem to make any progress.

We were exhausted and tired. Debbie and Violet had complained of having light headaches. I joined them in their feelings. No wonder! Our minds had been constantly thinking and deliberating. We had consumed every single drop of blood in our systems to concentrate fully and attentively while reading the instructions.

Finally, Marvin Connolly, looking directly at me and shouted out loud, "You've been sitting there and haven't said anything! We're all in this you know! Don't you have anything to say?"

Silence. Not a word was spoken. Every juror was staring at me. I felt their eyes upon my face. They had become aware of my silence and at that moment they wanted to hear my views and argument. They knew how I felt about Leslie's guilt and obviously it was up to me to say something convincing. Something which hadn't been said before and most important, something which would convey and prove to my fellow jurors, as well as myself, that Leslie Van Houten was guilty of first-degree murder. They all waited impatiently for me to speak.

Ray kept talking and repeating himself—he was struggling for words. Ray had brought a set of chopsticks from the Chinese restaurant where we had gone to eat lunch the day before. With the use of P-39—the buck knife that belonged to Linda Kasabian which was left inside the Tate residence by one of the female defendants—he kept himself busy carving miniature figures of various designs at the end of each stick.

"I'd also like to hear Bill's views," Mildred said, but her voice was grounded.

It seemed at that moment everybody had something to say but one couldn't hear clearly what was being said. Violet with Debbie and the foreman, Mr. Paine, were talking among themselves.

Next was Ray, still busy carving, and at the same time still repeating the same argument to convince Marvin, who was leaning on his chair with his feet on the edge of the table.

Then myself, just observing. At my left, Mr. Welch was rocking on his chair with a hand under his chin, his eyes closed and chewing gum.

Then Mr. White was busy writing the instructions on a pad. Following was Genaro talking with Mildred. Finally, Betty, who was smoking while covering her legs with a white towel to protect them from a cold draft stemming from the air conditioner.

"Yeah! Let's hear Bill express his opinion!" Frank shouted as he opened his eyes and straightened his chair.

Before speaking, I distinctly made an issue of not being interrupted especially by Ray who kept talking in the middle of everyone's speeches.

My objective was to show the jurors that Leslie Van Houten had premeditated thoughts before entering the La Bianca home.

Finally, I rose and walked to the end of the table behind the foreman. From there I began to speak.

One by one I enumerated the sequence of events and one by one, asked Marvin Connolly for confirmation—the juror who needed the most convincing.

Then I began to show the walking distance. At that point I pantomined the walk while standing in place, then walked towards the door out to the hallway leading to the rest rooms. Then, by chance, I noticed the aerial photographs of the La Bianca house standing on top of a file cabinet, which everyone could see clearly.

"Now, you all can see," I said. "Do you think that the distance between the car and the entrance to the door—a good half block—look, look at the photo," I said, pointing at the photograph, "see the distance? Would you say that Patricia Krenwinkel, Tex Watson, and Leslie Van Houten, while walking toward the house, didn't say a single word to one another?"

"They probably spoke," Marvin admitted.

"Is it possible then that these people, and especially Leslie Van Houten, didn't for one minute think that going into that house would cause some type of fear to the dweller of that house?"

Marvin nodded his head positively.

"Alright. Let's proceed," I continued. "It's dark. They are walking slowly. Perhaps Watson told one of the girls to go to the front entrance while he would enter the back—or maybe, they walked together. We don't know how it happened, but one thing for sure we do know: they went inside. We know it because of the testimony of Dianne Lake, and we have agreed that we believe her testimony. Right?"

"Yes," Marvin said.

"Okay now, watch this," I said before opening the door.

"Leslie Van Houten and the others surely stopped before entering and checked every direction. Then slowly, entered inside. Do you accept this?" I asked.

Marvin again nodded in agreement while the rest were following my demonstration.

Ray started to interrupt me, but flatly told him to let me finish. He did.

"Okay. They opened the door and went inside," I said. "We don't know what happened inside but suppose you or anyone of you (I pointed at Marvin first and then around the table for emphasis) go inside a house with two others with intentions to kill their occupants—and this we know because Linda Kasabian heard Manson telling them 'don't cause any panic' before he ordered them to go inside and also at the ranch, he told them 'last night was too messy.' Isn't that right? We know that because we accepted Linda Kasabian's testimony. Correct?"

Some confirmations were heard.

To illustrate Leslie Van Houten's awareness and participation in the La Bianca murders, I recurred the following demonstration, "Suppose you go inside," I said, opening the door and quietly stepping outside the jury room, closing the door behind me. Trying to prove my point, I gave indications of being involved in a situation of terror.

I screamed and pounded on the door and walls. I kicked a paper basket several times and even attempted to imitate the voices of agony as the victims might have yelled. I screamed for help and as a final stunt, I fell on the floor to give the indication of having been killed. Upon recurring these sources of speculation, I returned somewhat excited to the jury room.

Ray, Debbie and Violet were laughing but stopped when I questioned Marvin, "Now. *you* tell me if you were in Leslie Van Houten's place, wouldn't

386

you have premeditated thoughts before entering the La Bianca home? She certainly wasn't invited for *tea* and certainly, the hour they arrived was no hour to visit anyone. Wouldn't you say she knew what her friends' intentions were?

"Marvin, you must admit," I concluded, stepping forward, "that Leslie Van Houten knew ahead of time what she was getting involved in. Certainly, no one forced her to go. If she was innocent, she would certainly have never went there, or at least she'd have walked away. Anything! But no! She stayed and tried a new kick—that of killing people!

"No one! I repeat, no one, stabs anyone specially after that someone is supposedly dead. There's no question that she enjoyed it. She is guilty!"

"I've changed my mind!" Genaro shouted. "I believe she is guilty of first-degree murder."

Debbie and Violet followed suit.

"What about you?" Ray asked Marvin.

"I guess you're right."

"We don't want you to *guess*!" Genaro shouted. "If you *still* think she is not guilty of first-degree murder, it is your right to say so."

"That's right," Olivia added. "We can remain here longer if necessary. We want everybody to be surely convinced beyond the reasonable doubt that they are guilty of first-degree murder."

Everyone looked at the red-headed juror for an answer. We waited.

"I'm convinced," Marvin finally said. "She's guilty of first-degree murder."

"Let's take a break," Debbie said, somewhat exhausted.

We stopped for a few minutes and the jurors seemed more relaxed and congenial to one another. Everyone, including Debbie who hardly spoke to me, were curious to know what had gone through my mind at the time I was making all sorts of noise behind the door.

"I put myself in Leno La Bianca's place," I declared.

"For a moment I thought the deputies were going to think we were killing each other," Debbie remarked half smiling.

Ray added, "Yeah! I was going to get a straight jacket for you."

"I *made* my point, didn't I?" I replied while looking at Marvin. Ray got the message but continued making comical remarks which didn't agree with the majority of the jurors, except Debbie and Violet. The rest of the afternoon, we concentrated on Charles Manson's leadership.

The next day (Saturday), the jurors experienced a bit of excitement with the "outside world" when the bus transporting us slammed into a car upon entering the parking lot outside the Hall of Justice.

After scraping the parked automobile near the Temple Street entrance to the lot, the transportation officer backed the bus out and drove to the Spring Street driveway. The maneuver caused some momentary concern, especially when the driver wheeled the bus the wrong way on Spring Street (a one-way roadway in that area) and to add excitement, some nine or ten deputies dashed out into traffic to insure safety for the bus. Needless to say, the driver was terribly embarrassed afterwards as the jurors and the press outside were watching every move.

The jurors couldn't find any evidence which could set the hippie cult leader free. Jacobson, Watkins, Flynn, Poston, DeCarlo, Hoyt, Lake, and the State's star witness, Linda Kasabian, testified that Charles Manson led the family and he alone gave the orders.

Manson had made them believe he was Jesus Christ—the Messiah, and imposed his doctrine. He twisted the interpretation of Revelation 9 and gave the Beatles the rank of angels. Manson's philosophy about "the bottomless pit in the desert" was also brought out to light by the same witnesses and left no question in the minds of the jurors that Manson was their leader.

The ultimate issue of discussion was that Manson had effectively convinced and impressed the minds of the members of the family with his theory, "if you are willing to die, then you must live."

The theory, in itself, made the killers go on a rampage and slay the victims on those two consecutive nights. Manson was guilty.

"Okay, let's vote," Ray announced.

"It's alright with me," conceded the foreman.

The complexity of the twenty-seven charges against the four defendants and the fact that all charges were not applicable—individually—caused a rather slow process of voting.

To eliminate confusion, I prepared a chart which proved to be a simpler and faster method to vote.

Mildred, Paul, and Genaro, as well as Debbie, Violet, and Martin wanted to wait until Monday to reassure themselves that their verdict of guilty of first-degree murder was their final decision. Everyone agreed. The foreman closed the session by asking everyone to pray for thanks and guidance. We returned to the hotel.

Something that may have no significance at all but nevertheless I overheard, was a conversation on Friday evening between Mollie Kane and some other deputy. They were busy discussing right outside my room the possibility that the six-man jury of Lieutenant Calley's trial might reach a verdict at the same time we would. Mollie was deeply concerned.

She felt both trials were of equal-toned interest and would overshadow each other as far as headline publicity was concerned.

When Mollie knocked on my door to announce dinner, she indirectly expressed that it would be great if the jurors could hold from reaching the final verdict at least until Monday.

"Are you suggesting that I should hold the final vote?" I inquired, half serious.

"I didn't say that! Nor did I suggest such a thing!" Mollie snapped defensively. She smiled momentarily and immediately left.

As it happened, Lieutenant Calley was found guilty of massacring some twenty-two civilians in My Lai and it made the front page news on Saturday. I couldn't help thinking that the delay on voting in our case might have been the effects of an indirect but friendly persuasion.

Back in jury room following a brief discussion of the entire matter, we decided to vote. The defendants were all found guilty of first-degree murder. I filed and dated the twenty-seven verdicts, and the foreman signed them.

At long last... at 10:30 A.M.... on Monday, January 25, 1970, the jurors sent word that they had reached a verdict.

Violet happily pressed the buzzer three times and Deputy Taylor walked in to receive the news. We awaited word to return to the court room.

While waiting, everyone looked idly through the evidence submitted, including the color photographs of the victims. The jurors could see better through the photographs. A picture was worth a thousand words of testimony. The jurors could not disbelieve those pictures. It brought out a vision of what savage minds like those of Watson, Krenwinkel, Atkins, and Van Houten had done to the victims. To kill for... pleasure... senseless killings. At heart, we were a law-abiding people with a horror of killing.

At first, I looked at the case merely through the eyes of a juror. I tried hard not to be swayed by the inconceivable manner in which the crimes were committed. It is difficult to see bizarre photographs before your very eyes and at the same time retain your sense of perspective and justice. So, I controlled my sentiments and personal emotions.

I looked at the photographs as simply evidence, and weighed the amount of guilt and somehow managed to retain my feelings of disgust or vengeance for the human race.

As jurors we survived in one way or another, the presence of the photos and most were able to retain their mental balance and reveal no repulsiveness.

Those pictures were objects of curiosity at the time we had to see them; however, they will never be nearly forgotten. On the contrary, they will be firmly implanted in the minds of the jurors.

After an hour or so of waiting, Deputy Taylor opened the door and told us to be ready. As we walked downstairs, I felt that the excitement was extraordinary. The jurors filed back to their respective seats. The court room was jammed with spectators and a waiting line stretched interminably down the eighth floor corridor of the Hall of Justice Building. We had remained out for eight days. The entire nation waited impatiently for word of the verdict. Press, television, and radio coverage was exhaustive.

Many of the world's leading newspaper and magazine writers were present. Every gesture, every word, every flicker of an eyelash was duly noted, recorded, and hoarded.

All the defendants entered the court room smiling and remained calm. The girls were dressed in drab jail-blue dresses with dark blue sweaters. Manson came in dressed in a loose fitting, light tan shirt and dark pants. He wore a handkerchief around his neck. His hair was disheveled and he was sporting a full, pointed beard.

We waited for the Judge. There wasn't a sound in the court room.

Judge Older walked in and immediately cast the legendary question, "Ladies and gentlemen of the Jury, have you reached a verdict?"

"Yes, Your Honor, we have," Martin Paine answered.

Deputy Taylor took the twenty-seven counts bearing the verdicts of the defendants from foreman Paine and handed them to the Judge.

No expression of surprise seemed to flit across Judge Older's face. He, in turn, passed the slips of paper to the court clerk, Eugene Darrow, who read the verdicts aloud. A hush fell over the court room. Darrow, with a lump in his throat, began reading the verdicts:

"We, the Jury, find the defendant Charles Manson guilty as charged in the First Count."

As the verdict was read, a slight smirk spread across Charlie's face. The court clerk continued. The three girls just smiled and acted as though they didn't care throughout the reading of the verdicts, although the cult leader blurted out at the end:

"We're still not allowed to put on a defense... *you* won't outlive that, *old man!*"

The remark apparently was aimed at Judge Older who ignored the comment.

Mr. Fitzgerald and Mr. Kanarek requested and were granted that the jurors be polled as a group and then separately. Each juror responded clearly with "Yes" or "Yes, it is" when asked if the verdicts as read were our decisions.

Perhaps because I had, on various occasions, smiled to the defendants, the defense counsel had taken for granted that my vote and especially that of Marvin's would be "not guilty." Maybe they had decided what our final votes would be. None of them looked directly into the jury box but stared, in turn, into the eyes of one juror after another. Personally, from that day on I looked upon the defendants as killers and not as suspects.

When Judge Older announced that the penalty phase would begin two days later, the spectators swarmed their way out.

We then returned to the hotel.

Though half of our civic duty had been fulfilled, we still dreaded the length of time we would have to wait to deliberate.

The harmony among the jurors and between the deputies and the jurors progressed somewhat to the worst. The days seemed longer and fastidious. Luckily, I found refuge while writing my impressions.

Some of my notes follow:

January 28, 1971, 9:00 P.M.

It is difficult to concentrate on writing about what has happened. Perhaps it would be easier if I had the feeling that the reason for being sequestered was solely for the purpose of writing the most inner and intimate thoughts of the jurors—as if I were a spy and they were unaware that my function was to divulge their private lives or their little and insignificant complaints, or the details they volunteered of their lives either out of pure disgust in being sequestered or when in a good communicative mood.

Perhaps I should mention that although we jurors are normal, the fact of having been thrown together under the pressure of the law, has caused us to release our more intrinsic, personal, and sometimes unusual behavior to one another. We have been divided among ourselves to the extent that it is known who befriends who, who participates in what activity, and who encourages who if something is said or planned.

A joke is not a joke unless he who says it is in the presence of those who befriend him.

On the other hand, if one accepts such stupid and childish jokes, it would be only to pass time quickly and pleasantly, to bear the monotony of waiting day after day, or sitting hour after hour and not being able to concentrate on doing anything concrete or useful, or not being able to gain by it after we have returned to our homes.

The only thing that most of us had gained was the feeling or desire to get the hell out of here.

We had gained the rich experience that hopefully we can use later on; that of having survived amongst ourselves, having accepted each other momentarily and *only* momentarily.

Surely, some of us do not wish to see each other after the trial, either for a day or for a flashing moment. No, it is not hate. It is just simple arithmetic, a simple equation of sentiments. You meet someone and find you don't get along with that person. Why would anyone search out such a person? Why would anyone want to see or again meet a person whose character or philosophy does not appeal to his needs or personality? It would only cause despair. It would bring back memories of unpleasant moments and it would add, to say the least, more than we already have on our minds.

However, now would be the time to know each other, it would be the ideal occasion to discuss things and hobbies, it would be the time to have respect for each other, and try to understand what makes each one of us different.

As I put this into words, it is just impossible to search out each other's character and freely converse with any person on any wave of communication or on any subject. As we attempt to speak, we lack that urge; we do not want to be bothered with nasty remarks or be insulted; or even to the point of being ignored when one says, very distinctively, "Good Morning" to someone and there is none other around to warrant a misinterpretation. How can one explain such behavior? Would any one of you reading these lines say "Good Morning" to the same person knowing well in advance that this person would ignore you and pretend not to hear or be bothered to acknowledge one of the most basic amenities of our society today?

Place yourself in such a situation and see how far you would go; find out how many months you would spend before realizing the futility of your greeting. I would guess your endurance to be rather limited.

This is one of the many reasons why, once we are cleared from this "mess," that we would not wish to see one another. What for? To associate with someone who makes smart remarks, who smirks at you, and who makes fun at some serious observations? No! I am not being overly sentimental. I'm simply applying the rules of courtesy and consideration.

We are all in the same boat. We all have feelings and ideas of what it means to be away from our everyday way of life.

Anything would be better at home, but here... at the "Ambassador....

Mentally exhausted I felt the lids kindly closing over my eyes. I put on my pajamas and went to sleep.

We returned to court and when the penalty phase of the trial opened, things were back to what had been normal. Sitting at the counsel table, Charles Manson suddenly shoved and slugged his attorney Mr. Kanarek. Manson's violent objection came after he was denied permission to represent himself.

He argued that Mr. Kanarek could not know his thoughts and therefore could not adequately represent him.

Mr. Bugliosi called Bernard Crowe to the witness stand—a heavy-set Negro jazz trumpeter who admitted his friends called him "Lotsa Poppa."

The witness testified that he had been shot in the stomach by Charles Manson on August 1, 1969, with a long-barreled .22-caliber revolver at a Hollywood apartment house in a dispute stemming from a twenty-four hundred dollar marijuana transaction.

"Lotsa Poppa," under examination by Mr. Bugliosi, declared that late on July 31, 1969, he gave Tex Watson $2400 for some 24 or 25 kilos of weed but that Watson disappeared with the money.

According to the witness, he had Watson's girlfriend, "Rosina," try to reach Watson via telephone at the Spahn Movie Ranch. Describing the phone call, Crowe testified:

"She told him that everybody at the ranch connected with Tex was gonna be destroyed if I didn't get either my money or the marijuana."

It was an hour or so after the call was made that Manson showed up at the apartment with a gun.

"What happened then?" asked Mr. Bugliosi.

"Manson said he didn't believe Tex did what I said he did. Then Manson said 'I came prepared' and pulled out this gun. He pulled the trigger three times. I started to get up out of the chair to protect myself and the gun went off the fourth time."

"What happened next?" inquired Mr. Bugliosi.

"I fell to the floor and played possum," the witness replied.

Crowe then stated, "Manson, before leaving, ordered to be given a fancy suede shirt worn by one of my friends."

The black musician concluded by saying that he was released eighteen days later from the county general hospital with the bullet still lodged near his spine.

Unexpectedly Charles Manson started elbowing and pushing his attorny Mr. Kanarek. Judge Older firmly admonished the defendant to stop it. The prisoner ignored His Honor. Charles Manson then remained in a holding room listening to the proceedings through a loud speaker.

Under cross-examination, Mr. Kanarek conducted a series of questions in regard to marijuana and explored Lottsa 'Pappa's story suggesting that the witness knew a great deal about the illicit narcotics trade. As expected, Mr. Kanarek bored everyone because of the pace and monotony of his questioning. Mr. Kanarek ended his cross-examination by asking Crowe if he had been convicted of a felony and was awaiting sentencing. The witness indicated he was.

Court adjourned and we returned to the hotel.

"Cool it, Man! cool it!" That's what I told myself at exactly eleven-thirty P.M. I had to, otherwise, it would have cost me a hell of a time. How did I get involved in this? Why! Of all the people in the world, why did it have to be me? Of all the days, today would be the day, if any, that a dramatic moment would develop. This premonition had engulfed me since the moment of awakening this morning. I felt a funny, wonderous, and uneasy feeling.

The night before last had been restful. I'd gone to bed at almost one thirty in the morning. After having watched "Dan August," starring my ex-neighbor Burt Reynolds, on television, I had continued watching a color movie, *Blue-beard*. The script was atrocious. The entire film was badly edited, and the movie itself was slow and boring, but since there was nothing better to do, I had stayed up to see the end, half asleep.

Stubbornly, I had remained in the recreation room because of all the noise. Tom, his wife, Claudia, and their two children, Tracy (about thirteen years old) and Tina (nine or ten years old) had congregated with Violet and were running and playing as most children do. Danny was there sitting by himself, and, as usual, with his eyes closed and arms folded.

Walking in, I'd said hello and immediately sat in front of the television set. I wanted to see something to get my mind off the day's happenings.

Shortly afterwards, Deputy Tull came in accompanied by Mrs. Colvig and one of her daughters. The laughter combined with the children's noise became unbearable.

They all were so boisterous and hectically obnoxious that gradually I kept raising the volume on the television set until finally they got the message and moved to the next room.

Edith, my next immediate cell partner in the hotel, entered and inquired about the program. Before I could finish answering, she made a face of discontentment as to the noise. She sat down.

Danny rose and left, and after about five minutes Edith got up and closed the door to the next room, hoping perhaps to hear the dialogue. Needless to say, they didn't calm down, but continued even louder, slamming the doors of the refrigerators and really carrying on in an unpleasant and sarcastic manner.

"Do you know," Edith began, "that Ruth and two others are watching television outside in the hall? They couldn't take this noise. I thought this recreation room was for jurors who wanted to watch television or read. Why is it that Tom brings his family in here and makes all this noise? Why doesn't he keep his family in his own room?"

"I don't know," I replied quietly, "maybe he can't bear his family in his room alone."

Edith stood up and as she departed, she shouted, "As much as I hate to go to my room, I'm sure it is more quiet *there* than *here*!"

It was true. There was too much noise and running around, and no one was able to do anything, especially when the bailiffs in charge were participating full blast. They finally calmed down as the late hours arrived. Around midnight, Tracy brought a sleeping bag and laid it on top of the couch and almost instantly went to sleep with a very minor sort of snoring.

The picture was over. After shutting the television off, I walked to my room, half asleep and half awake. Once in bed I did not even intend to read or write. I was exhausted and somehow unevenly annoyed because during the day, while waiting in the jury room, the clique had done their best to disturb those wishing to rest. During most of the afternoon, I had a neuralgia on my right cheek and to add to that, an earache in the left ear. It ended up that we waited all afternoon and didn't go into court at all.

Before noon recess, we heard George being dismissed from the prospective jury box. The Judge had told us he was being excused for personal matters —someone was ill in his family. We all knew his wife had been in a minor accident, causing damage to her 1969 Mustang. Although she was not initially injured, she had received a bad whiplash and had not come to see him for the last ten or so days, even though we were allowed visitors.

For nearly two weeks, the jurors had not been taken on a Sunday outing, nor were dinners planned for those evenings. That was more than enough to put one in a bad and quiet mood, and that's what had happened to me. Everybody was uptight because of the length of the trial. I missed George.

Also, Deputy Taylor had cut considerably my weekly cleaners and laundry allowance, because of a personal altercation with Taylor himself in the coffee shop about two or three days before.

That incident in the coffee shop had stirred him defiantly toward me. It had made him aware of my attitude and behavior toward him. That had been the point where I really stood up against him and made him appear like an ass in front of the people dining in the main room of the coffee shop. The incident had occurred so fast that I was shaken by its results.

The jurors had been sitting and eating dinner for over one and one-half hours, and, as usual, some of us had been waiting for a deputy to take us up to the sixth floor. Now, that length of time for dinner may appear sensibly normal, but when one has been sitting practically all day in court or during the recess at the jury room or at lunch time and during transportation to and from...well, it gets your fanny flat and sore.

To avoid boredom at dinner and also to avoid an unexpected argument of any kind, I always brought a book along. *Fire Island* was the title and while dining, I had placed it on the cross piece of wood underneath the chair. There were four jurors, including myself, seated at the table. We had been carrying on a conversation about the current attraction at the "Now Grove"—the Connie Stevens Show. We all wanted to see her perform but that would be impossible we felt since we had been denied permission to go previously. They had told us the spontaneous jokes from the performers might inadvertently mention something about the Manson trial and that would give a good strong opportunity for the defense to call a mistrial.

At that time, someone said if anyone wished to go upstairs, they could do so. About four of us jumped and stood up ready to go. Shirley Metz, a Negro female deputy had been instructed by Taylor to lead us upstairs.

Since I had forgotten my book from underneath the chair, Shirley had told the jurors to stop and wait for me. I returned to my seat for the book and then rushed out to the waiting jurors.

Deputy Taylor, unaware that Miss Metz was waiting outside, ran after me and in front of the customers yelled:

"Bill! I'm not going to take this shit from you! When I call you, you better return!" I didn't hear him calling me. Rather excited I tried to explain to him but he didn't believe me. Everybody was watching and when the tall deputy discovered that I was telling the truth, he mumbled and went back to his chair rather embarrassed. Because of that and some other previous minor incidents, I kept quiet and to myself and tried not to show my unhappy and disgusted frame of mind. When I went to bed, my body collapsed and my brain was exhausted because of another confrontation with deputy Taylor early in the evening. I fell asleep momentarily.

I didn't sleep well. When I awoke, some strange feeling perturbed me. "What could it be?" I asked myself. I wanted to escape. I had a reason. I rose, washed, and dressed in casual clothes—levis, a plaid blue-and-red shirt, and my Capri sandals—and went to the recreation room for coffee and orange juice.

Just before I reached the end of the hall, from a distance, I noticed that Gertrude Goran, a tall, slim and atractive Negro female deputy, was seated and talking to Marvin Connolly and Dan Jackson. My empty stomach ached with repulsion and as I walked through them, I excused myself.

396

I avoided any friendliness since Miss Goran had previously told Albert Taylor that Betty Clark and I had stepped out in a hurry, had walked out of her sight and left her alone while she was escorting us for a walk on the grounds of the hotel. That, of course, was a lie. All these untruths had caused a big controversy between Deputy Taylor, Betty, and, particularly, myself.

Betty and I didn't leave Miss Goran. She left us. After Betty and I finally located Miss Goran, Betty wisely went back to her room immediately. Unfortunately, I went directly to the recreation room and sat among the other jurors to watch television. Miss Goran had gone directly to see the bailiff of record.

No more than three minutes had passed when Deputy Taylor entered the room at a very fast pace. Albert Taylor was six feet 2 inches tall, languid, had a pale-looking face. His walk denoted lack of body control, and the extra-large-sized shoes he wore were prominently visible as they tended to go sideways when he walked.

He was a family man. I understand he has ten children and that may account for his lack of patience with us jurors. He looks "doped," in fact. The first time I had visitors, they thought he was intoxicated and surely they were erroneous. I attempted to explain to them that he was that way, that I hadn't seen him drinking and stated he didn't smell of alcohol either.

But, all in all, his face was an enigma. His mouth was moist and at the edge of his lips, the saliva retained a foamy aspect. He looked sweaty and his eyes appeared somber, tilted, greasy and steady. Albert never looked into a person's eyes when he spoke. He avoided a straight forward look and that sometimes can be molesting, annoying, and unpleasant. Is he afraid to look into one's eyes? Is he perhaps there and yet... far away? One cannot trust someone like that.

Anyway... Al came into the recreation room as a bull runs into the center of a plaza of Toros. He stampeded in and furiously stopped in the center of the room, his eyes wandering and searching purposely for someone.

When he spotted his target, mandatorily, he commanded me by saying, "Bill,! Come to my room, I want to talk to you."

Taylor left in the same manner he entered. I got up suspiciously and as I walked to his room, Miss Goran was coming into the recreation room—her slim figure moved with assurance and her face was jubilant. I looked at her directly in the face and I could see she had reported the incident outside in the garden. We both looked at one another but her eyes gave it away, and then I knew that trouble was coming in the next few minutes.

When I walked into Taylor's room, he was seated, waiting impatiently.

397

He arose and slammed the door behind me. With an accurate flexibility, he paced across the room in long strides. In no time, he reached the window area which was built on a platform almost like an enclosed square balcony.

He spoke like thunder, "What is this of walking out on the deputy? Damn it! If you want to get out of this, *this is the time*! I can personally make sure of it! You ask for it and you can get it!"

Taylor kept on shouting and finally noticed himself that his attitude was far from rational, that he was getting his message across but his approach was unreasonable. He abruptly stopped and for the first time, he barely sustained an instant look in my eyes. Taylor waited for me to say something. Precise and well behaved, I uttered my opening reply by saying softly and showing an amazing state of ease and control, "Taylor, there are two versions to every story. Obviously you heard only her side. Would you let me tell mine?"

Quickly, he burst out again, repeating solemnly and majestically, "Damn it! You can get the hell out of here! Now is the time! I can tell the Judge and you'd be going out of here—*tonight*!"

"Albert," I said, "Betty was also with us and she can tell you what happened too."

Taylor continued by saying, "She can go to hell, too!" and just as he said that, he left the room and ran out into the hallway and passing through the Little Lobby in front of the elevator, he climbed the stairs leading to Betty's room, the only room, for above her's was the penthouse, rented to a middle-aged, well-tanned bachelor who smoked large cigars. Taylor, with an ability beyond description, arrived at the top of the stairs and knocked severely on the door. No response. Again he knocked but Betty didn't answer. Upset as he was, Taylor descended and asked the deputy on duty, seated beside a desk situated directly in front of the elevator, where Betty was. Before Taylor received an answer, Martin, who always chats with the deputy on duty, volunteered to tell Taylor that Betty was not in her room. I knew that was a lie because Betty had gone upstairs. I personally had seen her. Furthermore, she had mentioned to me something about washing her hair or clothes while we were walking on the hotel grounds. I didn't say anything. I stood there watching, not knowing what Taylor was going to do next. Then, as he returned to his room, he said, "I'll be damned if I go looking for her!"

I followed him immediately. He closed the door and with a tone of dislike, he shouted, "She has a foul mouth and damn it! If she wants to go, she can get her ass out of here, too! And I mean *fast*! One thing I can't stand is a woman with a foul mouth and she has the biggest one. She's always making smart remarks, remarks about us, about the conditions, and remarks about anything! What the hell does she think she is anyway? I'll tell you one thing, if Mollie didn't plan these outings on Sundays, you people would stay in the hotel every Sunday because no one wants to be bothered making arrangements or phoning or be concerned. And also, you may know that it is a lot of hassle trying to get to go to places and making reservations. Mollie volunteered for this job, but her job doesn't require her to go out of her way, so you people should be glad that she does it. And look at Betty, always complaining. If she only could keep her fat mouth shut, but she only opens it to insult and to say unkind comments and make herself known as being unhappy. Well, damn it! This time she can get her ass off her! Fast! Right now!"

When Taylor finally finished, he went to the king-sized bed and sat down by the phone. I just kept staring at him—rigidly speechless—unable to utter a single word, perhaps in a séance mood, waiting to think of saying something that would pacify and satisfy this man's mind.

Again, quite composed and controlled with assuredness and with a firm voice, I began by saying humbly, but proudly, "I realize you have the responsibility to cater to 17 jurors and, in addition, the supervision of the other deputies. It's a lot to be concerned about—you have your hands full and certainly you don't need any more trouble—especially coming from me."

At this moment Taylor interrupted me, "Bill," he said, "it's not that I—"

"No let me finish," I overlapped him. "You're right, I'm guilty for making remarks, for having perhaps made it uncomfortable, but bear in mind, that it has not been my desire to do so. I certainly didn't go out of my way to cause you this trouble, nor will it ever happen again—I promise you. From now on, I'll mind my own business and you'll hear no more from me. I'll stay in my room, and that way you shouldn't worry."

I returned to my room and I thought of escaping—leaving the hotel and returning home, for good—to be *free*. My thoughts of freedom stopped when I told myself, "Cool it man. Cool it!"

We returned to court. Michael Erwin a young man wearing glasses was called next to testify. He gave his occupation as busboy and student. "Did you know a man named Gary Hinman"?, asked Mr. Bugliosi as he showed him at the same time a picture of the victim. "Yes," answered the witness as he adjusted his glasses. Since there were no questions from the defense counsel, he immediately was dismissed.

The following witness, also wearing glasses, was an Oregon state policeman by the name of Thomas Drynan. He testified he had arrested Susan Atkins in 1966 in a town approximately 30 miles east of Salem, Oregon. "I was returning from a horse game patrol," said the witness under Mr. Bugliosi's examination, "when I received information by radio that the defendant, in connection with two other men, had escaped with stolen goods," when asked by the prosecutor if he had searched them, the soft-spoken witness replied: "Yes, I did." "Did you find anything?" Mr. Bugliosi wanted to know. "I found a .25-caliber automatic in her pocket. The others carried a .38-caliber revolver and a .32 automatic pistol". "On the way to town later" the officer related, "I asked Miss Atkins what she had intended to do with the gun and she told me if she had had the opportunity she would have shot and killed me".

Under Mr. Shin's interrogation, the witness stated that the information came on the radio about ten minutes before he spotted the prisoners and added, "A piece of the information was that they were white and that one of the fellows was wearing a military flight jacket." Drynan concluded by saying that he didn't have much information other than that the woman was just that: a female. No hair description, weight, eyes, etc. "But," he recalled, "It was my opinion that Susan Atkins was pointing something at me—I didn't know if they had weapons at the time but if it wasn't a weapon—she must have had awful long fingers."

A natural reaction of some of us jurors was to switch our attention to Susan Atkins. The prisoner defiantly stared at the jury box, concealing her hands under the table in front of her. Mr. Bugliosi out of the blue announced: "The Prosecution rests."

"Wow we're going home." I whispered to Mildred and Betty. "Isn't that great" whispered back Mildred while rubbing gently underneath her left eyelash. Betty simply nodded approvingly.

The defense lawyer Mr. Fitzgerald, to establish the background and character of the client, called to the stand Mr. & Mrs. Krenwinkel to testify in their daughter's behalf. He also introduced photos, letters, a yearbook, and a birth certificate as evidence.

Speaking about his daughter Mr. Krenwinkel said, "Patricia was born on December 3. She attended Windsor Elementary School for 2 or 3 years in 1952–1953, then went to Kenwood in Westchester until 6th grade, and to high school also in Westchester. In Mobile, Alabama, she went to Spring Hills Jesuit College and one semester at the University. She has an aunt and uncle and some cousins living in Mobile, Alabama," Mr. Krenwinkel, somber looking and with a controled voice continued saying, "Patricia was an extremely normal girl—she didn't require very much assistance. She was fond of animals, not like other girls that would go for stuffed dolls. She was gentle with animals—canary, parakeet, you name it, we had it. She was never ill.

Up until age 12 she participated in many activities. She became a camp girl and got along with everybody and with her half-sister. Mr. Krenwinkel retained his composure when he testified in a husky voice and when he mentioned that Charlene Krenwinkel, a step-sister seven years older than Patricia, 23, had accidently drowned in Alabama. "Did she do good in school?" questioned Mr. Fitzgerald.

"Most of the remarks from the teachers were admireable", answered Mr. Krenwinkel and continued, "She was a good student—not exceptionally excellent but she worked hard to obtain the grades given to her."

"Was she religious?" asked defense attorney.

"My wife and I were affiliated to the Dutch Reform Church—which is the head or should I say one of the Norman Vincent Peal's church association. Patricia was baptized in that church. She was enthusiastic about her religion and she seemed to derive a great pleasure in their programs—such as Christmas and whatever. She attended every Sunday on her own—it was her desire. She liked to read the Bible and she was awarded a plaque in Sunday school for having memorized a passage from the Bible. We were proud, as most parents would be in such circumstances. In March, 1967, after she attended Spring Hills College (she was 18 or 19 years old), she attended a Catholic Military School and sang in many choirs. She liked to go swimming. Her mother and I went with her to Honolulu and she enjoyed it very much.

"Did you have a close relationship with your daughter, Pat?" inquired Mr. Fitzgerald.

"I estimate we had a close relationship," said the concerned father. "She enjoyed going places with me we attended the music center together."
In a series of short questions the interrogation continued:

Q. "Did she have many friends?"

A. "Yes, but no more than one or two—they came to the house."

Q. "Did she ever appear to be a problem?"

A. "No she never presented any disciplinary problem. She enjoyed school."
When asked the names of the clubs his daughter belonged to the witness answered:

A. "Yes, she belonged to clubs and organizations—but frankly I cannot remember their names."

Q. "How would you describe your daughter's behavior?" asked Mr. Fitzgerald.

A. "Patricia was never hostile—nor quick or violent tempered. She never was depressed nor irrational. She appeared to be coherent."

The defendant, clad in a plain lavender dress, kept busy looking at her nails and occasionally would look at her father without any sign of interest.

Upon question after question related to the childhood of his daughter, the defense counsel finally asked Mr. Krenwinkel to explain why the defendant was in Alabama in 1967. He responded, "At that time Patricia was with her mother. You see, we divorced when Pat was about 16 years old. We departed as friends," and the witness pointing toward the audience added, "she's in court today."

Mr. Krenwinkel went on to explain that when his daughter moved back to California she took residence with her sister Charlene in Manhattan Beach. Patricia worked for Penney's in Santa Monica and she managed her own money. She was then employed by North American Insurance Co. in the same year.

Without interruption the witness explained in his own words, "But then something unusual happened. At that time Patricia was going to be given a vacation. She called me and said she was going to leave with two other girls on a vacation. She told me then that she was going in approximately a month or so and I asked her why. She left abruptly her Manhattan Beach apartment and even left her own car in a parking lot."

"How did you discover where she was?" interrogated Mr. Fitzgerald.

Mr. Krenwinkel responded, "I did not know whom she went with but by tracing a license number given to me by one of Patricia's friends, I found out she had left with a guy named Charles Manson."

Mr. Fitzgerald brought a letter postmarked September 25, 1967, to the witness for identification and then read it out loud. Among other things written to her father was, "For the first time in my life, I've found contentment and inner peace." She signed off with, "I love you very much. Take good care of yourself."

According to Mr. Krenwinkel: "It was not until 25 months later that I heard from her again. When I saw her I arranged for her to go to Mobile, Alabama. I took her personally to the airport in October or November of 1969. At the conclusion of his testimony he said, "To my knowledge, she was arrested in Mobile, Alabama. I did not go there but I have visited her weekly in the Los Angeles county jail."

There were no more questions. Mrs. Dorothy Krenwinkel, tear stained and nervous, followed more or less the same pattern of questions as her ex-husband. Mr. Fitzgerald asked the mother of the defendant questions regarding the childhood of her daughter. The witness stated she was married the first time in 1941. After her husband had died when Charlene was 18 months old, she married Pat's father. She and her new husband were never in a financial dear. She divorced him in 1964, but it was a quiet divorce—it didn't make the children suffer and did not seem to have a traumatic effect on Patricia. Mr. Fitzgerald then asked the witness to relate if Patricia was a disciplinary child.

"Yes," she replied, and went on saying: "Pat taught Bible School every summer and I assisted her in her errands to help with charitable organizations. She was a responsible child. She never ran away from home, neither as a child nor as a teenager. She never had any problem with the police."

Mrs. Krenwinkel, holding a handkerchief, would at intervals dry her tears and wipe her nostrils. She continued her testimony, "After my divorce I took Pat to Fort Lauderdale but it was too hot so I moved to Mobile, Alabama. Then I came to West Los Angeles where Pat went to school. Pat decided to get a job and then she moved with her sister. It was then that I returned to Mobile, Alabama, assured that Pat was going to finish school."

The witness, controlling her emotions, audibly added:

"Then I didn't see her for a long time. One time I went to get her at New Orleans and after Pat came to visit me—she came with some friends. They ate, slept, washed and dried their clothes. Pat never talked with me because she was now always with someone. She would say "I'm going to bed" and that was it. She was different. I can't explain how. Eventually she left home and I didn't hear from her until the time her father sent her by plane to Mobile, Alabama, and then she was arrested on December, 1969. I didn't ask anything because I didn't know she had done anything wrong."

Mrs. Krenwinkel wept again as she concluded saying, "I did love my daughter. I do love my daughter. I'll always love my daughter. No one can ever tell me that she ever did anything terrible and horrible."

The jury, needless to say, were moved by the pleas of innocence echoed from the lips of the mother of Patricia Krenwinkel.

On the following day the next witness was Jane Van Houten, mother of slender, dark-haired Leslie Van Houten. The defendant's attorney, M. Maxwell Keith, conducted the interrogation.

Mrs. Van Houten, very solemn and with her hands folded, told a story closely resembling the testimony of the parents of Patricia Krenwinkel. Mrs. Van Houten had divorced her husband. She testified that Leslie Van Houten was born in 1941 and living in San Francisco, California. She also testified to save her daughter's life by testifying in her behalf. Mr. Keith asked the witness a line of questions which all seemed to have a positive answer. "Yes," her daughter had attended church; "yes," she belonged to the Camp Fire Girls. "She played the saxaphone, took piano lessons, liked needlework, loved camping in the outdoors, she was a Bluebird, enjoyed elementary and junior high school and the first two years she attended Monrovia High School. Then the well-groomed Mrs. Van Houten said, "Les was small for her age and always fun to be around. She was a 'fiesty' child."

The witness, under questioning by the able Mr. Keith, stated that she and her husband held meetings weekly to rectify the needs and problems of the family. It was during one of these meetings they decided to adopt two Korean children. After Mrs. Van Houten, a teacher in the Los Angeles school system was shown a high school year book in which she identified her daughter in various pages she disclosed that, "Les was unhappy during her senior high school because things didn't go right—including a romance with a young man." "Of course", the witness added, "the divorce hurt Leslie very much—but she still went to see her father, who was living in one of the beach cities. The meetings ceased because it was too difficult at the time. Her grades became poor but she managed to pass at the end of school and graduated. During her senior year she didn't try out for school office."

Mrs. Van Houten, quite at ease proceeded saying, "In 1966, I took a trip but Leslie couldn't go because she was studying to make up a grade and I'll always regret that in 1967 Les couldn't go with me to Expo at Montreal because at the time she was attending business school."

"After that did you see much of Leslie?" asked Mr. Keith. (She had completed a course as a legal secretary).

"No," replied the witness. "And then in the summer of 68 I heard she was living in Victorville, California. She stayed there for several months, because she loved outdoors. She lived with a girlfriend whose parents owned a ranch which was empty. Then one day she called me and said she was going to San Francisco with the girls. Shortly after she called me and said she was going to drop out and I wouldn't be hearing from her. I couldn't understand why we couldn't keep in touch. We argued and we both hung up. We were both still angry." The witness stopped briefly to look at her daughter. Leslie just looked back half smiling and silently formed the words, "I love you."

"It was in April, 1969—several months later—before I heard from Leslie. She was picked up by the police for hitchhiking in Reseda. I brought her home and she stayed that night. Next day she left and promised to leave a phone number to get hold of her but she didn't—she only said she was going to see a friend in Hollywood. The next time I saw her at Sybil Brand Institute for women when she had been charged these matters. I was still shocked."

"Do you blame yourself for what happened?" asked Mr. Keith.

Mrs. Van Houten hesitated, then carefully replied, "Any thinking person must consider that possibility," and then doubtfully added, "You go over a hundred things you wish were different... for myself I never would have believed it, and still don't believe it."

The witness concluded by saying that she had received over 100 letters of people concerned about Leslie. "Do you love your daughter?" asked the defense counsel. "Yes, I love Leslie very much." She was dismissed.

Prosecutor Vincent T. Bugliosi did not cross-examine either of the Krenwinkels nor Mrs. Van Houten. Personally I felt no need for it and was glad because the trial was coming to an end.

The weekends had become very slow and this one was no different. Among my visitors on Saturday morning was a brother of mine. As in the past, he had just stopped in for a few days to say hello. Knowing him well, I knew there was going to be an argument between the two of us. I dreaded the thought but, being the oldest, I welcomed him.

My brother, a free-lance worker sort of handyman, is quite capable but unfortunately he has not made up his mind what he wants to become in our society, so he wanders from job to job and occasionally takes off to other cities.

Although he has responsibilities of his own, he has managed one way or another to support his own family. Like in the past, I knew my brother's visit was just one more escapade of his responsibilities. It stirred in him sudden anxious impatience. I confronted him with his duties but he didn't like it. I wanted to know what was worrying him, if anything.

"There's nothing wrong," he said defensively and added, "I just came to say hello—to tell you *Los viejitos* (the "little ones"—in reference to our parents) say hello."

"Yes, I talked to them last night," I replied suggestively. My brother, not a dumb person, understood the inflation of my voice and changed the subject by admiring the surroundings I was in.

"You want to drink something?" I asked in order to break the gap of silence.

"You know I don't drink," he answered half smiling as he looked around for an ashtray.

"Oh, yes I forgot" I said and added "What about a soda pop?"

"No thanks, I just came to say hello."

I resented his refusal and suddenly I couldn't control myself. I asked him to stop beating around the bush and tell me what was his reason for he being in Los Angeles.

"I tell you I just came to say hello, that's all," he said rather uncomfortable.

I felt somewhat guilty and didn't know how to get out of it but he aided me

405

by saying weakly, "I'll come back later."

"Yes, yes, please do so," I rushed saying in order to make him feel good and added, "You can stay in my house and sleep in my bedroom, you know?"

"I *am* staying in your house," he said as a matter of fact. "I hope you don't mind."

"Oh no, not at all." I quickly replied knowing well in advance that's where he was staying. He left. Shortly after, Mrs. Reid, my tenant's mother, phoned and informed me she was baking a wine cake and would bring it on Sunday. I thanked her but then the following conversation took place on the phone.

"And by the way, Bill," she said, "your brother is here."

"Yes, I know. He told me when he came over to visit me a few minutes ago."

"Is that right. Good... oh, the poor dear, he came last night. He complained he was broke and asked me to loan him ten dollars, so I gave it to him."

"You shouldn't have done it Mrs. Reid," I interrupted the charming lady.

"Well, he said he was going to mail it back as soon as he got back home."

"I'll give you back that ten dollars," I told Mrs. Reid rather upset, "and do me a favor, don't loan him anymore money and please tell your son to do the same. Understand?"

"Yes, yes, of course, if you say so. But why, Bill? I did it because he's your brother."

"I know and I appreciate it, believe me. But please don't do it again. Listen, I'll talk to you tomorrow."

Some other jurors were waiting their turn to use the phone. I didn't want them to hear me so I tried to conceal my feelings as much as I could. I was upset. Effectively, my brother returned to the hotel before dinner time.

Unaware of my findings he knocked on my door. He walked nonchalantly in the room still not capturing my accusing eyes. His free-and-easy attitude annoyed me immensely to the point I bursted right out and began to argue:

"You have the guts, don't you? The nerve you have to ask a total stranger like Mrs. Reid to loan you money. You don't care who, or what happens after—do you? As long as you get what you want, you're happy. Well, let me tell you something. You've done this before, but I won't let you do it again."

My brother had repeatedly and unexpectedly visited me and after he had left town I discovered he had borrowed money from some friends of mine. He never paid them back. I did.

"I'll pay her back... I'll pay her back, you'll see," my brother kept saying.

"Like hell you will!" I protested.

My brother resented my infuriating remarks to the point that he began to confess that our other brothers, like me, didn't like him and wanted no part of him. With tears in his eyes he called himself the "black sheep" of the family and started leaving the room hurriedly saying, "You'll never see me again!"

"Wait, wait a minute," I called him back. With my heart full of remorse, I ran and stepped in front of him but he continued, "You were the only hope I had left... and... now you too don't care for me. I respect you Bill, but I guess you don't love me." His eyes were red with tears and painfully he faced me.

"Come on you son of a gun, you know I love all my brothers—we all came out of the same place. You're no exception." Impetuously my brother and I embraced forcibly. I felt thick and warm tears running on my cheeks. Nervously we started laughing as we wiped our tears with the backs of our hands.

What a relief it was afterward. For years my brother and I had been distanced. We had little in common. When we saw each other in the presence of our parents we hardly spoke to one another. Now we had rediscovered each other.

Back in court, Lynette Fromme, also known as "Squeaky" and a member of the "family," testified next that she had resided at the Sphan Ranch for three years, on and off. The 22-year-old redheaded witness gave an insight into the life style and philosophy of Charles Manson's group. Without being prompted by Mr. Fitzgerald she mentioned, "My father is an aeronautical engineer and I come from an upper-middle class background." Then the freckle-faced girl stated that she resided with her family and was a student at El Camino Junior College at the time she had met the cult leader in the Spring of 1967. Relating the incident she said, "I had been kicked out by my father. I hitchhiked from where I lived in Redondo Beach to Venice where I thought there were some kids living free but instead there were the same people. I was sitting there crying and this man walked up and said, 'Your father kicked you out of your house today.' I was surprised by this man. That was Charlie."

Rather excitedly the fragile-looking witness added, "He told me to come along with him—I refused at first and told him I was going to college. Then Charlie told me: 'If you want to come—fine—but you have to make up your mind.' I had never had anyone talk to me like that before—so then and there I picked my things up and left with Charlie."

Defense attorney Mr. Fitzgerald continued asking, "Did Charlie give orders on what to do and where to go?"

"No, we were riding on the wind," Miss Fromme replied quickly, then added, "Charlie was never our leader. He would follow us." Then witness went on to describe him, "Charlie is a man who would be at our feet with his

407

love, but not let us step on him. All he had to do after getting out of prison was to see what we needed... he really cares about us. Charlie was always happy, he made a game out of everything. He was a man of a thousand faces, and he gave every living creature attention."

"Do you love Charlie" asked Mr. Fitzgerald.

"Charlie is in love with love, and I'm in love with love and so we are in love with each other," replied the young woman.

"Does Manson have any power" inquired Mr. Fitzgerald.

"He loves," she said and then added, "that's the only power that doesn't look like power. He's the only person I ever knew who has real power. He sees things as they are... and does not judge!"

The defense attorney then asked the witness twice whether she thought Manson was Jesus Christ. She avoided a direct answer, replying instead that she thought "Jesus Christ is love." Restlessly and gesturing from one side to the other the young woman explained Manson's philosophy loudly, "Charlie is right now looking at what's in front of you. This is all Charlie is. Look over there. See that? Look over here. See that? What does that mean to you? Life is for living without guilt, without shame, being able to take off your clothes and lie in the sun... like babies. When you don't have any philosophy, you don't have any rules. You might call that an "Alice in Wonderland world" but it makes sense. You get what you put out."

Prompted by Mr. Fitzgerald's questions, the ardent family member continued saying, "Charlie did not hate black people, he was only predicting what was going to happen when he spoke of a black-white race war called Helter Skelter." Then, quite surprisingly, she addressed the entire court by saying, "People, Charlie's trying to tell you. You set that time bomb a long time ago."

The witness was speaking so fast that for a moment I stopped and just listened to her. Her dynamic and blowing-off attitude was something to see. Her eyes shined with fury. I continued writing as she said Helter Skelter only meant confusion. It was the only way of the family to make the best of everything every day. Everyone could be whatever he or she felt like being that day—a cowboy or a rich man riding in a Rolls Royce.

Under Mr. Fitzgerald's questioning the witness told how she had been one of the earliest to join the family and testified about accompanying the cult leader and others on an odyssey that included the Haight-Ashbury district of San Francisco, Mendocino County, and Sacramento. She also stated that they traveled up and down the state in a bus acquiring followers before the "family" settled at the Sphan Movie Ranch in early summer of 1968.

408

According to the witness, they moved in the Sphan Ranch by invitation of Mr. Sphan. At first they occupied the area in the back of the ranch, but eventually they moved in front. They cleaned the place and painted it the way they liked it. Diminutive Miss Fromme concluded her testimony by protesting about what the trial was all about. The witness was dismissed and on her way out she exchanged smiles with the defendants.

Nancy Pitman, who had assumed the name Brenda McCan when she was arrested at the age of 16, testified next that she was a member of the "family" and that she also was kicked out of her house by her father. However, she was not living at home when she first encountered Charles Manson.

Under Mr. Keith's interrogation, the witness stated:

"I first met Charlie on a dirt road—I was walking with a girl."

"Who was this girl?" Mr. Keith wanted to know.

"The daughter of Angela Lansbury... I think her name was DeDe."

"We approached the bus," she continued. "They were singing so I listened and then began to talk to Pat [Patricia Krenwinkel]. Sadie was there and the others. I felt like they were my sisters. They asked me to stay—so I stayed forever. The bus remained about two weeks before it went someplace. Then I hitchhiked to San Francisco and lived at Haight-Ashbury."

"When did you move to the Sphan Ranch?" asked Mr. Keith.

"Sadie gave me a ride to the ranch. There were many people."

When asked what her duties were the green-eyed girl replied, "I had to take care of Tanya when Linda dropped acid every day for a week."

According to Miss Pitman, Linda Kasabian told her she stole a bag of LSD and $5,000 from her husband before joining the "family".

Mr. Keith conducted his well-planned interrogation but due to unpending answers from the witness, Judge Older asked to be removed from court.

Sandra Good, known as "Sandy," next stated that she was born in San Diego in 1944. She attended high school in San Diego and went to the University of Oregon and also attended San Francisco State College. The 20-year-old testified that her family was well to do. Her mother was dominating and her father was hardly at home. In her own words, she explained that her childhood was full of pretensions and lack of love at home. Her parents traveled with her to Europe, Hawaii, and Mexico but she always was left in custody of a black nanny.

Sandra Good was a very well-expressed young woman. She stated that she met Charles Manson at the same time as Susan Atkins in Topanga Canyon. The pretty honey blonde echoed the testimony of the other two previous witnesses when she stated, "Charlie was always the happiest, always singing, always living... he was the most active person around." Miss Good also accentuated the cult leader's special powers, "Charlie could see every single thought we had; he could read our minds... and he'd bring it out in the open."

Asked by Mr. Shin if she thought Manson was Jesus Christ, she replied promptly, "I never really thought about it. I saw him as a million things."

Again, by ruling of the judge, the counsel approached the bench due to the fact that the witness was volunteering information. Mr. Shin advised her not to talk unless he first asked her a question.

Under questioning by Mr. Kanarek she said, "Charlie did not dominate anyone with his leadership. We looked at the babies as our leaders... wherever they went we followed them. We don't play mother and father."

Asked by Mr. Kanarek whether it was not true that eleven babies had been born to family members and to list their children, mothers, and fathers, she replied, "There were perhaps 7 or 8 children born to the cult leader's family women, including Pooh Bear, Sun Stone Hawk, Zee Zoe, and her own child, named Chosen." Looking at the jurors she asked, "But what difference does it make who the fathers are? The baby is the father of themselves." Miss Good then denied that Manson had predicted the end of the white man, that he hated black people or that he planned to start a black-white race war. "Charlie is love" she said.

Manson's attorney asking: "Was it against the law to disagree with Mr. Manson?"

"No. He agreed with everybody... he had no opinions. He agreed with every single one of us."

Sandy, a beautiful girl with striking blue eyes, sparkling blonde hair, and sharply well spoken, moved constantly. She used her hands in front of her to express every detail of her testimony. I tried hopelessly to draw her face twice on my notebook but because of her constant moving I didn't do justice to her good looks.

The next witness, escorted by two female deputy sherriffs, entered the courtroom through the jurors door. Katherine Share, also known as "Gypsy," stated she was born in Paris, France, in 1942. Her father and mother separated when she was two years old. During the war her father was member of the underground. She was adopted and brought into this country. Asked by Mr. Kanarek where had she met Linda Kasabian, the witness replied, "At Topanga Canyon Beach." The husky short lawyer wanted to know if Manson was against black people. Gypsy replied, "No. Charlie has no prejudice against Negroes."

The witness, pointing out that Manson had been close to many black people while being in jail, added, "They were like his father... they taught him every-thing he knows." Prompted by Mr. Kanarek she stated, "I never heard Charlie use the word 'Helter Skelter' except while singing the song. Others used the phrase, but not Charlie." Still under questioning by Mr. Kanarek she said, "We saw what was happening but we didn't want to cause anything... not only the black people, but the brown people and white people, too, all the people at the bottom are breaking their chains." To close his interrogation Mr. Kanarek asked the eight-month-pregnant witness if she believed Manson was Jesus Christ. She answered, "No. There are a lot of similarities but Jesus Christ lived 2,000 years ago."

Under Mr. Keith's direct examination the witness testified that she had met Leslie Van Houten while she was in the San Francisco area. In her own words she explained, "I was with Bobby Beausoleil at the time and we went to an apartment. Leslie was there and she fell in love with Bobby and when we left she wanted to go with us. Nobody could have stopped her. So we left together along with a girl named Gale. We traveled up north on a credit card that belonged to Leslie."

"What happened then?" inquired Mr. Keith.

"I left them and came to the Sphan Ranch."

"Why?"

"The reason was that Bobby had been fighting a lot with Gale—also I wanted to leave them, hoping Bobby would come after me."

"Did Bobby follow you?"

"Bobby came with Leslie and Gale—but only stayed for one day. Leslie remained, although she was hung up on Bobby a lot more than I was." Miss Share, a very appealing brunette tried to restrain her emotions as she was under cross-examination by Mr. Bugliosi. With tears in her eyes she testified she saw Sadie and Leslie return to the ranch with stolen clothes, money, and jewelry on many occasions. Miss Share kept looking intensely at the three female defendants as if asking for forgiveness. She frequently whispered words silently in an apparent effort to explain to the three women what she was doing. The witness was pale and under obvious stress as she testified. Unable to control herself, she uttered as to relieve herself, "I don't know why I'm doing this."

I felt the witness wanted to expel everything she knew. One could feel her burden and exasperating need to tell everything. At one instant under Mr. Bugliosi's examination she wanted to elaborate on how things had changed a lot at the ranch in the summer of 1969 but due to objections from the defense counsel she didn't get a chance.

411

Before being dismissed, Miss Share admitted that the father of the child she carried was Steve Crogan (Clem Tufts), and that she was a prisoner in Sybil Brand Institute for women on a charge. The jurors were not allowed to know about it. "Just as well" I said to myself. "We had enough evidence to contend with. Who needs more?"

We returned to the hotel.

Shortly after dinner I invited the jurors to my room for an evening of spooky listening entertainment. To set the mood I slightly opened the bathroom door with the lights on and then turned off the lights in the room. It gave a silhouetted effect.

Jim Reid had brought at my request a tape of "Sorry, Wrong Number" as performed by Agnes Moorehead. Jim shrewdly had added a suitable fanfare and narrative introduction of his own. The jurors were delighted, however one of them suggested it was not appropriate under the circumstances.

The following day, on February 9, 1971, at exactly 2 minutes before six o'clock in the morning I was awakened by the strongest jolt I've ever felt in my life. My bed began to rock violently, almost like someone was shaking it to wake me up. Instinctively I raised my hands above to get hold of the headboard. Suddenly I saw the huge table lamp falling to the floor—on a nearby table soda pop and liquor bottles rattled and rolled down. Also some of my collection of souvenir glasses crashed and broke.

The surprise was overwhelming. A jarring shock rattled my teeth. I didn't know what to do except to get up and run for cover. "But where?" I told myself, "Where?" No answer.

Having been born in Managua, Nicaragua, a city that once was destroyed (1931) by a devastating earthquake, I had the premonition, like Managuans do, to go out into the middle of the street and wait until it was over. I felt it was the safest way. But there was a problem. I was on the 6th floor of the hotel. I got up and took a pace forward and fell down. I could not walk. Finally I managed to open the door. I braced myself on the threshold as the building shooked again and at the moment saw my Sony tape recorder fall to the floor with a thud, dragging with it the 2 attached speakers placed at each end of the window ledge. The chandelier swung, at the same time I saw and heard the ceiling crack. The agony wrenched my jaw, shoulders, and waist down to my legs. I fell on my knees and prayed humbly: "Forgive me, oh God." The words were difficult to utter—to pronounce them, say them with fervor, feeling and meaning.

I had started praying in English but then turned frantically to Spanish— I felt assured God would understand me better in my native language. For a moment my mind took me back to the hells of Korea in the hot summer of 1951. I was part of a batallion of soldiers who had been taken on trucks to a point from where we would walk toward the enemy. My duties as a soldier were to administer emergency treatment to any wounded soldier on the battle-field and to distribute medicine on other occassions. I carried a heavy bag full of first aid items, a stretcher, .45 pistol, and two 5-pound grenades for my own protection. I was loaded.

I had just spoken to another soldier named Dave, who confided his fear and felt he was not going to make it back. "Hey Doc, you want a couple more?" he said, offering me two of his grenades.

"No thanks, Dave. I've enough to carry." I said. "In fact I shouldn't have these two grenades. You keep yours, you may need them."

The youthful-looking face stared at me and once again disclosed his fata-listic feelings, "I feel deep inside... I'm not going to make it."

"Have faith... have faith in God," I snapped strongly. He just smiled back.

The line of trucks had stopped on a bend going up hill. The enemy was on the other side of the hill. All of a sudden artillery bombs were falling all over. Everyone jumped out of the trucks. On the far side I saw soldiers running everywhere in a wide and spacious meadow. I felt they were wrong.

Dave was petrified and wouldn't move.

"Come on, jump." I yelled. He did so and ran behind me toward the foot of the hill. We reached what I thought was a safe spot. Suddenly my comrade looked around and out of panic darted away towards the other men. More bombs came down. My ears ached. There was so much dust from the bomb-ing. For a moment I could hardly see. I paused and smelled the air. The air was filled with gun powder and... death. I froze to the ground praying to God, "Please, please, oh God save me—forgive my sins." Then I remembered a prayer I was taught while studying at the Christian Brothers Pedagogical Institute in Managua, "Hail! Holy Queen, Mother of Mercy, our life, our sweetness and our hope! To thee do we cry, poor banished children of Eve; to thee do we send up our sighs, mourning and weeping in this valley of tears...." I felt as I articulated the words—stretching them, almost like utter-ing them for the last time. The temperature was hot. I was perspiring and breathing hard. Then I saw my fingers clawing the ground amidst hundreds of black biting ants. They didn't bother nor did I care, so I continued praying, "Turn then, most gracious advocate, thine eyes of mercy towards us; and after this our exile, show unto us the blessed fruit of thy womb, Jesus...."

In unison with the sound of the exploding shells I went on s-c-r-a-t-c-h-i-n-g each word of the prayer: "O clement." *Bomb*! "O loving." *Bomb*!

"O sweet Virgin Mary...." *Bomb*! "Pray for us, O holy mother of God." *Bomb*! "That we may be made worthy of the promises of Christ." *Bomb*!

The crisis was over! I stood up and within 30 feet I saw Dave's body on the ground. I rushed to help him. Before I reached him, I staggered. His decapitated head was lying at my feet. I cried and tembled with fear.

Once again the ground shooked with a flurry of explosions. Suddenly I felt someone's hand on my shoulder. "Please, Please, oh God, save me—forgive my sin.."

"Are you alright Mr. Zamora?" asked a woman sheriff, Mrs. Kolvig.

"Yes, I'm alright, thanks," I answered still trembling.

Back in court, Pete Miller, an investigator reporter for Channel 11 News, testified he had had a conversation with Mr. Bugliosi and attorney Richard Caballero at the Metromedia offices in December, 1969. The witness stated that they talked about blood tests related to Susan Atkins. There were no more questions.

Charles Manson returned to his seat after Mr. Kanarek announced his client would observe courtroom decorum. The bearded, long-haired cult leader sat quietly staring at the jurors and occasionally smiling at the three female defendants.

Susan Atkins moved automatically to the witness stand to testify. Her testimony, in which she expelled her life story up until the murders, lasted two days.

Questioned by her attorney, Mr. Shin, if she had participated in the Tate-LaBianca killings, the volatile murderess admitted openly that she had. Mr. Shin then switched to her childhood and through a lengthy number of questions she stated, "I was born in San Gabriel, California. I lived in Mellbrae [near San Francisco] for approximately 4 years. I attended grammar school in San Jose, California.

"My mother died when I was 14 years old. I was raised in a middle-class family. My mother and father worked—it seemed like a normal life. I got along pretty good with everybody. I lacked attention—cause my mother worked for an investigating company and was away all the time. I attended church and discovered that what they were preaching was not what they did. I saw hypocrisy. I attended all types of churches; Protestant, Methodist, Catholic, etc.

"I left home when I was 18. I didn't finish high school. My mother was ill for one year before she died of leukemia. My mother's death hurt—I couldn't understand why she had left me. I was sent to my aunt's and was told I had a heavy responsibility of looking after my two brothers and my father. I wanted to help and felt like it but I left to Los Banos [California] mainly because my father and relatives told me I was in a big world. I didn't have the strings to hold on. Then I moved to San Jose where I found a job.

"I met a man who told me I had to go to San Francisco. He put me in an apartment with a woman about 35 years old. I worked for magazines but I didn't get paid. I left.

"I found myself in a big city. With no one. Alone. I tried to commit suicide. I discovered I wanted attention—I tried it again but I called the emergency hospital. At that time I began to drink a lot. I got a job as a waitress making about $ 11 a week. I ran away from San Francisco with a young man to Oregon. With him I drank all the sophisticated drinks—I drank heavily to the point to fall down. I tried to get myself together.

"Then I met a man named Robert something—a computer operator. I can't remember his last name. He told me he was in love with me and wanted to marry me. I said yes but then one night the manager where I was staying told me that six young men were being arrested nearby. I went out and saw one of them—a pretty one. I helped him out. He asked me if he could walk me home. I had to go only about 3 houses from work. I was afraid but I spent the night with him. The next day I found out he had stolen a car and had jumped his parole.

"I went with him to Stockton [Calif] where I first tried marijuana. I met Al and we 3 left to Oregon. On the way crossing the border Al and the other guy stole an automobile with money on it. Al gave me a gun—he taught me how to use it and shoot with it. Al told me he loved me and would do anything for me—he said he was doing all this for me. I believed him because I loved him too. The other guy threatened me and I was afraid. I didn't leave because I was in love with Al. Then we went to live by the river—I had everything I wanted. Al and I had each other.

"Then one day the battery of the car went dead and as we went to buy a new one to the nearest town, four cops came and stopped us. That was the first time I had contact with the police. I had a gun but I had it because we were in the woods and had many snakes around... but I heard on the radio that the police had classified us as dangerous criminals. When the police stopped us I didn't make any false move.

"Eventually after I was arrested and found guilty on many accounts I was sent back to San Francisco. I went back to the computer operator who wanted to marry me. He bought me a ring and kept me in an apartment. Later I returned the ring and left the man.

"I went to all sorts of places. Got myself an apartment and by then I had

415

taken LSD. My family kept telling me I was going down the hell! and I guess I was. Then I asked a hippie if he had LSD—he didn't have any and together we panhandled $ 3 and obtained LSD at Union and Powell streets. That was the first time I experienced a trip of LSD. I went to Haight-Ashbury. I began dancing and got money—I gave it away. I began to feel good—happy.

"Then I met a girl I had gone to school with, and who lived with a long family. They all had LSD—Marijuana. I stayed with them and there met a young man.

"I gave up my own apartment—I had a TV set, stereo, etc. I didn't want them anymore. I moved with a man to Lyon St., where there is access to a lot of LSD. Each one of my LSD experiences has been different.

"Then I moved from the place of the man whom I was in love with because he was taken to jail. I moved to North Beach where I met Charles Manson. He was playing and singing "The Shadow of His Smile." The only place to sit down was on the floor. I liked him. I liked his voice."

Susan Atkins, to emphasize her testimony, moved ceaselessly. She used her arms and eyes, most of the time taking her hair out of her face. She was a fast speaker. She continued saying, "I wanted to play the guitar—so he gave me the guitar and told me to play. I felt I was taking the attention from him. 'Your stiff' he told me. No one had told me that before. He taught me how to play even though I had never played before.

"He left but he came back later. I realized that everybody was happy when he was around. I wanted to be part of it. I asked the girls who the man was. "Charlie" they told me. They were leaving and although I was sort of happy —I decided to join them.

"They had a yellow school bus. All the seats had been removed and later we painted it black. I felt in love with Charlie. He talked funny. I wanted him for myself but he never did pay attention to me alone. I had to work it out with the other girls. Charlie showed affection to all of them. Eventually we moved to South California and went to the Sphan Ranch. That's where I first saw Linda Kasabian in the company of Gypsy.

"I heard that Linda had stolen $ 5,000. I wanted to leave the ranch but it was too good for me. The love-peace was getting to me.

"Linda and I became rather close friends, due to the fact that we had similar backgrounds. So we went to steal more money from 'Crazy Charlie'. Linda would tell me to go inside and talk to him and smoke pot while she was stealing the money. I asked Linda why she needed to steal money, and she told me 'to go to the desert.' We also went to other houses in Encino to steal. She showed me how to touch cars—that is to see if they were open. We went together for about 4 or 5 times."

Susan Atkins switched her testimony to disclose more details about Linda Kasabian, "I saw Linda make love a couple of times with Bobby Beausoleil, who was going through a lot of changes. He left and came back. He gave and stopped giving attention to Linda. Linda then was more involved with Tex Watson..she would go for one or two days away with him!"

The witness was stopped by her attorney Mr. Shin and was asked, "Do you remember the night of August 8, 1969?"

"I was there, yes" she said and looking out on the audience added, "Don't you see? This whole thing started because I was there. The reason that I am in this courtroom... the reason Patricia [Krenwinkel] and Leslie [Van Houten] and Charlie are in this courtroom. We all here, all these months and the reason Bobby Beausoleil is on the Death Row, is all because of what I did."

The dark-haired witness quite emotionally began crying. She clenched her fists and kept repeatedly pounding with them on her knees.... "This whole thing started when I killed Gary Hinman. I killed him because he tried to hurt my love. I saw it had to be done and I did it."

The pale-looking Susan Atkins stopped and lowered her head, still crying and said breathlessly, "I had to...." Suddenly she raised her head. With fiery eyes she looked straight on the face of Mr. Bugliosi, "Your whole thing, man, is just gone. Your whole motive is ruined. It is silly. All your work is spoiled."

Susan Atkins seemed to enjoy herself at seeing Mr. Bugliosi's prosecution come to nothing. However by doing so, she didn't realize how much relief she gave the jurors' conscience. It was obvious that the convicted murderess was trying to save herself by telling the truth. Her anger and disposition was a way to express her guilt. We the jurors knew and felt then that the verdict we had given her and her companions was the right verdict, that of *guilty of first degree murder.*

That day some friends of mine were in the audience. They couldn't have picked a more important day. I saw the excitement on their faces. Susan Atkins' testimony was surely a big spotlight during the trial. She said enough for observers to guess what was coming.

Newspaper reporters, TV newsmen, general expectators, deputies, counsel, jurors, and even Judge Older himself listened attentively to the testimony of the convicted murderess. Still questioned by Mr. Shin she testified,

"I have tried to tell you all the truth for so long. When I went to the grand jury I lied and I knew I lied, and I told Mr. Caballero I lied. And he told me:

417

'It's too late now, baby!' And I was held incommunicado. I couldn't talk to anybody. I have tried and tried and tried to tell you the truth, and now you all know.''

The well-dressed attorney pressed the witness for step-by-step details. He was about to stop asking questions when Susan Atkins, still crying, said, "I'm rather nervous—bear with me." Mr. Shin, glancing at the clock requested noon recess.

Susan Atkins didn't appear nervous. However, it was evident, palpable if you will, that she was willing to tell all. She showed a necessity to divulge the most intimate details of her adventures—her escapades—in total her entire life up to the killings in question. She appeared to be drunk with truth.!

Judge Older called for noon recess. For a moment the courtroom was quiet. I felt Mr. Shin was right. He wanted to stop Susan Atkins because she was crying and, according to my belief, perhaps because she may have said more than he wanted her to.

On the way out of the courtroom I waved hello at my friends but somehow I couldn't help thinking that Susan Atkins was going to tell the real truth— exactly as it happened during the night of August 8, 1969. Then I thought of comparing her story with that of Patricia Krenwinkel and Leslie Van Houten.

Let's see if they will contradict each other I told myself. This is the last time anyone will speak for or against Susan Atkins. She herself would have to tell the truth. All these months as a juror I have been sitting here watching her and now hopefully she'll tell in detail the sequence of the events as they occurred the night of the killings. Now for the first time she would uncover the passages leading to the performance of the murders. Would she tell how they planned them? How they got there? What was said before it happened or at the time it was happening? The chaos—their feelings of what they were doing...the reaction of the victims... what went on their minds... gosh, so many things we'll know....

Instead of going to the Hilton for lunch we went to the Los Angeles County Administration Building. Because of the excitement caused by Susan Atkins, to avoid photographers, and because of the proximity, we didn't go by bus. We walked underneath the streets through a tunnel that connects the Hall of Justice Building and the aforementioned building. It was a long walk. As we walked on the tunnel, my mind kept thinking if a jolt would occur. Wow, I said to myself, what would we do? Would we be buried alive? I was terrified at the thought of dying under those circumstances. I guess because to think of death is nothing enjoyable. Death might be easy to overcome if we didn't let it enter in our minds—but can we overlook it? Day after day we

418

read and hear of people dying. Our dear ones also have departed at one time or another... however, no sooner do we think of death than we change our paths of thought, especially when one is in the company of someone. It's a uncomfortable feeling. Why? I guess because we don't know nor can we tell what kind of death we will have at the end of our lives. Let's hope it would easy and peaceful.

We walked long tunnels—it felt strangely enclosing. Anyone with claustrophobia would die just to think of it. No windows, sun, or trees. No sea or birds flying in a wonderful blue sky. No colors to enhance the beauty of the flowers nor the fragrant smell of the eucalyptus tree during summer.

We kept walking. I heard the echo of the jurors' feet. Then I observed the perspective line of pipes along the length of the tunnel. There were at least 12 to 14 pipes on the ceiling. Four of them were large—about 30 inches in diameter. On the walls of the tunnel there were a set of 3 pipes recently installed. They appeared bright, clean, somewhat shinning. Looking at the pipes I thought of their destination, their purposes, and their multiple uses. I thought they were perhaps the pipes of the Central Heating System of the Los Angeles Civic Center, or were they used for drainage? Yes, thats right, they must be drainage pipes I told myself. Then I thought of the thousands of toilets being flushed, the excrement, and waste going through those tubes —I thought of all the bathrooms, kitchen sinks, washbowls, and water fountains being used and that water assimilating and flowing in one common pipe. Who knows what else.

We kept on walking. Then I looked the floor, and I noticed dried stains along the edges of the walls. I presumed one of the tubes had broken down and mixed with dirt had left those shaded spots. The center of the tunnel was clean—rubbed by the footsteps of the personnel using those subterranean passages.

There were intersections leading to other buildings. At various locations there were hot drafts of air and then would change to cold. The air was humid and somewhat unpleasant. The repugnant odor made me think of the time I visited the catacombs outside of Rome—the underground galleries and burial places for thousands of Christians during the Crusades. Having read in my childhood Cardinal Weesman's novel *Fabiola*, I was appalled to think anyone could possibly survive in those catacombs, especially without the modern facilities provided for the family nowadays.

The mumbling of the tourists and their questions to the guide at the catacombs brought a parallelism to the murmuring of the jurors.

At the end of the subterranean tunnel an elevator transported us up to the cafeteria. We went back to court the same way.

At 1:52 P.M. Susan Atkins resumed her testimony, "I met Gary Hinman in 1968, at the same time I had met Bobby. Shortly after I had been arrested in Mendocino. The time is very foggy for me now." Susan frowned as to recollect her memory and prompted by her attorney continued, "I was very fond of Gary—I loved him as much as I love myself. Bobby had asked me to go with him to get a pink slip at Gary's. Bobby had given $100 to Gary for a car and that's why we went there."

"What happened after?" Mr. Shin wanted to know.

"There was a phone call on Saturday. Gary told me to answer and say that he was in Colorado, visiting his mother, that he wouldn't be in for awhile. Bobby wanted his pink slip—but Gary was upset for something so we left.

"After two days, Bobby, Leslie, and I came back to the house. Gary said hello. He was in a better mood than the day before—more friendly. He went to make coffee and we got along. We could talk, maybe that's why Bobby took me along. I asked Gary if he had some grass and he told me where to get it. Leslie went with me. Then Bobby and Gary got into an argument. Something about the car. Oh its been so long..."

Susan stopped for awhile and, again through Mr. Shin's assistance, she continued, "Bobby told me to call Charlie—that he couldn't control Gary. For awhile they calmed down but later again they seemed to get into a fight. I saw Gary hitting Bobby, who in self defense hit Gary on the mouth and maybe broke a tooth. Leslie and I went to the kitchen and took a towel to wipe Gary's face.

"Charlie and Bruce Davis arrived and then I heard Charlie saying 'I'm splitting.' Gary came out with a gun and was going to use it—he was pointing at Charlie.

"Leslie and I were washing the cups at that time and other dishes in the kitchen when we saw what was happening. I had—I had to—he was going to kill my love. I couldn't let him do it." Susan Atkins stopped for a brief moment and added, "Charlie hit Gary with something and right after having the knife in my hands I went and killed Gary Hinman. I did it—I—and they have an innocent man in jail. After that—after I killed him—we left and remained inside at the ranch for two days.

"Then Bobby had talked with Leslie and told her to tell me just to cool it and see what happens. We didn't have money to hire a lawyer. When I told what happened to Katie—Leslie was present and then Linda came out and told me that she had heard everything that I said to Leslie. She told me that she heard me saying that I killed Gary Hinman."

420

Under questioning by Mr. Shin the witness also said that Bobby Beausoleil had been arrested and charged with the murder of Gary Hinman. She added, "We didn't know how to get Bobby out of jail so someone mentioned that we should do something equal as to make it appear like someone had done it and not Bobby, who wouldn't be present."

Susan Atkins quite obvious didn't want to incriminate Charles Manson as the person who suggested to commit an equal crime and opted to refer to him as 'someone.'

Mr. Shin brought again the question involving the incidents on the night of 8th of August, 1969. Upon question after question Susan Atkins seemed to be confused and stated she was unsure as the sequence of events—time or hour. That it was not clear to her and claimed that she was 'stoned,' that she had taken acid, and she only remembered and knew what she did and not anyone else.

The spectators in the audience were at intervals getting up from their seats to see the defendant. They didn't want to miss a word.

Susan Atkins stated under Mr. Shin's interrogation, "The night we drove to the house, I didn't know what house." Someone told me it was 10550 Ceilo Drive. I can't remember the car. I can't tell you whether anyone was carrying guns or rope. I only remember bits and pieces. I remember Tex climbing a telephone pole and seeing wires on the ground. I remember landing on the grass. Linda had climbed the fence. I don't remember what kind of fence. Tex went crazy. I heard four shots. That happened after I saw a car just beginning to move.

"Then we all went inside the house. Linda told me to go around the house. I've seen her telling me and doing so."

"Did you have a knife with you?" inquired Mr. Shin.

"I've always have a knife with me."

The short Oriental lawyer brought a buck knife for identification and placed it in front of the witness. Without thinking or caring he turned around and went back. After she confessed to killing Gary Hinman, I was a little uneasy about the proximity of my position and that of the witness stand. I thought it was very amateurish on the part of Mr. Shin to leave the knife in front of the witness and walk away. I dreaded the thought of what could have happened. Then I discarded immediately the thought of her doing any damages to anyone but it entered in my mind the thought of her killing herself. I was aware of the knife and couldn't take my eyes off of it. Unable to control myself I muttered in a very low voice "How stupid can he be," referring to Mr. Shin.

Oddly enough, Mr. Fitzgerald was looking at me and instinctively he seemed to read my lips. He was bending to tell Mr. Keith about what he saw me doing or saying when the judge snapped at Mr. Shin and said, "Mr. Shin remove the knife."

The absent-minded lawyer apologized and needless to mention I was relieved like everybody else.

Resuming his interrogation, Mr. Shin brought to Susan Atkins a photograph of the car where Steven Parent was shown slain. In another photo, she pointed out the Polanski house and the window where Tex Watson had climbed inside. She also described the light they saw on the house as they entered from the gate. She was shown the color photos depicting the other victims in their horrible final fates as the murderers had left them.

Emotion... remorse... Susan Atkins's face showed no signs of these feelings. She simply accepted the photos as they were and identified them.

Under Mr. Shin's questioning, Susan finally described how the killings occurred. Her testimony resembled that of Linda Kasabian:

When we entered in the living room, there was a man lying on the couch. He stretched out—like waking up. He began to open his eyes and said, "What do you want?" Tex was pointing a gun at him.

At that moment I felt like a current of electricity. Something told me to go and look at the rest of the house. That's when I saw the woman with the dark hair reading a book—and then went into the other room where I saw the lady with blonde hair talking to a man.

I went back to the living room and told Tex, "There are three more." "Bring them in," he told me. So I went and asked the woman in the bedroom to come along.

I had a knife in my hand—I warned her. Now I know that her name was Abigail Folger. I made her walk in front and then the other two, Sharon Tate and Jay Sebring, came along.

At that time, the man on the couch had his hands already tied up with a towel. Tex still had the gun.

The two women were screaming and the man on the couch told them to shut up—they did. Jay ran towards the door. Then I heard a shot and saw Jay Sebring falling down.

The soft-spoken voice of Mr. Shin plus the incoherent answers from the witness made the continuity of her testimony a little obscure and difficult to follow. There was some type of struggle—it was not clear. However, Susan Atkins continued:

I found myself alone with Sharon. She was begging for her life—that she just wanted to have her child. But I kept telling her to shut up. I told her I didn't want to hear her talk or say anything.

"What happened then?" asked Mr. Shin softly.

I think I pushed Sharon on the couch and at one time I had her head locked up with my right arm and a knife in my left. I saw Tex coming in and he told me to kill Sharon—so I killed her.

The jurors and audience were petrified at the simplicity of Susan Atkins's confession. It didn't seem to bother her nor did she seem to care what others thought or felt. The murderess continued. "Then after, I saw Tex clubbing Voytick Frykowski and, at the same time, Katie stabbing Abigail." Asked what she did before they left, she replied, "I grabbed a towel and soaked it on Sharon's stomach and then wrote the word 'PIG' on the entrance door." Then she explained her hair was pulled by Voytick and that during the drive back to the ranch, it hurt. Describing her pain, she said, "But it was a different pain—like it was there and wasn't." The dark-haired murderess also admitted:

On the way back to the ranch, we stopped at a place to wash our hands and drink water, but we were chased away. We also stopped at about three gas stations. When we arrived, I went to sleep in the bunk house.

The next day, I saw Barbara Hoyt watching TV and for the first time I saw who the people were—that is, the people we killed. Later that day, I went to the hills and stayed two days. I wish I had stayed longer...

The next day, Susan Atkins continued her testimony, but for some reason she appeared cautious when answering the questions. Pertaining to the second night, when asked if Charles Manson went along to the La Bianca house, she replied, "He didn't go."

Her testimony went as follows: "I stayed in the car when we arrived at Harold True's house. Linda wanted to steal from him." Then she described the next door house, which was the La Bianca residence, and added:

We left behind Tex, Katie and Leslie, and the rest of us went to the beach. Linda was driving and we went to see this man—an actor. Linda knocked on the door, but it was the wrong door.

Asked what they did with the gun they carried, she responded:

Clem tried to get rid of it, but he didn't because there were too many people on the pier. He chose the pier because he wanted to throw it in the water. Eventually we drove away and I buried the gun someplace in the sand.

Mr. Shin slowly spent the afternoon and morning of the next day asking Susan Atkins questions up to when she was apprehended in the desert—then taken to Inyo County—and then through the series of interviews with detectives and deputies leading to her former lawyer, Mr. Richard Caballero:

I was taken from Sybil Brand Institute for Women on the authority of a

423

Superior Court order. I was taken to the office of Richard Caballero. The court appointed him to represent me in the murder of Gary Hinman. Then he showed me some transcripts of statements I had made to Ronnie Howard and Virginia Graham. He told me: "The only thing that will save your life is if you go to the Grand Jury." Then he taped the interviews...

I told him the way it went at the Tate house. The whole story. He promised me he would destroy it, but he never did. He sold it. He taped my conversations and sold them for profit.

Susan Atkins then related her meeting with Mr. Bugliosi at Caballero's office about her pending testimony before the Grand Jury. She said she understood that if she testified, Mr. Bugliosi would seek life sentences not only for her but for the other defendants as well, if they were eventually indicted. She stated:

He [Mr. Bugliosi] told me that I might get immunity if I became a state's witness. I agreed to testify before the Grand Jury only because of the pressure. He told me also: "If you don't testify to the Grand Jury—if you don't cooperate—you'll probably get the gas chamber and so will everyone else.

Mr. Shin had no more questions. Under Mr. Fitzgerald's examination, the witness was asked: "For what reason, if any, did you go to 10050 Cielo Drive [Sharon Tate's house]?" Susan Atkins, with a melodic voice and rhythmical movements of her arms and sensual moving fingers, replied: "What feels right for me... at the height of my career... it felt good. I did what I did because I did it."

Mr. Kanarek and Mr. Keith asked questions to clarify the innocence of their clients—Charles Manson and Leslie Van Houten, respectively.

Under Mr. Bugliosi's cross-examination, she testified that Manson was not at the Spahn Ranch the night she and the others left for Sharon Tate's house. She also stated that as far as she could remember, she never heard Charles Manson talk about Helter Skelter, Revolution 9, or the Bottomless Pit. "We did," she said, "but not Charlie."

Mr. Bugliosi shrewdly asked her if she hadn't told the Grand Jury that it meant the last war predicted by Charles Manson.

Sweeping her hand to encompass her answer, Susan Atkins replied:

The only reason I lied to the Grand Jury was because I wanted attention from Charlie—but he wouldn't give me what I wanted. That's why I told them he was Jesus Christ returned to earth. That's why I called him "the Devil" and "the Soul". I told you before I wanted attention. I used that man [Manson] to gain attention.

Surprisingly, the prosecutor addressed the dark-haired murderess as "Sadie" or "Susan" and she in return sometimes called him "Vince" as Mr. Bugliosi questioned her.

"Sadie, why did you put an 'X' on your head? Was it because Charlie has one himself?"

"No. I did it because I have 'Xed' myself out of society."

"Is it true that Charlie told you once to go to Brazil for a coconut and you got up and started out the door?"

"Yes, it is true. But it was only because I thought it might be fun—and I would have done it if anyone had asked me."

"Do you think Charles Manson is a second coming of Jesus Christ?" asked Mr. Bugliosi.

I thought about that quite a bit."

Then the witness admitted that Manson might or might not be Jesus Christ. No more questions.

Court adjourned and we returned to the hotel.

To avoid future confrontations with deputy Taylor and "the Clique," who patronized the senior sheriff's company, I bought an electric hot plate. I stopped going to breakfast and dinners. My only hot meal during the day was at lunch time.

In the midst of my silence, I kept busy writing notes and checking details of importance about the jurors. Also, I cancelled my sports' activities. When in the company of other jurors, I offered no conversation but confined myself to writing and reading. That night I wrote:

Besides the continuous tremors we have been having since the big earthquake, the morale of the jurors is dispersed as far as the variety of moods. Genaro Swanson has become friendlier and more outgoing towards the non-clique jurors. I like him. Edith Rayburn had a discussion with Deputy Taylor because of her mail. She cried until Mollie and another female bailiff consoled her. Ruth Collingwood has not been feeling well. She misses her children terribly and wants to go home.

The "Clique" is also going through a change of pace. Their jokes no longer predominate the conversations and the reason is unknown to me. It sure shows a different attitude and behavior among them.

Oh yes, Violet, usually a close companion of Debbie, is seemingly drifting away from her friend.

What's going on?

Last week I overheard the tail end of an argument between Mollie and Ray, siding with Tom in the "Little Lobby". I left my room to go to the recreation room. At the end of the hall I noticed Ray sitting at the top of the stairs. He

425

was bouncing a rubber ball on the floor.

"Bullshit!" yelled the curly-haired man at Mollie.

"I'm sorry, but you cannot," replied Mollie as she started walking towards me.

"We don't know where our rights begin and where they end!" Ray shouted back.

"Yeah!" Tom yelled approvingly, "tell us what kind of rights do we have?"

Mollie ignored them. She continued walking to her room and winked at me as she passed. Suddenly, aware of my presence, Ray and Tom lowered their voices and stopped talking momentarily. The two young jurors appeared somewhat upset. Ray, unable to control himself, made a reference to "being fed up with everything" and that he'd "do something about it."

To avoid any confrontation with me, Ray directed his attention to Olivia Madison: "Get off the phone, Olivia," he shouted, "you've already been talking for a half hour." Olivia and Ray had an exchange of words for a while. They tried to make it appear as a joke, though it sounded more serious. The sarcasm and tone of their remarks were more insulting than casual.

Since that day, Ray and Olivia kept pretty much reserved to themselves.

The usual joke-pounding on the doors has ceased and even the gaiety-charming atmosphere which prevailed at mealtime has almost disappeared. There's small talk and even laughter among the jurors but the degree of it has been diminishingly considerably.

Because of the change of moods and aroused feelings caused by the slow navigation of the trial, everyone has experienced a sense of lost time and restless patience. We all have displayed our indignation, not necessarily by protesting or demonstrating, but by behaving quietly or remaining silent.

Returned to the courtroom. Patricia Krenwinkel was the second defendant to testify on behalf of herself. In a warm, almost friendly manner, she unfolded her story:

I was residing in Manhattan Beach with my sister Charlene. I was working for an insurance company as a file clerk. I was working like everyone else. I had my apartment, paid my bills, etc.

I had a friend and one evening went to his apartment and there I saw this man sitting on the floor, playing a guitar and singing. He played the guitar well and sang beautifully. I sat down and watched him. His name was Charlie. I loved what I saw and was very happy.

The hairy-armed woman said Manson stayed in her apartment for four days and then added:

I fell in love with him. Charlie showed me how to love because I had been

426

held in so long. I had been afraid of loving. It was the first time I started to feel free.

Charlie was with Mary Brunner and 'Squeaky' [Lynette Fromme]. One day, they said they were leaving and said good-bye. They started to leave and I asked them, "I want to go with you." So I joined them. I called my sister and also my father, got a change of clothing and left with them.

We traveled to the woods—Los Angeles is like a concrete madness—and in the woods we put flowers in our hair. Charlie would smoke his pipe. We felt free—happy from day to day.

Then in San Francisco, we stayed in this apartment and there were a lot of people. Sadie was there.

We had a white Volkswagen then, but in Sacramento a family with seven kids helped us to obtain a school bus because we were too many. This beautiful family gave us lodging and we helped them with their kids.

Eventually, we all came to the Spahn Ranch in Chatsworth. George [Spahn] lived there without anyone to care for him—he was blind. We helped George with paper work. You know, he was in business and renting horses' business requires a lot of paper work—it also requires feeding the horses.

The Spahn Ranch was like a magical place, having been used as a movie set. It had good places where one could be anything—a cowgirl, anything. But the most beautiful thing was to take care of the children. There were also 30, maybe 40 people—mostly young people—they came and went."

Mr. Fitzgerald shifted his line of questions, leading to the night of the killings. Patricia Krenwinkel stated that:

About August 4, 1969, Bobby Beausoleil got arrested for the murder of Gary Hinman. I had spoken before with Sadie and Leslie, and Sadie told me she had killed Gary Hinman. Then one day, the three of us were speaking about it and Linda was present. We thought about how to free Bobby—we put a lot of thought into it and one stayed in our minds. We thought of doing some killing like sidetracking the police to make them believe that someone else did it.

Remarkably serene, the convicted murderess with her long, brown hair parted in the middle and wearing a purple velveteen jumper, gazed calmly with folded hands at her attorney Mr. Fitzgerald, and indicated: "Some people just think, but we did it right away. We all got in a car and did it."

Mr. Fitzgerald wanted to know if they had taken LSD: "I don't know—but I remember we had dropped acid among ourselves. We all felt good—we all felt empathy for each other."

Mr. Fitzgerald continued his interrogation but unfortunately, in the eyes of this juror, the sequences of the murders were not clearly indicated, even though Patricia Krenwinkel bluntly admitted having killed Abigail Folger.

Under Mr. Kanarek's examination, the hippie cult leader extended his left arm above his head and pointed his left index finger toward the ceiling. As he stroked his beard with his other hand and stared at the acoustical tile high on the opposite courtroom wall, each of the two women defendants pointed an index finger upward.

"Mr. Manson seems to be disrupting the proceedings," commented Mr. Bugliosi.

Judge Older replied that he was aware of what Manson was doing. His Honor instructed Mr. Kanarek to proceed with his interrogation.

In the meantime Patricia Krenwinkel appeared to be distracted at first when Manson raised his hand, but she adapted quickly, pointing her left index finger upward for more than one half hour as she continued testifying.

Mr. Kanarek spent the morning asking questions regarding LSD. Asked why she had taken LSD, she said:

"I do it because its there and I like it. Its just good to me. I enjoy it. I like it. I have taken so much and I am acid. I never came down."

The questions that really got me were those which Mr. Kanarek probed about Patricia Krenwinkel's state of mind a couple of minutes before she plunged a knife into Abigail Folger. The stocky lawyer asking:

"What were you thinking of?"

"Nothing," she said, "I wasn't thinking about anything."

"What was your reason?"

"I don't understand what reason is. Everything is done because it's done. It still doesn't explain the reason."

"Why did you murder?"

"I don't know why... it just was."

"Did you have any feelings for those people?"

"None."

"Did you have hatred for the victims?"

"None."

"Now, Miss Krenwinkel, could you tell us if you—why? While you had a knife in your hand—what propelled you to do it?"

"Because it was—it was—and now doesn't even exist anymore."

"What is the reason you had no reason for committing murder?"

"Because I'm satisfied with myself... that night was my death. I killed myself and I judged myself. Everything done and has been done is perfect. To kill someone is to kill yourself because we are all one with ourselves."

Then looking at the jurors and rest of the spectators in the courtroom, she lectured:

It was you who judged your brother with thoughts that you don't understand; it was you who turned the Bible into lies; it was you who professed the Golden Rule, but don't help your brother.

Children are starving in the streets and you go to the moon?

Mr. Kanarek didn't try to interrupt Patricia—she continued her lecturing on morality using the all-inclusive term of "You":

It was you who are trying to destroy everyone who tried to get together and that everyone knows that, but it doesn't matter.

I know that I judge myself and all of you judge yourselves. Because it's all perfect and everyone has done right, whatever they've done.

Pertaining to the first night of the events, Mr. Kanarek asked such questions as:

"Did you all change clothes after you did... what you did?"

"I believe we did."

"Why?"

"I guess because we all had blood on our clothing."

After shown a color photo where Jay Sebring appears with a rope on his neck, she claimed:

"I didn't see any rope nor anyone suspended from it."

Pertaining to the second night, Mr. Kanarek wanted to explore in detail how the murders occurred. He asked the murderess how many people besides Sadie, Linda, herself and Tex were present at the La Bianca residence, but she reluctantly elaborated with a look of disbelief and claimed she couldn't remember. She appeared bored at the questioning of such important questions. However, when Manson's attorney asked her to describe the raid at the ranch on August 16, 1969, the witness pulled herself together and became alive. She described how Charlie was taken away, pushed down on the ground by sheriffs. She even quoted some of the deputies as yelling: "Where's Charlie? Where's Charlie?"

At that moment, a question came to my mind: "How come Patricia Krenwinkel remembers what was said during the raid and not during the two nights in question? When one stops to think there were only eight people on the first night and five people on the second night, and yet she claimed she could remember what was said among many people during the raid—how come?" It was hard to believe her. It was evident she didn't want to disclose nor relate the sequences of what happened during those killings.

"I have no more questions," said Mr. Kanarek.

429

After having taken a 15-minute recess, Mr. Bugliosi surprisingly asked Patricia Krenwinkel the very same questions I had on my mind. The prosecutor wisely also asked a number of pertinent questions specifically as to what the victims said at the time they were being murdered. He received the same negative response: "I don't remember."

Unexpectedly, Judge Older announced that due to family problems, Ray Harris was being excused from jury service. His dismissal was a surprise to most of the jurors. I guessed because of his grievances with the bailiffs, it made him decide to quit or simply because he was bored with the whole thing. I never found out why. Before leaving the courtroom, His Honor thanked the easygoing and likeable juror and immediately after, addressed the court clerk to draw another name from among the alternate jurors. For lack of space, Tom, Danny and Edith were seated in front of the audience, then the regular panel, and then Ruth at the other end, next to me.

Ruth appeared pale and quivered fearfully. Her eyes darted across the room waiting for the bald-headed clerk to call the name. The alternate juror didn't look well.

Ironically, Ruth Collingwood's name was called. She was petrified, almost glued to her seat. The sound of her own name was almost frightening for her to hear. Ruth managed to control herself enough to come out of her trance.

"Mrs. Collingwood, take your seat in the jury box," Judge Older ordered. Ruth made an effort to stand up but could not. She tried again—the lady juror gained strength very slowly and stood up for a second and fainted back on her chair.

I stepped from my seat and grabbed my notebook to use it as a fan. Ruth was breathing hard. Frantically, I asked Mildred to give me her wet paper towel to apply it on the lady juror's head. It was customary among some jurors to bring cold wet towels into court to rub their wrists and eyes to keep from falling asleep. I asked Ruth if she was alright. When she heard me, she opened her eyes and nodded. Judge Older called for a recess.

Ray Harris was waiting in the jury room. I wanted to ask him how come he was leaving, but he was flanked with questions by Tom, Debbie and Violet. Ruth didn't say very much—she cried and expressed she wanted to GO HOME. I didn't blame her.

Suddenly, Deputy Taylor came in and asked Ray to follow him. Judge Older wanted to talk with him in his private chambers. Nobody knew what was going on.

When we returned to the courtroom, Judge Older, with no explanation,

430

surprisingly reinstated Ray Harris as a regular juror and subsequently Ruth Collingwood was made an alternate juror again,

The trial continued.

Mr. Maxwell Keith called his client, Leslie Van Houten, to the witness stand. The able attorney took the slim, attractive convicted murderess through her childhood and teenage years prior to meeting members of Manson's hippie "family".

Leslie began her testimony by stating:

I was born August 23, 1944 in Altadena, California, but my parents lived in Monrovia. I have an older brother named Paul and a brother and a sister who were adopted. I love them and I think they have mixed feelings about me. My mother's testimony recollected my memory about a lot of things I didn't remember. When I was a child, I liked to play with dolls. Later on, when I was older, I played in the band using different instruments from elementary school through senior high school.

I was a proper teenage girl—I did everything as not to offend my parents. My father belonged to Alcoholics Anonymous for many years, but I was a very young girl to know or care for that matter.

It was during my junior year at school that my parents were divorced. When I first heard about it, it was shattering. But I felt, since they both wanted to divorce, I encouraged them not to wait until I grew up. So I told them if they would be happier divorced, they should do it.

There were a lot of things I was happy for while living at home, like playing in the trees on the back yard. My parents built a swimming pool. I remember we had a couch where I loved to lie down, but they changed it into a sofa with iron bars and plastic pillows.

In my first two years of high school, I ran for several student body offices and always won. I was also chosen by the football players as homecoming princess two years in a row.

The dimple-faced witness then stated that it was in her midteens when she first turned on with marijuana and began to drop acid (LSD). She added:

It felt good, so I decided to take as much as I could, then I lost interest in competing. I was happy with myself and saw no point to make myself recognized by anybody so I did not run for any offices in my junior or senior years. Nor did I get picked as a homecoming princess because I stopped smiling at the football players.

My grades dropped considerably. I felt no holding interest in books. I found myself among people who entertained me and I reciprocated with them.

There are three types of people: one, those people who read and write;

two, those people who drink and smoke cigars; and three, those people who smoke marijuana and take acid and just watch the other two types. I belonged to the last group.

"Did you have many friends?" asked Mr. Keith.

"Yes, I had a high school friend, Bobby Mackey, whom I was very fond of... and I still am... but I guess he doesn't want anything to do with me now."

Miss Van Houten also testified about studying with the Self-Realization Fellowship because of her love for Bobby Mackey, who she claimed "got kicked out of school because he had long hair." The long-haired witness said:

Bobby was going to be a monk there and so I decided if he was going to be a monk, I'd be a nun with them. But everything changed. At the church, they needed a secretary so I attended business school. I took bookkeeping and studied shorthand for 8 months and I meditated. I was very good at being a secretary, 160 words per minute in shorthand and 65 words per minute in typing.

I was supposed to spend, according to the Self-Realization Program, 2 or 3 hours without thinking. But the more I tried not to think, the more I thought. I did it because Bobby was to become a monk, so I followed it, but eventually I gave up.

Mr. Keith, ready to ask his next question, was stopped by Judge Older to remind him it was time to recess for the weekend.

We returned to the hotel once again.

We went back to court.

Mr. Keith, wearing a dark grey gabardine suit, cleaned his eyeglasses before resuming his questioning. Leslie Van Houten proceeded:

In June of 1968, I graduated from high school. I made all sorts of efforts to get a job. I would fill out applications, would be accepted, and then would go home and say nothing. I didn't work so I would ask my parents for money.

I went to San Francisco with a blonde girl by the name of Dee... something ... I don't remember her last name. We moved into the Haight-Ashbury area of San Francisco and there I met a boy and two girls.

"What were their names?" Mr. Keith wanted to know.

"Bobby Beausoliel and the two girls were Gypsy and Gail."

"What happened then?" insisted the defense counsel.

"The next day they started to go to Oregon. I felt such a feeling being around them—all my life I wanted people like them—I felt completely free—like giving of myself to them."

"Did you join them?" inquired Mr. Keith.

432

"Yes, I did... it was like a little caravan of people. I felt almost individually in love with Bobby—I still am, and more now. Bobby is extremely handsome and very talented. He plays all kinds of musical instruments and writes music."

Leslie Van Houten related her story with a constant smile on her face as she continued:

"At first I had to learn to live with them. We traveled all around in a pick-up truck which in the back, they built a sort of tent. We all used drugs. I liked Gypsy very much but she left for Los Angeles because of the constant arguments and jealousness of Gail."

"When did you meet Charles Manson?" asked Mr. Keith.

"Well, Bobby, Gail and I went to San Jose. There we met a man working in a tatoo shop, who had mistaken Gail and I as two other girls whom he had just left and who had been stranded on a broken school bus. The man told us where the bus was. Charlie was there. I was attracted to the group because of the great freedom and happiness, so we stayed in a prune orchard in San Jose. Eventually, we all moved to the Spahn Ranch."

Describing her life at the Spahn Ranch, the witness said:

"It was like having my very own country house, my own home place. It was a good feeling, just existing."

"Tell us about what you did at the ranch?" asked Mr. Keith.

"Well, I loved the ranch life in contrast to the city life. I felt the city was a big monster—noises, car horns—people rushing, etc., in contrast to the peaceful life where only the sniffing of horses or the roosters in the morning can be heard. The same when I went to the desert—where only the humming of the wind is what one can hear. I only went to the city to get food. At the ranch I would stay and bake bread, wash the diapers. I hardly went out."

"Did you believe Charlie is Jesus Christ?"

"On occasions, I made myself believe that Charlie was Jesus Christ. Charlie is good to me and I am good to Charlie."

"Does LSD make you sleepy?" Mr. Keith questioned.

"LSD does not make you sleepy—it makes you alert. I love acid trips. I like hash and marijuana."

Asked to relate the time she met Gary Hinman, Leslie openly stated:

"I've met Gary Hinman—I went to his house with Bobby and Sadie. I didn't know where Gail was.. maybe she was attending Berkeley University. Anyway, I went along because Bobby had asked me and I always liked to go with Bobby and because Sadie was a friend of Gary Hinman."

"What happened at Gary Hinman's?" interrupted Mr. Keith.

"Sadie and I spent most of the time in the kitchen. Bobby and Gary were

433

arguing and Bobby hit Gary very hard in the mouth and broke some teeth. Bobby called Charlie and Bruce. They came over.

"At one time, everybody was in the kitchen and Gary came from the other room with a gun. He shot among the men—no one was hurt—but it seemed like Gary aimed at Charlie. So, Charlie, carrying a sword, lifted his arm and cut Gary's ear.

"I told Charlie and Bruce to go but Gary came back to attack them. Then Sadie hit him with a gun." Leslie hesitated for a moment, then added:

"I don't remember. I wanted to take care of Gary, but for fear of the police, I didn't. Then, I went back in the kitchen and saw Sadie stabbing Gary."

Leslie also said she saw Sadie writing something on the wall with blood.

Finally, assisted by her attorney, Leslie Van Houten replied cautiously to questions pertaining to the second night of the forays. The convicted murderess cleverly developed a sudden dubious mememory about the events surrounding the death of Rosemary La Bianca.

Mr. Keith interrogating:

"Leslie, can you tell us what happened at the La Bianca home?"

"I can't describe the scene..." quickly replied the witness. "It's all clear in my mind... but somehow I can't describe it."

"Tell us what you remember," prompted her attorney.

"All I can remember is wiping everything with a towel, even things that we didn't touch."

"What else?"

"I also remember Patricia taking the towel from me... and oh yes... on the way out, I saw the body of Lino La Bianca lying on the floor."

"Where was Tex Watson?"

"I don't know where Tex was at the time... maybe next room... I don't know."

"Did you all change clothes because of blood stains before you left the house?"

"We didn't have any change of clothes nor do I recall any blood stains."

"How did you get back to the Spahn Ranch?"

"We hitchhiked back to the ranch—we got more than one ride."

No more questions.

We returned to the hotel.

On the bus, Edith sat next to Ruth to comfort her. The alternate juror fainted again and took for the worse. Shortly after arriving at the hotel, Mrs. Collingwood was transferred and hospitalized at the Granada Hills Community Hospital. The jurors sympathized with the lady juror and wished her well.

434

I never saw Ruth Collingwood again.

The fact of seeing Ruth leaving under those conditions brought a tumult of despair and agony among the jurors. We also wanted to go home.

Ray Harris, instead of feeling sad or angry for having been reinstated, appeared happier. Still, I didn't dare to ask him to tell me the reason of his gaiety nor why he had remained as a juror. He knew something I didn't. However, I noticed that Ray, in the company of Tom, Debbie, Mr. Paine and Violet, while sitting in the recreation room, all equally excited, were discussing the possibilities of leaving for home the next day. Mildred, Olivia, Betty and I tried to verify the rumor through Mollie Kane. The charming blonde bailiff conceded with a smile:

"Yes, most probably, but I'm not sure."

"When is it going to take place?" asked Olivia.

"Maybe tomorrow or the day after tomorrow."

"Why not tonight?" suggested Betty.

Because of Judge Older's orders.

"Shall we start packing now?" inquired Mildred.

"If you want to..."

"I don't need to pack," interrupted Betty, "I've packed a long time ago."

We all laughed. From that moment on, it was like a bomb had exploded. The jurors became more talkative and friendlier to one another. There was a great deal of excitement on account of going home. All the jurors were allowed to telephone their families to break the great news.

Frank Welch wanted to hold an informal meeting among the jurors. He wanted to find out if perhaps we could all ask Judge Older to vacate the order of sending the jurors home. He sustained that the Judge himself had changed his mind and ordered Ray Harris to return to the courtroom and to occupy the same seat as he held before. In all his efforts, Frank didn't succeed and could not even finish his proposal—most of the jurors left. There were only five or six jurors present and all of them, including myself, wanted no part of his proposal. We all wanted to go home and get the hell out of the shaky hotel.

That night I stayed late watching TV in the recreation room and subsequently joined the bailiff sitting in front of Debbie's room, watching the same movie. The sheriff had gone to speak with the other bailiff in the "Little Lobby". I had fallen asleep on and off. Suddenly I saw Tom coming out of Debbie's room. Not wishing to embarrass them I feigned sleep.

Out of the corner of my eye, I saw Tom smile with a kind of tenderness and his eyes blinked, and then as he was closing the door softly, I heard Debbie say "pleasant dreams". "I'm sure they couldn't be otherwise tonight. Same to you," Tom responded, and closed the door.

Tom was too keenly conscious of my presence and tried to analyze his situation and sensations. Everything seemed blurred and he was content to relax at last when he heard me snoring.

We returned to the courtroom.

Effectively, Judge Charles H. Older vacated his order sequestering the jury. We were admonished not to discuss the case with anyone and His Honor concluded saying we would be sequestered again when the time came to deliberate the penalty phase.

In the jury room, Mollie announced:

"The jurors and alternates will be transported to the Hall of Justice each morning. You will drive to the county jail and park your car, and from there we'll bring you here. After the day court session is over, we'll take you back."

She distributed xerox copies of Thomas Guides and circled the meeting place.

Happily, we returned to the hotel.

A mob of newspaper photographers and TV newsmen had congregated at strategic locations to interview the jurors. The news media were not allowed on the sixth floor—so they placed themselves outside the two elevators and at the bottom of the staircases.

Deputy Mollie Kane had arranged to have breakfast served in the recreation room so the jurors could enjoy the company of their families. As the jurors left the hotel, their relatives and friends helped them carry boxes, suitcases and shopping bags filled with belongings that they all had accumulated while being sequestered.

Good old Jim Reid, my contact with the outside world these many months, arrived with my car. To avoid being confronted with reporters, I sent him down with my luggage which allowed me the opportunity to be alone these last moments in my room. In a moment my mind jumped back to reality. I looked at my watch. I walked to the window and looked down on the East Garden and beyond to the city. There stood the building almost finished. Back in July it was only a skeleton. Now, a beautiful building.

I glanced at the hot plate in the bathroom and began to recall the times I had cooked Nicaraguan fried rice and the other times I had boiled water for coffee or tea. Then I turned from the window to look around the room which had been my "home" for so many months. It was haunted by a hundred memories. Laura, the beautiful South American girl had come here to confess her suicidal plans. Mrs. Reid had sat here before me to ask that I be sure to

436

pray every night. And her son, Jim, who many times had visited me just to bring me things that only a friend could think of—like my subscription issues of Playboy Magazine, letters, books and phone messages—and once, even brought my dog Bluffy. My brother had cried and pleaded with me to help him. And, of course, that wonderful birthday surprise party that my friends gave me.

Then I recalled the time when one of the bailiff bus drivers knocked on my door and was ready to hit me. Then I looked at my Sony Tape and brought to my memory the time I invited some of the jurors to listen in semi-darkness to "Sorry, Wrong Number."

Here, in this room, I had started to write notes for this book and also type the main issues of the Tate-La Bianca evidence to present them at deliberation time.

I noticed the bed. I stood there for some seconds gazing at it and visualizing mentally the many times I had used it for comfort and pleasure. On that bed, part of my projects and wishes and dreams and even depressing moods had been formulated while staring at the ceiling. Like a switch, I blinked my eyes and saw the ceiling. I could see the cracks caused by the earthquake. A cold chill ran down my spine.

A sharp knock on the door cut through my reverie. I had completely forgotten that Jim was waiting for me downstairs, and noticed that the watch on my wrist read ten o'clock. I dropped my hand, looked once more rather regretfully around the room, placed the room key on a dresser and hurried out of the room.

Mollie Kane escorted me down the hall and into the elevator.

An NBC cameraman in the company of newscaster Paul Gardner with a mike in hand attempted to interview me and followed me to my car. He wanted me to express my feelings and views about the case and also what I felt toward being sequestered. Needless to say, I adhered to Judge Older's warning and courteously but firmly excused myself, for the only thought on my mind was to get out of those grounds and go home. It had been a long time since I'd been behind a car wheel. I found myself excited and unable to drive, so Jim drove.

It felt great to be out on my own and not a prisoner. The scene outside in the streets was contagious—the sky, though misty looking, appeared blue and alive; the people, the traffic, the weather, everything looked and felt different. All of a sudden I realized I could roll down the window, stick my head out and yell or speak to anyone without having to worry of receiving a warning from any of the stern-faced bailiffs. I felt free and I felt happy.

437

Back in court once again.

Quoting from a transcript book, Mr. Bugliosi questioned Leslie Van Houten about the murder of Gary Hinman:

"Leslie, you testified that you sent Bobby Beausoleil away just before it happened. Is that right?"

"Yes."

"Why then didn't you join him?"

"Because I had to stay with my sister [Susan Atkins]."

"Why, then, didn't you come forward and testify on his behalf when he was tried for Gary Hinman's murder?"

"Because Bobby wouldn't have wanted me to."

"Leslie, wasn't actually Mary Brunner, not Sadie, the other woman who was at the house of Gary Hinman when he was murdered?"

"No."

The prosecutor continued his cross-examination and wanted to know whether she had told anyone outside the "family" that the cult leader had ordered the killings in order to start a black-white race war.

Miss Van Houten hesitated to answer the question when Mr. Kanarek interjected: "I object, Your Honor."

"Mr. Kanarek, would you shut up so I can answer that question?" snapped the witness angrily.

The witness then explained that she once had told Charles Part, her former court-appointed lawyer, that Charles Manson had ordered the Tate murders so he could support a plea of insanity by having a psychiatrist listen to her tape-recorded confessions.

Mr. Bugliosi questioning:

"Did you tell Mr. Part that Charles Manson had ordered these killings?"

"Sure I told him that, but I did it only to answer in the way Mr. Part wanted me to," and with a smile she added, "I fired him."

"How many tape recording sessions did you make with Mr. Part?"

"Three, at the Sybil Brand Institute."

The prosecutor switched his interrogation and proceeded to ask about the second night on August 9, 1969.

"Why did you go along to the La Bianca home?"

"I just wanted to go for a ride, but then Tex decided to stay with Pat so I stayed with them."

"Why did you go inside the La Bianca house?"

"I don't know."

"Why did you stab Mrs. La Bianca?"

"I don't know."

"Why didn't you just leave when you heard Mrs. La Bianca screaming?"

"I don't know."

"Are you saying you can just kill someone?" the prosecutor insisted.

"I don't know why it happened," said the witness. "It just happened."

"In other words," Mr. Bugliosi continued, "you can kill someone anytime for no reason; is that correct?"

"Anybody can kill anything they can kill."

The prosecutor, holding a picture of the victim before Leslie, inquired how many of the 41 stab wounds she had made. The murderess replied she didn't know.

"Why did you continue stabbing Mr. La Bianca?"

"Because I was obsessed with the knife—once it went in, it kept going in and in."

Mr. Bugliosi concluded his interrogation by asking the witness in a rather soft spoken manner:

"Leslie, are you sorry about killing Mrs. La Bianca?"

The slim dark-haired murderess, looking straight at the prosecutor, was pressed for words but made herself heard when she replied:

"Sorry is only a five-letter word." Then somewhat cynically, Leslie added: "I don't feel bad about helping to kill Mrs. La Bianca."

Witness number 13 for the defense was none other than the prosecutor himself.

Personally, I felt no need to jot down the grievances of the defense counsel, Mr. Kanarek, against the prosecutor. The questions pertained about things that had been said inside the corridors of the Hall of Justice and of no absolute importance. The jurors felt it was a waste of time and energy and irrevelant to the case. The jurors would have felt the same had Mr. Bugliosi called Mr. Kanarek to the witness stand. They felt none of the two attorneys were involved in the crimes in question, so why tamper with their patience and the taxpayer's money.

The following witness was Samuel Barrett, who was recolled to the stand. Charles Manson's former parole officer testified that the hippie cult leader was convicted in 1957 of attempting to escape from custody. He identified a document P-5 (Copy of Attempt to Escape). Linda Kasabian, looking a little heavier and wearing a purple cotton ankle peasant dress and her sandy hair pulled back and held with a clasp, was also recalled by Mr. Kanarek.

Under his questioning, she admitted that she knew Gary Hinman had been killed but could not remember how she found out about it.

439

"Did you discuss 'copycat killings' in order to free Bobby Beausoleil?" asked Mr. Kanarek.

"No, I never did," she answered.

The defense counsel then switched to establish that the seven murders were committed by the defendants under the influence of drugs.

"Mrs. Kasabian, could you tell us whether you or anyone else was under the influence of LSD on the evening of August 8, 1969?"

"Not to my knowledge."

"Are you sure?"

"Tex might have taken 'speed'... I don't know."

Unexpectedly, Mr. Kanarek requested that the trial be adjourned to the Tate-La Bianca residences so he could question Linda Kasabian at the murder scenes. Needless to say, His Honor denied the request.

"Your Honor is foreclosing me," insisted Mr. Kanarek.

"That's not true," snapped Judge Older, "ask your next question."

"Your Honor, I have no more questions."

Mr. Keith, interrogating Linda Kasabian for the first time, cleverly tried to obtain negative answers from the witness, as to the participation of his client during the second night. He did not succeed.

Mr. Aaron Stovitz returned to the courtroom as a witness. The sharp-spoken deputy district attorney responded to questions regarding the agreement of immunity for Susan Atkins. Mr. Kanarek insinuatingly asked:

"Is a fair statement to say that you and Mr. Bugliosi had been sort of gold-dust twins in this case?"

"Ridiculous!" objected the prosecutor as he stood up.

His Honor sustained the objection. However, Mr. Kanarek had one more question in the stove:

"Isn't it true that you play the role of God in the district attorney's office?"

"That will conclude your examination, Mr. Kanarek!" snapped Judge Older, and then added, "you may sit down."

"Well—Your Honor," Mr. Kanarek protested softly.

"Sit down," the Court Magistrate ordered firmly.

Mr. Shin called Attorney Paul Caruso to testify in regards to agreements made for Susan Atkins's Grand Jury testimony and for the literary rights to her story.

The oriental descent lawyer began his direct examination by asking the witness whether he had represented Susan Atkins in a document to obtain publication of her story. "Yes," said Mr. Caruso.

Mr. Shin established then that Mr. Caruso and his tenant, Richard Caballero (Susan Atkins's former attorney), had proposed to the district attorney not to seek the death penalty but life in prison if she told the truth to the Grand Jury.

In response to a series of questions, Mr. Caruso said that Lawrence Schiller, a literary agent, was to receive 25% of the revenue from the sale of the story, and Susan Atkins, ex-attorney Richard Caballero and himself were to divide the remaining 75%.

Mr. Caruso declined to say how much money was his total profit and also claimed that he had no knowledge where the Los Angeles Times, on December 14, 1969, had obtained the story referring to Susan Atkins's confession, but suggested that the newspaper should be sued because it did not have a right to the story.

Two more members of the "family", Ruth Morehouse, alias "Ouish" and Steven Crogan, also known as "Clem Tufts", were briefly interrogated.

Miss Morehouse stated, among other things, that her father had introduced her to Charles Manson. Steven Crogan, quite incoherent, testified that he joined the group after he had approached a bus and seen a bunch of people sleeping on the floor (Steve Crogan was found later guilty of first degree murder for the killing of Donald (Shorty) Shea, whose body has never been found).

Another witness, Lawrence Schiller, admitted to having met Attorney Paul Caruso in 1962, and Attorney Richard Caballero on December 5, 1969. The chubby long-haired witness, under Mr. Shinn's questioning, gave his occupation as journalist-communicator and claimed that he did not know the amount of money he had received from the publication of his book, "The Killing of Sharon Tate."

Dr. Andrew N. Tweed, a psychiatrist, testified that he had examined Patricia Krenwinkel. Mr. Fitzgerald, after a lengthy interrogation, had the witness state that Miss Krenwinkel could still have a late residual psychosis and that she could commit murder out of love.

Dr. Tweed, reading at times from a transcript of his interview, mentioned that Miss Krenwinkel demonstrated bizarre ideas about love life and death and right and wrong. Dr. Tweed speaking:

"I also found through my examination that Miss Krenwinkel lacked concern for her situation. Her answers were incomprehensible and she claimed to be able to communicate with her friends by sensory perception."

Then the witness quoted from his notes what Patricia Krenwinkel had told him:

"You can't kill anything... It's impossible to take life because life and death are one."

"You believed Patricia Krenwinkel when you examined her, Dr. Tweed?" asked Mr. Fitzgerald.

"Yes, I did."

"Did Patricia Krenwinkel tell you that she thought she was crazy?"

"No, she didn't."

"Did she lie to you?"

"I don't think so."

"Dr. Tweed, because of personal belief in regards to the death penalty, would you change your medical testimony?"

"No, sir."

"Thank you," concluded Mr. Fitzgerald.

Mr. Kanarek conducted his interrogation in a very derogatory manner. At one time, he brought a piece of paper to the psychiatrist and asked him to draw a diagram of the outer part of the brain. From where I sat in the jury box, I could see the doctor drawing what appeared to be a skull.

"Doctor, what is the weight of the brain?" asked Mr. Kanarek.

Dr. Tweed scratched his hand and looking helplessly said:

"I don't know, Mr. Kanarek."

"Then tell me where's the LSD location in the brain after someone has injected it?"

"I told you, Mr. Kanarek before, that it hadn't been proved yet where LSD goes in the brain... it has not been proven what organic damage may be caused to the brain."

Mr. Kanarek insisted to know why it is not possible to determine if there's brain damage and Dr. Tweed kept answering the same thing. Finally, Mr. Kanarek shouted out loud and said:

"Is it because we are not smart enough?"

Mr. Bugliosi and Mr. Fitzgerald objected that the question was beyond the expertise of the witness, irrelevant, immaterial and beyond the scope of the interrogation. Sustained.

Mr. Kanarek questioning:

"Dr. Tweed, would you say that a person under LSD use has hallucinations?"

"Yes, Mr. Kanarek and I must repeat to all similar questions that a person under the influence of LSD can recollect and describe what she saw—no matter how distorted were the images she saw."

"So, in fact," said Mr. Kanarek, "if she saw God, she could describe God. Is that right?"

"Well, yes because nowadays, we are suppose to have God within ourselves and if she desires to see God in that person, she's only expanding her belief."

"But why then, do you believe certain contents from the report and not others?"

"Because I consider them as facts, she tells me something and I believe them."

"But why do you believe that she committed these things she's accused of?"

Dr. Tweed scratched his head impatiently and not knowing how to answer, he replied:

"I wasn't there, I only know from what she told me and what I read in the papers."

Everybody burst out laughing, including the jurors and the judge himself.

"No more questions," said Mr. Kanarek, also laughing, and went back to his seat but instead sat on Mr. Fitzgerald's seat, who was occupied talking with Charles Manson.

Mr. Bugliosi asked Dr. Tweed if he had read the report submitted by Dr. Claude Brown—who examined Patricia Krenwinkel in Mobile, Alabama— and if he had taken his findings in consideration. Dr. Tweed said he had. Mr. Bugliosi interrogating:

"Did you also take into consideration that Patricia Krenwinkel had stated that she just had come out of a LSD trip when she committed these murders?"

"Yes, I did."

"Now, Dr. Tweed, are you aware that Patricia Krenwinkel is pending in the penalty phase in this case?"

"Yes."

"Is it true that you are opposed to the death penalty?"

"Yes, personally I am."

"No more questions."

Judge Older addressed the jurors and told them that the findings of Dr. Tweed and other doctors, through notes and reports supplied by the defendant's counselor, should not be taken as evidence but only the believability of the doctors.

Dr. Keith S. Ditman, a specialist in the study of alcoholism and drug abuse, was the next witness. Mr. Keith asked the psychiatrist whether the murders at the Tate-La Bianca residences could be attributed to a chronic LSD in an appropriate setting. The witness said "Yes." To prove that theory, Mr. Keith, assisted by some written notes, employed a lengthy hypothetical question outlining Leslie Van Houten's life from childhood up to the murders on the second night. The answers of Dr. Ditman were directed by Mr. Keith to the fact that those killings were committed under the influence of LSD.

No more questions.

Mr. Bugliosi asking:

"Doctor, are you a personal friend of Mr. Keith?"

"Yes."

"Did you read all the testimony of Leslie Van Houten?"

"No."

"Don't you think that it would have helped to have read the entire testimony?"

"No."

"You have no way of knowing if Leslie has any homicidal inheritance, is that correct?"

"That's right."

"Doctor, you have no way of knowing whether she was under the influence of LSD the night of the murders?"

"No."

"Assuming that she didn't have any influence of LSD, would your opinion change?"

"No."

No more questions.

Mr. Keith inquired:

"Doctor, the fact that you know me personally, does that affect your testimony?"

"No."

"You are telling the truth. Is that right?"

"Yes."

No more questions.

Dr. Joel Forte, after giving a lengthy explanation of his background, stated that he had examined Leslie Van Houten, and then he described what a "bad trip" was.

Under Mr. Bugliosi's cross-examination, the witness declared that he couldn't say if Leslie Van Houten had a bad trip at the time she committed the murders.

Richard Caballero, ex-attorney of Susan Atkins, testified under Mr. Shin's direct examination that he had been appointed by Judge Tom Keene as her representative.

Mr. Shin asked the elegantly attired attorney questions regarding factors between him and his ex-client, Susan Atkins, and his association with Paul Caruso and Lawrence Schiller as partners on the publication of the book, "The Killing of Sharon Tate." Mr. Caballero, as well as his associates, stated he didn't know the amount of her share.

Mr. Fitzgerald put a drastic question to the witness:

"Why did you allow a publisher—a non-lawyer such as Schiller—to 'run the show' and even let him write contracts pertaining to your client?"

The short-looking attorney didn't know how to answer and simply replied: "I didn't think the publicity could hurt her."

Mr. Kanarek tried restlessly to corner the well-spoken attorney by asking questions such as:

"Why didn't you do anything whatsoever to stop Mr. Schiller from publishing any part of the transcript confession of Susan Atkins?" and "Why didn't Miss Atkins get immunity?" and "Why didn't you acknowledge her from testifying on the Grand Jury?" and "Why didn't you tell her of her constitutional rights?"

Mr. Caballero cleverly escaped from incriminating himself and responded: "I didn't want to get myself involved."

Manson shouted out loud and said: "He got the money—that's all he wanted and we all know it!"

Mr. Caballero, smartly dressed and well-spoken, appeared as a man that knows his business—he constantly smiled— a smile on one side of his mouth, a sort of a smirk. His teeth are uneven and that might be the reason he held himself from laughing heartily.

Judge Older admonished the jurors to disregard what the prisoner uttered and the trial continued.

Mr. Keith always kept in mind his primary interest—that of his client. He asked:

"In talking about the Hinman case, I presume Susan Atkins told you who was present?"

"Yes."

"Did she tell you that Leslie Van Houten was present?"

"No."

"Thank you," Mr. Keith said and sat down.

Mr. Bugliosi asked the witness on cross examination to describe what Susan Atkins had said was Manson's part in the murders.

Attorney Caballero quoted the murderess as saying:

"She said that Manson had asked her to go to Gary Hinman's home, to tie up the musician, force him to sign over his property and then kill him. Then later on, they had been buying dark clothes for creepy crawling missions and that Manson advised Charles Watson to go to Sharon Tate's home and order his girls 'to go with Tex and do what they were told,' and she also said, 'we were instructed to go to the next door neighbor's house and do the same thing.'"

"What else did she tell you?"

"On the second night she said that when Charlie had gone inside the La

445

Bianca residence alone and tied both victims, he came back and told Tex, 'last night you blew it—this time make them think everything's okay and let them go in peace.' "

"Did Susan Atkins tell you what was the motive of these murders?"

"Yes."

"What did she say?"

"Oh one occasion she told me something about Helter Skelter."

Mr. Caballero elaborated on explaining the theory about a white-black race war Susan Atkins had told him about and concluded by saying:

"It wasn't until she received visitors, she began to tell me consequently, as a matter of fact emphatically, that she had lied to me."

Dr. Joel Simon, another psychiatrist, testified under defense counsel direct examination that he had examined the three female defendants. The witness found Leslie Van Houten, psychologically speaking, mentally unbalanced while committing the crimes.

Mr. Bugliosi asking:

"Dr. Simon, on your examination, did Leslie tell you she had sexual intercourse before the age of 14 years old with other than Bobby Mackey?"

"Yes, she did, and later she manifested that he was the first who really 'turned her on.' He impregnated her and she had an abortion which, by the way, is the only thing he won't forgive her mother, although it was the moral thing to do at the time."

The doctor continued saying that Leslie had told him she hit her sister without shame for what he believed was the beginning of her impulses and that, at the time of the murders at the La Bianca home, she used Rosemary La Bianca only as an object—an alien—to perpetrate her impulses.

Under Mr. Fitzgerald's examination, the witness disclosed that of the three female defendants, Patricia Krenwinkel was the most liable to fall into a severe psychosis and that she would be a difficult patient to cure or to take care of. Dr. Simon said that her disturbance probably started at infancy and that, as a child, she had little control of her development.

Mr. Fitzgerald asked:

"How old was she when she first injected LSD?"

"She told me she was in a car with some hippie friends who asked her to open her mouth. She questioned what it was—LSD they told her. After she looked around all their faces, she went to the restroom and saw herself in the mirror. She saw mirrors all around the place—she saw herself ugly. She went home and her mother looked as if she was the devil. The next day she felt bad and decided to go to college in Mobile, Alabama. She was 17 years old."

Mr. Fitzgerald asked if the witness thought Patricia Krenwinkel had psychosis at the time of the crimes. Dr. Simon responded he had read a report from a doctor in Alabama but her history didn't reflect any schizophrenia and consequently, he would be bound to say "no."

When Mr. Shin questioned Dr. Simon about his client, the witness replied:

"Susan described herself as becoming an alcoholic at the age of 16 years old like her parents. She told me she would 'bawd' with older men but that she would have to get drunk to face it. At 17 years old, she took marijuana. At 18 years, she asked a fellow by the name of 'Mike' to sell her LSD. The man paranoided and they went together to get some at Market Street in San Francisco. After taking it, the city looked like a big monster—cable cars and everything. At the hotel room, she felt like everything and that everybody was against her. Mike, who reminded her of her brother, told her that she could transform all her thoughts into what she wanted so she changed into vines and roses and everything became a paradise. She became a gangster-moll—even a prostitute—although she only thought herself like that. She said she felt relieved her mother died after nine years of suffering of leukemia. Her childhood was a deprived situation for lack of love and because her father was a drunken bum."

Mr. Shin asked if Susan had any remorse for the victims. Dr. Simon replied that he thought Miss Atkins would show more than the others, but that, again, he would be bound to say "no."

Evelle J. Younger, Attorney General of California, and former Los Angeles City District Attorney, testified he knew Paul Caruso, Richard Caballero and Mr. Bugliosi.

The ex-boss of Mr. Bugliosi answered questions regarding the publication of the book *The Killing of Sharon Tate*. The witness flatly emphasized that because of the reference through the prosecutor, he had decided to seek the death penalty for Susan Atkins. He felt that she didn't say the truth during the Grand Jury trial.

The hippie cult leader and the three defendants were ejected from court for disturbing the trial. They listened to proceedings over a loud speaker.

Carmela Ambrossini, a certified shorthand reporter, testified that she took a statement from Miss Atkins. Asked if she had heard of the gag order, she said:

"Yes, I heard it on the radio and I inquired about it while Mr. Caballero, Mr. Jerry Cohen and I were in the car going to Sybil Brand Institute."

The witness also stated she heard something about the book being published only in foreign countries and about some recorded tapes in regard to how the crimes had been committed.

At home, among my notes, I found the following:

"On Sunday, March 7, 1971, at 2:00 P.M., in the afternoon, the photographer from Life Magazine came over the house and took some pictures of myself and Bluffy, my dog. Bluffy, at my command, performed all the tricks that I taught him and I'm sure all the pictures will come out okay, especially when the photographer, as he laughed, mentioned 'He's marvelous.' Then he caught himself and looking at me added, 'And, of course, you too.' The interview didn't take place—they'll do it after the end of the penalty phase—hopefully soon."

Since the day we had returned home, the jurors had been driving to the County Jail parking lot and from there to the Hall of Justice Building in a jail bus.

There was an air of lack of friendliness—very few jurors spoke to one another and the rest stayed alone and minded their own business. Mr. Paine, Marvin, Tom and Larry would congregate at the entrance of the building and have a cup of coffee from a machine.

Inside the bus waiting were Mr. Welch, eagerly working up the solution of the daily newspaper crossword puzzle. Mildred would knit. Genaro would read a new western paperback book while smoking. Debbie, Violet, Edith and Danny would just wait. Everybody automatically sat in the same places. Betty, Mr. White and I would leisurely walk beside the bus until depature time.

One morning, the driveway at the entrance of the Hall of Justice was jammed with the early traffic of cars and buses. Our bus had parked along Spring Street, so Deputy Taylor suggested we step down and walk. We did but at that particular instant, a young attractive blonde was walking by and flirtatiously smiled at the jurors. Her blonde hair, partially covering her face, reminded me of Veronica Lake. Marvin and I couldn't resist the jerky and voluptuous movements of her walking. Her dress was tight and left very little to the imagination. Marv and I slowed down our pace and stayed last while Mollie noticed the girl and our intentions. Mollie made sure we kept on walking and ordered the girl to do the same. I didn't understand it and somehow I resented the tough looking bailiff's intrusion. "Why?" I asked Marvin, "It doesn't make sense, now that we go home, we can talk to anyone, without being harrassed by these deputies." "Unbelievable," Marvin said, still looking at the girl's derrière.

When we walked in the courtroom, Marvin and I looked at each other in

448

disbelief. The person seated on the witness stand was none other than the girl we had seen outside. Marvin and I understood Mollie's attitude and were glad we didn't speak to the girl. We both felt Mollie was right.

Catherine Anne Gillies, the girl on the stand, occasionally smiled at the defendants who returned to court after promising to behave. Manson refused to make the same promise and was kept in a holding room next to the courtroom.

Miss Gillies declared she was a member of the family and that she lived for months in a truck outside the Hall of Justice during the trial.

The young woman's testimony suggested an alibi for Charles Manson on the night of the La Bianca murders. She said that he was in Devil's Canyon with a girl named Stephanie Schram the morning her friend Katie [Miss Krenwinkel] arrived and told her about the two nights of murder.

Miss Gillies constantly combed her long hair with the fingers of her left hand and at one time I noticed her forehead still showed the faint scar "X".

"When Miss Krenwinkel told you about the murders, did you ask any questions?" inquired Mr. Kanarek.

"No, I didn't have to—it was evident to me why they took place."

Then she indicated the motive for the murders—previously discussed by the women at the ranch—it was to free Bobby Beausoleil, who had been arrested on a charge for killing musician Gary Hinman. She explained:

"If there was another murder identical to that, it would be obvious that the killer was not in jail. However, on that night, when they left the ranch and went to the La Bianca house, I thought they probably were going out to steal something."

Mr. Kanarek questioning Miss Gillies:

"Would you have gone with them and did what they did?"

"Of course, I would have killed that night if I had gone along, but I didn't go because they didn't need me."

"What would have been the reason for killing?" insisted the defense counsel.

"I'd be willing to kill for the love of my brothers and sisters."

"Are you talking about the first or second night?"

"It didn't really matter—its all one thing... because I don't see any distinction or division."

"How long do you know Mr. Manson?"

"Three years."

"Is Mr. Manson your leader?"

"He's his own leader. I'm my own leader." Then she added: "I've never

449

heard Charlie order anyone to do anything."

Mr. Kanarek's next question was daring and almost too shocking to answer: "Miss Gillies, would you do... would you do what they did had you the opportunity now?"

Miss Gillies' look suddenly went beyond the power of description. She turned her eyes toward the jurors and the audience and openly stated: "I'd be willing to kill for the love of my brothers and sisters."

When I heard her saying that, I dared not to tremble for fear of showing panic. But there was no doubt I was petrified and speechless. I wondered what the people in the courtroom were thinking. Were they concerned? Were they afraid of future consequences? As I looked at the audience, I noticed their faces were attentive and perplexed by the statements made by the witness.

The jurors, likewise, didn't try to react. They just sat motionless and somber looking. It was too much to listen and not be able to feel fear for our families and dear ones.

Yes, I thought of my parents, my own brothers and sisters. I thought what could happen to them because of my being a juror on the Manson trial. My hands were moist and my mouth fell dry. I had consumed all the wetness in my mouth and tried not to show any emotion. Gradually, I felt perspiration and a cold chill shot through my spine. Motionless, I looked at the witness and somehow her words were almost materializing in my mind—for a flash of a second that seemed like an eternity, I found myself at home—sleeping late at night...... Suddenly, I was awakened by a painful lament that sounded like it was coming from the hall. I rushed out of bed and saw my dog, Bluffy, lying and covered with blood, vainly trying to wiggle his tail upon my presence. I bent over to take care of him, took his head in my hands, but soon realized he was dead. I laid him down. Instantly, still looking down, before me I saw two or three barefooted people. I looked up and noticed as they moved around me their faces were masked with red mesh stockings. "Who are you? What the hell do you want?" I was asking them. They didn't utter a word, just motioned me to get up. I could tell they were two men and a woman. Following their orders, I tried to look behind me but a pair of strong hands had gotten hold of my arms and twisted them backwards. "What is this?" I was protesting unable to release myself. A hard blow to the back of my head and. . . .

Returning to reality again, I heard the court clerk asking the new witness to repeat her name.

Mary Brunner, originally from Wisconsin, was another member of the family who testified she met Charles Manson in April 1967. She has a bachelor's degree and was assistant librarian at the Berkeley University. Miss

Brunner, who was in custody of the authorities, claimed she had a son whose father is Charles Manson.

The next day:

Again we sat in the jury box, to hear the final arguments of the penalty phase. Mr. Bugliosi began his summation, first with a recapitulation of the evidence. He recalled the testimony of each of the witnesses. He defended the testimony of the prosecution's star witness, Linda Kasabian.

He maintained that her confession alone should be reason enough for a guilty verdict for all the defendants. Mr. Bugliosi said, among other things:

"When I said these defendants committed seven murders, it doesn't mean I included Leslie Van Houten. I do not have to tell you how much dlfficulty you will bear in you final decision. The defense counsel will not be able to assist you nor I nor Judge Older."

The prosecutor went on to give a fine recitation of what it meant to kill in the first degree. Mr. Bugliosi had prepared his case and he knew the law. His strength did not rest upon trickery. It was his intesnse and thorough preparation for the trial. It showed that he had done a lot of studying and that he had worked with the case long hours after each court session.

He continued:

"After the unbelievable, savage, ghostly and bizarre murders they committed—viciously, inhumanly taking seven human lives—there's no reason under the stars why these seven murders should have been committed. I know the counsel will try to give you the talk to have these four defendants given life in prison and I say that's commendable—they are their clients. They will also tell you that the three defendants are female and young. We, the Law in California, do not stipulate genders—it's APPLICABLE TO ALL REGARDLESS of who's guilty and certainly they are all guilty of first degree murder. They testified and confessed they had committed those horrible horrendous murders. There's no reason why these defendants should be given life in prison; if that is the case, they should be kept for only ten days.

"These defendants should be found guilty of death—these defendants committed murder in the most terrible manner. I've heard of animals and human beings killing for food, but these killed not for food, but for pleasure.

"Ladies and Gentlemen of the jury, I'm confident that you'll have no problem in finding these defendants guilty, to be put to death. I see twelve honest people who represent a community. The whole world is focusing on your verdict and expect you to give them the benefit of your only verdict—Guilty. Thank you."

OK-Good!! Mr. Kanarek stood up and began his final argument:

"The truth was so tarnished by the Attorney General, who was running for that office. When the prosecution has made its mind up like the public prosecutor has at this moment that Susan Atkins should get the death penalty —when in fact, it was a political movement—when the district attorney should say: 'I got a gold star because I got Charles Manson.'

"This case has become entertainment—it has become big business. We don't need it—it is the last thing we need—it has become a livelihood for some members of the press-TV media.

"Now, when we speak about who's going into the penalty phase, we must deal with the instructions of the court. The jurors have the discretion to find the penalty of death." Judge Older stopped the defense counsel and told him:

"Mr. Kanarek, stop using words I wouldn't use," then reflectively added, "in fact, I wouldn't use any of those words. Proceed with your argument."

"Yes, Your Honor," Mr. Kanarek humbly replied and continued saying that the prosecution had made Manson appear as a person of unbelievable attributes to the point of calling him a monster. Mr. Kanarek brought to our attention the "Lotsa Poppa" incident and went on to explain that his client was capable of doing his own thing rather than having someone else doing it for him. He questioned:

"What is this genesis? What is the beginning of all these matters?"

Then he approached the jury box with some photographs to show the jurors. He showed Gary Hinman's residence, and made point after point that the words written on one photo—"Death to Political Pigs"—and those written in the Tate-La Bianca residence surely indicated that his client was innocent of those charges.

Mr. Kanarek, aided by a blackboard which he placed in front of the jury box, wrote some points of interest which he stated were of vital participation for us, the jurors, to decide one way or another. He continued:

"The prosecution could put all the evidence they can but it is a known fact that Mr. Manson spent seventeen years in prison. Mr. Manson has no parents —biological yes, but parents in the physical aspect, no. He has not had the benefits and background that these female defendants have had. We can easily say that they are high school graduates and even Patricia Krenwinkel I believe has some college. But Mr. Manson has had less than desirable whatever level school we choose. So when we speak of human values, well, we can't ponder what the prosecution says that they are human monsters. Is this fitting in this case when we compare these defendants with Mr. Manson? Well, even Linda Kasabian, who lived comfortably with a reliable mother, although she didn't have too much school. So, we look at his background and we see that it's

452

incredible that one person who has been called an accomplice, it would be grossly unfair and we suggest that this should be considered at your discretion while deliberating.

"I'm sure that looking at it, it would be a reasonable assumption that he deserves life in prison and not death. Except for the tragedy of these events, we may not approve but, except for the life of Mr. Manson at the Spahn Ranch, there was no indication that he was doing anything or that he was violating any federal court.

"Now, about the victims. I'm not demeaning their passing away, but certainly we think that if they had been in control of their faculties, maybe something else would have occurred. Frykowski, Abigail Folger, and Sebring— had they not used narcotics, they could have been able to sustain their faculties. Maybe not Steven Parent, but certainly, it's just the circumstances. The fact of the matter is that people who use these narcotics do get the usual results. Also, the fact that Mr. Watson was dealing with narcotics, he may have taken a great quantity before going to the Tate residence. These are matters which bear some kind of attention, it may well be that Mr. Watson and Linda Kasabian might have had some kind of feeling of doing whatever they did."

Mr. Kanarek, in order to save his client's life, brought issues against the female defendants. Oddly enough, there were no objections and it became obvious that perhaps the other defense counsel expected mercy from the jurors on account of their clients were female.

Weekend recess.

I took off for San Francisco. I spent a very relaxing weekend. I enjoyed seeing my family and some friends but most of all, I was glad to see my parents. They were thrilled to see me. My father seemed to be holding his own after a series of heart attacks in addition to a line of complicated ailments. However, my mother was my main interest. She had been the issue of my concern and was worried about her condition. She hardly had ever been sick but during the months I was sequestered, she had been ill. Her letters had stopped coming in and like mothers are, she avoided letting me know about her health so as not to worry me. But mothers can overlook the intuition of their children sometimes and somehow I felt deep in my heart she was hiding something from me. She didn't look well. I discovered my mother was gravely ill with cancer. Brokenhearted, I returned to Los Angeles.

Returned to court.

A change flourished among the jurors. The distance of relationships was obvious and quite open. Everybody dispersed and there was very little talk.

We just looked at each other. The "clique" still remained together and maintained their together-ness about being noisy, uproarious and obnoxious to the rest of the jurors. The only difference was that the clique made the noises face-to-face—there was no longer a game of hide-and-seek. We all accepted one another and just waited until the end of the penalty phase.

Three days had passed and Mr. Kanarek still argued for the life of his client. The curly-haired defense attorney reiterated arguments previously offered, mainly that his client was the victim of politics, publicity and the desire to make money. He continued:

"The reason Mr. Manson has been in trouble is because of the old ancient desire—that he likes girls—that he may have some type of constant desire for girls—surely that has been his problem."

The chunky looking lawyer changed his line of thinking and said:

"Now, if we're going to deal with a race war concept and we have a very sophisticated group of people, why then did it not start at the Hinman house when Susan Atkins wrote 'Death to Political Pigs?' It would seem like that would have been the beginning of this race war and not after. The prosecution is going to repute this and even argue about it. These girls are saying the truth —its not easy to do, but it is an ingratiating thing to do."

Mr. Kanarek, assisted with court transcripts, read some passages. He shouted out loud and got involved in a series of contraceptions of words which he ultimately managed to utter. Mr. Kanarek's mind was full of thoughts but somehow they didn't come out as fast as he would have liked them to. Mr. Kanarek thanked the jury and sat down.

Unexpectedly, Judge Older announced that the jurors would be sequestered following the court session. We couldn't understand it.

The jurors were driven to the Alexandria Hotel in downtown Los Angeles. The hotel, an old landmark in the city, had been redecorated and the manager was most pleasant and helpful. However, the rooms were not as good as the Ambassador.

Mollie immediately selected a wall to use as a bulletin board and a T-square corridor section as the new "Little Lobby" for meetings. The jurors didn't seem to mind their rooms, except for Edith and Debbie, who exchanged rooms. No one cared what the rooms looked like since it was only for a short time.

An empty room, still being refurbished, was converted by Ray and Marvin into a place to play ping-pong. The recreation room, located at the end of the hall and designed totally in French renaissance style, was feminine and delicate—almost too uncomfortable under the circumstances.

We returned to court.

Mr. Shin began his final argument by stating he would concentrate solely on the meetings that took place between Evelle Younger, Attorney General, Mr. Bugliosi and Mr. Aaron Stovitz, both deputy district attorneys, and the two attorneys, Paul Caruso and Richard Caballero—a meeting in which was discussed the interest of Susan Atkins.

Mr. Shinn introduced some memoranda and agreements all related to the value of Miss Atkins and how good and truthful they were at the time in view of her full cooperation.

The short looking lawyer claimed that because his client had testified truthfully, they would seek life in prison rather than death. He further stated that he could make a fair inference by saying that the five people in the meeting actually conspired against the life of his client, Susan Atkins. He argued:

"I based this statement because of the previous association of the people involved in that meeting. They decided what to do with her life. If these five people had been legitimately honest, they would have made an attempt to save Miss Atkins's life. Doesn't it appear strange that these people didn't have any contracts, or tapes or any type of agreement? They had a meeting on December 4, 1969 and they had no intentions to save her life—but making an honest inference was to give Mr. Caballero and Mr. Caruso an opportunity to make money—they are the ones who got the money, and not because of what the attorney general said that Susan Atkins did not say 100% the truth."

Mr. Shin brought force to his argument when he stated:

"I don't know if Judge Keene had done something in regards to the violation of the gag order."

He finished saying:

"These five people got money and Susan Atkins didn't."

Mr. Keith followed immediately after, by uttering:

"Leslie Van Houten must live, Ladies and Gentlemen. I almost feel I must insist that she must live, but I can only wish that you must return the verdict of life in prison. You are individuals, Ladies and Gentlemen—you have strength—integrity. We don't know what the world wants when the district attorney says that the eyes of the world want death. Don't let yourself believe what the prosecution wants you to do. We're here today for justice—don't be swayed by what your friends and community want you to do—it'll be catastrophic—tremble if you do what they want you to do.

"I feel uneasy when it comes to the penalty phase. Doctors, lawyers, engineers, etc. and those we are in the solemnity of this court, and they have asked you to take life. I'm going to ask you again to give life to Leslie Van Houten. I'm not demeaning the loss of the life of Rosemary La Bianca, but you would be more humane than what the little girl did, and if you don't, you will, after I finish this argument. Don't measure your decision by the quantity of blood in this case—don't be influenced by the amount of blood. I'll give you an example:

"If a person dies by a pin in the heart and only bleeds internally, should not it be just as much a death as any other? The very insanity of these crimes shows the essence close to insanity. It doesn't take a doctor or psychiatry to see its insanity—it is illustrated to you how vain, how insane those girls must have been—the repetition of the mere facts; doesn't that lead you to conclude the insanity of these defendants? Why don't we try to help them? Give them therapy—try to give them rehabilitation to bring them back to society and not destroy them to give them death.

"Mr. Bugliosi read to you at the close of his argument the roll call of the dead. Let me read you the roll call of the living: 'Squeaky'—Brenda—Gypsy, etc., and no doubt many others—their destruction is beyond repair, let's hope not."

Mr. Keith, speaking softly, continued his argument in a powerful and emotional delivery. He hardly spoke a sentence without being moved and it was his sound knowledge of law and the preparation which made him appear like a professional veteran of his craft.

He continued:

"Look at Leslie Van Houten at the age of 14, already a drug addict, a lost personality—the more personal problems she had, the more intensified her mind became. I suggest to you that it was a vacuum—a vacuum for the intrusion of the devil—vulnerable—took nothing serious—living only for the day. She was not prepared for what happened—she had no chance.

"I wonder if anyone of us would have. Yes, she made a decision—some sort of decision. She alienated herself from society. No way, no contradictory force. None. What are we talking about? A human monster? No, we're talking about a little girl. Her systematical mental capacity has been destroyed. We can see it, you can see it."

Mr. Keith moved with force and decision and attempted to even use Mr. Bugliosi as being sympathetic to Leslie, to which the prosecutor objected as not having any foundation of evidence nor even an inference. The judge overlooked the objection and told Mr. Keith to continue. He did:

"She has been condemned like a soldier in battle. I know what I'm talking about. I've done it. This is not Leslie you know of—it's a caricature of a lovely homecoming princess—so LSD took hold of her much faster. She didn't want to stop.

"Ladies and Gentlemen, I'm not trying to say that some of the blame should't be attached when she was going downhill but she needed to turn to someone —there was no one—none—nothing. I don't want anyone of you to think that I don't like Leslie, on the contrary, I like her—I'm very fond of her. I feel better for what has been going on in this court. She really needs help. I ask you to give it to her. I used the analogy of war—for Leslie, the war is over, but maybe there's a spark left in her."

Mr. Keith solemnly ended his emotional argument:

"We don't give very often our society an opportunity—this is your opportunity—take it—grab it. What does it do to us? It makes killers of us—it makes us play God. That's not for us. What social benefit would society gain by putting Leslie to death? To put this little girl to death? The only thing we would accomplish would be to demean ourselves. Let her live—let Leslie live—she'll die slowly and painfully but Leslie will live again. Thank you, Ladies and Gentlemen."

It was obvious Mr. Keith had made an impact upon the jurors and those present. His words were still echoing in the courtroom as we exited for the day.

Mr. Fitzgerald began his summation. He looked pale and seemed tired. He spoke solemnly:

"It's been a long trial. I'll try to be brief as I can. I'll try to answer certain questions that you may have in your mind. You're like an emperor who can raise his thumb for life or down for death. You alone—each one of you—is the one to determine the death of these defendants. They cannot die without your approval or decision—you're the person to decide their lives or death."

Mr. Fitzgerald, tall and slim looking with one hand on the podium and the other in his jacket, increased the tone of his voice to a tremendous plateau. The seriousness of his presentation was somber and one may say it was like an erupting volcano that, instead of lava snaking on the ground and burning everything in its way, his words came out of his mouth like statements of meaningful thoughts—hitting our minds. His eyes searching the jurors' eyes, especially at this author when he related to a 1814 edict in Russia that called for the execution of bearded people, who refused to shave. I, at the time, had a full-grown beard. No, I didn't feel any uneasiness from that fact but it became obvious.

Mr. Fitzgerald went on to speak eloquently by reading a number of issues which pertained to the absolution of death in 93 counties but he was objected to promptly by the prosecutor and sustained by Judge Older. Mr. Fitzgerald changed his pattern of thinking to LSD.

457

"When you left home, you didn't leave your common sense in your homes. You didn't have to hear from a doctor for you to know that these defendants had an insanity in them. The testimony has indicated that the drugs injected and the effect—destination—mood and behavior is hallucination. Sometimes it causes fear and panic on terrifying occasions. Under the influence of these drugs, one is less responsible—also displays homicidal urges, which would appear very real. The religious mystical feeling is profound and the distinction between fantasy and reality is blurred.

"LSD also changes the personality often with disastrous results, particularly with those that have previous psychological and severe emotional personalities, attitudes and adverse instincts. Drastic complications can follow the use of the drug."

Mr. Fitzgerald suggested Diane Lake as an example when he claimed her psychosis occurred almost after she had taken LSD, and continued:

"Patricia Krenwinkel is suffering a chronic residual result of taking LSD and most important is the fact that she prolonged the use of LSD. She lacked the use of logical judgment. She was not responsible—she had a philosophical naivete, replete with bizarre beliefs, a feeling of brotherhood and love, even lifting her finger to indicate that she has demonstrable psychosis, and the rest of the witnesses demonstrated an impediment in rational logical thinking—incoherency. All because of the use of drugs and LSD. Bear in mind also the powerful preexisting personality and environment she had been committed to—the type of life she experimented at the Spahn Ranch."

When we returned from lunch recess, Mr. Fitzgerald informed the jurors that the proceedings in the penalty phase were quite different than the proceedings of the guilty phase. He explained:

"In the penalty phase, the prosecution summarizes and then the defense rests. However, if the prosecution chooses to answer those statements on the final summation, the defense is also entitled to answer again."

Then he returned to his argument:

"This is the first murder case caused by LSD in conjunction with a poor organized mental personality and if this doesn't convince you, ask yourself a question: Would you allow your children to take a dose of LSD? Would you take it yourself? Killing these children is just killing the potential resources of finding the cause of these murders. We can study these mentally-ill defendants. Don't let this opportunity go by. Save them from death. If we care not to cure the ill, then justice has not been vindicated, the noble history of this great country of ours has been denied of justice—justice for all."

Mr. Fitzgerald read a letter addressed to the City of Philadelphia—a letter written from a father whose three-and-a-half-year-old child had been killed by a fifteen-year-old boy. The contents of the letter sounded very profound and sincere. The father admitted the desire to kill the boy had he been present at the time of his child's murder. But because of the past demeanor—character and good behavior of the boy—he found himself unable to kill for vengeance. So he felt sorry for the boy. The finally signed letter read: "A Sick Father".

Mr. Fitzgerald, with moist eyes and sad face, concluded his argument by begging and imploring for the life of Patricia Krenwinkel. He thanked the jury.

The deputy district attorney asked Judge Older to approach the bench before he resumed his final summation. The prosecutor stated he would not take as long as the defense counsel but he would clear for the jurors certain attacks made, namely, by Irving Kanarek. Mr. Bugliosi, in an erudite style, called the accusations unbelievable and said that he was not going to answer the preposterous statements. He spoke:

"I don't know just how much influence you were taken in by Mr. Kanarek's accusations and so I would have to answer it all. I couldn't be bothered. Nor do I have the interest, but I certainly can make an inference—only one —because you know through this whole trial he has used 200 or 300 inferences to the point that we lost track of all of them. I'm allowed to make as many inferences but I will make an honest and fair inference just like he. My only inference is that the only trust—the whole bulk of his argument is based in accusing the prosecutor in this case: myself and my two assistants. He went on to accuse the Attorney General and the police and accused of false agreement with Mr. Caballero and Mr. Caruso. If you think, Ladies and Gentlemen, he even went so far as to insult your intelligence by calling you murderers if you come out with a verdict of death from the jury room. Nothing could be farther from the truth—to try to tell you that because of political reasons, we try to make it appear that man inside [Mr. Bugliosi directed his finger at the cell where Manson was locked] is a monster in order to get political power. He pointed out that Charles is innocent. Ladies and Gentlemen, this is not the guilty phase—he speaks as if he was innocent—the ball game is over. This is a new game—this is the penalty phase, Ladies and Gentlemen."

In a formidable and brilliant manner, Mr. Bugliosi delivered his final argument with sounding voice. The spectators were silent, but vividly attentive. The adjoining press section were concentrating and jotting down what the prosecutor was shouting, bringing impact, order and excitement to the court room.

In reference to life in prison or death, Mr. Bugliosi maintained that the defendants should automatically receive the death penalty. He stipulated:

"These crimes are so horrendous that when Mr. Keith, counsel for Leslie Van Houten, spoke of this crime, he himself held at least five seconds. He couldn't find other murders in the past that could equal the nature, the bizarre and brutal means by which these seven victims were murdered. Mr. Shin argues that the district attorney offered life in prison to Susan Atkins. I remind you, Ladies and Gentlemen, that the law of this state does not specify for you to consider any agreement and that is not the issue. Judge Older will instruct you on that."

Mr. Bugliosi then read part of a confession where Susan Atkins declared and signed a statement that she had lied during the testimony at the Grand Jury.

To answer Mr. Fitzgerald's LSD theory, Mr. Bugliosi argued:

"Having personality and mental disorder doesn't mean that these defendants should be spared. These defendants knew what they were doing. They premeditated these cold murders. The fact that Patricia Krenwinkel told Linda Kasabian: 'Listen for sounds.' That's why Charles Watson cut wires, climbed the fence and cut the screen window. They knew what they were doing—they knew reality from fantasy and consequently, they knew exactly what they were doing. Vicious? Yes, they are vicious. Weird? Yes. Strange? Yes. Way out? Yes. Bizarre? Yes. But Insanity? NO. Mental illness? NO.

"The four counselors of the defense brought four psychiatrists as witnesses and no one of them, Ladies and Gentlemen, no one of them asked if their clients had ever been insane nor if they had a mental or personality disorder."

Mr. Bugliosi's well prepared argument showed there was little about the defendants or witnesses that he did not know. He showed also that he had gone to an excruciating study and painstaking investigation of the testimonies by each of those psychiatrists resulting in evidence presented and interpreted dramatically for the benefit of the jurors and the public in the courtroom. He brought a sample and said:

"Among these samples is the fact that Linda Kasabian should be a way of believing—why should she be an exception? And she herself testified that they had not taken LSD and Susan Atkins had told me personally that they were not under the influence of LSD and you can bet your last dollar that Charles Manson would not allow his killers to plunge their knives in their victims under LSD. Furthermore, Dr. Ditman testified that these three female defendants were under the absolute influence of Charles Manson while they committed the crimes. During the years since LSD was discovered, millions of people had taken it and the results never had been homicidal instincts, but

460

peaceful, non-violent. One other factor and the main factor that Leslie Van Houten is a killer. Why? Because she killed. That's why."

Mr. Bugliosi then read from the report of a psychiatrist:

"'Dr. Detman: How come you killed?'

'Leslie Van Houten: Something inside of me—a rage, an emotional rage to kill someone. It's easier to kill someone you don't know than someone you like.'

"Dr. Detman testified that Leslie Van Houten had a feeling of anger and rage for a long time against the establishment. There's no section in the Penal Code of California where it says that a person who kills under the order of someone that shouldn't receive the death penalty. Mr. Keith told us that Leslie Van Houten was not always a killer. Of course, she was not a killer when she came out of her mother's womb... but she developed. Of course she was not born with a knife and a gun to go and kill, but she developed. There's always a reason why a particular defendant commits a murder—there's always a reason.

"Manson's influence was their reason. It's not uncommon. The Nazis committed murders, look at the thousands and thousands of prisoners murdered by the Nazis. The defendants belonged to the family. Notable gangs —they all have leaders and they all are responsible. Al Capone, who had hoodlums who committed murders and hid from the authorities. They all were guilty. They couldn't get away from being guilty. There's no evidence that Charles Manson forced anyone of these defendants or that they were pushed or forced to commit murder. In fact, there's ample proof of their desire to kill. Catherine Gillies stated that 'she wanted to go and kill for her brothers'—that she wanted to go but there wasn't room enough in the car. The defendants wanted to go to show their love to Charles Manson. There's no evidence that Charles Manson used force or fear—right to this day, they're still behind Charles Manson 101%. They love the guy. They think he's Jesus Christ. I'm not saying this for the first time—I said it the 23rd of July, 1970. Charlie's domination has been shown throughout the trial. Maybe we are all capable to kill, but no one can convince me to kill a totally strange person. It takes a person who has no value in human property. They would never have committed these murders if Charles Manson did not tell them to do it, they had it in their systems—they had murder in their blood.

"Susan Atkins, long before she met Charles Manson, with a concealed gun with one bullet told a sergeant in Oregon that if she had the opportunity, she would have killed him."

Mr. Bugliosi then read, from a transcript, the testimony of Dr. Detman about Leslie Van Houten that Charles Manson gave form and shape to what it was already there. The prosecutor added:

"When Leslie Van Houten, Susan Atkins and Patricia Krenwinkel plunged their knives, it was their will, not Charles Manson's. Look at Dr. Detman's testimony—it is very important—there is a very important point:

"'Question: Do you have any opinion whether Charles Manson's influence has any significance?

'Answer: Someone can tell you to shoot someone, but your decision comes from within you—inside of you.'

"In other words, Ladies and Gentlemen, the final decision was theirs and only theirs—the decision to plunge those knives into their victims' bodies. A classical example of what is to kill or not to kill is the fact that Linda Kasabian did not kill that actor in Venice, when she told Charles Manson: 'I'm not you, Charlie, I can't kill like you.'

"Ladies and Gentlemen, these defendants committed these crimes because THEY WANTED TO. I repeat it—THEY COMMITTED THESE CRIMES BECAUSE THEY WANTED TO. They liked each other. Why? Because deep, deep inside, they felt all the same. Why didn't they leave the family? The counsel for the defendants constantly repeats that everybody in the family would go and leave as they pleased—they could have left. Why didn't they leave? They didn't leave because they liked the brand-black diabolical hand of Charles Manson.

"These three girls, Ladies and Gentlemen, were not the girls-next-door type —don't confuse them with the next-door type. They hated society—they hated the establishment long before they met Charles Manson. They only achieved their hatred towards human beings under Charles Manson's guidance. Charles Manson only seasoned it, but they had it in them.

"Mr. Kanarek, Ladies and Gentlemen, seems to forget that the fact—that the reason of these killings was the 'Helter Skelter'—the multiple stab wounds on the victims is not an ordinary killing—it is not only one or two wounds —is the great number of stab wounds that predominates in the killings that gives the motive of 'Helter Skelter'.

"Brooks Poston testified way back in this courtroom what 'Helter Skelter' was going to do: cutting bodies to pieces and overkill. This is not a situation where Charles Manson sent these murderers to kill someone for hate—but it is a situation where they actually enjoyed it. 169 stab wounds, Ladies and Gentlemen.

"These girls knew exactly what they were doing. Linda Kasabian was aghast of these murders; she left immediately, but the three defendants and Charles

Watson stayed with Charles Manson to the last minute.

"Ladies and Gentlemen, Charles Manson should not have any objection for you to return the verdict of death—he should welcome death—he told it to Brooks Poston, Paul Watkins and Jacobson."

Mr. Bugliosi stated life in prison is not so bad and enumerated the activities of entertainment, although he emphasized that it "is not a country club." Then slowly but solemnly he pronounced the names of the victims one at a time and emotionally stirred the jurors and the public forum of the courtroom. His sincere and intense manner of presenting his argument made him reach a climax of enormous proportions. He concluded:

"If this case doesn't prove that these four defendants deserve death, they should abolish the death penalty in California."

Mr. Kanarek had a second round and his argument was totally distorted. He would start out on a point and leave it entirely for several days and would never get back to what he originally intended to say. It was difficult to follow his trend of thought. When I checked my note book, I found reading the episodes a laughing matter. It seemed that at many times, the stocky lawyer brought a blackboard in front of the jury box to stress some arguments. However, because of his lack of discipline, he would forget and never use it. The judge asked him to remove the blackboard since he was not using it. This scene happened about three or four times and brought laughter and relief from Mr. Kanarek's tedious final argument. He simply couldn't understand that the life of his client was a moral issue and not a vendetta against the assistant district attorney. Mr. Kanarek managed to write on the blackboard in large letters:

LIFE   DEATH

UNCERTAINTY

The defense counsel proceeded to tell us about a case where a man had killed two people with a rope and had been given life in prison. Mr. Bugliosi objected to this as being improper and Judge Older sustained the objection by stating:

"That's improper, Mr. Kanarek, and you know it—do you have anything else?"

"Yes, Your Honor," replied the defense counsel.

"What we are asking is that this case can be viewed like another case. The Tate-La Bianca case is different only in the publicity given. If there's one issue here, is the fact that for political reasons, this case has augmented a huge publicity. The prosecution has relied upon the atrocity of these killings, which is

463

true. But they are appealing to our emotions—this is in fact what happens here. The prosecution has forgotten the issue to discuss. He has given the victims a sense of sainthood if you will. I'm not trying to diminish the killings, but that's all the prosecution has in mind."

At that time, Mr. Kanarek took a sip of water from a glass placed underneath the podium and from which the prosecutor had drank some. He uttered nonchalantly:

"I'm going to take a chance with Mr. Bugliosi."

That obviously brought a big roar from everybody in the courtroom, except the judge. The laughter subsided for a while. Mr. Kanarek resumed his argument by bringing to our attention the Leopold Case in 1920. He started to proceed but didn't get to finish because the prosecutor objected, alleging that it was improper and that furthermore he could have used 100 other cases but he didn't. Judge Older, unable to decide, just stared at both counsels. Mr. Kanarek contested that the case was a historical case and that he was only using it for the purpose of... Judge Older interrupted Mr. Kanarek and told the counsel to approach the bench.

While the counselors were conferring, I noticed Leslie Van Houten and the other female defendants were engaged in looking at Marvin Connolly. Leslie, squinting her eyes and showing a permanent smile, finally drew a return smile from the juror in question. Marvin noticed that I was aware and simply looked at me. When Mr. Kanarek returned to the podium, he didn't continue with the inference of the Leopold Case but spoke of Linda Kasabian's immunity extensively.

We returned to the hotel.

The tension began to really build up among the jurors. When word came out that, because of the surroundings, the bailiffs denied permission to go down for a walk, the mood of the jurors darkened and some became increasingly outspoken. There were ups and downs.

Betty, Mildred and Edith used the corridors to exercise. Twice, Betty and I went up to the roof, unfortunately we couldn't even see the city down below. We felt frustrated and isolated. Once on the way down, we were shown some suites which were formerly occupied by some movie stars and celebrities and even a late U.S. President. The nights were boring. There was not much to do. My room was small and had no view. It was depressing.

Surprisingly, I was invited by Debbie to join the "clique" and play poker for pennies. However cordial Debbie and the others were on the surface, somehow I was not convinced of their true feelings. I sensed that they were not genuinely interested in me and consequently I was not taken in by their acts. The more they pretended to like and fellowship me, the more I distrusted them. I had my reasons. I had watched them for months and I felt they were incapable of consideration for their fellow jurors and their so-called courteous manners were merely a window dressing that screened their real personalities. Above all I liked them and made myself available to play poker. Tom was friendly and charming, Ray always chummy and jokeful, and Debbie extra talkative and somewhat sensitive. Violet refused to play and seemed distant to Debbie. I didn't know why. Marvin played for a while and left the room. They were all drinking. Ray offered me a beer and I gladly accepted it.

Through the game, Tom stood up many times and left the game. Something bothered him. Debbie would follow him with her eyes. I discovered the poker game was of no interest for her. Ray sensed the relationship of his friends was at stake. He probably never discussed it with Debbie, but surely with Tom—they were buddies. I felt sorry for Debbie. She had no one to confide in—no one to talk with. I liked her and knew she was in pain. Debbie rose and went to the refrigerator and brought one more beer to relieve herself. I couldn't help thinking while we were playing that Debbie knew she would have to go home. She hadn't been home for almost a year. She felt apprehensive. Somehow, her affair was coming to an end and the excitement of her secret love for Tom would soon be only a remembrance. Her jury duty hadn't been boring on account of Tom; however, all good things come to an end and it was time to return home. Then I thought that for Debbie at least, with her husband, there would be a relief from emotional complications. She would no longer try to pretend and time would erase the memory of her love for Tom Brooks.

"I'm going to hit the sack," announced Ray, and then added, "there's not enough of us to play." He picked up his winnings.

"Wait a minute, Ramon is here... and I... and Tom is coming back." Debbie spoke earnestly.

Ray stood up and walked to the door. Without stopping he turned and said: "Good night folks."

"Chicken!" Debbie yelled back and laughed.

I joined her in laughing but felt rather uncomfortable. For lack of words, I asked her what was wrong with Violet. We both knew Violet's husband had mentioned to the news media that his wife had taken to drinking a cocktail before dinner, which hadn't been a habit with her. Violet had taken it badly and developed an attack of asthma, especially in the courtroom.

"I'd kill my husband if he ever did that to me!" Debbie said. Still, she didn't tell me why Violet avoided her. While she lighted a cigarette, I turned the

465

television on.

Debbie went to the refrigerator and took more beer once again, and hurriedly left the room, carrying two cans of beer. She didn't turn back. She went directly to Tom's door. She knocked and Tom opened it. Debbie sensed that something was wrong. He did not invite her in, but Debbie was resolute. She stepped into his room and then closed the door. Debbie still wanted to have one more reunion with Tom. She wanted to express how much he had meant to her, having him as a companion.

I turned the television off and on the way to my room, I stopped at the T-Square corridor section to watch the TV set of the deputy on duty, who was not present. I sat down. A few minutes later, Tom came out of his room, slamming the door, and hurried to the recreation room. There was no one visible. I waited, pretending to watch television. Debbie—she also came out and slammed the door—ran and caught up with Tom and he pleaded with her "to forget the whole thing as if she had never seen him." A moment passed, a bailiff came out of "Lucy", and Tom and Debbie came back from the recreation room and returned to their own rooms.

I felt exceedingly sorry for Debbie but the trance had ended and although she was overwhelmed with grief for their separation, there was nothing she could do. They had spouses and children at home to think of and within themselves, however, they had difficulty to refuse this wonderful and marvelous opportunity. They thought no one would find out, no one would be hurt; so, with quiet persistence, they forgot about their homes and expressed their capacity to love.

Tom and Debbie became very happy and friendly amongst the jurors the following days. They spoke more than before and behaved themselves in a way that was nothing but decent until we went home. We stayed in the hotel because one of the counsels was ill.

We returned to the courtroom.

Mr. Kanarek continued all morning his argument in favor of his client. He read from the Bible according to St. Matthews's Chapter 27, which relates the events about the time Jesus was taken before Pontius Pilate and followed by his crucifixion. The reading was slow and lengthy—the press and the spectators were aware, as well as Judge Older, who suddenly stopped the attorney and asked the counsel to approach the bench. Mr. Kanarek never returned to the podium to finish his argument.

Mr. Shin tried to retaliate Mr. Bugliosi's argument by saying:

"Now, if you stop to think that the Grand Jury is picked by friends of the Supreme Court, don't you think that has some influence? But Mr. Younger

466

played with words; now, the only thing we can concur and agree and think is that the prosecution is trying to find peace of mind because Mr. Bugliosi has a guilty conscience. There'll always be voices haunting him, even to his grave, and the voice of Miss Atkins will keep asking him: Why? Why? Why? [Mr. Bugliosi laughed.]

"Now, the district attorney wants to find a way to wiggle out, wants to find an excuse to get out... now, if you feel that she deserves and you have some feelings towards Miss Atkins, give her life. Thank you."

Mr. Keith:

"Ladies and Gentlemen, Mr. Bugliosi made to you a very strong powerful argument. I'm not denying that. It sounded like a vengeance—he demanded death—revenge for more blood."

The well-spoken lawyer covered very thoroughly what the prosecutor argued and then he concluded:

"Mr. Bugliosi wants us to believe that death in the gas chamber is not one per cent of what the victims suffered. How does he know? For those who are in death row waiting months before they get their day, think about it. How inhuman it could be. Is this human philosophy? Is it reasonable? It's all passion and vengeance.

"Ladies and Gentlemen, shall we not be beyond that degradation? Save Leslie. Give Leslie a chance. Give Leslie LIFE! Thank you."

Mr. Keith swept his hand through his hair and walked to his chair and sank into it.

Mr. Fitzgerald:

"First of all let me apologize for the delay of my own illness. In answer to Mr. Bugliosi, let me tell you that Mr. Bugliosi represents the most glorious symbol of death. I'm embarrassed to have such a scholar of my profession —he used many times the words death penalty, murder, blood, bloodthirsty and adjectives such as monsters, despicable, and you name it. Such display of death desire gives me the feeling of shame and embarrassment."

Mr. Fitzgerald followed his final argument by reading passages from the Bible and sustained that he couldn't go on and added:

"God was not set to wish death. Mary Magdalene was saved from being stoned. Now, if you had Jesus Christ next to you, how do you think he'd vote? Don't wash your hands like Pontius Pilate, apply your own judgment."

Mr. Fitzgerald went on to discuss the life of Sadie Glutz [Susan Atkins], something that her own lawyer didn't do and by doing so, Mr. Fitzgerald overlooked his own client. He said:

"On behalf of Susan Atkins, I want to say that she didn't have anyone to

467

talk for her... the most needed... the girl who had abandonment and rejection... a girl desperately in need of love and attention. She searched for love from the wrong places and the wrong people. To replace the love of her father, she would have other men to love her. She thought she was worthless. She was worthless to the district attorney—Paul Caruso—Richard Caballero—Ronnie Howard—and to Virginia Graham. All rejected her. For lack of love, she was pushed into suicidal attempts and worse things. She would do anything —literally anything—she would do anything. She craved attention. Sexy Sadie Glutz would tell anything to anyone and if she'd run out of stories, she'd make them up. She searched for adulation from gruesome people, she even searched for your attention. She called her son ZI-ZE-ZU and also found people like herself—people desperately in need of love—full of loneliness— they all were the same—they all would find themselves like she is. It is obvious to you jurors that these girls love one another. Never saw anything like it. They actually relate to one another like brother and sister. It's incredible and you know I'm not fooling you. You've seen them smile—effervescent—decent people. I'm not trying to say that they didn't commit seven murders. Maybe you can help them now. We can help Patricia Krenwinkel. We can learn what a plain girl, rejected, with long hair and full of ugliness, unwanted—how you're going to feel when they'll ask you after they're executed. Mr. Bugliosi tried desperately to convince you that they were monsters, bloody murderers, etc."

Mr. Fitzgerald went on to tell us a story. The last mile of a prisoner on the way to be executed. He explained that an execution takes place at 10:00 A.M. and cleverly, to enlighten his point, he disclosed the salary of each individual participating in an execution: A priest gets paid $50.00. The guards, $75.00. The executioner, $150.00. Plus there are twenty-two witnesses. An execution room contains two chairs, not for economical use, but for practical use. Mr. Bugliosi objected to this as improper evidence. While the judge called the counsel to the bench, Olivia Madison bent over to my side and said: "We don't have to hear that—Fitzgerald is evading the issue."

The slim looking attorney had returned to the podium:

"I want to be careful that I'm not misrepresenting the facts. I want you to imagine the scene, if you will. Imagine that this courtroom is the gas chamber —imagine the ritual and everybody involved preparing the execution. The condemned man or woman sitting in his cell..."

Mr. Fitzgerald shrewdly read the "Last Night" before the gas chamber at San Quentin, using Patricia Krenwinkel and Susan Atkins as an example; thus, his final words were highly packed with emotion. Mr. Fitzgerald's final argument was aimed at creating more emotional upsets, rather than intellectual or moral issues.

The recitation was somber, dramatically described, solemn and precise—one almost felt as being present, witnessing the execution. We could visualize the prisoners belted to the chairs—their eyes—their looks and even the sound of the dropping of the pellets of cyanide—and death. Mr. Fitzgerald finished his recitation with tears in his eyes; such was the impact of his own words. Some jurors were also moved and showed moist eyes.

Deputy Taylor announced in the microphone that once Judge Older started reading the instructions, no one could leave; so if anyone wanted to leave, better leave then.

Judge Older walked in and read the instructions. They were almost identical as before except for a few changes.

Deputy Taylor led us to the jury room.

Then he opened the door for the jurors to enter and pointed to two piles of evidence. The lofty bailiff told us that one was for the guilty phase and the other for the penalty phase—that we needed both. A few minutes later, he rolled in a cart with coffee and paper cups. Ray took it upon himself to serve those who asked for it. Everybody began to take their previous seats so as not to cause any delay. The foreman, Mr. Paine, asked everybody to be quiet and to have a silent prayer for guidance in our decision. We all bowed our heads—some just closed their eyes. A big board with eight color photos was the central attention. Everybody wanted to see it. The board contained pictures of Gary Hinman's house. While everybody was busy looking at the pictures, I had gotten hold of the judge's instructions. I wanted to know how many there were. I looked at the little circled numbers on the upper right corner—there were 62 pages.

Among the judge's instructions was the statement:

"I have not intended by anything I have said or done, or by any questions that I have asked, to estimate or suggest what you would find to be the facts on any questions submitted to you, or that I believe or disbelieve any witness. If anything I have done or said has seemed to so indicate, you will disregard it and form your own opinion."

Marvin explained to Debbie:

"This instruction is regarding Linda Kasabian—you shouldn't be concerned with...."

"Yeah," Mr. White joined in, "Linda Kasabian has been given immunity and that's the decision of the court and not ours."

"Right," said Mildred, "whether she told the truth or not."

"We have gone through some of these instructions," Olivia stated, "and

I don't understand about the parole."

"You don't suppose to consider that," Ray responded.

"That's a hard thing to do!" Debbie cried out.

Marvin followed suit and said:

"I personally don't understand that either, and then the judge points out where it reads 'that we should fix the penalty as confinement in the state prison for life...'"

The discussion broke down in separate directions. Debbie and Olivia got agitated in regard to the Adult Authority, an agency empowered by statute to determine if and when a prisoner is to be paroled. Both lady jurors discussed the subject over the table and seemed agreeable to one another.

"The less we talk about that subject, the faster we can reach a verdict," Mr. Welch said.

"We have no limited time, Frank," snapped Olivia.

"That's right," admitted the elderly juror, "forget what I said."

"The more I think about the Adult Authority, the less I trust them," Debbie re-entered the discussion.

At that time, this juror-author hadn't said anything yet.

"May I remind you that," I started, directing my attention to Mrs. Hart facing me across the table and Olivia farther left, "in regard to 'Adult Authority' the instructions simply inform us as to the general scheme of the parole system, and if you read Instruction No. 16, you'll see that... here... let me read it." I searched among the pages.

"Oh, here it is, at the bottom of the page. It says: 'You are now instructed, however, that the matter of parole is not to be considered by you in determining the punishment for these defendants.'"

At that time, Debbie interrupted me but Mr. Welch broke in and said: "Let Bill read the rest of the instruction."

"Thank you, Mr. Welch," I said and continued: " 'And you may not speculate as to if, or when, parole would or would not be granted to them. It is not your function to decide now whether these defendants will be suitable for parole at some future date. So far as you are concerned, you are to decide only whether these defendants shall suffer the death penalty or whether they shall be permitted to remain alive.'" "As you can see" I added, "we shouldn't concern ourselves whether the Adult Authority will give parole or not to these people."

"I go along with that!" yelled Genaro and then said: "Why don't we start with Charles Manson? He's the biggest issue, then we can go on with the rest of the defendants."

Effectively, the discussion developed in Charlie's direction. Everyone had a chance to talk and we all seemed to agree that Manson was the family leader and that he had sent Tex Watson, Patricia Krenwinkel, Susan Atkins and Linda Kasabian to kill on the first night and that he had personally gone on second night to show them "how to do it."

We were ready to continue when Olivia said in regards to Charles Manson leaving behind Tex Watson, Patricia Krenwinkel and Leslie Van Houten at the La Bianca home:

"It would have been a matter of courtesy if he had given them a ride."

Mr. White laughed heartily and the others also. Up until then, no ballots had been taken, nor had anyone declared how they felt. Genaro was the first to express how he stood:

"I think Manson and Susan Atkins should receive the death penalty and Leslie Van Houten and Patricia Krenwinkel life in prison."

"Why?" I wanted to know.

Suddenly, there was a tumult of excitement and expectation and everyone focused their attention to hear Genaro's reply:

"Because I have my doubts and although they're no less responsible, I feel they were brainwashed."

Olivia, Betty, Frank, Ray, Martin and the others in unison began firing questions to Genaro. Genaro, who was seated between Mildred and Mr. White and across the foreman, explained that he had trouble making his decision, but he would welcome to discuss it because he still had some doubts. He wasn't sure.

"You asked me the question. How do you feel?" retaliated Genaro.

"I think under the circumstances the murders were perpetrated, they all deserve the death penalty," I commented.

"I agree with Bill," shouted Olivia, followed by Mr. Welch.

Olivia added: "If they wanted to go away, they could have done it. When they killed those people, it was their own decision."

Genaro ignored Olivia and said, "Well, that's how I feel at this moment."

Mr. White then suggested to go around the table because everybody was talking aloud. I motioned to the foreman that he should start, but he felt under pressure and replied:

"I don't care who starts first," and looked at the juror at his right, said "okay, I pass."

Ray also passed as well as Marvin. It was my turn to speak, so I said:

"I've already told Genaro how I feel about it; however, if there's anyone who can convince me otherwise, I'd be glad to change my verdict."

Mr. Welch followed me:

"I'd like to point out about Leslie Van Houten—the fact that she killed only one person—is no lesser."

Frank talked about the attitude of the general public and added, "If we're going to live in a safe society, we should do something about it. When you stop to think that during this argument, we should find out the way to protect the citizens."

Mr. White was next. He began reading a passage from a Bible but Olivia and the others stopped him. The pious looking juror then said: "Before, during the Guilty Phase, we had considerable difficulty in reaching the verdict of guilty on Leslie Van Houten. I personally couldn't buy that Rosemary La Bianca tried to butcher Leslie and that Leslie killed in self-defense—that was a fabrication of lies. Since we've been in this trial, I feel like Frank—about the safety of soceity—but apparently Charlie was capable of plotting and leading those murders, including Gary Hinman's."

Mr. White then openly asked: "Does anybody believe that Gary Hinman shot the first gun shot?"

No one responded.

"I'll let it go now and come back later to develop that point," he concluded saying.

Genaro Swanson's turn was next. "With respect to all of you, I agree with you, but then I have to disagree. Giving you my personal experiences about the time I was in World War II, I was afraid about the Japanese, even after the war. However, in this case, and applied to these two girls, they're not getting away from punishment the way I see it. I don't mean to mix the complexities of war with these murders."

Genaro then gave an example of a young man twenty-one years old, mentally ill who was brilliant, intelligent—until he committed a crime. The young killer was given life in prison. It was his contention that Leslie Van Houten and Patricia Krenwinkel should receive equal punishment.

"That's interesting," intervened Mildred, who followed Genaro. "I was thinking in the same line of thought, but then I remembered that Dr. Detman said that the three female defendants were sane and knew what they were doing at the time of the killings." Mrs. Osborne looked at Olivia to let her know she had finished.

"There were 30 or 40 people at the ranch," commented the blonde-haired juror. "Some stayed behind... but the defendants had the lust to kill. They wanted to do something, they wanted to identify themselves. There's no indication they were insane. As to my reaction, since I spent so many months

472

in this trial as you know— if I fail to society, I'd be guilty—it's my duty to protect the people. I wouldn't want to..."

Betty waited for Olivia to end, but apparently the ex-drama critic had finished. Mrs. Clark stated:

"I agree with Mr. Welch, I tried to give them the benefit of the doubt. I sat and listened for eight months. I thought death and life or life and death. Patricia Krenwinkel and Leslie Van Houten had a good education and probably didn't know what they were getting into. I don't know."

Violet Stokes, between short spells of coughing, managed to give her points of view:

"As far as Susan Atkins and Charlie, they should get death, but Patricia Krenwinkel and Leslie Van Houten—I think maybe they were insane. I side with Betty."

"I go along also with Betty about Leslie and Pat," said Debbie, "I find it hard to find an excuse. Mr. Fitzgerald's climactic scene made me sick to my stomach, especially after watching those big brown eyes of Leslie—it made me violently sick." Mrs. Hart then talked about the education of the two girls and finished saying: "Maybe they lacked love or whatever, but I have come to the conclusion they're guilty."

Deputy Taylor knocked on the door and announced:

"Okay, folks—leave everything as is. Take only what you need at the hotel. There'll be no work tomorrow Sunday."

I didn't realize that two days had gone by. Some jurors wanted to return and expedite the final verdict. Somehow I was glad we had the Sunday off. It gave me the opportunity to look deeper into my decision. I wanted to find a reason—a moral reason to give life to the killers in question.

The next day, a Catholic Priest came over to the hotel and celebrated mass in the recreation room in front of Mr. Paine, Marvin and this juror-author.

With tearful eyes, I asked God to give me the strength to make the right decision—I asked forgiveness for the accused and for myself. I cried... and prayed for the victims.

That night, I stayed in my room and transferred the instructions from my note book into typed form. I tried to obtain the ones I missed from Ray but he told me he had left his note book in the jury room. Luckily, Mr. White and I helped each other and we both ended up having a complete set.

That same night, Ray came to my room and suggested that if all the jurors could hold out from giving information to the reporters, we could sell our stories to *Life* magazine for $ 200,000. There were fifteen jurors at $ 10,000 each and $ 50,000 to a lawyer he befriended. I told him to count on me and not to worry. "Great," said Ray, "we'll talk more later."

We returned to court.

Again, the jurors paraded the witnesses one by one in their arguments. Each one brought force and assurance to their belief. However, there were still some jurors holding on from giving their final decision.

"Why don't we start using the testimony of each witness, including those of the defendants?" I asked, "and see if we find something that will give us a hint as to save their lives." Everybody agreed and then each juror spoke how they felt about the veracity of some witnesses.

It was accepted among the jurors that the ballistic experts who had testified calmly and objectively were qualified, respected technical men. They had no reason to lie on the stand.

About the psychiatrists, the jurors unanimously accepted that their testimony had generated considerable amount of questions answered about the lack of proof that the defendants had committed the crimes under the influence of LSD. In fact, their testimony had prepared the minds of the jurors as to erase that factor, that they killed because of LSD.

At someone's suggestion again I was selected to draw a sort of graph to record our individual verdicts.

"It'll take me at least one half hour," said, "why don't we try and find out how we stand first?"

"That shounds like a good idea," Mr. Welch said.

"How are we going to do it?" questioned Mildred.

"Go around the table," snapped Mr. Welch, "and have everyone say death or life, that'll do it."

The jury deliberation broke down again and everyone disputed in separate groups. There was no pattern of organization. Everybody was trying to speak at the same time and those who spoke loudest were able to command the attention, momentarily, until someone else would follow suit. The excitement continued until Mr. White, somewhat authoritatively, delegated orders and asked Genaro to define his position, and then around clockwise.

Genaro started: "Well, during the weekend, I still had my doubts about Leslie Van Houten."

Olivia seemed a little hazy as to how much weight we should give to conspiracy. She felt that Charlie was not at the scene of the crimes although he was responsible. She was confused about determining the conspiracy issue. Mildred and Debbie agreed and felt the defendants should receive death, but because of the manner in which we would have to vote, they felt that if one of the defendants should per chance receive one count of life and one of death,

474

what would be the ultimate penalty?

In the middle of drafting the assignment, I mentioned that the instructions specified to disregard such questions in our minds.

"I brought the question," retorted Mildred, "because I looked deep inside to find innocence in these people."

Violet, Martin, and Ray voted for death in all counts. Marvin couldn't reconcile his mind to give death to Leslie Van Houten. He stated, "I need more time."

It was now my turn to speak and in a few words I explained that it seemed to me the defendants had been proven guilty of murder beyond the reasonable doubt, and that's why I voted death. Frank agreed with me.

Mr. White said he needed more discussion and clarification about Leslie Van Houten. Mildred promptly sided with him.

Mr. Welch, during a break, wanted me to come out with something and prove the defendants guilty.

"But they are guilty and they know it," I said.

"I mean, if I could talk like you, I would convince them, but I don't know how. You do it."

"There's nothing I can tell them that they don't know," I replied. "This is a moral issue and they have to decide."

"You're right, Bill, however, I still think you can do it."

I was amazed at Mr. Welch's strong belief. The fact of having been a sheriff for many years had made him aware of lawless people and law breakers. However, he was a fair, honest individual, who wouldn't insult nor take advantage of anyone and for that I liked him.

After discussing over and over Leslie Van Houten's culpability, we made a count again and discovered there were only two holdouts: Genaro and especially Marvin.

We continued arguing and for a while we seemed stuck for words and unable to convince the two gentlemen. I had finished the graph, so I decided to look over the instructions once more for assistance.

Marvin and Genaro sustained that Leslie Van Houten was not as guilty as the others and consequently she should receive life in prison.

Ray said: "She stabbed Rosemary La Bianca 41 times—isn't that enough to make her guilty?"

"Leslie didn't know she was going to stab anyone, less yet 41 times," replied Marvin argumentatively.

"All right, just think for a moment," said Mr. White, "wouldn't one stab be sufficient to make her guilty?"

"I don't buy that. Still, she didn't know at the time."

"Like hell she didn't!" snapped Ray.

"OKAY!" Mr. Welch yelled. "YOU convince us!"

"I don't have to convince anybody," Marvin said with his feet on the table. "You're not going to change my mind unless..."

"We don't want you to change your mind. If you believe she's innocent, then stick to it," said Olivia, "but try to be reasonable to understand."

"You were going to say unless something..." Ray inquired.

"Ah yes, unless someone can prove to me that she's guilty. I don't see how, but anyway, you have to prove it to me."

The discussion broke down again as a result of Marvin. Obviously, we were unable to get to him to find the real possible explanation. Some jurors stood up and leaned against the wall for a moment, others were looking at the gruesome photos of the victims. There were comments made but of no value to Marvin.

"Hey Bill!" Mr. Welch shouted, "Have you found something in those instructions?"

"Maybe," I answered doubtfully.

"Let's have it," Ray cried.

"The last time we were tied up with the same thing and we couldn't convince Marvin. I think that deep in his heart he knows Leslie is as guilty as charged; however, it is our duty to see that he convinces us or we convince him. What would it be? Is it our burden or his? I really don't know how to go about it."

"Did you find something?" inquired Olivia.

"Well, if you read the instructions, you'll find one says one thing and the following contradicts. Its difficult."

"You're not kidding," Marvin admitted.

"Let's take a vote," Ray suggested.

We did and, surprisingly, Genaro had conceded to give death to all defendants.

We went out to lunch and upon returning to the jury room, everyone deliberated without stopping. Olivia brought out good points of why Leslie was guilty—such as:

"Leslie must have reflected before she killed Mrs. La Bianca; otherwise, she would have run away."

Mr. White added: "The evidence showed that Patricia Krenwinkel, Tex Watson and Leslie were told by Manson to go inside and kill the victims."

Ray's opinion was: "Leslie didn't have to be encouraged to kill Rosemary, she went and did it on her own free will."

Genaro looking at Marvin expressed his new decision: "Regardless of how many stab wounds she inflicted on Mrs. La Bianca, she killed her and that's enough for her to get death."

"Listen Marvin," I said, "you mentioned before that Leslie didn't know she was going to stab anyone; is that right?"

Marvin nodded and I proceeded while holding the bulk of instructions in my hand. "Somewhere in here, it says that the law does not guarantee to measure in units of time the length of period during which the thought entered before it developed into the desire for killing. In other words, it means that it doesn't matter the duration of time—one second in your mind would be sufficient to develop a thought or an impulse to kill in cold blood. I don't know if I'm making myself clear. What I mean is that Leslie had deliberated just like we're doing here—discussing—she deliberated with Tex and Patricia Krenwinkel before they decided to go inside the house. Now, premeditated because while she was walking towards the house, she forethought by herself what she was going to do."

"Let's try to vote and see how we stand," Ray suggested.

"Bill, you have the list," said the foreman, "go ahead."

"To make it easy," I started saying, "I'm going to call your names one at a time—then I'll pick Manson's name first, and go through each count, naming the victim. The same with Susan Atkins and the rest. Okay? Here we go:

"Frank Welch: how do you vote against Charles Manson on Count 1 for the killing of Abigail Folger—Death or Life?"

"Death," replied Frank and I placed an "X" on the box.

"Paul White: How do you vote against Charles Manson on Count 1 for the killing of Abigail Folger—Death or Life?"

"Death," responded Paul and again, I placed an "X" on the box.

The procedure was slow and tedious—if only to reassure the jurors of their final verdict.

Charles Manson, Patricia Krenwinkel, and Susan Atkins had been convicted of seven counts of first degree murder and one count of conspiracy to commit murder. Leslie Van Houten had been convicted of two counts of first degree murder and one count of conspiracy to commit murder.

We were instructed that each defendant may be sentenced to death or life imprisonment on each count of which he or she was convicted. Therefore, there were eight possible verdicts of life or death for the defendants Manson, Atkins and Krenwinkel, and three possible verdicts of life or death for defendant Van Houten.

There were 27 possible counts to ask each juror multiplied by 11 times—

477

excluding myself, this gave a total of 297 times I had to ask the jurors—324 X's I had to mark on the graph.

When I asked Marvin how he voted on Count VI, VII and VIII, there was an air of suspense at first, because we didn't know if he would still hold on. Marvin voted for death on all counts.

As before, I filled and dated the 27 verdicts and the foreman signed them.

It was 2:50 P.M. on Monday, March 23, 1971, when Violet Stokes again was commissioned by Martin to press the buzzer three times to let the judge know we had reached a verdict.

Deputy Taylor arrived and told us to wait and that he'd be back shortly after.

We scattered around the room and Ray immediately brought to our attention the $200,000 to be made from an exclusive magazine sale. The majority of the jurors accepted Ray's idea; however, some held back like Betty and Mildred who wanted no part of it. Violet was skeptical because of her husband. I was not aware of Genaro's opinion. The rest, including the foreman, were interested, and felt that there could be no harm in selling what would otherwise be given to the magazine free.

I heard Mr. Paine telling Ray: "I can't hold too long you know, I'm going on TV and they're going to ask me many questions."

The curly-haired young man sustained he had to verify the agreement with a lawyer friend of his. He wrote down our phone numbers and promised to call everybody to let us know if there was a deal or not.

"Okay, folks," said the familiar voice of Deputy Taylor and the jurors trooped downstairs. As we entered the courtroom, some of the jurors glanced at the defendants and others to the audience. The courtroom was packed with TV reporters, local and international newsmen; plainclothesmen and deputy sheriffs were ready in case of an unexpected incident.

"Mr. Paine," Judge Older asked the foreman. "Has the jury reached a verdict?"

"Yes, we have, Your Honor," Martin replied, handing a sheaf of papers to Deputy Taylor.

Everyone followed with their eyes as the sheriff walked towards the bench.

Judge Older with facial reaction was looking through the verdicts when Manson cried out:

"I don't see how you can get by with this without letting me put on some kind of defense. Who gives you authority to do this?"

"Be quiet, Mr. Manson or I'll have you removed from the courtroom," the Magistrate said patiently and firmly.

"I didn't ask to come back!" replied the hippie cult leader. The Judge ignored him and countinued reading the verdicts and then gave them to the court clerk.

"Hey, boy!" shouted Manson at Judge Older. Then, directing his attention to the jury box, he added: "You people don't have authority over me. Half of you in here ain't as good as I am."

Judge Older ordered two bailiffs to remove Manson and as he was being escorted to a holding room he turned and said: "It's not the people's courtroom."

Court Clerk Gene Darrow began reading the verdicts at 4:20 P.M. When he announced our verdict of death for Manson for the murder of Abigail Folger, the three defendants, staring at the jurors, cried out:

"You have just judged yourselves!" Patricia Krenwinkel said.

"Your whole system is a game," said Leslie Van Houten, "you blind stupid people, your children will turn against you."

"You'd best lock your doors and watch your own kids!" yelled Susan Atkins squeakingly, "you are removing yourselves from the face of the earth, you old fools!"

The prisoners were guided to the same room where Manson had been taken a few moments before.

While the court clerk read each verdict, the jurors kept grim-faced. I was the only juror writing notes—I was writing what one feels when one hears someone call—27 times—death... death... death... death... for another human being. I couldn't control my emotions, my eyes seemed to burn, my hands felt warm and they trembled as I wrote. I felt like crying. I felt a need of gasping for more air. I had a lump in my throat and my lips were rigid and dry. My tongue kept licking my lips to be able to sustain the inside feeling—the urge to and the need to cry—to cry for the victims—to cry for the defendants, and yet to be able to perform my duty as a citizen and to render a verdict in a manner that would aid society. I cried and I was not embarrassed.

Speaking about the defendants, I wrote:

"We got to know them in court; week after week and into months. We noticed their vanities and fears and arrogances and, believe it or not, we got to know them as people, as human beings and not as monsters. Only we who have watched them for so long a time and listened to all the evidence could make a qualified decision of death or life in prison."

Mr. Fitzgerald, generally considered to be the most competent of the defense attorneys, apparently not putting out anything like a maximum effort during the trial, stood up and asked the judge to have the jurors polled collectively

479

after each verdict on each count and individually on Counts One through Eight after the court clerk completed reading them.

We all answered: "Yes," "Yes," "Yes, it is" as we were asked if the verdicts were our own.

The defense counsel appeared somber and speechless. Mr. Keith, with one hand under his chin, seemed terribly upset and unhappy. Mr. Fitzgerald had tears under his eyes. Mr. Kanarek, still fighting, stood up and requested to impose a "gag rule" on the jury. The judge promptly denied and then turned to the jurors:

"Ladies and Gentlemen, the State of California owes you a tremendous debt of gratitude. To my knowledge, no jury in history has been sequestered for so long a period or subjected to such an ordeal. Your devotion on this trial has been above and beyond the call of duty. If it was within my power, I would award each of you a medal of honor. I want to thank you individually on behalf of the People of California."

Then Judge Older did something unusual: he stepped down from the bench and walked directly to the jurors and smilingly called them by name and shook hands with each one.

The trial was over.

Deputy Taylor and Mollie escorted us out of the courtroom and into the bus to the hotel. We were on our own to do as we pleased. On my way home, I noticed no one in the corridor except Martin Paine, who was coatless, chatting with a deputy. We both bid each other good-bye and that was the last time I saw Martin.

Downstairs in the lobby, the press was waiting. They took pictures and asked me questions but I declined by saying:

"What I'm holding from you are my inner feelings and the story of the association of the jurors. That's the thing that's never been disclosed to the public and that will be the key to my book."

Before sundown two policemen knocked on my door and informed me they'd patrol my house on the hour—also a police helicopter would check over my place of residence. "I have a gun," I told them. "Good" replied one of them and added, "I'll live across the street. I'll keep an eye out just in case."

"Thanks" I said and locked the door.

That night at home—I didn't answer the phone—instead I locked myself in my bedroom and watched television.

I was amazed to see Marvin being interviewed and also Violet.

The next day, Ray phoned me and said to go ahead and speak to the news media. I questioned him briefly about the others and he replied: "Martin

480

backed out, but the one who surprised me was Paul. You wouldn't think it —would you? Paul waited until the last minute. Thanks Bill, I'll see you sometime."

Baxter Ward, a well-known TV newscaster, invited me to appear in his sixty-minute program. Mr. Ward explained that the interview would last about five minutes, but that if he felt he had to cut it short, he would do it by thanking me, followed by a commercial plug. I agreed.

Mr. Ward was so successful interviewing me that he extended our meeting on the air for almost forty-five minutes. The capable Mr. Ward was aghast when I disclosed that there was promiscuity among the jurors and immediately stopped for a commercial spot. Off the air, he wanted to verify if I knew the meaning of the word "promiscuity." I replied yes and he continued with his program. The next day, I appeared on Tempo, another TV program.

The news had repercussioned and the news media, hungry for information, bombarded my home and place of work with messages and telephone calls, begging for details. I received phone calls from London, Paris, Frankfurt and Rome. They offered me up to $5,000 if I'd write a short story about the things I had stated on the air. I refused.

Mr. Paine, under pressure, held a press conference on the same grounds of the hotel where we had been sequestered. On the air, Martin Paine, assisted by two legal advisors standing behind him, failed to know what the word "promiscuity" meant. The lack of knowledge of his native language prompted the ex-foreman to lean back and search for help from one of the gentlemen. The white-haired mortician, his brow furrowed and fists clinched, said that he knew of no "hanky-panky" going on amongst the jurors and that I was "very small" for making such implications.

All the jurors knew it, including Mr. Paine. If he denies the existence of the romance, he either was blind or stupid, but deep in his heart, he knows I'm telling the TRUTH. That's why I was chosen to be a juror in this trial. I didn't make it up.

The Manson trial had all the elements essential for fascinating the public, the work—a Hollywood Movie Star had been slain. In addition to the other victims, a renowned Hollywood hair stylist, a wealthy coffee heiress, plus others, including a young man who was not connected with the "Beautiful People".

Among the many telephone calls offering me roles in pictures, I received one in particular that's worthwhile to relate.

Some four years ago, I was taking drama lessons at the Lawrence Merrick Studios in Hollywood. Mr. Merrick, a producer of Hot Rod and Bike Films

481

and a competent teacher, had a fascinating salesmanship. He taught me well and was satisfied with my progress—to the point he would use me regularly on a stage during the classes.

Mr. Merrick addressed all the would-be actors as "Baby" or "Sweetheart," accepted terms in show business, especially in Hollywood.

Three months after I had quit the Lawrence Merrick School, I found myself with the opportunity to do a three-minute scene with an actress before a casting director at Columbia Studios. The actress and I had worked diligently on the scene; however, I felt someone capable should see it and give us a constructive critique—possibly polish it. I went to see Merrick:

"I'm busy, Bill," he told me, "but I can squeeze in an hour. It'll cost you $100."

"Lawrence," I pleaded, "all I want you to do is see it and tell me where I can improve."

"Okay, Baby! Because of you, I'll give one half hour for $50." and he left his office.

I thought Lawrence was a true patron of the arts—one and a half years at his school at $85 monthly, once a week, and he wouldn't even take the time for three minutes. I didn't get the part at Columbia because I was "too good looking", they told me.

"Baby," Merrick said on the line, "I saw you on TV, read about you—it's great. You're on top of the world!"

"What do you want?" I asked coldly.

"Listen, Baby, I'm producing a picture about the Manson family—it's called 'The Manson Girls' and it'll be simultaneously premiered in London, New York and Los Angeles."

"Congratulations," I said.

"I want you to be in it—you don't have to do anything, as an ex-juror—you'll just sit in front of the camera and I'll ask you some questions about the trial. We'll shoot the scene on Sunday at 2:00 P.M. It'll be added at the end of the film."

I tried to explain to Mr. Merrick that I was tired and didn't know what to think at the moment.

"Don't waste this opportunity—this is what you've been waiting for—take it. I'll see you Sunday at 2:00 P.M."

"Let me call you back," I said, "I got to think it over."

That was Thursday.

On Sunday, at 2:00 P.M., the phone rang: "Baby, we're waiting for you," said Lawrence. "Baby, are you there? Listen, the crew is here—cameramen, lights—the whole works—hurry up!"

"Lawrence, Baby," I said, "how long did you say the scene is going to last?"

"Sweetheart, it is only five minutes—that's all."

"Five minutes you said?"

"Yes, Baby."

"Alright Lawrence, Baby, because of you, I'll give you five minutes for $5,000."

No answer.

"Hello... hello..." I said.

There was no answer.

BILL ZAMORA
Hollywood, California
April, 1973